Imperial Requiem

*Four Royal Women and
the Fall of the Age of Empires*

Justin C. Vovk

iUniverse, Inc.
Bloomington

Imperial Requiem
Four Royal Women and the Fall of the Age of Empires

iUniverse books may be ordered through booksellers or by contacting:

iUniverse
1663 Liberty Drive
Bloomington, IN 47403
www.iuniverse.com
1-800-Authors (1-800-288-4677)

ISBN: 978-1-4759-1749-9 (sc)
ISBN: 978-1-4759-1748-2 (hc)
ISBN: 978-1-4759-1750-5 (e)

Library of Congress Control Number: 2012907569

Printed in the United States of America

iUniverse rev. date: 8/1/2012

Also by Justin C. Vovk
In Destiny's Hands

*For my parents, without whom this book,
literally, would not exist.*

Contents

Part 1. Unlikely Empresses

Part 2. The Age of Empires

Part 3. The Great Tragedy

Part 4. Twilight and Shadow

Acknowledgments

I must take a moment to express my deepest thanks to all those who have helped me in writing *Imperial Requiem*. I have learned so much since writing *In Destiny's Hands* that I would like to think that I have corrected many of the mistakes I made the first time around. Once again, I would like to thank Dr. Otto von Habsburg, whose insights, recollections, and memories have proved invaluable. I was deeply saddened by his death in July 2011, and regret that he was not able to see this book completed. In addition, the interviews both he and Empress Zita conducted with the journalist and historian Gordon Brook-Shepherd were treasure troves of information that I could never have dreamed of uncovering on my own.

For sharing his experiences and insights with me regarding the Prussian royal family and the House of Hohenzollern, I would like to thank Paul Rizo-Patron. His reminiscences provided from the grandchildren and great-grandchildren of Empress Augusta Victoria have proved crucial. I am also deeply indebted to the authors and historians Julia P. Gelardi and Helen Rappaport, whose expertise on Tsarina Alexandra and the Romanovs helped make *Imperial Requiem* what it is.

A word of heartfelt thanks goes out to my stalwart editor, Cherylyn Donaldson, whose loyalty and commitment are inspirational. Not every editor is willing to endure personal criticism for supporting authors, but she did. I am also grateful for her advice, both supportive and critical, in helping me flesh out a strong story that made sense. I am also indebted to Sara, my professional editor at the publisher's, who provided tremendous assistance in unifying the style and voice of this book. Her attention to detail and the finer points in the book were vital. I am deeply indebted to my wonderful executive assistant, Diana Lozada, who not only made my burdens as light as possible, but also made working on this project with her a great joy and pleasure. Her professionalism, commitment, and encouragement were especially valued when this book was stalled by a family tragedy.

I owe a debt of gratitude to George Nedeff, my chief editorial consultant at iUniverse Publishing, who provided great counsel and direction, as well as tremendous patience with me when the process took much longer than expected. I also would like to thank the design and editing teams that spent so many long hours making *Imperial Requiem* the best it could possibly be. I would also like to thank Rebekka Potter for helping me smooth out the complex anscillary materials. To the staff of the numerous archives and university archives, a sincere thank-you for all your help. These include in Canada: the Mills Historical Library and Archives at McMaster University and the Scott Library at York University; in Germany: the Brandenburg-Preussisches Hausarchiv and the Langenburg Hausarchiv; in Austria: the Hausarchiv, Hofarchiv, and Staatsarchiv in Vienna; in the United Kingdom: the London Public Records Office and the Parliamentary Archives; and in Slovenia: the National Ethnographic Institute, the National Library, and the Kobarid War Memorial.

I would like to express my gratefulness to the staff at Indigo Books and Music. The staff at Home Office in Toronto has been crucial in getting my book into stores across Canada. Just as supportive have been my colleagues at Chapters Ancaster, whose commitment to my success has been ceaseless. The numbers of copies my colleagues have hand-sold have truly been touching. I would like to particularly thank LouAnne Disher, Kim Rochon, Lisa Belder, Michael Clemens, Laura Llewellyn, and Stephanie Seagrove.

A most heartfelt thank you goes out to my friends and family who have supported me throughout the entire writing process yet again. My friends have rallied around me with tremendous support and encouragement, especially during some of the more recent, difficult times. I am deeply grateful to Vanessa Rundle, Frank Borger, Steven LeClerc, Stefanyie Hamilton, Marc Murchison, Ryan Hashimoto, Lisa Wilson, Roberta Rayburn, Barbara Lancefield, Karen Corlis, Kim Doucette, Jeff Grivel, Christine Matthews, Cynthia Kay, Connor Prebianca, David Antunes, Beau Caza, Michael Van Arragon, and Barb Girvan. I thank my parents, Sharon and Stan Vovk, who supported me wholeheartedly the moment I told them I was writing another book. It would not be an understatement to say that *Imperial Requiem* would not exist without them. Many thanks belong to my brother and sister-in-law, Steven and Jolene; my aunts and uncles, Patricia and Andrew Price, Tom Vovk, Monika Vovk, and Roger and Patty West; as well as my immensely supportive cousins—not limited to, but including—Jessica, Caitlin, Andrea,

Miha, Maja, Marko, Kristina, and Andreja. I also wish to thank my cousin Gašper, who has been one of my biggest fans since the day I put pen to paper; I suspect I owe my European following to his support. To each and every one of you who has stood by me all this time, you have my deepest thanks.

Family Trees

Dona's family tree *(and how she was related to Wilhelm)*

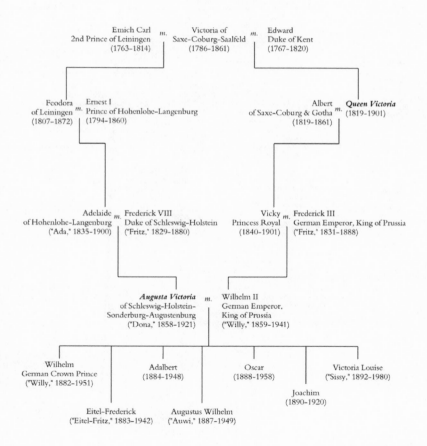

Emich Carl
2nd Prince of Leiningen
(1763–1814)

m.

Victoria of
Saxe-Coburg-Saalfeld
(1786–1861)

m.

Edward
Duke of Kent
(1767–1820)

Feodora
of Leiningen
(1807–1872)

m.

Ernest I
Prince of Hohenlohe-Langenburg
(1794–1860)

Albert
of Saxe-Coburg & Gotha
(1819–1861)

m.

Queen Victoria
(1819–1901)

Adelaide
of Hohenlohe-Langenburg
("Ada," 1835–1900)

m.

Frederick VIII
Duke of Schleswig-Holstein
("Fritz," 1829–1880)

Vicky
Princess Royal
(1840–1901)

m.

Frederick III
German Emperor, King of Prussia
("Fritz," 1831–1888)

Augusta Victoria
of Schleswig-Holstein-
Sonderburg-Augustenburg
("Dona," 1858–1921)

m.

Wilhelm II
German Emperor,
King of Prussia
("Willy," 1859–1941)

Wilhelm
German Crown Prince
("Willy," 1882–1951)

Adalbert
(1884–1948)

Oscar
(1888–1958)

Victoria Louise
("Sissy," 1892–1980)

Joachim
(1890–1920)

Eitel-Frederick
("Eitel-Fritz," 1883–1942)

Augustus Wilhelm
("Auwi," 1887–1949)

British Royal Family *(and how Mary, Alexandra, and Augusta Victoria were related)*

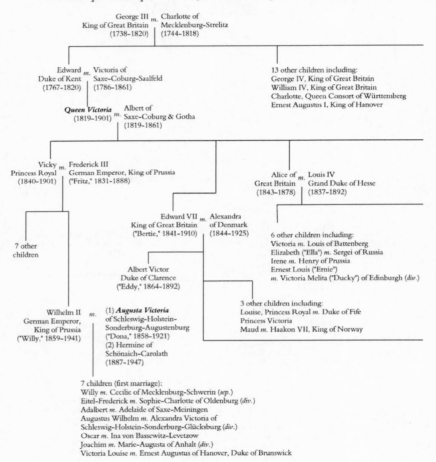

George III *m.* Charlotte of
King of Great Britain Mecklenburg-Strelitz
(1738–1820) (1744–1818)

Edward *m.* Victoria of
Duke of Kent Saxe-Coburg-Saalfeld
(1767–1820) (1786–1861)

13 other children including:
George IV, King of Great Britain
William IV, King of Great Britain
Charlotte, Queen Consort of Württemberg
Ernest Augustus I, King of Hanover

Queen Victoria *m.* Albert of
(1819–1901) Saxe-Coburg & Gotha
(1819–1861)

Vicky *m.* Frederick III
Princess Royal German Emperor, King of Prussia
(1840–1901) ("Fritz," 1831–1888)

Alice of *m.* Louis IV
Great Britain Grand Duke of Hesse
(1843–1878) (1837–1892)

Edward VII *m.* Alexandra
King of Great Britain of Denmark
("Bertie," 1841–1910) (1844–1925)

6 other children including:
Victoria *m.* Louis of Battenberg
Elizabeth ("Ella") *m.* Sergei of Russia
Irene *m.* Henry of Prussia
Ernest Louis ("Ernie")
  m. Victoria Melita ("Ducky") of Edinburgh (*div.*)

7 other
children

Albert Victor
Duke of Clarence
("Eddy," 1864–1892)

3 other children including:
Louise, Princess Royal *m.* Duke of Fife
Princess Victoria
Maud *m.* Haakon VII, King of Norway

Wilhelm II *m.* (1) ***Augusta Victoria***
German Emperor, of Schleswig-Holstein-
King of Prussia Sonderburg-Augustenburg
("Willy," 1859–1941) ("Dona," 1858–1921)
  (2) Hermine of
  Schönaich-Carolath
  (1887–1947)

7 children (first marriage):
Willy *m.* Cecilie of Mecklenburg-Schwerin (*sep.*)
Eitel-Frederick *m.* Sophie-Charlotte of Oldenburg (*div.*)
Adalbert *m.* Adelaide of Saxe-Meiningen
Augustus Wilhelm *m.* Alexandra Victoria of
Schleswig-Holstein-Sonderburg-Glücksburg (*div.*)
Oscar *m.* Ina von Bassewitz-Levetzow
Joachim *m.* Marie-Augusta of Anhalt (*div.*)
Victoria Louise *m.* Ernest Augustus of Hanover, Duke of Brunswick

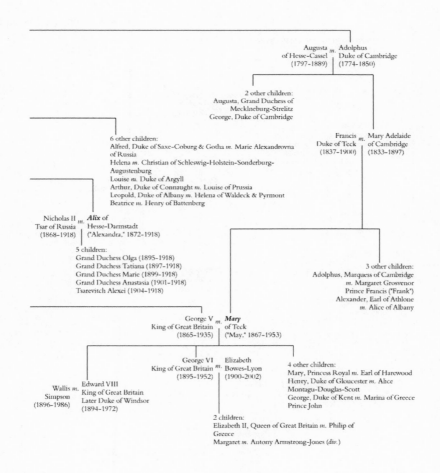

Augusta _m._ Adolphus
of Hesse-Cassel   Duke of Cambridge
(1797-1889)   (1774-1850)

2 other children:
Augusta, Grand Duchess of
Mecklneburg-Strelitz
George, Duke of Cambridge

6 other children: Francis _m._ Mary Adelaide
Alfred, Duke of Saxe-Coburg & Gotha _m._ Marie Alexandrovna   Duke of Teck   of Cambridge
of Russia   (1837-1900)   (1833-1897)
Helena _m._ Christian of Schleswig-Holstein-Sonderburg-
Augustenburg
Louise _m._ Duke of Argyll
Arthur, Duke of Connaught _m._ Louise of Prussia
Leopold, Duke of Albany _m._ Helena of Waldeck & Pyrmont
Beatrice _m._ Henry of Battenberg

Nicholas II _m._ **Alix** of
Tsar of Russia   Hesse-Darmstadt
(1868-1918)   ("Alexandra," 1872-1918)

5 children:
Grand Duchess Olga (1895-1918)
Grand Duchess Tatiana (1897-1918)   3 other children:
Grand Duchess Marie (1899-1918)   Adolphus, Marquess of Cambridge
Grand Duchess Anastasia (1901-1918)   _m._ Margaret Grosvenor
Tsarevitch Alexei (1904-1918)   Prince Francis ("Frank")
                                                          Alexander, Earl of Athlone
                                                             _m._ Alice of Albany

George V _m._ **Mary**
King of Great Britain   of Teck
(1865-1935)   ("May," 1867-1953)

George VI   Elizabeth
King of Great Britain _m._ Bowes-Lyon   4 other children:
(1895-1952)   (1900-2002)   Mary, Princess Royal _m._ Earl of Harewood
                                    Henry, Duke of Gloucester _m._ Alice
Wallis _m._   Edward VIII   Montagu-Douglas-Scott
Simpson   King of Great Britain   George, Duke of Kent _m._ Marina of Greece
(1896-1986)   Later Duke of Windsor   Prince John
            (1894-1972)

2 children:
Elizabeth II, Queen of Great Britain _m._ Philip of
Greece
Margaret _m._ Antony Armstrong-Jones (_div._)

xvii

Danish Royal Family simplified (and how they related to other royal families)

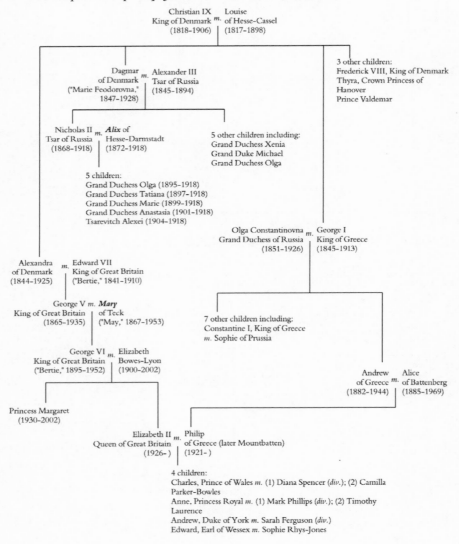

Christian IX
King of Denmark *m.* Louise
(1818-1906) of Hesse-Cassel
(1817-1898)

3 other children:
Frederick VIII, King of Denmark
Thyra, Crown Princess of
Hanover
Prince Valdemar

Dagmar *m.* Alexander III
of Denmark Tsar of Russia
("Marie Feodorovna," (1845-1894)
1847-1928)

Nicholas II *m.* **Alix** of
Tsar of Russia Hesse-Darmstadt
(1868-1918) (1872-1918)

5 other children including:
Grand Duchess Xenia
Grand Duke Michael
Grand Duchess Olga

5 children:
Grand Duchess Olga (1895-1918)
Grand Duchess Tatiana (1897-1918)
Grand Duchess Marie (1899-1918)
Grand Duchess Anastasia (1901-1918)
Tsarevitch Alexei (1904-1918)

Olga Constantinovna *m.* George I
Grand Duchess of Russia King of Greece
(1851-1926) (1845-1913)

Alexandra *m.* Edward VII
of Denmark King of Great Britain
(1844-1925) ("Bertie," 1841-1910)

George V *m.* **Mary**
King of Great Britain of Teck
(1865-1935) ("May," 1867-1953)

7 other children including:
Constantine I, King of Greece
m. Sophie of Prussia

George VI *m.* Elizabeth
King of Great Britain Bowes-Lyon
("Bertie," 1895-1952) (1900-2002)

Andrew Alice
of Greece *m.* of Battenberg
(1882-1944) (1885-1969)

Princess Margaret
(1930-2002)

Elizabeth II *m.* Philip
Queen of Great Britain of Greece (later Mountbatten)
(1926-) (1921-)

4 children:
Charles, Prince of Wales *m.* (1) Diana Spencer (*div.*); (2) Camilla
Parker-Bowles
Anne, Princess Royal *m.* (1) Mark Phillips (*div.*); (2) Timothy
Laurence
Andrew, Duke of York *m.* Sarah Ferguson (*div.*)
Edward, Earl of Wessex *m.* Sophie Rhys-Jones

Zita's family tree

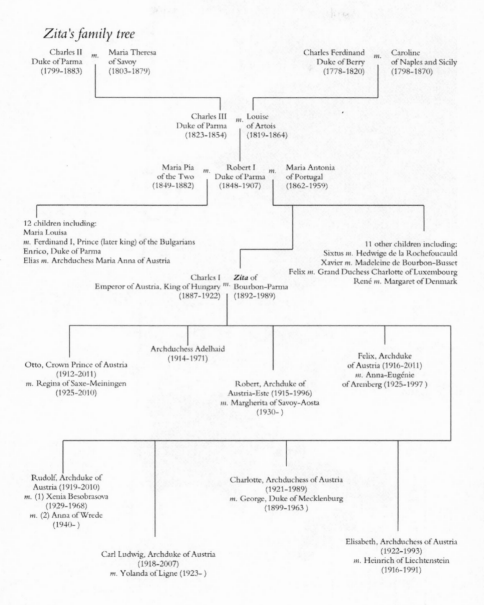

Charles II
Duke of Parma
(1799–1883)

m.

Maria Theresa
of Savoy
(1803–1879)

Charles Ferdinand
Duke of Berry
(1778–1820)

m.

Caroline
of Naples and Sicily
(1798–1870)

Charles III
Duke of Parma
(1823–1854)

m.

Louise
of Artois
(1819–1864)

Maria Pia
of the Two
(1849–1882)

m.

Robert I
Duke of Parma
(1848–1907)

m.

Maria Antonia
of Portugal
(1862–1959)

12 children including:
Maria Louisa
m. Ferdinand I, Prince (later king) of the Bulgarians
Enrico, Duke of Parma
Elias *m.* Archduchess Maria Anna of Austria

11 other children including:
Sixtus *m.* Hedwige de la Rochefoucauld
Xavier *m.* Madeleine de Bourbon-Busset
Felix *m.* Grand Duchess Charlotte of Luxembourg
René *m.* Margaret of Denmark

Charles I
Emperor of Austria, King of Hungary
(1887–1922)

m.

Zita of
Bourbon–Parma
(1892–1989)

Otto, Crown Prince of Austria
(1912–2011)
m. Regina of Saxe-Meiningen
(1925–2010)

Archduchess Adelhaid
(1914–1971)

Robert, Archduke of
Austria-Este (1915–1996)
m. Margherita of Savoy-Aosta
(1930–)

Felix, Archduke
of Austria (1916–2011)
m. Anna-Eugénie
of Arenberg (1925–1997)

Rudolf, Archduke of
Austria (1919–2010)
m. (1) Xenia Besobrasova
(1929–1968)
m. (2) Anna of Wrede
(1940–)

Charlotte, Archduchess of Austria
(1921–1989)
m. George, Duke of Mecklenburg
(1899–1963)

Carl Ludwig, Archduke of Austria
(1918–2007)
m. Yolanda of Ligne (1923–)

Elisabeth, Archduchess of Austria
(1922–1993)
m. Heinrich of Liechtenstein
(1916–1991)

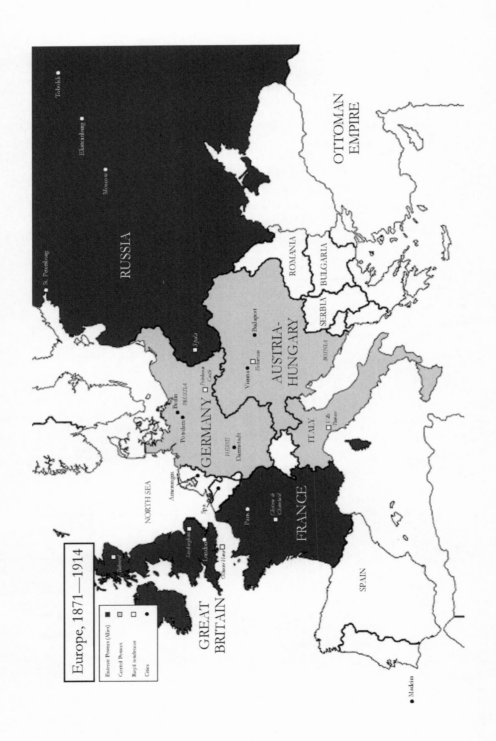

Europe, 1871—1914

Entente Powers (Allies) ■
Central Powers ■
Royal residences □
Cities ●

GREAT BRITAIN

Balmoral □
Sandringham ■
London ● Clarence House □

FRANCE

Paris ●
Château de Clarmont ●

SPAIN

Madrid ●

NORTH SEA

Antwerpen
Spa ●

GERMANY

Potsdam ●
Berlin ● PRUSSIA
Pottsdam Coda □

HESSE
Darmstadt ●

ITALY

Villa
Danese □

Spala □

AUSTRIA-HUNGARY

Vienna ● Tischerin □
Budapest ●

ROMANIA

SERBIA

BULGARIA

BOSNIA

RUSSIA

St. Petersburg ●

Moscow ●

Ekaterinburg ●

Tobolsk ●

OTTOMAN EMPIRE

Illustrations

1. The Hessian children with Queen Victoria in mourning for their mother, 1879. *Left to right*: Ella, Victoria, Queen Victoria, Ernie, Irene, and Alix.
2. Princess May with her mother, the Duchess of Teck, and her brothers Dolly, Frank, and Alge, c. 1880.
3. Princess May of Teck, 1893.
4. Princess Alix and Tsarevitch Nicholas in a formal engagement photograph, 1894.
5. The Prussian royal family in 1896. *Standing left to right:* Crown Prince Willy, Victoria Louise, Dona, and Adalbert. *Seated, left to right:* Augustus Wilhelm, Joachim, Wilhelm II (with Oscar seated in front), and Eitel-Frederick.
6. The Hessian princesses, 1906. *Left to right*: Alexandra, Victoria, Ella, and Irene.
7. Dona and Wilhelm looking stately and dignified in a formal portrait, 1910.
8. Tsarina Alexandra in formal Russian court regalia.
9. Dona and her daughter, Princess Victoria Louise, riding through the streets of Berlin, 1911.
10. Zita and Charles on their wedding day, October 21, 1911.
11. The Russian imperial family in 1913. *Left to right*: Marie, Alexandra (with Alexei seated in front of her), Olga, Tatiana, Nicholas II, and Anastasia.
12. Mary, queen of England and empress of India, c. 1913.
13. Augusta Victoria, German empress and queen of Prussia, 1913.
14. Tsar Nicholas II and King George V, 1913.

15. Queen Mary with her daughter, Princess Mary, as a nurse during World War I.
16. Zita in her coronation robes as queen of Hungary, 1916.
17. Emperor Charles I of Austria, king of Hungary, 1917.
18. Dona in exile at Amerongen, 1921.
19. Queen Mary, c. 1930.

The author and publisher would like to thank the Library of Congress, the Deutches Bundesarchiv, and the WikiMedia Foundation for permission to reproduce the illustrations contained herein. From the Library of Congress, illustrations are taken from the George Grantham Bain Collection. All illustrations are used under the GNU Free Documentation License.

Main Protagonists

Alexandra (1872-1918). Tsarina of Russia, 1894-1917, wife of Tsar Nicholas II of Russia. Born on June 6, 1872, in Darmstadt, Hesse, she was the sixth child and fourth daughter of Princess Alice of Great Britain and Prince Louis of Hesse-Darmstadt (later Grand Duke Louis IV). At the time of her birth, her full name was HGDH Princess Victoria *Alix* Helena Louise Beatrice of Hesse-Darmstadt. She married Nicholas on November 14, 1894, in Saint Petersburg and took the Russian names Alexandra Feodorovna.

Children:
1. Olga (1895-1918)
2. Tatiana (1897-1918)
3. Marie (1899-1918)
4. Anastasia (1901-18)
5. Alexei (1904-18)

Augusta Victoria (1858-1921). Empress and queen consort, 1888-1918, of Wilhelm II, German emperor and king of Prussia. More commonly known in her family as "Dona," she was born at Dolzig Palace, Brandenburg, on October 22, 1858, and given the names Augusta Victoria Friederike Louise Feodora Jenny. She was the second child and first daughter of Hereditary Prince Frederick of Schleswig-Holstein-Sonderburg-Augustenburg and Princess Adelaide of Hohenlohe-Langenburg. On February 22, 1881, she was married in Berlin to Prince Wilhelm of Prussia (Emperor Wilhelm II after 1888).

Children:
1. Wilhelm (1882-1951), German crown prince; married HH Cecilie, Duchess of Mecklenburg-Schwerin (1886-1954); 6 children
2. Eitel-Frederick (1883-1942); married HH Sophie-Charlotte, Duchess of Oldenburg (1879-1964); divorced, 1926
3. Adalbert (1884-1948); married HH Princess Adelaide of Saxe-Meiningen (1891-1971); 2 children
4. Augustus Wilhelm (1887-1949); married HH Princess Alexandra Victoria of Schleswig-Holstein-Sonderburg-Glücksburg (1887-1957); divorced, 1920; 1 child
5. Oscar (1888-1958); married Countess Ina von Bassewitz-Levetzow (1888-1973); 4 children
6. Joachim (1890-1920); married HH Princess Marie-Augusta of Anhalt (1898-1983); divorced, 1920; 1 child
7. Victoria Louise (1892-1980), Duchess of Brunswick; married HRH Prince Ernest Augustus of Hanover, Duke of Brunswick (1887-1953); 5 children

Charles I (1887-1922). Emperor of Austria and king of Hungary, 1916-18. The first son of Archduke Otto of Austria and Princess Maria Josepha of Saxony, he was born on August 17, 1887, at Persenbeug Castle in Lower Austria and given the names Charles Franz Joseph Louis Hubert George Otto Marie. In 1914, after the assassination of the Austrian heir apparent, Archduke Franz Ferdinand, Charles was designated the new heir apparent by his great-uncle, Emperor Franz Joseph. Charles married HRH Princess Zita of Bourbon-Parma on October 21, 1911, at Schwarzau Castle. He became emperor on December 16, 1916. *See* Zita.

George V (1865-1936). King of Great Britain and emperor of India, 1910-36. Born on June 3, 1865, at Marlborough House in London, HRH Prince George Frederick Ernest Albert was the second son of Albert Edward, Prince of Wales (later King Edward VII) and Alexandra of Denmark. Known from 1892-1901 as the Duke of York, he married HSH Princess May of Teck on July 6, 1893. After his father's accession in 1901, he was styled as Prince of Wales. He ascended the throne upon the death of his father in 1910. *See* Mary.

Mary (1867-1953). Queen and empress consort, 1910-36, of King George V of Great Britain, emperor of India. Born at Kensington Palace, London, on

May 26, 1867, she was christened Victoria Mary Augusta Louise Olga Pauline Claudine Agnes, although she was known simply as "May." At the time of her birth, Mary was the eldest daughter and child of HSH Francis, Duke of Teck, and HRH Princess Mary Adelaide of Cambridge. She married HRH Prince George, Duke of York, on July 6, 1893, at the Chapel Royal, Saint James's Palace, in London. Upon her husband's accession to the throne, she formally became known as Mary.

Children:
1. Edward VIII (1894-1972), King of Great Britain (later Duke of Windsor); married Wallis Simpson (1896-1986)
2. George VI (1895-1952), King of Great Britain (1936-52); married Lady Elizabeth Bowes-Lyon (1900-2002); 2 children
3. Mary (1897-1965), Princess Royal; married Henry Lascelles, Sixth Earl of Harewood (1882-1947); 2 children
4. Henry (1900-74), Duke of Gloucester; married Lady Alice Montagu-Douglas-Scott (1901-2004); 2 children
5. George (1902-42), Duke of Kent; married HRH Princess Marina of Greece (1906-68); 3 children
6. John (1905-19)

Nicholas II (1868-1918). Tsar of Russia, 1894-1917. Born at Tsarskoe Selo on May 6, 1868, as HIH Grand Duke Nicholas Alexandrovich, he became tsarevitch of Russia when his father ascended the throne in 1881. His parents were Tsar Alexander III and Princess Dagmar (Marie Feodorovna) of Denmark. Nicholas, commonly known as "Nicky," ascended the throne upon his father's death in 1894. He later married HGDH Princess Alix of Hesse-Darmstadt. *See* Alexandra.

Wilhelm II (1859-1941). German emperor and king of Prussia, 1888-1918. HRH Prince Frederick *Wilhelm* Victor Albrecht of Prussia was born on January 27, 1859, in Berlin. Wilhelm was the eldest son of Crown Prince Frederick Wilhelm of Prussia (Emperor Frederick III in 1888) and Princess Vicky of Great Britain, the eldest daughter of Queen Victoria. Wilhelm's father became the German crown prince after the formation of the German Empire in 1871. On February 27, 1881, he married HSH Princess Augusta Victoria of Schleswig-Holstein-Sonderburg-Augustenburg in Berlin. He succeeded his father as emperor on June 15, 1888. *See* Augusta Victoria.

Zita (1892-1989). Empress and queen consort, 1916-18, of Emperor Charles I of Austria, king of Hungary. Born at Villa Pianore, Tuscany, on May 9, 1892, she was the ninth daughter and seventeenth child of Robert I, Duke of Parma, and Infanta Maria Antonia of Portugal. Christened Zita Maria delle Grazie Adelgonda Micaela Raffaela Gabriella Giuseppina Antonia Luisa Agnese, she married HI and RH Archduke Charles of Austria (later Emperor Charles I) on October 21, 1911.

Children:
1. Otto (1912-2011), Crown prince of Austria; married HH Princess Regina of Saxe-Meiningen (1925-2010); 7 children
2. Adelhaid (1914-71)
3. Robert (1915-96), Archduke of Austria-Este; married HRH Princess Margherita of Savoy-Aosta (1930-); 5 children
4. Felix (1916-2011); married HSH Anna-Eugénie, princess and duchess of Arenberg (1925-97); 7 children
5. Carl Ludwig (1918-2007); married HH Princess Yolande de Ligne (1923-); 4 children
6. Rudolf (1919-2010); married [1] Countess Xenia Besobrasova (1929-68); 3 children; and [2] Princess Anna von Wrede (1940-); 1 child
7. Charlotte (1921-89), Duchess of Mecklenburg; married HH Georg, Duke of Mecklenburg (1899-1962)
8. Elisabeth (1922-93), Princess of Liechtenstein; married HSH Prince Heinrich of Liechtenstein (1916-91); 5 children

Introduction

(May 24, 1913)

The city of Berlin was alive with joyful exuberance. Thousands of people filled Unter den Linden from the Brandenburg Gate up the thoroughfare to the Stadtschloss, the imposing royal palace. In the skies above, the brightly decorated zeppelin *Hansa* buzzed loudly as it circled the palace, dropping large bouquets of flowers. Inside the Stadtschloss was one of the largest gatherings of royalty in the early twentieth century. They had come from the four corners of Europe to celebrate the wedding of Princess Victoria Louise of Prussia, the youngest child of Emperor Wilhelm II of Germany, to Prince Ernest Augustus of Hanover. At 5:00 p.m., a long line of pages, heralds, court officials, and military leaders led the bridal procession from the Electress's Hall to the palace chapel. The procession entered the chapel, with its marble walls, Roman arches, and high-domed cupola ceiling, led by the bride and groom. Immediately behind the young couple came an unprecedented collection of kings, queens, princes, princesses, dukes, and duchesses led by the imperial rulers of Germany, Great Britain, and Russia. Noticeably absent was eighty-two-year-old Emperor Franz Joseph of Austria.

Hosting so many reigning monarchs at one time was a first for Germany since its unification in 1871. At the wedding feast that night, some twelve hundred guests watched in awe as the blushing bride danced the *Fackeltanz*, the traditional candlelight Prussian royal wedding dance. As candelabras flickered, reflecting off the diamonds, emeralds, and medals of the enthralled guests, Victoria Louise danced with her father. The king of England and the tsar of Russia had the honor of dancing with her next. As radiant as the princess was that day, there were three women whose presence not only outshone the bride but also captured public attention. The three individuals in question were the highest-ranking women in the world at that time. They were the bride's mother, Augusta Victoria, German empress and queen of Prussia (1858–1921); Queen Mary of England, empress of India (1867–1953); and Tsarina Alexandra of Russia (1872–1918).

What was it about these women that caused such a stir? How did they manage to steal the spotlight at the biggest royal wedding of the decade? The wedding of Augusta Victoria's daughter marked the first and only time in history that these three women—the reigning consorts of three of Europe's four imperial powers—were together at the same time. Many historians have speculated what must have been going through their minds on that warm, sunny day in May 1913, for what would be the last gathering of the "royal mob" before the cataclysm of the First World War only fourteen months later. It is doubtful that they had any prescience about the disasters that lay ahead for each of them.

As I delved into the lives of the empress, the queen, and the tsarina, I could not help but reflect on what they each experienced as they stood witness to the decisive collapse of Europe's empires in the first half of the twentieth century. The rule of the tsars was brought to an end by the blood-soaked Russian Revolution in 1917, replaced with the equally repressive Soviet Union. The German Empire was dissolved and reorganized into a republic at the conclusion of the First World War in 1918. Without a doubt, Great Britain enjoyed the easiest—though by no means a bloodless—transition from a vast overseas empire to a commonwealth of nations, the provenance of which began at the Paris Peace Conference in 1919 and culminated after 1945. As I pondered these women's lives and their roles as the last empresses, my mind could not help but be drawn to the story of a lesser-known imperial consort whose life was just as impacting as her counterparts and whose legacy has made a profound impact on European affairs. This individual was Princess Zita of Bourbon-Parma, empress of Austria, queen of Hungary, Bohemia, Croatia, and so on (1892–1989). Her husband's reign—and her role as empress—came to an end when Austria-Hungary—like Germany—collapsed in 1918. With Zita's life and experiences coming into focus, I undertook to write this, my latest book. It is the tumultuous story of Europe's imperial past, a story that will take readers from the opulent world of nineteenth-century royalty to the catastrophic Great War, the various revolutions that swept the continent in its aftermath, and the decades of instability that followed.

For almost a century, historians, academics, novelists, and journalists have intricately studied the end of the imperial era. Equally scrutinized have been the significant lives and reigns of the husbands of these women—King George V, Emperor Wilhelm II, and Tsar Nicholas II. Despite this incomparable body of literature, there has never been a book that looks at the women who sat on the thrones of these great empires. To that end, *Imperial Requiem* is a collective narrative of the destruction of Europe's four empires—Austria-Hungary, Germany, Great Britain, and Russia—the turbulent aftermath, and the birth of the modern world, all filtered through the experiences of the last women who ruled them.

For all the political, diplomatic, and military factors that are brought to bear in this book, at its heart it remains the story of four extraordinary women. There were, of course, other imperial consorts who were contemporaries of these protagonists. However, my decision in choosing the empresses I did was deliberate. Initially, I had chosen to include Empress Eugénie, wife of Emperor Napoleon III, the last French monarch. Their deposition and exile in 1871 marked the permanent end of monarchy in France. After much thought, I chose to exclude Eugénie because there was a significant generational chasm between her and the other four women—she was already eighty-eight when World War I began, but her counterparts were relatively young women. There is also a generational gap between Zita and the other three. When she became empress, she and Augusta Victoria's daughter were the same age, but her role in the destruction of the Austro-Hungarian Empire and subsequent European events in the postwar period were too significant to be overlooked.

I also chose to exclude Queen Mary's daughter-in-law Queen Elizabeth, consort of King George VI. While technically she did become empress of India upon her husband's accession in 1936, it was a title she was forced to relinquish upon Indian independence eleven years later. Queen Mary rarely ever used her imperial title. She and the other consorts of British rulers almost exclusively referred to themselves as queens. Mary's role as empress of India and her de facto position as imperial consort of the British Empire made her inclusion in this book an obvious choice. I also did briefly consider including the beautiful yet tragic Empress Elizabeth of Austria, Franz Joseph's wife, who was assassinated in 1898, but she was not the last empress of Austria. Like Empress Eugénie, she did not have a place in the story of *Imperial Requiem*.

Throughout their lives, mostly after marrying, these women stayed in contact with one another. Their husbands wrote to each other, passing along news between their wives. They visited one another, sometimes on official state visits, sometimes on private holidays, and often for royal weddings, which at that time seemed to occur at least once a year. Some of the empresses—like Alexandra and Mary—were fond of each other. In other cases, such as with Augusta Victoria and Alexandra, they loathed their counterparts. Along with their shared experiences as consorts, these women were also connected through bonds of family, both by blood and marriage. Augusta Victoria, Mary, and Alexandra all had ties to Queen Victoria. Augusta Victoria's mother was Princess Adelaide of Hohenlohe-Langenburg, daughter of the queen's elder half sister, and Frederick VIII, Duke of Schleswig-Holstein. Mary was the daughter of Princess Mary Adelaide of Cambridge, Queen Victoria's cousin and a granddaughter of King George III, and Francis, Duke of Teck. Both Mary and Augusta Victoria would marry grandsons of the queen as well. Alexandra had a direct link with the British matriarch. Her parents were Princess Alice, Queen Victoria's second daughter, and Grand Duke Louis IV of Hesse. Zita was on a peripheral orbit when it came to familial connections with her three counterparts. Her parents were the deposed duke Robert I of Parma, and Infanta Maria Antonia of Portugal, one of Augusta Victoria's second cousins.

Each of these women came to occupy one of the four imperial thrones spread across Europe. In the far corners, there was Great Britain in the west and Russia in the east, where Europe merges into Asia. In the center, Germany was situated in the north, occupying the land between France and Russia. The dual monarchy of Austria-Hungary stretched toward Russia in the east and into the Balkans in the south. The countries and courts that these princesses married into bore striking similarities in spite of their differences, which could also be said of the women themselves. By the late nineteenth century, every European nation was governed by hereditary royalty, save for France and Switzerland. These royal states saw the rest of the globe as a frenzied game of imperialist conquest, with every Great Power scrambling to build an empire, both at home and overseas. This invariably led to conflicts, especially between Britain, Germany, and Russia, who were each struggling to become the ultimate power. But what drove these imperial monarchies? Why was it so important for them to be set apart as empires? One modern historian answered these questions this way:

> [In] the 1870s, Britain and Russia, along with the other Western Great Powers, had launched themselves into a violent phase of territorial acquisition, carving up the globe beyond Europe into colonies and "spheres of influence." There are many complex and conflicting arguments as to why the (mostly) Western, (relatively) developed powers all decided they needed an empire: the natural evolution of global power politics made it inevitable that the few rich, militarily superior, technologically developed powers would dominate and exploit the other, more "backward," weak territories; the need of the industrialized nations for raw materials, and for new places to put their capital; a sense of fierce competition among the Great Powers and a perception that new territories were the way to steal a march on their competitors. All these aspects played their role.[1]

These ideas were critical factors in the events that shaped Europe in the decades leading up to 1914. They also fueled the leaders who instigated the First World War. As we will see, in the end, it proved to be the imperial ambition itself that helped bring these empires down.

⁓

When I began writing this book in 2009, the issues I encountered were legion. Along with the normal burdens an author carries, I also found myself shouldering the legacy of my first book, *In Destiny's Hands*. It was an account of five children of Empress Maria Theresa—two were reigning emperors, and the other three were reigning consorts. In the months that followed that book's release, I was contacted by several readers who expressed concerns over the accuracy of the facts I presented. There are many factors an author has to take into account when writing nonfiction.

In compiling a biographical narrative, one always tries to use as many primary sources as possible—direct quotes from protagonists or contemporaries are an author's favorite source. But even into the nineteenth and early twentieth centuries, contemporary accounts of people or events have not always been trustworthy. They can be biased, hyperbolic, misleading, or all of the above. One witness may have recorded a series of events one way, but another witness may have a had a totally different recollection of the exact same event. It can be challenging for an author to discern which piece of information is most accurate. More than once was I forced to make a judgment call when sources were vague or contradictory.

Another important consideration is the concept of publishable materials. In this age when media is pervasive, information has never been more accessible than through the Internet. I received several correspondences from readers citing a fact on a website or forum that contradicted information I had presented. Simply because a piece of information is widely disseminated does not make it accurate. Furthermore, when a nonfiction author submits his or her manuscript, publishers and editors often examine the bibliography to ensure that credible sources are used. Websites—with exceptions, such as governmental, official, or academic—are rarely acceptable.

None of these are excuses for poor nonfiction. Authors have a responsibility to present the facts, ideally without bias. Professor Abbas Milani of Stanford University aptly describes the writing process and the challenges faced by nonfiction authors in his latest book, *The Shah*.

Though books often have the name of one person as their author, they are invariably a collective effort—every conversation, every question, every book or essay we read, every criticism, fair or unfair, that we encounter, combine to shape our vision and words and leave indelible marks on any narrative we form. I have made every effort to reduce the affects of these influences to a minimum and allow the facts, reflected first and foremost in primary documents, to speak for themselves....

There is an element of hubris in biography as a genre. It claims to illuminate the dark corners and the infinite complexities in the life of an individual [or individuals], a life invariably shaped by concentric influences, dreads, dreams, and pressures ... Any narrative of a life entails a constant process of cutting, encapsulating, eliminating, glossing, and sometimes surmising. A good biography is not one that forgoes these choices, but one that makes them without any a priori assumptions and in the humble recognition that the search for the truth of a life is ever-exclusive, yet never bereft of interest.[2]

With this in the forefront of my mind, and coupled with my goal to improve upon those areas of *In Destiny's Hands* that came under scrutiny, I have written *Imperial Requiem: Four Royal Women and the Fall of the Age of Empires*. I certainly make no claim that this book is a paradigm-altering work that could ever compete with or replace the many incomparable biographies of these women or their husbands and families. In fact, the opposite is true. I have drawn heavily on many splendid authors and historians to compose this work. Saying I am in the debt of authors like James Pope-Hennessy, Julia Gelardi, or Gordon Brook-Shepherd is an insulting understatement. In weaving my narrative I have had to accept the fact that dealing with four lives precludes the possibility of providing readers with the exhaustively-researched biographies that are so often craved, though I have tried to provide as much in-depth detail as possible. Throughout the writing process I was encouraged to discover that the story of these four women—which invariably encompasses many individuals, locations, and events—was greater than simply the sum of its parts. The stories of these four empresses can easily stand alone, but I cannot help but feel that their tales become more fully rounded out when they are set in the context of one another, what preceded their time as reigning consorts, what followed, and how cause and effect came into play.

I have done my best to wean out hyperbole without compromising the narrative epic, to present the facts on their own merit, and to discern proven facts, evidentially supported hypotheses, and reported but unsubstantiated claims in the hopes of showing every side of these women—their strengths, their weaknesses, their quirks, and even their contradictions. It is my desire that readers will see them as more than just two-dimensional women without depth or gradation. If that happens, I think I will have succeeded in my goal and done these incomparable individuals justice. Whether readers judge them as successful or failures as women, wives, mothers, and empresses, no one can deny the incredible impact they each have had. Their tales of duty, self-sacrifice, and inspiration are part of the special legacies they have left behind.

Justin C. Vovk
Ljubljana, Slovenia
July 11, 2011

PART 1

Unlikely Empresses

(1858–94)

1

Imperial Forge

(1858–73)

F ar removed from the imperial grandeur of the Berlin Stadtschloss, the first of Europe's last four empresses came into the world amid humble surroundings. She was born in the yellow Dolzig Palace, nestled in central Brandenburg in eastern Prussia, near the small riverside town of Sommerfeld (now Lubsko in Poland). The palace—which could better be described as a luxurious country villa at best—was the home of the infant's father, Hereditary Prince Frederick ("Fritz") of Schleswig-Holstein-Sonderburg-Augustenburg[1], who received Dolzig as wedding present in 1856 from his father. Fritz's wife, Princess Adelaide ("Ada") of Hohenlohe-Langenburg, was twenty-three when she gave birth to their second child on October 22, 1858. It was an excruciating delivery performed without the benefit of chloroform to dull the pain—a practice that Ada's aunt, Queen Victoria, began to champion since the birth of her son Prince Leopold in 1853; she described the effects as "soothing, quieting and delightful beyond measure."[2]

Happy though Fritz and Ada were for their daughter's arrival, their joy was quickly mingled with grief. Seven days later, on October 29, their first child, a son named Frederick, died at the age of fifteen months. The new baby girl was now an only child. Protocol dictated she be baptized as quickly as possible, which took place a few days later in a simple, Evangelical Lutheran ceremony in Dolzig's chapel. At that time, the infant received the names Augusta Victoria Friederike Louise Feodora Jenny, though she would always be known officially as Augusta Victoria. In time, her family gave her the diminutive "Dona," a nickname that would stick for the rest of her life and helped to distinguish her from the ubiquitous princesses named Victoria, Augusta, and Friederike that populated Europe. There are a number of theories regarding whom Dona was named after. The most widely accepted belief is that Augusta was for Princess Augusta of Saxe-Weimar, the wife of the future king of Prussia, and later, the first German emperor; and that Victoria was either for Dona's great-aunt, Queen Victoria, or Queen Victoria's daughter Vicky (who also happened to be Augusta's daughter-in-law and a close friend to Fritz and Ada). In reality, Victoria was probably for both women.

Fritz Holstein—as Dona's father was generally known among Europe's extended, interwoven royal family—was relatively tall according to the standards of the time, possessing a slight frame with dark hair and a matching beard. Labile, forward thinking, and a progressive constitutionalist, he was the son and heir of Christian August II, Duke of Schleswig-Holstein-Sonderburg-Augustenburg, the insignificant ruler of the microscopic city-state Augustenburg, located on Als Island near the Jutland Peninsula in southern Denmark. In 1852, at the end of the First Schleswig War, Christian August lost his family seat after unsuccessfully trying to claim the throne of the twin duchies of Schleswig-Holstein. Financially ruined after the war, he sold his ancestral lands in Schleswig-Holstein to the king of Denmark for 2.75 million thalers—less than half of their total worth. Now hugely unpopular and without any real prospects for the future, the middle-aged Christian August retreated into near seclusion at Augustenburg Palace, his pseudo-Baroque family home on Als Island.

Christian August's wife, Countess Louise-Sophie Danneskjold-Samsøe, was equally unpopular with monarchists since she was an illegitimate descendent of the Danish royal family. Her aristocratic title notwithstanding, Louise-Sophie was not considered truly *ebenbürtig*—of equal birth to marry into Europe's royal houses. Christian August's critics, most of whom were royals from Prussia or other German-speaking lands who fiercely guarded their prerogatives, argued that because of his marriage to a countess, his family was parvenu and therefore had no claim to the purple blood of royalty. Dona's grandfather was not the only member of her family to marry a commoner. Her great-uncle and a number of her father's cousins had similarly taken nonroyal wives. The fact that her maternal grandmother was a countess, and that some of her extended relatives were commoners was a sore spot on Dona's pride for the rest of her life. In later years, she would become overly concerned, almost obsessed, with royal rank, especially when it came to marriages.

Unlike Fritz, Dona's mother came from a more established royal lineage. Ada was the fifth of six children born to Prince Ernest I of Hohenlohe-Langenburg.[3] The Langenburgs were a relatively insignificant German house that ruled an equally insignificant German principality for barely a century until their territory was mediatised into the Kingdom of Württemberg by Napoleon in 1806. The Langenburgs lost their realm but were still considered *ebenbürtig* and were allowed to keep their rank and titles. Ada's mother, Princess Feodora, was the elder half sister of Queen Victoria from their mother's first marriage to the Prince of Leiningen.

As a young woman, Ada had a reputation for being beautiful. When she was seventeen, she captured the attention of Emperor Napoleon III of the French. The emperor was no Prince Charming. Already forty-four years old in 1852—compared to Ada's seventeen—his appearance did not fall short of the Bonaparte family reputation. At around four feet six inches tall, he possessed a disproportionately large head, was balding, had one eyeball that was reportedly more dilated than the other, a bird-like nose, a waxy mustache, and a noticeable limp caused by rheumatism. In light of such an unseemly appearance, one must wonder what a young princess might see in him. An arranged marriage for Ada was a given, but few suitors could offer her anything comparable to what she would experience as empress of the French, living in some of the most opulent palaces in the world. After all, Marie Louise of Austria was in a similar situation when she married Napoleon I in 1810, and she was quite happy in France, albeit her marriage only lasted four years.

Queen Victoria, a woman of incredible tenacity, took a serious view of her position as head of her family and the impact that the actions of her family members would have on British interests and the monarchy. In a letter to her sister Feodora, she outlined her opinion on the emperor's interest in Ada: "You know what *he* is, what his moral character is—(without thinking him devoid of good qualities and even valuable ones) what his entourage is, how thoroughly immoral France and French society are—hardly looking at what is wrong as more than fashionable and natural—you know how very insecure *his* position is—you know his age, that his health is indifferent, and naturally his wish to marry [Ada is] merely a political one, for he has never seen her … I ask you if you can imagine for a moment anything more awful than the fate of that sweet innocent child."[4] Tempted though Ada may have been by the prospect of the French throne—she said she was "dying to be Empress"[5]—her parents would have none of it, browbeating their daughter into refusing the proposal. In a letter sent to the emperor dated January 1, 1853, Ada wrote that she had to decline on religious and moral grounds—as empress, she would most likely have been required to convert from the Protestant faith to Catholicism. Princess Michael of Kent wrote that "too much stood against" the emperor in his campaign to win Ada: "his morals, his religion, his *parvenu* status as royalty, and the sad fate of so many Queens of France in the last sixty years."[6] Three years later, Ernest and Feodora married her off to Fritz Holstein, whose pro-German ideologies, and—most importantly to English dynastic interests in Europe—progressive attitudes, made him ideal.

Pro-German ideas were something Fritz Holstein espoused since his youth. Educated at the University of Bonn, he became close friends with the future crown prince of Prussia, Frederick Wilhelm, who was, naturally, also nicknamed Fritz. The two princes had a deep affection for one another, and Frederick Wilhelm's enlightened views on constitutional ruling made a profound impression on Fritz Holstein; the two men would remain close for the rest of their lives. When Fritz Holstein's first son was born in 1857, he was named Frederick in honor of the Prussian prince, who stood as godfather. And when the latter married Ada's cousin Vicky, the Princess Royal of Great Britain, in 1858, it only strengthened their bond. After completing his studies at Bonn, Fritz took up a commission in the Bavarian military. By the time Dona was born, Fritz and Ada had determined to raise their daughter to think of herself first and foremost as a German princess. They felt a special attachment to Prussia, the largest, most influential, and most powerful of the German states. This brought with it a sense of connection with the Prussian royal family, the Hohenzollerns, through Frederick Wilhelm and Vicky.

The Hohenzollerns were by the mid-nineteenth century the rising dynastic power on continental Europe. Their provenance as a strong royal house was a long process marked by continual dynastic evolution. Like the Habsburgs of Austria, they originated as counts sometime around the eleventh century. The family took its name from what is believed to be their ancestral home, Hohenzollern Castle. A typical German *burg* with high turrets, ramparts, and classic medieval architecture, it is located 768 feet on a mountaintop above Hechingen, in the Swabian Alps. The family tree branched off several times throughout the centuries, but the most prominent line eventually became rulers of Brandenburg, a frontier region in northeastern Prussia, in 1417. Through marriage, conquest, and inheritance, the Hohenzollerns transitioned from being margraves and electors of Brandenburg to also being dukes—and eventually kings—of Prussia.

By the 1850s, the Hohenzollerns were at the center of Prussia's authoritarianism, which, though decried by liberals as philistine and conservative, gave the country a functionality and stability that many of its neighbors lacked. Like many of Europe's Great Powers, Prussia was a nation of intense contrasts. In the 1750s, King Frederick II (more famously remembered as Frederick the Great) pushed Prussian ascendancy to terminal velocity. He spread Prussian influence across the continent through his support of art, philosophy, and modernization during the Age of Enlightenment. At the same time, he began establishing Prussia's military as a force to be reckoned with when he successfully tore from Austria its beloved, ore-rich province of Silesia in 1740, marking the beginning of the War of the Austrian Succession and leading to decades of Habsburg-Hohenzollern acrimony. In 1815, it was the Prussian military that helped shatter the armies of Napoleon at the Battle of Waterloo. This was not something the Prussians took lightly, since Waterloo marked the end of the Napoleonic Wars. It would also lead to decades of rivalry with the Russians, who believed it was their burning of Moscow in 1812 and the subsequent decimation of the French army that had truly sounded Napoleon's death knell. This history of triumph through its armed forces led to Prussia effectively becoming a military state. Following the uprisings in Berlin during the Year of Revolutions in 1848, all traces of liberal or reforming ideologies were swept away, cementing a threefold Prussian cultural identity of conservatism, militarism, and absolutism, all tied inextricably with the monarchy. In time, the overwhelming influence of the military would border on paradomania—an unhealthy psychological obsession with the military—becoming an inseparable part of Prussia's existence.

The efforts made by Fritz and Ada to impart into Dona a love for all things German was no easy task. Throughout her childhood, Germany was little more than an idea, a geopolitical concept desperately struggling to find a cultural and existential identity for itself. The root of the problem was that the German states had once been the Holy Roman Empire. Established in AD 800, this imperial brainchild of Charlemagne's was an attempt to resurrect the Roman Empire in Western Europe, mostly among the German-speaking realms. At its apex, the Holy Roman Empire encompassed more than four hundred states stretching from the English Channel to the Italian Alps. By the sixteenth century, the empire's elected throne had passed into the hands of the Habsburgs. For the next two hundred years, the two greatest German dynasties, the Habsburgs of Austria and the Hohenzollerns of Prussia, used the empire as a shuttlecock in their game of imperial politics.

This lasted almost uninterrupted until the French Revolution and the disastrous Battle of Austerlitz in 1805, in which French forces defeated the Austrians. The day after Christmas, Napoleon effectively dismantled the Holy Roman Empire, and through a complex process, the Austrian Empire was born. Nine years later, following the final defeat of Napoleonic France in 1814 and the Congress of Vienna, those lands that had not been placed under the control of the Austrian crown became a "loose confederation of thirty-eight duchies, kingdoms, and four free cities" that were "ruled by kings, princes, archdukes, dukes, electors, margraves, landgraves, archbishops, and so forth." So disparate were these lands that collectively called themselves "Germany" that some—like Prussia—covered thousands of square miles spread disconnectedly across northern Europe; others—like Augustenburg— "were smaller than Liechtenstein (sixty-one square miles) is today, and most were poor, rural, and sparsely populated."[7] Compared to modern, united countries like Great Britain, the northern European, mostly German states were feudal, undeveloped, and backward.

As a young toddler, the complex politics surrounding Germany, Austria, and the intricate lattice that kept them loosely allied meant little to Dona Holstein. Not until decades later would she realize how significantly these issues impacted her life. In the meantime, the death of her brother Frederick in 1858 meant she was an only child, but she soon became the eldest in a growing family. Her next sibling, a sister named Caroline Matilda, came into the world fifteen months after Dona was born. Nicknamed "Calma," she was considered the prettiest of all the Holstein girls. She was also the sister with whom Dona would always have the closest relationship. Queen Victoria, writing to her daughter Vicky in 1860 after Calma's birth, commented on Ada's frequent pregnancies after only a few years of marriage.

> How can anyone, who has not been married above two years and three quarters rejoice at being a third time in that condition? I positively think those ladies who are always enceinte quite disgusting; it is more like a rabbit or a guinea-pig than anything else and really it is not very nice … Let me repeat once more, dear, that it is very bad for any person to have them very fast—and that the poor children suffer for it even more, not to speak of the ruin it is to the looks of a young woman—which she must not neglect for her husband's sake, particularly when she is a Princess.[8]

Two years later, Fritz and Ada were thrilled when two sons, Gerard and Ernest Günther, were born in 1862 and 1863, respectively. The hereditary prince and princess's efforts to model their family after the German royals they so idolized were encouraged by Ada's family, especially her mother, Dowager Princess Feodora of Hohenlohe-Langenburg. Feodora often passed on advice to her daughter on how to raise her family, advice that came from her half sister the queen.

As was often the case with Victoria, she freely dispensed advice, opinions, or criticisms with a noticeable lack of sensitivity for other people's feelings or circumstances. This was the case when it came to managing the Holsteins' finances. Fritz insisted on maintaining a comfortable lifestyle, but German royals were famous for exorbitant spending and, as a consequence, debt-ridden courts—the king of Bavaria was rumored to be so poor that his weekly pocket money amounted to only twenty cents. "Poor and unimportant in the eyes of the world, the German royal families of the eighteenth and early nineteenth century were at their historical nadir," wrote one of Queen

Victoria's biographers.[9] Despite the fiscal tribulations faced by many of their contemporaries, the Holsteins were not entirely destitute. Christian August was exceptionally frugal with what was left of the settlement he received for his territories in Schleswig-Holstein, enabling him to provide Fritz with Dolzig and a small palace in Gotha. His finances were also augmented by the modest revenues he received from Augustenburg.

Dona's uncomplicated life lasted a mere five years before the Holsteins were overtaken by calamity. Prince Gerard, who had been born at Dolzig in the early weeks of 1862, died four months later. Eighteen months after that, in November 1863, the German Confederation declared war on Denmark over the already battle-scarred twin duchies of Schleswig-Holstein. Later known as the Second Schleswig War of 1863–64, this conflict would have great ramifications for not only Dona's family but also for German and European history. The confederation used the treaty from the First Schleswig War as their casus belli, claiming Denmark violated the accord by trying to absorb the duchies directly into their sovereign borders. For the most part, ethnic Germans "in Schleswig, Holstein, and throughout Germany wanted only the restored independence of the duchies under a prince of their choosing."[10] Overwhelming public opinion looked to the liberal Fritz Holstein as the prince with the most lawful claim to the ducal throne. Following in his father's footsteps, Fritz announced his intention of assuming the throne and began styling himself Frederick VIII, Duke of Schleswig-Holstein.

When it looked as if a German victory over the Danish was imminent, Fritz—believing he would promptly be invested with the mantle of government—departed Dolzig for his Thuringian estate with the goal of being ready to move into the ducal capital, Kiel, at a moment's notice. The decision to leave his family was a difficult one for a man who cared so deeply for his wife and children. If things went according to plan, Fritz reasoned, he would send for his family as soon as he was installed as duke. It is difficult to ascertain exactly when Ada and the children joined Fritz, but it is reasonable to conclude that, given the volatility of the situation and how much the duke cared for his family, he did not want to risk their safety by bringing them so close to an active war zone.

In Fritz's absence, the person who bore the greatest burden of responsibility was Dona's mother, who was now being called the Duchess of Schleswig-Holstein. With her husband shuttling back and forth across Germany trying to shore up support for when he would actually assume the government in Kiel, Ada was left with few resources with which to care for herself and her three young children. Their meager finances evaporated as the duke struggled to pay for his expenses abroad. Coming to Ada's rescue during this period was her cousin Prince Chlodwig of Hohenlohe-Schillingsfürst. A prominent politician who would one day be appointed German chancellor, Chlodwig took an active role in managing what was left of the duchess's money and ensuring her children were provided for. Some thirty years later, Dona's brother Ernest Günther wrote an embittered letter in which he said Prince Chlodwig was the only person who saved their family while their father was away in Kiel squandering their money.

When the Danish surrendered to the victorious German Confederation in 1864, Prussia was given administration of Schleswig, while Austria received Holstein. As the weeks and months rolled by, Fritz Holstein was disconcerted to find that Prussia had still not consented to his entering Kiel and assuming the throne. The person standing in the duke's way was the balding, mustachioed Prussian minister-president, Otto von Bismarck. At first glance, he appeared to be a saturnine, middle-aged statesman entering his political twilight. In reality, he was fiercely ambitious, obsessively conservative, unprogressive, and reactionary. He agreed to Prussia's participation in the Second Schleswig War to further his goal of *Realpolitik*—his unfaltering commitment to establishing Prussian hegemony in German Europe through conquest and annexation; and because Fritz was pro-German, Bismarck saw him as a convenient puppet. Once Prussia had control of Schleswig, Bismarck used the duke to set into motion the next phase of his plan: war with Austria. An integral part of *Realpolitik* was forcing Austria out of the German Confederation—the Austrian emperor had been president of the confederation since 1850—and, by extension, German affairs altogether, since Bismarck believed the Habsburgs were no longer worthy of being leaders of German Europe. Hoping to chum the waters in an effort to get Austria to make a military strike against Prussia, Bismarck launched a vicious campaign to destroy Fritz Holstein and his family. Bismarck openly derided the duke, whom he called "that idiot of Holstein."[11]

By May 1865, the duke had grown tired of Prussian false promises. Using his personal authority as Duke of Schleswig-Holstein, he made his way to Kiel, took up residence in the castle there, and established a provisional government with ministers loaned to him by the Duke of Coburg. It appears that it was at this point that Ada and the children joined Fritz. But even with the presence of his attractive wife and young family, German public opinion began to turn against the duke. Bismarck managed to convince the general public that Fritz's government was illegal under the terms of the treaty that ended the war. He then began a public relations campaign to destroy the duke. By the time the Holsteins were settled in at Kiel Castle, Bismarck had succeeded in spreading so much anti-Augustenburg propaganda that no foreign ambassadors would receive Fritz, and King Wilhelm I of Prussia even accused him of treason.

Fritz managed to keep his government operating in Kiel for almost another year. He was also hesitant to uproot his family again because his wife was into the third trimester of another pregnancy. In April 1866, she gave birth at Kiel Castle to a daughter named Louise Sophie. Contemporary accounts indicate that within a matter of weeks of Louise Sophie's birth, Fritz's government fell apart. Prussia declared it would never recognize his reign, German public opinion was against him, and his support from the international community evaporated. Dejected and utterly defeated, Fritz and his family had returned to Dolzig by June 1866. Children, even young ones, can sometimes sense drastic changes in their parents' moods. It is probable that for a number of months, Dona could see the morose depression that weighed on her father. But if Dona's parents—who, as a courtesy from the King of Prussia, were allowed to continue using the titles Duke and Duchess of Schleswig-Holstein—hoped their return presaged the end of a long, difficult period, they were wrong.

With Fritz out of the picture, there was nothing standing in Bismarck's way from proceeding with the next step in his plan. In June 1866, his coveted Austro-Prussian War began and progressed exactly as he had predicted. States like Hanover and Hesse were told Prussian troops would be marching through their territories to attack Austria. Should they offer any resistance, Prussia would take it as a de facto declaration of war. Hanover and Hesse did just that. Their plight at the hands of Prussia elicited the support of Saxony, Bavaria, Württemberg, and Baden, all of whom categorically sided with Austria.

The decisive hammer stroke was the Battle of Königgrätz, which took place in July. Half a million soldiers fought on both sides that day. It seemed at first that the Austrians were winning, until the Prussian crown prince showed up later in the day with eighty thousand reinforcements, tipping the scales decisively in Prussia's favor. Austrian losses were more than forty-four thousand, while the Prussian casualties were just under nine thousand. The defeat at Königgrätz brought the war to an end with the total defeat of Austria. In the aftermath, Bismarck's short-term ambitions came to be realized when Prussia was able to take full control of both Schleswig and Holstein, and Austria was forced out of the German Confederation permanently. Austria's German allies paid a high price for their choice and were forced to yield large portions of their realms to Prussia. To emphasize one last time the penumbra that was cast over Austria and their allies, the victorious powers reorganized themselves into the Northern German Confederation.

For the Holsteins, the Prussian victory was ruinous. Now in full control of the twin duchies—including Als Island—Prussia confiscated Augustenburg for compensation owed by the family. They evicted Dona's grandfather from his palace and turned the Holsteins into nothing more than mediatised (or fourth-rank) royals at best. Christian August's lifestyle at Augustenburg had continued to be a modest yet comfortable one, and he was able to purchase a new home, Primkenau Castle, in Silesia. Fritz and his family, bereft of their inheritance, settled permanently into their rural palace at Dolzig, uncertain what the future would hold. As with so many important events in European history, no one at the time could have foreseen the far-reaching consequences of conflicts like the Second Schleswig War and the Austro-Prussian War. The Schleswig wars and even Bismarck's campaign to ruin Fritz Holstein would directly alter the course of Dona's life. For the moment, though, as the daughter of a disgraced, dispossessed duke, there was little indication her life would be tapped for greatness. The same was also true for the lives of two other future empresses who had not even been born yet.

As Dona's family struggled to carve out a permanent life for themselves at Dolzig, in England, Princess Mary Adelaide of Teck was enceinte with her first child. Her husband, Prince Francis of Teck, had been making arrangements for the delivery for months. "I am looking over Kensington Palace," he wrote to his sister from his mother-in-law's house in Kew Gardens, "as I want to be established there by at least the 6th.... Let us hope that a nice baby will be born there in the lovely month of May."[12] As if on cue, Mary Adelaide gave birth to a daughter just before midnight on May 26, 1867. Her physician, Dr. Arthur Farre, released an official statement the next day: "Her Royal Highness the Princess Mary Adelaide was safely delivered of a Princess at one minute before midnight on the 26th inst. Her Royal Highness and the infant Princess are doing perfectly well."[13] The girl was named Victoria Mary Augusta Louise Olga Pauline Claudine Agnes. Each of the names chosen had significance for the new parents. Victoria was for the queen of England; Mary was for the infant's mother; Augusta was for Mary Adelaide's mother and also her sister; Claudine was for Francis's mother; and Agnes was for his grandmother. The other names—Louise Olga Pauline—were for various women in the princess's family tree. A less widely known account suggests the infant was initially named Agnes Augusta, which was later switched with Victoria Mary. At her christening on July 27, the infant became officially known as Princess Victoria Mary of Teck, though her family called her simply "May," for the month of her birth. In family correspondences and casual conversations, she was often referred to as May Teck, following the English custom of using peerages as surnames. An impressive royal panoply was in attendance for the July christening at Kensington Palace. Charles Thomas Longley, the archbishop of Canterbury, performed the ceremony, which was presided over by May's godparents: Queen Victoria—whose own birthday was two days before the baby's; Albert Edward ("Bertie"), Prince of Wales; and her maternal grandmother, Augusta, Duchess of Cambridge.

Princess May brought much joy to her parents, Prince Francis of Teck and his wife, Mary Adelaide. Throughout his life, Francis had been a pariah in royal circles. His father, Duke Alexander of Württemberg, had broken one of the sacrosanct laws of royalty in 1835 when he married a commoner, Countess Claudine Rhédey von Kis-Rhéde, a descendant of the great Hungarian king Saint Stephen. The gravitas of this was greater than when Dona's grandfather married his commoner wife because Alexander was in line for the throne of the German kingdom of Württemberg. Not only was Alexander exiled from the obsessively hierarchical German courts, his children were forbidden to use any royal styles or titles—a fact that made Francis overly sensitive to matters of rank. In a gesture of kindness, Emperor Franz Joseph of Austria, with whom Alexander had cultivated a friendship while serving as a captain in the Austrian military, gave his wife and children the titles Count and Countess von Hohenstein. It took nearly thirty years, but Alexander's cousin King Wilhelm I of Württemberg eventually recognized the former's marriage to Claudine and elevated Francis to royal rank by creating him Prince of Teck, a medieval title from the Holy Roman Empire that had not been used since the 1430s. Along with it came the style of Serene Highness, the lowest possible rank royalty could have. Claudine never lived to see that day. She was trampled to death by horses at a military review in 1841.

Claudine's morganatic blood meant that Francis was most likely destined to remain a bachelor. Most princesses wanted nothing to do with him, since he had no fortune and was not in line to inherit any thrones. The little income he did receive came from his meager soldier's pay or the occasional handout from the Austrian emperor. Undaunted, he searched Europe for any meagerly royal bride who would take him. After unsuccessfully trawling the German courts, he crossed paths with Mary Adelaide, daughter of Adolphus, Duke of Cambridge. While the princess was famous for her effervescence, it was frowned upon that she was four years older than Francis. She was also notoriously overweight. One estimate placed her weight at 252 pounds, earning her the unkind nickname "Fat Mary." Her father, Adolphus, once the viceroy of Hanover, was a son of King George III and an uncle of Queen Victoria. Her mother was Princess Augusta of Hesse-Cassel, an aunt of Queen Louise of Denmark. Some contemporaries have claimed that Emperor Napoleon III considered proposing to Mary Adelaide shortly after he was rebuffed by Dona's mother, but the plan fell through when the princess revealed she was unwilling to leave England. A number of other suitors—Prince Wilhelm of Baden, the dukes of Brunswick and Saxe-Meiningen, and a number of others—came and went, but the princess was adamant that she would not leave her home.

By 1859, Mary Adelaide had admitted to the statesman Lord Clarendon that she had made up her mind "to be a *jolly old maid*."[14] However, her relatives within the British royal family were working behind the scenes to play matchmaker on her behalf. So when Francis and Mary Adelaide met for the first time in 1866, it was not by chance. Mary Adelaide's cousin Bertie, Prince of Wales, and his wife, Alexandra, had arranged it all. During a visit to Vienna in 1865, the Prince and Princess of Wales had taken a liking to Francis, whom they thought perfect for Mary Adelaide. "You see, they all wanted to find a husband for my Mother," May said later in life. "So once when King Edward (then Prince of Wales) was out in Vienna he met this handsome young officer in the Austrian Army, liked him, invited him to come to England on a visit, introduced him to my Mother—and everyone seemed to think it would *do*—and it did."[15]

To say that Francis and Mary Adelaide's courtship was brief would be an understatement. "The wooing was but a short affair," Mary Adelaide herself admitted. "Francis only arrived in England on March 6th and we met for the first time on the 7th at St. James's [Palace]. One month's acquaintance settled the question [of marriage], and on April 6th he proposed in KEW GARDENS and was accepted."[16] The fact that Mary Adelaide accepted Francis after knowing him for only a month may seem like desperation, but it proved to be a testament to the high esteem the couple had for one another. In an era marked by disastrous arranged marriages littered with infidelities, May Teck's parents were surprisingly happy. Shortly before May's birth, Mary Adelaide wrote to a friend, "I long to tell you how happy I am, and with what confiding hope I can look forward to a future of bright promise, as *he* is not only all *I* could wish for, but all Mama's heart could possibly desire for her child."[17]

The world in which little May Teck grew up was centered in London, the thriving capital of the British Empire which, by the 1860s, controlled almost one-quarter of the planet. As members of Britain's extended royal family, the Tecks were familiar faces at Queen Victoria's court, though their presence usually caused a stir. As a niece of two former kings, Mary Adelaide was a fairly high-ranking member of the royal family, but Francis was painfully conscious that he remained close to the bottom of the royal totem. This prompted him to overcompensate and throw fits of petulance when he felt he was not being treated with proper royal deference. On many occasions, he sent his wife to plead with Queen Victoria to grant him the higher rank of Highness, which the queen refused each time, for fear of setting a dangerous precedent.[18] Shortly before May was born, Mary Adelaide sent one of her requests to the queen, also asking that her husband receive the Order of the Bath, an honorary chivalric medal created by King George I in 1725. Queen Victoria was growing weary of these constant requests. "The [Order of the] Bath, Prince Teck shall certainly have," she promptly wrote to Mary Adelaide, "but the Title of 'Highness' I think wld be of little use."[19]

The issue of titles and rank was not the only problem facing the Tecks. Although May's parents enjoyed a happy marriage, they were constantly neck-deep in debt. Mary Adelaide received an annual stipend of £7,000. Of this amount, £5,000 came from the Civil List thanks to the efforts of Lord Palmerston, and the other £2,000 came from Mary Adelaide's mother. In today's American dollars, Mary Adelaide's stipend amounted to approximately $656,000, but it was barely enough to cover the family's expenses.[20] Mary Adelaide was famous for her generosity and charitable endeavors, but she always spent more than she had. By the late 1860s, the Tecks managed to bolster their income to £8,000, but they were still spending £15,000 each year.

When May Teck was four, the new king of Württemberg, Charles I, elevated her parents to the rank of Duke and Duchess of Teck. Queen Victoria's foreign secretary, Lord Clarendon, had earlier approached the queen to try and persuade her to use her influence with King Charles to grant Francis a dukedom. She flatly refused. It took five years after King Charles ascended the throne to confer the duchy of Teck on May's father. This thrust Mary Adelaide into a much more visible position in British society, since her husband had now moved up to being a mid-rank royal. Even though she derived satisfaction from vigorously carrying out charitable works and creating improvements for the welfare of her countrymen, the duchess insisted on maintaining a lifestyle she believed was necessary for an English princess. This only worsened the family's debts, and the Tecks were hounded more than ever by creditors. This deeply worried Queen Victoria, who clearly remembered how her uncles, the profligate sons of George III, damaged England's economy by accumulating tens of millions of pounds in debt. The Duchess of Teck's repeated pleas to the queen for money were denied. Eventually, they went unanswered.

Like Dona Holstein, May Teck found herself the eldest child in her family. Her own birth in 1867 was followed by the prompt arrivals of three brothers: Adolphus in 1868, Francis in 1870, and Alexander in 1874. "Mary Teck was safely confined yesterday with another & *still* bigger boy!" Queen Victoria wrote to her daughter the day after Alexander was born.[21] Royalty, especially in the Victorian era, was obsessed with nicknames, no matter how strange they sounded. Consequently, May's brothers became known as Dolly, Frank, and Alge, respectively. The Teck children enjoyed a degree of stability in their lives that Dona and the Holsteins did not. When in London, they resided in the south wing of Kensington Palace. Their use of the palace had been a gift to them from the queen. They shared it with a number of other members of the royal family who occupied flats spread throughout the palace's different wings. Tall and spacious, Kensington Palace's most famous occupant was Queen Victoria herself, who had been born there in 1819—in the same room, in the same bed in which Princess May had been born—and spent the first eighteen years of her life there under the watchful eye of her mother, the Duchess of Kent, and her vile henchman, Sir John Conroy. It was not until her accession in 1837 that she left Kensington Palace.

When the Tecks were not at Kensington Palace, they could be found at their well-loved Richmond Park estate, White Lodge. This grace-and-favor country home came into the Tecks' possession only after Mary Adelaide harangued the queen over the fact that her young children needed a rural estate. The queen acquiesced, partly because Princess May almost died as an infant after contracting a feverish illness from the squalid, unsanitary living conditions in London at that time. Though not a lavish home, White Lodge had a rich heritage. Originally built as a hunting lodge by King George II in 1727, the palatial residence was two stories tall with four Roman pillars on the front facade. Like many of Britain's royal estates, White Lodge changed hands numerous times in its one-hundred-and fifty-year history. Since its construction for George II, the building had been owned by a king, two queens, a princess, and a prime minister. It was here that Horatio Nelson mapped out his attack plans for the Battle of Trafalgar. Later, after Queen Victoria gave it to the Tecks, it would grow to become one of the most familiar homes Princess May would ever have.

Two months after May Teck's third birthday, another German war took place. Unlike the Second Schleswig War and the Austro-Prussian War, which were relatively limited in their impact beyond continental Europe, this third conflict would completely reshape the course of history and would directly impact all four of Europe's last empresses in one way or another. In July 1870, France declared war on Prussia. Not only did the North German Confederation ally with Prussia against France, but so too did the other, nonaligned German states. Even Fritz Holstein obtained semi-redemption by taking up his military commission once again and serving on the general staff of his old friend Crown Prince Frederick Wilhelm of Prussia. The entire war, which began with manipulating France into making a first strike so that Prussia would not look like the aggressor, was strategically planned by Bismarck in the pièce de résistance of his *Realpolitik*. At the Battle of Sedan in September 1870, French forces were quickly defeated by the Prussians, and Emperor Napoleon III personally surrendered. Though he was later released, his government promptly dethroned him, abolished the French monarchy for the last time, and declared the Third Republic on September 5. The broken, battered Napoleon III fled into exile in England, followed later by his wife and son. The last Bonaparte rulers of imperial France spent the remainder of their lives living as guests of their old friend Queen Victoria.

Decisive though the Battle of Sedan was, it did not immediately end the war. The end did not take place until 1871, after a five-month siege of Paris by the Germans led to France's surrender. Out of the innumerable armed conflicts fought in Europe since the beginning of the Late Modern Period, the outcome of the Franco-Prussian War had one of the most significant impacts on both the state of Europe at the time and the course of its future. Along with handing over the provinces of Alsace and Lorraine to German control, which would be a sore spot in French national pride for decades to follow, France was also forced to yield up its status as a great imperial power. The structure, order, and politics that had existed in Europe since the Congress of Vienna were now gone. This opened the door for Otto von Bismarck to see his ambitions for *Realpolitik* bear their long-awaited fruits. During the siege of Paris, German military command had been established in the Palace of Versailles. It was here, in the Hall of Mirrors, that Prussia, the North German Confederation, and the smaller, unaligned states united to form the German Empire. Throughout the ceremony, the windows in the Hall of Mirrors rattled from explosions as gunfire rained down on Paris twelve miles away. While watching the unification ceremony at Versailles, Fritz Holstein remarked to the poet Gustav Freytag, "Such a time changes the opinions of men and imposes new challenges."[22]

At the center of Europe's newest imperial power was the Prussian royal family, the Hohenzollerns. Selected by popular vote, King Wilhelm I of Prussia became the first German emperor—this specific wording was chosen rather than emperor of Germany, which was deemed unacceptable by the empire's other rulers, as it offended their own statuses as heads of state.[23] The Hohenzollerns, now both kings of Prussia and German emperors, became the foremost dynasty on the continent, ruling the preeminent imperial power. With its provenance in Bismarck's *Realpolitik* and its foundation established through militarism, German-speaking Europe's imperial forge was now complete. Germany was no longer an existential anomaly but was now a physical, geopolitical empire whose borders were vast, covering more than three hundred thousand square miles. In the west, it bordered France, Belgium, and Luxembourg and ran along the entire Baltic Sea up to Lithuania and Russia. It shared its southern border with Switzerland and Austria-Hungary.

Governing this vast new empire was no small feat, since united Germany now faced the same internal problems as the other great empires. Ethnic divisions required monitoring, since smaller states like Hesse and Mecklenburg felt little affection for Prussia or the Hohenzollerns. Religious sentiments were also volatile. Many of the northern states were fanatically—and in the case of Prussia, militantly—Lutheran. The south, however, was still Roman Catholic and felt some remaining connection with the nearby bastion of Catholicism in Europe—Austria. Keeping Germany's new political system together was a series of complex royal, national, and federal trellises based around its constitution. Progressives snickered at the word's use in this case, since the German "constitution" was not so much a constitution "in the traditional sense" as much as a "treaty between those sovereign territories that had agreed to form the German empire." In essence, it could be described as "little more than a confederation of principalities (*Fürstenbund*)."[24] Since it was now a federated empire, Germany was comprised of its constituent member states, each of whom still enjoyed a measure of autonomy. States as diverse as Bavaria, Mecklenburg, or the Ernestine duchies[25] retained a certain legal and constitutional independence but only as part of a larger body. The independence of these states was pronounced enough that they still maintained their own ambassadors. Conversely, foreign courts sent their own envoys to Dresden, Munich, and the other constituent capitals.

From among these states, it was Prussia that became the standard-bearer of the empire. As part of Germany, Prussia comprised "65 per cent of the surface area and 62 per cent of the population," giving it "*de facto* hegemony."[26] The Prussian capital of Berlin was the natural choice for the seat of the new imperial government, which was now responsible for foreign policy, the military, and other imperial matters. The individual rulers of the constituent states still maintained domestic and ceremonial duties as their royal prerogatives, but the political, administrative, and monarchical composition of the new German Empire was more or less grafted onto the setup of the Hohenzollern monarchy in Prussia, which had already been in existence for 170 years. While the empire did have something akin to a parliamentary body, the Reichstag, it was merely an evolution of the increasingly superfluous Prussian *Landtag*. It had little authority to govern beyond budgets and taxation, though it could enact some legislation. Its official power was also heavily counterbalanced by the Bundesrat, the council of the empire's sovereign princes, whose approval was required to enact legislations. The ultimate power rested with the emperor. He was something of a neoabsolutist ruler. Even the imperial chancellor—the first of whom was, naturally, Otto von Bismarck, who was created a prince in 1871 by Wilhelm I for his role in uniting Germany—was answerable only to the crown rather than the Reichstag. Almost half a century later, this structure would prove to be imperial Germany's Achilles' heel.

⊸⊰⊱⊸

In the year following the end of the Franco-Prussian War, when Dona Holstein was thirteen and May Teck was five, another child joined the rarefied circle of Europe's last imperial consorts. On June 6, 1872, a baby girl was born to Prince Louis of Hesse-Darmstadt and his wife, Princess Alice, at the New Palace in Darmstadt, capital of the small German state of Hesse.[27] The baby's proud parents named her Victoria Alix Helena Louise Beatrice, or simply Alix for short. At her Lutheran christening on July 1, Alix's godparents were chosen: her maternal uncle and aunt the Prince and Princess of Wales; the Tsarevitch and Tsarevna of Russia; her maternal aunt Princess Beatrice of England; her great-great-aunt the Duchess of Cambridge; and Princess Anne of Prussia.

The baby's mother, Alice, was the third child of Queen Victoria, and she chose the names in honor of each of her sisters—Alix was the Germanicized form of Alice. Little Alix's father, Louis, was the nephew of the Grand Duke of Hesse, and he was second in line to the throne after his father. He and Alice were married, almost sight unseen, in 1862. The union had been largely orchestrated by Alice's father, Prince Albert, who dreamed of the day Germany would be unified under a liberal, parliamentary monarchy following Britain's example. Queen Victoria and Prince Albert used their greatest asset to help bring about their Pan-German vision: royal marriages. Their eldest daughter, Vicky, had married the heir to the Prussian throne, but it did not take long for that dream to flounder; she was viewed with bitterness and suspicion in Berlin for her unwillingness to forsake her Englishness and become a true Prussian. Alice, it was hoped, could redeem the dream, but when Prince Albert died unexpectedly from typhoid fever in 1861, Germany's champion was gone, and the possibility of marriage between the royal houses of England and Hesse looked bleak. In response to her father's death, and to escape her mother's intense mourning, Alice hastily agreed to marry Prince Louis. The ceremony on July 1, 1862, was held in the dining room at Osborne House on the Isle of Wight, off the southern coast of England. Queen Victoria described it as being more like a funeral than a wedding. So consumed was the queen by her own continuing grief over Albert's death that she barely noticed Alice's departure from the family circle: "Much as she has been to me ... and dear and precious as a comfort and an assistance, I hardly miss her at all, or felt her going—so utterly alone am I."[28]

Though their marriage was loving and genuine, a gulf emerged between the couple—Princess May's maternal grandmother, the Duchess of Cambridge, described it as "an insignificant match." Like her father, Alice was intellectual, cultivated, and a gifted erudite. By contrast, Louis, in the words of one British politician, was a "dull boy" from "a dull family in a dull country."[29] It was well known that the prince was shy, tongue-tied, and easily influenced by others, especially by his mother-in-law, Queen Victoria. Life in Darmstadt was also a far cry from the abundant surroundings of Alice's childhood in England. The semipenurious nature of the Hessian court was highlighted by the fact that Louis and Alice's first home was a little house on some dingy street in Darmstadt's Old Quarter. They would be forced to wait until a proper residence could be built for them.

Though their marriage lacked the intellectual stimulation Alice craved, she and Louis were blessed with many children, each of whom they adored. When Alix was born in 1872, she joined three sisters—Victoria (b. 1863), Elizabeth ("Ella," b. 1864), and Irene (b. 1866)—and two brothers, Ernest Louis ("Ernie," b. 1868) and Frederick ("Frittie," b. 1870). She was later joined by another sister, Marie ("May," b. 1874). The birth of seven children so close together did not stop Alice from pursuing projects to improve the quality of life in Hesse. She was vitally important to the establishment of modern nursing practices in Germany. She established such a high reputation for nursing that some of the more progressive minds in Britain compared her to Florence Nightingale. In Darmstadt, she established her own facility, the Alice Hospital, which treated the city's poor at no cost. Alice's pioneering efforts in Hessian medical care in the 1870s proved invaluable during the Franco-Prussian War, when hundreds of wounded soldiers were sent to Darmstadt for medical attention.

The first years of Alix's life were similar to those of May Teck's. Both princesses were raised by loving parents who lavished upon them affection. In this atmosphere, little Alix of Hesse-Darmstadt thrived. So warm and loving was her disposition that many who met her could not help but call her "Sunny." Princess Alice once described her daughter as "a sweet, merry little person, always laughing and [who had] a dimple in one cheek."[30] Others in the family, especially Queen Victoria with her infatuation for nicknames for her grandchildren, took to calling her Alicky.

Alix's life in Hesse centered on Darmstadt, a medieval city of seventy thousand people located just a few miles from the bank of the Rhine River. Its narrow cobblestone streets wove through the city, converging in the center at the New Palace, which had been designed and built specifically for Alice and her family and was subsidized mostly by Queen Victoria personally. The parks that surrounded the palace were thickly dotted with trees and bushes. For vacations, Louis and Alice enjoyed taking their family to the closest thing they had to a holiday home—the gray, turreted castle of Kranichstein, forty miles northeast of Darmstadt. Its bucolic setting, with its dense forests, private lake, and free-roaming wildlife, afforded the family a respite from the hustle and bustle of Darmstadt.

At the time Alix was born in 1872, Hesse was ruled by her paternal great-uncle Grand Duke Louis III. The nation had changed shape numerous times throughout the centuries and had experienced a long and colorful history. For more than six hundred years, it was an important member of the Holy Roman Empire as a landgraviate, a feudal state ruled by an imperial count (or landgrave) that was answerable to the emperor. After the empire was dismantled in 1806, Hesse threw in its lot with Napoleon. As a reward for supporting the French Empire, Napoleon elevated Hesse to a grand duchy. Later, it was a partisan member of the German confederations until it joined with the other states as part of the German Empire.

The rulers of Hesse were known mainly for two traits. First, they had a talent for making bad alliances. In the Thirty Years' War of 1618–48, the landgrave of Hesse sided with the Holy Roman emperor, who suffered a long, drawn-out, humiliating defeat. Two centuries later, the landgrave of Hesse took up the cause of revolutionary France during the Napoleonic Wars. When the Bonapartist forces were defeated, Hesse was forced to give up huge swaths of land at the Congress of Vienna in 1815 but was allowed to keep its grand ducal status. The final humiliation came when Louis III sided against Prussia in the Austro-Prussian War of 1866. The outcome was nothing short of a disaster for the grand duke and his country. When Prussia emerged victorious after only two months, it seized the entire northern half of Hesse and deposited a regiment of Prussian soldiers in Darmstadt for six weeks. Thankfully, the general population was spared from violence by their Prussian occupiers, but the country was forced to pay an indemnity of 3 million florins. Princess Alice was forced to use most of her £30,000 dowry to go toward payment of this. The situation became so difficult for Darmstadt's citizens that their burgomaster hung himself. As a consequence of all these factors, Alix grew up in the firm belief that Hesse was completely isolated "from the rest of Germany, which she looked on as Prussia and as a different country."[31]

The second trait that the Hessian dynasty was famous for was its royal connections. Over the centuries, the family had succeeded in forging a number of matrimonial alliances. Alix's father had married an English princess. The family tree also included a long list of reigning consorts, which included a queen of Prussia, an empress of Russia, an imperial electress, and four grand duchesses. This connection with Russia—Louis III's sister was the Russian empress—was what saved Hesse from being permanently swallowed up after the war in 1866. One day, Alix would be able to add herself to this list of Hessian marital triumphs by becoming the last empress of Russia.

Shortly before Alix's first birthday, her pleasant childhood came to an abrupt end. Her brothers Frittie and Ernie were playing together when the two-year-old Frittie slipped from a windowsill and fell twenty feet onto a balustrade. He died a few hours later from a brain hemorrhage. The fall itself was not enough to kill the toddler. His cause of death was far more sinister. Frittie suffered from hemophilia, the dreaded disease that prevents blood from clotting. Had he not been a hemophiliac, he may have survived the fall. The confirmation of Frittie's illness came shortly before the accident when a small cut on his ear bled unstoppably for three days. What was even more tragic about his death was the fact that he inherited the disease from his mother.

In the makeup of hemophilia, it is carried by women but is suffered only by men—only in infinitesimally rare cases, when first cousins married, had female sufferers been reported. Princess Alice had herself inherited the defective gene from Queen Victoria. Alice's brother Leopold, Duke of Albany, was a hemophiliac. Leopold had defied the odds and survived into adulthood—and even married and started a family. Moved by Frittie's death, he sent Alice his condolences. "I know too well what it is to suffer as he would have suffered, and the great trials of not being able to enjoy life or to know what happiness is," he wrote. "I cannot help saying to myself that it is perhaps well that the dear child has been spared all the trials and possible miseries of a life of ill health like mine."[32] Princess Alice was overcome with grief over the fact that she was partly responsible for her son's death. She described to Queen Victoria the pain of losing her child: "The horror of my darling's sudden death at times torments me too much … He was such a bright child … I miss the little feet, the coming to me … and Ernie feels so lost, poor love."[33]

At the time Frittie died in 1873, hemophilia was a little-understood disease that had only recently been acknowledged by medical science. A more comprehensive understanding of it did not emerge until after 1918. Frittie's diagnosis as a hemophiliac brought with it a moment of grim realization not only for Alix's parents but for all of Queen Victoria's descendants. There was no doubt that the Duke of Albany's case was not an isolated incident within the royal family. The defective genes causing hemophilia were being passed on by the queen of England herself. The fact that hemophilia was not apparent in the families of either of her parents has led many to wonder whether or not the disease actually began with Queen Victoria. John Van der Kiste, one of the most widely known modern royal biographers, made this assertion about hemophilia in his book, *Queen Victoria's Children*: "Medical and scientific theory [*sic*] have singled Queen Victoria out as the first royal carrier of haemophilia. The gene may have originated in her by spontaneous mutation, or it may have been inherited through her mother, though no instances of it have been traced in the Duchess of Kent's relations. Leopold was the only victim among the Queen's children and therefore the only male carrier." Van der Kiste also asserted that because her father was a member of the British royal family, had he or any of his relatives been hemophiliacs, it is doubtful they could have hidden it from the public.[34]

Surprisingly, out of Queen Victoria's four sons, Leopold was the hemophiliac, but over time, it would be discovered that three of her daughters—Vicky, Alice, and Beatrice—were all carriers who passed it on to some of their children. It was eventually proven that two of Victoria's grandsons and six of her great-grandsons were hemophiliacs. It has been generally agreed upon that Victoria never knew that she was the source of the defective gene, instead blaming her husband's lecherous Coburg relatives. On a personal level, Alice realized in the wake of Frittie's death that any of her daughters could be carriers. What no one knew at the time was that Alix was indeed a carrier, and the consequences of that fact would one day help destabilize one of the most powerful empires the world had ever known.

2

"Sleeping Beauty!"

(1873–83)

In Britain, Princess May and her siblings continued to enjoy a relatively stable family life untainted by political upheaval, war, or illness. Like most Victorian children, their first years were spent largely in their nursery. From an early age, May and her brothers showed ample proof that they had inherited their father's volatile temper. The boys were especially boisterous and could be regularly spotted wrestling on their nursery floor. These opportunities afforded young May the chance to hone her natural tact and diplomacy, as she was often required to play peacemaker between her rowdier brothers.

Unlike other upper-class families of the era, who gave the care of their children almost exclusively over to governesses, the Duke and Duchess of Teck were actively involved in raising their children. This was due, at least in part, to their strained finances, which meant their children could never be formally educated or cared for in the same way other royals were. Their parents did make a concerted effort to bring in some household staff—they were eventually able to hire a single governess, the Hanoverian-born Anna Mund. When the children were little, this absence of formal staff suited the duke very well, since he loved nothing more than to poke his head into the spacious, airy nursery at Kensington Palace, or to play on the floor with his sons; formal nurses and tutors would have frowned upon such indecorous intrusions. While Mary Adelaide was somewhat less hands-on than her husband, she was keen to ensure her children grew up with great probity. Thanks to her influence, paramount in May's formative years was a strong sense of noblesse

24

oblige, which suited the kindhearted princess, who was praised for being "a personable young woman, thoughtful, studious and observant."[1]

When the family went off to White Lodge, their Richmond Park estate on the outskirts of London, an even less disciplined atmosphere prevailed than at Kensington. Visitors to White Lodge often found May and her brothers playing with their more famous cousins, the children of the Prince and Princess of Wales. As children of the future king, they were in the spotlight far more often than the Teck children and were much more conscious of their vaunted position. More rambunctious than the Tecks, it was not uncommon to see "the Wales brood on the warpath, sliding on tea trays and ringing bells to call the servants endlessly."[2] Their behavior, though, was not always endearing. The Wales cousins had become so unruly that the Teck children—and most of their other childhood friends—got into the habit of putting their best toys away in the nursery cupboard before a playdate to ensure they were not manhandled, damaged, or completely destroyed.

Playdates were not the only time May saw her more famous cousins. The Duchess of Teck and the Princess of Wales were regularly seen out and about doing charity work with their daughters in tow. During one charity bazaar at Kew Gardens, May and her mother ran their own booth with Princess Alexandra and "the Wales girls"—Maud, Victoria ("Toria"), and Louise. When a wealthy lady bought a fan with Princess May's portrait on it, she asked the young girl to autograph it. "With pleasure," she replied excitedly, "but are you not mistaking me for one of my cousins of Wales?"[3] These childhood memories that May created with her cousins marked the beginning of some ultimately historic relationships. She became lifelong friends with Princess Maud and got to know two young princes who would change the course of her life. These boys were Princess Alexandra's sons Albert Victor ("Eddy") and George ("Georgie"). The two brothers would have a profound impact on May Teck's life, with one of them destined to be her fiancé and the other her husband.

In the years following the death of Alix's brother Frittie, her mother, Alice, did everything in her power to give her children as loving and secure a home as possible. The greatest support for Alix's family during this time was the redoubtable Queen Victoria. She and Alice wrote to each other on a regular basis. The princess asked her mother for advice on everything from proper eating habits for her children to her choices of tutors and governesses.

As Alix grew into a young girl, her cheeriness did not dwindle. She was allowed to prosper and thrive in the cultivated atmosphere that prevailed in Darmstadt. Princess Alice insisted on modeling life in Hesse after the British court. Alice emphasized to her mother her attempts to mimic life in England: "I try to copy as much as is in my power all those things for my children that they may have an idea when I speak to them of what a happy home ours was."[4] The New Palace was decorated with British trimmings. Meals were thoroughly English with common staples like rice puddings and baked apples. Alice boasted to Queen Victoria that "the decoration and domestic arrangements were so English that it was hard to realise one was in Germany."[5] Even the head of the children's nursery, Mary Anne Orchard, came straight from England. A bare-bones, straight-laced woman who had no taste for extravagance, Mrs. Orchard made sure Alix and her siblings were brought up with simple tastes. "The children's bedrooms were large and airy, but plainly furnished," wrote Robert Massie in his definitive biography, *Nicholas and Alexandra*. "Mrs. Orchard believed in strict daily schedules with fixed hours for every activity."[6] Mrs. Orchard was not the only Englishwoman employed at the Hessian court. Princess Alice also brought a woman to Darmstadt named Miss Jackson, who served as Alix's governess. It was under Jackson's tutelage that the young princess first took an interest in politics, "which later was to prove fatal."[7] Alice's efforts to model Darmstadt after the British court came at a high price. The expenses she incurred were well beyond the financial resources available to her and Louis. Eventually, her requests to Queen Victoria for money put a difficult strain on their relationship.

In 1877, Alix's family underwent two drastic changes. First, Louis's father, the heir to the Hessian throne, died in March. "These have been most painful—most distressing days, so harrowing," Alice wrote to her mother. "The recollections of 1861 [when Prince Albert died], of dear Frittie's death, when my dear father-in-law was so tender and kind, were painfully vivid."[8] Three months later, Alix's great-uncle died, making her father Grand Duke Louis IV. With the accession of Alix's father, her mother was now the Grand Duchess of Hesse, but it was not a role Alice relished. She told her mother that, when it came to being the new first lady of the land, "I am so dreading every thing, and above all the responsibility of being the first in every thing."[9] Her new position was not without its benefits, though. As the heads of state, Louis and Alice received a moderate improvement in their finances, since they now had access to the small Hessian treasury. Louis's accession to the grand ducal throne only widened the chasm separating him and Alice. In a telling letter, Alice explained to Louis how happy she would have been "if I had been able to share my intellectual interests, and intellectual aspirations with a husband whose strong, protective love would have guided me round the rocks strewn in my way by my own nature, outward circumstances, and the excesses of my own opinions." She added that she had tried to talk to him about more serious matters, but "we have developed separately—away from each other; and that is why I feel that true companionship is an impossibility for us—because our thoughts will never meet."[10] The difficulties Alix's parents faced, both in their marriage and as the first couple of Hesse, were soon overshadowed by the greatest tragedy their family would ever endure.

A deadly strain of diphtheria invaded Darmstadt in November 1878, cutting straight to the heart of the grand ducal family. The entire family, save for Alice and Ella, fell ill. Queen Victoria sent her chief physician, Sir William Jenner, as did her daughter Vicky in Berlin. Alice nursed her family with the utmost care. It was the second time in her life she played the role of nurse. The first time, she lovingly took care of her father during his fatal battle with typhoid fever in 1861. Now, as she tended to her children, she wrote to Queen Victoria that the pain of "knowing all these precious lives [are] hanging on a thread, is an agony barely to be conceived."[11] On November 16, Alix's sister May died from the illness. The poor toddler literally choked to death from the effects of the infection. Devastated, the grand duchess, who was exhausted and worn down from caring for her family, went to break the news to her son Ernie. Against her doctors' orders, she tearfully embraced him, but this act of a grieving mother would cost Alice her life. She fell ill with diphtheria on December 7. On Friday, December 13, Grand Duke Louis was told his wife would not recover. The next morning, just before 8:30 a.m., Alice died. The date was December 14, "the horrible day" when her father died seventeen years earlier at Windsor Castle. The last two words Alice murmured were: "Dear Papa."[12]

The Duchess of Teck, whose own children had once been ill with diphtheria, was grieved by the loss of Princess Alice. She wrote the following to the Countess of Hopetown:

> Now again the shadow of a great sorrow has fallen upon us, in which the whole country warmly and touchly [*sic*] sympathises. Those poor bereaved ones, in that once so *happy* home, are never out of my thoughts, and my *very heart* bleeds for them. God help them! for He alone can! The poor Queen is so sadly shaken, though more composed than I expected, and very resigned.... I have just been summoned to Windsor to-morrow, to be present at the religious service which the Queen is going to have in the private

Chapel of the Castle at the same hour (2.30) as that at which the last sad ceremony at Darmstadt is to take place.[13]

With her mother gone, Alix's world imploded. The very heart and soul of her family was gone. Queen Victoria's heart broke for her Hessian grandchildren. She poured out her grief in a letter to them: "Poor dear children for I write this for you *all*—You have all had the most terrible blow which can befall Children—you have lost your precious, dear, devoted Mother who loved you—and devoted her life to you & your dear Papa!"[14]

The deaths of her mother and sister were among the most important events that shaped Alix's life. Before this, she was warm and loving, though possessing a stubborn streak. After these tragedies, she began to shut down, cutting herself off emotionally from other people. Even those objects that all children would cling to for comfort—toys, playthings, and clothes—were taken away from her during this horrible time. To prevent the spread of the diphtheria, they were burned. "In one fell swoop," wrote one historian, "everything that had been familiar and comforting to the six-year-old Alix was suddenly and permanently wrenched from her. Alicky withdrew into herself—setting a pattern that would mark her propensity to withdraw and brood."[15] This behavior was not purely spontaneous. When Alice was a young girl, she demonstrated a melancholy, oversensitive personality that, while giving her greater compassion for people than most of what Queen Victoria's other children possessed, birthed somewhat darker moods that she ostensibly passed on to Alix.

A month after the grand duchess's death, Alix and her family visited the queen in January 1879, once the doctors decided it was safe for them to travel. "Next week the dear Queen expects the poor Grand Duke and his motherless children over," the Duchess of Teck wrote, "and I shall be most thankful for them all when the dreaded painful first meeting is over."[16] A few days later, Alix's aunt Beatrice, Queen Victoria's youngest daughter, sent the Duchess of Teck a note when the Hesse family arrived: "I cannot tell you how sad the meeting yesterday with Louis and the Children was. For the first time to miss darling Alice, and to see him alone [*sic*]. It all brought our terrible loss so vividly before us."[17] During the visit, Grand Duke Louis came to Kensington Palace to see Mary Adelaide. The duchess was deeply moved by his demeanor, which she described as "utterly broken hearted."[18]

Grand Duke Louis found himself at a loss caring for his five young children alone. One of his family's few refuges was Wolfsgarten, a hunting lodge between Darmstadt and Frankfurt. The grand duke purchased the building after Alice's death. In time it became the family's preferred residence over the New Palace. In Alice's absence, Queen Victoria stepped into the role of loving matriarch. She embraced the grand duke as her own son and frequently invited him and his children to stay with her in Britain for prolonged periods. She also decreed that Alice's sister Helena would visit Darmstadt every year to provide the family with a maternal presence. The children, in turn, would spend part of every holiday they took in England with Princess Helena and her family. In time, Balmoral Castle in the fog-laden Scottish Highlands and Osborne House, the queen's vacation home on the Isle of Wight, became as comforting and familiar to Alix as the New Palace in Darmstadt. Alix later said her visits to Balmoral and Osborne were "the best part of the year."[19] The years that Alix spent at her grandmother's side shaped the very foundation of the woman, and eventually the empress, she became.

She visited Windsor Castle in March 1879 for the wedding of her uncle, the Duke of Connaught, to Princess Louise of Prussia. Unlike Buckingham Palace, which was a relatively new building, Windsor Castle had been an iconic home of the English monarchy since the eleventh century. A fortresslike abode with high stone walls, it remains the longest-used royal residence in Europe. Princess Alix's visit here revealed to her for the first time the true opulence of her maternal ancestry. Before this, she had only known the isolated but comfortable world at Darmstadt, where she and her sisters sewed their own socks and waited on themselves. In Britain, as a granddaughter of the queen, Alix was fondled over and treated to incomparable luxury. Despite the glamour of London, she preferred peace and quiet. While she was in Britain, she enjoyed playing quietly with her siblings or having personal time with her grandmother, who was affectionately known as "Gangan."

Princess Alix became a true by-product of the Victorian court who espoused the highest morals of the era. She was conservative in her personal and political views—withdrawn, almost cold, when out in public. But in private, she burned with well-guarded emotion. She also echoed her grandmother's extremely shy personality by hating one of the most integral duties of royalty: being on display. Once, when Alix was asked by the queen to play the piano for a room full of dinner guests, she was overcome with anxiety. Her "clammy hands felt literally glued to the keys," she told a friend later in life.[20] She described it as "one of the worst ordeals of her life."[21] Even in the relative quiet of the Hessian court, Alix's shyness showed itself. Her "shyness became so crippling that visitors to Darmstadt sometimes took the little princess's tied tongue for arrogance."[22] Princess Marie of Edinburgh, her cousin, wrote that Alix's "attitude to the world was perpetually distrustful...strangely empty of tenderness and, in a way, hostile...She held both great and small at a distance, as though they intended to steal something which was hers."[23]

Alix's aunt Vicky, Queen Victoria's eldest daughter, was less sympathetic toward the princess than her grandmother. Vicky felt the death of Alix's mother left her spoiled and overindulged, leading to her being obdurate, melodramatic, and self-centered. Vicky's opinion of Alix was somewhat ironic, given her failure raising her three eldest children, but not everything she said was inaccurate. What Vicky perceived as self-centeredness was actually Alix's intense insecurity. She was terrified to open up and care for others out of fear she would lose them. In the end, the only person who seemed to fill that void in her life was Queen Victoria. It is not surprising Alix came to idolize her grandmother. She began using English as her first language in an effort to distance herself from the painful memories of Darmstadt. The queen, in turn, became Alix's English refuge. She described the queen as "a combination of a very grand person and Santa Claus."[24] Queen Victoria undoubtedly became the woman she loved most in the world, and the queen was just as devoted to Alix. She was very affectionate toward her Hessian grandchildren, even more so than toward many of her English grandchildren—the Prince and Princess of Wales' children never enjoyed the same level of intimacy with the queen that Alix and her siblings did. Not until the arrival of other grandchildren years later did the queen come to be affectionately known as "Gangan" by a wider group of her descendants. As the years passed, the queen's love for her Hessian grandchildren grew deeper. She hoped they would come to see her as a second mother. She emphasized this point when she wrote to Alix's sister, Princess Victoria, hoping she would look upon the queen as "a loving *Mother* (for I feel I *am that* to you beloved Children far *more* than a Grandmother)."[25]

Dona Holstein's parents struggled to carve out a life for their family at Dolzig Palace in the years following the end of the Second Schleswig and the Austro-Prussian wars. Duke Frederick VIII was overcome with depression but—like the Duke of Teck—was tenderly attached to his children and sought comfort and consolation with his son and daughters. The Duchess of Schleswig-Holstein was unable to cope with her family's misfortunes as easily as her husband—a quality that would later be recognized in Dona. The birth of her daughter Louise Sophie in 1866 only worsened her somber ennui. Ada became moody, erratic, and gloomy. What we now know as postpartum depression is a possible explanation of what was causing havoc on the duchess's personality, creating a chasm between Ada and her children that would only widen with time. Contemporary accounts show that Dona and her sisters were much closer with their father than they ever were with their mother.

At this point in her life, Dona's day-to-day activities were still overseen by the ducal chaplain and her English governess. The governess's efforts allowed Dona to become fluent in English by the time she was ten. Whether playing in the nursery or sitting through Bible lessons with the chaplain, discipline reigned supreme in the Holstein household. Like most princesses of that period, especially the German ones, Dona and her sisters were trained to be reserved, submissive, and obedient. The rare times that Dona misbehaved, the governess would use Otto von Bismarck's name to scare her into obedience. All she had to do was "say 'Bismarck kommt!' when her charge was not amenable to nursery authority. The little Princess was at once ready to do anything she was told, for fear the enemy of her house might appear."[26]

A few months before Dona's eleventh birthday in 1869, her paternal grandfather, Duke Christian August II, died. The Duke of Schleswig-Holstein-Sonderburg-Augustenburg's last years had been disheartening ones. Increasingly infirmed, he and his wife rarely left their isolated estate, Primkenau Castle, where they had moved to following the end of the Second Schleswig War. The misfortunes that had fallen upon the House of Augustenburg became even more unbearable for Christian August when his wife died in March 1867. In a twist that truly evokes notions of a fateful romance, Christian August and his wife died on exactly the same day, March 11, two years apart. The duke's death in 1869 meant Dona's father now inherited his father's entire estate. This included a small fortune and Christian August's impressive Silesian castle, Primkenau, located near a town of the same name. Following his father's funeral, Fritz sold Dolzig Palace to produce enough money to facilitate the move to the grander Primkenau. Located in the present-day, southwestern Polish town of Przemków, Primkenau was an iconic fairy-tale castle that sat deep in a verdant forest, nestled on the shores of a tiny lake. Visitors always described it as a "fair castle, looking, turret for turret and battlement for battlement, as if torn bodily from the pages of some quaint, beautifully illuminated volume of legends."[27]

During Dona's first summer at Primkenau in July 1870, the Franco-Prussian War broke out. Fritz was invited by his old friend Crown Prince Frederick Wilhelm of Prussia to serve in the military forces of the North German Confederation The offer was tantamount to semi-redemption for the duke, who was eager to fight for Prussia and Germany against France. The duke returned home from war in 1871 after the unification ceremony at Versailles and the eventual French surrender. By the time Fritz returned, Dona was nearly thirteen years old. She was slender, though perhaps a bit short for her age, with thick, golden-blonde hair, a smooth, porcelain complexion, but with tiny, round ears and a short, stout chin. Despite having a slim figure, observers always remarked on her round, pudgy cheeks and jaw, a trait all of her sisters inherited. She was never considered a classically beautiful child, but her regal bearing and queenly manner were unmistakable. Of all the children of the Duke and Duchess of Schleswig-Holstein, it was Dona who was described as possessing the most graceful, dignified carriage. The staff at Dolzig, and later Primkenau, observed that the princess was always aware of any situation she was in and the necessary behavior that was expected. A later contemporary of Dona's noted that "she was always dignified; she never forgot herself."[28]

As a young girl, Dona had a natural artistic ability for drawing and sketching, though this was not stressed heavily at any point in her education. Her taste in music was typical for the period, embracing traditional German composers and operas. She showed little interest or taste for the more classical Italian pieces. A good and disciplined student, though not terribly bright, she did her best to be attentive in her lessons. History most appealed to her when it revolved around Germany, especially Prussia—proof that the indiscretions of the past, courtesy of Otto von Bismarck, had by now been more or less forgotten by her. Books and newspapers were noticeably omitted from her education. Religious tutoring in the Evangelical Lutheran faith impacted her greatly. The black-and-white nature of God, the devil, sin, and salvation appealed to her way of looking at the world. All indicators are that German was her first language, though she spoke English fluently. She may have been tutored in French, but how long these lessons were carried out is hard to determine. Like most princesses, she also excelled in handicrafts like knitting, sewing, and crochet. Beyond the formal lessons in the schoolroom at Primkenau, Dona was being taught other lessons by her father. The idea of a German prince personally educating his daughter was truly a modern one in the nineteenth century. The duke insisted on taking an active role in Dona's upbringing. He insisted on a vigorous exercise regimen that began early each morning. In good and bad weather alike, Fritz took Dona and Calma on long walks in the vast forests surrounding the castle.

Money continued to be a problem, even as Dona entered her adolescent years. Maintaining their large castle and its expansive grounds required so much money that the family could not even afford a formal carriage if they wanted to travel. When they wanted to go anywhere, the duke was forced to hire a local farmer to chauffeur them in a hand-drawn wooden cart sometimes pulled by a cow or a mule. Their own financial troubles did not stop the Holsteins from working to improve the quality of life for the peasants living around their estate. When the Holsteins arrived at Primkenau, the level of poverty was quite high. To help those less fortunate, Fritz provided jobs on his estate for those that wanted them. He later began donating considerable sums of money for the ducal chaplain to use to help those living nearby who suffered from serious needs. Even the meager pocket money Dona received was often saved up and distributed in large amounts by the local pastors at Christmas. Most of the time, Dona and her sisters went with the chaplain to give out money and tend to the needs of the local populations. It was normal for them to make long treks into the countryside on foot, loaded with money, gifts, and medicine. One particularly touching story about Dona recalled her "walking with her sister in the country lanes near Primkenau, [when] she saw an old woman dragging a little cart with great difficulty. The Princesses ran to her, and themselves dragged the cart up the hill."[29]

It was in this humble, picturesque setting in the summer of 1875 that seventeen-year-old Dona and her sister Calma were confirmed in the Evangelical Lutheran Church. The simple ceremony, which was presided over by a certain Pastor Meissner, was attended by only the duke, duchess, and their family and household. Meissner commented that he was "delighted at the answers given by his pupils" during the service.[30] Now that Dona was officially recognized as a young woman, the duke and duchess decided it was time for her to appear at more well-connected courts. Since Fritz and Ada had little disposable income beyond what they needed to maintain Primkenau, these trips were often financed by their relatives in Coburg, Baden, and Carlsruhe. Dona was especially fond of visiting her uncle and aunt the Prince and Princess of Hohenlohe-Langenburg. The Holsteins were not so poor that traveling was limited to Germany. On more than one occasion, Dona visited the south of France, which had only recently become a popular vacation spot for royals. She seemed to display little affection for the French Mediterranean; her tastes were unfalteringly German.

Dona's travels also invariably took her to England to visit her uncle Prince Christian of Schleswig-Holstein-Sonderburg-Augustenburg and his wife, Princess Helena. As the third daughter of Queen Victoria, Helena was extremely wealthy—compared to Dona's family. This wealth paid for the couple's seventeenth-century home, Cumberland Lodge, in Windsor Great Park. As a guest at Cumberland, Dona naturally gravitated toward Helena, who was only twelve years older than herself, rather than her unseemly, middle-aged uncle. Christian—like many of the other Holsteins—had no claim to fame. The closest semblance he ever had to a career was serving in the Prussian army. He was stripped of his commission and banished from Prussia after the Second Schleswig War simply for being Fritz Holstein's younger brother. Now middle-aged, he had no money, little hair, bad teeth, and smoked incessantly. In later years, he became especially eccentric after losing one of his eyes when he was accidentally shot in the face by his brother-in-law the Duke of Connaught. He amassed a large collection of glass eyes that he brought out at dinner parties to show his unlucky guests. "He would explain the history of each at great length," recalled one witness, "his favourite being a blood-shot eye which he wore when he had a cold."[31]

During Dona's prolonged stay in England in 1878, she became acquainted with the tall, handsome Prince Wilhelm ("Willy") of Prussia. He was the eldest child of Fritz Holstein's old friend Crown Prince Frederick ("Fritz") of Germany, and his wife, Vicky, Queen Victoria's eldest daughter. Dona and Willy had first met in 1868, when the Holsteins visited Willy's parents in Potsdam, but it was not until their encounter at Cumberland Lodge that they first really noticed each other. "It was there [at Cumberland], that William and I fell in love with each other," Dona recalled later in life.[32] Vicky had hoped for some time that her son would cross paths with Dona, whom she thought would make an excellent wife. "I hear much about your Cousins of Holstein!" she wrote to Willy in May 1878. "Victoria [Dona] is the favorite of Uncle Christian & Aunt Helena, & they also think her the prettiest which I fancy you do also!"[33]

Dona and Willy's relationship took a decisive turn in 1879. The prince was on a hunting trip at Görlitz, near Primkenau, when he received an invitation from Dona's father to join him for a pheasant hunt. Willy accepted—at his parents' insistence—and arrived in late April. One afternoon, when Willy was exploring the gardens around the castle, he came upon Dona, dressed in a white muslin gown with flowers in her golden hair. She was napping in a hammock tied between two rose garland firs. As she lay there, her "softly chiselled features, hair sombre gold in the shadow," her lips were "half parted in a smile, as if her dreams were singularly pleasant ones." Willy was instantly in love. "*Dornröschen!*" ("Sleeping Beauty!") he muttered.[34] Later, he penned a note to the Duke of Schleswig-Holstein, confessing, "Your daughter Dona, whom I so dearly adore, has so delighted me and carried me away with her whole being and her nature that I immediately resolved with great clarity and firmness to devote all my efforts to *fighting* for her hand. I can hardly describe to you how dear she has become to me over the last few days, and how difficult it was for me taking my leave of her to only be able to press her hand."[35]

Willy—officially named Frederick Wilhelm Victor Albrecht—was tall and handsome, with dark eyes and fair hair, but he and Dona had led radically different lives. Unlike the princess, he had spent his entire life being groomed for greatness. He was born on January 27, 1859, in Berlin—making him four months younger than Dona, an unusual occurrence in royal romances. At the time of his birth, he was second in line for the throne of Prussia. After the Franco-Prussian War and German unification of 1871, he also became second in line for the German imperial throne after his grandfather was crowned emperor. Thanks to the intermarriages of Europe's royal houses, Willy was a first cousin on his mother's side to Alix of Hesse-Darmstadt; the future king of England, George V; and the future queens Marie of Romania, Maud of Norway, and Victoria Eugenie of Spain. His own sister Sophie would become queen consort of Greece. As a grandson of Queen Victoria, he and Dona were second half cousins. By the time Willy was twenty, his good looks and seemingly kind nature proved intoxicating to the impressionable Dona. This was hardly a surprising development considering the somewhat limited upbringing Dona experienced in which she was never really exposed to royal opulence. But like so much else in the Holstein family, the blossoming romance between Willy and Dona was overshadowed by tragedy.

While staying at an inn near Wiesbaden in January 1880, Dona's father, Fritz, died from cancer. His long and painful battle had been made worse by his doctor prescribing arsenic as a treatment. The strain of Fritz's death pushed Ada over the edge. Still reeling from yet another blast of postpartum depression from the birth of her last child (a daughter, Feodora, who arrived in 1874) and plagued by an increasingly unstable and depressed personality, the death of her husband sent the Duchess of Schleswig-Holstein into a dark tailspin of grief. During Fritz's funeral at Primkenau, her hysterics were so dramatic that her cries kept interrupting the vicar's speech. Her relationship with Dona fell apart completely in the weeks that followed. Ada's grief was made all the worse by her now-obvious bipolar disorder, causing her moods to become violent and erratic. According to one witness, the "situation leads daily to unpleasant scenes which the young lady [Dona] rides out with exemplary grace and submissiveness."[36] Little wonder then that Willy—and imperial Germany—proved alluring to Dona or that she accepted when Willy proposed on February 14, 1880, Saint Valentine's Day.

The complex marriage negotiations went forward under Ernest Stockmar, son of the famed Baron Christian Stockmar, who had negotiated the marriage between Willy's grandparents, Queen Victoria and Prince Albert. The queen was quite supportive of Willy marrying Dona, since she knew that Dona's father had been a close friend of Fritz and Vicky's. She also felt a personal connection to Dona's family, beyond the one she already shared through her half sister, Dona's grandmother Feodora, and her son-in-law, Dona's uncle Christian. This was because, during the Second Schleswig War, she had vehemently supported Frederick VIII's claim to the throne. Unlike in London, news of the romance was not received so well in Berlin, where most of the Hohenzollerns looked down on Dona as not being *ebenbürtig* enough to marry the heir to the German and Prussian thrones.

The only person whose voice really mattered was Willy's grandfather and namesake. As head of the House of Hohenzollern, Emperor Wilhelm I's approval of the marriage was required. If Prussia orbited the Hohenzollerns, then the Hohenzollerns orbited the emperor. Wilhelm I was a shockingly simple man. Unquestionably a soldier, he had little use for the trappings of royalty. He slept on an army cot, ate off a card table, and marked the level of wine in his bottles to make sure the servants did not steal any of it. Born in 1797 just after the outbreak of the French Revolution, he was raised at a time when both Prussia and monarchism were under attack. As a young man, he became fiercely protective of both his homeland and the sanctity of royal blood. As such, when he was approached in 1880 with the news that his grandson wanted to marry the daughter of the Duke of Schleswig-Holstein, he shared his countrymen's concern for her insufficiently royal family. He was further unnerved by Prussia's—and Otto von Bismarck's—history with the Holsteins. At one point, Bismarck was heard to unkindly call Dona "the cow from Holstein."[37]

The emperor acquiesced only when Bismarck, who had become indifferent to the match after Frederick VIII's death, admitted that by marrying Dona, the sins they had committed over Schleswig-Holstein might be somewhat forgotten, if not forgiven. With his chancellor's obsequious blessing, Wilhelm I gave his approval for the complex marriage negotiations to continue apace on one condition: Dona's family must sign away all rights to the throne of the twin duchies forever, with the explicit understanding that Dona's brother Ernest Günther, who was now the titular Duke of Schleswig-Holstein, and any descendants they might have would never again try to reclaim their lost rights. This was agreed upon, and the emperor offered the family an annual stipend of $75,000, an impressive sum for that era.

The German emperor's final approval put an end to any official anti-Holstein propaganda in Berlin, though a certain level of grassroots hostility toward Dona would continue for some time. With the emperor's approval now official, the Hohenzollerns embarked on a summer vacation at the medieval Babelsberg Castle, on the banks of the river Havel near Potsdam. One night in June, the royal family, led by Wilhelm I and his cantankerous wife, Empress Augusta, officially announced their grandson's engagement to a small party of fifty-four. That night, Willy recorded in his diary his feelings about the match. Though his words do not reveal any trace of love, they do show his admiration and respect for Dona. His entry also hints at some of the political undercurrents of the union.

> My marriage with the Princess Augusta Victoria of Schleswig Holstein Augustenburg [*sic*] has been decided upon and declared. I like the Princess. She is a charming, fresh, German girl, who will make a perfect Empress, and at the same time an excellent wife. My mother and father, as well as the Emperor and Prince Bismarck, are quite pleased at ... my betrothal, which in a certain sense is a

political event, because it puts an end to a feud [with the Holsteins] that has lasted for something like fifteen years, and has reconciled our House with one of the minor dynasties that have had to suffer through the rise of Prussia. I have thus fulfilled the injunction given to me by Prince Bismarck one year ago, to marry a German princess, and not to introduce another foreigner in our home [e.g., his English mother, Vicky].... As for my future wife, she need not fear that I shall ever be wanting in respect and consideration in regard to her. I shall know how to treat her, and honour in her a German Empress, and the mother of future German Emperors. But I shall certainly not allow her to have anything to do with my private affairs or those of the State.[38]

Willy's grandmother Empress Augusta understood all too well the difficulties faced by marrying a Hohenzollern prince. She cautioned Dona that Willy "needed much understanding love" and that it was "the serious and difficult task of his wife to help him understand the true nature of his high office."[39]

The apparently warm, congenial atmosphere at Babelsberg concealed a deeply divided family whose troubled epicenter was Willy himself. As a child, he "came under the influence of his tyrannical German grandmother, the Empress Augusta, who spoiled him, bribed him and stimulated the development of that 'terrible Prussian pride' that his parents had hoped to discourage."[40] As Willy grew older, his German grandparents used him as a weapon against Fritz and Vicky especially, whom they disliked and distrusted for her liberal ideologies. By the time Dona met Willy, he was a deeply flawed individual caught in a perpetual love-hate relationship with his parents that would only get worse with time and, in the process, would suck Dona in until she was a part of the struggle herself. Those around Willy considered it a stroke of luck that he had found someone as loving and supportive as Dona. Georg Hinzpeter, his childhood tutor, elatedly wrote to Dona when he heard the news of their engagement: "May I tell Your Royal Highness how greatly relieved I went home, convinced that my dearly beloved problem child has had the inestimable fortune to unite himself for life with someone who understands him and sympathizes with his weaknesses."[41]

Over the next few months, Willy carried out a trothplighting campaign through a daily exchange of letters. The bride-to-be, who was not normally given to public displays of affection, poured out a wellspring of emotions to her fiancé. She addressed him in a plethora of loving clichés like "heart's treasure," "Herzblatt," or "Schatzi." She ended her letters just as passionately. She closed one letter by writing, "I *so* look forward, my heart's treasure, to the moment when I can kiss you again so ardently and look into your dear beautiful eyes."[42] During a visit to Cumberland Lodge after her engagement, Dona expressed her impatience to Willy at having to wait for her wedding.

> I thank you with my whole heart for your last 2 letters ... I have kissed them instead of you, for you wrote me so many loving and kind things that my longing for you became all the greater. I too cannot *express* how I am looking forward to the moment when after all the ceremonies we are *completely* alone with each other and I can flee into your arms after all the turmoil & excitement. It will truly be a happy feeling. And to obey, it will probably not be so bad, my heart's treasure?[43]

Leading up to her wedding, Dona could not contain her excitement. In one of her last letters to Willy before becoming his wife, she wrote, "Your sweet words did me such good that it was as if you gazed into my heart and had discovered the longing which so completely and especially fills my heart at this time in particular."[44] Willy was just as anxious as Dona was for the wedding day to approach. Shortly before the big day, he wrote to one of his aunts, "I hope with God's help together with the incomparable Princess to make a Christian and good house like the one I see and revere of my grandparents."[45]

On Saturday, February 26, 1881, Dona made her triumphant entry into Germany's capital. The procession in the streets of Berlin to welcome the princess proved to be a brilliant imperial pageant watched by tens of thousands of clamoring spectators. The black-and-white Prussian flag with its black crowned eagle decorated the buildings along Unter den Linden. The bride was preceded by unending lines of military officers, troops, and officials marching down Berlin's main thoroughfare, led by the city's master butchers as part of an ancient tradition. Next came the imperial carriage carrying Dona and Vicky, which was resplendently covered with gold and glass and drawn by horses dressed in the Prussian military livery. The smiling bride-to-be graciously waved to her future subjects, emanating a youthful enthusiasm that belied the fact that she was freezing cold wearing a dress that left her shoulders uncovered—a piece of traditional etiquette demanded by the uncompromising Prussian court. Behind Dona and Vicky's carriage was Willy on horseback, dressed as a Captain of the Bodyguard. As they passed through the Brandenburg Gate, white doves were released from atop the monument as a seventy-two-gun salute boomed across the winter sky. The royal family made their way to Berlin's primary palace, the Stadtschloss, with its awe-inspiring colonnaded grand entrance built beneath an equally impressive Romanesque dome. Waiting to welcome Dona when she arrived at the palace at 3:00 p.m. was the emperor, Fritz, and a full military honor guard. On entering, everyone signed the final marriage contract between the bride and groom. That night, celebrations took place "throughout the city, and dense joyous crowds paraded the streets until a late hour."[46] Few countries could match the magnificence of the welcome that Germany extended for the woman who would become its last empress.

The next day, Sunday, February 27, 1881, Princess Augusta Victoria became the first of the four special women to marry. It was only the third time in history that a Prussian prince had married a member of the House of Schleswig-Holstein. Breaking with the tradition of many other Hohenzollern weddings, Willy and Dona were married in the marble chapel of the Stadtschloss. A mustachioed pastor performed the solemn, extraordinarily complex Lutheran service, which lasted six interminable hours. During the nuptial sermon, the pastor told the young couple, "And now abideth faith, hope, charity, these three; but the greatest of these is charity."[47] These would be three qualities Dona would carry with her always. Because of the chapel's relatively small size, hundreds of guests stood in the palace's other gilded halls awaiting the conclusion of the ceremony. As Willy took his vows, he turned to his grandfather, Wilhelm I, and made the traditional bow, as if to ask the old emperor one last time for his permission to marry. Dona wore a dress of gold-and-light-blue fabric with diamonds adorning her head and neck; her train was so long that it had to be carried by six bridesmaids. Vicky happily reported to Queen Victoria that "Dona looked charming and everyone was taken with her sweetness and grace."[48] At the crown princess's request, the wedding reception included a massive English wedding cake surrounded by orange blossoms.

The day ended with the spectacular *Fackeltanz*, a torchlight dance performed at Prussian royal weddings that could only be danced by the bride and men with the style of Royal Highness or higher. As the grand hall was bathed in blazing reds and oranges, Dona danced with her new father-in-law, Fritz, while pages held aloft glowing candles set in silver candelabras. The only person who did not seem to bubble over that day was the groom. Willy's diary entry was simple and nondescript: "I was married to-day in the chapel of the Castle. We shall settle in Potsdam, where I am to continue my service in the Hussars of the Guards."[49]

The nuptial festivities in Berlin lasted for days. On Monday, February 28 Dona and Willy made their first public appearance together as husband and wife during a carriage ride through Berlin. Along the entire route, crowds of people clamored for a glimpse of the newlyweds. For Dona, a woman so unused to being the center of attention, these were heady days. But through it all, the new princess of Prussia was radiant, smiling, and genuinely enthusiastic about everything she did and everyone she met. This exuberance was an asset to Dona immediately after her wedding. During the first week of March, she and Willy received the more than two hundred royal deputations that had come to Berlin for their wedding, including Willy's maternal uncles, the Prince of Wales, the Grand Duke of Hesse, and the Duke of Edinburgh; his great-uncle the Duke of Saxe-Coburg-Gotha; and the king and queen of Saxony. These audiences were held for several reasons. Etiquette demanded that these senior members of reigning families be properly received; many of them were related to the groom, bride, or both; and it was also intended to give Dona her first taste of life in Prussia.

The Prussia of the 1880s in which Dona went to live was a kingdom that Vicky described as full of "thorny people ... with their sharp tongues [and] their cutting sarcasm about everybody and everything."[50] Thankfully for Dona, her new home was not the intrigue-ridden Berlin but the city of Potsdam, almost fifteen miles away. Potsdam was often called the Windsor of Prussia for its magnificent royal residences. Poultney Bigelow, a childhood friend of Willy's, remembered it as "a wilderness of palaces, barracks, fountains, temples, [and] esplanades with innumerable marble divinities waving their naked arms and legs as though begging in vain for warm clothes in the damp and cold of the Brandenburg swamps."[51]

Potsdam's main attraction was the awe-inspiring Neues Palais. Used by Willy's parents as their official residence, it was built by Frederick the Great in 1763 to impress his enemies. It was more than three stories tall and contained over two hundred rooms, multiple gathering halls, and a theater. The suites were filled with ornate silver furniture, silk tapestries, and Savonnerie carpets. Keeping with his unpredictable personality, once Frederick the Great completed the palace, he declared it to be an architectural monstrosity and refused to ever live there. Most people who visited it agreed that it was a cavernous old building that was meant to do little more than impress, which was evidenced by the fact that it exited out onto a military parade ground on the western side of Sanssouci Park.

Located nearby was the less imposing but equally beautiful Marble Palace, which was set aside for Willy and Dona. They spent almost all their time here in the first years after their wedding, since they were given no other official residences—the only accommodations they had outside Potsdam were a few austere, unfurnished rooms at the Stadtschloss in Berlin. For Dona, the Marble Palace was more than commodious. The palace, nestled on the shore of the Heiligen Sea, derived its name from its interior design. Its rooms were decorated with black-and-white marble floors, statues, and columns stretching high to its frescoed ceilings painted in the neoclassical style that was popular in nineteenth-century Germany. Considered warm and intimate by Prussian standards, the palace actually had working bathrooms and limited plumbing, which were added in a recent renovation. There were few royal residences in Germany that were equipped with modern amenities. In most castles and palaces, the carpets were threadbare, floors were dirty, and lavatories were few and far between. Princess Marie Louise of Schleswig-Holstein-Sonderburg-Augustenburg, Dona and Willy's mutual cousin, wrote about the poor living conditions: "It is very hard to convey to English readers the medieval conditions in which people in our state of life lived in Germany."[52]

Unlike the close family atmospheres enjoyed by the Teck and Hesse families, the Hohenzollerns were rife with discord. Nowhere was the contrast more evident between the loving family ties of May and Alix's intimate families and Dona and the Hohenzollerns than following the latter's wedding in 1881. One woman in particular made herself the bane of Dona's existence for the first few years of her married life. She was none other than Willy's eldest sister, Charlotte ("Charly").

For most of her adult life, Charly lived in a constant state of manic frenzy. She suffered violent moods swings and acute health problems that baffled her doctors. She outlined her symptoms to the world-renowned physician Dr. Ernest Schweninger. "My nerves are in shreds, although my appearance does not show it," she wrote. "But a terrible headache on one side & dizziness on the left side *so* depress [*sic*] me, & completely irregular feelings of malaise, with a rash & itching."[53] Most historians now agree that Charly suffered from a disease she inherited from Queen Victoria known as porphyria. The disease, which—like hemophilia—is genetic but is suffered by both men and women, is believed to be responsible for driving Charly's great-great-grandfather—King George III—mad. And when Dona married into the Hohenzollerns in 1881 by becoming Willy's wife, it brought out the worst in Charly, sending her unstable personality soaring to new heights. She resented Dona for being "silent, barely communicative and very shy."[54] Charly's venomous personality grew worse when she married Prince Bernard of Saxe-Meiningen in 1878. He was brutal in his assessment of Dona. He became something of a polemicist toward her, claiming she was stupid, tactless, and virtually illiterate compared to the modern, fashionable lifestyle he and his wife shared.

As hurtful as the insults hurled upon Dona by her sister-in-law and brother-in-law may have been, by September 1881, they mattered little. She excitedly told her family that a baby was on the way. On May 6, 1882, the guns of Berlin fired off a salute to mark the arrival of Dona's firstborn child, a son, who came into the world at the Marble Palace. The delivery at the Marble

Palace was a difficult one. Had it not been for the intervention of adroit doctors, both mother and child could have been lost. Waiting outside the delivery room were Fritz, Vicky, the emperor, and his aides, all dressed in full military uniforms. When Willy came out to announce the birth, he walked across the room directly to the emperor and said, "Grandfather, it is a boy!"[55] There, surrounded by his son, grandson, and great-grandson, the emperor exclaimed, "Hurrah, hurrah! Four Kings!"[56] Willy confided to his diary his pride over being a father and the significance of the birth for Germany.

> My son was born to-day. He is the first heir to the German Empire, and I feel that I have performed my duty towards this Empire, in providing our dynasty with a successor in the direct line. My grandfather is so happy, far happier than my father, at least outwardly. He never expected to have this wish of his granted before he died, to see his family continued by me. In the country, also, the event has been hailed with immense joy, and I have received any amount of congratulations. The Reichstag even sent a deputation to assure me of its satisfaction and that of the whole Empire. Now I can think of the future with a certain amount of pride which I could not feel before, when I had not done anything for the welfare of my country or of the dynasty of which I am one day to be the head.[57]

In keeping with the tradition of the Prussian court, Dona's firstborn son was given the names Frederick Wilhelm Victor August Ernest, which was later shortened to Wilhelm. His family took to calling him "Little Willy," to distinguish him from his father; while the English-speaking world perennially dubbed him Frederick William, to avoid any confusion with his progenitors. The birth of another great-grandchild to Queen Victoria was received well in England, where a solemn photograph was distributed depicting the old emperor seated with Little Willy on his knee and Fritz and Willy standing behind them.

With the German succession now secured indefinitely, and her dynastic role fulfilled, Dona began to take on an air of haughtiness that she had not displayed before. Many people felt she developed this attitude from her husband, who was obsessed with his position as heir to the Prusso-German throne. Dona's growing sense of her own importance is not at all surprising, given the environment in which she lived. In a country that had very clearly defined views on gender roles, she was becoming the ideal embodiment of everything a woman, wife, and mother was to be. Eager to please the Hohenzollern men, she was a willing pupil of the more seasoned members of the royal family. Otto von Bismarck was also pleased to find her receptive to his own self-serving brand of guidance. The fact that the royal family was the very nucleus of Prussia meant Dona was surrounded by hordes of sycophantic ladies, servants, and other staff. As the increasingly popular wife of the heir presumptive—and having given birth to another heir only a year after her wedding—meant Dona had ample reason to feel proud of herself, at least, according to Prussian standards.

The princess's growing sense of her own importance and popularity may have fit perfectly with the Hohenzollerns and the aristocrats in Berlin or Potsdam, but it caused a great deal of friction within her own family when she returned to Primkenau in March 1885 for the wedding of her sister Calma. Since before Dona's own marriage, a search had been underway to find a suitable husband for her next sister. At one point, Calma had been the leading candidate to become the wife of Queen Victoria's youngest son, Leopold, Duke of Albany. A marriage with the duke would have been difficult for Calma because of his hemophilia, but as a son of the queen, his position would have ensured his wife's comfort for the rest of her life. Before the couple could run off and get married, a letter was discovered, written by Fritz Holstein before his death, forbidding the union. In the end, Calma settled on a distant relative—Prince Frederick Ferdinand of Schleswig-Holstein-Sonderburg-Glücksburg.[58] Although most of the guests at the wedding were royalty, they all ranked considerably lower than Dona, a fact she repeatedly made clear to everyone, especially Frederick Ferdinand's family.

Dona's growing hauteur not only alienated some of her immediate family, it also caused increasing tensions with her in-laws, Fritz and Vicky. Fritz, despite his friendship with Dona's late father, still had difficulty accepting her as being sufficiently *ebenbürtig* for a German heir. Dona's morganatic lineage was something she shared with May Teck, though the former never spoke of it publicly. Willy and Dona's attitudes also damaged their relationship with his British relatives when, later in 1885, his aunt Princess Beatrice married Prince Henry of Battenberg. It was an event that brought together much of Queen Victoria's family. Fourteen-year-old Alix of Hesse-Darmstadt was a bridesmaid for her aunt. The princess from Hesse stood at the altar alongside her cousins Marie of Edinburgh (the future queen of Romania) and Maud of Wales (the future queen of Norway). Dona, who was growing increasingly obsessed with royal rank—possibly having been left somewhat unnerved by the relatively low company at her sister's wedding—made it known to everyone that she disapproved of the marriage on the grounds that Henry possessed morganatic blood.

When Beatrice and Henry paid Vicky and Fritz a visit while on their honeymoon, Willy and Dona made it a point to snub them. Their reaction could, at least in part, have something to do with the fact that Beatrice was only a year and a half older than Willy, who saw her more as a contemporary rather than his aunt. It may have seemed easier for him to pass judgment on her marriage, though it was by no means justified. Queen Victoria was incredulous, writing to Vicky of their "extraordinary impertinence and insolence." She commented, "that if the Queen of England thinks a person good enough for her daughter what have other people got to say?"[59] She reiterated this sentiment when she wrote to Vicky, "As for Dona, a poor, little, insignificant Princess raised entirely by your kindness to the position she is in, I have no words."[60]

⇋

To outsiders, the Duke and Duchess of Teck were a study in contradiction. Loving, selfless, and charitable, Mary Adelaide freely gave to all who were in need, especially the poor. She was adamant that her children visit the poorer communities in London to see how others lived. Carr Glyn, the vicar at Kensington Palace who was responsible for giving the Teck children Bible lessons, recalled one of the family's outings. "On one of these expeditions," he wrote, the duchess "sent a dinner to a destitute family, and gave instructions that the children were to stop and see the poor people eat it, showing at once her practical mind and her goodness of heart."[61] Though the duchess was socially conscious, Francis continued to be worldlier. He lacked the social graces that could have made his difficult qualities more manageable. His elevation to the rank of Duke of Teck did nothing to improve his petulance. He flew into wild public rages when he felt he had been snubbed in some way. He found himself shunned by London's social leaders, who feared one of the duke's temper tantrums at their parties. More often than not, the duchess was seen attending official functions without her husband.

The Tecks also continued to be plagued by financial woes. They never seemed to have enough money to cover their surfeit spending. Royals visiting London made the requisite courtesy visits to the Tecks at Kensington Palace, where Mary Adelaide insisted on throwing extravagantly expensive dinner parties in their honor. The family's money problems were not the duchess's fault alone. Francis's fanatical obsession with being treated properly according to his rank as a royal duke was also a contributing factor. He insisted on having as many servants as possible, filling their Kensington Palace flat with a ludicrously oversized entourage. Since the duke found himself on few social guest lists, he threw expensive parties to ensure he was not entirely shut out of the London social scene. He paid for the servants and the parties with most of his wife's annual allowance and on credit. "Poor man," May later wrote of her father, "if only he was less proud and foolish about that sort of thing, what can it matter how many servants one has as long as one can live comfortably?"[62]

After nearly twenty years of marriage, the Tecks were worse off than ever. They could no longer afford tutors to educate their children. Their lessons had to be taken over by Mary Adelaide's mother, the Duchess of Cambridge. By 1883, the debts of May's parents finally caught up with them. Their bills exceeded £68,000—more than $7.3 million today.[63] Requests to Queen Victoria for emergency loans were refused. Gone were the days of Parliament fronting the bills for squandering members of the royal family. Creditors were seen constantly lurking around Kensington Palace and White Lodge. When bailiffs showed up in the summer to reclaim their property, the duke and duchess—influenced heavily by their frustrated relatives—had no choice but to temporarily leave England. Since they could not even cover the most basic expenses at either of their homes, Kensington Palace had to be vacated completely, and White Lodge was only to be maintained as the building required. "Well, you see, my parents were always *in short street*, so they had to go abroad to economize," May explained years later.[64] Her parents' financial ruin made a profound impact on seventeen-year-old May. She realized for the first time just how fallible her parents were and how royalties were just as vulnerable to money problems as ordinary people. From that point on in her life, she made it a priority to never live beyond her income so as to never lack money again. For the Duchess of Teck, their very public, humiliating bankruptcy was almost too much to bear. "I do my best to keep up my spirits," she wrote to a friend, "for alas! a great trial is before me. On Saturday next we are going up … to Kensington Palace to wind [*sic*] there, and break up the beautiful, happy home, that has sheltered us for the last *sixteen* years, in which all our children were born. You can guess the wrench it will be to us."[65]

The Tecks, traveling incognito as the Count and Countess von Hohenstein, decided upon Florence as their home-in-exile. Compared to the rest of Europe at the time, Italy's cost of living was relatively low, but Florence was also remote enough to keep Mary Adelaide's luxuriant spending at a minimum—or so it was hoped. The Tecks left Britain on the evening of Saturday, September 15, 1883. They faced "a vastly different life from the life they had led for the past twenty years … they had dispensed hospitality to almost every royal and distinguished visitor who had visited London during that time."[66] Not surprisingly, though "somewhat to the embarrassment of her family," the Duchess of Teck did not make straight for Florence. Ever conscious that "she was the daughter of the Viceroy of Hanover, niece of the [formers kings] of Great Britain and" had once been "fifth in line to the throne," she promptly shed her innocuous pseudonym and insisted on paying semiofficial visits to numerous royals en route to Italy.[67] They spent their first few weeks at a villa on the shores of Lake Constance in Switzerland that belonged to Francis's Württemberger relatives. In mid-October, the Tecks could no longer delay their journey into Italy. Although the family had traveled to Switzerland together, May's brothers Frank and Dolly returned to England to finish their educations at the Wellington School in Somerset—this did not last long, since Frank was soon expelled for throwing the headmaster over a bush.

Once the Tecks and their suite entered Italy, they still showed no signs of altering their ways. Shortly after crossing the border, May's parents were invited to dinner with the king and queen of Italy. When they finally reached Florence, the Tecks settled into some rooms at the Hotel Paoli, but even this became a difficult situation. Incensed that other guests were allowed to stay on the same floor as the cousin of the queen of England, Francis insisted the other rooms be kept empty. Naturally, the duke and duchess were charged for this, leading Francis to experience "one of the uncontrolled fits of temper which were becoming more and more frequent in his life." May was just as unhappy about being in Florence as her parents. David Duff, one of her biographers, commented on the way it impacted her.

> This exile had a deep effect on May, altering not only her adolescent years but lasting through the rest of her life. It was the humiliation which hurt … she had reached an age when she could think for herself and she realized that she was under a handicap in life. Her contemporaries were completing their education and beginning to think of parties and "coming out" and boyfriends, while May found herself backward in learning, totally unfitted for the ballroom and obviously without the financial background necessary for launching her into the social round…. Her brothers being younger than herself, she was held back in sophistication, causing her to be treated as younger than she really was.[68]

These thoughts were foremost in May's mind as she settled into her new Florentine life. She made it her goal to enhance her education, which was helped with the departure of the stern, authoritarian governess Fraulein Gutman, who had been selected to oversee the princess's education in Italy. Gutman was ardently anti-Italian and discouraged May from embracing the culture or the lifestyle of the country. May and Alge—who pushed Gutman into a fountain in his sister's defense—loathed the woman, and Mary Adelaide found her insufferable. So when she was sent packing in late 1883, there were no tears shed.

May's new governess, Signora Zucchelli, could not have been more different from her predecessor. Vivacious and cultivated, she stimulated in

May a renewed interest in her own education. This was partly accomplished by selecting young ladies of the same age to come and share May's lessons with her. It was the first time she had ever interacted with girls her own age in that type of environment. Much to May's satisfaction, her daily lessons began to include music and drawing, as well as tutoring in languages—she quickly mastered German and became proficient in French. Her studies were not limited to indoor lessons. Perhaps her favorite part of this whirlwind of new experiences was the expeditions to museums, the opera, and academic and historic locales. Visits to places like the Basilica of San Lorenzo, the Via Camillo Cavour, and the Pitti Palace cemented a permanent love in May Teck for traveling and sightseeing, especially to places of historic significance. Her time in Italy proved to be one of the most fruitful, productive periods in her life. When she left Britain, she was shy, awkward, and introverted, but after only a short time in Florence, she had turned into a lively, vivacious young woman. For May, "Florence was overwhelming" at first, but by 1884, she "proceeded deliberately to make it her own."[69]

By the time she reached adolescence, Princess Alix of Hesse-Darmstadt had grown into a ravishingly beautiful young woman with gray-blue eyes, flowing chestnut hair, and a flawless complexion. Her beauty became well known in royal circles. Queen Victoria told her daughter Vicky that Alix was "the handsomest child I ever saw."[70]

The year that Alix turned twelve, 1884, three family weddings took place. The first two occurred in April, when Alix's eldest sister, Victoria, married Prince Louis of Battenberg. Most of Europe's "royal mob," including Queen Victoria, had congregated in Darmstadt for the ceremony on April 30, which was held in the Marble Chamber in the New Palace. What no one knew at the time was that the bride's father, the Grand Duke of Hesse, was planning his own secret marriage to Alexandrina von Kolemine, the Polish ex-wife of the Russian chargé d'affaires in Darmstadt. The same day that Louis and Victoria were married, the grand duke slipped away to a smaller, quieter room "and there married his divorcée in a clandestine little ceremony that was a threadbare simulation of the main event a few hours earlier." One royal biographer has concluded, "Though there was no question of Madame Kolemine becoming the new grand duchess of Hesse, Louis must have known that his actions were, by the overarching rules of nineteenth-century European royal conduct, scandalous. He also must have been truly besotted to think that making Kolemine even his morganatic wife was going to be easy."[71] When word leaked out three days later that the grand duke had married his mistress under everyone's noses, there was outrage. Most of the guests immediately fled Darmstadt and declared Louis persona non grata at their courts. Queen Victoria was stupefied that the father of her grandchildren would marry morganatically, and using her own personal authority, she forced him to have it annulled less than a year later. Alexandrina was paid off by the grand duke, given a title, and married a Russian diplomat.

Two months later, Alix took a journey that would change her life forever. In June 1884, she and her family traveled to Saint Petersburg for the wedding of her sister Ella to Grand Duke Serge Alexandrovich of Russia, one of the brothers of Tsar Alexander III. Ella was also a beautiful woman but was not as dour or cold as Alix was reputed to be. As a young woman, Ella had caught the eye of her first cousin Prince Willy of Prussia. At the time, Willy was studying at Bonn University and visited Ella in Darmstadt on the weekends. Flattered though she was, Ella politely refused Willy's romantic overtures. It was a rejection from which he never recovered. For the rest of his life, he would keep her photograph on his desk. In the end, it was Grand Duke Serge who won her heart. The pair had little in common at first, but after Serge lost both his parents in a single year—his mother to a terminal illness and his father to an assassin's bomb—the nurturing Ella saw a more sensitive side of him. When he proposed to her in 1883, she accepted.

The experience of traveling to Saint Petersburg for Ella's wedding opened Alix's eyes to royal opulence like she had never known before. Despite her visits to Queen Victoria in Britain, the Russian imperial court was unparalleled in magnificence and scale anywhere in Europe. The Romanovs reportedly employed more than fifteen thousand servants across their many palaces. This drew a stark contrast with the humble surroundings in Alix's native Hesse. Alix's family's very arrival at the train station in Saint Petersburg was carried out with radiance. Alix watched in awe as her sister was chauffeured through the city in a gold carriage drawn by horses dressed in imperial livery. Queen Victoria wrote to one of her granddaughters that she hoped "Darling Ella won't be spoilt by all this admiration & adulation & all this flitter of jewelry & grandeur etc."[72]

Ardently Russophobic, Queen Victoria felt nothing but contempt for the Romanovs and their empire. Queen Victoria's feelings reflected the opinions of many of her countrymen. Russia was viewed as a direct threat to British imperial interests. The queen summed up her feelings to Benjamin Disraeli by declaring, "Oh, if the Queen were a man, she would to go & give those horrid Russians, whose word one cannot trust, such a beating."[73] Like many of her contemporaries, the queen ascribed moral traits to situations that otherwise had none. In the case of the Russians, she believed their moral bankruptcy was contributed to by the fact that they did not keep their homes properly ventilated; Victoria insisted on keeping all of her homes bone-chillingly cold, which she believed crucial to good health. Her antipathy for Russia was not only political. It was a deeply personal sentiment. Her son Alfred, Duke of Edinburgh, married the formidable Grand Duchess Marie Alexandrovna, the daughter of Tsar Alexander II. She was reputed to be the wealthiest woman in the world at the time. Many hoped that the marriage would bring about a thaw in Russo-British relations, but Marie created constant headaches at the English court. To begin with, Queen Victoria insisted on seeing Marie before the wedding, but her father refused to bring her over for inspection, which Victoria took as a personal insult. Once Marie settled into Clarence House in England after her wedding, it was obvious that she was demanding and obdurate. She insisted on being given precedence over other higher-ranking women in the family, including the Princess of Wales. Her behavior only confirmed Queen Victoria's low opinion of the Romanovs, which only got worse when Marie and Alfred's marriage fell apart. When Ella announced she was marrying Serge, the queen was revolted. In August 1883, her daughter-in-law Marie wrote regarding Ella and Serge's marriage: "I knew that from the very first she [Queen Victoria] sett [*sic*] her heart against it saying that she had only heard his [Serge's] praise, but he had the greatest of all misfortunes, he was Russian and she had enough of *one Russian* in the family (meaning me of course)."[74]

The wedding ceremony was held on June 15 in the gold and marble chapel of the famously opulent Winter Palace. Alix looked like a vision of beauty in her white muslin dress, with roses decorating her long hair that sat draped over her shoulders. As she stood off to one side during the ceremony, a handsome young prince of sixteen found he could not keep his eyes off the angelic princess from Hesse. The young man was Grand Duke Serge's nephew, the timid but thoughtful Tsarevitch Nicholas Alexandrovich ("Nicky"), heir to the Russian throne. The young royals met for the first time after the ceremony at the Alexandria cottage, a small villa on the grounds of the Peterhof Palace in the Gulf of Finland. Like the pair themselves, their first meeting was simple and devoid of pretension.

"I'm Nicky," the tsarevitch said when he walked over to Alix.

"I'm Sunny," replied the shy princess.

"Yes," Nicky said with a little smile, "I know."[75]

At the parties that followed the wedding, Alix and Nicky became enamored with one another. Born on May 16, 1868, Nicholas was the son of Tsar Alexander III and his Danish-born wife, Marie Feodorovna—who was known as Minnie in the family to distinguish her from the hundreds of other Maries that populated both the Romanov clan and royal Europe.

Like Willy of Prussia, Nicky was directly related to many of Europe's royal houses. His mother's family was especially well connected. Minnie's siblings included Queen Victoria's daughter-in-law the Princess of Wales, the king of Greece, the crown prince of Denmark, and the crown princess of Hanover. Nicky could also boast of being a first cousin on his mother's side to the future kings of Denmark, Greece, Norway, and Great Britain. On his father's side, he was a cousin to Princess Marie of Edinburgh, the future queen of Romania; this was the same Marie who had stood alongside Alix at their aunt Beatrice's wedding in 1885. These complex intermarriages meant that Nicky and Alix, besides sharing numerous cousins in common, were also second cousins themselves.

Brought up by his doting mother and exacting father, Nicholas Alexandrovich had a reputation for being mild mannered from the time he was very young. Both parents insisted on isolating Nicky and his siblings— George, Xenia, Michael, and Olga—from the outside world as much as possible. This prevented Nicky from ever developing a strong resolve in the face of real-world problems. He was known for kindness, gentility, and his sympathetic eyes, but he also lacked the formidable Romanov demeanor that his father and uncles possessed. Until the day he died, Nicholas was hampered by a crippling indecisiveness in the face of opposition.

Those qualities that others criticized in the tsarevitch were what endeared him to Alix. She was drawn to his quiet personality. There was little doubt that she was smitten with him. Even members of Alix's extended family could see a budding romance between the two young royals. Princess Maud of Wales, who was a first cousin both to Alix and Nicky, wrote to the tsarevitch during Alix's visit, "Do you like little Alix?.... She is my best friend, we always go for walks together when we meet. They say I am very much like her, but I do not think I am like her at all."[76] Before Alix left Russia, the pair carved their initials into a windowpane. Nicky wrote in his journal, "Alix and I wrote our names on the rear window" of a nearby house. He added at the end, "We love each other." On June 21, Alix and her family left Saint Petersburg. As a parting gift, the tsarevitch gave Alix a diamond brooch. She handed it back to him though, because as a granddaughter of Queen Victoria, she knew that any exchange of gifts would be scrutinized for any political undertones. Nicky wrote dejectedly in his diary, "I am very sad the Darmstadts are going tomorrow and even more so that dearest Alix is leaving me."[77] Later that day, he pasted a photograph of Alix into his diary. No one could ever have realized that this adolescent romance would become one of the greatest love stories of the twentieth century.

3

Ninety-Nine Days

(1884–88)

The exhilarating, stimulating lifestyle May Teck was experiencing after only six months in Florence received a sudden, frightening interruption on March 5, 1884, when her father suffered a massive stroke. Those close to the family were shocked by Mary Adelaide's efforts to downplay the gravitas of the situation—the duke's left arm and leg were paralyzed, and his mouth was noticeably crooked. With the Duchess of Teck unwilling to accept the reality of the situation—or more accurately, her unwillingness to allow it to interfere with her highly prized social life—the arduous responsibility of caring for Francis fell on her daughter. May, who was only a teenager, was left profoundly altered from caring for her demanding father around the clock. The tempestuous duke took his dark moods out on his daughter. But instead of lashing back at her father, May "determined to keep her emotions strictly under control and not to allow her father's quirks to upset her."[1] This decision to keep up a strong front regardless of her internal emotions would become one of the most defining characteristics of May's personality. From 1884 onward, she rarely lost her temper and never did so in public. It set a pattern for the rest of her life; she reserved her emotions more the worse a situation became.

In April, the Tecks moved out of their hotel and into their own private residence, the Villa I Cedri. A fifteenth-century house three miles outside of Florence, May's family was offered use of the house, rent-free, by its owner, Bianca Light, whose brother was the president of the English Club in Florence.

It was a picturesque Tuscan villa with a flat, tiled roof and yellow-tinged walls. Surrounding it was an elaborate English country garden filled with ilexes, cedars, and magnolias. From the balcony, May could see beyond I Cedri's walls across the vineyard-covered Tuscan landscape. Moving into her own private residence suited the Duchess of Teck quite well, who used it as an excuse to continue her exorbitant spending by hosting her now-customary parties. Telegrams apprising the British royal family of the duchess's behavior flew between Florence and London regularly. Most of the ones arriving from Britain were from either the queen or the Duchess of Cambridge, imploring Mary Adelaide to learn some self-restraint. But after years of such unrepentant profligacy, the Duchess of Cambridge began to see her daughter as a financial delinquent of sorts.

After nearly two years in Florence, in April 1885, messengers arrived at I Cedri informing the Tecks that permission had been granted for their return to Britain. The decision had been in the works for some time. Mary Adelaide's brother, the Duke of Cambridge, made the point to the queen that there seemed little point to keeping the Tecks abroad any longer, since his sister seemed uninterested in mending her ways. It was also hurting the prospects for her children. May, he argued, was not receiving the education necessary for an English princess, while Alge was barely being educated at all. On the evening of May 24, 1885, the Tecks left Florence by train, arriving in Paris the next day for a brief layover. This afforded May the chance to visit the Louvre, stimulating her newfound historic and academic curiosity. "I admired the Rubenses and some of the Murillos immensely," she wrote about her day in Paris. "The rooms are beautiful ... We lunched with Lord Lyons (the British Ambassador), who was kindness itself ... We left Paris at eight, and our crossing [the English Channel] was so-so, rather a swell."[2] At dawn on the morning of May 26, the Tecks disembarked at Victoria Station in central London's Belgravia district. It was Princess May's eighteenth birthday. She was thrilled to be home, writing to a friend that same day, "we reached London about seven, to find the dear boys waiting for us at the station." The "dear boys" May spoke of were her brothers Dolly and Frank. "They are so grown," she wrote, "Frank much taller than Mama.... I am so glad to be in London again."[3]

An important milestone in Princess May's life took place two months after she returned to England. On August 1, 1885, her confirmation was held in the Chapel Royal of Saint James's Palace. With this acknowledgment that her youth was over, May was invited to take on more official responsibilities as a member of the royal family. In 1886 alone, she was present at the opening of Parliament, attended the ceremony for the laying of the foundation stone when construction began on the Tower Bridge, and accompanied Queen

Victoria to the opening of the Colonial and Indian Exhibition. The grandest occasion that May participated in was one of the country's most highly anticipated affairs of 1887: Queen Victoria's Golden Jubilee, marking the fiftieth anniversary of her reign. All of London came alive for the first great celebration of monarchy since Prince Albert's death in 1861. Jubilee fever was epidemic. Coins were minted, medals were created, and jubilee brooches and tie pins were sold. In some cases, convicts were even released from prison, while others had their sentences remitted. Foreign royals flooded into the English capital to celebrate Victoria's momentous reign. Along with her grandfather George III, only two other English monarchs—Henry III and Edward III—had ever ruled that long. On June 20, Princess May joined nearly forty other members of the royal family as they rode in state to Saint Paul's Cathedral for a service of thanksgiving. The response from the general public was literally overwhelming. Lady Geraldine Somerset, a lady-in-waiting to May's grandmother the Duchess of Cambridge, wrote,

> [Of the] masses and *millions* of people thronging the streets like an anthill, and *every* window within sight and every roof of every house, men hanging on the chimneys! There was never anything seen like it ... And their enthusiasm! The Duke [of Cambridge] ... told us he had never seen anything like the enthusiasm anywhere!! It was one continuous roar of cheering from the moment [the Queen] came out of the door of her Palace till the instant she got back to it: Deafening.[4]

Along with Queen Victoria's numerous relations was a guest list of nearly fifty other reigning monarchs, dignitaries, and royals. At dinner that evening—a "large family dinner," as the queen called it—she sat between King Christian IX of Denmark and his son King George I of Greece. Across from her sat her infamous first cousin King Leopold II of the Belgians.[5]

Twenty-year-old Princess May was in awe of this great royal pageant. Most of the British population had never witnessed a Golden Jubilee before. The last English monarch to reign for anything beyond a decade was King George III, who had died in 1820. There were few people still alive who remembered his reign. Those that did would have been infants when George III ruled under his own name. They most likely recalled the governance of the king's enormously unpopular son, who became prince-regent—and later King George IV—when George III was left incapacitated by his mental and physical illnesses in 1811. For the jubilee festivities, London came alive in a "bright and beautiful" atmosphere that "was particular clear" and had "a glow and colour about everything."[6] Writing to her friend Emily

Alcock, Princess May described the excitement of the jubilee. "I really cannot describe all the fêtes," she wrote. "The excitement here in London was something not to be imagined, & I believe it was this that kept us up thro' that fatiguing time when we were on the go from morning till night—*sans relâche*."[7]

Two guests who cast a dark shadow over the festivities were Willy and Dona. The queen originally planned to not invite them. Officially, Germany was to be represented by Vicky and Fritz, but the real reason behind Victoria's decision was Willy and Dona's conduct toward the queen's daughter Beatrice and her husband, Henry of Battenberg, on their honeymoon. "You know *how* ill he [Willy] behaved, how rude, to me, to Liko [Henry]," the queen wrote to Vicky. "*Bertie wants* me to invite William & Dona, but … I fear he may show his dislike and be disagreeable."[8] In the end, Bertie and Vicky convinced their mother to invite the couple, saying that Willy really *"ought* to be present" since he was the "eldest Grand Child."[9] In appealing to her mother, Vicky explained that not inviting them could do more harm than good.

> [They] need only stay for a very few days. He [Willy] has behaved very badly to you – and to us – but I fear it would only do harm in every way to appear to take more notice of his behaviour than it is worth! It is well *not* to give him a handle for saying he is ill treated! … He fancies himself of immense importance & service to the State – to his country, thinks he is indispensable to Bismarck and the Emperor! As he has little heart or *Zartgefühl* [tact] – and as his conscience & intelligence have been completely *wharped* [*sic*] by the … people in whose hands he is, he is not aware of the mischief he does … His staying away would *only* be used by the [ultraconservative] Party against you & Fritz & me!"[10]

Willy and Dona arrived in June, bringing with them their eldest son, Little Willy. The grandeur of the event made a lasting impression on the young prince. His first meeting with his great-grandmother the queen remained especially vivid in his memory for many years. "It was at a great garden fête in St. James's Park that I first saw the Queen," he wrote in his memoirs. "She was very friendly to me, kissed me and kept on fondling me with her aged and slightly trembling hands."[11] Little Willy may have been received by his English relatives with open arms, but his parents were less welcome. One German lady-in-waiting recalled how "Pr. W[illiam] and the Princess [Dona] were received with exquisite coolness" and "bare courtesy." When it was announced that, during the royal procession, Dona would take precedence after the visiting queen of Hawaii, she nearly exploded. "*She* was always placed behind the black Queen of Hawaii!!" one witness observed with some satisfaction. "Both [Willy and Dona] returned not in the best of tempers."[12] Dona would never forgive Britain, or the royal family, for this slight.

In the wake of the jubilee festivities, Princess May's family found a new lease on life. Their participation in the official ceremonies showed that their financial indiscretions had been somewhat forgiven. With a new outlook, they made their permanent home exclusively at White Lodge. Although the Tecks were now more conscious of the money they spent, Mary Adelaide never completely gave up her spendthrift habits. Even after settling in at White Lodge, May spent little time there. Her time in Florence left her with an indelible curiosity about the world around her. For the rest of her life, she would take a profound interest in exotic places and the people who lived there. Eager to mix with people of all classes, she was always keen to ask questions and to get to know others. When she was not learning more about London's history, she was busy with charity work or lobbying for social reforms alongside her mother. "She never forgot anyone," wrote one of the Duchess of Teck's biographers, "high, low, rich or poor—while the slightest act of kindness is remembered." The people who lived around Richmond Park thought very highly of Princess May. A daughter of one of the locals recalled, "The Royal carriage never went by our gate without Her Royal Highness looking to see if my father was in the garden or at the window, and a gracious cordial greeting was invariably given."[13]

Now a young woman, May's parents became concerned about her eligibility in Europe's highly contested royal matrimonial stakes. The fact that she was a great-granddaughter of King George III, or that she was born and raised at the English court, seemed overshadowed by the fact that she had morganatic blood in her veins. Although not a great beauty like the Princess of Wales, May's handsome features won her some admirers. Undaunted by her daughter's shortcomings, the Duchess of Teck launched her into society. May's diary from this time is a testament to how active she was. It is filled with passages that echo one another: "Mama opened an industrial exhibition;.... Mama opened an exhibition at King Ward ragged schools, Spitalfields;.... Went to L[ad]y Wolverton's where Mama read & I sang to some poor men from Westminster;.... drove to Camberwell where Mama opened the Institute & Gymnasium which Ly Wolverton gave to the Parish. The Dean & Mr Chapman made charming speeches & Mama's speech was so touching that we nearly wept."[14] In accompanying her mother on all these outings, May became her de facto private secretary.

As May settled into a round of official engagements, tragedy struck her family in April 1889 with the sudden death of her maternal grandmother, the Duchess of Cambridge. Mary Adelaide described the "great sorrow" of her mother's "irreparable loss" to a friend: "We have thus far been wonderfully supported by the feeling that our beloved mother has at length been released from all her weary pain and suffering, and is now, as we dare hope, enjoying the rest, peace, and joy she so longed for!"[15] Queen Victoria, who had been close with her aunt, mourned the loss deeply alongside her cousin. "The last one gone," the queen commented, "who had the right to call me Victoria!"[16]

The official mourning period for the duchess did not last long because London was soon atwitter with the news that the queen was looking for a wife for her grandson Prince Albert Victor ("Eddy") of Wales, who was second in line to the throne. Searching for a bride for the British heir typically involved something of a royal beauty pageant. Since the Royal Marriages Act passed by George III prevented a British heir from marrying a Catholic, a suitable bride had to be, and traditionally was, found in the German or Scandinavian courts. German princesses had been supplying English queen consorts for hundreds of years, but in this case, Queen Victoria was willing to look closer to home. Princess May—as a relative of the royal family, a Protestant princess with a German title, and a woman whose upstanding character and moral integrity were well established—was at the top of the list of candidates to be Eddy's bride. Queen Victoria took notice of May's fine qualities. She told her daughter Vicky, "May is a particularly nice girl, so quiet & yet cheerful & so vy carefully brought up & so sensible."[17] Along with other eligible princesses from Prussia, Mecklenburg, and Anhalt, May was in line for one of the most vaunted positions in the world: queen of England.

After a few years in Germany, Dona's fairy-tale romance was beginning to lose its luster. Like most newlyweds, she and Willy began to discover each other's idiosyncrasies—she was somewhat alarmed to learn that her husband kept a loaded pistol in his desk drawer at all times. She also found that he could be remarkably high strung. He was a hypochondriac who exasperated his retinue with one imagined ailment after another. For his part, Prince Wilhelm began to chafe with married life and looked for reasons to be away from his wife. Not long after the wedding, he started realizing Dona lacked the sophistication he craved in order to keep his attention. Willy opined that his wife's simple tastes reflected her modest provincial upbringing, away from the fast-paced life of more fashionable, mainstream royal courts. He said publicly that you could always tell that Dona "was not brought up at Windsor but rather in Primkenau."[18] By Hohenzollern standards, Willy was considered a faithful husband, even though he kept a handful of mistresses in Vienna and Strasbourg that he visited when he was away on military exercises. These women nearly caused a scandal for the royal family when they threatened to publicize the details of their relationships with the prince after "he was notably ungenerous over recompensing them for services rendered."[19] Only after Otto von Bismarck paid these women off did they back down. There were also rumors that Caroline Seiffert, one of Willy's mistresses, became pregnant in 1882 and gave birth to a daughter, but this has never been proven conclusively.

Making matters worse for Dona was her family's recurring presence. It irritated Willy that his bipolar mother-in-law, Ada, made frequent visits to Potsdam, where she created one problem after another. Recent studies into neurology have led some to speculate that the eccentric Dowager Duchess of Schleswig-Holstein could also have instead suffered from encephalitis, the symptoms of which—hallucinations, headaches, and violent or antisocial tendencies—were consistent with her behavior. Whether bipolar or encephalitic, Ada Holstein was the archetypal nightmarish mother-in-law. She took to bathing herself publicly at the Marble Palace. She detailed for the palace staff her "remarkable system of washing" herself, which involved dividing her body into twenty-four "'hemispheres,' and required a complete set of bowl, ewer, soap dish and towel for each one." At formal functions, Ada's manic behavior caused more than one public relations catastrophe. On two different occasions, she "made unspeakable assaults upon her male neighbours at table." When Dona and her ladies-in-waiting made efforts to calm the duchess, she responded by losing her temper, breaking glasses, and swearing "most obscenely." In the end, Willy—probably with Dona's full consent—declared that his mother-in-law could only visit three times a year. When she did, she could stay no longer than "one, two or three weeks, or as long as the household could stand it." Willy found it easier to get along with Dona's sisters, Calma, Louise Sophie, or Feodora. Although her brother Duke Ernest Günther of Schleswig-Holstein was pleasant enough, "he was also the sort of man who could not take a hint when it was time to terminate his visit. He was a clinger."[20]

When Dona's difficult relatives were not around, the daily routine that she and Willy settled into was perfect as far as the prince was concerned. His wife was forced to make the best of it. On a typical day, she would see her husband at breakfast. He would then dash off to his beloved military post, commanding the First Regiment of the Foot Guards, to which he was promoted by the emperor shortly before his wedding. The prince's duties with the foot guards usually revolved around maneuvers, parades, or other similar activities. On rare occasions, he returned to the Marble Palace for lunch. On those afternoons, he took Dona for a ride into the countryside around

Potsdam, but even these excursions were in the company of Willy's aide-de-camp. Dona was forced to accept early on that hers would always be a crowded marriage. Since childhood, Wilhelm had a deep need for the company of men to receive their approbation, praise, and encouragement. The form that this took in his life was his paradomaniac obsession with the military. From the age of twenty, he wore almost nothing but military uniforms. For centuries, the Prussian court had been fiercely militaristic, with princes and kings spending their entire lives devoted to the army. Prussia's very identity was its inextricable link between the monarchy and the military. Willy, in turn, idolized his warrior grandfather, Emperor Wilhelm I, and he strove to be exactly like him. Usually he saw his soldiers more frequently than his wife.

The happiness Willy and Dona did enjoy was overshadowed by the political and personal dramas that played themselves out in the Prussian royal family. Willy's bitter struggle with his parents, especially his mother, was like a poisonous cloud engulfing Potsdam. Before long, Dona found herself involved in the clash between her husband and his mother. The relationship between the two women began amicably enough. Vicky took it upon herself to mentor and guide Dona through life at the Prussian court, but what she failed to realize was that, through "shyness and fright," Dona did not possess the psychological capacity to respond to her mother-in-law's efforts.[21] Vicky became "impatient with Dona's slow mind and with occasional stupidities." Since the crown princess did not hide her feelings, "Dona saw this and resented it."[22] This only reinforced the negative gossip Dona heard about Vicky and soon began criticizing her mother-in-law the same way Willy did. She was especially indignant at the way the crown princess was constantly interfering in every aspect of their lives. Nothing seemed to be off-limits. Dona wrote that she was "in complete despair" over her mother-in-law's meddling. It especially bothered her, she told Willy, that Vicky openly declared "everything which you ... have arranged with such trouble and such careful consideration and finally perhaps to your satisfaction to be ugly."[23]

In what was shaping into a battle involving two strong-willed women, the crown princess let it be known that she disapproved of Dona's ultraconservative nature. The problem between these two women was a clash of ideologies, one that played itself out in the prejudices and intricacies of the Prussian court. It was also a microcosm of the political divisions of Europe in the 1880s. Dona, conservative and increasingly distrustful of other ethnic groups, represented Prussia and Germany; while Vicky, with her liberal, parliamentary ideas, was the embodiment of all things English. When Queen Victoria asked her daughter why she had supported Willy's marrying Dona if the princess was so difficult, Vicky replied, "Dona seemed to me the most likely to make an excellent wife & mother. We had great affection & esteem for her father. I *then* hoped and thought she might be grateful & affectionate to me ... in *that* my hopes have been *completely* disappointed."[24]

As time went on, Dona and Willy's relationship with Vicky remained uneasy. In September 1886, Willy was struck with an excruciating inner ear infection after returning from a visit to Russia. His physician, Dr. Trautmann, informed Dona that the illness was "relatively insignificant," but a few days later the infection spread.[25] For a while, Willy's life appeared in peril. An emergency surgery to save his life was barely successful; it took nearly two more weeks for him to show any sign of improvement. Terrified for her husband's life, Dona perched herself at his bedside, holding his hand as she waited and prayed. "Dona is most devoted to him and never leaves him for one minute," Vicky admitted to her mother. By the end of October, Willy had rallied. Dona stayed close to her husband throughout his convalescence. With his recovery, a degree of intimacy returned to their marriage. The drama of Willy's illness also exacerbated the quarrel with his mother, who tried to take over as his nurse. "A little civility, kindness and *empressement* go a long way ... but I never get them from him," Vicky complained to her mother, "it is very painful to a soft-hearted Mama to feel so plainly that her own child does not care whether he sees her or no, whether she is well or ill, or away, etc."[26]

Amid the ongoing frustrations of Dona's life in Potsdam with her in-laws, her one refuge was her children. She fulfilled Willy's paternal dreams by delivering four sons, one after the other. Little Willy was followed by Eitel-Frederick ("Eitel-Fritz") in 1883, Adalbert in 1884, and Augustus Wilhelm ("Auwi") in 1887. One courtier observed of Dona that "so frequent were the stork's visits in the young household that [she] was unable to appear at the great Court festivals for three winters in succession."[27] Regardless, Dona "loved above everything else the numerous children who were born to her in quick succession, and was never so happy as when playing with them in their nursery."[28] From an early age, the little princes were inculcated with the traditional Prussian passion for the military. They "grew up surrounded by lead solders, by little cannons that discharged peas, and by every kind of plaything that had some near or remote bearing on real military science." Little Willy "was allowed to run along the carefully raked walks of the parks with his noisy companions, to play at war in miniature; he was permitted to construct strongholds of sand, fortresses of pounded earth, and, by digging up the flower beds or grass plots sacrificed to his youthful and bellicose whims, he was able to enjoy a foretaste of the trenches of 1914."[29]

Exactly eight weeks before Little Willy celebrated his sixth birthday, everything in his mother's life changed forever. Ninety-one-year-old Emperor Wilhelm I died on March 6, 1888. His last words included an endorsement for Dona's husband: "I have always been pleased with you, for you have always done everything right."[30] Willy, now crown prince of Germany and Prussia, confided in his diary, "William I., King of Prussia and First German Emperor, passed away this morning. At eight o'clock he passed into eternity so quietly that it was only when Doctor Leuthold approached him and closed his eyes that I knew that all was over."[31] Willy's parents ascended the throne as Emperor Frederick III and Empress Victoria. "The sad news has just come that dear Emperor has passed away!" Vicky tearfully wrote to her mother from San Remo, where she was staying with Fritz, who was battling excruciating laryngeal cancer. She continued, "Fritz is deeply affected ... I cannot tell you how anxious I feel and how nervous.... To think of my poor Fritz succeeding his father as a sick and stricken man is so hard!!"[32] The next day, Vicky and Fritz held a brief ceremony in the drawing room at the Villa Zirio where the new emperor was sworn in. During the ceremony, he took off his Order of the Black Eagle and placed it on the shoulders of his wife, who burst into tears—along with Dona later on, Vicky was the only woman to ever be invested with the Black Eagle. The great tragedy for Fritz and Vicky was that they had so many dreams to reform Germany, but Fritz was so near death from cancer when he became emperor that everyone knew he would not last long.

When the imperial train bearing the new monarchs on their return from San Remo pulled into the Charlottenburg station in the west end of Berlin's old quarter, Dona, Willy, and his brother Henry were there to meet Fritz and Vicky. The winter that year was especially unforgiving, with large snowdrifts and howling winds sweeping through the station. When the emperor and empress got off the train, the scene that unfolded was heartrending. After embracing his son, Fritz turned to Dona, who, with tears streaming down her face, threw herself into the towering emperor's arms. One witness at the station recalled that the "whole scene was exceedingly affecting, and many of the onlookers were moved to tears."[33] A few days later, the city of Berlin gathered to mourn the death of the man who had forged the German Empire. The royal family, dressed in furs and pelts, walked behind the gun carriage bearing the old emperor's coffin—the use of a gun carriage in state funerals was a sign of the deceased's status as a great military leader. Fritz's wretched health was devastated by the harsh winter, forcing him to watch the funeral procession from a raised dais so he could see through the palace windows while he wept. One witness noted that there was nothing "more pathetic, more tragic, than the spectacle of the funeral *cortège* wending its solemn way through the snow-drifted park, with the death-stricken Emperor Frederick looking on from an upper window of the Palace, because [he was] unable to follow the body of his father to the tomb!"[34]

Willy chose this opportunity to step up his attacks on his mother. Even though Vicky's husband was the reigning emperor, Germany's social elites were inclined to side with her truculent son. Bismarck made sure Willy was named deputy emperor on March 23, along with arranging for him to chair a number of government committees and take up a position at the German Foreign Office. "So they already look upon me as dead," Fritz muttered to Vicky.[35] Willy's supporters quickly expanded to include Vicky's older children, Charly and Henry. She wrote bitterly to her mother, "People in general consider us a mere passing shadow soon to be replaced by *reality* in the shape of William!!"[36] Queen Victoria had "no words to express" her "indignation and astonishment" at how coldly Willy was acting during this time.[37] Frederick III was nearly incapacitated. He had endured a painful tracheotomy, could barely speak, and issued his orders by scrawling them onto pieces of scrap paper. His own chancellor, Otto von Bismarck, unscrupulously jumped ship and threw his support behind Willy.

To help shore up support for her daughter, and to remind Willy that she was still a powerful woman, Queen Victoria made a rare visit to Germany on her way back to England after a holiday in Italy. After arriving at the Charlottenburg station on April 25, where the queen was met by Vicky, her daughters, and all their children, she was taken to Vicky's home, the Neues Palais. Once she had readied herself, Victoria accompanied her daughter to see Fritz. In her diary, the queen recorded the emotional reunion with her beloved son-in-law: "He was lying in bed, and he raised up both hands with pleasure at seeing me and gave me a nosegay. It was very touching and sad to see him thus in bed."[38] It was the last time Fritz and the queen would ever meet. Afterward, Victoria made a visit to the nearby Marble Palace to see Dona and the children. Although she enjoyed the presence of her great-grandchildren, the two women were icily cold to one another, stemming from the latter's anger over the precedence issue from the jubilee the year before.

Of all the meetings the queen held during her brief German visit, it was her face-to-face audience with Otto von Bismarck at Charlottenburg Palace that was the most memorable. After the forty-five-minute confrontation, the politically battle-hardened Bismarck walked out of the meeting wiping the sweat from his forehead. According to Arthur Bigge, the queen's assistant private secretary, Bismarck declared, *"Mein Gott! That* was a woman! One could do business with her!" The next day, Victoria returned to the railway station bound for the coast. She described in her diary that night the wrenching good-bye from her daughter: "I kissed her again and again. She struggled hard not to give way, but finally broke down, and it was terrible to see her standing there in tears while the train slowly moved off, and to think of all she was suffering and might have to go through. My poor child, what would I not do to help her in her hard lot."[39]

The highly charged atmosphere in Potsdam was slightly interrupted a month later when Willy's brother Henry married Alix's sister Princess Irene of Hesse on May 24. Everyone made a valiant though transparent effort to seem happy. Fritz donned one of his elaborate military dress uniforms, leaning heavily on a cane during the ceremony. Vicky, dressed in a pale green silk dress accented with diamonds around the neck, did everything within her abilities to set aside her feelings for Willy and Dona. This bitter struggle between Dona, Willy, Vicky, and her meager number of supporters resumed after the wedding, but it did not last long. After a reign of only ninety-nine days, Fritz's agonizing battle with cancer came to an end on June 15, 1888, making him the shortest-reigning monarch in Prussian history. It was a bittersweet day for the immediate royal family, as only hours before they had put on brave faces to celebrate the eighteenth birthday of Willy's sister Sophie. "What a birthday for the poor child!" Vicky recorded, "what a recollection for the whole of her life! The last day on earth of her beloved father!" In the moments after his death, Vicky placed on his chest the wreath she had given him during the Franco-Prussian War. After placing a sword in his hand, she collapsed beside his bed, consumed by her grief as Dona, Willy, and her daughters looked on in silence. Upon hearing the dreadful news of Fritz's passing, Queen Victoria immediately sent a letter to her grandson. "I am broken-hearted," she wrote. "Help and do all you can for your poor dear Mother and try to follow in your best, noblest, and kindest of father's footsteps."[40]

If his early years had shown Willy to be a selfish albeit young man, his accession to the throne as Emperor Wilhelm II revealed how truly flawed his character was. Within an hour of his father's death, Wilhelm sent his soldiers to ransack the Neues Palais in search of documents to incriminate his parents. Rooms were torn apart, desks were overturned, and belongings were destroyed. When the new emperor finally returned, dressed in his full military uniform, "he gave his shocked mother no explanation. More high-ranking officers came to ransack the palace and rifle through Fritz's desk again while Vicky huddled with her three youngest daughters, the dead emperor's body still lying nearby."[41] Queen Victoria was horrified by his actions and shuddered to think about Germany under his rule. She wrote to her granddaughter Victoria of Battenberg, "It is too dreadful for us to think of Willy & Bismarck & Dona—being the supreme head of all now! Two so unfit & one so wicked."[42]

The new emperor immediately set about consolidating his power. He wanted to ensure there was no question that he reigned supreme by the will of God. On June 25, he made his first throne speech to a crowded Reichstag. Keeping with his theatrical personality, Wilhelm spoke with bravado and rhetoric. He was explicit that the entire powers of the Prusso-German monarchy were embodied in him, along with the empire's complex constitution, which he swore to "watch over and protect."[43] His words were quickly to put to the test. Less than ten months after becoming emperor, Wilhelm was faced with his first major crisis in the form of massive, nationwide labor strikes. The crisis began in May 1889 in the empire's heavy industry core, the Ruhr basin, situated on the Westphalian plain near the Lower Rhine. In a relatively short period, the unrest spread into Aachen, the Saar region, Saxony, and eventually to Silesia, one of the richest mining regions in the eastern empire. It was a tremendously violent uprising that lasted for nearly a year. Direct mediation was required between the emperor, the chancellor, and the industry leaders before some sort of equilibrium was restored months later.

Vicky, somewhat naively and with her usual poor choice of timing, felt that during the heavy industry crisis of 1889–90 was an appropriate time to enlist Dona's help in deflecting some of her son's wrath. She hoped her daughter-in-law, who was now German empress and queen of Prussia, would be able to step into the fray in a direct manner on her behalf. But at the time of her husband's accession, Dona could do little. At thirty years old, she was almost nine months pregnant with her fifth child. Many were afraid that the stress of two deaths and two accessions in three months would cause Dona problems during her pregnancy. These concerns were put to rest a month later. After what turned out to be a particularly harrowing six months, Empress Augusta Victoria was blessed with another son. Vicky, who was now styled as Empress Frederick, wrote to her mother, "William is overjoyed that it is a boy ... He was afraid it might have been 'only' a girl!! *She* is pleased too."[44] When the baby prince was christened that summer, he was given the name Oscar, in honor of his illustrious godfather, King Oscar II of Sweden.

The official mourning period prescribed by etiquette for the death of Emperor Frederick III was insultingly short—at Wilhelm's insistence. With Fritz's calming presence gone, the battle within the royal family turned decisively against Vicky and in favor of the new emperor and empress. Wilhelm funded a vituperative public campaign to smear his mother. Accusations against her ranged from "passing military secrets to the French during the Franco-Prussian War" to contributing "to her husband's death because she had supposedly ignored the German doctors." The accusations against her prompted her to write to her mother, "I am no longer astonished at any *lies* or impertinence. The most imprudent gang in the world, without principles or conscience, is now in power! I feel *utterly without any protection* whatsoever!" She accused her son of trying "to wipe out all trace of Fritz's reign, as of an *interlude* without importance.... William II succeeds William the 1st—in *perfect* continuity."[45]

With her husband now the head of the German Empire and the Prussian royal family, Dona found herself somewhat relegated to the sidelines, less involved in the battle between her husband and her mother-in-law. Dona took a less direct stand against Vicky and instead focused all of her energies on her children, whom she kept isolated from the dowager empress, which left her mother-in-law speechless. "They are kept entirely away from me, though I am so passionately fond of children," Vicky wrote to a friend.[46] She could not believe Dona would not unite with her against Wilhelm's outrageous behavior. Vicky wrote to Queen Victoria, "She has *quite* forgotten me, or does not like to remember, or really does not understand what she owes me.... She has a great sense of duty, but she does not seem to see *what* her duty towards *me* is!"[47] The environment at the Prussian court quickly became toxic. The Empress Frederick publicly disapproved of everything Dona and Wilhelm did. This left Dona, who always felt somewhat intimidated by Vicky, feeling more insecure than ever. She overcompensated by becoming obsessed with her role as empress and the prerogatives that came with it. The problem was that she had never been properly educated about wielding power, and Wilhelm's egocentric personality greatly enhanced her own less appealing qualities. In time, Dona would develop a dichotic personality, marked by narrow-mindedness and haughtiness but also by loyalty, honor, and devotion. The question was, which traits would prevail, and what would Empress Augusta Victoria's lasting legacy be?

4

"Bitter Tears"

(1889–92)

In January 1889, Princess Alix of Hesse-Darmstadt returned to Russia for six weeks to visit Serge and Ella. Unlike her first visit for Ella's wedding, this time Alix was the center of attention. A small crowd of royals gathered at the train station to welcome the princess, including Ella, Serge, Tsar Alexander III, and his besotted son Nicky. When he saw Alix again, Nicky enthusiastically wrote in his diary that she "has grown up a lot and become much prettier."[1] Alix stayed at Ella's home, the pink-tinged, "grandiose" Beloselsky-Belozersky Palace, on the banks of the Neva and Fontanka rivers in Saint Petersburg. Ella's home embodied all the magnificence of imperial Russia. Everywhere inside the palace there was a "profusion of wealth and splendour ... Silks and velvets, marble and ormolu, gilding and tapestry, plate and pictures, inlaid floorings and mosaic tables, were all literally scattered everywhere."[2]

Alix's first day in Russia was packed with activities in Saint Petersburg, whose winter social scene was reportedly the most extravagant in the world. Ice-skating and tobogganing in the afternoon were followed by a candlelit ball at the Winter Palace. Alix recalled that after dinner that evening, she and Ella "went to the Winter Palace where we dressed for the ball (white diamonds, white flowers and sash)."[3] The thousand-square-foot marble White Ballroom was decorated in sparkling diamonds for the occasion. During Alix's visit, her constant companion was the young and handsome Tsarevitch Nicholas, whose parents, Alexander and Minnie, watched her closely, scrutinizing her every move. Whatever adolescent feelings Nicky and Alix may have had when they first met had since fully blossomed into love. When Alix returned to Darmstadt, she left her heart in Russia. She and Nicky began writing to one another in English, the only language they shared. "It was so good of you to write and it gave me great pleasure," Alix wrote after receiving one of Nicky's letters. "Thank you so much for your dear little letter," came the reply from Nicholas, who made no secret of his feelings for Alix by closing with the words, "With much love, your ever loving Nicky."[4]

Nicholas became determined to make her his wife. What he did not realize was that he would have to contend with the most powerful force in Alix's life: her grandmother, who was against the match. Queen Victoria had hoped to pair Alix with her grandson Prince Eddy. He was a young man to whom historians have been somewhat ungenerous. While certainly not a pillar of the monarchy or a man who inspired great confidence, the listless, indolent Eddy became the subject of a historical feeding frenzy when an article appeared in the periodical *The Criminologist* in November 1970. The author, Dr. Thomas Stowell, began a decades-long belief that Eddy was not only a sybaritic, syphilitic lethario, but that he was also Jack the Ripper. This also led to speculation that Eddy was involved with the notorious Hundred Guinness Club on Cleveland Street, which was embroiled in a scandal in 1889 alleging the club was a male brothel.[5]

In pairing Alix with Eddy, Queen Victoria was also in love with the idea of Alix one day becoming queen of England. When Alix was seventeen, Queen Victoria brought her and Eddy to her Scottish home, Balmoral Castle, to give them a chance to take a liking to one another—this was something the queen did often, as she fancied herself her family's matchmaker. Strained lectures on Eddy's virtues, coupled with his own protestations of love for Alix all came to naught. It became quickly obvious that Alix had no interest in Eddy, despite the tantalizing prospect of becoming queen. Queen Victoria was resolute until the end. She wrote to Alix's sister Victoria in March 1889, trying to convince her to intervene: "Is there *no* hope abt. E[ddy].? She is *not* 19—& she shld. be made to reflect seriously on the folly of throwing away the chance of a very good Husband, kind, affectionate & steady & of entering a united happy family & a very good position wh. is second to *none* in *the world*!"[6]

A few months later, the queen wrote again to Princess Victoria, frustrated by Alix's lack of interest in Eddy: "We have just a *faint lingering* hope that Alicky *might in time* look to see what a pleasant home, & what a *useful* position she will lose if she ultimately *persists* in not yielding to Eddy's *really earnest* wishes. He wrote to me he shld. *not* give up the idea (tho' it is considered for the *present at an end*)—and: 'I don't think she shows how I love her, or she cld. not be so cruel.'"[7] In the spring of 1890, Alix sat down to write Eddy a letter. Once and for all, she wanted to put an end to any notion of their getting married. Although it "pained her to pain him," she wrote that she could not marry him, nor would they ever be truly happy as husband and wife. She reaffirmed her cousinly affection for him and left it at that.[8] Her words did little to soothe the sting of rejection Eddy was feeling. He wrote to Prince Louis of Battenberg, Alix's brother-in-law.

> For I can't really believe Alicky knows how much I love her, or she would not I think have treated me quite so cruelly. I can't help considering it so, as she apparently gives me no chance at all, and little or no hope; although I shall continue loving her, and in the hope that some day she may think better of what she has said, and give me the chance of being one of the happiest beings in the world. For I should indeed consider myself so, if I would only call her my own.

> ....Perhaps later you might be able to find out if there is any real reason why Alicky does not care for me, and if I have offended her in any way. For Ernie said there was none, which makes it all harder for me to understand.[9]

"It is a real sorrow to us," Queen Victoria wrote to the Empress Frederick once the matter was settled, "she [Alix] says – that if she is *forced* she will do it – but that she would be unhappy & he – too. This shows g[rea]t strength of character as all her family & all of us wish it, & she refuses the g[rea]test position there is."[10] One of the great historical ironies of Alix's life was that she probably would have been much better as the queen of England than the empress of Russia. Trained by Queen Victoria, she fit the British idea of royalty exactly. It remains uncertain whether or not Alix ever realized how incredibly different her life—and history as a whole—would have been had she married Eddy.

In truth, Eddy was never a contender for Alix's affections. Her heart belonged to Nicky of Russia. Their romance was encouraged by her sister Ella, who enjoyed playing matchmaker between her sister and her husband's nephew. When Queen Victoria caught wind of this, she was livid. She wrote Alix and Ella's sister Victoria to "take care & *tell* Ella that no marriage for *Alicky in Russia* wld be *allowed*, then there will be *an end of it*."[11] By the end of the year, no one had been able to dissolve the prospect of marriage between Nicky and Alix. Frustrated with the whole thing, the queen told Princess Victoria, "Papa must put his foot down and there must be no more visits of Alicky to Russia—and he must and you and Ernie must insist on a stop being put to the whole affair." Later, she explained to her granddaughter why she was so adamant about Alix not marrying Nicky: "The state of Russia is so bad, so rotten that at any moment something dreadful might happen and though it may not signify to Ella, the wife of a *Thronfolger* [heir to the throne] is in a most difficult and precarious position."[12]

Determined not to see her favorite granddaughter married to the Russian heir, Queen Victoria hatched another plan to get Alix married off to someone else. The new incumbent was Prince Max of Baden, a cousin of Emperor Wilhelm II. Tactless and unpopular but otherwise acceptable, Max was brought to Darmstadt on the queen's order and was under the distinct impression that Alix had already accepted him. Alix—who had been completely unaware of the scheme up until that point—was horrified when she was told that Max had come with the explicit purpose of proposing to her. "I vividly remember the torments I suffered," Alix told a friend years later. "I did not know him at all and I shall never forget what I suffered when I met him for the first time."[13] Sensing another forced romance, Alix summoned all of her defenses. Her icy outward demeanor became stronger than ever, prompting her to withdraw into herself. It took a combined plea from both herself and her sister Victoria to convince Max that she had no interest in him. His visit made a profound impression on Alix because she realized that the matchmaking would never come to an end until she was engaged or unless she made a declaration to never marry.

At the same time that Princess Alix was visiting Russia, Europe was hit by one of the biggest royal scandals of the nineteenth century. On the morning of January 30, 1889, the heir to the Austrian throne, Crown Prince Rudolf, was found dead along with his mistress, Baroness Marie Vetsera. Their bodies were discovered at the crown prince's hunting lodge in the tiny village of Mayerling, fifteen miles southwest of Vienna. Rudolf's father, the ultraconservative Emperor Franz Joseph, ordered his government to release an official statement in the Austrian newspaper *Wiener Zeitung* claiming the cause of death was apoplexy. This was later edited to be heart failure. No mention was made of the baroness whatsoever; she was quickly buried privately at the abbey cemetery in nearby Heiligenkreuz. Few people believed the official story, and it did not take long for rumors to begin to circulate. One of the more outlandish conspiracy theories was that Freemasons had perpetrated the murder to seek revenge on the Habsburgs for their devoted adherence to Catholicism. The more popular theories claimed that Rudolf "had been seriously wounded out shooting and could not live; that he and his mistress had been found in bed dead from cyanide poisoning; that he had died after a duel; that he had been killed by a forester for seducing his daughter; that he had been hit over the head with a bottle by his cousin the Archduke John ..."[14]

Investigators who arrived at Mayerling were eventually forced to conclude that Rudolf killed Marie, then shot himself in the head in a grisly murder-suicide pact. Various explanations for what could have possibly motivated such a tragedy were put forward. Some claimed Rudolf had been suffering from depression. Others mentioned the fact that his mother, Empress Elizabeth, came from the Wittelsbach dynasty of Bavaria, whose members reportedly suffered from mental instability for a confounding forty generations.[15] A more widely circulated rumor, even to this day, was that the crown prince had contracted a venereal disease and found killing himself preferable to a long, lingering death from his supposed illness.

The blood-chilling details of the Mayerling Incident left royals and commoners alike shaking their heads in disbelief. Murders and assassinations were one thing, but for a crown prince to take his own life was a tragedy that no one ever imagined. Wilhelm and Dona took the news quite badly—Dona broke down sobbing when she was told. The emperor and empress had been close friends with the crown prince and had even attended his wedding to Princess Stéphanie of Belgium in 1881 as honored guests. One of Wilhelm's staff reported how "very shocked" he was and that he could "even now scarcely believe that it was suicide." When Wilhelm later made his first visit to Rudolf's grave, Dona wrote to him, "A friend of your youth in the same position in life, and *how* different, thank God, the course of your lives! One can easily see there what a difference it makes whether someone has built on the right ground or not!!"[16]

After Crown Prince Rudolf's death, Emperor Franz Joseph was hard-pressed to find an heir to the throne, since Rudolf had been his only son. The laws of succession in Austria decreed that the succeeding heir should have been the emperor's next brother, Maximilian, but he had met an equally sad end as Rudolf. A die-hard adventurer who "had been tempted to become an Emperor of sorts,"[17] the blond, handsome Maximilian became the first and only emperor of Mexico in 1864 after the country declared its independence from Spain. Sadly, Maximilian's reign lasted only three turbulent years before he was overthrown and executed by firing squad on a hilltop in Querétaro, Mexico. Since Maximilian had no children, the succession passed to Franz Joseph's next brother, Archduke Charles Louis, but he renounced his rights to the throne in favor of his eldest son, Archduke Franz Ferdinand, on February 1. If Franz Joseph thought that his dynastic affairs would settle down in the months and years after his son's death, he was terribly mistaken.

꧁

When Wilhelm II ascended the Prusso-German throne in 1888, Dona became the first of Europe's last imperial consorts to become an empress. Only twenty-nine at the time, she was the youngest reigning consort in Europe, as well as the youngest empress of modern Germany.[18] Only a year after Frederick III's death, the new empress hosted her first major public event. In the summer of 1889, a coterie of royals converged on Berlin for the wedding of her sister Princess Louise Sophie to Prince Frederick Leopold of Prussia, one of the emperor's many extended relatives. The grand but brief ceremony at the Stadtschloss was followed by a glittering wedding banquet attended by hundreds of guests. After a brief honeymoon, the newlyweds became familiar faces at the Prussian court. Unlike Dona's mother and brother, Louise Sophie's presence in Berlin and Potsdam was welcome. The princess, besides being beautiful, was well received by the people and only increased their rising affection for their young empress.

The popularity Dona enjoyed was sharply countered by the continuing tensions within the Prussian royal family. Unlike her husband, who had been trained all his life to one day wear the crown, Dona was learning as she went, having had only a few years in Prussia to learn what was expected of her. As a consequence, she clung to Wilhelm more tightly than ever to guide, influence, and protect her. This had the understandable effect of widening the gulf of hostility that separated her and Wilhelm from Vicky and her side of the family. "I am sorry to say poor Dona is not a help but an obstacle," Vicky told Queen Victoria. "Her pride is so great that she thinks she knows better than everyone, because she is the Empress, and she is always on the defensive, and ridiculously *exigeante*."[19] This pride Vicky sensed from Dona—usually in response to some criticism from the dowager empress—also alienated Wilhelm's sisters, who resented Dona's interfering in their lives. "She meddles in *every* thing the family does," Vicky wrote later, "*every little* trifle is reported to her & she orders & directs in a way very galling for the others."[20] Lamar Cecil, one of Wilhelm II's biographers, agreed with Vicky's assessment of Dona. "By almost all accounts," he wrote, "including those of her admirers, the Kaiserin was very self-conscious of her high position and determined that everyone acknowledge it." He concluded that this was "undoubtedly a legacy of her being descended from a minor house scorned by Wilhelm's Hohenzollern and Hanoverian ancestors."[21]

This Hohenzollern family war was not purely a domestic Prussian issue but would also have a lasting impact on German foreign relations. The seeds of future international discord were sown in October 1889 when the Prussian royal family traveled to Athens for another family wedding. This time, Wilhelm's sister Sophie was marrying the heir to the Greek throne, Crown Prince Constantine ("Tino"). The ceremony was truly an affair *en famille* that brought together Sophie and Tino's cousins from Britain, Germany, Denmark, and Russia. It was the first time in centuries that Athens had seen so splendid a naval display. Dozens of yachts, cruisers, and battleships from Britain and Germany anchored themselves near the port at Piraeus. When Wilhelm and Dona arrived on their imperial yacht, the unimaginatively named *Hohenzollern*, they created a debacle. Accompanied by a deliberately oversized suite of sixty-seven attendants for the emperor alone, the pair made it a point to offend almost every member of the Greek royal family. Dona was icily cold to Tino's mother, the affable and pious Queen Olga. As a former Romanov grand duchess, Olga was on the receiving end of Dona's antipathy for all things Russian—an antipathy possibly rooted in a perceived snub her husband had received on a trip to Saint Petersburg. Her husband did not fare any better. Wilhelm II infuriated Tino's father, King George I, when he brought his own Lutheran pastor to perform the wedding, insisting that no sister of the emperor would be married in a Greek Orthodox ceremony. The king was so furious he refused to even meet with Wilhelm or Dona face to face, "a slight for which Wilhelm never forgave him."[22]

During the Greek trip, Dona began to show signs of health problems. Still a relatively young woman, she suffered muscle weakness, exhaustion, a general frailty, and nervous anxiety. The emperor was not surprised by her fragile constitution. He generally viewed women as weaker than, less robust than, and generally inferior to men—a true Hohenzollern misogynist. It is also likely that he knew when he married Dona that her health would be an issue, given her father's death from cancer and her mother's litany of maladies. The empress's five pregnancies in six years—each of which was more difficult than the last—did not help her situation. At the time of the visit to Greece, Dona was in between pregnancies, but it was still tiring.

Once she returned to Germany, Dona had little time to rest or recover herself. Shortly before Christmas 1889, Wilhelm's uncle the Prince of Wales and his son George arrived for a state visit. Wilhelm, who dressed in a British admiral's uniform for most of the visit, insisted that Dona throw as many grand parties as she could for them. The presence of Wilhelm's English relatives did not appeal to the empress. Since her marriage, she began subscribing to the Anglophobia that saturated the Prussian court and was made worse by Vicky's unabashed English patriotism. On a personal level, Dona still resented being forced to take precedence after the queen of Hawaii at Queen Victoria's jubilee. She also despised Wilhelm's aunt—the Princess of Wales—for her very public anti-German views. As the daughter of King Christian IX of Denmark, whose accession to the throne in 1863 sparked the Second Schleswig War, Princess Alexandra never forgave the Holsteins or Prussia for "stealing" the duchies from her father, which she believed were his rightful inheritance. Whereas Dona and Vicky represented disparate ideologies, Dona and Alexandra loathed one another for deeply personal reasons.

By the time Bertie and George visited Germany, the empress's views toward Great Britain bordered on Anglophobia. In her estimation, both that country and its royal family "meant immorality, hypocrisy and liberalism."[23] She felt there was no greater embodiment of that hypocritical liberalism than her uncle-in-law, the popular and charismatic Prince of Wales, whom she decried as "disgusting and immoral."[24] During Bertie's visit, Dona's low opinion of him was confirmed when he declined Wilhelm's invitation to be made an admiral in the German navy. The move was driven by the Princess of Wales, who insisted her husband refuse any such offers. This was an unforgivable offense in the empress's opinion. Always the peacemaker, Prince George accepted an honorary commission in a Prussian dragoon regiment. It is interesting to note that Dona held George in esteem, despite her dislike for his mother and father. Perhaps it was because he could not have been more different than his fashionable, forward-thinking parents. Whatever the reason for it, when George accepted the honorary commission, the Princess of Wales was furious. The letter she wrote to her son about it accurately conveys her feelings: "So my Georgie boy has become a real filthy blue-coated Pickelhaube German soldier!!! Well, I never thought to have lived to see that! But never mind; as you say, it could not have been helped—it was your misfortune and not your fault—and anything was better—even my two boys being sacrificed!!!—than Papa being made a German Admiral—that I could not have survived—you would have had to look for our poor old Motherdear at the bottom of the sea."[25]

Once Bertie and George returned to London, Dona's life still continued to be a whirlwind. At the start of the New Year, she informed her husband she was pregnant for the sixth time. This coincided with the downfall of Wilhelm's chancellor, Otto von Bismarck. Since Wilhelm ascended the throne, he and the Machiavellian chancellor had constantly been at loggerheads. Eventually, Wilhelm forced Bismarck's resignation after years of growing hostility toward Russia. Wilhelm, who strongly disliked Tsar Alexander III, was convinced that Russia was preparing an invasion of Germany. Bismarck—who had once been the Prussian ambassador to Russia—was not so shortsighted and realized Germany's survival depended on cooperation between Berlin and Saint Petersburg. In the end, the emotionally driven Wilhelm won out after Bismarck's government, the Kartell, was smashed in the most recent elections in the Reichstag. A few days later, the emperor visited Bismarck and demanded his resignation. Wilhelm was relieved by Bismarck's dismissal, writing that it felt like "at last I had gotten rid of the tutor who wished to rule me with the same iron hand he had used in ruling Prussia and, later on, Germany."[26] Desperate to remain in power, the elderly Bismarck visited his old nemesis the Empress Frederick to ask for help. "I am sorry," Vicky replied, "you, yourself, Prince Bismarck, have destroyed all my influence with my son. I can do nothing."[27] Surprisingly, the foreign press was ambivalent about Bismarck's departure from the political scene. He may have annexed hundreds of thousands of miles of land to Prussia, but he also had a strong ability to keep the German government in check. He was also fiercely devoted to the German nationalist cause, so when peace served Germany's purpose, he supported it. No one was certain what impact this would have on the future. Even the emperor was forced to admit that dismissing Bismarck may have been a faulty move: "I have discovered in regard to foreign politics the retirement of Prince Bismarck has not left the German Empire upon the best of terms with its neighbours, nor with any definite policy."[28]

As her husband worked to steer the German ship of state, Dona continued to devote herself to being a model empress and *Landesmutter*. Though, after a decade in Prussia, Dona continued to be viewed by the country's elite as provincial and unsophisticated, the same could not be said for the greater German population. In many ways, these ordinary citizens were the people with whom Dona connected the most. Her sparse childhood gave her great sensitivity to the hardships endured by others, especially women and children. Where the masses were concerned, their empress was a bridge between them and the monarchy. Her religious views were especially important in developing a rapport with the German people. Southern states like Bavaria may have been Roman Catholic, and though Wilhelm II tried to win German Catholic public opinion by making symbolic gestures, it was Prussia and the more dominant northern kingdoms that were almost fanatical in their adherence to German Lutheranism.

Known as both the Prussian Union and the Evangelical Christian Church, German Lutheranism melded extremely well with Empress Augusta Victoria's devoted, serious nature. Its forms and beliefs, bred into her since she was a small child, continued to strike a deep chord in Dona's heart, even into adulthood. She was especially receptive to the core Lutheran belief in salvation by faith alone, not by good works and prayer. Unlike so many other rulers, the empress's faith was at the very core of her being, and she looked upon matters of life, salvation, and eternity with seriousness. She interpreted biblical scriptures literally. According to one member of the Prussian court, "her view is that without religion no people can really be great, nor do they deserve the protection of Providence."[29] Not everyone saw Dona's faith as a strength. Foreign observers, certain members of Berlin high society, and some southern Catholic political groups accused the empress of using Lutheranism to promote narrow-minded bigotry. It was reported by a contemporary that Dona dismissed those members of her household who were not committed members of the Evangelical Church. A more widely known incident took place in 1893, when the empress nearly caused an international incident when, during a visit to Rome, she refused to meet with the pope. Her feelings went well beyond the political arena. Wilhelm became friends with Albert Ballin, passenger division chief of the Hamburg-America Line. Ballin was responsible for naming his company's newest ship, the *Auguste Victoria,* in the empress's honor. Dona was impressed but disapproved of her husband's friendship with Ballin because he was Jewish.

As a woman who strictly subscribed to the tenets of Lutheranism and divinely appointed monarchy, the empress naturally believed that she and Wilhelm were called to rule by God's will. In Prussia, the connection between the monarch and God was so strong that coronations were often forgone because it was an accepted fact that the king, the state, and God were already as one, and no ceremony was needed to show this. Wilhelm II took this ideal to a new level. His "belief in himself as the divinely appointed mediator between God and his subjects was absolutely central to his conviction that it was the emperor's task, and his alone, to concentrate and reconcile in his person the divergent interests of regions, classes and confessions."[30] He and Dona were among the last rulers in Europe to claim they reigned by divine right. "We Hohenzollerns," Wilhelm once announced, "are the bailiffs of God."[31]

The empress had a less self-centered but equally grandiose view of divine right as her husband. This belief in God-given authority extended into Dona's general political views. Lamar Cecil, Wilhelm's American biographer, described her conservatism this way:

> Dona's ideas were undeviatingly conservative. She protested that she understood "little about politics," which was probably true enough, and she never attempted, as had Wilhelm's mother, to play a central role in affairs of state. But that did not mean that Dona cut herself off from politics, for she believed ardently in the maintenance of Hohenzollern prerogative, German superiority, and conservative principles. Modernity, whether in the arts, in religion, or in social behavior, was beyond the pale, and Dona was swift to view with suspicion all that was not solidly old-fashioned

and German. When the Kaiserin thought that any traditional values were threatened, she did not hesitate to intervene, urging Wilhelm to act decisively to ensure their preservation.[32]

At this point in her life, Dona's faith was a source of strength because she was living through a difficult period that taxed her already sensitive nerves. In the summer of 1890, the Russian tsar sent Wilhelm a troika accompanied by three wild Asiatic stallions. It was clear that the horses had never been properly broken in, making riding in the troika especially dangerous. Dona begged Wilhelm not to use it but to no avail. Only when the Russian driver who had arrived along with it asked for more money was he let go, a German driver brought in, and the horses properly trained. Hot on the heels of the troika episode came a state visit by King Leopold II of the Belgians, a man Dona thoroughly hated. Disaster nearly struck when Leopold was seriously burned by boiling water while taking a bath; some historians have argued the king blamed Dona for his injury. During the visit, Leopold behaved so reprehensibly that Dona ordered the court chaplain to perform an exorcism on his apartments when he left. The final contretemps for Dona came that autumn. Against Wilhelm's wishes, she surprised him and his retinue during a hunt at Hubertusstock. Dressed in a snow-white outfit, Dona's arrival frightened the deer being hunted, causing the men to not catch anything that day. Wilhelm was furious and ordered Dona to eat alone that night with her lady-in-waiting.

No sooner had she been returned to grace in her husband's affections than her convictions brought her into direct conflict with Wilhelm's more moderate sister Sophie, now the crown princess of Greece. In November 1890, Wilhelm's other sister, Moretta, was getting married to Prince Adolf of Schaumburg-Lippe. Tino and Sophie, who were now expecting their first child, came from Greece for the wedding. Once Moretta and Adolf had left for their honeymoon in Cairo, Sophie quietly told her family that she planned to convert from Lutheranism to the Greek Orthodox faith. Wilhelm took this as a personal affront. Furious, he could not find the words to confront his sister, so he asked Dona to do it. It is possible the emperor "thought Sophie would be more open to her sister-in-law than to him, and perhaps he thought she would not dare to argue with the heavily pregnant Empress," who was well into her third trimester by now.[33]

The meeting that followed was a disaster. Dona summoned Sophie to her apartments.

"I hear you are thinking of changing your religion," she said. "We shall never agree to that. If you have no feeling about it yourself, William, as Head of the Church and of our family, will speak to you.... You will end up in hell."

"That does not concern anyone here and I do not need to ask anyone," Sophie shot back.[34] "As for William," she snapped, "I know him better than that, he has absolutely no religion. If he had, he would never have behaved as he did [when Fritz died]."[35]

A disgusted Sophie stormed out of the meeting, slamming the door behind her. Dona became so hysterical that doctors had to be called in to calm her down. "The audacity of Dona to speak to Sophie like that!" Queen Victoria wrote indignantly.[36] Angry at being humiliated, Dona implored her husband to intervene. The next day, he showed up at the Neues Palais dressed in full imperial regalia and threatened, "If my sister does anything like [converting] I will forbid her [from entering] the country."[37] Later, Wilhelm sent an angry letter to Vicky and to Sophie's father-in-law, King George of Greece. He said that if Sophie went ahead with her conversion, she would be forbidden from entering Germany for the rest of her life. Both Queen Victoria and the Empress Frederick were fuming. In the queen's eyes, it was not Wilhelm who was at fault but Dona. In a letter to Sophie, Vicky relayed the queen's opinions: "I cannot say how grieved and distressed I am at what has happened, and which was so entirely unnecessary and uncalled for. I think it was all Dona's love of interference."[38]

Two weeks later, in December 1890, Dona went into premature labor with her sixth child. At the time, Wilhelm was attending a performance of *Tannhäuser* at the Opera House on Unter den Linden. During the performance, the emperor received a note that his wife was in labor. He shot up out of his seat and immediately departed. The opera manager was informed why the emperor was leaving so abruptly, who then went and announced Dona's accouchement to the audience. At the news, the people erupted into applause, cried out, "God save the Emperor and Empress!" and "long live the emperor and empress," and sang the national anthem.[39]

The onset of Dona's labor pains brought with it greater anxiety than in the past. Her almost consecutive pregnancies made each successive birth that much more difficult; she had a particularly difficult time coming back from her delivery in 1888. Since then, she had suffered at least two miscarriages, maybe more, and her doctors had advised her to not have any more children—a warning she obviously did not heed. Whether or not Wilhelm ever knew of his wife's miscarriages is not recorded. It is consistent with Dona's character that she may have hidden her medical difficulties from her husband. What is certain, however, is that her latest accouchement was quickly becoming perilous. She fought to keep her screams under control as she struggled through some of the worst labor pains she had ever experienced. An entire team of doctors and nurses waited upon the laboring empress, who was forced to submit to paddles and forceps to retrieve the infant when it became lodged in the birth canal. The attending physicians were hesitant to intervene directly, since there was a dangerous precedent for those doctors who chose to do so. In 1817, when the delivery of Princess Charlotte—the heir to the British throne before Queen Victoria—turned perilous, the doctor at the time intervened, but when both mother and child perished, he committed suicide. Eventually, the decision to intervene in Dona's delivery was made, and the child was saved—but at a high price.

For nearly two days afterward, the doctors feared for the empress's life because of constant hemorrhaging. It took another month for her to begin to show signs of recovery. The child was Dona's last son, whom Wilhelm named Joachim Francis Humbert, or simply Joachim for short. Wilhelm blamed the premature birth on Dona's confrontation with Sophie. Vicky, with more than a touch of sarcasm in her writing, explained the situation to Queen Victoria: "The version here ... is that *I* made a scene to Dona, announcing to her that Sophie had turned Greek, and in consequence, Dona had fallen ill, & the baby had been born too soon."[40] One of Wilhelm II's biographers has noted "William instantly blamed his sister for upsetting Dona; though the probability is that Dona's accumulated anxieties plus far too much riding and tight corseting had caused the premature birth."[41]

Even the happy occasion of a new baby, Dona's recovery, and her manifold popularity for giving Prussia and the empire a sixth prince, was overshadowed by the immutable Hohenzollern family politics. When Joachim was christened, the Empress Frederick offered to hold her new grandson, "as the Empress Augusta or Emperor Wilhelm held *all* mine," she recalled. But Dona denied her this, claiming, "William does not wish it as you are not the godmother."[42] Months after Joachim's birth, there was continued hostility even toward Crown Princess Sophie, especially after she converted. Five months after the fact, Wilhelm wrote to his grandmother that "Sophy [*sic*] made poor Dona—in the highest state of expectancy—an awful scene [*sic*] in which she behaved in a simply incredible manner like a naughty child which has been caught doing wrong. My poor wife got ill and bore too early and was for two days at death's door." He finished with his usual melodramatic style, writing in big letters, "If my poor Baby dies it is solely Sophy's fault and she has murdered it."[43]

Wilhelm and Dona's intransigence toward Sophie's conversion may have been consistent with Prussian ultraconservatism, but it did not earn them any points with their extended family. This fact was obvious when the emperor announced that he and his wife would travel to Britain in July 1891 for their first official state visit to the country. No one in the British royal family was happy about the visit. Queen Victoria was in the midst of hosting the wedding of one her granddaughters—Princess Marie Louise[44]—to Prince Aribert of Anhalt. The queen rightly believed that Wilhelm and Dona's presence would upstage the bride and groom, but the imperial couple insisted on coming anyway. Victoria was livid, but her daughter-in-law the Duchess of Edinburgh pointed out that although the queen might decry "that dreadful tyrant Wilhelm who always takes things so badly and makes rows about anything," once she saw him in person, the trouble would "all disappear."[45]

On July 4, the imperial yacht *Hohenzollern* arrived at the port town of Sheerness in Kent. Traveling abroad was never a small affair for the emperor and empress. Dona's suite alone was typically smaller than her husband's. It consisted of "ladies and gentlemen in waiting, marshals, equerries, masters of the hounds, valets, chamberlains, treasurers, her overseers of the plate, gun-chargers, mouth-cooks, and the cloud of footmen, couriers, coachmen, and grooms." When Dona's foreign tours did not include royal stops, she also brought her own linens for her bed and bathroom.[46] On this particular visit, Dona's personal suite numbered almost a hundred individuals. When they docked at Sheerness, they were met by the three highest-ranking men in the British royal family: the Prince of Wales, his son Eddy, and his brother the Duke of Connaught. As a sign of respect, all three were dressed in the uniform of the Prussian Hussars, accented by the gold sash of the Order of the Black Eagle. Upon taking the train to Windsor, Wilhelm and Dona were received by the rest of the royal family.

On July 10, the emperor and empress were hosted by the Lord Mayor of London. They were cheered by thousands of people as they drove through the city streets. Dona calmly waved while Wilhelm returned the salutes of the crowd. Wilhelm felt he was greeted with the proper respect due to "the most powerful of Continental monarchs." He was equally pleased to learn "that no foreign ruler—not even Napoleon III on his visit after the victorious war in the Crimea in 1855—had ever been greeted with anything approaching" this level of enthusiasm. There was no doubt that Wilhelm was a smashing success with the British people, but Dona—who was dressed in frumpy brown and gray dresses—managed to offend almost the entire royal court. She created "a very disagreeable impression by her stiffness, rudeness and arrogance towards the royal family and even towards the Queen."[47] Wilhelm's cousin Princess Marie of Edinburgh described Dona's attitude toward foreigners as a "stereotyped graciousness which too much resembled condescension to be quite pleasant."[48] Her growing Anglophobia took hold, prompting her to compare everything to life in Germany. She also made no effort to hide the fact that she distrusted non-Germans. Given Dona's performance during the visit, it surprised many when she decided to remain privately in England for a few weeks while Wilhelm embarked on a trip to Norway aboard the *Hohenzollern*. This is perhaps the only time in Dona's life—aside from childhood visits to her family—that she took a holiday in England. Declaring it a personal family vacation, she took her six sons, their tutors, governesses, and staff to Felixstowe in Suffolk.

Personal time with her children was tremendously important to Dona, whose family life was contented. She was devoted to each of her six sons yet had a unique relationship with each of them. Crown Prince Willy was brought up with more exacting discipline than his brothers, since he was the heir. There was a long-standing tradition of discord between fathers and sons in the Hohenzollern family. As far back as Frederick the Great and his father, King Frederick Wilhelm I, in the 1720s, Prussian rulers and their heirs had been viciously at odds. Wilhelm II had a difficult relationship with Frederick III, who had a difficult relationship with Wilhelm I, and so on. The Hohenzollern women tended to fall in line with their husbands as it pertained to raising their children, but Dona was more hands-on and affectionate with her sons than many of her predecessors. She was overly anxious and protective of Joachim, whose premature birth had left him sickly. Oscar was undoubtedly the empress's favorite because she felt he had a chivalrous, brave personality. She also could not help but have compassion when his older, stronger brothers picked on him. Auwi and Adalbert gave their mother little frustration. Her second son, Eitel-Fritz, though Dona unquestionably loved him, was showing signs that concerned her. Even at a young age, the prince—who was ironically Wilhelm's favorite son—was becoming willful, stubborn, and mischievous, all traits that his mother could not abide. They were also traits that would get substantially worse with time.

The birth of six sons meant that Dona was truly living in a man's world. When she discovered at the end of 1891 that she was pregnant again, she earnestly hoped it would be a daughter. On September 13, 1892, she went into labor at the Marble Palace. Early the next morning, the Guards Field Artillery fired twenty-one shots over Potsdam to announce the birth of a daughter. Dona was overjoyed. She had a tradition that with the birth of each child, she kept a special diary for each day of their lives. "After six sons, God has given us our seventh child, a small but very strong little daughter," she wrote in her daughter's diary. "The pleasure over this little ray of sunshine was great, not just for us as parents and the nearest relatives, but indeed the whole nation rejoiced at the birth of the little girl. May she some day become a joy and a blessing for many and—as she has created happiness by her appearance—let her have happiness in life. Her father, who up to now had always wanted sons, was very happy and is marvelling still."[49] The following month, the infant princess was christened. The date chosen, October 22, was doubly significant:

it was Dona's thirty-fourth birthday. The baby was named Victoria Louise Adelheid Mathilde Charlotte. Like her mother, she was known officially by her first two names, Victoria Louise, but her family would affectionately call her "Sissy."

~

By 1891, May Teck had blossomed. Although not a classical beauty, she was stately and regal, standing at five feet seven inches tall. Her hair was most often described as light brown, but in the sunlight, it was noticeably golden. At her mother's insistence, she wore her hair tightly braided atop her head, which had the unfortunate effect of making her appear more masculine and severe than she really was. It was her personality, which turned out so unlike either of her parents, that earned May a great deal of popularity. She was now nearly twenty-four, but despite her upstanding qualities, she had failed to garner very much attention from eligible bachelors. Her potential suitors were deterred by her family's previous financial ruin and her morganatic blood. Most princes were obsessively concerned with royal rank and money and wanted nothing to do with her. Many people believed that May had a better chance of marrying a wealthy English aristocrat than ever finding a royal husband who would accept her family's penury and low rank. Those who discouraged the idea that Princess May could ever have a glittering future were soon silenced because, in the winter of 1891, London was alive with gossip over the news of her engagement to Prince Eddy, whom the queen had created Duke of Clarence in 1890.

Queen Victoria "was quite delighted" to hear of the engagement. She confided to her journal that Eddy came to see her. "I suspected something at once," she wrote. "He came in and said, 'I have some good news to tell you; I am engaged to May Teck.'" The queen concluded that her grandson "seemed very pleased and satisfied, and I am so thankful, as I had much wished for this marriage, thinking her so suitable."[50] Grand Duchess Augusta of Mecklenburg-Strelitz, May's aunt, was quick to offer her opinion on the engagement. "How well the Queen *worded* her *consent* given in Council. 'Pss Victoria Mary, Daughter of H R H The Pss Mary Ad. *and* of H H Duke of Teck' quite as it is *correct*," she wrote with her usual grandiose style with many words underlined for emphasis, "*thus* proving May's *descent* from a *Royal* Mother; *brave Queen!* and just what *May truly is*, according to English notions."[51]

Some people expressed misgivings about the match. The Prince of Wales strongly disliked the Duke and Duchess of Teck. The Duke of Cambridge,

May's uncle, could not fathom how Eddy would make a suitable husband. The duke described him as "an inveterate and incurable dawdler, never ready, never there."[52] Dona sneered at the idea as well, since May's parents could not afford to offer a dowry. The Empress Frederick wrote to Queen Victoria that she "cannot help laughing … when I think of … someone mentioning to Dona what a charming girl May was, & how nice it would be if her [Dona's] brother thought of [marrying her]!" Vicky then bluntly added, "Dona was most offended & said to me that her brother would not dream of making such a mésalliance!!!"[53] The queen shared her daughter's reaction to Dona's attitude toward May: "I am much amused that Dona turned up her nose at the *idea* of her *charming* brother thinking of May whereas I *know it* as a *fact* that he *made demarches* to obtain her hand wh. *May refused* at *once!*"[54] Some twentieth-century historians like David Duff have argued that the Empress Frederick may have been transferring some of her own ill feelings onto Dona, since the former may have been "put out because of her daughters had not been chosen" as a bride for Eddy.[55]

Dona was not the only person to look down on May and her family. Queen Victoria's daughters Helena and Louise were against the match. Helena was especially hostile toward May, as Queen Victoria described in a letter dated December 16, 1891.

> [Helena] is not at all pleased at May's Engagt. to Eddy, & does *not* unfortunately keep it to herself—& was (to my horror) positively rude to Mary [Adelaide] & May at Marlborough House when we went there on Monday 7th & both Mary and Alix [the Princess of Wales] were distressed at it (it made me so hot) & she has been imprudent enough to speak to other people abt. it. *I can't* understand *it.* Louise also does not much like it, tho' she admits May is a vy nice girl & L. was quite kind & civil.—But both sisters are *jealous* of Mary [Adelaide]'s popularity. May will I am *sure* be a very nice Niece & cousin.… she is a vy pretty girl,—*very* sensible & well informed, a *solid girl* wh. we want.[56]

May and Eddy had grown up together. They played together as children at White Lodge and attended the same royal events. Eddy was born January 8, 1864, two months prematurely, the cause of which was believed to be stress and anxiety endured by his mother during the Second Schleswig War. Eddy knew May well enough, but they never perceived one another in romantic terms. She always thought of his family, the Wales brood from her childhood, as friends and playmates. And even in that context, she still had not thought highly of him. As children, Eddy bullied May and her siblings repeatedly.

For his part, Eddy saw the Tecks as amiable if poor relations at best. Most of the time, he seemed apathetic to the world around him. According to one contemporary, he "never seemed to mind what he did or what happened to him."[57] By most surviving accounts, May had little inclination that she was seriously being considered for Eddy. Her father could certainly not afford a dowry. And the taint of her morganatic blood was not easily overlooked by princes on the continent. May seems to have resigned herself to being a spinster, an old maid who would spend her years caring for her invalid of a father.

The Princess of Wales and the Duchess of Fife had been prodding Eddy toward May for some time though. Queen Victoria was also keen on seeing Eddy and May together: "I think & hope that Eddy will try & marry her for I think she is a superior girl—quiet & reserved *till* you know her well,—but she is the reverse of *oberflächlich* [shallow or superficial]. She has no frivolous tastes, has been very carefully brought up & is well informed & always occupied."[58] All these questions about Eddy's feelings for May prompted the Empress Frederick to write, "I wonder whether Eddy—will ever marry May?"[59] By the winter of 1891, he decided to propose by candlelight at a ball in Lutton Hoo, at the home of the Danish ambassador. "To my great surprise Eddy proposed to me during the evening in Mme de Falbe's boudoir," May recorded in her diary. "Of course I said yes—We are both very happy."[60] Once she heard of the engagement, Queen Victoria immediately sent a letter to May at White Lodge welcoming her into the family. She rejoiced that May was becoming "My Grandchild" and assured her of

> how much confidence I have in you, to fill worthily the important position to which you are called by your marriage with Eddy.
> Marriage is the *most* important step which can be taken & should not be looked upon lightly or as *all roses*. The trials of life in fact *begin* with marriage, & no one should forget that it is only by mutually giving way to one another, & by mutual respect & confidence as well as love – that true happiness can be obtained. Dear Eddy is a dear, good boy …[61]

Once the date was set for the wedding, May excitedly sent a letter off to Aunt Augusta in Strelitz: "Our wedding is fixed for Feb 27th at Windsor and afterwards we are to drive thro' the principal streets of London on our way to St Pancras to Sandringham for the honeymoon."[62]

Like Dona Holstein with Wilhelm's proposal, May Teck accepted Eddy on the spot. What most appealed to her was that since her fiancé was expected to ascend the British throne, her family's financial future would be secure, and her parents would never have to worry about money again. The engagement did not come as a surprise to everyone, though. "We are much excited and delighted about the happy event of May Teck's engagement to dear Eddy," the Empress Frederick wrote to her daughter Sophie. "Aunt Mary Teck will be in the 7th heaven, for years and years it has been her ardent wish, and she has thought of nothing else. What a marriage, and what a position for her daughter!"[63]

After the proposal was made, however, doubts about the match began to surface. May found to her dismay that Eddy's listless side shone forth. She was soon being asked by the Prince and Princess of Wales to take an almost mothering role with their son. "Keep Eddy up to the mark," Bertie reminded her, which was usually followed with, "See that Eddy does this, May," or, "May, please do see that Eddy does that." Within a month, she had taken on the role of her fiancé's private secretary, answering stacks of correspondence. At one point, it proved too much for the princess, who cried to her mother, "Do you think I can *really* take this on, Mama?"[64] The duchess's reply was blunt and direct: "Of course you can. If I can put up with your father for twenty-five years, you can handle the Heir Presumptive of Great Britain."[65] May's aunt Augusta was under no illusions about the future that lay ahead of her niece. "It is an immense position and has ever been your heart's desire," the grand duchess wrote to Mary Adelaide, "but it is a serious, great undertaking for poor May."[66]

In January 1892, in the midst of wedding plans, the British royal family gathered at Sandringham, their seven-thousand-acre estate in the Norfolk countryside, to celebrate Eddy's twenty-eighth birthday—his last as a bachelor. Everyone seemed to be sick that winter. The Princess of Wales and Princess May both had heavy colds. Eddy's sisters were virtually quarantined in their rooms with influenza. Toria had some type of lingering infection. And Prince George was recovering from typhoid fever. At first, Eddy seemed in the best health—relatively—with only a slight cold.

During a celebratory hunt, he caught a chill and came down with influenza. After only a few days, Eddy was on his deathbed. A simple bulletin was posted outside Marlborough House.

Sandringham, 9:30am

Symptoms of great gravity have supervened, and the condition of his Royal Highness the Duke of Clarence is critical.[67]

83

Pneumonia set in, his fever skyrocketed to 107 degrees, and he fell into fits of delirium. The royal family—save for the queen, who was deemed too ill to make the journey from Osborne—stayed at Eddy's bedside for days, racked with anxiety and fear. During this difficult time, it was observed that Princess May often sought consolation with Eddy's brother, Prince George. Dr. Manby, the physician in attendance on the royal family at Sandringham, was gazing out the window one day and noticed George and May walking hand-in-hand. Lady Willens, Manby's daughter, later said in an interview that her father "appears to have suspected that the prince and princess were, in reality, much closer than protocol made out."[68]

Eddy's suffering ended after a six-hour vigil at 9:35 a.m. on Thursday, January 14, one month before his wedding to May. A few moments after Eddy died, May rose slowly from her chair and, coming around side of the Princess of Wales, leaned in and kissed her beloved's brow. Eddy's mild-mannered brother George was now heir to the throne, though it was a role he never wanted. "Gladly would I have given my life for his, as I put no value on mine," George wrote to his mother. "Such a tragedy has never before occurred in the annals of our family."[69] The day that Eddy died, the Duchess of Teck wrote a grief-stricken note to the queen describing the suffering everyone was enduring.

> *I clung to hope* even through the terrible watch of that awful *never* to be forgotten night of agony. It wrung one's heart to hear Him [Eddy], & to see Alix's [the Princess of Wales] wretched, imploring face, Bertie's bowed head, & May's *dazed misery*. It seemed *too much, too hard* to bear! ... All today telegrams have been *pouring in* & I have been much with darling Alix & the dearest girls and *angelic* George who is the *tower* of strength to us all! & in His room (where he lies amid flowers, chiefly *Maiblumen*—*Her* flower *now* being woven for the wedding train!) ... his adoring Mother & poor May could not tear themselves away—they have just 11 o'clock borne him to the church ... Bertie & Alix kindly wished to keep us on [at Sandringham], united as we all are in common sorrow—Our presence seems a comfort to them!—Of course their kindness to our May, I cannot say enough. They have quite adopted her as their daughter and she called Alix "Motherdear"—& hopes you will allow her to call you "Grandmama"? These privileges & *two rings* are all that remain to her, poor child! of her bright dream of happiness.[70]

May was devastated, but even in the midst of her grief, she still thought of others first. Her heart went out to Eddy's family. She wrote to Queen Victoria, "How too dear & touching of you in the midst of your sorrow to write to poor little me.... Never shall I forget that dreadful night of agony and suspense as we sat round His bed watching Him get weaker & weaker.... I shall always look back with gratitude to your great kindness to darling Eddy and me at Windsor last month."[71] Queen Victoria's thoughts and prayers went out to Eddy's heartbroken fiancée. She confided to her journal about how tragic it was for "poor May to have her whole bright future to be merely a dream!"[72] The nation, shocked by Eddy's sudden death, went into deep mourning. It was not long after that a ballad began circulating to the tune of "God Bless the Prince of Wales." At one village in East Anglia could be heard the song:

> A nation wrapped in mourning,
> Shed bitter tears today,
> For the noble Duke of Clarence,
> And fair young Princess May.[73]

It was the first death of an heir to the throne in nearly a century. As such, it was treated with appropriate dignity. Eddy's body was laid out for five days at the small church near Sandringham, surrounded by exotic flowers and the silken Royal Standard. From Norfolk, the unpolished oak coffin was ceremoniously taken by gun-carriage to Saint George's Chapel at Windsor Castle, the royal family's traditional parish church. The mournful procession was led by the Prince of Wales and Prince George and included the Royal Horse Artillery, the foot guards, and the Tenth Royal Hussars—Eddy's own regiment. When the coffin reached the Albert Memorial Chapel at Saint George's Chapel, Princess May—wearing a long black dress with a white collar and cuffs—placed a wreath of orange blossoms on her beloved's tomb.

Perhaps for the first time in her life, May was utterly at a loss. She did not know how her life could possibly go on. Two days after the funeral, she wrote to her friend Emily Alcock, "It is so difficult to begin one's old life again after such a shock. Even reading, of which I am so fond, is a trouble to me & I cannot settle down to anything—As for writing I simply *cannot* write ... for it is so dreadful to have to open the wound afresh."[74] What she failed to realize was that she would have a greater role in life than to grieve for Eddy and step off into the shadows. Princess May of Teck was truly born to rule and one day would still be queen of England.

5

A Touch of Destiny

(1892–94)

The 1890s was a decade of tremendous change for Empress Augusta Victoria, May Teck, and Alix of Hesse. Dona, increasingly conservative but popular with her people, was reigning over the German Empire alongside her larger-than-life husband; May was grieving the unexpected loss of her beloved Eddy; and Alix longingly pined for her darling Nicky. In a remote corner of northwestern Italy, a new life was set to come into the world, which would complete the circle of the four royal women who were destined to preside over the fall of the age of empires.

In the spring of 1892, Maria Antonia, Duchess of Parma, was in labor with her fifth child. Her husband, Robert I, Duke of Parma, already had twelve children from his first marriage to Princess Maria Pia of the Two Sicilies. So many hopes had been attached to Robert and Maria Pia's union that their wedding was performed by Pope Pius IX himself in the Sistine Chapel. But because of the close blood ties between the couple[1], three of their children died in infancy, while another six were mentally disabled. Maria Pia died shortly after giving birth to a stillborn child in 1882. So when Robert married Maria Antonia of Portugal in 1884, he made sure he and his new wife were not even distant relatives. The outcome was highly successful. Their first four children—like Maria Pia, Maria Antonia would eventually have twelve children—were lusty with strong constitutions. The Duchess of Parma had delivered her first four children in Austria. Her latest accouchement took place at Villa Pianore in Tuscany, Robert's red-roofed, two-story Italian estate located between Pietrasanta and Viareggio, only a few miles from the Ligurian Sea. After a long delivery, the duchess delivered a healthy baby girl on May 9, 1892.

At her baptism, the infant received the lofty names Zita Maria delle Grazie Adelgonda Micaela Raffaela Gabriella Giussepina Antonia Luise Agnese, which were made at the suggestion of her aunt and godmother, Princess Adelgundes of Bourbon-Parma. The first of her eleven names, Zita, proved prescient. It was chosen for the thirteenth-century saint who became the patron of servants, the pious, and the laboring poor, all qualities that would come to be associated with this future empress of Austria and queen of Hungary. Officially known by her first name, Princess Zita of Bourbon-Parma was more than thirty years younger than Augusta Victoria of Germany—the empress with whom Zita's political fate would be the most connected—and she could not have been more different. While Dona could be neurotic, prudish, haughty, and was convinced that she had been born to rule, Zita was the spitting image of her namesake and was content to lead a quiet life doing good works.

Unlike Dona, May, or Alix, Zita had no real connection with Germany or the British royal family. Although she was born in Italy and her father was the Duke of Parma, Zita and her family thought of themselves first and foremost as Frenchmen. "We are French princes who reigned in Italy," Robert once told Zita.[2] Robert's father had been assassinated when he was six, leaving the young duke to be raised by his French mother, Princess Louise of Artois, who inculcated into her son a deep love for France. After leaving Parma during the turbulent Italian unification of the 1850s and 1860s, the *Risorgimento*, Robert spent most of his life living at the home of his uncle Henry, Count of Chambord. As the great-nephew of King Louis XVI and Marie Antoinette, Henry was the sole heir to the entire French royal fortune. When the unimaginably wealthy Henry died in 1883[3], he left his entire estate—a priceless treasury of monies, jewels, and palaces—to Robert. The connection Robert had with his ancestral home can be seen in the fact that many of his children were born in France and were given French names. Where Dona was unequivocally German, and Alix and May were fiercely British, Zita was devotedly French.

Similarly to May Teck's parents, there is little doubt that Zita's parents were in love and shared many things in common. Like her husband, Maria Antonia came from a deposed family. Her father was the one-time King Michael I of Portugal, who had led a revolution against his brother King Peter IV in 1828. Michael reigned for six years before Peter reclaimed his throne, sending Michael into permanent exile in Germany in 1834. As he approached middle age, the still-unmarried Michael decided it was time to start a family. He may have hoped that if he produced a son, that son might one day reclaim the Portuguese throne. In 1851, Michael married Princess Adelaide of Löwenstein-Wertheim-Rosenberg. Whereas Michael was forty-nine, his new German wife was only twenty at the time of their marriage. After the wedding, Adelaide assumed the courtesy title queen of Portugal.

This eclectic mix of French, Italian, and Portuguese influences gave Zita's family an inimitable flavor. As an adult, Zita recalled that her family "grew up internationally. My father thought of himself first and foremost as a Frenchman, and spent a few weeks every year with the elder children at Chambord, his main property on the Loire." She later realized that "of the twenty-four children, only three including me, were actually born in Italy."[4] Of the four imperial consorts, the blissfulness of Zita of Bourbon-Parma's childhood was unmatched—she herself described it as *"particularly joyful and happy."* She and her siblings, including her half brothers and sisters from her father's first marriage, were a close-knit group. The Duchess of Parma was a loving mother who doted on all twenty-one of her children equally. Robert was just as dedicated. Unlike other royal fathers, he preferred to pass much of the day in the company of his children. A gifted academic, he encouraged his children to spend hours on end with him in his study, listening to him read from his library of books in French, Italian, German, and English. Their education "was a mixture of austerity, charity, and profound piety."[5]

The homes that the Bourbon-Parma children grew up in were hardly what one expected for a deposed duke; they were more suited to a reigning monarch. Thanks to Robert's French family, he owned half a dozen awe-inspiring castles, mansions, and villas spread across central and southern Europe. There was Frohsdorf, a castle-like estate in Lanzenkirchen in eastern Austria; Villa Pianore in Tuscany, a typical Mediterranean manor house; and Schwarzau am Steinfeld, an old, somewhat intimidating castle in Lower Austria on the edge of the Neuenkirchen Forest and less than twenty miles from Vienna. But all of these residences paled in comparison to their most luxurious home, their iconic French palace of Chambord, in the Loire Valley, where Robert spent many happy years as a young man. Famous for its French Renaissance architecture, Chambord was commissioned by King Francis I in the sixteenth century. The five-story limestone palace accommodated the Duke of Parma and his family nicely, with more than four hundred rooms, three hundred fireplaces, and a dozen towers. It even dwarfed the Neues Palais in Potsdam and some of the British royal family's homes. Trips to Chambord were not as frequent as the family would have liked, though. Despite their enormous fortune, Zita's parents were keenly aware of living within their means—a quality learned by both Zita and May Teck. The duke and duchess realized that the cost of moving their entire family and court from Italy to France was often prohibitively expensive.

The times they did move, however, left a vivid impression on the young Princess Zita. "We spent about six months of the year at Schwarzau," she recalled, "usually beginning in July, when the heat got intense in Italy, and staying over Christmas and the New Year until early January, when the real winter cold set in in Austria. Then we would go down to Pianore and stay there through the spring and early summer until moving north again." When the family moved, it was always an adventure for the children. "And what moves they were!" Zita reminisced. "Every year and for each journey back and forth we had our special train. When fully assembled for the trip, it must have had fifteen or sixteen coaches and two engines were needed to pull it over the Semmering Pass just south of Schwarzau."[6] Zita's happy childhood, an intellectual wonderland presided over by her passionate father and loving mother, laid the best possible foundation for the rest of her life. "It was a peaceful, happy time," she said later in life.[7] Decades later, it would give Zita the strength to hold together not only her family but her empire.

It was the norm for many Victorian widows to shy away from public life. In fact, Victorian England essentially wrote the book on mourning. It was a morbid cult for many people, carried out with an almost thespian flare. When one's loved ones died, society expected them to mourn for them with a fanatical obsession. Princess May was no exception to this. For the first few months of 1892, she and her mother stayed in near seclusion at White Lodge. Many in London's social circle who had been close to Eddy felt it was May's responsibility to spend the rest of her days pining for her lost love, wearing only black and setting up a shrine to his memory. The Princess of Wales did just that, turning the room where he died into a memorial to her firstborn. For the rest Alexandra's life, she visited Eddy's room every day she was at Sandringham, often bringing flowers to place on the bed in which he died. May was expected to be no less devout in her grief.

In the aftermath of Eddy's death, there was genuine concern in Britain for the future of the monarchy. Eddy's brother George was now heir to the throne, but he was somewhat sickly and was recovering from deadly typhoid at the time of his brother's death. Typhoid fever—not to be confused with typhus, a lice-spread illness—made an indelible mark on the British royal family. It had killed George's grandfather Prince Albert in 1861 and nearly claimed his father's life a decade later. Many feared in the winter of 1891/92 that George would succumb too. If he did, the throne would pass to his eldest sister, Princess Louise, and her commoner husband, the Earl of Fife.

Louise was not generally esteemed in England; many took notice of her dim intellectual accomplishments and listless nature that seemed endemic to the Wales family. The idea of Louise as queen regnant left many people unsettled. It became imperative that George marry as quickly as possible so as to produce an heir of his own. A number of brides were considered. George would have preferred his cousin Princess Marie of Edinburgh, whom he had romanced while stationed with the Royal Navy on Malta. Marie's Anglophobic mother quickly ended their teenage romance. The Empress Frederick, George's aunt, had hoped he might marry one of her daughters—perhaps her youngest, Mossy—but the prince expressed little interest. There appeared to be one other candidate, though.

A year after Eddy died, May commemorated his passing by visiting the Chapel Royal at Windsor Castle. "How beautiful it is … and how calmly and peacefully our Loved One lies there at rest from all the cares of this world," she wrote to Prince George. "God be with us and help us to bear our cross is the fervent prayer of your very loving cousin—May."[8]

In 1893, the Empress Frederick visited Queen Victoria at Windsor Castle. While she was there, the grieving Tecks arrived for a visit. Those who were privy to the details of May and Eddy's relationship expressed their sympathies to the princess. "Aunt Mary Teck was here with May whom I thought very nice indeed," Vicky wrote. On the day planned for the wedding, February 27, the Prince and Princess of Wales presented May with a dazzling group of diamonds, along with a beautiful handbag covered with gold and jewels, all of which had been intended as wedding gifts. Saddened by May's tragedy, the Empress Frederick did not mince words: "Her position is most difficult and embarrassing. She is still in mourning for our poor darling Eddy, and the newspapers are constantly writing about her becoming engaged to Georgie, and the whole public seem to wish it ardently."[9]

Not long after Vicky wrote these words, her predication came true when May became engaged to George in the spring of 1893. Vicky's instincts proved correct when she said that the British people wanted May and George to marry. The couple was immensely popular with the general public. May was the grief-stricken princess whose dreams were shattered, and George was the noble, honorable brother now bound by duty to fill his brother's shoes. Soon after the engagement was announced, the *Morning Post* published an article about May, noting, "Not only by birth, but by education and by domicile, she belongs to England. She possesses every qualification for the high place that awaits her."[10]

George—who was born June 3, 1865—was eighteen months younger than Eddy. Since he and Eddy were raised extremely closely, their childhood experiences with Princess May were similar. George was quiet, withdrawn, and used to blending into the background. He admired Eddy and was more than happy to let him have the limelight. When the Duke of Clarence died unexpectedly, George was overwhelmed by all the attention he received when he became heir to the throne of Britain and its empire. Since he was now second in line to the throne, George was forced to give up his active position in the Royal Navy, which he had held since 1877. Queen Victoria gave him the title Duke of York on May 24, 1892. This peerage, which like all others included a seat in the House of Lords, is typically given to the next male heir when there is still a Prince of Wales. Queen Victoria wrote to George when she conferred the York peerage on him, "I am glad you like the title of Duke of York. I am afraid, I do not and wish you had remained as you are. A Prince *no one* else can be, whereas a Duke any nobleman can be, and many are! I am not very fond of that of York which has not very agreeable associations."[11]

As a child, Princess May took little notice of George, who was usually off playing with his big brother. When George joined the Royal Navy and left for prolonged periods, May did not give his absence a second thought, especially once she became swept up in her engagement with Eddy, who was the first real love interest of her life. For George, his feelings for May were just the opposite. He had admired her for many years—and even more so once Eddy died. By the spring of 1893, he was prepared to take the risk of proposing, though he was scared he might be rejected. Family trips to the French Riviera had the effect of lightening the mood for one and all, including May. A few weeks later, while May and her mother were visiting Strelitz, her last palpable link to Eddy was symbolically and dramatically severed when a fire in the palace where they were staying destroyed all the pictures she had of him.

A flurry of letters soon began flying between the members of the British royal family. Queen Victoria wrote to Vicky; the Princess of Wales wrote to George; and the Duchess of Teck wrote to the queen. The only two people who kept things on an uncomplicated level, at least for them, were George and May. "Goodbye Miss May," George wrote to her in March 1892, "ever your very loving old cousin Georgie."[12] It took him more than a year to work up the courage to propose, and it required prodding from a number of his relatives. One person who was instrumental in pushing George in May's direction was his maternal aunt Queen Olga of Greece. "I'm sure, tootsums, that she will make you happy," Olga wrote encouragingly. "They say she has such a sweet disposition & is so *equal* and *that* in itself is a great blessing, because nothing can be more disagreeable in everyday-life, than a person which is in high spirits today & low tomorrow."[13] Queen Victoria also strongly hoped for the match, writing to her grandson, "Have you seen May and have you thought more about the *possibility* or *foundout* [*sic*] what her feelings might be?"[14] On May 29, 1893, George decided to do just that. It was a misty but comfortable afternoon. After they had tea together, he invited May for a walk through the Richmond garden of his aunt Princess Louise, the future Duchess of Argyll. May recorded in her diary her recollections of what happened next: "We walked together afterwards in the gardens and he proposed to me, & I accepted him.... I drove home to announce the news to Mama & Papa & Georgie followed.... We telegraphed to all the relations."[15] Once it was done, Queen Victoria reported happily, "Received a telegram from Georgie ... to say he was engaged to May Teck, and asked for my consent. I answered that I gladly did so."[16]

At the time of the engagement, George's mother, Alexandra, was away in Venice. A week after the news broke, she sent May the following message:

> *God bless* you *both* & let me welcome you back once more as my dear daughter & grant you all the happiness here on Earth—which *you* so fully deserve—with my Georgie—which was alas denied you with my darling Eddy. I am sure ... his spirit is watching over you now and rejoicing with us & that the clouds have been lifted once more from your saddened young life and that you may yet look forward to a bright & happy future with the brother he loved so well ... I know we two will always understand each other & I hope that my sweet May will always come straight to me for everything ... Ever yr most loving & devoted old Motherdear.[17]

May was happier than she had been for a long time, but both she and George had difficulty overcoming their natural timidity. "I am very sorry I am still so shy with you," she wrote to him. "I tried not to be the other day, but alas I failed, I was angry with myself!" She thought it was "so stupid to be so stiff together and really there is nothing I would not tell you, except that I LOVE you more than anybody in the world, and this I cannot tell you myself so I write it to relieve my feelings." Touched by his fiancée's letter, George replied, "Thank God we both understand each other, and I think it really unnecessary for me to tell you how deep my love for you my darling is and I feel it growing stronger and stronger every time I see you; although I may appear shy and cold."[18]

By the summer of 1893, much to Queen Victoria's satisfaction, preparations were well in place for the much-anticipated wedding of Princess May of Teck to the Duke of York. On July 4, the British royal family attended a performance at the Royal Opera House at Covent Garden in honor of the upcoming nuptials. Roses of every color decorated the building. Box seats were decorated with pink roses; the proscenium was lined with them as well. Bouquets of pink, white, and crimson roses were supplied to every balcony. When May arrived, dressed in an ice-blue brocade with two rows of perfect pearls around her neck and a diamond tiara and earrings, the three thousand people gathered rose to their feet and gave her a standing ovation.

Two days later, on July 6, May and George were married in the Chapel Royal of Saint James's Palace, just down Pall Mall from Buckingham Palace. It was the biggest event for the royal family since Queen Victoria's jubilee in 1887, and it brought together some of the continent's most illustrious royals. George's cousins came from Saint Petersburg, including Tsarevitch Nicholas. So too did his other cousin, Emperor Wilhelm II. King Christian IX and Queen Louise of Denmark, the groom's maternal grandparents, arrived from Copenhagen; the wedding registry alone was signed by twenty-seven royals. The guests marveled at the lavish wedding gifts the couple received. The more than fifteen hundred presents—including horses, ponies, carriages, sleighs, boats, and a cow from India—were so numerous that they had to be stored at the Imperial Institute near Kensington Palace. Their worth was estimated at more than £1 million at the time. On the morning of the wedding, May penciled a note to her soon-to-be husband: "What a memorable day in our lives this will be. God grant it may bring us much happiness. I love you with all my heart. Yrs for ever & ever—May."[19]

An estimated two million excited spectators filled the streets of London to catch a glimpse of May and Queen Victoria as they rode together in a glass carriage pulled by four cream-colored horses. As she entered the Chapel Royal, the bride was escorted by ten bridesmaids, nine of whom were Queen Victoria's granddaughters. Among the bridesmaids were two future queens: George's twenty-three-year-old sister, Maud of Wales, the future queen of Norway; and little six-year-old Ena of Battenberg, who was destined to be queen of Spain. During the ceremony, May appeared serene as she took her vows. Tsarevitch Nicholas recorded that she looked "radiant" and was "much better looking than her photograph."[20] Following her family's tradition, all the silk for her dress came "from England, all the flannel from Wales, all the tweeds from Scotland, and every yard of lace and poplin from Ireland."[21] Her cloth-of-silver wedding gown was embroidered with roses, orange blossoms, and other flowers. On her head sat a stunning arrangement of diamonds, courtesy of Queen Victoria. "The great day, so anxiously looking forward to, was very bright and fine," Queen Victoria wrote. "To describe this day fully would be impossible.... I could not help but remember that I had stood, where May did, fifty-three years ago, and dear Vicky thirty-five years ago, and that the dear ones, who stood where Georgie did, were gone from us! May these dear children's happiness last longer!"[22]

In her diary entry for that day, Lady Geraldine Somerset captured the true atmosphere that prevailed.

> May's Wedding Day! The greatest success ever seen or heard of! not a hitch from first to last, nor an if or a but!! everything went *absolutely à souhait*! first of all it was the *most heavenly* day ever *could* be…. The town was alive!! swarms everywhere! … Piccadilly was beautifully decorated; but anything to equal the loveliness of St. James's Street I never saw – it was like a bower from end to end … garlands of green across and between the Venetian masts with bracelets of flowers suspended from them, *too* pretty.
>
> I went to the Household pew in the Chapel Royal … It was all so admirably arranged I think everybody in the Chapel could see well! The first to enter the Chapel was the Queen followed by P[rincess] M[ary Adelaide] who drove *in* the Queen's carriage from Buckingham Palace!! will her head be still on her shoulders tomorrow! I believe it will have expanded and blown to the moon! The Princess of Wales looked *more lovely* – than ever! – none can approach her! but I was so sorry for her today. May with the Duke of York standing at the Altar!! and for the Princess *what pain*.[23]

The "pain" that Lady Somerset wrote of regarded the Princess of Wales and George. Alexandra was close with all of her children, but even more so with George, as he became her only son when Eddy died. It was no secret that Alexandra was both happy and saddened by her son's marriage to May, which she knew would change their relationship forever.

The honeymoon was spent at York Cottage, their new home on the Sandringham estate. During the few days the Yorks spent alone there, they constantly wrote love notes to one another. George found it much easier to express his love for his wife in writing. In one letter after their wedding, he poured out his belief that his love for May had grown so much since their engagement.

> You know by this time that I never do anything by halves, when I asked you to marry me I was very fond of you, but not very much in love with you, but saw in *you* the person I was capable of loving most deeply, if you only returned that love … I have tried to understand you and to know you, and with the happy result that I know now that I do love you darling girl with all my *heart*, and am simply *devoted* to you … *I adore you sweet May*. My love grows

stronger for you every day, mixed with admiration and I thank God every day that he has given me such a darling devoted wife as you are. God bless you my sweet Angel May, who I know will always stick to me as I need our love and help more than ever now.[24]

Although their honeymoon at Sandringham was meant to be a vacation, George and May spent the time answering piles upon piles of correspondences and notes of congratulations. A few weeks later, they rejoined the royal family at Osborne House on the Isle of Wight, where triumphal arches covered in flowers and garlands had been built in their honor. To welcome the Duke and Duchess of York, a crowd of nine hundred schoolchildren cheered them from carts draped in green branches. At dinner one night, May found herself seated next to Wilhelm II. "I sat next to William," she wrote to her mother, "who made himself most agreeable … Fancy me, little me, sitting next to William, the place of honour!!! It seemed so strange … I talked my *best* German."[25] May soon found herself somewhat taken with the emperor, who treated her deferentially, though she did admit that, at times, he made "royalty ridiculous."[26]

As the decade progressed, Alix's congenial life in Darmstadt was undergoing some significant changes. She was increasingly worried about her father, Louis. The bearded, thickset grand duke had been in failing health for several years. His children became troubled in the winter of 1892 when they noticed that he was short of breath, pale, and struggled to keep his balance. He felt the cold German winter terribly, forcing him to stay confined to his room for days on end. As the months passed, there was little change. Then, one afternoon in March while the family was having lunch, Louis collapsed at the table. He suffered a massive stroke. Alix sat at his bedside for the next nine days, anxiously praying. Irene and Victoria rushed to Darmstadt, joining Alix and Ernie in their round-the-clock vigil. Only Ella had been unable to make it from Russia in time for his death on March 13, 1892. At the age of nineteen, Alix was now an orphan. "Death is dreadful without preparation," she recalled years later, "and without the body gradually loosening all earthly ties."[27] Although the grand duke and Queen Victoria had not always gotten along, she was deeply saddened by his passing. She later described Louis as "so dear and joyous—so loving," whose death came too "young for his age."[28]

With the death of Alix's father, there seemed added urgency for her to find a husband as soon as possible. Her brother, Ernie, was now Grand Duke of Hesse and would be expected to marry quickly. This meant there would be a new first lady of the land, rendering Alix obsolete. Her old governess, Mrs. Orchard, murmured that she should have married Max of Baden while she still had the chance. Alix's grief over her father's death only fueled her longing for Nicky, which came to the fore once again when she journeyed to Berlin for another family wedding in January 1893. This time, her cousin Frederick Charles of Hesse was marrying another cousin—Mossy of Prussia, Wilhelm II's youngest sister. The reception, which was hosted by Wilhelm and Dona at the Stadtschloss, was so overcrowded that one of the guests fainted from the heat. During the festivities, Dona found herself trying to clean up her family's messes when her brother Ernest Günther caused several high-ranking royals to miss a number of the formal gatherings because he had kept them all night out partying. The wedding gave Alix a chance to see Nicky again (who happened to be one of those royals caught up with Dona's brother). The pair shared afternoon tea and a family dinner, but they did not spend any time alone. For his part, Nicky was more determined than ever to marry Princess Alix of Hesse, despite pressure from some implacable foes. Queen Victoria had set herself against the marriage, and she was not the only one. Nicky's parents, Alexander and Minnie, did everything in their power to dissuade their son from marrying the German-born Alix.

The tsar and his wife had two serious objections to Nicky's making Alix his wife. The first was her personality. They believed her dour, somber moods were unsuited to the role of empress of Russia. Where Alix brooded and withdrew from the public, a Russian empress was expected to sparkle in society, and Nicky's mother was the embodiment of that. Born Princess Dagmar of Denmark, she was the sister of the Princess of Wales. When she married Nicky's father in 1866, she took the names Marie Feodorovna; Minnie was a nickname she adopted later on. With her petite figure, dark eyes, and strong personality, Minnie became a trendsetter in Russian society, the same way her sister Alexandra did in Britain. She enjoyed rubbing shoulders with Saint Petersburg's socialites, wearing fine clothes, and showing off the breathtaking jewels of the imperial treasury. As a young man, Nicholas recalled watching his mother dress for a ball, surrounded by six ladies-in-waiting helping her into her silver brocade dress and attaching ten rows of pearls around her neck. Alix of Hesse could not have been more different. She disliked most aristocrats, whom she believed phony and insincere. She also disliked appearing in public. "I am not made to shine before an assembly," she told a friend. "I have not got the easy nor the witty talk one needs for that. I like the *internal being*, and that attracts me with great force."[29] Minnie wrote to the Princess of Wales that "it would never do for the youngest daughter of an undistinguished grand duke to marry the heir to the Russian throne. Besides, Alix was personally not suited to be tsarina. She was too hard, she lacked grace and tact, she did not have the gift of making people like her."[30]

The second obstacle Nicky faced was undoubtedly the most difficult: Alix's faith. Born and raised a devout Lutheran like Empress Augusta Victoria, she was devoutly religious, but as a Russian empress, she would be expected to convert to the Orthodox faith. Alix was "too attached to her Protestant faith to contemplate converting." She felt as though she would be turning her back on God, and that was something she could never do. "I have tried to look at it in every light," Alix said, "but I always return to one thing. I cannot go against my conscience." To do so would be "a sin ... and I should be miserable all the days of my life, knowing that I had done a wrongful thing." She concluded, "what happiness can come from a marriage which begins without the real blessing of God?"[31] Her faith was a critical part of who she was, and she could not forsake it; this was in stark contrast to her late mother, Alice, who looked snidely upon religion and was regarded by other German royals as "a complete atheist."[32] In a pleading letter to Nicky, Alix poured out her feelings: "I should never find my peace of mind again, and like that I should never be your real companion who should help you on in life; for there always should be something between us two, in my not having the real conviction of the belief I had taken, and in the regret for the one I *had* left." She ended her letter by poignantly writing, "I can *never* change my confession."[33] If there was any doubt, she wrote a similar letter to Nicky's sister Xenia: "I cannot become untrue to my own confession ... I don't want him [Nicky] to go on hoping, as I can *never* change my Religion."[34]

Alexander and Minnie spent months trying to dissuade Nicky from his mission. They suggested he marry someone else—Princess Hélène of Orléans. As a French royal, a marriage to Hélène was picture-perfect, cementing years of growing friendship between Russia and France. "Mama made a few allusions to Hélène, daughter of the Comte de Paris," Nicky wrote in his journal. "I myself want to go in one direction and it is evident that Mama wants me to choose the other."[35] Hélène was soon out of the running though. Like Alix, she was unwilling to forsake her Catholic faith for Orthodoxy. Nicky's parents soon became frustrated with him. "She won't have you. She's a confirmed Lutheran," an impatient Alexander told his son. "And what in the world do you see in her?" he asked his son in desperation. "Everything," Nicky shot back. Minnie was just as resolute. "Alix of Hesse does not wish to have you," she insisted to Nicky. "You are the heir. It is your duty to marry." Exasperated, Nicky replied, "And I shall. And she'll have me yet."[36] His last words to his mother on the subject were, "It's Alicky of Hesse—or nobody—for me!"[37]

In April 1894, Nicky's opportunity finally presented itself. Alix's brother, Ernie, was marrying Princess Victoria Melita ("Ducky") of Edinburgh in

Coburg. He seized his chance. After months of arguing, he finally secured his parents' permission to join his uncles Serge and Vladimir in going to Coburg. Part of the reason Alexander and Minnie finally acquiesced was because the tsar's health was beginning to wane. It reminded everyone of the utmost importance of Nicky's finding a wife and producing an heir. Once in Coburg, Nicky planned to propose to Alix and make her his wife. So confident was he of his powers of persuasion that he brought with him a priest, Father Yanishev, to instruct Alix about the Russian Orthodox faith, and a tutor, Catherine Schneider, to teach her the language.

The wedding of Ernie and Ducky in the tiny German city of Coburg promised an august display of personages. Most of the royal mob was attending, since both the bride and groom were grandchildren of Queen Victoria. The old icon herself, now seventy-five, was coming from London, as was most of the extended British royal family, including Wilhelm, Dona, and the Empress Frederick. With the exception of Queen Victoria, few people at the wedding were in high spirits. It was an open secret that the queen herself was the only reason Ernie and Ducky were getting married. For years, she had been trying to set the couple up. She regularly reminded Ernie that it was his responsibility to provide Hesse with an heir. Since Ducky was rich, young, attractive, and available, their grandmother decided it was her duty to see them married. Victoria was so enamored playing matchmaker for many of her other grandchildren that she failed to realize that Ernie and Ducky were hopelessly incompatible. So when news reached Coburg that Nicky was on his way, everyone was relieved for a diversion. By the time the imperial train arrived in Coburg, the wedding festivities had taken a backseat to the juiciest piece of gossip in years: would the resolute Alix accept Nicky's proposal?

Even before Nicholas had a chance to see Alix, a cloud of gossip swirled around the city. "All the relatives one after another asked me about her," Nicky told his mother.[38] Most of the royals hoped Alix would accept Nicky, but not everyone was in agreement. "Even my dear Mama thought she would not accept him, she was so pointed about it," the Empress Frederick wrote about the queen.[39] When the couple finally came face to face the day after Nicky arrived, it was an exhausting experience. For over two hours, Nicky pleaded and begged while Alix sobbed, "No! I cannot." Nicky described the meeting in a letter to his mother: "I tried to explain that there was no other way for her than to give her consent and that she simply could not withhold it ... Still I went on repeating and insisting ... though this went on for two hours, it came to nothing."[40] Even a letter Nicky gave to Alix written by his mother, another Lutheran princess who had converted to Russian Orthodoxy and was quite happy, failed to sway her.

For the next two days, Alix would not even see Nicky. At Ernie and Ducky's wedding on April 9, she seemed to be "in a troubled trance."[41] That night, Emperor Wilhelm invited Alix to his residence in order to convince her to accept the tsarevitch. The emperor egotistically fancied himself Europe's matchmaker and did not want to pass up a golden opportunity. It was no secret that Nicky's parents loathed Wilhelm and Dona, but if he could get Alix and Nicky together, a German-born empress of Russia might just lead to a much-desired alliance between the two empires. Wilhelm mistakenly believed that since Alix was "entirely German," then she would not allow German imperial interests to "suffer."[42] He manipulated his position as head of the Lutheran Church by pressuring Alix to accept. Her destiny was by Nicky's side, he told her. It seemed to be enough.

The day after Ernie and Ducky were married, April 10, Wilhelm drove Alix to the house where Nicky was staying. They met in a room overlooking the palace gardens as a spring thunderstorm roared outside. Nicky presented Alix with a bouquet of flowers he swiped from a nearby table. It was here that she told him she accepted his proposal. "The first thing she said was … that she agreed!" wrote an ecstatic Nicky. "Oh God, what happened to me then! I started to cry like a child, and so did she, only her expression immediately changed; her face brightened and took on an aura of peace."[43]

The first thing Alix did after accepting Nicky was to write a note to Queen Victoria. "Please do not think that my marrying will make a difference to my love for You," she wrote. "Certainly it will not, and when I am far away, I shall long to think that there is One, the dearest and kindest Woman alive, who loves me a little bit."[44] Later in the day, Nicholas and Alix went to the queen's room to receive her blessing, which she gave wholeheartedly. Afterward, the queen wrote,

> [I was] quite thunderstruck, as though I knew Nicky much wished it, I thought Alicky was not sure of her mind. Saw them both. Alicky had tears in her eyes, but looked very bright, and I kissed them both … People generally seemed pleased at the engagement, which has the drawback that Russia is so far away … But as her mind is made up, and they are really attached to one another, it is perhaps better so…. He is so sensible and nice, & expressed the hope to come quietly to England to see Alicky at the end of June.[45]

Alix and Dona's mutual cousin, Princess Marie Louise of Schleswig-Holstein-Sonderburg-Augustenburg, recalled seeing her after she accepted the proposal: "I remember I was sitting in my room. I was quietly getting ready for a luncheon party when Alix stormed into my room, threw her arms around my neck and said, 'I'm going to marry Nicky!'"[46] "I am more happy than words can express," Alix wrote to her old governess. "At last after these five sad years!"[47] Perhaps for the first time in his life, Nicky "displayed a sustained effort of will, carrying forward, until victory against strong parental opposition, his personal battle for happiness."[48] Shortly after Alix accepted the proposal, Nicky and a number of his relatives attended a service of thanksgiving in the private Orthodox chapel of Ducky's mother, the Duchess of Coburg.

"Alicky is quite radiant and beaming with joy," the Empress Frederick wrote to her daughter Sophie. "The moment Nicky arrived I saw by her face that she would [accept him]—though it was so strange to refuse him first, and to swear to everyone that though she was very fond of him, she would never take him.... I could not help chuckling to myself that William did not think Alicky so very sinful to accept Nicky, and with him the necessity of conforming to the Orthodox Church. Of course, I made no remarks!"[49] It struck many as hypocritical but not overly surprising that Wilhelm pushed Alix toward Nicholas. When her sister Ella converted from Lutheranism after marrying Grand Duke Serge, Wilhelm and Dona branded her a "traitor to her faith and her Fatherland" for embracing the Russian Orthodox faith.[50] In reality, Wilhelm's influence actually had very little to do with Alix's change of heart. For one, the fact that Ducky was now the Grand Duchess of Hesse meant Alix would just be in the way in Darmstadt. She and her sister-in-law respected one another but were never friends. Her staying on would only cause problems between herself and the newlyweds. "I would only be in their way here," Alix said forlornly.[51] Ducky was not the only person's influence Alix feared in Darmstadt after the wedding. Ducky's mother, Marie, was the formidable Russian-born wife of Queen Victoria's son, the Duke of Edinburgh, who became the Duke of Saxe-Coburg-Gotha in 1893. Alix was worried that her aunt Marie would end up "playing the dictator around Darmstadt" once Ducky had settled in.[52]

When it came to the question of religion, "Ella's painless religious conversion undoubtedly helped settle her younger sister's mind. But in the end, Alix's unbounded love for Nicholas was the strongest factor in her decision to agree to his proposal." That love meant she was committed to helping him rule Russia, for better or worse. Nicholas was a weak-willed man who was easily dominated by others. The resolute Alix saw this and was determined to be a strength to him. She believed "she could best serve

God by helping Nicholas become a better tsar."[53] In the end, Alix accepted Nicky

> because it came to her that she and she alone could make him envisage duty from the only possible point of view; that her very passion for him was strong enough to evoke qualities she considered dormant; that in marrying him she would be able to guide and to counsel; that in their joint happiness they would fulfill their high duty to the utmost. And, as she reflected on those points, she came to see that she would not violate her conscience … it was her true vocation to love and to serve him. Therein lay God's will for her.[54]

She knew her destiny was, as Wilhelm said, at Nicky's side. She wanted every day of her life to be spent serving God's purposes for her family and for Russia: "Thus, in reconciling herself to her conversion to Orthodoxy, Alix wielded this irrevocable decision to a greater calling. She was to be an instrument of God, sent to transform the future Nicholas II and the Russian Empire. In tandem, she and Nicky would work for the greater good of Russia."[55] The union of Nicholas of Russia and Alix of Hesse-Darmstadt would permanently reshape the course of history.

PART 2

The Age of Empires

(1894–1914)

6

"A Little Scrubby Hessian Princess"

(April–November 1894)

Once Alix accepted Nicky's proposal, a team of advisers began sedulously planning the biggest wedding of the last quarter century. The marriage of a Russian heir to the throne was a once-in-a-lifetime event, and Saint Petersburg was preparing for it to be a day of special magnificence. Nicky's mother, Empress Marie Feodorovna, had experienced all the fanfare when she arrived in Russia from Denmark for her own wedding in 1866. She was greeted in Kronstadt by an exuberant imperial family and feted with parties, parades, and tributes before a glittering wedding at the Winter Palace. Now that Tsarevitch Nicholas was preparing for his own nuptials, Russia's imperial family determined to make his wedding to Princess Alix just as grand.

A few weeks after the engagement became official, Alix made it a point to contact her future mother-in-law. In a letter dated April 21 and addressed to her "Darling Auntie," Alix thanked Marie for her touching letter. After saying "how happy" she was, Alix wrote about the struggle she endured with her conscience over converting and her hope that she "would grow to love the Orthodox religion and make Nicholas a good wife." Marie later told Nicky to tell Alix to call her Mama or Motherdear, rather than Auntie, since she "is already like a daughter to me."[1] As an engagement present, the empress sent her an emerald bracelet and a jewel-encrusted Fabergé egg.

By the summer of 1894, Alix was beginning to come to terms with her religious conversion, but Queen Victoria was ill at ease about the upcoming wedding. She detested the idea of her favorite granddaughter marrying into their "barbaric court," as she called it. It helped that she thought highly of Nicholas, whom she asked to call her "Granny." She already felt a family connection to him as well. His mother, Minnie, was the sister of the queen's daughter-in-law the Princess of Wales. And although the queen spoke kindly of Minnie and Nicky, she detested the Romanov family as a whole. In a telling letter to one of her granddaughters, she poured out her anxiety about Alix's fate.

> All my fears abt. her future marriage now show themselves so strongly & my blood runs cold when I think of her *so* young most likely placed on that vy. unsafe Throne, her dear life & above all her Husband's constantly threatened & unable to see her but rarely; it is a great additional anxiety in my declining years! Oh! how I wish it was not to be that I shld lose my sweet Alicky. All I *most earnestly* ask now is that *nothing* shld be *settled* for her *future without* my *being told* before. She has *no Parents* & I am her only *Grandparent* & feel I *have* a *claim* on her! She is like my *own Child* ...[2]

Queen Victoria reiterated this in a letter to Nicky: "As she has no parents, I feel I am the only person who can really be answerable for her. All her dear Sisters ... looked to me as their second Mother."[3] Her fears about Alix's future in Russia were well founded. Over the previous fifty years, the tsarist empire had become a breeding ground for revolutionaries, making it the birthplace of what, in modern parlance, we call terrorism. Those who took up the Russian revolutionary cause came to be known as Nihilists, because along with totally rejecting "authority as well as religious and moral values," they advocated "the destruction of social and political institutions."[4] These Nihilists succeeded in several of their deadly missions. The Winter Palace had been blown up once before, and Nicky's grandfather, Alexander II, had been targeted for assassination six times. Eventually, the Nihilists succeeded in murdering Alexander II, whose broken body was returned to the Winter Palace. The assassins tried three times to blow up the tsar's carriage with bombs. In the process, they wounded dozens of spectators. Only when the sympathetic, liberal Alexander attended to the injured did the Nihilists succeed in their mission.

In the late nineteenth century, Russia was a land of incredible contrasts infused with vibrant mixtures of European and Asiatic cultures. The imperial family, nobility, and the society elite tended to follow European trends, while many of the population living outside the larger cities were inclined to semimystic cultural traits more indicative of Russia's neighbors in the Far East. Even the natural world in Russia was dichotic. In the summer months, known as the White Nights, the sun went down only for a few short hours. The opposite was true in the long winter. Endless nights blanketed the vast, snow-covered landscape as the wealthy and elite traveled around in muffs and heavy fur coats. The country was so vast that an old proverb claimed that the sun never set on the Russian Empire. Imperial Russia, or *Rossiiskaia Imperiia* as it was known in the Russian language, "was a colossus anchored to traditions a hundred years out of date. At 8.6 million square miles it covered almost one-sixth of the world's surface, had a population of 120 million (the combined populations of Britain, France and Germany) and a standing army of over 1 million men. Its tsars lived on an unparalleled scale of public splendour; its grand duchesses staggered under the weight of their diamonds, its social season was more spectacular than anything in Europe."[5] By the end of the nineteenth century, the Russian tsar "was undoubtedly the wealthiest monarch in the world."[6]

Of the 120 million people living in the Russian Empire, more than 80 percent were peasants, made up primarily of Slavs, Poles, Ruthenians, and a melting pot of nearly eighty other ethnic groups living on a vast, relatively unpopulated swath of land stretching from Moscow to Saint Petersburg; smaller groups inhabited the eastern provinces, such as Siberia. The people themselves mostly lived in poverty. In 1894, fewer than 20 percent of Russians could read or write. The country's power rested solely with the tsar and his court, punctuated by the influence of the incredibly powerful Russian Orthodox Church. Priests dominated the larger cities but virtually controlled the tinier parishes, where loyalty to the imperial family was preached on a regular basis. For the Russian people, the tsar was God's personal representative on earth. He was the *Batiushka Tsar*—the father-emperor—whose very existence was tied into the lives of Russia and its people. Even Russian folksayings were anchored on the relationship between God and the tsar: "Without God the world cannot be; without the Tsar the earth cannot hold."[7]

This belief stretched back four hundred years to the fall of Constantinople to the Ottomans in 1453. Ivan the Great, the Grand Prince of Moscow, married a niece of the last Byzantine emperor, Constantine XI, and adopted many of their practices in order to strengthen his new claim as the tsar—or Caesar—of All the Russias in the latter half of the fifteenth century. Moscow itself came to be seen as the Third Rome, after the First and Second (Constantinople), rising like a phoenix from the ashes of history. It received greater prominence when Peter the Great assumed the title *emperor* and declared Russia an imperial power in 1721.[8] From then on, it became the mission of all the tsars not only to defend Christendom by recapturing Constantinople from the Turks but to protect all Slavs in the Balkans. This became known as Pan-Slavism. Catherine the Great had planned to take this vision a step further. Not only did she plan to retake Constantinople and resurrect the Byzantine Empire, she also intended to unify Russia with the Slavic Balkans, thus creating the largest empire in the world at that time, stretching from the Sea of Japan to the Adriatic. Although the practicality of a Russo-Balkan empire fizzled out, it was an ambition to which the Romanovs held. Pan-Slavism became a central tenet in Russian politics by the 1840s. It would eventually set the country on course for war in 1914.

This dual mission inexorably tied the Russian Orthodox Church to the monarchy, giving the tsars absolute power over church and state, the likes of which few other dynasties ever experienced. "Theoretically the tsar's power was unlimited," wrote one of Nicholas II's biographers, "the Romanovs liked to think of Russia and its empire as one enormous feudal estate in which everything derived from them."[9] This absolutism went a step further in Russia and became autocracy, the total supreme power of the state concentrated in the hands of one individual—the tsar. Romanov autocracy could be seen in the details of the day-to-day business of ruling. Unlike other monarchs, the Russian tsar "had neither a personal secretariat nor a private secretary, stamped his own envelopes and communicated with staff and ministers through hand-written notes."[10] The chimeric nature of the autocratic power wielded by the tsars turned Russia into a hotbed of revolutionary ideologies over the centuries. Unwilling to give up a drop of power, the Romanovs were vehemently opposed to liberal ideas, which they perceived as a direct attack on their God-given prerogatives. In response to this autocracy with which the Romanovs became synonymous, revolutionary attacks against members of the imperial family became commonplace by the 1890s; half a dozen tsars had been murdered since the dynasty came to power in 1613. This was the world into which Alix of Hesse was marrying. It was a world Queen Victoria understood all too well.

Unwilling to part with her beloved granddaughter forever, the queen invited Alix to stay with her at Windsor Castle immediately after the engagement. She spent many days questioning Alix about every detail of her relationship with Nicholas, which the princess duly reported in letters. The correspondence that began between Nicky and Alix was voluminous, to say the least. They wrote back and forth to each other daily, sharing their hopes, fears, trials, and anxieties. Alix made it a particular point to express her thoughts on God and man's lot in life. "What sorrows this life does bring, what great trials and how difficult to bear them patiently," she wrote. "Suffering always draws one nearer to God, does it not, and when we think what Jesus Christ had to bear for us, how little and small our sorrows seem in comparison, and yet we fret and grumble and are not patient as He was."[11] Letters like these reveal Alix's deep love for God and her commitment to her Christian faith. That faith sustained her through many ordeals, including the most perilous, which were yet to come.

The love Nicholas and Alix had for one another only grew stronger with each passing day, prompting them to open up to each other about every aspect of their lives. In the summer, Nicky told Alix about some of the more sordid dalliances of his youth. He mentioned a liaison he had with a ballerina named Mathilde Kschessinska, which was widely known among Russian courtiers. But Alix was quick to forgive his indiscretions.

> What is past is past and will never return. We all are tempted in this world and when we are young we cannot always fight and hold our own against the temptation, but as long as we repent, God will forgive us.... Forgive me for writing so much, but I want you to be quite sure of my love for you and that I love you even more since you told me that little story, your confidence in me touches me oh so deeply.... [May] I always show myself worthy of it.... God bless you, beloved Nicky ...[12]

During Alix's time in England, the tsarevitch paid her a visit. Her met here at Walton-on-Thames, where her sister Victoria had a holiday cottage. From there, they drove to Windsor where the tsarevitch met with the queen. Nicky's arrival coincided with the imminent arrival of George and May's first child. Before the due date, the Duchess of York had the satisfaction of returning to White Lodge for the delivery, where she would be in familiar surroundings. There had been a great deal of speculation over where the birth would take place. May immediately dismissed Buckingham Palace because it was too public. York Cottage was more private, but moving in there for the delivery meant the duchess would be under the thumb of her domineering mother-in-law. In the end, George agreed to White Lodge. It was no small sacrifice, since he was often frustrated by the Duchess of Teck's indecorum and the duke's growing invalidity and surliness. And so it was at White Lodge, just shy of their first wedding anniversary on June 23, 1894, that the Yorks became the proud parents of a healthy baby boy.

"Yesterday at 10 o'clock a son was born to Georgie and May," Nicholas reported happily in his diary. He and Alix were chosen as godparents. Queen Victoria—whose dislike of newborn infants was well known—even admitted that "the Baby, who is a vy. strong Boy" was "a pretty child."[13] The baptism was held on July 16 in the Green Drawing Room at White Lodge. As the archbishop of Canterbury held the baby at the font, he was christened Edward Albert Christian George Andrew Patrick David. Each of his names had illustrious forebearers. Edward was for his late uncle Eddy; Albert for his great-grandfather the prince consort; Christian was for another great-grandfather—the king of Denmark; and George, Andrew, Patrick, and David were chosen for the patron saints of England, Scotland, Ireland, and Wales, though he would always be known simply as David. Nicky recorded of the ceremony, "Instead of plunging the infant into the water, the archbishop sprinkled water on his head.... What a nice, healthy child."[14]

The following day, more than fifteen hundred visitors came to White Lodge to see Queen Victoria's latest great-grandchild, who was now third in line to the throne. So many visitors flocked in after a few days that a tent was set up on the lawn of White Lodge to accommodate everyone. The queen wrote to her daughter Vicky that it was the first time in English history "that there should be three direct heirs, as well as the sovereign [still] alive."[15] All the ceremoniousness of David's birth could not wipe away May's shock and exhaustion at carrying and delivering her first child. Childbirth in the Victorian age was never easy. Nor was it any easier for royal mothers, who were forced to submit to stupefying etiquette at the expense of their own comfort and, sometimes, the health and safety of both themselves and their children. For May, her "nerves had been shattered by the birth and she was suffering from post-natal depression."[16] Only after a holiday at the Hotel Victoria in Saint Moritz did she recover herself.

While the Duchess of York was convalescing after her first delivery, Alix was enjoying a contented life at Windsor Castle throughout the summer of 1894. With Nicky by her side—and accompanied by the Yorks when May felt up to it—she set off for picnics at Richmond Park, excursions into the countryside near Sandringham, and river cruises down the Thames. Alix also made it a point to take Nicholas to Henley to visit her sister Victoria. Alix's brother-in-law Prince Louis of Battenberg was an up-and-coming officer in the Royal Navy who renounced his German national identity at the age of fourteen and became thoroughly English. According to Nicky, the time he and Alix spent together was filled with "paradisiacal happiness" for them both.[17] Like so many other times in Alix's life, the idyll did not last long. In the autumn, news arrived that Nicky's father, the immense, herculean Tsar Alexander III, was dying. For months, he had been suffering from insomnia, headaches, and weakness in the legs. The doctors diagnosed him with nephritis, inflammation of the kidneys. The news greatly alarmed the Romanovs because the tsar, towering at six feet five inches tall, had always been in the best of health; Alexander was so strong that he had been known to bend metal fire pokers with his bare hands to amuse his children. In October, the imperial court had moved to the warm climate of the Crimea where the tsar was expected to recuperate. Queen Olga of Greece offered him the use of her Villa Mon Repos on the island of Corfu, but it was considered too unsafe to move the tsar. In no time, Nicky's father was on his deathbed, nearly blind and incapacitated.

Nicky immediately summoned Alix to Livadia, the Romanovs' palace on the Black Sea, where the imperial family was holding a vigil. Ordinarily, the arrival of a future tsarevna into Russia would be treated with the utmost care and ceremony, but the court was entirely wrapped up in the drama surrounding the tsar's declining health. But Nicky was overjoyed to have Alix with him. "My God, what a joy to meet her in my country and to have her near," he wrote. "Half my fears and sadness have disappeared."[18]

For the next ten days, the court held its breath. Alix was Nicholas's great strength and support. Timid and weak-willed, he had never been properly trained as a tsar. He struggled with making the simplest decisions. The doctors virtually ignored him as heir, instead going straight to the empress or the tsar's brothers. "Be firm and make the doctors ... come alone to you every day ... so that you are the first to know," she told him. "Don't let others be put first and you left out.... Show your own mind and don't let others forget who you are."[19] These words began Alix's lifelong exhortation of Nicholas. "Tell me everything my soul," Alix wrote to him in a note. "You can fully trust me, look upon me as a bit of yourself. Let your joys and sorrows be mine, so that we may ever draw nearer together."[20]

On October 20, 1894, the day Nicholas dreaded all his life finally arrived when Alexander III died. One of his last acts had been to summon Nicky and Alix to his bedside to give them his blessing. Despite being unable to stand, the tsar insisted on donning a full imperial uniform, stating it was "the only fitting garb in which to greet a future Russian empress."[21] With Alexander gone, his son was now Tsar Nicholas II, the eighteenth ruler of the Imperial House of Romanov. That night, he wrote in his diary, "God, God, what a day. The Lord has called to him our adored, our dear, our tenderly loved Papa. My head turns, it isn't possible to believe it.... It was the death of a saint, Lord assist us in these difficult days. Poor dear Mama."[22] The Duchess of York was deeply saddened when she was told. "This news is too awful," she wrote to George, "& I feel for you all with all my heart.... My head gets quite bewildered in thinking of all our dear ones [Nicky and Alix] in their sorrow & misery."[23] The Prince and Princess of Wales arrived a few days later to find that Minnie, now the dowager empress, had locked herself in her rooms in grief. Princess Alexandra would not leave her sister's side for the next nineteen days and even slept in her bedroom at night. She described the Romanovs' crisis as an "unspeakable agony."[24]

Queen Victoria, who had watched over Alix and Nicky with so much loving care, was grief-stricken by the news. She noted in her diary, "Poor dear Nicky and darling Alicky. What a terrible load of responsibility and anxiety has been laid upon the poor children!" She concluded in her usually perceptive manner, "I had hoped and trusted they would have many years of comparative quiet and happiness before ascending to this thorny throne." In a letter to the Empress Frederick, she expressed the same worry: "What a horrible tragedy this is! And what a position for these dear young people. God help them! And now I hear that poor little Alicky goes with them to Saint Petersburg and that the wedding is to take place soon after the funeral. I am quite miserable not to see my darling child again before, here. *Where* shall I *ever* see her again?"[25]

In his grief, the truth of Nicholas's feelings came out. He sobbingly asked his brother-in-law Grand Duke Alexander ("Sandro"), "what am I going to do.... What is going to happen to me ... to Alix, to mother, to all of Russia? I am not prepared to be a Tsar. I never wanted to become one. I know nothing of the business of ruling. I have no idea of even how to talk to the ministers."[26] The panicked frenzy in the Crimea was quelled by the efforts of Nicky and Alix's uncle Bertie. According to Nicky's sister Olga, it was he who "quietly began calming down the tumult that met them on their arrival ... The last days at Livadia would have been beyond anyone's endurance were it not for the presence of the Prince of Wales."[27]

At 10:00 a.m. on the day after Alexander III died, Alix converted from Lutheranism into the Russian Orthodox Church. After the set of questions and responses, Alix was given absolution by the priest. He then anointed her with oil on her temples, eyes, nose, lips, ears, hands, and feet. Those spots were then touched by a sponge dipped in holy water. Once the service was over, Alix, Nicholas, and the dowager empress took Holy Communion together. Contrary to her worries, her conversion was remarkably painless. Her sister Ella made it a point to reassure a concerned Queen Victoria that the ceremony was "so beautiful and touching," and Alexandra looked "very calm."[28] That day, Nicholas issued his first official decree as emperor. He signed an imperial decree that confirmed Alix in her new faith, along with a new name and title. She was now "the truly believing Grand Duchess Alexandra Feodorovna."[29] These were her official Russian names, but to friends and family she would always remain Alix.

The funeral for Alexander III was on a scale never before seen in Russian history. Sixty-one royals, including the kings of Denmark, Serbia, and Greece, made the long journey to Russia to pay their last respects. The Duke of York was summoned at his father's behest to be a pallbearer at the funeral. It was the first time since their wedding that George and May were separated, and it was a difficult time for them both. To ease his homesickness, George wrote some twenty letters to May in the few weeks he was away. In each of them, he begged her to give him some news from home. In one of his letters to May, George described some of the funeral practices of the Russian court in the days leading up to the funeral: "Every day, after lunch, we had another service at the church. After the service, we all went up to [the] coffin which was open and kissed the Holy Picture which he [Alexander's body] held in his hand. It gave me a shock when I saw [his] dear face so close to mine when I stooped down. He looks so beautiful and peaceful, but of course he has changed very much. It is a fortnight today."[30] From the Crimea, the tsar's body made a seventeen-day journey to the Cathedral of Our Lady of Kazan—the largest church in Saint Petersburg—where it was laid to rest after a four-hour ceremony. Tens of thousands of soldiers lined the streets of Saint Petersburg, which were packed with sobbing peasants. The city itself was draped in black, with funeral arches lining the procession route. George wrote to May about the experience of assisting with the emperor's final interment. "We carried him and lowered him down into the vault," he wrote, "and it was most impressive and sad, and I shall never forget it. Darling Aunt Minny was so brave and stood the whole time and never broke down once."[31]

A week after Alexander III's body was laid to rest, plans went ahead for Nicholas and Alexandra's wedding. Under normal circumstances, Alix would have returned to Darmstadt to await the end of the official mourning period for Alexander III before marrying the new tsar. This was changed not out of disrespect for the late tsar but to consolidate Nicholas's reign. As the new monarch, it was imperative for him to begin his rule with stability and solidarity. The best way he could see that happening was to make Alexandra his wife as quickly as possible. Nicholas was determined that they should be married in the relative privacy at Livadia. His mother agreed, but it was his uncles—Serge and the other brothers of the late emperor—who quashed such a notion. It was the duty of a tsar to marry in the splendor of Saint Petersburg, they insisted. Burly and intimidating like Alexander, Nicky's uncles were a force to be reckoned with. He relented. Queen Victoria was racked with anxiety over Alexandra's fate. "Tomorrow morning poor dear Alicky's fate will be sealed," she wrote on November 13. "No two people were ever more devoted as she and he are and that is the *one* consolation I have, for otherwise the dangers and responsibilities fill me with anxiety and I shall constantly be thinking of them with anxiety.... I daily pray for them."[32]

The wedding took place on the cold, gray morning of November 14, 1894, at the Winter Palace in Saint Petersburg. At 8:00 a.m., a twenty-one-gun salute was fired across the Neva River, signaling the start of the nuptial procession. Nicholas II, accompanied by the Prince of Wales, made the mile-and-a-half journey to the Winter Palace from his mother's home, the Anichkov Palace. Behind the tsar and his uncle were a dozen state carriages transporting the various guests, including the king and queen of Denmark, the king and queen of Greece, the Grand Duke of Hesse, the Duke and Duchess of Coburg, the Princess of Wales, the crown prince and princess of Romania, and numerous other princes and princesses. "The list of the palace procession does not give a full idea of the scene," wrote one witness. "Representatives of many nationalities were present in the halls [of the Winter Palace]. These consisted of Turks, Japanese, Chinese, Parsees, Bohkarians, and men of all colors and diversified garbs."[33]

Alexandra arrived at the Winter Palace separately from the guests. She had been staying with Ella at her palace but traveled to the palace that morning with the dowager empress. Their arrival was met with genuine exuberance from the people who had packed the streets. Inside the palace, she was dressed for her wedding by the women of the Russian imperial family, the Princess of Wales, and the dowager empress. The beautiful gold mirror Alexandra stood in front of was used by every Russian grand duchess on her wedding day. Her wedding gown properly befitted an empress. Made from cloth of silver, it included a double ermine-lined mantle. Over her shoulders rested a brocade of white silk trimmed with strawberry velvet and a gold inlay. Her jewelry was equally dazzling. Atop her head sat the sparkling nuptial crown surrounded by sweet-scented orange blossoms brought from Poland. Most special of all was the ring she wore on one of her fingers, which was a gift from Queen Victoria.

"I don't think I can move," Alexandra muttered at one point. "I'm pinned to the ground."

"Yes, I know how heavy it all is," the dowager empress told her. "But I'm afraid it's only one of the lesser weights that need to be borne by a Russian empress."[34]

During the dressing, a ceremonial catastrophe almost took place when the court hairdresser—the only person prescribed by imperial etiquette who could fasten the bride's crown upon her head—was over an hour late, having been denied entry to the palace by police. Rumors quickly spread that something was amiss. They were only silenced when, finally, a resplendent Alexandra emerged from her dressing room.

Walking side by side with Minnie and followed by the Romanov women and the imperial courtesans, Alexandra made her way to the green Malachite Hall where the tsar was waiting. It was Nicholas II's first major public appearance as tsar, and he showed signs of nervousness. He trembled with anticipation in his red Hussar uniform knowing that—in just a few short hours—his darling Alexandra would be his wife. Alexandra wrote to her sister

Ella that day, "One day in deepest mourning lamenting a beloved one, the next in smartest clothes being married. There cannot be a greater contrast, but it drew us more together, if possible."[35]

Once the bride and groom arrived, the entire imperial court assembled in the hall for the procession to the chapel. "The gentlemen of the court were all in gala uniform," reported the *New York Times*, "and the ladies were dressed in court costume of strawberry color, trimmed with velvet of a similar shade, with long trains, and wearing long white veils."[36] The first member of the wedding procession to enter the chapel after the 150 Gentlemen of the Chamber was Empress Marie Feodorovna, on the arm of her father, King Christian IX of Denmark. It was a bittersweet day for Minnie, who was also celebrating her forty-seventh birthday. Alexandra was not unsympathetic toward her mother-in-law's plight. She later described to Queen Victoria that "poor Aunt Minnie is alone. She is an angel of kindness and is more touching and brave than I can say."[37] After Minnie and Christian IX entered, Nicholas and Alexandra followed them, arm in arm, walking under an honor guard with sabers high in the air. When the entire procession filed into the chapel, the ceremony began. It was an exotic, almost mystic service conducted by the metropolitan of Saint Petersburg, the Holy Synod, and the clergy of the court. As the bride and groom held lighted candles at the altar, an estimated eight thousand guests watched them in silent awe.

The two-hour ceremony went off perfectly and was concluded with yet another gun salute, this time numbering 301 shots, shortly before 1:00 p.m. George sent Queen Victoria a glowing report.

> Dear Alicky looked quite lovely at the Wedding … she went through it all with so much modesty but was so graceful and dignified at the same time, she certainly made a most excellent impression … I do think Nicky is a very lucky man to have got such a lovely and charming wife … I must say I never [saw] two people more in love with each other or happier than they are. When they drove from the Winter Palace after the wedding they got a tremendous reception and ovation from the large crowds in the streets, the cheering was more hearty and reminded me of England.[38]

George did not forget to send a report to May. "I think Nicky is a very lucky man," he wrote. "I told them both that I could not wish them more than that they should be as happy as you and I are together. Was that right?"[39]

Queen Victoria's thoughts were on Russia and Alexandra that day. In the evening, the queen gave a banquet at Windsor Castle in honor of the new tsarina. Alexandra's new position instantly made her one of the most powerful women in the world, which filled her grandmother with a sense of awe: "How I thought of darling Alicky, and how impossible it seemed that gentle little simple Alicky should be the great Empress of Russia!"[40] Charlotte Knollys, wife of the private secretary to the British royal family, felt the same as Queen Victoria, but hers was of a much more scathing opinion: "What a change! A little scrubby Hessian Princess—not even a Royal Highness & now the Empress of the largest Empire in Europe!"[41] Knollys's comment seems more an insult to Alexandra than actually attacking the House of Hesse, since Hessian and other low-ranking German royals had been supplying Russian empresses for over a century.

The day after the new tsar and tsarina were married, people were still talking about the wedding. In Saint Petersburg, some forty thousand soldiers took off their hats simultaneously as a sign of respect. When they appeared in public, both Nicholas and Alexandra strained under the weight of so many onlookers. It was a painful experience for the painfully shy Alexandra, who recorded that she felt like a bird in a cage. Some of the people, many of whom were superstitious because of the nature of the Russian Orthodox faith, began to distrust their new empress. "She comes to us behind a coffin," they murmured.[42]

In the days and weeks that followed, the newlyweds were busy answering messages of congratulations. It took nearly a week for them to escape for anything close to a honeymoon. They managed to spend four days at Tsarskoe Selo ("the tsar's village") fifteen miles outside Saint Petersburg. One of the most magical places in Europe, Tsarskoe Selo was its own imperial town filled with gardens, palaces, and parks. It was eighteen miles in circumference and dotted by lakes, forests, and other creations. It contained "a collection of boats of all nations, varying from a Chinese sampan to an English light four-oar; from a Venetian gondola to a Brazilian catamaran."[43] It was also one of the most state-of-the-art locations in all of Russia. Guarded by a garrison of five thousand soldiers, it possessed "the only town-wide electrical system in the country, the first railway, a telegraph and radio station, and the most advanced water and sewage system in the whole of Russia." By contrast, "Most Russian villages had no running water or drains."[44] When in residence at Tsarskoe Selo, Nicholas and Alexandra stayed in one of two enormous buildings: the Catherine Palace, built in 1752 by the Empress Elizabeth; and the Alexander Palace, constructed by Catherine the Great in 1792. The tsarina took a liking to the heavily colonnaded Alexander Palace and truly made it her own, decorating it with English chintz. Most of the furniture itself was ordered from Maples in London. Outside of Windsor and Balmoral, the Alexander Palace was the happiest home Alexandra would ever know.

7

"Only Give Me a Chance"

(1895–1901)

Tsarina Alexandra's private life in Russia was filled with contentment. She and Nicholas enjoyed a love-filled marriage overflowing with passion. They constantly wrote love notes to one another. In Alexandra's diary, Nicky poured out his feelings: "Ever more and more, stronger and deeper, grow my love and devotion, and my longing for you. Never can I thank God enough for the treasure he has given me for my VERY OWN—and to be called yours, darling, what happiness can be greater? ... No more separations. At last united, bound for life, and when this life is ended we meet again in the other world to remain together for all eternity. Yours, yours!"[1] Alexandra was just as head over heels. "I can assure you that I never thought one could be as happy as I am now," she wrote to her brother-in-law Prince Louis of Battenberg. For the first time since her mother died, Alexandra felt loved and secure, as if all the sorrows of the past were washed away at her wedding. She admitted this to Louis: "life is so different to what it was in the past—though there may be many difficulties, and all is not easy when one comes first into a new country and has to speak another language yet in time I hope I shall be of some help and use."[2]

The love Nicholas and Alexandra shared soon expanded to include their first child. In November 1895, the tsarina went into labor at the Alexander Palace in Tsarskoe Selo. So anticipated had this birth been that a bevy of doctors and nurses waited on the empress, including the court accoucheur, Professor Ott, and the imperial chief surgeon, Dr. Girsh. The delivery was an agonizing one, largely due to the fact that the baby was a number of weeks late, and Alexandra was a slim woman with tiny hips. At one point, the doctors gave Nicholas the horrifying news that they may lose both mother and child without direct intervention. After sixteen hours of labor, a cesarean section was successfully performed. A healthy ten-pound baby girl was delivered, who was named Olga Nicholaievna. A sense of disappointment swept through Saint Petersburg when the 101-cannon salute signaled the birth of a daughter. Sons were more highly prized than daughters, since women had been ineligible to rule Russia since Catherine the Great. She was so loathed by her son, Paul I, that he changed the law so that no woman could ever rule unless all other male members of the dynasty, from great uncles to third cousins, were dead. This did not dampen Nicky and Alexandra's spirits. Princess Maud of Wales, the couple's mutual cousin, wrote, "Nicky is now a happy father, but it is a pity it was not a boy!"[3]

There was a general excitement in Britain over the birth, since Olga was a great-grandchild of Queen Victoria. It was hoped Olga's birth would lead to better relations between Great Britain and Russia. The *Daily Telegraph* wrote that Olga's arrival was "received with much friendly interest in this country, where all that concerns the present and future of Russia is the subject of intelligent and sympathetic appreciation."[4] Few were surprised when Queen Victoria was asked to be the godmother. Alexandra's recovery was incredibly slow, and many in Russia did not expect her to survive. To the surprise of many, she rallied and was soon able to enjoy her new daughter. "You can imagine our intense happiness now that we have such a precious little being of our own to care for and look after," Alexandra wrote to one of her sisters.[5]

In autocratic Russia, the accession of a new tsar was a deeply significant event that impacted all facets of society, including politics, religion, and foreign affairs. There was nothing greater to cement the unitary nature of the tsar with all aspects of Russian life than the coronation. It was the sort of event that Alexandra had always dreaded. The thought that she was to play such a public role in the spectacle undoubtedly preyed upon her fears. When the time came, she and Nicholas set off on the four-hundred-mile journey to the city of Moscow. If Saint Petersburg—founded in 1703 by Peter the Great—was Russia's link to its future with Europe, Moscow was its tie to the past. The city's iconic onion-domed buildings framed a cityscape of churches, palaces, and other ornately designed buildings decorated in mosaics of red, blue, and gold. In the backdrop, the mighty Kremlin complex was a silent reminder of the power of the Orthodox Church and the state. The coronation would bind the new sovereigns to the people in a most religious way, cementing the idea of Nicholas as the *Batiushka Tsar*, but signs of the already emerging gulf between Alexandra and the Russian people were evident when the imperial family made its ceremonial entrance into Moscow. The tsarina rode alone in her own carriage behind her husband and mother-in-law. Nicholas was greeted with cheers; Minnie received shouts of hurrah; but when Alexandra came through, a hush fell over the crowds, reducing her to tears. "Silence—an ominous silence," wrote one of her biographers. "Not open jeering, or insults, but the quiet of rejection."[6] One witness to the early days of Nicholas II's reign wrote that his wife "was not born to be Empress of one of the largest countries on the face of the earth."[7]

The scale of the coronation was extraordinary. "A gang of princes" came from all over Europe, but in keeping with court tradition no reigning monarchs were invited so that no one with equal rank to the tsar would be in attendance.[8] Seven thousand invited guests flocked into Moscow. Almost a million more stood in the streets to watch the procession. To run smoothly, the event required no less than "1300 full time servants and 1200 part time. The livery division required 600 horses and 800 coachmen with horses and carriages. Guards came from 83 battalions, 47 squadrons and hundreds of batteries."[9]

Nicholas was the first to be crowned on May 26, 1896, in what would turn out to be a five-hour ceremony at the Cathedral of the Assumption. After receiving the diamond-and-ruby crown that had first been worn by Catherine the Great, Nicholas II's grand titles were announced by the deacon: "Nicholas Alexandrovich, Emperor and Autocrat of All the Russias, Tsar of Moscow, Kiev, Vladimir, Novgorod." The list went on to include all the provinces, territories, and fiefs over which the tsars claimed lordship: "Poland, Finland, Bulgaria, Tver…Semigalia, Samogotia, Armenia and the Mountain Princes."[10] After Nicholas's crowning and proclamation, it was his wife's turn. When the moment came, Alexandra acquitted herself well, though her nerves were certainly tested. For most of the long ceremony, the tsar and tsarina sat on their thrones, staring out into the crowds, their faces motionless and without expression. One witness drew a sharp contrast between the tsar and his wife. While Nicholas looked overwhelmed by his imperial mantle, Alexandra, "stood steadily upright, her crown did not appear to crush her…. [but] even at this supreme hour no joy seemed to uplift her, not even pride; aloof enigmatic, she was all dignity but she shed about her no warmth. It was almost a relief to tear one's gaze from her."[11] The dowager empress also wrote about the coronation, telling her mother "how *gripping* and solemn it all *was*! My heart truly bled to see my Nicky at this, *so young*, in his beloved father's place."[12] That night, as the tsar and his wife stepped out onto the balcony of the mighty Kremlin before an excited crowd of thousands, the palace's facade was illuminated by thousands of tiny bulbs.

What should have been an otherwise joyous event was marred by disaster. A few days after the coronation, a mob of four hundred thousand people assembled at the Khodynka field to celebrate the tsar and his wife. By the evening, an estimated one million people had converged on the field for the revelry. What started out as a festive atmosphere, with hundreds of thousands drinking from mugs adorned with the imperial crest, soon erupted into bedlam when a rumor circulated that the officials ran out of food and drink. Almost immediately, the masses panicked. Drunk and unruly, they threw off their restraints and went into a frenzy. Men, women, and children were literally trampled to death by the alcohol-induced panic on a field lined with artillery trenches. Vladimir Giliarovsky, a reporter for the *Russian Gazette*, was at Khodynka that day. His account from several days later is a haunting description of the tragedy. "Steam began to rise," he recalled, "looking like the mist over a swamp.... Many felt faint, some lost consciousness." All around him people were "fighting for breath, vomiting, succumbing to the irresistible pushing and jostling. There was no wind, no moon. Only the suffocating congestion, which worsened as dawn approached." One of the survivors of the massacre recalled what happened next. "A mass of people half a million strong staggered with all its unimaginable weight in the direction of the buffets," he wrote. "People by the thousands fell in a ditch and ended up literally on their heads at the bottom. Others fell straight after them, and more, and more...."[13] When the dust on the field finally settled, witnesses became ill at the sight of hundreds of lifeless, bloodied corpses. The official death toll was estimated at 1,389, with another 1,300 injured.

The imperial family was horrified beyond words. "The *dreadful* accident ... was appalling beyond all description, and has ... draped a *black veil* over all the splendor and glory!" Minnie wrote to her mother. "Just imagine *how many* poor unfortunate people were *crushed* and fatally injured."[14] In the aftermath, Nicholas and Alexandra rushed to the hospitals to be with the injured. Nicholas paid out of his own pocket for the burial of every person who died at Khodynka. The finger of blame was pointed squarely at the tsar's uncle Grand Duke Serge, who had been responsible for the preparations that day. It was widely known that Serge neglected to properly prepare the field because he quarreled with another court official over protocol for the event. When the tsar announced he was launching an investigation into the tragedy, Serge browbeat him into calling it off by threatening to boycott the imperial court if he was implicated. "How outrageous can you get!" wrote the tsar's incredulous cousin Grand Duke Constantine Constantinovich. "If only the Emperor were sterner and stronger!"[15]

Neither the tsar nor his wife felt it was appropriate to hold any further coronation festivities, but once again, Nicholas II's formidable uncles pressured him into submission. They practically forced him and Alexandra to attend a ball held by the French ambassador. It was imperative that the tsar attend, the grand dukes insisted, since the ambassador had spent more than half a million rubles on the ball and Nicholas's absence could be taken as a snub. France was Russia's only European ally—the two powers had signed a treaty in 1892. Nicky's uncles warned him that snubbing the French ambassador would earn bitter recriminations from Paris. Browbeaten, Nicholas agreed to make an appearance at the ball. Many criticized Alexandra for agreeing to attend with her husband, but her heart was broken for the victims and their families. Crown Princess Marie of Romania, one of her cousins who was no fan of the tsarina, wrote years later, "No doubt many that night considered the Empress heartless because she went to a ball on the evening of the great disaster, yet God alone knows how much rather she would have stayed at home to pray for the dead!"[16]

The months that followed the coronation were particularly miserable ones for Alexandra. A few weeks before leaving for Moscow, she excitedly told Nicholas she was pregnant again. Early reports from her doctors indicated she was carrying a boy. In an effort to avoid the close scrutiny brought about by her first pregnancy, Alexandra chose to tell only her husband, their immediate family, and a few of her ladies-in-waiting. Sadly for Alexandra, the emotional strain of the coronation and her overwhelming grief from the Khodynka tragedy taxed her body. According to one historian, her "body rebelled," and she miscarried the baby. "What had begun in joy," the same historian wrote, "and celebration was ending in a season of disaster, with the crown of the Romanovs tarnished by tragedy and the heir to the throne, the boy whose existence Alix had kept as her secret, lost in a swirl of blood."[17] Her critics used this tragedy as an excuse to heap insults upon the empress. They claimed she had become pregnant by a lover and aborted the fetus to cover up her infidelity—"a malevolent distortion of the reality of her miscarriage."[18]

The emotional turmoil of Alexandra's failed pregnancy was soothed when she and Nicholas accepted an invitation from Queen Victoria to visit Scotland. It became a major continental tour that included a visit to France and finished with a much-awaited trip to see Alexandra's brother, Ernie, in Darmstadt. At the beginning of September, Nicholas, Alexandra, and their entourage of several hundred docked in the port town of Leith, a district in northern Edinburgh. The tsar and tsarina were welcomed by the Prince of Wales, their mutual uncle, but they still had much traveling to do before they reached journey's end. From the dockside at Leith, the royals drove in a downpour to Edinburgh Station, where a train took them more than seventy-four miles west to Ballater. From there, an entire squadron of Scots Greys escorted the group for the eight mile drive to Balmoral in open carriages. When they finally reached the castle, everyone was soaking wet from the pouring rain. Despite the cold, damp climate, the imperial couple received a tenderly warm welcome from the queen. And although she had early reservations about Alexandra's marrying into the Russian imperial family, Queen Victoria soon became quite fond of Nicholas II. "It feels funny to me," Nicholas wrote to his brother, "the extent to which I have become part of the English [royal] family. I have become almost as indispensable to [the Queen] as her Indians and her Scotsmen; I am, as it were, attached to her and the best thing is that she does not like me to leave her side ... She exudes such enormous charm."[19]

The accommodations that had to be set up at Balmoral for the imperial family and their entourage were enormous. Their security detail alone included hundreds of "plainclothes secret servicemen, plus twenty-four constables and four sergeants from the Metropolitan Police."[20] Outside the castle walls, an entire man-made village had to be built to handle the overflow of servants. Even the British royal family was not immune to the hardships imposed by the imperial visit. Accompanying the queen had been the Prince and Princess of Wales, George and May, and numerous other relations. So crowded was Balmoral that the Duke and Duchess of York had to lodge at an inn down the road. Even the castle servants were forced to sleep three or four to a bed.

For the month of September, Nicholas and Alexandra were swept up in a whirlwind of activities planned by their British relatives. Nicholas went hunting with the Prince of Wales and the Duke of York—a pastime the tsar did not enjoy. He was left feeling even more miserable because of a toothache and a cheek that was "much swollen from irritation at the stump of a decayed molar."[21] Meanwhile, Alexandra spent long hours in the company of her grandmother. Queen Victoria was relieved that, after two years as empress of Russia, Alexandra had not let the position go to her head. She wrote to the Empress Frederick, "Dear Nicky and Alicky are quite unspoilt and unchanged and as dear and simple as ever and as kind as ever. He is looking rather thin and pale and careworn, but sweet Alicky is in great beauty and very blooming. The baby is magnificent, bigger than she and Ella ever were, and a lovely, lively [great-]grandchild;"[22] but privately, the queen later admitted that Alexandra's recent experiences in Russia had made her distant and aloof. Courtiers at Balmoral during the visit could not help but be swept up in the grandeur of the occasion. While attending church one Sunday morning, Lady Lytton observed that it was "very interesting seeing the two pews full of the Royalties and the Emperor and Empress standing by the Queen even in the Scotch [Church] where all is simple and reverent."[23]

The last day of the visit was emotional for Alexandra and Victoria. They passed the rainy, misty day quietly in one of the castle's salons. When the rain finally broke, Nicholas and Alexandra planted a tree in the garden to commemorate their visit. The queen recorded in her diary, "in the afternoon [we] drove out with them, alas! for the last time."[24] Nicholas and Alexandra's generosity shone forth in the parting gifts they left for the Balmoral staff. The tsar left a staggering tip of £1,000 for the master of the household to distribute among the staff. To the queen's physician, Sir James Reid, who cured his toothache, he left a gold cigarette case decorated with the imperial crest studded with diamonds. The empress left a sachet of flawless diamonds and pearl jewelry for the ladies-in-waiting. These gifts, though, were not as lavish as one would think under the circumstances. When the tsar's ancestor and namesake, Tsar Nicholas I, visited Queen Victoria early in her reign, he left £2,000, a diamond parure worth another thousand, and freely distributed rings, brooches, and other jewels.

When the time finally came for the Romanovs to depart, Scottish attendants dressed in formal kilts held blazing torches aloft to illuminate the imperial family's departure into the night. Both the tsar and tsarina—Nicholas in a gray Scottish uniform and Alexandra in a glittering pink dress trimmed with white fur—looked stately and dignified as they said their farewells. "It has been such a very short stay and I leave dear kind Grandmama with a heavy heart," she wrote shortly before her departure. As if she had some preternatural instinct that she would never see Victoria again, she added, "Who knows when we may meet again and where?"[25]

Capping the Russian imperial couple's tour abroad was the highly anticipated state visit to France, the tsarist empire's newest ally. When Nicholas and Alexandra drove through the streets of Paris, they were greeted with cheering crowds. French president Félix Faure bestowed a number of gifts on the imperial family. To two-year-old Grand Duchess Olga, he gave a set of accessories that included a tiny comb, brush, and mirror for one of her prized toy dolls. To the tsarina, Faure presented a Gobelin tapestry of Marie Antoinette and her children. This ironic piece of décor, based on the portrait done by Madame Vigée Le Brun, later hung in Alexandra's drawing room in the Alexander Palace on the grounds of Tsarskoe Selo. Nicholas was well received in Paris, but once again, despite her best efforts, Alexandra was a flop. Painfully self-conscious, she shied away from the people's thunderous welcome. Her only effort to align herself with France's republicanism backfired when she refused to meet a group of *grande dames* with ties to the old monarchy. What she did not realize was that France enjoyed an unusual mixture of republican and royalist elements. There were still many facets of French society connected to the old Bourbon and Bonaparte dynasties. In response to this slight, the French people withdrew their acclamations of Alexandra. The press promptly started criticizing everything about her. Even her accommodations came under scrutiny. She had been staying in Marie Antoinette's apartments at Versailles, but after this incident, the public declared she was no longer worthy of that honor. For all her failed efforts in France, Alexandra Feodorovna meant well. But fatigued, nauseous, and weak, she had little energy to carry her through the visit. The news of her condition arrived shortly before leaving Balmoral. Alexandra was pregnant again.

As a young wife and mother, May York's life centered on a variety of homes. While in London, her family resided at the deceptively named York House. It is actually an entire wing of Saint James's Palace on Pall Mall, a street in central London between Westminster and Buckingham Palace. Their main residence continued to be York Cottage, at the royal family's Sandringham estate in the Norfolk countryside. Located six miles away from the port town of King's Lynn on England's east coast, York Cottage was a two-story manor house that was originally built as an annex known as the Bachelor's Cottage for male guests visiting Sandringham. Much as May tried to personalize the place, she never came to see York Cottage as a true home, not in the way she did Kensington Palace or White Lodge. Being located only a few hundred yards from George's parents' Grand Manor, it offered the duke and duchess little privacy. During the daytime, there were nearly three dozen servants in the cramped house. May once said it was "so very nice but so small for my needs."[26]

The house had few modern amenities. Bathrooms were in short supply. With the exception of the master bedroom and a few dressing rooms, the rooms contained no indoor plumbing for lavatories. George felt differently than his wife about the house. The subdued, demure Duke of York cherished its remoteness from London. He also liked being close to his parents, especially his mother, whom George and his sisters affectionately called "Motherdear." What also appealed to George was the fact that Sandringham possessed thirty thousand acres upon which he could indulge his favorite pastime: hunting. George's official biographer, Harold Nicolson, noted that "when he was Duke of York ... he did nothing at all but kill [hunt] animals and stick in stamps."[27] Sandringham was so vast that it contained a menagerie of free-roaming animals, including an elephant, a bear, and a miniature Indian pony.

For nearly two decades, May's husband would insist on making Sandringham their family's true home largely for that reason.

Life at York Cottage was a far cry from Tsarina Alexandra's extravagant palaces in Saint Petersburg and Tsarskoe Selo, Augusta Victoria's austere surroundings in Berlin and Potsdam, or even Zita's homes in Chambord and Tuscany. Regardless of its inconveniences, May still grew attached to her Norfolk home. It was at York Cottage that she gave birth to her second child on December 14, 1895. That afternoon cannons boomed from the Tower of London, and guns were fired in Hyde Park to announce the birth of a son. George recorded in his diary that day, "A little boy was born weighing 8lb at 3.30 … everything most satisfactory, both doing very well. Sent a great number of telegrams, had something to eat. Went to bed at 6.45 very tired."[28] The Duchess of Teck was thrilled at the arrival of another grandchild. *"A Boy!!! What Joy!!!"* she squealed with delight to her son Alge.[29]

The infant's date of birth, December 14, was a deeply symbolic one for Queen Victoria. It fell on Mausoleum Day, the thirty-fourth anniversary of the death of her husband, Prince Albert. For Queen Victoria, December 14 was a sacred day, which she looked upon with a strange mix of reverence and apprehension. Her thirty-nine years of mourning for her beloved Albert has since become iconic. Since the day he died, she wore nothing but black and had his clothes laid out each morning as if he were about to walk into the room and start his day. When the queen's newest great-grandchild was born on the hallowed day of her husband's death, "the child's grandfather, the Prince of Wales, announced the news of the birth with a kind of apology." Queen Victoria was "rather distressed that this happy event should have taken place on a darkly sad anniversary for us."[30] "This terrible anniversary returned for the thirty-fourth time," she wrote. "When I went into my dressing-room found telegrams saying dear May had been safely delivered of a son at three this morning. Georgie's first feeling was regret that this dear child should be born on such a sad day. I have a feeling it may be a blessing for the dear Little Boy, and may he be looked upon as a gift from God."[31] In the end, May and George decided the child should be named Albert, in the prince consort's honor. "I really think it would gratify her if you yourself proposed the name *Albert* to her," wrote May's father-in-law.[32] Two days later, the queen received the news that the baby would indeed be named Albert, which she recorded gave her "the greatest pleasure."[33] At the infant's christening three months later, he was given the names Albert Frederick Arthur George ("Bertie"). In consequence, Queen Victoria gave the child a marble bust of Prince Albert as a gift. The Duchess of Teck, however, did not approve of the child's first name. She wrote prophetically that she hoped the infant's last name, George, "may supplant the less favoured one [Albert]."[34]

Only a few months after Bertie's birth, George and May traveled to Coburg in April 1896 to represent the aging Queen Victoria at another family wedding. They journeyed to Coburg via Darmstadt, where they visited Tsarina Alexandra's brother, Ernie, and his wife, Ducky. It was May's first official foreign tour as the Duchess of York. Once they reached Coburg, George and May stayed as guests of the Duke and Duchess of Coburg, George's uncle and aunt. Their daughter Princess Alexandra ("Sandra") was marrying Prince Ernest of Hohenlohe-Langenburg. Although it was not nearly as grandiose as Ernie and Ducky's wedding two years earlier, it still brought together the venerated royal mob. The Yorks were reunited with Wilhelm and Dona.[35] George was undoubtedly excited to see Sandra's sister, his old flame, Crown Princess Marie of Romania, though it is unrecorded what affect the presence of her husband, Crown Prince Ferdinand, had on the reunion. From Coburg, May penned a note home to her mother describing their first day.

> We arrived here at 2.30 on Thursday. Ernie & Ducky came with us in our carriage, & we were met at the station by U[ncle]. Alfred, Missy [Marie] & Ferdinand, Sandra, Baby [Sandra's sister], etc.— General embracing & presentations of suites—Drove to Palais Edinburgh, comfortable nice house, where A[un]t. Marie received us. Lunched & then we came over to this nice large Schloss where we are installed in the rooms Grandmama had 2 years ago—They are furnished in a terribly old fashioned style but we are quite comfortable and have lots of room.… Sandra is delighted with your & Papa's present which is very pretty & will be most useful to them, they have *very* few presents, such a contrast to our mass [from their wedding].[36]

The formal portrait that was taken to commemorate the occasion bears a striking similarity to the one from Ernie and Ducky's wedding in 1894. In the photograph, May and Dona cut contrasting figures. The duchess, though rigidly formal, is tightly surrounded by grinning cousins locked arm in arm. The empress, however, stands in the front, aloof, as the highest-ranking woman present. Unlike May, Dona is given a wide berth by those standing around her. And rather than looking at the camera, the empress is glaring austerely at Marie, the Russian-born Duchess of Coburg. Dona's disdain for the haughty duchess—and all things Russian, for that matter—was no secret. One can only speculate what she was thinking at the time this portrait was taken.

The pleasure the Duchess of York received from visiting Germany and the Coburg wedding was fast eclipsed by a prolonged period of familial adversity spanning 1895–96. After years of gambling, mounting debts, and scandals, May's brother Frank was sent into exile in India. Queen Victoria could no longer tolerate the damage Frank was doing to the monarchy, and she would not approve of members of the royal family paying off any more of his debts. The final straw came "when he incontinently wagered £10,000 on a ridiculous bet when he probably could not have raised 10,000 pence."[37] The task of gathering the money fell to May, who somehow managed to pay off the debt. The government decided Frank should "rejoin" his military regiment, which was now stationed in India. Perhaps for the first time, a major gulf emerged in the Teck family. Frank grew estranged from his mother and sister, who had always adored him. His letters home from Mahabaleshwar and Ganeshkhind were superficial, unrepentant, and sometimes tinged with bitterness—he described India "as being the nearest place to hell."[38]

The grief Frank caused his family was temporarily brushed aside for a happy occasion. In April 1897, May gave birth to another child, a daughter. It was no secret that George and May had longed for a girl for years. "Heard from Georgie that May had given birth to a little girl, both doing well," Queen Victoria noted.[39] George was especially delighted to have a daughter. The couple's eldest son, David, was now old enough to be curious about where his little sister came from. The answer he received from his unprepared parents was timeless: "He was told that she was a little angel who had flown in through the window and had her wings cut off."[40] April proved to be a month of particular turmoil for the Tecks that year. While May was still recovering from her accouchement, she was informed that her mother had undergone emergency surgery to remove kidney stones. Mary Adelaide seemed to be doing well after the operation, but no one could deny that her health was failing. Even once she was discharged from hospital, doctors warned that, because of her size, there was the very real possibility her heart could give out. Dire warnings such as this did not slow down the sixty-three-year-old Mary Adelaide. A few weeks after surgery, she was spotted at one of Queen Victoria's garden parties, being pushed around in a wheelchair.

The Duchess of Teck insisted on being present at the christening of her granddaughter. Held at the tiny church at Sandringham on June 7, it was performed by the archbishop of York, who used a golden bowl that had been a wedding present to George and May. The godparents included the queen; the Duchess of Teck; and the baby's paternal great-aunt and uncle the dowager empress of Russia and the king of Greece. Whereas Queen Victoria looked upon Bertie's birth with sadness because it fell on Mausoleum Day, she saw the arrival of May's daughter as a good augury because it fell on the year of her Diamond Jubilee—the sixtieth anniversary of her accession to the throne. So excited was the queen about her "dear little Diamond Jubilee baby"[41] that she even suggested the Yorks' new daughter should be named Diamond. That idea soon fizzled out when she realized the child would spend the rest of her life being known as Princess Diamond. Instead, the Duke and Duchess of York made Victoria the first of her four names, but she would always be known as Mary, after her maternal grandmother.

The Diamond Jubilee of 1897 was a milestone that was significant not only for the British royal family but for the British Empire itself. It was an unprecedented moment in history. The British Empire directly controlled more than a quarter of the world's landmass, boasting a population of 444 million people. Its imperial dominions included Canada, India, Australia, Jamaica, the Caribbean, the Malay Peninsula, Sierra Leone, parts of present-day South Africa, Ceylon (now Sri Lanka), Malta, New Zealand, many of the South Pacific islands, Cyprus, Sudan, Nigeria, the Gold Coast (modern-day Ghana), the Gambia, Malawi, Zambia, and Zimbabwe. The British territories were not limited to vast countries on the largest continents. Piles of rocks scattered throughout the world's oceans were part of the imperial spectrum. The farthest reaches of the British Empire stretched to the Falkland Islands off the coast of Argentina and Saint Helena and Ascension Island in the Atlantic, nearly a thousand miles west of Africa.

In England, the jubilee marked a defining moment in the history of the monarchy. The diminutive Queen Victoria—known sarcastically at the beginning of her reign as "Little Vic" because she was barely five feet tall—sat upon what was now the most powerful throne in Europe, a throne that had weathered a number of incredibly turbulent events throughout the centuries. The Wars of the Roses (1455-85) had placed a distant scion of the Lancaster dynasty named Henry Tudor on the throne of England. His son Henry VIII would become the most famous ruler in English history by breaking ties with the Roman Catholic Church and giving birth to the Church of England in 1534. The full effects of Henry's actions were not felt until the Glorious Revolution of 1688, when any chance of Catholicism being reestablished in England was permanently ended. It was also decreed that the monarch could neither be Catholic nor marry a Catholic.[42] Of greater import to the long-term survival of the monarchy was the Glorious Revolution's end to absolutism in the kingdom. Never again could the monarch rule absolutely. The Bill of Rights, passed by Parliament on December 16, 1689, gave Europe one of its earliest forms of constitutional monarchy. All of these events culminated in creating a throne that had endured. The ingredients for revolution—absolutism, corruption, oppression—were largely kept in check by the balance established between the monarchy and Parliament. And because of these parliamentary advances throughout English history, when Queen Victoria—who was Britain's first queen regnant since Queen

Anne in 1714—celebrated her Diamond Jubilee in 1897, she was the head of an unbroken royal line dating back nearly a millennium. Since the Battle of Hastings in 1066, England has been ruled by a total of six dynasties, all directly related to one another. As a result, England has the longest-reigning successive monarchy in European history.[43]

On June 22, the entire royal family attended a thanksgiving service at Saint Paul's Cathedral. On the way to the cathedral, thousands of soldiers who had arrived in London from the four corners of the globe followed Queen Victoria's carriage through the streets. Estimates placed the number of spectators as high as one million. That day, the queen refused to wear her crown or the robes of state. Instead, she preferred her typical black dress topped by a bonnet accented with diamonds. The Duchess of York was in awe of the grandeur. She was especially overwhelmed and flattered by the public response she received. "A never-to-be forgotten day," she wrote in her diary. "No one ever, I believe, has met with such an ovation as was given to me, passing through those six miles of streets ..."[44]

The arrival of little Princess Mary of York and Queen Victoria's jubilee coincided with the birth of Tsarina Alexandra's second child, a daughter named Tatiana, who had been conceived around the time of her stay in Scotland with Queen Victoria. Helping Alexandra through this time was her sister Irene, who was by far the most amiable of all her sisters. When Irene heard from Ernie that their sister was pregnant again, she immediately left her estate, Hemmelmark, near Kiel, to be at Alexandra's side during the last months of her pregnancy and for the delivery. When the cannon salute in Saint Petersburg heralded the arrival of a second girl, the news was greeted with disappointment. After the delivery, when Alexandra had awoken from the effects of the chloroform used to dull the pain, she looked around the room and saw the expressions of sadness on everyone's faces. Overcome, she began to cry. "My God, it is again a daughter," she wailed. "What will the nation say, what will the nation say?"[45]

Once both Alexandra and Tatiana were sufficiently recovered from the delivery, Emperor Wilhelm II decided it was time to make a state visit to Russia. Unlike many of his previous trips abroad, the emperor chose to bring his wife with him this time. It was Dona's first visit to Saint Petersburg and was one of the few interactions she ever had with Alexandra after both women were married. Wilhelm, who had been denied permission to attend Queen Victoria's jubilee celebration, mostly planned the visit as an attempt to reingratiate himself with his extended family; a string of political blunders, family insults, and direct confrontations had damaged Germany's—specifically Prussia's—relationships with both Britain and Russia. Still falsely believing he played Cupid in getting Nicholas and Alexandra together, and with the empress making a concerted effort to hide her Russophobia, Wilhelm and Dona arrived in Saint Petersburg in the autumn of 1897.

To his surprise, Nicholas found he and Wilhelm got along better than expected. At a banquet given for the visiting couple, the tsar made a lofty speech in the hope of building on his friendship with Wilhelm.

> The presence of your majesties among us causes me very lively satisfaction. I desire sincerely to thank you for the visit, which is a fresh manifestation of the traditional bonds uniting us and the good relations so happily established between our two neighboring empires. It is at the same time a precious guarantee of the maintenance of the general peace, which forms the object of our most fervent wishes. I drink to the health of the Emperor-King William and the Empress-Queen Augusta Victoria, and to the health of the august members of their family.[46]

Wilhelm raised his glass and, in typical fashion, made an even more grandiose speech about friendship and unity, heavy on circumlocution. But no political headway was achieved in creating the Russo-German alliance Wilhelm had hoped for; and unlike her husband, Alexandra did not get along with Wilhelm. She detested his flamboyancy, to which she responded with utter disdain. "He thinks he is a superman," she once said, "and he's really nothing but a clown. He has no real worth. His only virtues are his strict morals and his conjugal fidelity."[47] When Wilhelm gave her a silver toilette set that once belonged to the famous Queen Louise of Prussia, Alexandra was indignant. She declared that only a gold toilette set would be sufficient for an empress. Understandably insulted, the German emperor said that by giving his cousin such a gift, he was "paying her a great compliment." Incensed by Wilhelm's remark, she shot back that "it seemed to her that her cousin William still thought her the little Hessian princess of as little importance as she had been before her marriage."[48]

Things were just as bad between Alexandra and Dona. The two empresses never got along, and this latest visit only reminded them of that. In fact, Alexandra's hatred for Dona was one of the only things she had in common with the members of the Russian court, whom the latter failed to impress with her lack of style. "Thank God the German visit is over," Nicholas wrote to his mother afterward. "On the whole Wilhelm was very cheerful, calm and courteous, while she [Dona] tried to be charming, and looked very ugly in rich clothes without taste; the hats she wore in the evenings ... were particularly impossible."[49] At the end of the visit, Wilhelm and Nicholas were better off than they had been before, but there was no doubt that Dona and Alexandra were worlds apart.

⤜⤚

By the autumn of 1897, the Duchess of Teck's health was once again failing her. In her heart, she knew her time was growing short. "Oh, I don't want to die," she cried. "My children, my husband, need me."[50] In October, tests revealed a malignant tumor, prompting her doctors to perform emergency surgery. Follow-up tests revealed the operation was unsuccessful. The doctors decided to perform another emergency surgery, less than forty-eight hours after the first. The combination of two high-risk operations in only two days proved too much for the elderly duchess. She passed away from heart failure at 3:00 a.m. on October 20, 1897. In a letter to the duchess's sister, Grand Duchess Augusta, the Princess of Wales described the scene after Mary Adelaide died.

> Everyone plunged in the most terrible grief – poor man [Duke of Teck] heart-broken utterly crushed, poor darling May & her two brothers calm but in perfect despair – Uncle George [Duke of Cambridge] very much upset – Bertie was also there having come up from Newmarket with the former – [Bertie's] Sister Louise also there ... so nice & feeling – We had a long talk together. Darling May who so far bears up wonderfully well took me upstairs at once into Mary's room! Where she was lying in her *last* sleep. She looked *so* beautiful & peaceful with such a happy expression on her dear face.[51]

"I dread to think how we can live without her," May wrote to her aunt Augusta. "For Papa it is cruel & his sad state makes it so much worse. He was so dependent on Mama for everything & now God knows what he will do."[52] Queen Victoria wrote to one of her granddaughters, "You mourn dear Aunt Mary Teck with us, as I'm sure you wld. She was a true, warm friend & so clever and charming ... Poor Uncle Teck is in a most sad & anxious state which is a terrible trouble to the poor sons & dear good May."[53]

Consumed with grief, May York rushed to be with her aunt Augusta, who was in the south of France at the time. The death of her sister came as a crushing blow to the grand duchess, who was living through an already unbearable period in her own life. Her granddaughter Princess Marie became pregnant by a palace servant and was being blackmailed. In this situation,

131

the Duchess of York's giving nature came to the fore once again. She took it upon herself to care for her Mecklenburg cousin, bringing her back to England with her and allowing her to be in an environment where she felt safe and protected.

As the twentieth century dawned, May learned she was pregnant again. This news was especially welcome because her family was deeply saddened by the death of her father, the Duke of Teck, in January 1900. The death of his wife in 1897 had precipitated the duke's final collapse. In his last three years, he retreated entirely from public life. After spending some time with relatives in Germany, he returned to White Lodge and lived in near seclusion under the care of a doctor and two male nurses. He even refused to see his children except for brief periods every few months. To console herself during her pregnancy and in an effort to keep her spirits up, May remained in close contact with her aunt Augusta, who became a second mother to the duchess after her parents died. The Grand Duchess of Mecklenburg-Strelitz wrote to her niece that her "old loving heart will be with you in the ensuing century as it is and ever has been in this."[54]

Just five months after her father died on May 17, 1900, May went into labor again. She delivered a son, Henry, whom the family affectionately called "Harry," a common British nickname for Henry. Emperor Wilhelm II was asked to be the godfather as a sign of the closer relationship George and May had with Wilhelm and Dona. Things were going so well between the two couples that, later that year, the Yorks were invited to Germany for Crown Prince Willy's confirmation in the Lutheran Church. "I think I have done my duty and may now *stop*," May wrote to Aunt Augusta after this delivery, "as having babies is highly distasteful to me ..."[55] Queen Victoria, once again chosen as godmother, recorded in her journal that Harry "is a very pretty little boy."[56]

The queen grew to love her York great-grandchildren immensely. She even insisted that they take long holidays with her at Osborne House. May's eldest son, David, had vivid memories of his great-grandmother. As an adult, he recalled that "such was the majesty that surrounded Queen Victoria, that she was regarded almost as a divinity of whom even her own family stood in awe. However, to us children she was 'Gangan,' a childish interpretation of 'great-grandmama.'"[57] The birth of Prince Harry was not the only great-grandchild the queen received at that time. Less than a year earlier, on June 26, 1899, Tsarina Alexandra gave birth to her third daughter, Marie, at the Peterhof Palace, Russia's eight-hundred-foot-long answer to Versailles. The arrival of another girl was deeply upsetting in Russia. Alexandra's sister-in-law Grand

Duchess Xenia summed up the public sentiment: "What a disappointment that it isn't a son. Poor Alix!" Queen Victoria likewise understood the dynastic misfortune of another daughter. "I regret the 3rd girl for the country," she wrote to the tsar. "I know that an Heir would be more welcome than a daughter."[58]

In England, May York found that, despite her consistent pregnancies, Queen Victoria began relying upon her more than ever. The queen was now nearly blind, and although she had innumerable relations upon which to rely, there was something about May that attracted her. The duchess's critics accused her of being too simple and unaffected, too attached to the common man, to be a proper queen and empress. But Victoria saw her as a mirror for herself and had the utmost faith in her. "Every time I see them I love and like them more and respect them greatly," the queen wrote of the Yorks. "Thank God! Georgie has got such an excellent, useful, and good wife."[59] May was eager to please, admitting as much to her old governess: "Only give me a chance, & I will do things as well as anybody—after all, why shouldn't I?"[60] Queen Victoria's opinion of "Dear May" was that she was "so dear & *und passt so gut zu uns*" ("and fits in so well").[61]

While the Duchess of York was being groomed by Queen Victoria, Empress Augusta Victoria was weathering a difficult period in her life, one that has been studied by historians and psychologists alike for decades. Stress, overwork, and constant childbearing were taking their toll on the thirty-nine-year-old empress. She was also becoming concerned about her marriage. Though there was no doubt of the love between the emperor and empress, Wilhelm had taken to regularly traveling abroad, usually without his wife. For a woman whose identity was so intimately connected with her husband, this was upsetting. All these factors led the empress to a minor breakdown in 1897. Her children's military governor, Major General Adolf von Deines, reported, "H.M. broke down from exhaustion and suffered not only a slight influenza attack, but such a nervous shock, that simply taking it easy will no longer help her."[62]

Although Wilhelm and his staff had hoped otherwise, Dona's behavior did not improve after she recovered from her bout of influenza. On the contrary, the atmosphere within the Prussian royal family became even more highly charged. It comes as little surprise that one of the major catalysts continued to be Wilhelm himself. His announcement that he would be making his first visit to Britain in 1899 after five years sent Dona—normally the model of submissive, wifely behavior—into such a nervous fit that she claimed she was too ill to go. In what was becoming a common occurrence, she pressured her husband to cancel the trip altogether. As with his mother, Wilhelm had a complicated relationship with his English relatives and their country. Perhaps more than any other nation or its people, the emperor desperately craved British affections. Dona had come to resent having to share her husband with a country for which she held little love. In the broader picture, Dona's refusal to join her husband in visiting Britain was based upon the ongoing, politically charged Boer War. The empress publicly sided with the Dutch against the British, who were portrayed as violent aggressors. She told Bernhard von Bülow, the German chancellor, that British "mammonism" was strangling "the brave and godly Boers."[63] In the end, Wilhelm refused to accept Dona's recalcitrance. He flat out ordered her to accompany him, which she did in November along with two of their sons. The state banquet given for the Hohenzollerns in Saint George's Hall of Windsor Castle was "unusually brilliant" but "very formal."[64] Dona sat next to the Prince of Wales, the person in the British royal family she hated the most.

The situation had not improved any later that year when Nicholas II and Alexandra paid a visit to Potsdam. It was one of the rare times that the tsar and tsarina ever set foot in Germany. Achieving the visit was no easy feat. It took Bernhard von Bülow months to convince the tsar to come to Potsdam. The visit was a failure at best. Wilhelm's unpredictable personality took hold, which led him to overshadow the visit by signing a treaty with Britain over the disputed Samoan Islands in the Pacific. Nicholas, who had agreed to come out of familial loyalty to Wilhelm, was not impressed by this snub and responded with jokes that did not go over well at the Prussian court. Alexandra, whose health was poor the entire trip, was deeply offended when Dona personally insulted her by refusing to escort the tsarina to the Charlottenburg station when she and Nicholas returned to Saint Petersburg. This served as the last straw for Alexandra, who never wanted to lay eyes on Dona again.

Two family deaths in 1900 only worsened Dona's high-strung personality. The first loss was her mother, Ada, who died at Dresden in January, reportedly from pleurisy. "Now poor dear Aunt Ada has died," the Empress Frederick wrote to her daughter Sophie, "and Dona seems in great grief, and to feel her poor Mother's death even more than I expected. I am truly so sorry, she was an old friend of mine since our young days, she was 3 years older than I am. She was so kind-hearted and good-natured, and very pretty in her youth."[65] The second family death that affected the empress was that of her cousin Prince Christian Victor of Schleswig-Holstein-Sonderburg-Augustenburg, who died in October from enteric fever while he was serving with the British Sixtieth Rifle division in South Africa. "I could not believe it," Queen Victoria wrote when she heard of her grandson's death. "It seemed too dreadful and heart-breaking, this dear, excellent, gallant boy, beloved by all, such a good as well as a brave and capable officer, gone."[66]

For a woman so seriously concerned with matters of faith and eternity as Dona, the deaths of her unbalanced mother and soldier cousin may have plunged the empress deeper into emotional crisis. So what was the cause of Augusta Victoria's apparently unbalanced mental state? Often considered the most demure, docile member of her family—both the Holsteins and the Hohenzollerns—her behavior in recent years seemed entirely out of character. When a closer look is given, one realizes that many factors were coming to bear on the empress's life by this point. In October 1900, she turned forty-two. She began to suffer from a number of the ailments that befell her parents. In spite of these, she insisted on remaining physically active. In summer, she walked, played tennis, and went horseback riding. In winter, she and her sister Louise Sophie ice-skated. Out of love for her husband, she accompanied him as often as she could on as many of his long, hectic foreign trips to places she sometimes hated. She also delivered seven children in ten years, as well as suffering at least two miscarriages, possibly more.

The personal activities, health problems, and frenetic lifestyle account for a certain amount of short-temperedness and irritability in Augusta Victoria; it has never been reported that she suffered from any mental disorder to the same degree as her mother. At most, she is consistently described as having a nervous disposition. This is a highly speculative but vague description. When all the factors are brought to bear, it is most likely that as the empress entered her forties, she was suffering from extended postpartum depression. It is probable that each successive pregnancy and delivery took its toll. These, followed by the miscarriages and Sissy's birth in 1892, were the ultimate contributing factors. Casual observers assume postpartum depression simply means the new mother is melancholy. In a literal sense, this is something from which Dona never suffered, but her other symptoms are more telling. In their 2008 book *Our Bodies, Ourselves: Pregnancy and Childbirth*, the Boston Women's Health Collective describes a number of possible symptoms that can be present in postpartum depression, including low self-esteem, sleeping or eating irregularity, an inability to be comforted, exhaustion, withdrawal from social situations, little energy, and being easily frustrated or irritable[67]—all of which completely fit with Dona's personality during this period of her life.

Ultimately, trying to analyze the state of mind of an individual more than a century after the fact is fraught with difficulties. Writing in a similar vein in his semiacademic study of Wilhelm II, author Christopher Clark described the pitfalls this way: "as a means of accounting for behaviour, the psychoanalysis of dead persons is a fascinating but highly speculative exercise.

The inherent difficulty of assessing the applicability of diagnostic categories ... is compounded by the ambiguous and *sometimes even contradictory character of the sources* [author's italics]."[68] Rather than relying solely on subjective accounts, one must also look at physical evidence. Suffering from postpartum depression or not, Dona's aforementioned symptoms led to a change in her physical appearance. Her blonde hair turned white. Her once flawless complexion became blotchy and wrinkled. "Poor dear," said the courtesan Princess Daisy of Pless, "she looks more like the Emperor's mother than his wife."[69] Even the *New York Times* ran a brief article on Dona's condition: "From a high court official it is ascertained that Empress Augusta Victoria has greatly aged as of late, her hair being now entirely gray and thin, and her forehead furrowed."[70] Long sensitive about her appearance, she went on a drastic diet in a hurried effort to lose extra weight she thought she had gained.

Her husband made a show of being concerned for his wife's well-being, but those close to the family suspected his motives were more from the public embarrassment Dona was causing him—at a moment's notice, she would fly into a wild rage, directing most of her hostility at her husband. "The Kaiserin's nerves are in a condition which worries me very much," Wilhelm wrote.[71] She accused him of not loving her and instead—and not entirely off the mark—of escaping her as often as possible. When Wilhelm announced he was planning on taking a Mediterranean cruise on a British yacht, she was "*in despair* and begged me to do what I could to prevent the journey," Wilhelm recalled.[72] The insecurity Dona endured in her marriage made her suspicious of the individuals who shared Wilhelm's attention, his entourage. She even accused him of having a liaison with his closest friend, Count Philip zu Eulenburg (later Prince zu Eulenburg). Although this is almost certainly untrue, Eulenburg was so close to the emperor that Dona's jealous reaction is not surprising. An older aristocrat—he was fifty-three to Wilhelm's forty-one—who patiently indulged Wilhelm, Eulenburg gave him something he had lacked his entire life: a loving father figure. Despite the kindliness of Frederick III, Wilhelm had been raised in the shadow of his academician grandfather—Prince Albert—whom both his mother and grandmother treated with reverence approaching apotheosis. As a child, Wilhelm received the same vigorous, constricting education that had worked marvelously on Vicky but backfired on both himself and his uncle the Prince of Wales, who had been forced to attend both Oxford and Cambridge, as well as the Curragh military camp in Ireland. The outcome was that Dona's husband was a man who desperately craved the approval of his contemporaries, especially older men.

A tense atmosphere entered Dona's marriage that had not been there before. For the first time, she reproved her husband in public for his decisions. During a trip to the imperial hunting district at Rominten in the autumn of 1900, there were "appalling scenes" between the emperor and empress over the educations of their sons Auwi and Oscar. "The poor dear Kaiserin really seems to be in a bad nervous condition," Eulenburg reported to Chancellor von Bülow. Eulenburg watched in shock as Dona ran after her husband "like a madwoman" who was screaming and raving so much that the emperor did not know what to do.[73] Later, Eulenburg noticed "all night long, the Empress made scenes with her weeping and screaming." In another conversation, he told Bülow "with feverish agitation that the Empress was in such a nervous state that it would be very advisable if she were separated from the Kaiser soon."[74] Major General von Deines reported similar scenes when he spoke with Dona about her sons' educations. "I have to deal with a nervously ill woman and an unreasonably anxious mother, who, despite many excellent qualities, hurts as least as much as she helps—strictly from anxiety."[75] Philip Eulenburg resented Dona's relationship with Wilhelm, feeling it encroached on his personal status as the close friend of the emperor. Some three years after the incident at Rominten, he said that the empress's "love for His Majesty is like the passion of a cook for her sweetheart who shows signs of cooling off. The method of forcing herself upon him is certainly not the way to keep the beloved's affection."[76]

According to one court observer, Wilhelm "was alarmed that his wife might be suffering from a hereditary disorder which would make it necessary for her to be confined in a sanatorium, a development that would render the dynasty less an object of sympathy than one of enduring shame." Later, when "he confided his woes to Eulenburg, he advised him to sleep in a separate bedroom and lock the door."[77] By the time winter came, Dona's battle with postpartum depression seemed to have reached its end. What exactly happened to bring this about remains unclear, but by December, she appeared calmer and less easily agitated. Surviving historical evidence suggests the empress never again suffered from a clinical form of depression as it is recognized today; but for the rest of her life, her behavior would exhibit signs of an anxiety disorder of varying intensity.

As this personal crisis began to wind down for Wilhelm and Augusta Victoria, another royal scandal involving the Austrian imperial dynasty, the Habsburgs, came to the fore. This latest upheaval was caused when Emperor Franz Joseph's nephew and heir, Archduke Franz Ferdinand, fell in love with a commoner. The object of his desire was the thirty-two-year-old Countess Sophie Chotek, a lady-in-waiting to the formidable Archduchess Isabella, whose husband, Archduke Frederick, was a senior member of the

Austrian imperial family and one of the highest-ranking officers in the Austro-Hungarian military. Sophie, though descended from an aristocratic Bohemian family, was deemed wholly unacceptable to be an empress one day because she did not come from a royal house. In 1899, Franz Ferdinand told the emperor of his determination to make Sophie his wife, regardless of the imperial laws. Franz Joseph refused to consent to the controversial wedding because "by no stretch of the Habsburg family laws or standards could the Choteks be accepted as eligible for marriage into the Imperial house."[78]

After a few months, an impatient Franz Ferdinand took matters into his own hands and publicly declared he would marry no one but Sophie. The Austro-Hungarian monarchy nearly cannibalized itself as the imperial court divided into two factions—the traditionalists who were loyal to the emperor and wanted to stop the marriage at all costs, and the progressive liberals who were in favor of the match. With the prospect of permanently damaging the monarchy, and facing pressure from the German emperor, the tsar of Russia, and Pope Leo XIII, the emperor agreed to allow the wedding—but on one condition: it would be morganatic. Sophie could never share her husband's titles or rank, she could never be empress when he ascended the throne, and any children they might have would be subject to the same restrictions.

The emperor summoned his Crown Council, Privy Council, the Prince-Bishop of Vienna, the Prince-Primate of Hungary, and all the senior members of the imperial family to a special, elaborate ceremony at the Hofburg Palace in Vienna on June 28, 1900. With his hand on the Gospels, Franz Ferdinand swore the "oath of renunciation" on behalf of his wife and future children.[79] Three days later, on July 1, Franz Ferdinand married Sophie in a private ceremony at Reichstadt in Bohemia. Neither Franz Joseph nor any other male members of the imperial family were present, including the groom's brothers. The only members of the dynasty in attendance were Franz Ferdinand's stepmother, Archduchess Maria Theresa, and her two daughters.

Now that there was no possibility of Franz Ferdinand's children ever inheriting the throne, attention shifted once again to a new heir: Franz Ferdinand's younger brother, the dissolute playboy Archduke Otto. The notion that this archduke might one day rule as emperor was relished by no one. A member of the Prussian court remarked that Otto was a man "whom the nations of the dual monarchy, fearful of his possible succession to the throne, include in their daily prayers under the head of 'Deliver us from all evil.'"[80] For all the possible evils Otto could unleash upon Austria-Hungary, he offered the monarchy future security with his two healthy sons, Charles and Max, both of whom were eligible heirs to the throne, untainted by scandal. The boys were raised almost entirely by their pious mother, Archduchess Maria Josepha, the youngest daughter of King George of Saxony. Under his mother's influence, Charles became respectable and unassuming. He was a boy of only thirteen when his uncle Franz Ferdinand married Sophie. At the time, there was little indication that this adolescent archduke would have a direct hand any time soon in charting the future of the Austro-Hungarian Empire.

By the winter of 1900/01, once the dynastic crisis of Franz Ferdinand's controversial marriage had passed, things seemed to be settling down for Augusta Victoria and the Prussian royal family. They had finally taken up residence at the massive Neues Palais in Potsdam after the Empress Frederick relocated to a new home she had built—Friedrichshof, named for her late husband—near Kronberg, west of Berlin. The Hohenzollerns also began spending more time at the Stadtschloss in Berlin. Located at the end of Unter den Linden, the palace was designed by Andreas Schlüter in the late 1690s before Prussia was even a kingdom (that honor would not come until 1701). With its 650 rooms, the building was massive; the kitchens were nearly a mile away from the dining rooms. At the turn of the twentieth century, it underwent a badly needed, multimillion-dollar renovation. For decades, Prussian castles had been notoriously medieval. Upon moving to Prussia after her marriage in 1857, Dona's mother-in-law, Vicky, was horrified by the lack of bathrooms, heating systems, or even sufficient lighting.

Around the same time that the Stadtschloss was renovated, so too was the royal family's transportation upgraded. Millions were spent on a new royal train. Designed to show off the Hohenzollerns' imperial dignity, the train comprised eleven gilded carriages that could seat at least twenty-four people around a formal dinner table at any one time. With the German navy's star in the ascendant, the emperor and empress naturally declared themselves to be sovereigns of the sea. They commissioned a new royal yacht, the *Hohenzollern II*, colored in shades of cream and gold—it was the first time a member of the Prussian royal family ever commissioned a private royal yacht. The biggest private vessel on the seas, it was so well armed that, upon first sight, many observers thought it was a battleship. The *Hohenzollern II* was the royal family's official yacht, though Dona was given her own private vessel, the *Iduna*, complete with a cook from Brighton who always addressed the empress as "Mum."[81] The *Iduna* came in especially handy for Dona when Wilhelm purchased the Achilleion, a villa on the Greek Ionian island of Corfu that became one of their favorite getaways. All of these—palaces, trains, yachts—were meant to impress. Wilhelm and Dona wanted to create an image that theirs was the greatest imperial power in the world.

At the beginning of January 1901, the Hohenzollerns were out in full force in Potsdam and Berlin for the celebrations marking the Prussian monarchy's bicentennial. Thousands of soldiers marched past the Stadtschloss in the freezing cold as they saluted Emperor Wilhelm II and Empress Augusta Victoria. One of the special guests at the celebrations was the emperor's uncle the Duke of Connaught, one of Queen Victoria's sons. During the festivities, the emperor made a speech in which he declared his resolve to make the German Imperial Navy "as mighty an instrument" as the army.[82] As Wilhelm stepped off the podium after his speech, he was informed that a telegram arrived for the duke from Osborne House. Queen Victoria—the larger-than-life matriarch, the woman who had lent her name to an era—was dying. As many of the relatives as possible were summoned to Osborne House on the Isle of Wight, where the British royal family was holding the death vigil.

The last years of the queen's life had been tinged by deeply painful tragedies. The Boer War in South Africa, which showed no signs of concluding any time soon, overshadowed the twilight of her reign. Her family had also been plagued by trials. Her youngest, the Duke of Albany, died after a hemophilia attack in 1884. Her second son, the Duke of Coburg, died from tongue cancer in 1900. The death of her favorite son proved too much for the queen to bear. She poured herself out in her journal: "Oh, God! my poor darling Affie gone too! My third grown-up child, besides three very dear sons-in-law. It is hard at eighty-one!"[83] Less than a year later, she was told that her daughter Vicky was succumbing to excruciating cancer of the spine. By the dawn of the twentieth century, Queen Victoria had also outlived eight of her grandchildren.

Wilhelm II immediately cancelled all the bicentennial celebrations. Accompanied by his eldest son and his uncle, he rushed from Berlin to be at his grandmother's bedside, leaving a disconsolate Dona to care for their family. The empress tried as much as possible to discourage her husband from spending so much time in England. She later told one of his ministers that she took special care to make sure "that her sons would think differently."[84] Dona was commensurately unpopular in England. Marie Mallet, one of Queen Victoria's ladies-in-waiting, wrote in her diary that Wilhelm was a "poor man" because "he has a most insipid and boring wife who he does not care for and from whom he escapes by prancing to the four corners of the world." Wilhelm ignored his wife's entreaties to stay away from England. For him, there was no question about it. He had to go. "At heart," Dona later admitted about her husband, Wilhelm was "enthusiastic about England and everything which is England, it is in his blood."[85]

The German emperor's arrival on the Isle of Wight educed a strong reaction from his British relatives. The queen's daughters Helena and Louise had been caring for their mother during her final weeks and tried to keep him away. Unimpressed, Wilhelm remarked that "the petticoats," as he called his aunts, were "fencing off poor grandmamma from the world." When he finally arrived, the emperor impressed everyone with his grace and tactfulness. The Prince of Wales wrote to the Empress Frederick, who was now too ill to come to Osborne, "William was kindness itself and touching in his devotion."[86]

Gathered at Osborne House for the death vigil were four generations of Queen Victoria's family, including George and May, who arrived from Sandringham only an hour before the end. To ease the queen's final hours, her grandson Prince Leopold of Battenberg played his violin. Wilhelm and the queen's physician, Sir James Reid, held her up in their arms for two hours straight as she drifted in and out of consciousness. Next to her bedside knelt the unusually pensive Prince of Wales. Winter darkness descended on the Isle of Wight around 4:00 p.m. that day. It seemed symbolic that with the setting of the sun that day, so too was the sun setting on the life of this unparalleled woman. In his diary, the Duke of York recalled the queen's last moments: "She looked just the same, not a bit changed. She was almost asleep and had her eyes shut … I kissed her hand, Motherdear was with me. She was conscious up til 5.0 [o'clock] and called each of us by name and we took leave of her. I shall never forget that scene in her room with all of us sobbing and heartbroken round her bed. It was terribly sad."[87]

At 6:30 p.m. on January 22, 1901, Victoria, queen of the United Kingdom of Great Britain and Ireland, the first empress of India, passed away at the age of eighty-one. The last word she muttered was "Bertie," her son's name, before a look of peace fell upon her face.[88] A hushed silence fell upon the room as those gathered realized that this special little lady was gone. Exhausted from holding up his grandmother for two hours, Wilhelm turned to his youngest cousin, little Ena of Battenberg, and said cryptically, "I am the eldest grandchild and you are the youngest."[89] The queen had played a role, in some form or another, in uniting Willy and Dona, George and May, and Nicky and Alix, and her loss was a crushing blow to all of them. "The thought of England without the Queen is dreadful," May confided to her diary. "God help us all."[90]

That night, after a twilight memorial service in the queen's bedroom, her body was lifted by her sons into a coffin that, at Wilhelm's request, was draped with the Union Jack. Later, her iconic diamond-encrusted crown, which she wore with her black widow's dress for decades, was placed on top of the coffin, along with six massive candles, representing the six children who had assembled for the death vigil. The dining room where her coffin was placed was turned into an otherworldly shrine to her memory. Four guardsmen kept a round-the-clock watch over the coffin, which was surrounded by funeral wreaths of white lilies and blue hyacinths. The Duchess of York recalled the almost mystic aura in a letter to her aunt Augusta: "Now she lies in her coffin in the dining room, which is beautifully arranged as a chapel, the coffin is covered with the coronation robes & her little diamond crown and the garter lie on a cushion above her head—4 huge Grenadiers watch there day and night, it is so impressive & fine & yet so simple ..."[91]

It is not an understatement to say that countless millions of people around the world mourned this tremendous loss. Newspapers from Newfoundland to Berlin to Beijing ran touching tributes to the queen, while governmental agencies on every continent offered their condolences. For ten days, Victoria's body was laid out in state in the dining room at Osborne House. From the Isle of Wight, her body was taken to Portsmouth on February 1 aboard the royal yacht *Alberta*. The Duchess of York, sitting at a window in Osborne House, watched the yacht move toward the mainland as it traveled between endless rows of battleships. It was from Portsmouth that the military escort took the queen's coffin to London. At train stations all along the route, vast crowds gathered in silence. Men removed their caps, others fell on one knee.

On the freezing cold morning of February 2, Queen Victoria received a military funeral in the capital of the British Empire. More than one million people lined the streets in silence to bid farewell to the doyenne of sovereigns. In the funeral procession, the coffin was followed on horseback by Bertie, Wilhelm II, King George I of Greece, and King Charles I of Portugal. In accordance with Victoria's wishes, London was not draped in mourning black. Ironically, the woman who had worn nothing but black for forty years of her life detested the idea of mourning for herself. Instead, purple cashmere accented by a white stripe was used to commemorate the passing of one sovereign and the accession of another. The funeral procession was equally awe inspiring. Along with the four kings on horseback were carriages ferrying King Leopold II of the Belgians, and the crown princes of Germany, Greece, Romania, Denmark, Norway, Sweden, and Siam. These were then followed by royal heirs representing the emperors of Austria and Russia and the king of Italy. Years later, May's son David wrote that Queen Victoria's funeral "was mournful beyond description, and no doubt the elderly and the sage who witnessed it must have shared a sense of the passing of a great era of peace and security, and a foreboding of the inevitable changes that would profoundly affect their own lives while altering Britain's destiny."[92]

Mourning was not confined to the British Empire. In faraway Russia, Tsarina Alexandra was shattered by the news of her beloved grandmother's death. The queen had truly been a second mother to the empress, and the thought of a world without her was frightening to Alexandra. She had wanted to set off for Windsor Castle immediately, but because she was pregnant again, such a trip was ill-advised. At a memorial service in Saint Petersburg attended by the imperial family, Alexandra and her sister Ella broke down sobbing. "I cannot really believe she has gone, that we shall never see her anymore," she wrote to her sister Victoria. "Since one can remember, she was in our life, and a dearer, kind being never was." She echoed May York's feelings when she added, "England without the Queen seems impossible."[93]

8

The Weight of the World

(1901–04)

With the death of Queen Victoria, the curtain descended on one of the most important reigns in British history, marked by propriety, conservatism, and traditional values. The accession of George's father as Britain's first king in almost sixty-four years ushered in an equally grandiose era, presided over by a more fun-loving, gregarious monarch and his wife, the soigné Queen Alexandra. This meant that May's husband, George, was now heir to the British throne. George was carrying the weight of the empire on his shoulders. One of the new king's first acts was to take the name Edward VII. It had been his mother's wish that he should reign as the German-sounding King Albert Edward, to honor the late prince consort, but as he reminded his mother, no other king of England had ever used two names.

Although Queen Victoria's death was met with sincere grief, high hopes were attached to the reign of Edward VII, who was the first and only heir apparent ever to be born to an English queen regnant. Since it was the first time in almost seventy years that England had a king, many were optimistic that the new sovereigns would breathe new life into the monarchy. They would not be disappointed.

Almost immediately, Edward VII became a sensation despite the hand fate had dealt him. Just shy of his sixtieth birthday when he came to the throne, Edward had inherited his mother's Hanoverian looks. He was short and overweight with a receding chin that he covered with a pointed beard. His health was poor as well. At the time of his accession, he could barely walk up a flight of stairs without losing his breath. Once, at the opera during a visit to Germany, Edward became so exhausted from climbing the stairs to the royal box with his wife, Wilhelm, and Dona that he fell asleep partway through the performance. Later, when the actors lit several fires on stage as part of the show, Edward awoke with a startle and, seeing the flames, assumed the building was on fire. He began bellowing for everyone to calmly evacuate the burning opera house. Only after a lengthy reassurance by Dona that it was part of the show did he calm down. His obesity and chronic respiratory troubles were the direct result of his gourmand lifestyle of eating five or six meals a day, each of which was between eight and ten courses. He also smoked dozens of cigars. Edward's health was so poor, in fact, that his coronation on June 26, 1902, had to be postponed. The ordeal started earlier that month when he began complaining of stomach pains. He later told his doctors he would attend his coronation even if it killed him. The doctors replied it very likely would. Thus, it was postponed, and the king underwent surgery for what was revealed to be severe appendicitis. A briefer, curtailed coronation was held two months later.

Unlike his father, the prince consort, or his precocious sister Vicky, Edward was not overly intellectual. In a society that placed handsomeness and intelligence on a pedestal, the new king was an anomaly. He broke the mold through his urbane charisma, but "because he was 'intensely human,' and because 'he never attempted to his hide his weaknesses,' Edward succeeded in winning over most of his critics."[1] The Liberal politician Lord Esher shared this sentiment when he admitted, "The King is kind and debonair, and not undignified – but too human!"[2] Queen Alexandra was equally popular. Like her sister Dowager Empress Marie Feodorovna of Russia, she was regal and stately, with a slim figure and a swan-like neck. She was a trendsetter in British society who looked every inch a queen. She also earned a place in the history books by becoming the last foreign princess to be queen of England.

In the immediate aftermath of Queen Victoria's death, London was overcome by a wave of controlled chaos. Most of the population had lived and died under Victoria, Regina et Imperatrix. There was a finely tuned social order that many people had known all their lives, with Victoria at the top, followed by her son, the Prince of Wales. But Edward VII had held that title—which is traditionally given by the monarch to the heir to the throne but is not an automatic title—since he was a month old, and most of the British population was uncomfortable having a new Prince of Wales so quickly after Edward's accession. Even letters and memos intended for Princess May, as wife of the heir to the throne, were accidentally sent to Queen Alexandra.

Almost from the moment he became king, Edward made it a point to depart from the traditions that his mother had held to so vehemently. One of the ways he did this was by not immediately making George Prince of Wales. The king correctly argued that the public had been so used to himself in that role that it would cause confusion for there to suddenly be a new Prince of Wales after sixty years. Having an heir apparent styled as Duke of York was inappropriate, but since the king was unwilling to grant George the Wales title, he granted him the duchy of Cornwall. Typically given to the heir apparent along with being created Prince of Wales, Cornwall was the first ducal peerage ever created in England. It also brought with it tremendous revenues. The fact that she was now a very wealthy woman seemed to interest May very little. Long accustomed to keenly observing others, she was sensitive enough to understand the significance of the king's decision. "We are to be called D. & Dss of Cornwall & York and I don't think the King intends to create G. Pce of Wales," she wrote to her old governess Hélène Bricka in January 1901.[3] Later, in a letter to her aunt Augusta, she was more candid about her feelings: "I believe this is the first time that the Heir Apparent has not been created Prince of Wales! I dislike departing from traditions."[4] However the duchess may have behaved outwardly, the king's choice offended her sense of tradition. It was one of the few times she explicitly displayed her father's fanatical obsession about royal rank.

To help alleviate some of the administrative confusion in London, George and May were sent on a lengthy tour of the British Empire, with stops in Canada, Australia, and New Zealand. The visit had been planned since before Queen Victoria's death. King Edward had always been close to his son, especially after Eddy died. He insisted on canceling the tour because he could not bear being parted from his son and daughter-in-law at such a difficult time. The colonial secretary Joseph Chamberlain, along with the prime minister Lord Salisbury, convinced the king to go ahead with the expedition as planned. It was the largest international tour ever undertaken by a member of the British royal family. King Edward may also have been waxing sentimental about sending George and May abroad. In 1860, when the king was still Prince of Wales, he had made his own official visit to Canada, marking the first time a British heir apparent had ever crossed the Atlantic. Remembering how much of a hit he had been, the king may have hoped that sending his shy son and daughter-in-law might do them some good.

Not keen on leaving her children, May was encouraged to take the trip by Queen Alexandra, who felt it was important for the world to see a fresh, youthful face representing the monarchy. The British politician and statesman Arthur Balfour argued it was imperative for George and May to take the tour. "The King is no longer merely King of Great Britain and Ireland and of a few dependencies whose whole value consisted in ministering to the wealth and security of Great Britain and Ireland," he told Edward VII. "He is now the great constitutional bond uniting together in a single Empire communities of free men separated by half the circumference of the Globe."[5]

On March 16, 1901, the Duke and Duchess of Cornwall left England. That day, they brought their children down to the harbor at Portsmouth to say good-bye. "Pretty!" little Princess Mary exclaimed when she saw their newly redecorated, black-and-white-striped steamship, the *Ophir*.[6] The children, left in the care of the king and queen, watched from shore as the *Ophir* gave three long booms on the horn before slowly pulling away. As the duke and duchess stood on the bridge waving, their eyes filled with tears. George later wrote to his mother that, after the departure, he and May "came down to our cabins and had a good cry and tried to comfort each other."[7] A few days after leaving England, May wrote to an old friend, "Those dreadfull [*sic*] farewells nearly killed me. I am always thinking of the children, and must thank you so much for the sweet picture of baby Mary; it is too nice, and looks so pretty on my table."[8]

～

In Germany, Empress Augusta Victoria's battle with postpartum depression and anxiety seemed to have little effect on her continued popularity with her subjects. The death of Queen Victoria and the accession of Edward VII cemented her Anglophobia. It also strengthened her resolve to be as moral and pious and she believed the English royal family was not. That the Prussian court was filled with narrow-minded, fanatical conservatives who revered the empress and praised her virtues only added to her sense of self-righteousness. She was now the undisputed *Landesmutter*.

The household Dona picked for herself was entirely made up of Evangelical Lutherans, all from high-ranking aristocratic families, none of whom could have the slightest blemish against their reputations. In this regard, the empress followed in Queen Victoria's footsteps, who had similarly conservative opinions on who was worthy of serving on her personal staff. Like most ladies-in-waiting, the women Dona surrounded herself with mimicked their mistress— though in this case, they tended to be more ridiculous exaggerations. Prudish bordering on bigoted, hypersensitive, and tending to be melodramatic, these women became Dona's closest friends. The countesses Mathilde Keller, Claire von Gersdorff, and Therese von Brockdorff never left Dona's side. Along with her, they became known—sometimes derisively by Wilhelm's entourage—as the "Hallelujah Aunts" for their obsessive devotion to Protestantism; Vicky referred to them as "a blessed set of donkeys."[9] Dona's critics accused her ladies-in-waiting of being as "conservative, agrarian and strictly evangelical" as she was. Wilhelm took special delight in tormenting the countesses, especially Claire von Gersdorff, whom he described as "naively silly." Not everyone reproached the Hallelujah Aunts, though. The countesses were constantly out and about working on behalf of one charity or another. Their piety also helped protect the immediate royal family and the court from many of the scandals that befell other Hohenzollerns. Karl Treutler, one of Germany's ambassadors, admitted, "They did innumerable good works, and if they were perhaps not very young, not very elegant, not overly intelligent, and not very modern, this was all compensated for in that they gave their all in the service of their mistress and shielded the Court from any not quite correct note."[10]

Like Tsarina Alexandra and the Duchess of Cornwall, Augusta Victoria's sense of moral propriety was in keeping with the standards of the Victorian era. The empress did not tolerate impropriety, and she would not easily forgive those who had sinned against the strict code of etiquette that enveloped the Hohenzollern court. One witness described her as having a *"great aversion to divorced women"* in particular. When Count Paul von Hatzfeldt, the German ambassador to London, divorced and remarried in 1895, the empress refused an audience with his second wife. Writing to one of his close friends, Wilhelm said he regretted "that nothing could be done in this matter. The Kaiserin had *refused in such decided* terms to receive the Countess that it was useless to make any further attempt." He later admitted, "in these questions I cannot give orders to the Kaiserin. It is her domain. I cannot command her to receive someone who has made herself unacceptable to society."[11] A member of the German court later observed that "William II. never interferes with anything his wife has decided concerning her household and its management, and accepts all her arrangements with absolute submission."[12]

Prussian court life had not always been so closeted. The winter social season of 1893/94 was considered one of the country's most lavish. Prince Philip zu Eulenburg recalled a fashionable concert given in the opulent Marble Hall of the Neues Palais. In a letter to his mother, he described Dona as wearing "a gown of blue velvet combined with yellow muslin, large diamond and sapphire jewellery" though despite her grand outfit, he thought she was "not very well dressed."[13] By most contemporary accounts, 1893/94 was an anomaly during the Wilhelmine era. For the most part, Prussian court life was never spectacular. Like Great Britain, Germany relied heavily on its aristocratic families spread throughout the empire, but they rarely appeared in Berlin or Potsdam. Most of them hated the Hohenzollerns and resented their hegemonic role in German affairs. Tradition stated that court entertainments were strictly the province of the empress, but as the first lady of the land, Dona brought German high society to something of a halt. She never learned at Dolzig or Primkenau how to properly entertain or throw fashionable parties.

Wilhelm II's constant traveling abroad meant foreign visitors were seldom seen in Berlin. Dignitaries were also a rarity, since most of them loathed the emperor and were harshly scrutinized by the empress. Her attitudes toward moral propriety meant she almost never agreed to hold audiences with men without her husband there. This pallid court life "was partly due to the rigidity of the court, and partly to the novelty of Berlin as a national capital: many of the grander German families still kept away, and the Junkers who lodged in hotels for the short season were provincial bumpkins who hardly lent any glamour to the occasion."[14]

The aristocrats scattered throughout Germany's federal states may have viewed the empress as a rural prude, but the German population at large continued to see her as a paragon of virtue. Motivated by her own upbringing, Dona was very active in promoting charitable causes. She received dozens of petitions every day from people or organizations "begging" for her help. According to one witness, the empress read every letter that was "addressed to her, and never misses making inquiries as to the truth of the tales of distress brought to her notice."[15] She was deeply interested in the welfare of the poor and sick. In 1884, she became the matron of the Elizabeth Children's Hospital in Berlin, where she frequently visited the patients. She was actively involved with the Berlin City Mission. Feeling that the mission was not broad enough to help all those in need, she founded the Aid Society of the Evangelical Church in 1888, which became the Protestant Women's Mission in 1897. The advocacy for young women was a cause that was especially dear to the empress's heart. In an era when the rights of women were few, Dona showed great forward thinking when she founded the Elberfeld House of Refuge, designed to care for neglected infants and young girls at risk.

With the help of her ladies-in-waiting, Augusta Victoria succeeded in making the etiquette at the Prussian court rigidly strict. The atmosphere was so restrictive that the "latest American dances were outlawed and it was hard even to smoke, eat or drink." Everything from the polka to the two-step was forbidden. At a ball given for the Prince and Princess of Wales, a nasty verbal exchange broke out between two of Dona's sons—most likely Eitel-Fritz and Willy—and the band, which had been ordered by the emperor not to play any modern songs, since it was his firm belief that court balls were not held for personal pleasure but for lessons in personal diplomacy. Matters of etiquette went so far that Dona even forbade her sister Calma and her daughters from learning to ride bicycles, a sport that the empress decried as "indecent."[16]

In some ways, the etiquette was even more rigid than in the famous courts of Spain or Austria. The court rules became so inflexible that at formal functions involving a meal, "the emperor and empress were served first and everyone had to yield up their plates when they finished. Those who had been served last often hardly touched their food." The children, "who were seated the farthest away from the royal pair, were left hungry, and had to cultivate good relations with the servants below-stairs in order to fill their bellies."[17] The rules that governed the Prussian court kept the members of the various households in an imperial prison, which was dominated by an intolerable list of small, arbitrary rules that were designed to inculcate complete adherence to the emperor and empress. Even the personal lives of courtiers were regulated. They could not use public transportation or even wear glasses, since it was forbidden to view any member of the royal family through spectacles. Staff attached directly to the households of the emperor or empress "were reminded of their position in the hierarchy. They were graded and classified by colour-coded passes; these decided, among other things, which room they stood in at balls and how large a Christmas present they received from the imperial couple."[18]

Day-to-day activities in Dona's household were uncomplicated. Most evenings were spent with Wilhelm going off to an innumerable military review, diplomatic meeting, or official function, while Dona oversaw affairs at the palace. These meetings were usually insufferable for the old generals in Wilhelm's entourage, who were forced to stand in his presence for hours on end. If no important events were happening, the emperor and empress might sit down for tea. Wilhelm would read reports while his wife sat near the fire, knitting clothes for the poor. But even Wilhelm, who enjoyed state functions where he was the center of attention, chafed from time to time under his wife's strictures. Late one evening, Dona asked him, "Are you not going to go to bed at all?" The emperor shot back sharply, "Well, what else could I do, it is so incredibly dull here."[19] To break up the tedium of court life, Wilhelm continued to spend much of the year traveling abroad. Between the months of June and October, he usually only spent twelve days in Potsdam. In his first eighteen months as emperor, he visited Saint Petersburg, Stockholm, Copenhagen, Vienna, Rome, London, Monza, Athens, and Constantinople. One of his biographers went a step further and asserted that "Wilhelm spent less than half his reign in Berlin and Potsdam."[20] This did not mean that Dona was always stranded at home. In March 1905, she traveled alone to Italy on a state visit to King Victor Emmanuel III and Queen Helen. It was highly successful. Ten thousand spectators stood in the pouring rain to greet the empress when she arrived at the harbor of Civitavecchia, almost fifty miles northwest of Rome. She later told the king "she was very happy to be in Italy."[21]

Life at the Prussian court received a severe interruption in the summer of 1901. At 6:00 p.m. on August 5, the Empress Frederick died at her home, Friedrichshof, after an excruciating battle with spinal cancer. She was surrounded by her three youngest daughters—Sophie, Mossy, and Moretta—who had been at her side for months; Wilhelm, Dona, and Crown Prince Willy joined them only twelve hours before the end, but it gave Vicky the chance to speak to them one last time. During her final months, Wilhelm had written to Edward VII of Vicky being "weak" and feeling "absolutely miserable.... We are all fearfully pained by what we see & hear.... Poor mother's simply in a horrible state of suffering & discomfort."[22] For twenty years, Dona had hardly known a week without the presence, whether in letter or in person, of her formidable mother-in-law. Theirs had been an initially cordial but never peaceful relationship. They had endured rocky patches, especially once Wilhelm ascended the throne. But by the time of Vicky's death, Dona—already in her forties and comfortable in her role as German empress and queen of Prussia—had come to empathize with the woman who had held her own against so many attacks from Wilhelm II. In the weeks before the end, Dona became a more frequent face at Friedrichshof, usually arriving in her carriage with her children. For Wilhelm, the death of his mother was a profound loss but not enough to change him for the better. In a repeat episode of Frederick III's death, Wilhelm had Friedrichshof torn apart by his soldiers, looking for anything to incriminate his mother. But always one step ahead of her son, Vicky had her papers spirited away to England during Edward VII's last visit by his private secretary Sir Frederick Ponsonby. Even in death, the Empress Frederick refused to concede defeat to her flawed, immoral son.

As Russia marched into the twentieth century, Alexandra Feodorovna was overcome with anxiety. After nearly a decade of marriage, she had still not delivered a son. In June 1901, she gave birth to a fourth daughter, Anastasia Nicholaievna, whose name came from an old Russian word meaning resurrection. "What a disappointment!" said Nicholas II's sister Xenia when she received the news from her mother. "A fourth girl! They have named her Anastasia."[23] In six years, Alexandra had produced four daughters: Olga, Tatiana, Marie, and Anastasia, but the all-important male heir was still something she could only dream of since her miscarriage. The internal struggle Alexandra was waging played itself out around the world. In England, the *Daily Mail* ran a boldly underlined headline at Anastasia's birth: ILLUMINATIONS, BUT DISAPPOINTMENT. The newspaper noted, "There is much rejoicing, although there is a popular undercurrent of disappointment, as a son had been most keenly hoped for."[24]

151

Alexandra became obsessed with having a son. Part of this could be traced back to 1900, when the tsar fell dangerously ill with typhus and almost died. Without any sons, the throne would have passed to Nicholas's brother Michael. Alexandra's obsession was not only political, it was deeply personal too. She blamed herself for the lack of an heir. Thanks to modern science, "we know that it is the father who determines the sex of a child by passing on his Y or X chromosome, but at the time, a mother felt responsible if she produced only girls."[25] Alexandra believed there must have been some divine reason she had not been blessed with a son. Perhaps she had done something wrong? Her desperation, mixed with a growing mysticism that had been born out of her devotion to the Orthodox faith, fostered by her pious sister Ella, left her prey to two eccentric spiritualists. They were the royal sisters Stana and Militza. The daughters of King Nicholas I of Montenegro, the two sisters had married into the extended Romanov clan as part of an arrangement between the king and the tsar. Militza was the wife of Grand Duke Peter Nicholaievich, and Stana married the Duke of Leuchtenberg, a distant cousin of the tsar. They grew up in the southern Balkans, where the exotic Orthodox faith collided with Muslim Turkey's rule. Often given to strange, almost occultist practices, Stana and Militza traveled in several fringe Orthodox circles that were known primarily for their belief in holy men, individuals chosen directly by God to be His emissaries. The sisters often held strange spiritual gatherings at their homes in Znamensky or Sergeevsky, leading to their being called the Black Sisters. It was at these gatherings that they introduced Alexandra to a string of unsuccessful—and ultimately fraudulent—"holy men." One in particular, Philippe Vachot, assured Alexandra he could secure God's direct intervention on her behalf for a son. The dowager empress believed Vachot was a fraud after receiving reports about him from the Russian police. She was furious with Stana and Militza for drawing Nicholas and Alexandra into their circle. "It is more Alicky who is under this horrid man's influence than Nicky," the Duchess of Cornwall told her husband. "Aunt Minny is in despair."[26]

Vachot was only exposed as a charlatan after a humiliating episode. For months, it appeared that Alexandra was pregnant again. Her waistline was increasing, she had a healthy glow as any expectant mother normally does, but her stomach did not take on the wholesome roundness that so often accompanies pregnancy. Then one night in August, she appeared to go into labor, except there was no child in her womb. The truth was revealed: medicinal herbs Vachot had given her to encourage conception actually made her anemic. The swelling in her abdomen and change in her physical condition was a result of amenorrhea. "At last a natural way out of this unfortunate situation has been found," wrote Grand Duchess Xenia. "She is in bed—as a precaution, as there can sometimes be bleeding in such cases. Thank God so far she is in good health."[27] Enemies of the tsar and tsarina claimed that Alexandra had actually given birth to a fifth daughter. According to the theories, Nicholas was supposedly so ashamed that he had the child smuggled out of Russia to spare the monarchy further embarrassment.

Alexandra's mystic obsession with having a son and the subsequent damage it was doing to the Russian monarchy attracted the attention of many, including the German government. Prince Henry VII of Reuss, whose niece Grand Duchess Marie Pavlovna ("Miechen") had married into the Romanovs, recounted the unsettling situation in Russia to Chancellor von Bülow.

> All that I have managed to gather has left a very disturbing impression ... certain influences, which can only be described as pernicious, are beginning to make themselves felt. These influences ... with a very dubious admixture of mysticism, emanate from the Montenegrin princesses ... wielded so decisive a power over the reigning Tsarina that even the Dowager Empress cannot combat it.... The Russian people sense corruption and the Little Father's [Nicholas II] prestige suffers accordingly. All this is being carefully used by the Nihilists to undermine Imperial prestige still further. Revolution, to-day, has changed its tactics. The *mot d'ordre* is no longer to assassinate a sovereign, but to discredit dynastic infallibility with the people. At the top there is utter ignorance of this danger ... Everybody else is ignored. No one who tells the truth can get a hearing, but is jealously watched and pushed aside.[28]

Her obsession with having a son was not the only matter that caused Alexandra anxiety in 1901. Less than a year after Queen Victoria's death, the unbelievable news broke that her brother the Grand Duke of Hesse and his wife, Ducky, were divorcing. Ducky announced to her family almost immediately after Queen Victoria's funeral that she would not be returning to Darmstadt.

The revelation sent shockwaves rippling through royal courts. Until the early twentieth century, divorce was a scandalous affair, and despite ubiquitous unhappy royal marriages, it was a practice wholly unheard of amongst proper upper-class society. But for Ernie and Ducky—who had been forced together by Queen Victoria—divorce was the only answer. They were maddeningly unhappy together, and their tiny court in Darmstadt was tainted with one scandal after another. "I do not think they were at all happy together," May's husband wrote to Nicholas II, "but I never thought it would come to this; I am very sorry as I like them both. You and I, thank God, are both so happy with our wives and children, that we can't understand this sort of thing."[29] Empress Augusta Victoria was aghast at the idea, blaming the divorce on a lack of morality within Ducky's family. "The last time I saw her," Princess Antoine Radziwill wrote to a friend, Dona "spoke to me with great severity about the duchess of Coburg [Ducky's mother], who, according to her, must have raised her daughters very badly." In Saint Petersburg, Nicholas II was at a loss for words. "Can you imagine," he wrote to his mother, "getting divorced, *yes*, actually *divorced!*... In a case like this even the loss of a dear person is better than the general disgrace of a divorce."[30]

Darmstadt was "shrouded temporarily in dishonor," according to one historian. Alexandra's enemies used the scandal in their ongoing campaign of vilification against the empress. The "Romanovs discovered a fresh reason to be contemptuous of Ernie's sister Alix, who could not, they supposed, have been ignorant of her brother's unmentionable proclivities."[31] Not everyone was ready to use the scandal against Alexandra, however. Her mother-in-law, Minnie, offered her support. "It is simply awful," she wrote after a sleepless night. "I am also *extremely* sorry for poor Alix, knowing well how dear Ernie is to her ..."[32]

What made her brother's divorce so much more painful for Alexandra (which she blamed solely on his now ex-wife) was that Ducky had run off with Grand Duke Kyril Vladimirovich, one of the tsar's cousins. Alexandra's Victorian sensibilities were offended when the divorced Ducky was admitted into Russia's ruling family—Ernie remarried in 1905 to Princess Eleonore of Solms-Hohensolms-Lich. So too was Nicholas. He stripped Kyril of his title, rank, honors, and commission in the navy. Despite a violent altercation with Kyril's father, his uncle the Grand Duke Vladimir, Nicholas refused to back down. Kyril's mother, Miechen, blamed the tsar's reaction on Alexandra's contempt for Ducky. "And why all this?" she wrote to her uncle Henry VII of Reuss. "Because the Tsarina does not want her hated ex-sister-in-law in the family."[33] In the hopes of winning the tsar's favor for Ducky, her sister the Crown Princess Marie of Romania named her newborn son Nicolas. This gesture seemed to have little impact on the tsar's decision, which included forcing the newlyweds to live in exile. It would be another eight years before Kyril and Ducky were allowed to return to Russia.

~~~

Dubbed by the international press as "the Colonial Tour," the Duchess of Cornwall's trip around the world began inauspiciously. Her passage aboard the *Ophir* only increased her aversion to sea travel. Seasickness left her bedridden in her cabin for most of the first few weeks. "I *detest* the sea," she wrote home from the Indian Ocean. "I like seeing the places and being on land, the rest of it is purgatory to me."[34] The *Ophir*'s first official stop was Gibraltar, followed by Malta, where George had made many visits during his youthful naval days. Malta held a special place in George's heart because it was here that he experienced first love. His uncle the Duke of Edinburgh was stationed on the island when he commanded the Royal Navy's Mediterranean Squadron. George fell in love with the duke's beautiful daughter Marie ("Missy"), but her mother would have none of it. The formidable Duchess of Edinburgh loathed the English court and quickly put an end to George and Missy's adolescent romance. She later saw to it that Missy married Crown Prince Ferdinand of Romania.

From Valletta, the *Ophir* sailed on to Sri Lanka, then known as Ceylon. May deeply enjoyed her time on the exotic island. She became the first English princess to visit a Buddhist monastery. She also received the unique honor of observing a procession of Peraharu priests, an ancient sect of Hindu. Their next stop was Singapore. During lunch at the Government House, the Duke and Duchess of Cornwall were introduced to the four sultans of the Federated Malay States, a British-protected political union on the Malay Peninsula. In the afternoon, May held a private audience with the numerous wives of the Perak sultan and some of the tribe's lesser chiefs.

Singapore was the last stop before the much-anticipated visit to Australia. "It seems so wonderful to be actually in Australia," the duchess wrote home. "It is like a second England, with the same people and the same towns, only the scenery is different."[35] May's first glimpse of Australia was fittingly that of Melbourne, the bustling embodiment of English influence stretching to the other side of the globe. The city was named for Lord Melbourne, the famous British prime minister who had once been a close friend and adviser to Queen Victoria in the first few years of her reign. This city, renowned for being built in less than fifty years, welcomed the Duchess of Cornwall and her husband with such exuberance that it nearly eclipsed the fanfare that surrounded her own wedding. The route from their hotel to the Parliament House was lined with triumphal arches erected high above excited crowds numbering in the thousands. The royal couple was present at the opening session of Parliament for the newly formed Commonwealth of Australia, which had united for the first time the provinces of New South Wales, Victoria, South Australia, Queensland, Tasmania, and Western Australia.

May was immensely popular in Australia and New Zealand. She was the embodiment of the word *royal*. Her tall, stately beauty was even greater than what the populace had believed. She also greatly impressed everyone by her knowledge of the region. Lady Mary Lygon, one of her ladies-in-waiting,

wrote home, "Her Royal Highness has quite got over all her shyness abroad ...
Her smile is commented on in every paper and her charm of manner: in
fact, she is having a *'success fou.'"* Lady Lygon wrote later, "Every state has
successively fallen in love with her looks, her smile, and her great charm of
manner. She is at last coming out of her shell and will electrify them at home
as she has everyone here."[36]

For the final and most in-depth part of the colonial tour, the duke and
duchess headed to Canada. The *Ophir* skirted around Cape Town and up the
coast of West Africa before crossing the Atlantic and docking in Montreal.
It was here that May received one of her most treasured possessions: a gold
maple leaf covered with enamel and diamonds. It would remain one of her
favorites, especially once she became queen. May and George's Canadian visit
soon turned into a real adventure. Political parties, dignitaries, and ordinary
folk clamored over one another for the Duchess of Cornwall's attention. But
it was with the last group, ordinary people, with whom she was most at ease.
When she visited the home of one of the local dockworkers, the hostess was
somewhat tongue-tied and embarrassed. Seizing the opportunity, May asked
if she could see her children's nursery and suddenly asked, "And may I show
you my children's pictures?"[37]

Ottawa was next on the itinerary. The duke and duchess were impressed
by the towering buildings. Later, they watched an awe-inspiring evening of
entertainments on the sprawling lawn of the Parliament building, where
Edward VII laid the foundation stone during his 1860 visit. Actors recreated
a lumberjack's life and the discovery of Canada by French explorers, followed
by a dinner of pea soup and pork and beans to add a dose of reality to the
local flavor. After a walking tour of Hull—just across the provincial border
in Quebec—it was back to Ottawa for a presentation ceremony in the Senate
Chamber. More than a thousand people were paraded past George and
May, who had taken up seats on the thrones normally occupied by the
governor general and his consort. The Senate Chamber ceremony, in which
May was seated beneath a glistening diamond-studded canopy surrounded
by thousands of miniature lamps, was exhausting but a success. According to
one witness, both George and May "were uniformly gracious to all, without
exception, who came with their tribute of respect and duty."[38]

The rest of the hectic journey was loaded with speeches, luncheons,
banquets, and public ceremonies. In Winnipeg, May presided over a rose-
themed ball decorated with sparkling lights awash in pinks and yellows,
followed by a torchlight procession to the train station.

> The entire route ... was lined with cheering spectators, determined
> to get a good view of the Duke and Duchess, which the gaily

illuminated streets rendered an easy matter. Along Assiniboine avenue and down Donald street as far as St. Mary, were stationed lines of torch-bearers. As the royal carriage passed by, these fell in behind, and with the bands at different points playing spirited airs, presented a spectacular appearance along the whole route extending over a mile and a half.[39]

May and George always tried to write home to King Edward and Queen Alexandra about their experiences. "Darling May is of the greatest possible help to me & works very hard, I don't think I could have done all this without her," George wrote to his mother. "Everybody admires her very much which is very pleasing to me. I hope you are as proud of your daughter in law as I am of my wife."[40]

The list of places visited continued to mount—Calgary, Banff, Vancouver, Victoria, Toronto, Hamilton, London, Niagara Falls, Belleville, and Kingston. Thousands flocked to local train stations as the royal carriage made one stop after another. The royal couple visited many of the same places that Edward VII had when he visited Canada more than forty years earlier. The most interesting part of the colonial tour was May's encounter with nearly two thousand representatives of North America's western native tribes. Anticipation of the royal visit prompted a gathering of the Black Foot, Blood, Piegan, Sarcee, Stony, and Cree natives, the likes of which had not been seen in Canada in two decades. The couple was welcomed at a marquee built by the tribes themselves bearing the inscription "*Kitaisimatsimpmom*—We Greet You." George and May entered a pavilion, where they were met by six tribal chiefs. The only blemish that marred the day's theatrical events occurred when Joseph Samson, chief of the Cree Nation, refused to shake hands with May, since "a woman was deemed unworthy in their eyes of consideration upon an occasion of such solemnity."[41]

After boarding a train for Halifax, the duke and duchess sailed from the East Coast back to England in November 1901. When the *Ophir* arrived, May was somewhat pale because the Atlantic crossing had been a stormy one. On the eight-month voyage across the globe, they "covered 45,000 miles, laid 21 foundation stones, received 544 addresses, presented 4,329 medals, reviewed 62,000 troops, and shook hands with 24,855 people at official receptions."[42] In a speech to the Lord Mayor of London, George expressed his happiness at returning home and what the journey meant to him.

We rejoice at being home again, and our hearts are full of thankfulness for the protection which has been vouchsafed to us during our long and deeply interesting journey.... Our journey has extended over 33,000 miles by sea and 12,500 by land. Everywhere we have been profoundly impressed by the kindness and affectionate enthusiasm extended to us, by the universal declarations of loyalty to the Throne, and by the conscious pride in membership of our great Empire which so unmistakably declared itself. We have gained great, pleasant, and profitable experience, and we have made many friends.[43]

George was under no illusions as to who really deserved the credit for the success of the 1901 colonial tour. Shortly after their return, he wrote to May, "Somehow I can't tell you, so I take the first opportunity of writing to say how deeply I am indebted to you darling for the splendid way in which you supported and helped me on our long Tour. It was you who made it a success."[44]

Much to the delight of Edward VII and Queen Alexandra, the couple's return coincided with the king's birthday on November 15. A few days after the celebration, Edward VII conferred on George and May the coveted titles Prince and Princess of Wales. "May purred with pleasure at her elevation ..." wrote one of her biographers.[45] Many felt it was long overdue and that the couple should have been feted immediately when George's parents ascended the throne. Unlike his own parents, the king wanted to ensure that his heir was properly trained for the day he would become king. Throughout his six decades as Prince of Wales, Edward was denied all but the most cursory role as heir to the throne. Queen Victoria was fiercely protective of her sovereign prerogatives, and it was widely known that, for many years, she felt her son was not up to the task of being king. In contrast, Prince George was given access to state documents by his father, which he in turn presented to May for her insights. Along with their elevation in status came an increase in the standard of living for May and her family. Parliament voted on providing the couple with an annual income of £100,000. To put this amount in context, in 1901 "a farm labourer earned no more than forty pounds a year, and a domestic servant half that."[46] In today's money, George and May enjoyed an annual income of more than $11 million.[47]

Their new titles and fortune meant a change of address for the new Wales family. They moved from their modest yet comfortable official residence, York House at Saint James's Palace, to the palatial, red-brick Marlborough House, located a few blocks away from Buckingham Palace. George's parents had lived there for decades, after Queen Victoria asked Parliament in 1849 to allow the Prince of Wales to live there when he turned nineteen. After £60,000 worth of renovations, George's parents moved in after their wedding and remained there until they ascended the throne in January and, naturally, took up residence at Buckingham Palace. Now, it was home to May as she raised the next generation of Britain's royal family, which expanded on December 20, 1902, with the birth of her fifth child at York Cottage, a son whom she named George Edward Alexander Edmund.

❧

As Princess Zita of Bourbon-Parma grew into a vivacious, kind young woman, one of the things that made a profound impact on her life was religion. Years later, she would take as her personal motto "More for you than for me."[48] Her family was devoutly Roman Catholic. From the age of eight, Zita undertook catechism lessons under a certain Father Travers, which were followed by her First Communion in 1902 in the chapel at Pianore. Faith was more than just a religious practice to the Duke and Duchess of Parma. They encouraged Zita and her siblings to seek after God with all their hearts and to make prayer and faith the very foundations of who they were. To help make this a reality for their children, the duke and duchess took their family to Rome in 1903 for the Silver Jubilee celebrations in honor of Pope Leo XIII. Only ten years old at the time, Zita recalled "the splendid ceremony, the chants, the grandeur of it all."[49] Like Alexandra of Russia, religion for Zita was not simply a pair of gloves to be taken on and off. It was a serious commitment to God. She and her sisters were trained from an early age to serve and minister to those in need not in spite of their royal position but because of it. Duke Robert I was one of those truly remarkable, enlightened royals who believed it was the duty of all people of high position to benefit and help those less fortunate. He made it a point to donate 10 percent of his income to the poor.

The Bourbon-Parma princesses made regular visits to textile factories where they bought up unused pieces of fabric and then personally sewed them into clothes to be handed out to peasants living in the villages near their estates. Around Pianore, where the standard of living was especially low and the people were desperately poor, Zita and her sisters routinely handed out clothing, food, and medicines to many who were sick with tuberculosis. The Duchess of Parma insisted her daughters think of themselves as "Little Sisters of the poor." Each night after returning home, she made sure her daughters promptly changed all their clothes and disinfected themselves with alcohol. When someone once asked the duchess if there was any danger of infection to her daughters, she famously replied, "Love of one's neighbour is the best disinfectant."[50]

For the Bourbon-Parma family, religion truly began at home. Three of Zita's sisters—Adelaide, Francesca, and Maria Antonia—became nuns, as did her maternal grandmother, Queen Adelaide of Portugal, whom she called "Mère Adelheide." In light of such a devout upbringing, it came as no surprise that Princess Zita's education was thoroughly religious. In 1902, Duke Robert sent her to a boarding school at Zangberg in Upper Bavaria to complete her formal schooling. Her parents felt it was suitable since the school itself was administered by Salesian nuns from the Order of the Visitation of Holy Mary. Though most children would have been terrified to be sent off to a strange school at the age of ten in a country they did not know, for Zita, it was just another family affair. Her sisters were studying at Zangberg as well, and it was close to the homes of so many of her French and Austrian relatives. At Zangberg, from dawn until dusk, every part of Zita's studies in history, art, languages, and music were submitted to the careful eyes of the nuns. "She always kept others at a certain distant [*sic*]," one of the nuns recalled of Zita, "and, though she had a fiery temper, never gave the slightest difficulty to the nuns or teachers."[51] She learned to play the piano but actually preferred the organ, which she played every Sunday at Mass. The princess fit in perfectly, and she felt safe and content during her time in Bavaria.

The grief that Tsarina Alexandra experienced over not having produced a son only grew worse with time. In spite of the damaging episode with Philippe Vachot, she still was drawn to the circle of mystics to which Stana and Militza belonged. It did not take long for Militza to introduce Alexandra to the teachings of another holy man, this one a monk named Seraphim of Sarov, who died in 1833. According to the Montenegrin sisters, it hardly mattered that he had been dead for decades. They claimed Alexandra must seek Seraphim's intercession to conceive a son, but more than that, it "was imperative," insisted Militza, "that Seraphim be declared a saint in order for Alexandra to benefit from his prayers. Never mind that it was too soon for Seraphim to be made a saint, never mind that there was opposition from the church against such a move." Determined against all odds, Alexandra pleaded with Nicholas to use his position as head of the Russian Orthodox Church "to press for Seraphim's case."[52]

Against the concerns of the chief procurator of the Holy Synod, the tsarina succeeded in having Seraphim made a saint. At a moving ceremony in Sarov, a Baroque monastery east of Saint Petersburg, the relatively unknown Seraphim was canonized amid strong-voiced choirs and priests burning incense. Thousands of peasants walked for days to reach the monastery at Sarov, hoping with fervent prayers that Seraphim could heal their lame, sick, and infirmed. And by all accounts, he did. According to a number of witnesses, mute children became able to speak, people with crippled limbs could walk again, and even those appearing to suffer from insanity were healed. On the last night of Seraphim's canonization ceremony, Alexandra "bathed in the waters of the Sarov River in hopes that she would at last conceive a male child." In this, she was not alone; she was joined by Nicholas, the dowager empress, Ella, the tsar's sister Olga, and many other members of the imperial family who made their way down to the river under the moonlight in groups of twos and threes. In the end, the "efforts seemed to have reaped their intended rewards, for within months of Seraphim becoming a saint Alexandra Feodorovna found to her satisfaction that she was again with child."[53]

During her fifth pregnancy, she was racked with anxiety over whether or not she would deliver a boy. This undermined the empress's already-fragile health. She was never well during her pregnancies, and her added anxiety afflicted her with very real pain in her back, legs, and head—her mother, Alice, had endured very similar symptoms, leading many to speculate about the genetic predisposition for illness in Queen Victoria's bloodline. For days at a time, Alexandra would withdraw to her now-famous Mauve Boudoir in the hundred-room, white-and-yellow, neoclassical Alexander Palace at Tsarskoe Selo. Of all the rooms in all the palaces Alexandra called home, it was her Mauve Boudoir that was truly her refuge. Decorated entirely in mauve—the curtains, the linens, the flowers spread throughout the room—it was filled with books, chintz, lounges, and two pianos. She spent many hours alone resting or on her knees in prayer beneath jewel-encrusted icons. She would not see anyone, save for her husband, daughters, and a handful of close friends. "Why, *why* will God not grant me a son?" she sobbed to Nicholas.[54]

His wife's insularity did not strike Nicholas II as unusual. Growing up, his parents had insisted that family life and governance were to be kept mutually exclusive. This extended to sheltering Nicholas and his siblings, even into their twenties. Alexander III "would not even have Nicky sit in the Council of State until 1893," wrote his sister Olga. "My father disliked the mere idea of state matters encroaching on our family life."[55] Nicholas and Alexandra were united in their desire to isolate themselves from the outside world. "I feel very sorry for the Emperor and Empress," wrote the British ambassador to Russia. "They live at Tsarskoe Selo in a world apart, and are almost like prisoners since it is not considered safe to come even to Saint Petersburg."[56] By all appearances, Tsarskoe Selo was a fortress against the difficulties of life. By 1905, the fences were ten feet high and capped off by barbed wire and razor-sharp spikes.

Alexandra and Nicholas's growing isolation from other members of the Romanov family—and the imperial court as a whole—earned them a reputation for being haughty and difficult, especially the tsarina. Her natural timidity was mistaken for aloofness, prompting many to think she was cold, distant, and uncaring. Whispers, from within the court and without, grew louder and louder claiming that Nicholas and Alexandra should never have been permitted to ascend the throne. But where Nicholas II was easily influenced by members of the imperial family, especially his larger-than-life uncles, Alexandra stood resolute against their influence. She closed in around Nicholas, making a concerted effort to shield him from their advice. Sadly, when she did this, she also prevented him from receiving the help he so desperately needed to rule Russia. Even Alexandra's own brother, Ernie, commented on this issue during a visit to Livadia. When a woman asked him about his sister, he replied, "My sister? She is splendid. Only you people here don't know how to treat her. The Tsar is an angel, but he doesn't know how to deal with her. What she needs is a superior will which can dominate her, and which can, so to speak, bridle her."[57] To outsiders, Alexandra seemed mad. She rejected the opinions of those who were truly wise in favor of others whom she believed possessed some small merit. On both sides of what became the Alexandra issue, misunderstanding reigned supreme. It was not long before most of the Romanovs wanted nothing to do with the empress.

Alexandra did not care what people thought of her, especially Russia's hypocritical courtiers of whom, in the early days of her marriage, she had drawn embarrassing caricatures of in an act of defiance against their criticisms. They became just as scathing of her. "What else could we expect from Victoria's grand-daughter," her critics opined. "Hemming red-flannel petticoats on weekdays and reading the Bible on Sundays—there's an Englishwoman for you!"[58] One of the tsarina's friends later remarked on the chasm that separated Alexandra from those around her: "The Russian aristocracy could not understand why on all the earth their Empress knitted scarves and shawls as presents for her friends. Their conception of an Imperial gift was entirely different, and they were oblivious of the love which had been crocheted into the despised scarf or the useful shawl."[59]

Alexandra's only concerns were helping Nicholas rule the Russian Empire and raising their children. Their four daughters were charming young girls who brought great joy to their parents' lives. Alexandra was a devoted mother who loved her children beyond words. Unlike Princess May, Alexandra took a hands-on approach to parenting, rather than give the care of her children entirely over to governesses. Whatever grief she may have experienced at the Russian court, Alexandra received ample rewards for it in the blessedness of her family life.

The happiness Nicholas II and Alexandra enjoyed was soon overshadowed by talk of war. During the empress's fifth and final pregnancy, Russia found itself embroiled in war in the Far East. The problem began internally. Conflict in the tsarist empire had been brewing for years. Work stoppages, strikes, and riots were becoming commonplace in Moscow and Saint Petersburg as a result of the poor living conditions, rampant poverty, and illiteracy among the masses. These problems only added to the maelstrom when Russia went to war with Japan in 1904, which proved to be Nicholas II's *annus horribilis*. The conflict had been brewing ever since Russian imperial ambitions branched out into Asia by targeting Manchuria. But when the first volley was fired, it caught the Russian Empire totally unprepared. After breaking off peace talks with Russia in February 1904, Japan sent a group of torpedo boats to attack Port Arthur, Russia's Asian military command center in China and its only seaport on open, warm water. After making it into port, the torpedo boats sank two of the most advanced warships in the Russian fleet. "Yes, it is a trying time," Alexandra wrote to her sister Victoria, "but one must put all one's trust in God, who gives strength and courage. Unluckily I cannot get about at all and spend my days on the sofa … walking and standing causes me great pain."[60]

Despite Russia's lack of preparedness, the war was met with enthusiasm by the population at first. It diverted the nation's attention off its own problems and onto the war effort. The French military attaché in Russia reported on the people's reaction to the war: "All the Russians, apart from a handful of fanatics, are prepared to make any sacrifice to bring it to a victorious conclusion and avenge the insult to the Russian flag. We are witnessing a great outburst of national vigour and the grim determination which animates even the lowest classes—particularly the lowest classes—is most impressive."[61] There was an inflated sense that the tsarist empire would quickly vanquish the forces of Japan; many in Russia considered the Japanese an inferior race. Alexandra wrote about the war to her brother, Ernie, how "we did everything to avoid it, but it seems it had to be, & it has done our country good."[62] Wilhelm II supported Russia in the conflict by allowing Russian ships to be refueled with coal at German stations en route to the Far East.

The early weeks of the war also brought about a resurgence in the imperial family's popularity, which had taken a serious hit in the first years of the twentieth century. Undoubtedly, the imperial couple was relishing their popularity when, in the summer of 1904, the day Tsarina Alexandra had hoped and prayed for finally arrived. On the stiflingly hot afternoon of August 12, Nicholas and Alexandra were at the Peterhof Palace, on the outskirts of Saint Petersburg in the Gulf of Finland. Just as the couple sat down to lunch, the empress went into labor. After a surprisingly short delivery of only one hour, the empress delivered an eleven-pound son at 1:15 p.m. Holding the child in his arms, Dr. Ott turned to Nicholas and announced, "I congratulate Your Majesty on the birth of a tsarevich!"[63] When Alexandra awoke from the effects of the chloroform, she looked around the room and saw her husband's beaming face. "Oh, it cannot be true; it cannot be true," she cried out in joy. "Is it really a boy?"[64]

A thunderous 301-gun salute announced to the people of Saint Petersburg that an heir had finally been born—this may seem like overkill, but in 1537 when Jane Seymour presented Henry VIII with his much coveted son, the future Edward VI, the Tower of London guards fired off two thousand rounds of artillery as a tribute. It was the first time in nearly three hundred years that an heir had been born to a reigning tsar. In his diary, Nicholas described it as a "great and unforgettable day ... during which we were clearly visited by the grace of God."[65] The reaction across Russia was rapturous. Church bells rang out in parishes from Kiev to Siberia as people celebrated into the small hours of the morning. Nicholas, his mother, and his daughters attended a *Te Deum* to thank God for the birth of a son.

Eleven days later, Alexandra's son made his first public appearance for his christening. The tiny infant was paraded through the streets of Saint Petersburg resting on a cloth-of-silver cushion in a gilded carriage drawn by six cream-colored horses. The four-hour ceremony was held at the ornate Peterhof Palace, famous for its gold-plated, eight-tiered fountain system that reminded visitors of Versailles. In a fitting move during a time of war, the entire armed forces were named godparents to the tsarevitch, along with the Prince of Wales and Emperor Wilhelm II. The christening brought together the entire Russian imperial court. Hundreds of men and women, dressed in dazzling medals and jewels made of gold and diamonds, watched as the metropolitan of Saint Petersburg baptized the little boy, who was given the title tsarevitch and publicly proclaimed heir to the throne. During the ceremony, Nicholas II and Alexandra named their only son Alexei, after the seventeenth-century tsar of the same name. Some people looked upon the choice as a bad omen: "others shook their heads and saw the name as foreboding; it was an unlucky name. According to a seventeenth-century prophecy, the Romanov dynasty would end with an Alexey as heir."[66]

Nicholas and Alexandra thought nothing could dampen their happiness, but they were dreadfully mistaken. In September, Alexandra was horrified when she noticed her baby son was bleeding from his navel. "Alix and I are very disturbed at the constant bleeding in little Alexei," Nicholas confided to his diary. "It continued at intervals from his navel until evening."[67] For the next three days, Nicholas and Alexandra watched in terror as their son bled intermittently from his navel. It was then that they reached a horrifying conclusion: little Alexei was a hemophiliac. That dreaded blood disease that had killed Alexandra's brother Frittie and her uncle Leopold had shown up in her son. The slightest bump or bruise could lead to a fatal bleeding episode. The long-term prognosis was equally grim, since the disease's bleeding effect destroys tissue, bone, and cartilage. The empress then had a sickening revelation: it was she who had passed the disease on to Alexei. As a granddaughter of Queen Victoria, she was a carrier of what the imperial court dubbed the "English bleeding disease." Now, she passed the disease to her only son. "Oh, what anguish it was," she wrote after Alexei's first attack, "and not to let others see the knife digging in one."[68] Although the tsarina was somewhat familiar with the disease—her sister Irene's two sons were both hemophiliacs—she did not realize how widespread it was in her family. Emperor Wilhelm II lost one of his brothers to hemophilia and would later watch a nephew die from it as well.

Once the truth of Alexei's condition was revealed, the tsar and tsarina made the fateful decision to keep it a state secret. The truth of the tsarevitch's illness was never to be revealed, not to the public, not even to other members of the imperial family. Everyone from the dowager empress to the tsar's sisters to the palace servants were kept in the dark. The decision to hide the truth of Alexei's condition was twofold. First, it was a long-standing tradition in Russia to never discuss the health of the imperial family. Second, Nicholas and Alexandra were afraid that if the truth were known, it would cast doubt on Alexei's position as heir and thereby threaten the future of the monarchy. From the moment the decision was made, Tsarina Alexandra would not know a moment's peace. Every moment of every day for the rest of her life would be tinged with anxiety and worry over her son's delicate health.

9

A Mother's Heart

(1905–06)

The new year brought with it an unending string of challenges for Russia. The country's infrastructure continued to be undermined by strikes, work stoppages, and protests. The winter of 1904/05 was particularly unbearable for the people of Saint Petersburg. No longer able to endure rising food prices, falling wages, and the inevitable starvation that followed, the people took matters into their own hands. An assassination attempt on the tsar's life was made that winter during a ceremony to bless the waters of the Neva River in Saint Petersburg, leading to a tangible increase in security at all imperial facilities. Nicholas II's uncles, who were particularly hated for their brutality and graft, were often the targets of assassins. Ella's husband, Serge, was so terrified of being murdered that he slept in a different palace in Moscow every night, surrounded by a constantly changing contingent of guards lest an assassin infiltrate their ranks. Dona's son Willy was in Russia at the time. In his memoirs, the crown prince recalled the tense atmosphere: "The fear of assassins was very great at the court. Among the many precautionary and preventive measures which I saw taken everywhere, one that I met with on paying the Tsar a late evening visit made a deep impression upon me. In the vestibule of his private apartments, the Emperor's entire body-guard of about one hundred men were posted like the pieces on a chess-board. It was impossible for anyone to pass; and my entrance created the greatest alarm and excitement."[1]

On January 9, 1905, a group of exasperated workers gathered in the streets of Saint Petersburg. They were desperate for Nicholas II to reform his

166

tottering empire. Their list of demands included a constituent assembly for the people and better working conditions, such as an eight-hour workday. As the crowd moved through the city streets toward the Winter Palace, it grew in size. Mostly made up of peasants—workers, women, and children—the mob's size soared to more than two hundred thousand. Their leader, Father Gregory Gapon, was a priest loyal to the tsar—until recently, Gapon had been secretly working for the interior ministry. The crowd he now led was undeniably devoted to Nicholas II. "We workers and residents of the city of Saint Petersburg," so went their petition to the tsar, "of various ranks and stations, our wives, children and helpless old parents, have come to Thee, Sire, to seek justice and protection."[2] As they hovered outside the gates of the palace, they held up portraits of the tsar and tsarina while singing the national anthem. What happened next has since gone down as one of imperial Russia's grisliest political rallies.

> As the hymn-singing, icon-waving, noisy but entirely respectful mass of humanity closed in on the [palace] and showed no sign of withdrawing, the commander of the guard finally panicked and ordered his men to fire their first volley not over the heads of the crowd, as was the customary dispersal procedure, but slap [*sic*] into their bodies. Volley after volley followed and the killing continued late into the afternoon as Cossacks and other mounted troops of the Petersburg garrison hunted down groups who had fled the corpse-strewn palace square. 'Bloody Sunday' had entered its mark on the Russian calendar, and the stain was never to be removed.[3]

The irony was that neither Nicholas nor Alexandra was at the Winter Palace that day. They were instead at Tsarskoe Selo at the urging of their ministers, who felt it was an easier location to protect against the strife in the capital. Charles Hardinge, the British diplomat and statesman, could not hide his disgust at the massacre. He believed that the tsar had "missed the chance of his lifetime ... if he had received at the Winter Palace a small deputation and promised to give them what has been sincerely promised to them in his name, he would have obtained the undying loyalty and admiration of the lower classes."[4]

Alexandra was horrified at the bloodshed that day, which amounted to more than two hundred people killed. Her comments on the massacre are a chilling reminder of the repressive nature of autocracy in Russia: "The poor workmen who had been utterly misled, had to suffer, and the organizers have hidden as usual behind. I love my new country. It's so young, powerful, and has much good in it, only utterly unbalanced and childlike."[5] In a letter to one of her sisters, she was more candid: "It is a time full of trials indeed. Things are in a bad state and it's abominable [*sic*] unpatriotic at the time when we are plunged into war to break forth with revolutionary ideas." Unfortunately, the empress refused to believe things were as bad as they really were. "Don't believe all the horrors the foreign papers say," she continued. "They make one's hair stand on end—foul exaggeration."[6] This myopic quality would stay with Alexandra until the bitter end.

The situation in Russia remained dire. Any previous loyalty Gregor Gapon may have had toward the monarchy was now washed away in blood. "We have no tsar anymore," he declared ominously. "Rivers of blood separate the Emperor from his people."[7] The day after the Bloody Sunday massacre, the Russian Social Democratic Party issued a bold statement against the monarchy: "Yesterday you saw the savagery of the monarchy. You saw the blood running in the streets ... Who directed the soldiers' rifles and shot against the breasts of the workers? It was the Tsar! the Grand Dukes, the ministers, the generals, the scum of the Court! ... may they meet death. To arms, comrades! Seize the arsenals, depots and magazines of arms ... destroy the police and gendarme stations and all the Governmental buildings. Down with the monarchic government!" Bloody Sunday proved to be "the first in a series of events to shake the tsarist empire." The Marxist revolutionary Leon Trotsky declared, "The Revolution has come."[8]

A few weeks later, revolutionaries succeeded in assassinating one of Nicholas II's hated uncles. Grand Duke Serge, Saint Petersburg's notoriously brutal governor, was murdered when his carriage was destroyed by a bomb thrown by Ivan Kalyaev, a member of the Social Revolutionary Party. In her grief, Serge's wife, Ella, demonstrated true Christian integrity by going to visit Kalyaev in prison and even forgiving him. She went to the tsar begging him to pardon Kalyaev. "I admire this act," recounted one of the grand dukes, "but I cannot grasp this incredible piety." Ella's plea to Nicholas II was to no effect. Kalyaev was executed shortly thereafter. Ella's niece Grand Duchess Marie Pavlovna recalled that she "gave proof of an almost incomprehensible heroism; no one could understand whence came the strength so to bear her misfortune."[9]

Kalyaev's execution did not deter the rapidly increasing revolutionary fever in Russia. A few weeks later, the secret police uncovered a plot in which assassins planned to masquerade as members of the imperial court choir. They intended to hide grenades under their robes during the upcoming Easter service and then later throw them into the midst of Nicholas, Alexandra, and their family. Even more jarring was the fact that the plot was discovered only a few short hours before the would-be assassins planned to carry out their mission.

Added to this ferment were the setbacks Russia was enduring in its war with Japan. The Russian economy had been weak for years and began to erode. The war already cost the empire nearly two billion dollars, and even that was not enough to provide meals for the soldiers or ammunition for their guns. The country's overwhelming size compared to their tiny island adversary made Russia notoriously difficult to resupply, while the military leaders struggled to keep up with their Japanese counterparts. This fact came to the fore at the Battle of Mukden. Lasting from February into March 1905, 330,000 Russian soldiers fought, and almost 90,000 were killed: "Mukden was, in terms of the numbers involved, the biggest battle until then recorded.... Over six hundred thousand men, more than were ever engaged in any nineteenth-century battle, fought desperately for over two weeks instead of for a day."[10] The Russians were forced to retreat forty miles north and lost ninety thousand additional soldiers in the process.

Nicholas was anxious about the war's outcome but was resolute in his determination to win it. "You may be sure that Russia shall fight this war to the end, until the last Jap is driven out of Manchuria," he wrote to Wilhelm II.[11] The war was indeed about to end, but in a disastrous defeat for Russia. Desperate to secure a massive victory after the fall of Port Arthur, the tsar's Baltic Fleet took a nine-month, eighteen-thousand mile journey through the Arctic to Japan to wipe out their naval forces. But when they arrived at what became known as the Battle of Tsushima in May 1905, the Baltic Fleet was utterly annihilated in such a spectacular way that it sent shockwaves around the world. The "decisive battle" lasted "an incredibly brief forty-five minutes ... The barrage of Japanese firepower resulted in the mind-boggling loss for Russia of six destroyers, twelve cruisers, eight battleships, and thousands of men."[12] According to one historian, the "battle of Tsushima was the greatest and most decisive naval action since Trafalgar a century before. Its effects, as far as the loser was concerned, were even more drastic. Not only did it end the war almost at once ... it also marked the beginning of the slow end inside imperial Russia itself."[13]

The news of the Russian defeat at Tsushima came as a crushing blow to Nicholas II, who was at a picnic with his family that afternoon. His sister Grand Duchess Olga Alexandrovna was with him and Alexandra when they received word of Japan's devastating victory. She recalled that when Nicky was told, he "turned ashen pale ... and clutched at a chair for support." Alexandra, meanwhile, "broke down and sobbed."[14] With no alternative, Russia sued for peace with Japan, culminating in the Treaty of Portsmouth of 1905, which was negotiated by President Theodore Roosevelt. The Russo-Japanese War brought nothing but humiliation to Nicholas II and his reign, striking a blow from which the imperial dynasty would never recover.

❦

The death of the Empress Frederick meant that Dona was no longer living in her predecessor's shadow. She now felt that she could spread her wings and expand her influence into different areas without fear of criticism or comparison to Vicky. Her Christian faith provided an easy outlet. She became actively involved in building and restoring dozens of churches in and around Berlin. She also attended numerous rallies put on by the Reichstag's right-wing Christian Democratic Party. Her flurry of activity was motivated by a strong desire to "not to be a nonentity, as people had prophesied would be the case." She took up managing the Red Cross, as well as other charitable organizations that had been patronized by the first German empress, Wilhelm's grandmother Augusta. She also became passionate about the education of women. She was credited for doing "more than anyone else in Germany to make public careers open to women as well as men, encouraging them to work for their own living."[15]

By the time she was forty-seven years old, Dona's famed regal bearing remained undimmed; she still looked "every inch a queen." One of her contemporaries observed, "Her face has become quite lovely, with its wealth of snow-white hair, which she wears piled up high on the top of her brow, and which she likes to ornate with a diamond tiara or crown."[16] Her head and neck were often adorned with some of imperial Germany's finest jewels; one of her ladies-in-waiting once remarked that her "only claim to beauty" was that she had "a neck and shoulders modelled [sic] by an artist's hand to support the burden of crown jewels."[17] This was one way in which Dona created something of a unique style in Prussia, even though she was not generally a trendsetter. Her predecessors, the empresses Augusta and Vicky, were modest women when it came to fashion and rarely made use of the stunning crown jewels. Wilhelm was lavish in the gifts he showered upon his wife, who loved wearing the finest diamonds and gemstones. In particular, her pearls were "worth millions, for they are so large, so perfect in color and shape, so lavish in their profusion that few Regalias [sic] contain such treasures."[18]

When it came to her family, Dona remained the center of their world. For her husband, she became his rock. Her moments of frantic anxiety had grown few and far between, replaced by a quiet submissiveness and determination to add strength, prestige, and stability to the imperial and royal House of Hohenzollern. For Emperor Wilhelm II, a man who was driven by sentiment and emotion, Dona's influence started having a calming effect on him. One contemporary observed that the empress "acquired a considerable influence over her husband precisely by the way in which she effaced herself and subordinated all her thoughts and actions to his." Dona made it a point to never offer advice to her husband but rather waited for him to come to her, which began to happen frequently. Count Axel Schwering, a member of the Prussian court, concluded that Wilhelm "learned, in consequence, to look up to" his wife "in many of the difficulties in which he found himself not infrequently entangled."[19]

Dona's support of her husband was not limited only to emotional issues. At some point in their marriage, she had realized how fragile his ego truly was. In her efforts to be Wilhelm's helpmate, she "did everything she could to ingratiate herself into her husband's life, memorizing the uniforms of his various regiments, forcing herself to read books on military subjects that she knew interested him, and accompanying him on his daily horseback rides, his early morning calls on his officials, and (when he would permit it) his trips."[20]

Like her husband, the empress was a creature of habit that rigidly followed a daily routine. She awoke every morning at 6:00 a.m. and joined Wilhelm for breakfast in their private dining room. This was their own personal space, into which even servants were not admitted. One member of their court described this as "the one hour which the All-Highest [Wilhelm] ... devoted to domesticity, when husband and wife could gossip and discuss matters alone and in secret."[21] After breakfast, the empress reviewed the daily kitchen menus and consulted with each member of the household on the day's plans. She then checked in with her children before the start of their lessons. Much of the day was then spent working at her desk. In her memoirs, Dona's daughter, Sissy, recalled how busy her mother was: "My earliest childhood recollection of my mother evokes the picture of her never-ending writing. I can still hear the continuous scratch of her pen on her diary as I went into her sitting-room."[22]

Dona's children deeply loved and respected her. When it came to the children, she made it clear to her husband that she was in charge. She once told Poultney Bigelow, a childhood friend of Wilhelm's, that though her husband was "German Emperor I am Empress of the nursery."[23] This was supported by a contemporary who observed that Dona, "even in the intimacy of her home life never forgets or allows others, even William II., to forget that she is an Empress."[24]

No matter how busy or tired Dona was, she always made it a priority to check in on her children in their nursery before she went to bed. One evening, the princes were eager to receive a goodnight kiss from their mother, who was attending a function with Wilhelm and would not be home until late. The princes assured their mother they would remain awake for her, which they did until after midnight. When Dona asked the boys how they were able to stay up so late, Little Willy explained that he and his brothers tied a string to each other, and when one started falling asleep, the others would tug on the string to wake him up. It is not difficult to imagine that Dona's children worshipped their mother. In their memoirs, letters, and reminiscences, they seem to have nothing but praise for her. Of all her children, Willy and Sissy left the most vivid recollections. In his memoirs published in 1922, the crown prince wrote of his relationship with the empress.

> As far back as I can remember, the centre of our existence has been our dearly beloved mother. She has radiated a love which has warmed and comforted us. Whatever joy or sorrow moved us, she has always had for it understanding and sympathy. All that was best in our childhood, nay, all the best that home and family can give, we owe to her. What she was to us in our early youth, that she has remained throughout our adolesence and our manhood. The kindest and best woman is she for whom living means helping, succoring and spending herself in the interests of others; and such a woman is our mother.[25]

For Dona's sons, she was their confidante, advisor, and intercessor. One of the main reasons for this was her accessibility. Any of the children could approach Dona at any time, but to speak to Wilhelm, they needed to apply for permission first from either their tutor or their military governor. A true soldier, Wilhelm was a strict disciplinarian who rarely indulged his sons, especially the oldest three. This strictness was somewhat surprising, given his own rowdiness as a child. At the wedding of George's parents—the future King Edward VII and Alexandra of Denmark—young Willy, then aged four, caused a long string of embarrassments for his family. On the way to Saint George's Chapel, he hurled his aunt's muff out the carriage window. During the ceremony, he tried to toss the cairngorm from the head of his dirk across the choir. He bit his uncles Leopold and Arthur when they tried to restrain him. He also caused a shock by publicly addressing Queen Victoria as "Duck."

The emperor's unflinching, demanding attitude toward his sons eventually led to strained relationships between the boys and their father. When any of them had committed some transgression, it was always the empress who went to her husband to smooth things out. When it came to these intercessions, Dona never made more than on behalf of her eldest son. The emperor and the crown prince never saw eye to eye, and it almost always fell to Dona to mediate. The concern of a loving mother, though, could not cover over Willy's multitude of sins. Like Eddy of Clarence, Willy was famous for his libertine lifestyle, which was almost certainly a rebellion against his father's dictatorial style of parenting. Just to annoy his father, Willy very publicly aligned himself with the Reichstag's extreme political Far Right "who criticized the Kaiser for being insufficiently nationalist and aggressive, and upset his father even more by deliberately modelling himself on Edward [VII] and his English playboy style." He made Wilhelm and Dona especially angry the last time he visited England, where he and King Edward were "unseemly romping in unlighted corridors" and a lady had "removed her slipper,"[26] behavior that Dona decried as inappropriate. "My wife," Wilhelm told his chancellor in 1908, "has a fanatical hate for the British majesties."[27] "The old fat king," was how Dona once described Edward VII.[28]

Part of the princes' deep love for Dona was rooted in her strong moral character, which time and experience began to make more balanced and less fanatical. When her children were young, the princes received Bible lessons. One day, when the teacher said, "There is no one without sin," little Eitel-Fritz popped up and declared, "That is not true, for my mamma has never sinned."[29] Dona took delight in her close relationship with her children. All of the empress's children grew to love outdoor activities like their mother. Dona was especially fond of tennis, which she played with her family. Wilhelm ensured that tennis courts were installed at each of the family's residences. Her favorite outdoor activity, though, was riding. She made it a point to ride every day if possible. "She was a superb horsewoman," Sissy recalled, "and it was from her that I inherited the passion for riding. But she had to put up with a lot of anxiety, particularly when I galloped away and jumped over obstacles she considered dangerous and which I did not."[30] The empress's exemplary equestrian skills did not mean that accidents never happened. While riding in Sanssouci Park in Potsdam one afternoon in June 1908, Dona's horse tripped and fell on its knee, throwing the empress. "Staff Surgeon Dr. Wiemuth and Prof. Wolff instituted an examination as soon as her Majesty arrived" back at the palace, reported the *New York Times*. "They found that she suffered no injury, except a severe bruise on the back of her right hand, which was bleeding." Even though Dona was lucky that time, the same article reported that this was not an isolated incident.

> This is the fourth time the Empress has had a fall within the last seven years. On one occasion she fell down an incline while in the upper Bavarian lake region. In 1903 she injured her arm in falling from her horse while riding in the Tiergarten, in Berlin ... In the summer of 1907 her Majesty sustained another fall from vertigo while playing lawn tennis at Wilhelmshohe. It is understood that

her Majesty is obliged to take unusual care of herself because of the fact that she is subject to sudden spells of faintness.[31]

Dona's health, which had grown increasingly delicate, prevented her from taking a more hands-on approach with her younger children. Among her most crippling ailments were excruciating migraines that left her incapacitated for days. In this way, her life was strikingly similar to Alexandra of Russia's. Both women were loving wives and mothers, but both were limited in their scopes of activity because of their health problems. Unlike Alexandra, who took morphine, arsenic, and Veronal for her pain, Dona allowed her physician to administer only chloroform in large doses. She suffered so much that sometimes she was given chloroform eleven times in a single day. As much as she railed against her infirmities, the ordinarily tireless empress was forced to reduce her busy schedule from time to time. In those instances when she could not be present at official functions, she was frequently represented by her sister Princess Louise Sophie, who was available whenever her husband, Prince Frederick Leopold, was away on active duty with his regiment in the Prussian army. To help ease her symptoms, Dona also visited the mineral spa at Bad Nauheim in Hesse every year. Although her health would continue to decline in the coming years, she counted herself fortunate that she did not suffer as severely as the empress of Russia. Nor did she let her illnesses interfere with her life the same way Alexandra did; Dona rarely succumbed when her husband or her family were around.

As the heir to both the Prussian and German thrones, Crown Prince Willy naturally received more attention than his brothers from their parents. Following in the Hohenzollern tradition, Willy received a strict education at the military academy at Plön in Schleswig-Holstein. Dona hated being separated from any of her children, but both she and Wilhelm believed firmly in all their children being taught strong discipline. After completing his studies at Plön, the crown prince attended university, but once this period in his life began, he shed all his inhibitions. Since the late 1890s, Willy had told his parents half a dozen times that he intended to marry one woman or another. This was especially painful for Dona, who was a firm believer in the sanctity of royal blood. For any of her sons, let alone the crown prince, to marry morganatically was unforgivable. One woman in particular, an American singer named Geraldine Farrar, caught the crown prince's eye shortly after Queen Victoria's death. When Willy told his parents he planned to marry her, the emperor exploded in shock, anger, and indignation. Dona used all her influence to dissuade her son from marrying his commoner fiancée. After an exhausting meeting that lasted more than two hours, the empress had succeeded.

In 1904, Crown Prince Willy became involved in another romance, but this one led to the altar. This time, Dona was thrilled because Willy's bride-to-be was a princess who came from one of Germany's most prominent royal families. The woman who had caught the profligate crown prince's eye was Cecilie of Mecklenburg-Schwerin, whose pedigree and connections rivaled even the Hohenzollerns—the Mecklenburgs were reportedly "the oldest sovereign house in the Western World." Cecilie's brother, Frederick Francis IV, had been the reigning Grand Duke of Mecklenburg-Schwerin since the age of fifteen; her sister was married to Crown Prince Christian of Denmark; and her mother was a Russian grand duchess and cousin of Alexander III. The official engagement announcement was made in September 1904 during a state dinner Wilhelm and Dona were giving for officials from Schleswig-Holstein. "The announcement was received with great enthusiasm," reported the *New York Times*.[32]

The wedding took place at the Stadtschloss in the unusually hot June of 1905. The official festivities began when Cecilie, accompanied by Empress Augusta Victoria, made her inaugural entry into Berlin on June 4. They rode in the gold carriage of the Prussian kings, used only on the most important occasions. Their carriage took the traditional route through the Brandenburg Gate. As they rode down Unter den Linden, thousands of well-wishers threw roses at the couple. Willy was the first crown prince of the German Empire to get married, prompting so many royal guests to flood into Berlin that it was "one of the most distinguished assemblages that could be gathered in Europe."[33] Sissy wrote how "Cecilie's beauty, grace and charm filled me with astonishment."[34] In keeping with the traditions of the Prussian court, the empress took an active role in each stage of the wedding ceremony. On the morning of the wedding, June 6, she accompanied Cecilie in a gold state landau from Potsdam into Berlin. Just before the wedding, she placed the glistening Prussian bridal crown on the princess's head. When Dr. Ernst von Dryander, the court chaplain, concluded the Lutheran ceremony, Willy and the new crown princess knelt to receive the emperor and empress's blessing. As Dona embraced Cecilie, kissing her on each cheek, she turned to her son and said, "My dear boy, you have made a good choice."[35]

Like so many things in the Hohenzollerns' lives, the wedding was overshadowed by family politics. George and May planned on attending the ceremony, but owing to the fickle relationship between Edward VII and Wilhelm II, their visit was cancelled on the grounds that the Prince and Princess of Wales had "other commitments." Furious, Wilhelm responded by refusing to allow Crown Prince Willy to attend King Edward's birthday celebrations that year. In the end, George and May were barely missed from Willy and Cecilie's nuptials. The wedding went off smoothly, and it did not take long for the new crown princess to become loved in Berlin. She was an "uncommonly favourable" woman whose "grace and natural amiability charm everyone."[36]

Initially, the crown princess joined Dona in promoting charitable causes. One of the more forward-thinking philanthropic organizations they supported was the Central Association of German Actresses. One contemporary wrote that this group, under Dona's tutelage, "has of late years done more toward elevating the stage than has ever been accomplished by members of the aristocracy who have seen fit to join the dramatic profession with that avowed object in view."[37] Cecilie hoped to forge deeper relationships with her new family in Berlin. She naturally looked to Dona for companionship, but the crown princess found her mother-in-law lacking in the ability to do so. The empress was "an excellent, kindly and extremely good and indulgent woman," but she was too "absorbed in her housewifely duties" to truly be a close friend to the crown princess.[38]

Since the Duchess of Teck's death in 1897, the Princess of Wales had appointed herself the matriarch of the Teck family. Periods of grief as well as joy came with this role. One of the happier moments May experienced was the wedding of her favorite brother, Alge, to the king's favorite niece and Prince George's cousin Princess Alice of Albany, in February 1904. It was a propitious match that cemented the Tecks' ties within the British royal family.

If Alge was May's favorite brother, the black sheep of the family continued to be Frank. He enjoyed making fun of royalty, something which offended Princess May's sensibilities. He took particular delight in mocking his sister. Shortly after her wedding, Frank began calling May and George Master and Mistress York. He had earned Queen Victoria's enmity by refusing to participate in or take seriously Mausoleum Day, December 14, the anniversary of Prince Albert's death. The Tecks were aghast by Frank's similar response to the funereal gatherings of Mary Adelaide's family to commemorate the Duchess of Cambridge's death.

Frank publicly embarrassed his family and the monarchy when his name was splattered across the tabloid press when he started up an affair with an older, married woman. The situation threatened to tear the Tecks apart when Frank started giving the woman some of Mary Adelaide's jewels, which had been bequeathed to May. These were no mere trinkets but consisted of a tiara, earrings, a necklace, stomacher, brooch, bracelets, and ring—all of which were covered with the emeralds that had once belonged to the Duchess of Cambridge.

As this personal battle between May and Frank was taking place, a professional gambler approached the Tecks. He informed them that Frank owed him £10,000 and that he "threatened scandal if the loss was not made good."[39] Realizing something had to be done quickly to avoid a scandal, Princess May went to the king. The payment was made, but the royal family had reached the end of its rope with Frank Teck. Edward VII ordered Frank sent back to India for a second exile under the pretense of rejoining his regiment. Frank humiliated his sister when he promptly resigned from the army and refused to leave England. May's place in the royal family, the expectation that she would one day be queen, and her absolute adherence to the monarchy meant there was no choice but for her to sever ties with her unrepentant brother. It was important that the Princess of Wales not be tainted by scandals, personal or otherwise. Along with her official duties, she was also the mother of the next generation of the royal family. She needed to be seen as pure, untainted, and ideally maternal.

On July 12, 1905, she gave birth to her last child after an excruciating labor. The child, born at York Cottage, was a son whom the parents named John. Sir John Williams, the physician in attendance, remained at Sandringham for eight days after the birth to monitor the princess. During her convalescence, George brought her breakfast every morning at nine and then spent much of each day reading to her aloud from her favorite books. John was baptized nearly a month later, on August 3, at Saint Mary Magdalene Church at Sandringham. A dazzling array of godparents were chosen from the four corners of Europe—from the southwest, the king of Portugal; from the southeast, George's cousins Crown Prince Constantine and Crown Princess Sophie of Greece; from the northeast, George's brother-in-law the king of Norway; and from the northwest, Princess Alice of Teck, May's new sister-in-law. There are conflicting reports over whom the prince was named for. One theory states that it was in honor of George's Danish cousin Prince John of Schleswig-Holstein-Sonderburg-Glücksburg. A more widely publicized account is that he was named for George's brother Alexander John, who died shortly after he was born in 1871.

By the time of Prince John's arrival, May was an active, attentive, though noticeably unaffectionate mother who took a dim view of pregnancy, childbirth, and the raising of small children. She echoed Queen Victoria's sentiments and did not enjoy being "with child." May detested how ill she felt during each pregnancy, as well as the limits it placed on her official duties. "Of course it is a great bore for me & requires a great deal of patience to bear it, but this is alas the penalty of being a woman!" she once wrote to her husband.[40] Like other high-ranking women of that era, she saw her children on a limited basis, usually twice each day in the morning and at tea time. She also entrusted the care of her children to a governess. Some of these women were inept.

One of them was even abusive. Mary Peters harbored an almost obsessive desire for May's two eldest sons, David and Bertie, but in different ways. With David, Peters was obsessively controlling. She always needed to have him with her. During her time employed by the Wales family, she did not spend even one day away from him. With Bertie, things took on a more malevolent tone. Peters obsessively resented the prince, whom she would summarily punish by refusing to feed him. Evidence has since emerged indicating that Peters misfed Bertie "so badly that he was afflicted for the rest of his life by digestive problems."[41] Determined to keep the children in her care as much as possible, Peters would twist and pinch the children's arms when they were taken to have tea with their parents. When they began to cry in front of May and George for no obvious reason, they were quickly returned to Peters' care. This abuse had a profound impact on Bertie. He developed a crippling speech impediment around the age of four or five, which lasted well into adulthood. It was only when a new, much-loved governess named Charlotte Bill was brought into the household that the abuse came to an end after the shocking length of three years. Bill—who, unlike the rest of the Wales' staff, was not afraid of Peters—reported what was going on to the head of the household, who in turn informed an incredulous and furious Princess May. At first, Peters refused to vacate the premises, though she was gone by that night. A week later, she ended up in hospital after suffering a complete nervous breakdown.

Once word of the Mary Peters imbroglio leaked out, criticism for May and George's parenting erupted like a mushroom cloud. "The tragedy was that neither had any understanding of a child's mind," admitted May's friend the Countess of Airlie. "They had not succeeded in making their children happy."[42] In private, the Princess of Wales could enjoy some shared activities with her children. There was no question that between herself and her husband, it was the princess who could be more fun-loving. According to David, when his father was not around, his mother "was an amusing woman."[43] This is rather surprising given George's rowdy childhood. In his youth, he and his siblings shocked visitors at Marlborough House with their antics. Queen Victoria considered George and Eddy to be among the most ill-bred, ill-trained, raucous children she had ever seen. Young George once received a reprimand from Queen Victoria for some minor infraction and was ordered to sit under the dining room table. When the queen summoned him a few minutes later, the little prince reportedly emerged completely naked.

The then Princess Alexandra was largely responsible for George's unbecoming behavior, regularly encouraging her children to play practical jokes. When a stunned onlooker questioned her children's behavior, Alexandra merely shrugged and admitted she had been worse at that age. By the time George was a father, he had shed the frivolous gaiety of his childhood. As an adult, the Prince of Wales had little use for jokes or lightheartedness. According to his son David, George "retained a gruff blue-water approach to all human situations. I have often felt that despite his undoubted affection for all of us, my father preferred children in the abstract."[44]

Compared to her husband, May was seen as much more affectionate. David once fondly wrote of his mother, "Her soft voice, her cultivated mind, the cosy room overflowing with personal treasures were all inseparable ingredients of the happiness associated with ... a child's day ... Such was my mother's pride in her children that everything that happened to each one was of the utmost importance to her. With the birth of each new child, Mama started an album in which she painstakingly recorded each progressive stage of our childhood."[45] The infanta Eulalia of Spain, a famous European courtesan, thought very highly of May's parenting: "As a mother she stands unequalled; well may her children arise and call her blessed! Her heart has been their home since their birth; to them she has always been the mother and friend ... and no shadow of the throne has ever darkened the happy youth of her charming sons and her idolized daughter."[46]

In October 1905, George and May set off for another extended international tour. This time their travels took them to India and the Far East. May was determined to go forward with as much knowledge as she could possibly have. She wrote before the trip, "We ... are having a nice restful time. I am reading books on India which are most interesting, I read nearly all morning when I have not letters to write."[47] For this second trip abroad, the royal couple would be gone for eight months. Their children were once again being left in the care of King Edward and Queen Alexandra, who lovingly called her grandchildren "the Georgie pets." The accommodations for this trip would be a cut above the colonial tour. Instead of the scrappy steamship *Ophir* to ferry them, George and May traveled on the HMS *Renown*, Britain's newest ship of the line. They made their way to Genoa, where they boarded the *Renown* for India.

When they arrived in Calcutta in late October, the British viceroy Lord Minto already had the Government House ready and waiting for them. It was the first time a Princess of Wales had set foot in India, and May was very glad that she had taken the time to read up on this ancient and beautiful country. "Thanks to the amount of Indian reading which I have done I really am not so ignorant about India as most of the English women here are," she wrote back to Hélène Bricka, her old governess.[48] May's arrival in India was truly unique and went a long way to establishing the credibility of both herself and the monarchy in the eyes of the Indian people.

> The visit of the then Princess of Wales to India was an innovation of which many an experienced official was admittedly afraid ... The presence of a woman where a woman had never been before, in a land where the status of women is so different ... might easily have spoilt the issues most desired from the tour;... The ardent interest in the life of the people which the Princess showed won at once an eager response from them, and completed in a manner which India had never known its sense of gratitude to Royal favour ... the Princess added a womanly sympathy which as a regal quality only existed for India as a tradition of the Great Queen [Victoria].[49]

The Prince and Princess of Wales were awestruck by India's majestic beauty, as well as by the incredible welcome they received from the people. At the opening ceremony of their visit, George made a moving speech about the deep impact the country had made on himself and his wife: "Here we are truly in a new world, and, from the moment when we arrived in your State to this hour, one charming impression has been quickly followed by another."[50] Along with Calcutta, the royal couple made visits to Bombay, Peshawar, Rangoon, Mandalay, Mysore, Benares, and Chaman. India made a deep and lasting impact on May, who later said, "when I die India will be written on my heart."[51]

The voyage home was in itself another international tour. The first stop was Egypt, complete with a visit to the Pyramids. "I did not ascend the Pyramid, it was too much of a climb," May wrote to Aunt Augusta, "but I did ride a camel and rather really liked it."[52] From Egypt, the royal party moved on to Greece, where it truly turned into a family affair. George's uncle was King George I of Greece. Known in the family as "Uncle Willy," this brother of Queen Alexandra and Marie Feodorovna of Russia was chosen to be king of the Hellenes in 1863 at the age of eighteen. Thanks to the ambitious matchmaking of their father, King Christian IX of Denmark, the Danish royal family had a monopoly on Europe. They were directly connected with the royal families of Britain, Russia, Greece, Norway, Sweden, Serbia, and Germany. Edward VII once remarked that at the Danish royal family's famed reunions at Fredensborg, one could hear seven different languages being spoken at any given time. George's aunt Queen Olga of Greece—like so many of Europe's other royal consorts—was a Romanov grand duchess and cousin to Alexander III. She was very fond of May and had been one of the voices encouraging George to propose to her. It was in Athens that George and May also met up with his parents and his sister Toria. Princess May, true to her academic nature, could not help but take advantage of the opportunity to see some of Greece's historic monuments. In the company of her husband's Greek cousins, she spent a day touring the Parthenon, the Propylaea, and the Nike Temple. George preferred to visit one of his favorite spots in the country, the Tatoi Palace, located three miles north of Athens, which he said reminded him of Scotland.

Of all the exotic places Princess May visited on this tour abroad, it was her visit to Spain in May 1906 before returning to England that had the greatest significance politically, dynastically, and historically. While still in India, the Prince and Princess of Wales learned of the engagement of George's cousin Princess Victoria Eugenie of Battenberg ("Ena") to King Alfonso XIII of Spain. As a young girl, Ena had been a bridesmaid at May and George's wedding. Now it was young Ena's turn. The only daughter of Queen Victoria's youngest daughter, Beatrice, Ena was marrying the spindly, twenty-year-old king of Spain. However dazzling a dynastic marriage it may have been, it was still littered with obstacles. There had not been a union between the royal houses of England and Spain in more than four hundred years, not since Henry VIII's daughter Queen Mary wed Philip II of Spain. Although it was undoubtedly an illustrious union between two powerful reigning houses, the greatest question to be overcome was that of religion. By the dawn of the twentieth century, the royal houses of Europe had divided themselves more or less into chiefly Protestant and Catholic camps. With few exceptions, the Catholic courts of Portugal, Austria, Spain, and Italy only married among themselves. The same was true for the predominantly northern Protestant nations like England, the Netherlands, the Scandinavian courts, and Germany. An Anglican English princess marrying the Catholic king of Spain was controversial enough to begin with, but when Ena—a favorite granddaughter of Queen Victoria—converted to the Catholic faith, a public relations nightmare ensued. Anti-Catholic sentiments in England were so strong that, after Ena and Alfonso became engaged, George wrote to May, "Beatrice is advised on her return to England to keep Ena quiet somewhere, at Osborne, and not to bring her to London as the feeling is so strong."[53]

Religion was not the only challenge facing Ena. Like Princess May, Ena of Battenberg had morganatic blood on her father's side. Grand Duchess Augusta thought little of May's Battenberg relatives, prompting her to write, "So Ena is to become Spanish Queen! A Battenberg, good gracious!"[54] Ena also shared similarities with another of her reigning cousins—Alexandra of Russia. Like the tsarina, Ena's life in Spain would be stained by tragedy. She too was a carrier of hemophilia and would pass it on to two of her sons, albeit with far less calamitous consequences for the Spanish royal family.

For this significant wedding, George and May were representing the British royal family. Ordinarily, an event of this magnitude would have required the presence of the king and queen, but their presence at such a controversial event was unfathomable. The death of the queen's father, the king of Denmark, in January 1906 gave the monarchs a get-out-of-jail-free card to send the Prince and Princess of Wales instead. When they arrived in Spain, it became clear that the country's reputation as the most rigidly formal court in Europe was well earned. Their apartments at the Royal Palace in Madrid—which contained more than 250 suites for visiting dignitaries alone—were guarded by halberdiers standing at each of the marble pillars stretching down the wide hallways in every direction. Every time the Wales' left their rooms, the guards would sound a clap and shout to one another, *"Arriba Princesa! Arriba Principe!!"*[55]

The morning of the wedding, May 31, 1906, was pristine with a sunny, cloudless blue sky. Thousands of people congested the streets of Madrid. In the courtyard of the Royal Palace, bejeweled state carriages ferried their royal passengers to the Church of San Jeronimo, near the famous Prado Museum. As heirs to the British throne and cousins of the bride, George and May were seated in the front row of the long, narrow church. The ceremony was a strict but haunting Catholic service, followed immediately by a nuptial mass performed by Cardinal Sancha, the archbishop of Toledo. After the three-hour ceremony, as the bridal carriage made its way through the crowded streets, tragedy struck when a madman, perched on the fourth-floor balcony of an overlooking house, threw a bomb at the king and his new queen. Ena and Alfonso were unharmed, but dozens were wounded, and a number of people were killed. By the time Alfonso and Ena arrived at the palace, the queen was hysterical. "I saw a man without any legs! I saw a man without any legs!" she kept muttering.[56] The reception that followed was eerily silent, despite the presence of five thousand guests. Ena's aunt Princess Marie of Erbach-Schönberg recalled how "every attempt at cheerfulness failed miserably." The one person who shone out was the Princess of Wales. She "was superb and remained calm, giving Ena the support that she badly needed." According to Princess Frederica of Hanover, May "was the only one to show proper feeling."[57]

After lunch, the guests retired to their rooms to inform their relatives they were safe. May wrote the following to her aunt Augusta:

> Well we have been thro' a most unpleasant experience & we can
> only thank God that the anarchist did not get into the church in

which case we must all have been blown up! Nothing could have been braver than the young people were, but what a beginning for her [Ena].... I saw the coach one day, still with blood on the wheels & behind where the footmen were standing—apart from the horror of this awful attempt the visit to Madrid was most interesting but oh! the heat was nearly as bad as India & made one feel quite exhausted.... I liked seeing the fine pictures, palace, Escurial, Armoury etc.[58]

It was three days before Ena and Alfonso's would-be assassin, Matteo Morral, was apprehended. When cornered by police, Morral shot and killed a police officer before committing suicide. For those three days while Morral was still on the loose, tension among the visiting royals remained high. Princess May was one of the few guests who ventured out in public, unafraid that Morral would make another attempt on the lives of the king, his new queen, or their guests. Even Prince George refused to be seen in public, but his wife's courage made a profound impact on everyone around her. "She was magnificent, as brave as a lion," remarked Ena's brother Alexander of Battenberg. "She was frightened of nothing."[59] May's experiences in Spain were once-in-a-lifetime preparations for her future as queen and empress. Her actions under these circumstances, demonstrated in the presence of some of the highest-ranking royals in the world, established her reputation for bravery, dignity, and levelheadedness.

Only a matter of days after the Wales returned to England from Spain, they were off again. This time, they were aboard the royal yacht *Victoria and Albert* bound for Norway, where George's sister Maud and her husband, Haakon[60], were being crowned the first queen and king of Norway, which had recently declared its independence from Sweden after nearly a century. "A letter this time from the far North! we do love to travel about to be sure," May wrote to Aunt Augusta. "We had lovely weather at first but then it turned cold & we had much wind & rain which was unpleasant for landing from the yacht in evening dress when the boat jumps up & down!"[61] In the months leading up to the ceremony, May and Maud were in close contact. As early as March 1906, a full three months before the coronation, Maud confided to May her fears about the very public ritual. "It all haunts me like an *awful* nightmare this Coronation and that it is *just* to be ours of all people," Maud wrote. "Think of me *alone* on my throne, having a crown to be shoved on my head which is very small and heavy by the aged Bishop, and a Minister and also has to be put on by them before the *whole* crowd!! and oil to put on my head, hands and *bosom*!! Gracious, it will be awful!"[62]

The coronation was performed at Trondheim, the site of Norway's medieval coronations. The local fjordic scenery lent itself well to creating a festive atmosphere in Trondheim, which was only a few hundred miles from the Arctic Circle. The ceremony on June 22, 1906, tested the easily rattled nerves of May's demure sister-in-law. The new queen consort of Norway shared May's dislike of public attention, but unlike the Princess of Wales, Maud had much more difficulty acquitting herself with ease in the spotlight. One witness thought Queen Maud looked quite pale "as she walked up the long choir, returning the salutations on each side of her." Not surprisingly, Aunt Augusta did not approve of May's attending the coronation. After separating from Sweden in 1905, Norway had voted to elect Maud's husband as king, but such a notion proved too much for the grandiose Augusta. She bluntly told May, "A *revolutionary* Coronation! such a *farce*, I don't like your being there for it, it looks like *sanctioning* all that nasty Revolution.... How can a future K. & Q. of E. go to witness a Coronation '*par la grace du Peuple et de la Révolution!!!*' makes me sick and I should say, *you too*." May did not feel as strongly as her aunt, though, and wrote back that "the whole thing seems curious, but we live in *very* modern days."[63]

This latest separation from her children brought May's parenting into the public eye yet again, once more earning her no shortage of criticism. Shortly before Ena and Alfonso's wedding, May was faced with a parenting crisis of sorts with each of her children. David began showing signs of deafness in one ear; Bertie's stammer was becoming worse, as too were his knock-knees, which required him to wear painful splints day and night; Mary had become a disruptive influence on her brothers during their lessons; Harry had uncontrollable fits of both crying and laughing; and George broke down sobbing in his mother's presence. Unlike most modern-day parents, May refused to address these issues, at least until after the visits to Spain and Norway. One of May's biographers observed the following:

> Modern psychologists believe that George and Mary took too little trouble to understand their children. Whereas Edward and Alexandra spoiled the grandchildren, their son and his wife wished to see a return to sound Victorian educational standards and moral behaviour. Implicit obedience was exacted from sons. Disobedience brought instant retribution. It seemed as though in rooting out the bad they sometimes overlooked the good in their offspring.... Consequently they committed blunders over their sons' training which, except in degree, differed little from the academic extremism which made George III's sons what they

became and was incredibly repeated by Victoria and the Prince Consort in the case of Edward.[64]

The Empress Frederick once wrote that May "does not seem to have the passionate tenderness for her little ones wh. seems so natural to me." She also said May "has something very cold and stiff—& distant in her manner—each time one sees her again one has to break the ice afresh."[65] This was an ironic statement coming from Vicky, since she herself had been on the receiving end of some very harsh criticism for her own mothering in the way she raised Wilhelm II, Charly, and her other children. May was not a hands-on mother who ever made maudlin displays of affection the way Queen Alexandra did. The princess's distaste for and repulsion of illnesses meant she took a stiff, inflexible, sometimes even unsympathetic approach with her children when they were sick. Her expectation was for them to respond to it the same way she would.

It would be ungenerous to say that the Princess of Wales was a cold, distant mother and nothing else. She made an effort to create a tranquil home life for her children—free from scandals, drama, and the other tribulations that plagued her own childhood. Nonetheless, her parenting style is somewhat ironic given how affectionate her own parents were. Historians seem to be divided over Princess May as a mother. Some praise her virtues like her strength, others criticize her aloofness. Few seem to have found middle ground. A careful review of all the facts shows that Princess May was both. There certainly is no doubt that she lacked maternal instincts toward young children—the same was often said of Queen Victoria, but in her later years the queen became very affectionate with her grandchildren. Affectionate is a word that would never be associated with May—even later in life. But those qualities for which May was criticized—her reserved emotions, outward calm, and ostensible aloofness—would become invaluable assets in the decades ahead. These qualities would even help the British monarchy survive one of the greatest crises in its history.

10

Life's Unexpected Trials

(1905–10)

The humiliating end to the Russo-Japanese War was only the beginning of Alexandra's problems in Saint Petersburg. The war had once and for all stripped away the facade of impenetrability that surrounded the Romanov dynasty. In June 1905, the crew of the battleship *Potemkin*, docked at Odessa on the Black Sea, mutinied. In no time, the revolt spread into Odessa itself, where fighting to suppress the uprising resulted in two thousand people dead. Before the crew of the *Potemkin* could be apprehended, the "crew sailed the ship to Romania and liberty."[1] For the first time, Russia's disaffected masses began to see that autocracy was more vulnerable than they had been led to believe. Things got so bad that "between Bloody Sunday and the late fall, Nicholas and his military advisers assigned 15,297 companies of infantry and 3,665 squadrons of cavalry, with 224 cannon and 124 machine guns, to suppress strikes and peasant riots."[2]

Almost all essential services in Moscow and Saint Petersburg shut down. Banks, grocery stores, public transportation, telegraph stations, and even running water stopped functioning because the workers had walked off their jobs. Mob violence swept cities and towns as people sang "La Marseillaise" and began crying out for a republic and an end to autocracy. Instead of fighting pockets of revolutionaries, the government was forced to contend with a mutinous population that numbered in the millions. Unrest soon spread beyond Russia into its imperial territories. Within a few months, Riga and Warsaw were on strike.

There was little doubt that control was slipping from the government's hands. Throughout the summer, foreign newspapers were reporting rumors that the tsar would be deposed, with Alexei taking his place under the regency of four senior grand dukes. In the end, it was Count Serge Witte, one of Russia's most able statesmen, who devised a solution. He called it the October Manifesto. This document promised the people civil liberties, such as freedom of religion and speech, as well as Russia's first elected assembly, whose votes would be required to make law. When Witte presented the manifesto to Nicholas, only one other person was present: Alexandra. "The Empress," the count recalled, "sat stiff as a ramrod, her face lobster-red, and did not utter a single word." Determined to preserve autocracy, Nicholas II was unwilling to sign the manifesto. It fell to his cousin Grand Duke Nicholas Nicholaievich ("Nikolasha"), the levelheaded, tall, imposing commander of the Russian military, to force the tsar to accept progress. Furious that his cousin was unwilling to accept reforms, Nikolasha stormed into the Winter Palace and declared, "I'm going now to the Czar and I will beg him to sign the manifesto and the Witte program. Either he signs or in his presence I will put a bullet through my head with this revolver."[3] Pressed between a rock and a hard place, the tsar accepted the manifesto on October 17, 1905. With the stroke of a pen, he ended three centuries of absolute rule by the Romanovs. In a letter to his mother, Nicholas II poured out his justification for accepting the end of autocracy in Russia.

> There were only two ways open: To find an energetic soldier and crush the rebellion by sheer force ... that would mean rivers of blood and in the end we should be where we started ... The other way out would be to give the people their civil rights, freedom of speech and press, also to have all laws confirmed by State Duma— that of course would be a constitution. Witte defends this very energetically.
>
> From all over Russia they cried for it, they begged for it, and around me many—very many—held the same views ... There was no other way out than to cross oneself and give what everyone was asking for. My only consolation is that such is the will of God, and this grave decision will lead my dear Russia out of the intolerable chaos she has been in for nearly a year.[4]

The reactions to the manifesto were swift and sharp. "That was the end, the end of the dynasty and the end of the empire," wrote Sandro, Alexandra's brother-in-law. "A brave jump from the precipice would have spared us the agony of the remaining twelve years."[5] The Russian aristocrat Princess

Galitzine observed that "something great was crashing—as if all Russian tradition had been annihilated by a single blow."[6]

Under the October Manifesto, Russia convened its first parliament, the Duma, in April 1906. Dressed in her imperial finery with pearls, diamonds, sash, and a flowing train, Alexandra accompanied Nicholas and Minnie to the opening session in the Saint George Room of the Winter Palace. As the imperial party entered the hall, the looks of hatred for the tsar and tsarina from the Duma members were unmistakable. "They looked at us as upon their enemies, and I could not make myself stop looking at certain faces, so much did they seem to reflect an incomprehensible hatred for all of us," the dowager empress admitted.[7] This was a sentiment that Sandro agreed with. "I saw burning hatred in the faces of some of the parliamentarians," he recalled.[8] Members of the imperial family were not the only ones to notice the hostility in the Duma. Count Vladimir Fredericks, the head of the imperial household, observed, "They gave one the impression of a gang of criminals who are only waiting for the signal to throw themselves upon the Ministers and cut their throats. What wicked faces! I will never again set foot among those people."[9] The reaction of the Duma was not surprising when its composition is examined. One contemporary noted that "out of the nearly 493 members, 380 have been elected. Of these, the Government can count on the support of 20."[10] The existential realities of both the Duma and the Romanov monarchy meant that these two forces would be diametrically opposed. "The Romanovs ruled Russia by dint of superstition disguised as religious faith," wrote one Russian historian. "As democrats, they made no sense at all."[11]

Russia's mounting woes weighed heavily on Tsarina Alexandra, but there were more than political tribulations burdening her. She was deeply troubled by Alexei's hemophilia, which Russia's forty court doctors were powerless to combat. There was nothing that medical science could do for the heir to the throne. If Alexandra was going to find any relief for her son—whom she and Nicholas affectionately called "Baby"—she would have to do it herself. That relief came in the form of an unkempt, scraggly peasant from Siberia named Gregory Rasputin. Born Gregory Efimovich Novik and raised in the distant village of Pokrovskoie in the remote Russian wilderness, Rasputin—a epithet which meant "Vagabond" or "the Debauched"—was tall and burly with mysterious, dark eyes and a long, disheveled black beard. His meeting with Alexandra and Nicholas came in 1905, after it was arranged through a mutual friend, Anna Viroubova. "We've made the acquaintance of a man of God, Grigory from the Tobolsk Guberniya," the tsar wrote in his diary.[12]

Rasputin's arrival on the scene provided an answer to the empress's prayers. Day in and day out, she was consumed by grief over her son's health. Her feelings were largely ones of guilt for having passed the defective genes for hemophilia on to Alexei. This only exacerbated her own health problems, which were getting worse: "For days on end, she could be found in the Mauve Boudoir lying on her sofa, suffering from very real and acute pains in the head, back, legs, or heart."[13] Added to these were difficulty breathing, panic attacks, neuralgia in her facial muscles, and constant earaches. The distress over her son's dangerous disease caused Alexandra to suffer a complete breakdown, both physically and mentally. Her ailments, many of which had come and gone throughout the years, completely overtook her. There were many theories as to their origins. Her physician, Dr. Eugene Botkin, believed the symptoms were psychosomatic. Others ascribed them to a childhood injury that had never healed properly; shortly after her mother's death, little Princess Alix fell through a glass window, leaving her legs shredded and bleeding. This caused her to walk with a pronounced limp for many years. Others—mostly modern scholars—have theorized she was a victim of porphyria, the genetic disorder that is believed to have afflicted King George III and Dona's sister-in-law Charly. Whatever the source, Alexandra's symptoms had a very real impact on her body. Her five pregnancies, almost back to back, also took a heavy toll on her. These pregnancies were almost constant for ten years, and each proved worse than the last. Under circumstances such as these, it is not surprising that Alexandra succumbed to an endless list of maladies. Her poor state of health was also a constant source of worry for Nicky. He once admitted to his mother that he was "completely run down mentally by worrying over her health."[14]

In her moments of despair, Alexandra turned to her faith. She was convinced that all was in God's hands, and according to Anna Viroubova and some of the other mystic members of the Romanovs, so was Rasputin. Father Gregory, as they called him, reputedly had the power to perform miracles. These included (but were not limited to) curing disease, healing wounds, and even stopping the flow of blood. This ability, combined with his own personal endorsement as a supposed miracle worker from God Himself, made this Siberian monk, this cipher, invaluable to Alexandra of Russia.

With Crown Prince Willy married, it was not long before the Prussian royal family expanded again. In February 1906, Dona's son Eitel-Fritz married Sophie-Charlotte ("Lotte") of Oldenburg at the Stadtschloss. At both the civil and religious ceremonies held on the wedding day, the bride wore a pearl-white silk dress with a four-yard-long train and a crown of diamonds set in green velvet. The couple had met at Willy and Cecilie's wedding when they were introduced to each other by the empress. Augusta Victoria considered Lotte a suitable choice for her son because not only was Lotte's mother a Prussian princess but the empress considered the Oldenburg women to be "quiet, inoffensive, and suitable for a prince."[15] Their engagement was announced in October 1905 at Glücksburg, where the emperor and empress were attending the wedding of Dona's niece to Wilhelm's cousin the Duke of Coburg. Unlike Willy and Cecilie, Eitel-Fritz and Lotte were mismatched from the beginning. Since reaching adulthood, Wilhelm II had been concerned about rumors surrounding the wayward and immoral Eitel-Fritz. Dona was equally troubled. She even encouraged her son Oscar, who was by then serving in the Prussian army, to avoid visiting Potsdam too often because she was afraid that Eitel-Fritz would be a negative influence on him. The only remedy Dona and Wilhelm could think of was for Eitel-Fritz to get married as quickly as possible.

There was no facade that his marriage to Lotte was a love match. It was one of convenience over anything else, especially for the attractive and wealthy bride. Lotte had lived most of her life under the watchful eye of her burdensome stepmother, the Grand Duchess of Oldenburg. Eager to escape her life in Oldenburg, the prospect of marrying into the Prussian royal family appealed to her greatly. But it became clear within a matter of weeks of the wedding that the union was not a happy one. Eitel-Fritz continued his dalliances with other women, leaving his wife to occupy herself for days at a stretch. Gracious and proud, Lotte did not utter a word of complaint or animosity toward the prince or his family at the time. She simply retreated to her castle in the Tiergarten and painted, read, and entertained a few close friends. According to one contemporary, when Lotte "found out what a sorry personage she had linked her fate with she withdrew into a kind of haughty reserve, from which she has never emerged."[16]

While Eitel-Fritz and Lotte were on their honeymoon, Augusta Victoria and Wilhelm celebrated their twenty-fifth wedding anniversary. The actual date of their anniversary fell on the day Eitel-Fritz and Lotte were married, so festivities were postponed for a few days. The royal publicity machine was hard at work producing memorabilia to commemorate the milestone. The most popular item created was a photograph of the emperor and empress "in a sort of cloud floating above a bird's-eye view of Berlin, with the palace and the cathedral dimly seen below."[17] The official celebrations in Prussia were suitably grand. King Edward VII sent his brother-in-law Prince Christian of Schleswig-Holstein-Sonderburg-Augustenburg as his personal representative. As Dona's uncle, the choice of Christian was a personal one designed to highlight the bonds between their two empires. On February 26, the emperor and empress received deputations from the Reichstag and several other government organizations offering their best wishes. In lieu of gifts, the couple asked for money to be donated to German charities. The mayor of Berlin proudly told Wilhelm that the city raised $125,000 for a number of charitable organizations.

After a quarter of a century, Dona and Wilhelm enjoyed a strong marriage. They endured difficulties that other couples would not have been able to weather. As they grew older, they became more devoted to one another, realizing their need for each other's strengths. When they attended a banquet during a visit to Dona's ancestral homeland of Schleswig-Holstein in 1890, the emperor presented a speech in which he devotedly sung his wife's praises: "The bond that unites me to this province, and chains me to it in a manner different from all others of my Empire, is the jewel that sparkles at my side—Her Majesty the Empress. Sprung from this soil, the type of the various virtues of a German princess [*sic*] it is to her that I owe it that I am able to meet the severe labours of my office with a happy spirit, and make head against them."[18] On another occasion, Wilhelm proudly called his wife a "pearl among women ... [forged] from her works of charity to the poor and suffering, and from her strengthening and fostering of the security and domestic life of our people."[19]

In some ways, their relationship mirrored that of Nicholas and Alexandra, who wrote touching love notes to one another. Though Dona and Wilhelm were not given to public displays of affection, they were deeply emotional in their private letters. "Last night I dreamt of you so vividly, darling," Dona wrote in one such letter. "At first you were quite out of my reach, then you came to me and I clung to you so tightly so as not to let you go again. You were wearing something very strange on your head, but in my dream I told you how well it suited you, and then of course you had to go away again."[20] One historian noted that, even after so many years, the emperor and empress were still "very good friends. They have two things in common, an intense love of religion and their children." Dona shone as an example of strong moral character: "Intellectually she is not the Kaiser's equal, but she is a good mother and is ever busying herself with work among the poor. The Kaiser is very proud of her; he still believes her beautiful."[21]

The revelry for Wilhelm and Augusta Victoria's silver wedding anniversary created a celebratory atmosphere in Prussia that helped remind the public of their interest in the royal family. The birth of the emperor and empress's first grandchild on their twenty-fifth anniversary year helped further cement the monarchy's popularity that year. On July 4, 1906, Crown Princess Cecilie gave birth to a son that was named—what else?—Wilhelm. At the time, the crown prince and princess were living at the Marble Palace until their new home, the Cecilienhof Palace, could be completed. At the time of the delivery, the emperor was on a Norwegian getaway, and the crown prince was off on a hunting trip with his friends. Willy returned home when Cecilie went into labor but made his annoyance at having to leave his friends apparent to everyone. In the end, the only person who was there "to encourage and soothe" the crown princess "during her trial" was Dona.[22] When the infant was only a few hours old, the crown prince left the Marble Palace and returned to his hunting trip, leaving the empress to comfort her exhausted daughter-in-law and new grandson. The succession to the Prusso-German throne was now secure for another two generations. The fact that Dona's first grandchild—and a boy, no less—was born on the twenty-fifth anniversary of her wedding to her beloved Wilhelm helped to assuage, somewhat, the guilt of seeing Eitel-Fritz's marriage collapse. Dona's growing guilt over his marriage came from the role she played in getting the couple together.

Something else that helped take Dona's mind off her son's failing marriage was yet another visit to Britain. Unlike in previous years, this time Wilhelm had no desire to see his British relatives. Anglo-German relations were at an all-time low, and the emperor tried to get out of the visit by using the false excuse of suffering from bronchitis. Edward VII was not amused by his nephew's antics. "Your telegram has greatly upset me," he wrote to Wilhelm, "as your not coming to England would be a terrible disappointment to us all—my family—and the British nation. Beg of you to reconsider your decision." The emperor knew Edward's telegram was an attempt to discredit him diplomatically, so Wilhelm relented. The original plan was for the emperor to go alone; his daughter was sick with chicken pox, and the empress insisted on caring for her herself. At the last minute, when Sissy showed some improvement, Dona "changed her mind ... and decided at a late hour to-night to accompany Emperor William on his visit to England."[23]

He and Dona arrived at Victoria Station on November 13, 1907. Prince George, dressed in his Prussian field marshal's uniform, met them. Despite the ebbing relations between the German and British monarchies, the people of London gave the emperor and empress a hearty welcome. "There were great crowds in the street and they got a splendid reception," George wrote.[24] Wilhelm recalled the visit in his memoirs more than a decade later: "In the late autumn of 1907 the Empress and I paid a visit to Windsor, at the invitation of King Edward VII. We were most cordially received by the English royal family and the visit went off harmoniously."[25]

The English visit became a royal affair *en famille*, with a horde of other royals coming to Britain at the same time. Visiting Windsor Castle at the same time as Wilhelm and Dona was Queen Maud of Norway, Edward VII's daughter; Queen Amélie of Portugal; and King Alfonso XIII and Queen Victoria Eugenie of Spain. The *New York Times* described it as "a larger assemblage of royalties than had ever taken place" at Windsor Castle."[26]

In a formal portrait taken at Windsor to commemorate the visit, Dona is seated between the much-younger queens Ena and Amélie. She is turned away from the camera, in what is most likely an attempt at striking a formal stately pose. Unlike Wilhelm, who could still charm his relatives, Dona's haughty demeanor made her no friends among the queens of Norway, Spain, or Portugal.

The weeklong visit was a whirlwind. The town of Windsor put on a medieval pageant for Dona and Wilhelm, who told the crowds gathered there that they made him feel as if he were "coming home." King Edward was the epitome of hospitality. He commented on what "good health" Their Majesties appeared to be in but was greatly relieved when the visit was over. "Thank God he's gone!" he muttered crossly as he watched the emperor and empress depart.[27] Lord Esher was equally unimpressed with the German sovereigns. "Our King makes a better show than William II," he wrote. "He has more graciousness and dignity. William is ungraceful, nervous and plain. There is no 'atmosphere' about him."[28] At the end of the visit, the emperor left a $10,000 tip for the staff, gamekeepers, and stable attendants at Windsor Castle. Before returning to Germany, Wilhelm went up to Highcliffe Castle in Dorset, while Dona traveled on to the Netherlands to meet with Queen Wilhelmina.

As an attempt at improving Anglo-German relations, the British visit ultimately proved futile. Three days after Dona and Wilhelm returned to Berlin, the proposals were published for the historic German Navy Bill that the Reichstag passed in 1908. The controversial legislation raised eyebrows across the continent and was one of imperial Germany's most significant steps toward provoking a war with Britain for mastery of the seas. The bill called for an increase in the production of battleships and a shorter lifespan on vessels, so they could be replaced more frequently. During this period, Dona paid little attention to domestic politics because her energies were focused on another family wedding. Her son Auwi married his first cousin Princess Alexandra Victoria of Schleswig-Holstein-Sonderburg-Glücksburg on October 22, 1908—Dona's fiftieth birthday. The wedding, held at 5:00 p.m. in the Berlin palace, was attended by more than eight hundred guests. Like previous Prussian royal weddings, a civil ceremony was carried out in one of the palace's private apartments. When this ceremony was completed, Dona placed the bridal crown upon Alexandra Victoria's head, and everyone proceeded to the chapel for the religious service. The bride wore "a white silk dress trimmed with lace, and her train, which was richly embroidered with silver and thirteen feet long, was borne by four pages."[29] At the reception that followed in the palace's White Hall, the number of guests swelled to two thousand.

As the matriarch of the House of Hohenzollern, Augusta Victoria went to great lengths to see her children married to suitable partners. If the crown prince's marriage was dynastic, and Eitel-Fritz's was to stave off gossip, then Auwi's was of a more personal nature. The empress herself had arranged the union, since Alexandra Victoria was her sister Calma's daughter. Dona's daughter Sissy admitted that though she and Calma "were vastly different personalities ... they clung together with a deep, inner love which was later strengthened by the marriage of Calma's daughter, Alexandra, to my brother Auwi."[30] Alexandra Victoria was considered the most beautiful, and the favorite, of Dona's daughters-in-law. Princess Catherine Radziwill observed that the princess "had always shown herself willing to listen to her mother-in-law. She is a nice girl—fair, fat, and a perfect type of the 'Deutsche Hausfrau' dear to the souls of German novel-writers."[31] But after being married for a short time, Alexandra Victoria quickly earned a reputation for being sarcastic and snide. Beyond the empress's circle of friends, who were watching Alexandra Victoria closely, most people at court were concerned about the serious blow that Anglo-German relations suffered with the creation of the Navy Bill. Any pretext of amity between the two empires was fading, marking the beginning of an antagonistic relationship between London and Berlin that would only get worse over the next six years.

The tranquility Princess Zita experienced at her boarding school in Bavaria was shattered in November 1907 when her father died from heart disease. According to the *New York Times*, the Duke of Parma bequeathed his children, in addition to their many homes, a fortune in cash that was worth $40 million at the time.[32] This was one of the largest cash inheritances in royal history, estimated at approximately $942 million today.[33] Settling the late duke's estate caused a serious break within the Bourbon-Parmas. The head of the family and new titular duke was Zita's thirty-five-year-old, mentally disabled half brother Enrico. An Austrian court eventually ruled that six of the other children from Robert's first marriage were mentally unfit to care for themselves. Prince Elias, one of Zita's many half brothers, became the legal guardian of those six siblings, including Enrico. This meant that almost all of the Bourbon-Parma fortune was given over to Elias and the other children from Robert I's marriage to Maria Pia. Two of Zita's full brothers—Sixtus and René—sued Elias for a greater share of the family fortune but lost in court.

For Zita, who was only fifteen years old, the money was of little interest. What was probably the most hurtful to her during this already difficult time was the significant schism from her older half siblings. Robert's death and the messy court battle that followed marked a turning point in her life, effectively ending her happy childhood. In the weeks that followed the emotional funeral, Zita was at a loss, perhaps for the first time in her life. She idolized her father with great zeal. His death left her with a void with which she was unprepared to cope, but she was not alone. Her maternal grandmother, Queen Adelaide of Portugal, stepped into the fore as a second parent to the heartbroken children, reflecting Queen Victoria's maternal concern for Tsarina Alexandra when Princess Alice died.

Queen Adelaide urged that Zita and her sister Francesca be allowed to finish their schooling in peace and stability. She invited her granddaughters to join her at Saint Cecilia's Abbey, which was run by the Benedictine nuns of Solesmes on the Isle of Wight, a stone's throw away from Queen Victoria's beloved Osborne House. Adelaide personally took charge of Zita's education, which covered a wide range of subjects from Latin and history to philosophy and art. But as much as Zita enjoyed studying in Britain, the damp climate on the isle affected her health badly, forcing her to return to the more comfortable climate of southern Europe in November 1909.

In August 1909, Tsar Nicholas II, Tsarina Alexandra, and their family made their first visit to England in eleven years. They were received on August 2 at Spithead with full military honors. As the Russian imperial yacht *Standart* crossed the Solent, it was escorted by twenty-four battleships, sixteen armored cruisers, forty-eight destroyers, and fifty other ships. It was a rare opportunity for George, May, Nicholas, and Alexandra to all be together. "Dear Nicky looking so well and Alicky too," George wrote.[34] Being back in her beloved England, Alexandra was happier than she had been in years. Touched by Edward VII's warm hospitality, she wrote how "dear Uncle" was "most kind and attentive."[35]

Much to May and Alexandra's relief, their children got on very well. It was also the only time that the two groups of children got to meet one another. David recalled that it "was the one and only time I ever saw Tsar Nicholas.... Uncle Nicky came for the regatta with his Empress and their numerous children aboard the *Standart*. I do remember being astonished at the elaborate police guard thrown around his every movement when I showed him through Osborne College." The children especially enjoyed teasing George and Nicholas about how similar they looked. The two cousins looked so alike with their deep eyes and Vandyke beards that many mistook the cousins for twins.

Noticeably absent from the festivities was May's son Bertie, who had come down with a nasty case of whooping cough. Fearful that if Alexei caught the virus it would lead to internal bleeding, Bertie was quarantined at his boarding school.[36] Alexei was wide-eyed with enthusiasm listening to David's stories of life at the Royal Naval School at Dartmouth. David, in turn, was smitten with Tatiana who, though only twelve to his sixteen, was tall, elegant, and exotically beautiful. More than once did Queen Alexandra hint at a possible dynastic marriage between David and Tatiana, though he was less than enchanted with the idea of Tsarina Alexandra—whom he remarked "wore such a sad expression on her face"—as his future mother-in-law.[37] One of the more poignant moments of the trip came when Alexandra went to the Hampshire town of Farnborough to visit Eugénie, the octogenarian former empress of the French, who had been living in exile since her husband, Napoleon III, was deposed in 1870. The tremendous courage Eugénie had displayed facing down the hostile mobs in France as she fled to England had earned her the respect of people throughout Europe. Alexandra's interest had long been captivated by deposed royalty, but it struck many as ironic that, though she could perceive Eugénie's mistakes in the buildup to the collapse of the French monarchy, she remained oblivious to her own role in Russia's deteriorating situation.

The visit by the Russian imperial family and the rest of 1909 may have gone smoothly, but 1910 became King Edward VII's denouement. Even at 12:01 a.m. on January 1, 1910, things did not augur well for the British royal family. They spent the holidays at Sandringham as they always did. Just before the stroke of midnight on New Year's Eve, the king and queen had all their family and staff assemble outside so that the monarchs could be the first people to open the door of their home in the new year—a ceremony they called the "first footing." Without noticing, David ran around back and ran through the garden door, flinging it open in triumph. Usually the epitome of jocularity, King Edward remarked gravely that David's prank boded ill for the rest of the year. The king was not wrong. Within a few weeks, he was faced with a series of governmental crises ranging from the growing invidious relationship with Germany to an explosive struggle with Herbert Asquith, the Liberal prime minister. Among other things, Asquith demanded sweeping reforms of the House of Lords in the hopes of bolstering his minority government, something that never would have been considered during Queen Victoria's lifetime. In the end, Edward and Asquith reached a compromise, but the hard-fought negotiations took a heavy toll on the sixty-eight-year-old king.

Physically worn down and emotionally exhausted, the king took a curative holiday at Biarritz, on the Bay of Biscay in southwestern of France. The queen took the opportunity to visit her brother and his family in Greece. In April, King Edward suffered a violent attack of bronchitis, forcing him to cut short his trip and return to Buckingham Palace early in the evening on April 27. Witnesses commented that he looked worse than when he left for Biarritz. After holding a few audiences and attending the opera, Edward moved to Sandringham. A few days later, he returned to Buckingham Palace, unalleviated by the Norfolk air. Within four days, his condition had deteriorated so badly that Queen Alexandra returned from Corfu. When she arrived at Victoria Station, George, May, David, and Bertie met her. This was a sign of just how serious the king's illness was, since he had never missed greeting the queen himself. At the beginning of May, Edward collapsed in his apartment, having suffered a series of heart attacks. This prompted a concerned May to write, "We felt very much worried about Papa."[38]

On Friday, May 6, Edward realized his end was near. He "had himself fully and formally dressed in a frock coat and propped up in a chair, where as king and head of the family he could receive relations and friends for a final good-bye."[39] Efforts by the doctors to stabilize the king with oxygen and hypodermic injections of strychnine, tyramine, and ether were unsuccessful. Princess May kept a constant vigil along with her husband and his family. She was in the next room when King Edward VII died at Buckingham Palace later that night, at 11:45 p.m. In a move that showcased Queen Alexandra's magnanimous nature, she gave orders that Edward's longtime mistress, Alice Keppel, should be sent for immediately to grieve alongside the queen. "What a loss to the Nation & to us all," May wrote tearfully.[40] Her timid and mild-mannered husband was heartbroken over the loss. Edward once told a staff member that he and his son were more like brothers. George confided the following in his diary that night:

At 11:45 beloved Papa passed peacefully away, & I have lost my best friend & the best of fathers. I never had a [cross] word with him in his life. I am heartbroken & overwhelmed with grief, but God will help me in my great responsibilities & darling May will be my comfort as she always has been. May God give me strength & guidance in the heavy task which has fallen on me. I sent telegrams to the Lord Mayor & the Prime Minister. Left Motherdear & Toria & drove back to M[arlborough] H[ouse] with darling May. I am quite stunned by this awful blow. Bed at 1.0.[41]

The general public was first made aware of the king's death early Saturday morning when they saw the Royal Standard above Buckingham Palace flying at half-mast. At Marlborough House that morning, May and George summoned their children downstairs to break the news to them. "My father's face was grey with fatigue, and he cried as he told us that Grandpapa was dead," David later recalled.[42] At 9:00 a.m. on Monday, May 9, May's husband was proclaimed King George V on the balcony of the Friary Court at Saint James's Palace. From Russia, Tsarina Alexandra's heart went out to her cousin George. She sent the new king a letter of condolence.

> Only a few words to tell you how very much we think of you in your great grief. Besides your heart being full of sorrow after the great loss you have entertained, now come the new & heavy responsibilities crowding upon you. From all my heart I pray that God may give you strength & wisdom to govern your country.... I think so much of you, as Nicky & I began our married life under similar trying circumstances.
>
> Thank God we saw yr. dear Pap still last summer—one cannot realise that he is gone.[43]

Nicholas II wrote his cousin George a heartfelt message, but now that they were both rulers, he could not help but comment on the development of stronger Anglo-Russian ties.

> Just a few lines to tell you how deeply I feel for you the terrible loss you and England have sustained. I know alas! by experience what it costs me. There you are with your heart bleeding and aching, but at the same time duty imposes itself and people & affairs come up and tear you away from your sorrow. It is difficult to realize that your beloved Father has been taken away. The awful rapidity with which it all happened! How I would have liked to have come now & be near you!
>
> I beg you dearest Georgie to continue your old friendship and to show my country the same interest as your dear Father did from the day he came to the throne. No one did so much in trying to bring our two countries closer together than Him. The first steps have brought good results. Let us strive and work in the same direction. From our talks in days past & from your letters I remember your opinion was the same. I assure you that the sad death of your Father has provoked throughout the whole

of Russia a feeling of sincere grief & of warmest sympathy toward your people. God bless you my dear old Georgie! My thoughts are always near you.

With much love to you & dearest May,
ever your devoted friend,
Nicky.[44]

With her husband's accession, May was now Queen Consort of Great Britain and Ireland and of the British Dominions beyond the Seas, Empress of India.[45] She was the first English-born queen consort since Henry VIII married Catherine Parr in 1543. There was a conscientious discussion about the name of the new queen. All her life, May was formally known as Victoria Mary, but her husband asked her to choose a single name for herself. Victoria was immediately ruled out as a possibility for obvious reasons. The only option was to go with simple Mary. "I hope you approve of my new name Mary," she wrote to Aunt Augusta. "George dislikes double names & I could not be Victoria, but it strikes me as curious to be rechristened at the age of 43."[46]

After four days of lying in state in the Throne Room of Buckingham Palace, Edward VII's large oak coffin was ceremoniously taken to Westminster Hall for the funeral. Held on May 20, 1910, the funeral for King Edward VII brought together the largest group of royals in history up until that time.[47] One of the first people to arrive in Britain was the widowed Queen Alexandra's sister Empress Marie Feodorovna. Attending the funeral was the new king, along with eight other reigning monarchs, all of whom were directly related to Edward in some way. There was his nephew Emperor Wilhelm II; his brothers-in-law the kings Frederick VIII of Denmark and George I of Greece; his nephew and son-in-law King Haakon VII of Norway; King Alfonso XIII of Spain, a nephew by marriage; and his second cousins the kings Ferdinand I of the Bulgarians, Manoel II of Portugal, and Albert I of the Belgians. Beyond these nine reigning monarchs were also seven queens, seven crown princes, thirty princes and heirs, and royals representing Turkey, Austria, Japan, Russia, Italy, Romania, Germany, Sweden, the Netherlands, Montenegro, Serbia, France, Egypt, and Siam. According to one historian, "who, seeing this self-confident parade of royalty through the streets of the world's greatest metropolis on the occasion of Edward VII's funeral, could imagine that their future was anything but assured."[48]

The funeral was a pageant lifted from the pages of history. England had never seen a funeral on such a scale before, and it would not see anything like it again until the death of Diana, Princess of Wales, in 1997. The procession made its way from Buckingham Palace to Westminster Abbey. More than two million hushed onlookers watched the awe-inspiring sight of the nine reigning monarchs, dressed in gold-braided uniforms with plumed hats and resplendent medals, riding three by three behind the funeral cortege. Behind this grand display "came five heirs apparent, forty more imperial or royal highnesses, seven queens—four dowager and three regnant—and a scattering of special ambassadors from uncrowned countries."[49] Writing to Nicholas II, Minnie said the funeral was "beautifully arranged, all in perfect order, very touching and solemn. Poor Aunt Alix [Queen Alexandra] bore up wonderfully to the last. Georgie, too, behaved so well and with such calm."[50]

The legacy of King Edward VII was a profound one. The echoes of his reign would carry Europe forward as it marched headlong toward the summer of 1914. Thanks to Edward VII's efforts, Queen Mary and King George now occupied a throne that was stronger than it had been at Queen Victoria's death and was more respected than ever. Edward was also a talented diplomat. His easygoing, gregarious nature won over even his staunchest of critics. The Italian foreign minister remarked that he had been the most powerful personal factor in world diplomacy. Not only did he forge alliances with France and Russia, he also strengthened the ties between the British crown and its counterparts among the continent's royals through their shared bonds of family.

> Edward ... was often called the "Uncle of Europe," a title which, insofar as Europe's ruling houses were meant, could be taken literally. He was the uncle not only of Kaiser Wilhelm but also, through his wife's sister, the Dowager Empress Marie of Russia, of Czar Nicholas II. His own niece Alix was the Czarina; his daughter Maud was Queen of Norway; another niece, Ena, was Queen of Spain; a third niece, Marie, was soon to be Queen of Rumania. The Danish family of his wife, besides occupying the throne of Denmark, had mothered the Czar of Russia and supplied kings to Greece and Norway. Other relatives, the progeny at various removes of Queen Victoria's nine sons and daughters, were scattered in abundance throughout the courts of Europe.[51]

This far-reaching influence was what King Edward VII bequeathed his son and daughter-in-law upon his deathbed. It was now up to King George V and Queen Mary to carry the torch that Edward VII had lit during his lifetime into the twentieth century.

Once the funeral was over, it did not take long for discord to seize the royal family. To Mary's disappointment, George's sister Toria was becoming possessive of the king and critical of her. "Do try to talk to May at dinner,"

Toria told a guest during a party, "though one knows she is deadly dull."[52] The real struggle, though, was with her mother-in-law, Alexandra, the queen dowager, who at first refused to relinquish her position as first lady of the land and "quibbled about questions of precedence."[53] In a total break with tradition, Alexandra demanded precedence over Mary, which she only gave after being harangued by her mother-in-law for weeks. "I am now very tired after the strain of the past weeks & now as you know come all the disagreeables," Mary wrote to Aunt Augusta, "so much to arrange, so much that must be changed, most awkward & unpleasant for both sides, if only things can be managed without having rows, but it is difficult to get a certain person [Alexandra] to see things in their right light." Alexandra had to be practically forced to vacate Buckingham Palace and return to her old home, Marlborough House. She was unwilling to give up many of the crown jewels that were now rightfully Mary's. "The odd part," Mary wrote to Augusta, "is that the person causing the delay and trouble remains supremely unconscious to the inconvenience it is causing, such a funny state of things & everyone seems afraid to speak."[54]

There were undeniable shadows of the tumultuous relationship between Alexandra of Russia and the fiery, stubborn Marie Feodorovna. As Mary's lifelong supporter, Grand Duchess Augusta placed the blame for this rift between Mary and Alexandra squarely on Minnie's shoulders, a woman who had become used to remaining in the public image during her widowhood. One of the dowager empress's biographers felt the problem was that, since Alexander III's death, she became "used to the prestige and influence of a Dowager Empress and she could not (or would not) understand that in England things were very different. Alix was now expected to give way to the new Queen Consort but Dagmar [Minnie], viewing things from her own experience, encouraged her sister to claim precedence."[55] Alexandra had always been known for her graciousness and civility, so Grand Duchess Augusta believed she was being egged on by her imperious sister. "May that pernicious influence soon depart!" Augusta wrote to Queen Mary with her usual dramatic flair.[56]

Mary's quarrel with Queen Alexandra took a backseat to an even more personal family episode involving her brother Prince Frank of Teck. After retiring from the army and refusing to leave England in 1901, Frank had been living a carefree bachelor life in London paid for by credit. Following the debacle he caused by giving the Cambridge family jewels to his mistress, Mary did not speak to him for years. In the last few years, Frank showed glimpses of redemption, working assiduously to raise money for the Middlesex Hospital, a cause the queen found honorable and respectable, thus paving the way for a reconciliation between her and her prodigal brother. In the summer of 1910, Frank Teck underwent a minor nasal operation. He was prematurely released from hospital, after which Mary invited him to join her at Balmoral in the hopes of furthering their reconciliation. Within days, pleurisy set in, and Frank was dead.

Mary was heartbroken. She wrote to her husband, "Indeed you were more than feeling & kind to me about dear Frank, whose death is a great sorrow & blow to me, for we were so very intimate in the old days until alas the 'rift' came. I am so thankful I still had that nice week with him at Balmoral when he was quite like his old self & seemed to be so happy with us & our children."[57] The funeral was held in Saint George's Chapel at Windsor Castle. The queen, who rarely showed emotion in public, broke down sobbing. Writing to Aunt Augusta, she was relieved at her brother's final resting place: "Dear Frank's coffin lies with that of dear Mama. I think she would have wished this as she was especially devoted to him."[58]

The Hessian children with Queen Victoria in mourning for their mother, 1879. *Left to right*: Ella, Victoria, Queen Victoria, Ernie, Irene, and Alix.

Princess May with her mother, the Duchess of Teck, and her brothers
Dolly, Frank, and Alge, c. 1880.

Princess May of Teck, 1893.

Princess Alix and Tsarevitch Nicholas in a formal engagement photograph, 1894.

The Prussian royal family in 1896. *Standing, left to right:* Crown Prince Willy, Victoria Louise, Dona, and Adalbert. *Seated, left to right:* Augustus Wilhelm, Joachim, Wilhelm II (with Oscar seated in front), and Eitel-Frederick.

The Hessian princesses, 1906. *Left to right*: Alexandra, Victoria, Ella, and Irene.

Dona and Wilhelm looking stately and dignified in a formal portrait, 1910.

Tsarina Alexandra in formal Russian court regalia.

Dona and her daughter, Princess Victoria Louise, riding through the streets of Berlin, 1911.

Zita and Charles on their wedding day, October 21, 1911.

The Russian imperial family in 1913. *Left to right*: Marie, Alexandra (with Alexei seated in front of her), Olga, Tatiana, Nicholas II, and Anastasia.

Mary, queen of England and empress of India, c. 1913.

Augusta Victoria, German empress and queen of Prussia, 1913.

Tsar Nicholas II and King George V, 1913.

Queen Mary with her daughter, Princess Mary, as a nurse during World War I.

Zita in her coronation robes as queen of Hungary, 1916.

Emperor Charles I of Austria, king of Hungary, 1917.

Dona in exile at Amerongen, 1921.

Queen Mary, c. 1930.

11

"We Must Help Each Other Get to Heaven"

(1910–11)

As Zita of Bourbon-Parma reached her late teen years, she had grown into a pretty young woman. Though not a classical beauty like Tsarina Alexandra, Zita inherited many fine features from both her parents. Like the Duchess of Parma, she possessed dark hair and deep-set chestnut eyes. From her father, she received the defined chin and jawline of her French Bourbon ancestors. With this type of exotic beauty and distinguished pedigree, it came as no surprise that as Zita stood upon the brink of womanhood, her admirers multiplied. The leading candidate for her hand was the pretender to both the French and Spanish thrones, her highly eligible yet overage cousin Jaime, Duke of Madrid, who was twenty-two years older than Zita. This Spanish prince's infatuation with the teenage Zita grew from time he spent with his Parma cousins at Frohsdorf while he was on leave from his position in the Russian army.

Always a welcome guest at the Austrian home of his aunt the Duchess of Parma, Jaime spent many hours in Zita's company. A mutual attraction took hold, though it was always stronger on Jaime's part. Jaime, then in his early forties, was smitten with the young princess, who was still only nineteen. Though a frequent companion to Zita and all her sisters, Jaime did not hide his preference for the elegant, vivacious younger sister. It was not long before Zita sensed her much older cousin's feelings.

Far from growing weaker, as time and distance might normally have been expected to do, Jaime's infatuation grew as Zita reached an age when she could start to think about marriage. His commission with the Russian army took him to the front lines on more than one occasion during the Russo-Japanese War. Jaime saw combat in one of the war's most decisive campaigns—the Battle of Liaoyang—which foreshadowed the fall of Port Arthur to the Japanese. When the duke returned from the front, it was always to Frohsdorf and to Zita, but because of his position as a pretender to the French throne, he was away in Paris for months, forcing him to settle for writing letters to his dear Zita.

This union was very much to the liking of Jaime's stepmother, the Duchess of Madrid, as well as the Carlist community in Spain who hoped to one day see him sit on the throne as King Jaime III. His hopes of marrying his Italian cousin, however, were dashed. His outspoken criticism of King Alfonso XIII and Queen Victoria Eugenie did not earn him any points with the Bourbon-Parmas, who were sympathetic to the couple. He was further hampered in his pursuit by other major obstacles, including his advanced age and the implacable opposition of Zita's mother, who protested on the grounds that Jaime and Zita were too closely related. He eventually discovered he could not make Zita his wife. As Jaime's visits increased, the Duchess of Parma watched her daughter carefully. Her tempered opposition to the match doomed any plans for marriage between her daughter and the duke.

Like the late Duke of Parma, who could not bear the thought of any of his daughters being forced into a loveless marriage, Maria Antonia prevented her daughter from being roped into an arranged union. This decision may have had something to do with the disastrous outcome of the marriage of Robert I's eldest daughter from his first marriage, Maria Louisa. Robert personally arranged her marriage to Prince Ferdinand of Bulgaria (later king of the Bulgarians); the couple did not meet until their wedding at Pianore in 1893. Unfortunately, Maria Louisa and Ferdinand were deeply unhappy together, largely because Ferdinand found his wife unattractive, paid her little attention, and was bisexual. It cannot be said for certain whether or not Maria Louisa's failed marriage was the Duchess of Parma's only impetus for not forcing Zita into an arranged union, but it did play a part. Thankfully, the duchess's decision destroyed any plans Don Jaime may have had for marriage, thus ending any chance of her daughter being locked in a marriage with a man who was old enough to be her father.

This episode spurred the Duchess of Parma into action. Maria Antonia knew that she had to act quickly to obviate an unsuitable romance. Although she hoped Zita would marry for love, Maria Antonia wanted a glittering future for her beautiful daughter. Though the political furor surrounding the Spanish and defunct French thrones was not to her liking, the Austrian throne was another matter entirely. Fortunately for this caring mother, Emperor Franz Joseph of Austria was also on the prowl for an ideal wife for his great-nephew and heir presumptive Archduke Charles. A pious, gentle young man with aspirations of being a career soldier, Charles was the son of the playboy Archduke Otto and the stocky, conservative Princess Maria Josepha of Saxony. Charles's remarkable character was almost shocking in light of his father's disreputable lifestyle. He came into his position as second in line for the throne after his father's death in 1906. Before Zita realized it, and while Charles was on leave from his dragoon regiment, the machinations of Emperor Franz Joseph and the Duchess of Parma would work to unite the destinies of these two young people.

The head of the Imperial and Royal House of Habsburg, Franz Joseph was an extremely conservative man who detested change. After the invention of telephones and elevators, he refused to use either. When he was sick, he would not let his doctor see him unless the physician was dressed in formal court attire. The emperor was a paradigm from a different era of royalty that was becoming extinct. He came to the throne in 1848 when he was only eighteen after his uncle Emperor Ferdinand—a hydrocephalic epileptic whose neurological problems were legion—was forced to abdicate.

From that day forward, Franz Joseph's reign was crippled by one calamity after another. In 1854, he married the stunningly beautiful Elizabeth, Duchess in Bavaria. Six years later, the nonconformist Elizabeth separated from her husband. She spent the next four decades wandering Europe, living on yachts and at resorts, trying to escape the pain of her life in Vienna. Franz Joseph's brother, the emperor of Mexico, was executed. His only son, Rudolf, killed himself. When it appeared that the emperor and his wife were on the verge of reconciliation in 1898, Elizabeth was killed in Switzerland when a lunatic stabbed her with a nail file. Two years later came Franz Ferdinand's historic decision to marry Sophie. In the hopes of conceding some ground to his heir, the emperor elevated Sophie to the rank of princess and, later, to Duchess of Hohenberg. These courtesy titles were the minimum requirements for Sophie to appear at court. Despite this token, the "marriage was awkward for Sophie. Even as the consort of the heir to the throne, her rank was lower than that of all the archdukes and archduchesses, including the children. She entered the halls of the Hofburg after little boys and little girls. The Hofburg was drafty in the best of times, but Sophie felt a special chill."[1] For the rest of his life, Franz Joseph reminded his nephew and his wife of the eternal shame that their marriage brought upon the dynasty. But undaunted by his tragedies and misfortunes, Franz Joseph threw himself wholeheartedly into his role as Austria's leader for more than sixty years.

This determination was all the more poignant because of Austria's waning influence as a Great Power. The decline and fall of the Holy Roman Empire, the rise of Prussian hegemony, and the embryonic ethnic groups gestating within Austria significantly weakened its imperial integrity.

> Austria-Hungary ... was territorially the dominant force in central Europe ... But in power terms it was regarded as an empire on the way down. Within its borders a dozen nascent nationalist movements were threatening to pull it apart. Respect for the inscrutable, irreproachably correct, dutiful and patient emperor Franz Joseph ... was increasingly cited as the only thing holding the different groups—among them Croats, Czechs, Poles, Hungarians and Ukrainians—together. Though he presented himself as an autocratic monarch with one of the most stiffly hierarchical courts in Europe, Franz Joseph had kept the empire together through a series of peaceful compromises which had turned him into a constitutional one. The empire had been further weakened by the loss of Italy after 1848, and Bismarck himself had sent it into eclipse by kicking it out of Germany in the Austro-Prussian War of 1866.[2]

The Habsburgs had ruled Austria for some sixteen generations. Their monarchy truly embodied the word *empire*. Centuries of conquest, royal marriages, and hereditary possessions meant that the Habsburgs, in addition to already being emperors and archdukes of Austria, were also the kings, grand dukes, margraves, princes, and counts of more than fifty territories that had been added to their monarchy since the 1400s. In the sixteenth century, Hungary, Poland, and Bohemia were added to their possessions through a marriage pact between the Habsburgs and the Jagiellonians, eastern Europe's most powerful ruling family at the time. Around the same time, the Habsburgs were called upon to rule Spain until their line died out almost two centuries later. By the beginning of the twentieth century, their empire was made up of present-day Austria, Hungary, Bosnia, Slovakia, the Czech Republic, Croatia, Slovenia, Liechtenstein, and parts of Italy, Switzerland, Romania, Poland, and Ukraine. Aside from Russia, Austria-Hungary was the largest power on continental Europe. "Within our Empire, the small nations of central Europe find a refuge," Franz Joseph said in 1868. "Without this common house their fate would be a miserable one. They would become the plaything of every powerful neighbour."[3] The emperor's statement, though somewhat disconnected from the true reality of central Europe, does reveal the mantle of responsibility that many of the Habsburgs felt was their duty to carry.

Throughout its long and volatile history, Austria (or more specifically, the Habsburgs) had learned to compromise to survive. In 1713, Emperor Charles VI essentially bribed Europe's other rulers to allow his daughter Maria Theresa to inherit his thrones. At the time, it seemed promising, but as soon as the emperor died, the heavily pregnant Maria Theresa was forced to rally her subjects to her side to defend against the Prussian-led invasion of the Habsburg crown lands. In 1810, Maria Theresa's grandson Emperor Francis I married his daughter off to Napoleon to cement the Franco-Austrian Alliance that was put in place after France's victory in the War of the Fifth Coalition. After the Austro-Prussian War, the Habsburgs were forced to create the Austro-Hungarian Compromise of 1867, granting the empire's Hungarian Magyars equality with its German citizens. The dual monarchy of Austria-Hungary was born.[4] Fifty-years later, it would be this compromise that would help unravel the Habsburgs' monarchy.

The Compromise of 1867 was not the only significant matter of policy that affected the course of Austria's future. By the late 1870s, the transgressions of the Austro-Prussian War were slowly being forgotten. The elimination of France as an imperial power in 1871 seemed to have eased tensions between Germany and Austria, paving the way for a level of rapprochement. By the end of that decade, Bismarck—the man who had been the single-greatest proponent of the 1866 war—had negotiated a mutual defense treaty between the two Germanic empires, known as the Dual Alliance. Upon his accession to the throne in 1888, Wilhelm II made it a priority mission to mend fences with Austria even further. He held deep respect and admiration for the aging Franz Joseph, whom he viewed as an archetype of his own venerated grandfather Wilhelm I.

The closer Germany and Austria became in the Wilhelmine era, the more apparent were the differences between the two empires. Where Germany was a homogenous state driven by a single nationalist agenda, Austria was quite the opposite. It was a true example of a vast empire made up of more than a dozen divergent, often volatile, ethnic groups; Zita once said that the Austrian Empire "incarnated the spirit of European civilisation as did no other state."[5] And unlike the homogenous, nationalistic Germany, where hundreds of dispossessed, mediatised royals searched to find their place in the monarchical hierarchy centered on the Hohenzollerns, Austria was the personification and embodiment of the Habsburg dynasty itself. It comes as no surprise, then, that their family motto was "Let others fight wars! Thou Happy Austria marry. What Mars gives to others, Venus bestows on thee."[6] Centuries-old tradition reigned supreme in Austria, where the dynasty "was always superior to the state. Family laws in old Austria-Hungary had precedence over state laws, and the provisions of the Family Charter, drawn up in 1839, are still unpublished and secret."[7]

Archduke Charles (who was known in German as "Karl") became heir presumptive at the age of nineteen when his father died. Charles's life from that point forward took on a decidedly different tone. His education now included political matters, whereas before it had revolved mostly around the military. For most of his teen years, he had his own household that moved from one palace to another. When he finished school, he took up the traditional Habsburg occupation of being a career soldier. Unlike many of his relatives, Charles remained free from scandals, but in 1910, he embroiled himself with the wrong crowd of friends from his dragoon regiment. A minor incident they caused with a young woman was the catalyst that launched the emperor on the search for a wife for Charles. For a brief period, his name was romantically linked with a number of princesses, including the emperor's granddaughter Ella and Princess Hohenlohe, an Austrian courtesan. Charles and Ella were already twice related, so a marriage between the two was stretching it. It also became noticeable that he had no interest in Princess Hohenlohe. Eventually, the emperor caught wind of the duchess's efforts to find a husband for Zita, so the two matchmakers arranged for the couple to meet in Lucca.

Dressed in a white muslin gown trimmed with lace, Zita was seated next to Charles at a dinner they both attended. They soon found themselves attending the same parties, which gave them the chance to become better acquainted. They spoke in German—a language Zita spoke since childhood—and the archduke soon charmed the princess. When they met in 1910 at Villa Wartholz, the home of their mutual relative Archduchess Maria Theresa, their interactions turned from charm to romance.[8] They were afforded the chance to spend more time together when Zita and her sister were invited to a ball given by Charles's mother, the Archduchess Maria Josepha. Later, they were guests of Maria Theresa at her hunting lodge, Saint Jacob, where Charles and Zita got to know one another on more intimate terms. They spent the next two years meeting together, primarily at Wartholz, where they developed a deep connection. Charles's kindness and gentility aroused admiration in Zita, while her "personality was a happy combination of Italian vivacity and German training."[9]

Just shy of his twenty-fourth birthday, Charles was five years older than Zita. Intelligent, generous, and loyal, Charles, who had brown hair and blue eyes, had inherited some of the good looks of his playboy father. In the very large Austrian imperial family, the moral character of Archduke Charles was highly respected. "If one does not know how to pray," recalled one the archduke's relatives, "he can learn from this young gentleman."[10] In character, he and Zita harmonized perfectly. Zita recalled of the time they spent together that they "were of course glad to meet ... and become close friends," but on her part, "feelings developed gradually." Although these do not sound like words of passion, Zita came to genuinely love Charles, and it was enough for the nineteen-year-old to accept his proposal on June 13, 1911. The engagement was an early modern example of public interest in the personal lives of royalty. The Austrians were conscientiously interested in this upcoming wedding, since it was a fact that Charles and Zita's children would one day inherit the throne, not Franz Ferdinand's. Zita herself became an object of interest partly because of her "most unusual name" and partly because of her "semi-Italian background."[11] Some observers noted that it was "the feast-day of an important Italian saint, St Anthony of Padua: a good day for a former ruling family of an Italian duchy to mark this new and significant chapter in its history."[12] The couple looked happy and in love as they posed on the balcony at Pianore for a formal engagement photograph. Zita's arm was gingerly wrapped around her fiancé's with an unpretentious smile on her face. The proposal was largely prompted by Archduchess Maria Theresa. Zita later recalled the following of the engagement:

> He [Charles] seemed to have made up his mind much more quickly, however, and became even keener when, in the autumn of 1910, rumours spread about that I had got engaged to a distant Spanish relative, Don Jaime, the Duke of Madrid. On hearing this, the Archduke came down post haste from his regiment at Brandeis and sought out his grandmother, Archduchess Maria Theresa, who was also my aunt and the natural confidant in such a matter. He asked if the rumor was true and when told it was not, he replied, 'Well, I had better hurry in any case or she will get engaged to someone else.'"[13]

Before he actually proposed, Charles went to ask for Zita's hand from her mother, the Duchess of Parma, who expressed concern since Zita was still so young and because of the responsibilities she would be taking on by being so close to the throne as the archduke's wife. Charles managed to reassure her that the emperor was still in good health, and there was no reason to think Franz Ferdinand would not reign for many years.

Once the proposal was actually made, Franz Joseph found himself taken aback, wondering whether or not it was a good idea. The "fact that Princess Zita belonged to a deposed Italian royal house did not strike the Emperor as a good augury."[14] In the end, the emperor accepted Zita because she was descended from two of the proudest royal dynasties in history, and for the first time in generations, a Habsburg was marrying a woman who actually strengthened the dynasty instead of destabilizing it. The famous nineteenth-century royal apologist Princess Catherine Radziwill noted that the "Austrian Imperial House has seldom been lucky in its choice of brides, and the public or private scandals which have arisen from time to time have been far too numerous for it to be possible to keep count." She also noted that "one Archduke after another tried to emancipate himself from the thraldom in which the exigencies of a merciless etiquette kept them confined."[15]

The Habsburgs were one of the unluckiest dynasties when it came to royal marriages. Most notoriously was Franz Ferdinand's recent morganatic marriage in 1900, but there were many others. The emperor's son, Crown Prince Rudolf, had married the highly strung, overly sensitive Princess Stéphanie of Belgium. There was constant animosity between the crown princess and her in-laws. Charles's uncle Archduke Ferdinand fell deeply in love with Berta Czuber, a university professor's daughter. The couple married, but with consequences. Franz Joseph ordered Ferdinand's name stricken from the official imperial family tree, stripping him of all titles, styles, and prerogatives. When he died in 1915, he was buried in Munich in an unremarkable grave marked "Ferdinand Burg." The Habsburg women were not immune from marital woes either. One of the most disastrous marriages in recent memory was that of Archduchess Louise, who married the crown prince of Saxony in 1891. By 1903, the marriage had been rocked by one scandal after another and eventually resulted in Louise divorcing her husband. Her conduct was considered so damaging to both the Saxon and Austrian monarchies that Franz Joseph stripped her of her imperial titles, which the *New York Times* called an act "without parallel in the Imperial house."[16]

Once Zita and Charles formalized their engagement, they had little time to spend together. Along with her mother, siblings, and an official Austrian escort, Zita headed for Rome where the new pope, Pius X, had asked for a special audience with the bride-to-be. It was the first time in almost two hundred years that a Habsburg archduke was marrying a Bourbon-Parma princess. The symbolism was not lost on the pontiff that their wedding would unite two of Europe's leading Catholic dynasties. Zita's visit began with a private Mass for her family in the pope's private chapel. "I am very happy with this marriage and I expect much from it for the future," Pius told Zita. "Charles is a gift from Heaven for what Austria has done for the church."[17] The pope nearly caused a diplomatic incident among Zita's Austrian escort when he referred to Charles as the heir apparent, forgetting his place after

Franz Ferdinand. It was only Zita's calm, quick reminder of her fiancé's place in the succession that prevented any offense.

While Zita was in Rome, Charles was off on his own mission. He was sent to England to represent Austria-Hungary at the biggest royal event of the year: the coronation of King George V and Queen Mary. The choice to send Charles was made both to call attention to his position as the heir presumptive and also to obviate the awkwardness that would have arisen from Franz Ferdinand's presence with his morganatic wife. They were forbidden by protocol from entering a room together, sharing a table at an official banquet, or even riding in the same carriage during the procession.

Planning for the event was a monumental undertaking. At Edward VII's coronation, Queen Alexandra threw tradition out the window by disregarding a number of important etiquettes. Even her choice of trainbearers ruffled feathers. Queen Mary, the archtraditionalist, saw to it that these were set right. To remedy Queen Alexandra's faux pas, she studied history books for hours, absorbing, analyzing, and dissecting all the various traditions that had been used for coronations of previous English kings. Mary wanted to be a statelier, less glamorized queen than her mother-in-law. One of the ways she set herself apart was in the clothes she chose for the coronation. The dress she chose for the ceremony was subtle, with silver, gold, and white woven throughout. Unlike her worldlier mother-in-law, Mary found the process of dress fittings burdensome. She wrote to Aunt Augusta of her "tiresome trousseau of clothes which has meant endless trying on. The fashions are so hideous that it has been a great trouble to evolve pretty *toilettes*."[18]

The city of London found itself playing "host to a huge number of foreign royals for what was to be, although no one involved in it was to know, the last gathering on the world stage of the royal houses of Old Europe before the wholesale social disintegration that was to come in the aftermath of the 1914–18 war."[19] There was an extraordinary display of dignitaries gathered for the event. Some fifty-eight delegations arrived from countries as far-off as Argentina and Zanzibar. The event had such a global impact that when the new shah of Persia came to the throne in 1925, he asked for a copy of King George V's coronation upon which to model his own. As the greatest symbol of royal power in the world, London proved to be the ideal—not to mention the traditional—venue for the coronation. To further celebrate the event, the Festival of Empire was opened at the Crystal Palace on May 12, showcasing exhibitions from around the world. On the dull, chilly day of Thursday, June 22, 1911, the king and queen made their way to Westminster Abbey, the site of past coronations of some thirty-eight English monarchs, which was founded in AD 965 by Saint Dunstan and built up in the tenth century by Edward the Confessor. The procession from Buckingham Palace to Westminster Abbey made a vivid impression on the queen. The embroidered coronation coach, pulled by eight cream-colored horses dressed with scarlet leather and touches of blue and lavender, was cheered on by hundreds of thousands of spectators standing behind decorated military officers from across the British Empire. Immediately behind the carriages of the British royal family was the coach that carried Archduke Charles, Crown Prince Willy, and Crown Princess Cecilie of Germany.

The queen entered Westminster before her husband's grand entrance. Her six-yard-long train was carried by a team of six earls' daughters. As she made her way up the abbey on the three-minute long procession to the altar, the altar boys cried out *"Vivat Regina Maria! Vivat, vivat, vivat!"*[20] First to be crowned that day was the king. After receiving the scepter, orb, and crown, George V made his way back to the throne. Once he was seated, the queen's crowning followed. Dressed in her white satin gown embroidered with gold and wearing a purple robe, Mary looked every inch a queen. When the moment came, she acquitted herself with dignity and grace, even though she had been crying as her husband was crowned. After being anointed, upon her head was placed a specially made crown sparkling with twenty-two hundred diamonds set in silver arches above a purple coronet. Once she returned to the throne, she and the king received tributes from the royal family and the other assembled dignitaries before exiting the church to the tune of "God Save the King."

One guest at the coronation, the First Viscount Murray, noted Mary's transformation that day from when she entered the church to after being crowned.

> The Queen looked pale and strained. You felt she was a great lady, but *not* a Queen. She was almost shrinking as she walked up the aisle, giving the impression that she would have liked to have made her way to her seat by some back entrance: the contrast on her "return"—crowned—was majestic, as if she had undergone some marvellous transformation. Instead of the shy creature for whom one had felt pity, one saw her emerge from the ceremony with a bearing and dignity, and a quiet confidence, signifying that she really felt that she was Queen of this great Empire, and that she derived strength and legitimate pride from the knowledge of it.[21]

After the ceremony, the queen sent a heartfelt letter to Aunt Augusta, whose old age prevented her from attending. In it, she shared her own feelings about the ceremony.

You may imagine what an intense relief it is to us that the great and solemn Ceremony of Thursday is well over for it was an awful ordeal for us both especially as we felt it all so deeply and taking so great a responsibility on our shoulders—To me who love [*sic*] tradition & the past, & who am English from top to toe, the service was a very real solemn thing & appealed to my feelings more than I can express—Everything was most perfectly & reverently done—The foreigners seemed much impressed & were most nice & feeling.... Everyone regretted yr enforced absence & no one more than I did but you wld have found it most agitating—I never ceased thinking of you the whole time.[22]

At the festivities that were held across London, Archduke Charles was immensely popular with both the British public and the hundreds of other dignitaries gathered. He stayed late at the parties "but was never seen to dance with anyone. This was interpreted as a gallant homage to Princess Zita, whose portrait he showed with pride to the newly-crowned Queen Mary."[23] Charles's meeting with the queen, at which he was introduced to the king, was a great historical irony. It was the only time Charles would meet the British monarchs face to face, even though the king and queen would one day become directly responsible for Charles and Zita's safety.

The coronation revelry went on for weeks. The king and queen took the customary seven-mile-long drive through the streets of London, attended the ceremony in which their son David was created Prince of Wales, held a review of the Royal Navy at Spithead, attended a thanksgiving service at Saint Paul's Cathedral, and ate the traditional luncheon at the London Guildhall. These public appearances sent Mary's popularity soaring. A joke began to circulate renaming the king and queen "George the Fifth and Mary the Four-Fifths."[24] The British press was relentless in its coverage of the royal events. A ball hosted by the Duke and Duchess of Sutherland at Stafford House was attended by one of the largest gatherings in history of foreign royalty on British soil. The newsmagazine the *Lady* offered in-depth coverage and also took special note of Charles and Zita's romance.

The Royalties began to arrive about half past eleven and of course those we looked for most were the German Crown Prince and Princess who arrived together, the latter tall, erect, smiling and very smart, with a beautiful tiara pointed with pearls in her hair.... Then there were Princess Louis of Battenberg [Alexandra's sister], Princess Frederick Charles of Hesse [Dona's sister-in-law Mossy], the Hereditary Princess of Saxe-Meiningen [Dona's sister-in-law

Charly], the Princess Militza of Montenegro, and the Crown Princess of Bulgaria. Amongst the most interesting men present, of course, were the Grand Duke Boris of Russia who represented the Czar, the Hereditary Prince Yousof Effandi representing Turkey (who, by the way, is second in precedence amongst the coronation guests and, I was told, had never been to a ball before!) and the Infante Don Fernando of Spain, the handsome Italian Prince, the Duke d'Aosta and the Archduke Charles Francis Josef of Austria representing his [great-]uncle the Emperor, a handsome young prince who, by the way, was formally betrothed the day before he came to England to the Princess Zita of Bourbon-Parma, a daughter of the late Duke of Parma and sister of the present. The bride-elect is only 19 and very pretty, and she is the 12th child in a family of 20 brothers and sisters, all born of the same parents![*sic*][25]

Crown Prince Willy and Crown Princess Cecilie were among the most senior-ranking royals visiting London. As honored guests, the couple was housed at Buckingham Palace. On more than one occasion, the queen "was noted in deep and informal conversation with" Willy.[26] This was taken as a sign of the continuing amiable relations between the British and German sovereigns, in spite of the floundering of Anglo-German relations as a whole.

The festivities ended on June 28 with a ball given by the politician Lord Derby. After everyone went their separate ways, George and Mary traveled throughout Great Britain. In Wales, their son David received his official investiture at a special ceremony at Caernarfon Castle on July 13. In the meantime, Charles returned home to his beloved Zita and his upcoming nuptials.

Nearly five months after the British coronation and the visit to Rome, one of the twentieth century's greatest tragic love stories began as Charles and Zita were united in matrimony on Saturday, October 21, 1911 at the white Baroque castle of Schwarzau am Steinfeld. Outside the castle walls, large crowds gathered to wish the archduke and his bride every happiness. The night before, villagers made a torchlight procession up to the castle, followed by a colorful fireworks display. It was during this dazzling display that Charles took Zita by the hand and told her, "Now, we must help each other get to heaven."[27] On her wedding day, Zita prepared herself in one of Schwarzau's salons. A full-length train embroidered with the Bourbon fleur-de-lis was attached to her iridescent cloth-of-silver dress. Resting on her head was a diamond crown surrounded at the top by large pearls, a gift from Emperor Franz Joseph, accented with sprays of myrtle and fresh orange blossoms.

Around her wrists were sparkling bracelets covered in precious stones, a gift from her mother. Together with Charles, the emperor, and her soon-to-be mother-in-law, Archduchess Maria Josepha, Zita made her way to the white-and-gold chapel for the wedding service.

The wedding itself was a vivid tapestry of tradition and progress, royal splendor and quiet dignity. The wedding gifts alone filled two of the castle's rooms from floor to ceiling. Part of the ceremony was filmed on cine cameras, a first for a royal wedding. The footage that still exists a century later captures the occasion. Everyone who appears on film, from the bride and groom to their illustrious guests, appears supremely happy, including Franz Ferdinand—who arrived without his controversial wife—and the Duke of Madrid, Zita's old flame. Although Zita never sought public acclaim, her grace and bearing commanded the attention of everyone who saw her walk down the aisle that day. Her dress, made of Duchesse satin embroidered with Bourbon lilies, was high necked with a wide waist. Charles was dressed in the blue uniform of the Lorraine Dragoons. His chest was covered in various medals, including the Order of the Golden Fleece—one of the highest honors in the world—and a Jubilee Medal given to him by the emperor on the sixtieth anniversary of his reign. Officiating the ceremony was Monsignore Bisletti, the personal representative of Pope Pius X and an old friend of the Bourbon-Parma family. According to the *Tablet,* London's weekly Catholic magazine, Bisletti "was also the bearer of a present from the Pontiff to the Royal pair, and an autograph [*sic*] letter in which His Holiness expressed his paternal affection and good wishes."[28] At the couple's request, the service was performed in Italian, but they took their vows in French. At the altar, Zita's voice was so strong and happy that it brought a smile to the emperor's usually stern face. When Bisletti declared the couple married, the guests erupted in cheers and applause. As the wife of a Habsburg archduke, Zita now enjoyed the styles and titles of Her Imperial and Royal Highness, princess imperial and archduchess of Austria, princess royal of Hungary and Bohemia.

For the reception that followed in Schwarzau's Theresa Hall, hundreds of guests—including Emperor Franz Joseph and Charles's maternal uncle King Frederick Augustus III of Saxony—dined on the late Duke of Parma's fine gold china. The emperor, normally cold and dour, was the epitome of joviality that day. He took it upon himself to make the wedding toast. With a champagne glass held high, he proclaimed, "And now I want to extend to the newly-weds on their great day my heartiest congratulations in the confident hope that they will both find in life that happiness which they are destined to achieve. May God guard and protect Archduke Charles and Archduchess Zita: long may they live!"[29] Charles and Zita were happy to get away for a tranquil six-week honeymoon tour of southern Europe. Starting at Villa

Wartholz in Reichenau, they made a pilgrimage to pray at the altar at one of the holiest churches in Austria, Mariazell. From there, Italy was next on the itinerary, with a stop at Kostanjevica in modern-day Slovenia to visit the tomb of King Charles X of France and Zita's other Bourbon relatives. This close time with Charles proved to be some of the happiest moments in Zita's life.

Like her imperial counterparts, Queen Mary's accession to the throne was greeted with the highest expectations. She now joined the rarified circle of Europe's imperial consorts. She was now the royal doyenne of the greatest imperial power the world had ever seen. Almost from the moment she became queen, Mary captured her role—she owned it; she embraced it. The shy awkwardness of her youth was gone. The years of training at Queen Victoria's side, the colonial tour, carrying out official duties as Princess of Wales—it all came together for the new queen-empress.

For the first time in fifty years, the queen of England was also the matriarch of a young family. David was seventeen, Bertie was sixteen, Mary was fourteen, Harry was eleven, George was nine, and John was six. But shortly after George's accession to the throne in July 1910, the unexpected happened: Mary announced she was pregnant for the seventh time at the age of forty-four. Most of the details surrounding the queen's last pregnancy have been obscured by history, but it is relatively certain that she was probably not happy about this. Mary made no secret of her dislike for pregnancy, especially once women reached a certain age. This, combined with her strong desire to be an active, useful queen could not have sat well with her. But the pregnancy of an English queen was still a celebrated event in Britain. Not since Queen Victoria gave birth to her last child, Beatrice, in 1857 had such an event taken place. In December, the *New York Times* reported, "Queen Mary's accouchement is expected in March. This will be the first birth at Buckingham Palace in fifty-four years."[30] This was the last official, publicly reported statement on Queen Mary's final pregnancy. There are no further newspaper articles, no public bulletins. Most likely, sometime between December 1910 and March 1911, the queen miscarried, and the details and circumstances surrounding it were evidently kept closely guarded secrets within the royal family.

During Queen Victoria's reign, Great Britain became a vast overseas empire that could proudly boast of being a superpower. Industrially, the country was unmatched. It "produced two-thirds of the world's coal, half its iron, well over half its steel, half its cotton and was engaged in 40 percent of its trade."[31] Geographically, the British Empire had a foothold on almost every continent, stretching from Canada in the West to Australia and India in the Far East. It was the last of these territories, India, which truly gave Britain its imperial identity. Its three hundred million inhabitants were "policed" by Britain's standing army in India of only seventy thousand. An English territory for more than a century, the subcontinent provided the empire with exotic, highly prized resources.

Queen Victoria had a deep, personal affinity for India. One of her favorite servants was an Indian man named Abdul Karim, similar in many respects to the now-famous John Brown. By the latter half of the nineteenth century, the queen became irked by the proliferation of emperors in Europe—specifically in Russia, Austria, and Germany—and she decided it was time to take an imperial title for herself. By definition, Great Britain was an empire: a diverse group of nations and peoples united under a single monarch. But as Queen Victoria put it, she "knew the British wouldn't stomach an empress at home," so she persuaded her prime minister Benjamin Disraeli to pass an act in Parliament on May 12, 1876 that granted her the title and style of empress of India. One of Victoria's biographers explained why gaining the imperial title was so important to her.

> She had long wanted this imperial title which so many sovereigns like the King of Prussia had acquired and which enabled those who held it – as it enabled the Emperor of Russia whose designs in the Far East were notorious – to arrogate to themselves and their children dignities and precedence which she felt demeaning to herself and her own. "I am an Empress," she announced one day in 1873 when she was certainly not, "& in common conversation am sometimes called Empress of India."[32]

It was a title that did not sit well with Edward VII. "I could never consent to the word 'Imperial' being added to my name," he disapprovingly told Disraeli."[33] But George and Mary, who shared Queen Victoria's love for India, had little trouble taking up the imperial mantle.

Once she became queen-empress, Mary had to adjust to yet another change of address. Throughout the course of her life, she had lived at Kensington Palace, White Lodge, York Cottage, and Marlborough House. But all of those were eclipsed by her latest home: Buckingham Palace, now one of the most recognizable royal residences in the world. The three-story palace, with its 775 rooms, was originally known as Buckingham House. Built by the Duke of Buckingham in 1703, it came into the royal family's possession when King George III purchased it in 1761. The palace earned the nickname "the queen's house," because for many years it was the home of George III's wife, Queen Charlotte. King William IV planned to move into the palace, but the necessary renovations to it were not completed before his death. It was not until 1837 that Queen Victoria moved the official royal residence from Saint James's to Buckingham Palace. Despite being the royal family's official London residence, Buckingham Palace was described as "a soulless office with residential rooms attached, which has inspired little affection among members of the Royal Family since it was transformed in the nineteenth century from an unassuming house into a grandiose official residence."[34]

Thankfully for the queen, her job had largely been done before she moved in. During Edward VII's brief reign, Queen Alexandra spent a great deal of time furnishing the palace with tasteful antiques and works of art, leaving Mary to only add personal touches here and there. The new queen moved into the palace four days before the rest of her family. She found the building somewhat daunting. "It is rather strange & lonely here without you & the children & I feel rather lost," she wrote to George. "Here everything is so straggly, such distances to go & so fatiguing. But I ought not to grumble for they have been very anxious to make me as comfortable as possible & these rooms are very nice & I have a good many of my own things round me."[35]

After a year on the throne, Mary was beginning to establish her own identity as queen. Unlike Queen Alexandra, who was always in the spotlight with her trendy wardrobe and vivacious personality, Queen Mary was becoming symbolic of a renaissance of Victorian values. Instead of being a social butterfly like her mother-in-law, she was the epitome of quiet dignity and grace. Wherever she went, she was met with enamored spectators who were in awe of her elegance. Even her dresses, noted for their soft pastel colors and simple designs, sparked a nostalgic note in British society.

Politically, George and Mary were set apart from their imperial counterparts. Unlike Nicholas and Alexandra and Wilhelm and Augusta Victoria, the king and queen were not absolute monarchs. In Russia and Germany, the new Reichstag and Duma were designed to curtail the powers of the sovereign through the democratic process. In Great Britain, the real power had rested with Parliament for centuries. This meant that, although George and Mary played hugely significant roles, they were not necessarily much more than figureheads. It was this existential reality that would separate the British monarchy from those of Germany, Austria, and Russia in the years to come. Ironically, the parliamentary nature of the British monarchy would be one of the very factors that contributed to its survival.

When it came to the political arena, Mary made it a point to stay out of it, but she nonetheless exercised a strong influence over her husband, though perhaps not to the extent that Tsarina Alexandra did over Nicholas II. Some accused the queen of trying to boss her husband around. Others claimed that she was browbeaten and intimidated by George, who was known to have a volatile temper. James Pope-Hennessy, one of Mary's most well-known biographers, interviewed her son David many years later. According to David, his parents did not always experience "a happy marriage." He told Pope-Hennessy "his father had a filthy temper and would humiliate his wife, attack her verbally in front of the children."[36] "Truth lay somewhere in between," wrote another of the queen's biographers. "Her attitude was that the King must reign, and in order to reign he must be sheltered from the importunities of daily life ... She was always to draw a firm line between the King's duties as Head of State and as *paterfamilias*."[37]

Regardless of whatever influence Mary may have had over the king, it remains certain that she was uncompromising in her support of him. "First and always she was his wife," one contemporary wrote. Though sometimes described as docile, George V was not without his dark moods. He often worried himself sick over important decisions or became depressed when things turned out badly for him. During these times, Mary was "by his side in anxiety and despondency, consoling him, greatly ambitious for him; with mind, heart, and soul ready for his service at any moment." It comes as no surprise, then, that in his first speech after ascending the throne, George declared, "And I am encouraged by the knowledge that I have in my dear wife a constant helpmate in every endeavour for our people's good...."[38]

King George V was unimpeachably faithful to his wife, despite a few, almost farcical, scandals. Shortly after his accession, the radical propagandist Edward Mylius circulated a pamphlet claiming that the king had secretly taken a wife when he was stationed on Malta with the Royal Navy. As early as 1893, salacious rumors were rampant that George had married an English admiral's daughter. Three weeks before their wedding, George told May, "I say, May, we can't get married after all! I hear I have got a wife and three children!"[39] Mylius's pamphlet further alleged that the king's marriage to Queen Mary was bigamous and therefore invalid. Nobody took it seriously, but to avoid further accusations against the new king, Mylius was arrested, tried, found guilty of libel, and sentenced to a year in prison. George's strict moral character and widely known conjugal fidelity were two of the main factors that contributed to his weathering the Mylius crisis. This was one area in which he was very different from his own father. Edward VII, though very much in love with his wife, was famous for his paramours. Some of his most famous mistresses included Lady Churchill, Winston Churchill's mother;

Daisy Greville, Countess of Warwick; and the actress Sarah Bernhardt. According to a 2007 report, Edward VII was believed to have had as many as fifty-five mistresses, since "he was the very model of genial but remorseless infidelity."[40] In an example of historical irony, one of the king's longtime liaisons was with a woman named Alice Keppel, whose great-granddaughter Camilla Parker-Bowles married Edward's great-great-grandson Charles, Prince of Wales.

Edward's liaisons were not as harmless as he may have hoped. In 1870, he was called to appear at the divorce trial of Sir Charles Mordaunt. Although Edward was not directly named in an affair with Lady Mordaunt, he was still booed one evening when he and Alexandra arrived at the Olympic Theater. Queen Alexandra often took her husband's infidelities in stride, even joking about them with some of her ladies-in-waiting. When Edward became involved with the American debutante Miss Chamberlayne, Alexandra nicknamed her "Chamberpots." This did not make Edward's unfaithfulness any less painful. He kept so many mistresses that he earned the nickname "Edward the Caresser." In this respect, the new king was the complete opposite of his father, who even described his affairs to George. In an 1881 letter, Edward boasted about the stage debut of his latest mistress Lillie Langtry. In contrast to Edward VII, George V remained completely loyal to his wedding vows. "We have seen enough of the intrigue and meddling of certain ladies," he once said, referring to his father's mistresses, "I'm not interested in any wife but my own."[41]

In November 1911, King George and Queen Mary traveled to Delhi for their coronation *durbar* as emperor and empress of India. The decision to go came as something of a shock, since "such a novelty as the King's visit to India had never occurred to more than ten in half a million" people.[42] "I think it a grand idea," Nicholas II wrote to George. "I do not doubt that it will produce a tremendous impression on the whole world."[43] No British monarch had ever been crowned in India, even though the title had been passed down from Queen Victoria. There was a tremendous sense of solemnity to the occasion. It was only the third time an imperial *durbar* had been ever held, and it was the only one ever to be presided over by a reigning monarch. The decision to hold the coronation was not merely a monarchical one but an imperial one as well. Contrary to the opinions of Britain's Conservative Party, the sun had begun to set on the British Empire over the last decade. Unrest in Ireland and India had given rise to the idea of home rule—self-sustained autonomy within the empire. Religion remained one of the greatest obstacles. The Irish parliament in Dublin was Catholic, but other counties like Ulster were

Protestant. Ireland was an ongoing problem, but India, George V believed, could be ameliorated with a display of empire that brought back memories of Queen Victoria's reign.

The official party left England on November 11 aboard the HMS *Medina*. A brand-new vessel, it was designed to carry 650 passengers, but for this voyage, it carried only the royal party—some two dozen people. During the monthlong trip, Mary's seasickness resurfaced. A stormy crossing on the Bay of Biscay left her bedridden for three days. The skies cleared by the time they passed Gibraltar, and the queen spent most of her time from then on writing letters on deck to her children and Aunt Augusta. The *Medina* reached Bombay on December 2. When the queen went ashore, she wore a yellow, flowered chiffon dress, punctuated by the Order of the Garter's bright blue ribbon. Her flat, straw-sewn hat was covered with artificial roses. "It is marvelous being in India again," she wrote. "I who never thought I should see it again. I am so glad I came."[44]

From Bombay, the king, queen, and their group boarded a train for Delhi. The king entered the city on horseback through the massive Gate of the Elephants dressed in a full field marshal's uniform. Next came the queen, who rode with her ladies-in-waiting in the first of a long line of state carriages. "It was a wonderful sight," she wrote to Aunt Augusta. "George rode and I followed in a carriage with the Mistress of the Robes & Lord Durham— Very grand & I felt proud to take part in so interesting & historical an event, just the kind of thing which appeals to my feelings of tradition—*You* will understand."[45] In the words of one of Queen Mary's biographers, "The preparations at Delhi were on a scale without precedent in the history of British India."[46] A vast canvas covering forty-five square miles was set up to accommodate the quarter of a million people who converged on Delhi for the historic event. A six-tent suite was set up for George and Mary's personal use. It was an elaborate construct that included a drawing room, anteroom, office, boudoir, bedrooms, and dining room that opened into a formal reception area.

At noon on the day of the *durbar*, December 12, King George, with Queen Mary at his side, entered the amphitheater wearing a crown specially made for the ceremony. It cost more than £60,000 to create—around $6.5 million today.[47] The Imperial Crown of India, as it became known, was covered in emeralds, rubies, sapphires, and 6,170 diamonds. George later wrote that he became "tired from wearing the Crown for $3^{1/2}$ hours, it hurt my head, as it is pretty heavy."[48] The newly crowned emperor and empress of India were seated on silver thrones beneath a gold dome upon a golden dais. On either side of them stood five-foot-tall maces, ornamented with lotus flowers, golden king cobras, and the Tudor crown. The correspondent for the London *Times* vividly described the coronation in their December 13 issue.

> Enthroned on high beneath a golden dome, looking outwards to the far north from whence they came, their Majesties, the King-Emperor and Queen-Empress were acclaimed by over 100,000 of their subjects. The ceremony at its culminating point exactly typified the Oriental conception of the ultimate repositories of Imperial power. The Monarchs sat alone, remote but beneficent, raised far above the multitude, but visible to all, clad in rich vestments, flanked by radiant emblems of authority, guarded by a glittering army of troops, the cynosure of the proudest Princes of India, the central figures in what was surely the most majestic assemblage ever seen in the East.[49]

The day after the coronation, Mary wrote, "Yesterday's Durbar was simply magnificent & too beautifully arranged, I am still quite under the influence of Imperialism it inspired."[50] King George was just as rapturous, writing to his mother, "The Durbar yesterday was the most wonderful & beautiful sight I have ever seen & one I shall remember all my life."[51] The high note on which the imperial coronation ended did not last. A week after the *durbar*, Sir Charles Hardinge, the new viceroy, was wounded when a bomb was thrown at his procession, killing one of his aides. Thankfully, George and Mary were on their way to Nepal and out of harm's way.

Always thoughtful and introspective, King George took this opportunity to look back and take stock of his life. When he did, the one person who was always there for him, to whom he owed unending gratitude and love, was his wife. He wrote the following to her while she was sightseeing in Jaipur:

> Each year I feel we become more & more necessary to one another & our lives become more and more wrapt [*sic*] up in each others. And I am sure that I love you more each year & am simply devoted to you & loathe being separated from you even for a day. Especially now in my present position with the enormous amount I have to do & with all my many responsibilities I feel that I want your kind help & support more than ever. And I must say you invariably give it [to] me, I greatly appreciate it & thank you from the bottom of my heart for all the love & devotion you give me.... very proud of being your husband & feel that our coming here to India as the first Emperor and Empress has certainly proved itself to be what I always predicated, a great success.[52]

The Indian coronation marked a turning point in Mary's life. She became more confident in her role as queen and empress. This was buttressed when she and George returned to England. The crowds gathered to greet them cheered like had never been done for a British monarch before. There was little doubt at the close of 1911 that, with few exceptions, King George V and Queen Mary were the most popular monarchs in the world.

12

"The Little One Will Not Die"

(1912–14)

When Charles and Zita returned from their honeymoon, they settled down to the quiet life of a provincial soldier and his wife. The archduke resumed his position in the Austrian military, beginning with the Seventh Dragoons at Brandeis, a small town on the Elbe River in what is today the Czech Republic. A few weeks later, Charles was transferred to the regiment at Galicia, located in the uppermost corner of the Austrian Empire near what is now Ukraine. The time that Charles and Zita spent in the company of their countrymen earned them immense popularity. One story that circulated during their first winter as husband and wife is ample testament to this.

During a car journey they had to stop while some repairs were carried out, and they took shelter in a nearby house where the housewife gave them hot drinks and chatted comfortably. When she heard where they were headed she was pleased—her son was a young soldier in the regiment [at Galicia]. Would they take his clean washing back to him for her? And also this small envelope of money that he needed? The Archduchess cheerfully took charge of the laundry, and the Archduke promised to deliver the money safely. Only later, when both had been handed over to the young soldier—the money with some extra added—did the story emerge, and the country woman realise who her guests had been … The

friendliness and naturalness of the young couple who were second
in line to the throne were beginning to win hearts.[1]

In 1912, Charles and Zita relocated to Vienna, bringing an end to his
tour of duty in the provinces. The move was prompted by an accident that
nearly put an abrupt end to Charles's life. Earlier that year at Lemberg, he
was thrown off his horse and hit his head on the ground, causing a severe
concussion. The field hospital in Galicia was not equipped to treat this type
of injury, so Charles was moved to a hospital in Vienna. After several days
gripped with anxiety, Zita was finally able to see an improvement in her
husband's condition. Within a matter of weeks, he was back on his feet.

Once Zita's husband recovered, the couple's relocation was made
permanent by his promotion to the rank of major in the Thirty-Ninth Infantry
Regiment, with command of the First Battalion in Vienna. The move had
been in the works for some time, since Zita was expecting their first child.
In the early morning hours of November 12, 1912, the archduchess went
into labor at Villa Wartholz, her aunt's home near Schwarzau. The old castle
was chosen because both of the parents wanted their child to be born in
peace, away from the public spotlight of the imperial court in the capital.
After a lengthy delivery, a healthy son was born. He was named Otto for his
paternal grandfather. Outside the castle, the townspeople gathered to sing
and celebrate the baby's safe arrival. So thunderous were the celebrations
that Zita's mother-in-law and brothers went out to greet the people. At Otto's
baptism on November 25, Cardinal Franz Nagl, the prince-archbishop of
Vienna, poured water from the Jordan River over his head. One of Vienna's
leading newspapers wrote an article extolling the highest hopes for Otto's
future: "In the new-born child ... is an emperor who, in all probability, will
only be called upon to guide the destiny of this state in the last quarter of the
twentieth century, and then, hopefully, in calmer times than we are living
through now."[2]

Otto's birth only enhanced Charles and Zita's popularity. Their reputations
for being down-to-earth, unaffected people spread across Austria. Archduchess
Zita garnered particular acclaim for making an effort to learn every major
language of the empire, beginning with the notoriously difficult Czech.
During a state dinner at the Hofburg, she charmed the different delegations
from across the empire by greeting each of them in their native languages. The
elderly Franz Joseph used every excuse he could think of to be in her company,
and even Franz Ferdinand and his wife, Sophie, enjoyed the company of this
attractive, wholesome young family. Zita was only nineteen.

The first home Zita and her family settled into in Vienna was Hetzendorf
Castle, on the western edge of the city. Although it was still attractive with

its Baroque architecture and its lush, verdant parklands, Hetzendorf was a far cry from the stateliness of the Hofburg and Schönbrunn, the two principal residences of the Habsburgs in Vienna. Situated on the western edge of the city, the Rococo-decorated Schönbrunn contained more than one thousand rooms. It was beloved by Habsburgs for centuries for its beautiful gardens, menagerie, orangery, and the Dutch Botanical Gardens. Schönbrunn may have been a pastoral Xanadu on the outskirts of the capital, but the Hofburg was the imperial family's symbol of power and authority. Built in the heart of Vienna on what is now the Ringstrasse, the Hofburg was the Habsburgs' main residence since the late thirteenth century. With its several thousand rooms and more than half a dozen wings, it easily dwarfed most other European palaces, putting it on par with Versailles or the Winter Palace.

When it came time for Charles and Zita to take up permanent residence in Vienna, they did not allow the splendor of the imperial court to affect them. They continued to win over the people they met with their charm, kindness, and grace. One contemporary noted that, during Charles's tour of duty in the provinces, "his boyish simplicity and the girlish charm of Archduchess Zita won all hearts, and when they left the Galician garrison to take up more responsibilities in Vienna – the Emperor Franz Josef fitted up for them the old castle of Hetzendorff near Schönbrunn – they had become the most popular of the younger members of the Imperial family."[3]

When Wilhelm I died in 1888, he left a throne that was consolidated and stable. The first emperor's antithesis was his grandson. Since the day he ascended the throne, Emperor Wilhelm II was noted for his erratic decisions and questionable behavior. Dona was forced to watch him make one poor decision after another, usually in the realm of foreign policy. Wilhelm, who was widely known as the kaiser—the German word for emperor—had succeeded in damaging Germany's relations with most of the world's other major powers. Tensions between the empire and Britain escalated after Queen Victoria's death and Edward VII's accession. Wilhelm had resented his English uncle, who had been a much more popular monarch.

Anglo-German relations did enjoy a brief resurrection when Wilhelm, Dona, and their daughter visited England in May 1911 for the unveiling of the now-iconic monument to Queen Victoria outside Buckingham Palace. After arriving at Sheerness on the evening of May 15 aboard the *Hohenzollern II*, the emperor, empress, and Sissy arrived in London the next day by train, where they were met at Victoria Station by George, Mary, and other members of the royal family. Mary's direct connection with the various German royal families—and George's amiability toward Wilhelm—ensured that the new king and queen enjoyed a more amicable, stable relationship with Wilhelm and Dona than had their predecessors. In the procession down Pall Mall to Buckingham Palace, Wilhelm, George, and the Prince of Wales rode in the first carriage, followed by the second carrying the queen, the empress, and their daughters Sissy and Mary. "Enormous crowds thronged the route from the railway station to the palace, and cheers greeted the party throughout the ride," reported the *New York Times*.[4] "The reception on the part of the English royal family and the people of London was cordial," Wilhelm later wrote in his memoirs. This "cordial.... very magnificent" visit was the last one Wilhelm and Dona would ever make to Great Britain.[5]

Despite this reprieve, the Prusso-German monarchy suffered further blows in the early years of the twentieth century, notably when Wilhelm II made an unannounced appearance in French-controlled Morocco. His hope was to escalate that people's incendiary desire for independence from France. The escapade was a foreign policy debacle. France's position in the region was strengthened. So too was Britain's, who stood behind their republican ally.

The second blow occurred in 1908 when an English officer named Colonel Edward Montagu-Stuart-Wortley published a series of private interviews with the emperor at Highcliffe Castle as a single article in the newspaper *Daily Telegraph*. An attempt to show Wilhelm as a lover of England, the article backfired, making it "the biggest and most damaging of the many media sensations of Wilhelm's reign."[6] Wilhelm's slightly deluded, unbalanced sense of humor came across as a personal insult to the British public. "You English," he said, "are mad, mad, mad as March hares."[7] He then went on a diatribe describing an unending list of mostly fictitious selfless acts he supposedly performed on Britain's behalf. With characteristic braggadocio, he also proclaimed that it had been himself personally who prevented France and Russia from siding against Britain in the unpopular, unsuccessful Boer War, a continuing sore spot in Britain's cultural pride. The entire fiasco sparked a two-pronged response. In Britain, it was met with slightly amused ridicule. Wilhelm genuinely seemed somewhat of an Anglophile, and the newspaper *Westminster Gazette* described it as "well meant" but "embarrassing."[8] Lord Esher added that it was "amazing" that the emperor "thinks himself immortal and omnipotent." The reaction in Germany was darker. German bitterness toward England had been rising for decades, and the *Daily Telegraph* article inflamed those feelings. The people resented their emperor's admiration for his mother's homeland. This was one area where Dona's personal feelings made her very visibly more popular than her husband. Her strident Anglophobia reflected public sentiment in Germany, helping to cement her already-excessive popularity. The former German chancellor Bernhard von Bülow described the article as a "dynamite bomb … [full of] sad effusions, which could scarcely have been surpassed in tactless stupidity." At the time, even Edward VII understood the damage Wilhelm was doing to his monarchy. "Of all the political gaffes which HIM [His Imperial Majesty] has made, this is the greatest," he said.[9]

The *Daily Telegraph* affair was a turning point in Wilhelm's reign. Public opinion turned against him in a striking way. For the first time, people openly questioned his sanity. Theories began to arise trying to ascertain the cause of the emperor's unbalanced personality. Some suggested it was overcompensation due to his physical shortcomings—during his perilous birth in 1859, in which his brain failed to receive oxygen for several minutes, his left arm was permanently damaged, rendering it useless to him for the rest of his life. Author Miranda Carter suggested that his erratic personality was possibly, though improvably, due to "those first few minutes without oxygen [which] may have caused brain damage. Willy grew up to be hyperactive and emotionally unstable; brain damage sustained at birth was a possible cause."[10] This hypothesis has since been supported by several other royal historians like Jerrold Packard in his book *Victoria's Daughters*. After two days of intense deliberation, some members of the Reichstag and Bundesrat called for his abdication. The federal princes' attitude devastated the emperor, but there was little love lost between himself and the Reichstag. As early as 1883, Crown Prince Rudolf of Austria remarked that Wilhelm "never speaks of the parliament except as 'that pig sty' or of the opposition deputies other than those 'dogs who must be handled with a whip.'"[11] The emperor's general sentiments about Germany's parliament were evidenced by the fact that he dissolved the Reichstag four times, in 1878, 1887, 1893, and 1906.

With a semiunified parliamentary voice calling for his abdication, Wilhelm fell into an emotional crisis. On November 17, Chancellor von Bülow hurried to Potsdam to meet with the emperor and empress. They awaited him on the terrace in front of the Neues Palais. As Bülow approached, Dona hurried to him first.

"Be really kind and gentle with the Emperor," she whispered in his ear. "He is quite broken up."

The next day, Wilhelm announced he was considering accepting the Reichstag's call to abdicate. Frantic, Dona immediately sent for Bülow to find out whether or not he would pressure the emperor to abdicate. She received him on the ground floor at the Neues Palais, her eyes red from crying all night.

"Must the Emperor abdicate?" she desperately asked the chancellor. "Do you wish him to abdicate?" He assured the empress he would not and that abdication would not be necessary because "the storm had begun to abate," thanks to his efforts in the Reichstag.[12]

The damage was already done. Overwhelmed, Wilhelm suffered a small nervous breakdown, collapsing on the floor of his office shortly after returning from a visit to Baden-Baden. One witness described the fifty-year-old emperor as being paralyzed by a "psychic [*sic*] and nervous depression."[13] In her diary, Dona wrote, "In November this year there arose very many difficult and serious political repercussions.... I went to Baden-Baden, found my husband very depressed and we returned to Potsdam together. Suffering from overwork and assailed by many mental conflicts at this, he fell ill."[14]

This was not the first time Wilhelm suffered a nervous breakdown. When Count Leo von Caprivi resigned as German chancellor in 1894, the "shock of his resignation seems to have triggered a nervous collapse lasting some two weeks."[15] His breakdown in 1908 seems to have lasted of similar duration. For approximately two weeks, Crown Prince Willy took over much of his father's responsibilities. The person who brought Wilhelm back from the depths of hopelessness was his wife. Dona guided and counseled her husband, urging him not to abdicate too rashly. Although the emperor soon abandoned any plans to do so, his self-esteem took a permanent blow. The crown prince recalled that Wilhelm "had lost his hope, and felt himself to be deserted by everybody; he was broken down by the catastrophe which had snatched the ground from beneath his feet; his self-confidence and his trust were shattered."[16] He was never quite the same after 1908 and required more support than ever from his patient wife. It would also not be his last nervous breakdown.

By the early 1910s, there was little doubt that the Prusso-German monarchy was struggling. Once the most fiercely monarchical people in Europe, the Germans—especially the Prussians—had become disillusioned not only with Wilhelm II but his sons and many others members of the royal family too. Dona and Sissy were exceptions. Muckraking newspapers in Berlin openly criticized the government's antiquated system of taxes for weighing heavily on the average citizens and almost not at all on the aristocracy, rising food prices, and growing national debt thanks to Wilhelm's exorbitant spending on the imperial navy. Between 1905 and 1913, some 2,226,000 workers went on strike "against the three-class franchise in Prussia."[17] In the hard-fought elections of 1912, the Far Left and the Catholic Center Party—both of which were polarized against the Hohenzollern monarchy—became the two largest parties in the Reichstag with a combined majority of 201 seats. Support for the Wilhelmine government was at an all-time low. Murmurs could be heard calling for an end to the reign of the Hohenzollerns.

Wilhelm II had not only alienated political leaders but other royals as well. By the time King George V ascended the throne, none of the several dozen royal families that made up Germany's upper strata wanted anything to do with the Hohenzollerns. Nicholas II's aunt Grand Duchess Marie Pavlovna, who was originally from Mecklenburg-Schwerin, expressed her contempt for Wilhelm II: "I am only a Mecklenburger on one point: in my hatred for the Emperor William. *He* represents what I have been taught from my childhood to detest the most—the tyranny of the Hohenzollerns. Yes, it is the Hohenzollerns who have perverted, demoralized, degraded and humiliated Germany and gradually destroyed all her elements of idealism and generosity, refinement and charity."[18] It was a similar story with foreign dynasties. Wilhelm offended the king of Italy by making crude jokes about his "extraordinarily small" physique.[19] In 1910, he nearly caused an international incident by playfully slapping King Ferdinand of the Bulgarians on the buttocks in public, who then promptly left Berlin "white-hot with hatred." He reportedly struck Grand Duke Vladimir of Russia across the back with a field marshal's baton.[20] Even Wilhelm's extended family loathed him. The Greek royal family despised the German emperor, who had gone out of his way to make things difficult for Greece in its recent war with Turkey, even though the country's future queen was his own sister Sophie. His cousins Tsarina Alexandra and Crown Princess Marie of Romania detested his arrogance, immaturity, and condescension.

Some of these sentiments changed for the better in 1913 when Wilhelm and Dona's daughter, Princess Victoria Louise ("Sissy"), became engaged to Prince Ernest Augustus of Hanover. The choice of the extravagantly wealthy prince from Hanover as a husband was a controversial one, given the years of enmity between the Hohenzollerns and the Hanovers. The conflict dated back decades to before the formation of the German Empire when Prussia annexed Hanover and deposed its king following the Austro-Prussian War. So when Sissy declared she wanted to marry the grandson of the last Hanoverian king, many hoped it would heal the rift between the two dynasties.

For most of her life, Sissy was a contradiction who had caused her mother much consternation. Like her grandmother Vicky, she was quite intelligent. When Sissy was young, Dona once wrote in her diary that she "interests herself a great deal in political events."[21] She had inherited the empress's statelier qualities—her dignity, carriage, and grace. She had also inherited an imperious, willful streak from her father. She was one of those "girls who think that they know everything better than their elders, and who, under the pretext of being romantic, sometimes sacrifice considerable advantages for the sake of asserting themselves in opposition to their elders."[22] As the youngest child in a family of seven—and the only girl at that—she knew she was the center of attention and took great pains to have the entire court revolve around her. According to Crown Prince Willy, she was "the only one of us who succeeded in her childhood in gaining a snug place" in the emperor's heart.[23] One of Wilhelm II's biographers described her as the emperor's little "sunshine princess."[24] But it was her flippant attitude that caused fights between mother and daughter. When it came to her daughter, the "Empress had many an anxious moment." Dona "had very decided opinions on propriety," and as a result, "she often felt sincerely alarmed at the extremely modern spirit which her daughter displayed."[25] Sissy took a measure of delight in causing havoc, especially with her pious mother. She found an eager ally in her sister-in-law Cecilie. Once, when the latest fashions from Paris had arrived, Dona decried the impropriety of the short, slit skirts the women were wearing. Within a few days, Sissy and Cecilie horrified the empress when they walked into a room wearing the tightest, shortest skirts they could find. Though at times frustrated by these qualities in her daughter, Dona nonetheless understood them well. The princess was the only girl in a household of boys, and she was spoiled by a father who made clear his preference for his daughter over his sons. She was also the only person in the family, including the empress, who could influence her father with great ease. When Sissy informed her parents that she wanted to marry Ernest Augustus, Dona was overjoyed—and relieved—that she was settling down to a life of her own.

Victoria Louise and Ernest Augustus met in 1912 when the prince came to Berlin after his brother's death in an automobile crash. The latter had been on his way to Denmark to attend the funeral of his uncle—King Frederick VIII—when his car skidded off the road near Nackel in Brandenburg. At the emperor's insistence, his sons Willy and Eitel-Fritz were part of the honor guard that escorted the body to its final resting place. Ernest Augustus came to Berlin to meet with Wilhelm II and thank him for his gesture of sympathy in sending his sons. Dressed in his light-blue uniform of the Bavarian military, Ernest Augustus was invited to an audience with Dona, who was greatly impressed by him. "How nice it is to see a Bavarian uniform here," she remarked. "It's just like the one in which my father went to war in 1870." The empress felt a certain affinity for Ernest Augustus and his family because—like her own—they had been dispossessed during Bismarck's military expansion of Prussia. The greatest impression Ernest Augustus made was on Sissy, for whom it was "love at first sight." He was equally smitten when he laid eyes on the emperor's daughter. It took a number of months to overcome all the political issues—which were very similar to those faced by Dona when she married Wilhelm—and required the help of most of Sissy's brothers and especially her sister-in-law Cecilie. When the betrothal finally became official, Dona was thrilled for her daughter. She wrote in her diary, "My child, her father, and I were radiantly happy."[26] After much deliberation, the wedding was set for May 1913.

Planning the marriage of the only daughter and youngest child of the reigning German emperor was steeped in etiquette. "During those weeks we were beset the whole time by people," Sissy later wrote, "particularly by the ladies-in-waiting and Court officials. Everyone wanted to give advice concerning the Princess's wedding."[27] As the mother of the bride, it fell to Dona to shoulder the responsibility of planning all the arrangements, but the inundation of unsolicited suggestions, corrections, and opinions was almost too much for the empress to bear. Ernest Augustus had great sympathy for her situation, both as a mother and a reigning consort. Before the wedding, he wrote the following to Sissy:

> I'm sorry for your mother. Do try to get her to keep calm. I'm very angry with these ladies [of the court] for they are to blame for making her so nervous. When you consider that none of these women is married, how can they want to involve themselves in such affairs?... You know, I understand your mother perfectly. She naturally wants the best for you, but she is an Empress and wants to have you just as she is, but she forgets that she is still an Empress.[28]

In a gesture aimed at furthering the emperor's belief in the success of international relations through personal diplomacy, he invited to the wedding King George V and Queen Mary, Tsar Nicholas II and Tsarina Alexandra, and almost all of his extended family. Wilhelm's choice to invite his imperial counterparts was a natural one because, despite years of building tension between Germany and Russia and Britain, Ernest Augustus was a first cousin to both the king and the tsar.[29] George wrote to Nicholas in April 1913, "May and I have accepted William's kind invitation to be present at his daughter's wedding next month. I also understand he has invited you and I trust that you may be able to come as it would give me the greatest pleasure to meet you there. I hope nothing will prevent this. Our best love to Alix and the children. Georgie." The response Nicholas sent back was simple and to the point: "I'll go if you go."[30]

George and Mary were the first guests to arrive in Berlin in May 1913. Their arrival was treated with the greatest ceremony, since they were the most highly regarded, highest-ranking visitors. After being met at the train station by Wilhelm and Dona, they passed under the Brandenburg Gate, driving down Under den Linden in an "awe-inspiring" ceremony. For the remainder of the day, the zeppelin *Hansa* circled above imperial Germany's capital. The next day, Nicholas and Alexandra arrived, accompanied by a hundred plainclothes police officers. "The arrival of all the wedding guests turned Berlin into a magnificent showcase, a display of Royalty rarely seen before," Sissy recalled in her memoirs. "Masses of people gathered in the streets of the capital to witness the parade of princes. They had come from everywhere to line the route the wedding guests would pass, and the sight of the tremendous throng in Under den Linden Opera Place, and in front of the castle was indescribable."[31]

The constant flow of royals arriving at the train station in the subsequent days was reminiscent of Ernie and Ducky's wedding twenty years before and brought together many of the same people. Alexandra was reunited with her sisters Irene and Victoria, whom she had not seen in more than four years. Many of the guests were housed at the Stadtschloss, where the strict etiquette reigned. Outside the rooms of every royal woman was a majordomo dressed in gold and scarlet, whose sole duty was to empty the washbasins. At a welcoming party that commenced the wedding celebrations, Dona, Wilhelm, George, Mary, Nicholas, and Alexandra were together again. Dressed in the uniforms of each other's armed forces as a sign of affection, the members of this imperial triumvirate put on a united front. Wilhelm and George visited Potsdam to review the Prussian regiments. Mary and Dona accompanied their husbands in an open carriage together. It was ostensibly one of the only times that these two women were ever together while both of their husbands were reigning.

A few days later on May 24, 1913, Sissy's wedding was carried out in two stages at the Berlin Stadtschloss. That morning, King George issued a proclamation in honor of the bride and groom: "We are especially pleased that we are the guests of the Sovereign of this great and friendly nation in order to celebrate the union of two young lives, which we earnestly pray may be fraught with all possible blessing."[32] The civil ceremony was held in the Electress's Hall, while the religious ceremony was carried out in the chapel. Augusta Victoria looked every inch an empress that day, dressed in a light-green, robe-style dress adorned with long strings of pearls and a diamond-encrusted crown. Queen Mary, who reportedly "was so overcome by the ceremony that she broke into a flood of tears,"[33] also attracted a great deal of attention. She wore a gown of Indian cloth of gold. Atop her head sat the same coronation tiara she had worn to the *durbar*. Her jewelry included six diamond brooches, two diamond necklaces, diamond earrings, and nine necklaces made up of strings of diamonds once owned by Queen Victoria, along with the Lesser Star of Africa—a 317-carat diamond—as a pendant. In Neustrelitz, the capital of Mecklenburg situated northwest of Berlin, Aunt Augusta kept abreast of Mary's German visit. She wrote to her niece, "a Lady (in Attendance there) told me, she never saw anything like your magnificent Dresses and Diamonds, and your regal appearance, the Wedding Toilette surpassing all!"[34]

The official wedding feast was attended by twelve hundred guests. Four emperors and empresses, four kings and queens, and dozens of princes sat crowded around massive tables filling the entire Grand Hall of the Stadtschloss. For dinner, Dona sat next to George and across from Nicholas and Alexandra. The highlight of the wedding reception was the *Fackeltanz*, the traditional Prussian torchlight ritual in which the bride danced with all the men bearing the style of Royal Highness or higher. It was this same dance, in this same room, that Dona herself performed decades earlier at her own wedding. Sissy, dancing with her father first, began by making a deep curtsy to the emperor. Then, one after the other, she danced with Nicholas, George, and all the other visiting kings and princes of sufficient rank. Once the bride had danced with the three emperors, the other senior women joined in. Dona looked joyous and regal as she danced with George, but Queen Mary stole the show. As she danced round and round with Wilhelm, the countless diamonds adorning the gold fabric of her dress flickered in the candlelight. It was such a beautiful, incomparable sight that newspapers in Canada and the United States reported every detail. At the end of the night, the newlyweds boarded a train for their honeymoon. The parting was especially hard on Dona, who broke down sobbing. "I shall say nothing about myself, except that it seemed that my heart was breaking," she wrote in her daughter's commemorative diary. "I could only pray, particularly as I knelt at my child's bed during the night, God protect my child, my youngest. Make her happy, O Lord."[35]

The celebrations in Berlin and Potsdam were some of the rare events that saw Alexandra and Augusta Victoria together after their dismal state visit almost twenty years earlier, but neither of them sought to make amends with the other. Both women preferred Queen Mary's company to each other's, which is a great irony considering how similar both women were. The empresses of Russia and Germany were deeply religious, distrustful of outsiders, fiercely loyal to their husbands and immediate family, and plagued by similar chronic health problems. They each claimed to suffer from weak hearts, which were exacerbated by anxiety or nervousness. Though Alexandra constantly referred to her heart problems, there is little evidence she suffered any physical cardiac disease. In the end, it proved to be their similarities that drove these two women apart.

During the exhausting round of parties, parades, and military reviews that etiquette demanded be put on for the visiting royals, Dona's health appeared in fine form, but Alexandra was struggling through one of her bad periods of health. Her suffering was obvious to many people, who described her being "bent with sciatica and totally absorbed in grief that her only son had haemophilia."[36] Despite her afflictions, Alexandra's spirits were lifted by the visit. Here in Berlin, she was among her friends and family, her equals. She may have disliked Wilhelm and Dona, but they were still kindred spirits, reigning monarchs who understood her plight as a wife, mother, and consort better than anyone in Saint Petersburg. No one there realized it then, but that was the last time that George and Mary, Wilhelm and Augusta Victoria, and Nicholas and Alexandra would ever see each other. It was also their last chance to try and make some type of détente between the three empires, but their efforts came to naught. George and Nicholas left closer than ever, surer of their need to stand united against expanding German influence. But Wilhelm became paranoid that George and Nicholas were not only uniting against Germany but were directly plotting against Prussia and the Hohenzollerns. George recalled that every time he and Nicholas tried to have a private conversation, Wilhelm was constantly "lurking around" with his ear "glued to the keyhole."[37]

For Queen Mary, her reunion with Dona and Alexandra went off very well. Since the Tecks were descended from the royal family of Württemberg, Dona was more gracious to the queen than toward many others. "We left Berlin at 5.35 for London," Queen Mary wrote in her diary on May 27, "William & [Augusta] Victoria accompanied us to the station—Took leave of them all with regret after charming visit."[38] A few days later, she described the visit in a letter to Aunt Augusta: "I cannot tell you how very much we enjoyed our visit to Berlin or how touched we were at the kindness shown us by William & [Augusta] Victoria & indeed by everybody. It was a most interesting time & so beautifully arranged in every way, nothing could have gone off better."[39]

The wedding celebrations of 1913 were some of the last happy moments in the life of Empress Augusta Victoria and arguably also for the German people for the foreseeable future. According to one of Wilhelm II's biographers, the wedding "was a public sensation; recorded using an early version of colour film and viewed by millions across the empire, this was perhaps the last occasion before the outbreak of the war on which an event in the life of the monarch could provide the occasion for mass emotional identification."[40] After the wedding, Wilhelm granted a further concession to the Hanovers in November 1913 by making Ernest Augustus the reigning duke of Brunswick, whose throne had been vacant for decades. Upon being invested with the dukedom, Ernest Augustus and Sissy relocated to the city of Brunswick in Lower Saxony, where they fashioned a charming and vivacious court. Less than a year later, Dona was blessed with another grandchild. In May 1914, Dona, Wilhelm, and their suites moved to Brunswick for the christening of

Sissy's first child, a son. Keeping with the traditions of the Hanoverian royal family, the eldest son was named Ernest Augustus. His godparents included the emperor and empress, Emperor Franz Joseph, Nicholas II, George V, the king of Bavaria, and many others. The ceremony "was solemnised in great state, in the presence of the Emperor and Empress, the Crown Prince and Princess ... and representatives of the crowned heads of Europe."[41]

❧

By the time he was nine, Alexei Nicholaievich had grown into a mischievous, outgoing child. He was very much aware that he was different from other children. The simplest of activities that his friends enjoyed—running, jumping, and playing—were potentially lethal for him. Alexandra watched her son like a hawk, sometimes to the point of obsessively smothering him. One contemporary observed that, given the difficulties faced by her only son, she "must have envied Charles and Zita their healthy baby son."[42] The tsarina's trusted friend and lady-in-waiting Anna Viroubova once saw her break down into hysterics when Alexei's leg became caught in a chair. When she saw him screaming "like a wounded animal," she ran over to him, shouting at Anna, "Leave him, stop, his leg's caught in the chair!" Later, Anna noticed how badly "bruised and swollen" the boy's leg was.[43]

Alexei was a child of contradictions. His illness gave him great sensitivity, which made him more acutely aware of the sufferings of others than the rest of his family. On other occasions, he was indulged by his parents, making him willful and selfish. He was Alexandra's only child who refused to speak English at home, the language the imperial family spoke in private. His tutors remarked that the tsarevitch had little interest in his lessons, except when they concerned matters of the military or trains. It helped his demeanor that he had been in relatively good health recently. A dangerous hernia operation he underwent in 1912 went well. It also helped the general atmosphere in the family that the tsarina made the decision to inform her in-laws of the true nature of his condition. This relieved some of the burden Alexandra had been carrying for so long. There was a glimmer of hope in her life again. Some of the imperial doctors even began speculating that the tsarevitch might be one of those lucky few hemophiliacs who survived into adulthood like Alexandra's uncle the Duke of Albany.

More than any of her other children, Alexandra felt a special connection with Alexei because, in her eyes, he was "the direct result of prayer, the Divine condescension of God, the crowning joy of her marriage." Alexei represented the best qualities of Nicholas and Alexandra hybridized into one. He had the gentleness and kindness of his father coupled with the devotion and loyalty of his mother. Julia ("Lili") Dehn, another of the tsarina's friends, recalled a touching scene one evening after Alexei had finished his bedtime prayers. Before Alexandra had left the room, he turned out the light over his bed. "Why have you done this, Baby?" the confused Alexandra asked. "Oh," he replied, "it's only light for me, Mama, when you are here. It's always quite dark when you have gone."[44]

The attention Alexandra gave to her only son in no way diminished her love for her daughters. The four grand duchesses, who were collectively known as OTMA for the first letters of each of their names, brought great joy to their mother's life. Largely brought up by Alexandra herself, the girls were dignified, gracious, and deeply religious. The girls' insularity preserved their virtues and morality, but it also left them with something of a maturity handicap. Even into their teen years, the grand duchesses often thought and acted like little girls.

Baroness Sophie Buxhoeveden, a family friend, was a firm supporter of the empress's style of parenting. She wrote, "It is not possible to imagine more charming, pure and high-minded girls. The Empress really brought up her daughters herself, and her work was well done."[45] This did not mean that there was never discord in the family. Alexandra's moral probity meant she left her daughters little breathing room for their own individual and often highly divergent personalities. "The children with all their love have quite other ideas and rarely understand my way of looking at things," Alexandra wrote. "The smallest, even—they are always right and when I say how I was brought up and how one must be, they can't understand, find it dull. Only when I speak quietly with Tatiana she grasps it....And when I am severe—sulks me."[46]

Growing up, the girls naturally divided themselves into two groups: Olga and Tatiana ("the big pair"), and Marie and Anastasia ("the little pair"), though all four of them were tenderly close. Olga and Tatiana, by virtue of being the eldest, took more after their father. Like Nicholas II, they possessed dark features and deep eyes that revealed passionate souls. Olga could be stubborn and experienced intense emotional highs and lows: "In temperament and appearance she most resembled her father, whom she adored."[47] Olga was also the daughter with whom Alexandra was most often in conflict. "Olga is most unamiable about every proposition," the empress wrote, "though she may end by doing what I wish."[48]

In contrast, Tatiana was the closest of the four girls with their mother. Like Alexandra, Tatiana was stately, elegant, refined, and inherited much of the empress's regal nature. More than any of her sisters, Tatiana also possessed a total acceptance of their family's royal position and the privileges that came with it. Her self-assurance and commanding nature made her the natural leader among the four sisters—even though Olga was the eldest. The other three girls nicknamed Tatiana the Governess. Nonetheless, she was still a modest, down-to-earth girl who embarrassed easily. She once kicked a lady-in-waiting for addressing her publicly as "Your Imperial Highness."[49]

The younger grand duchesses, Marie and Anastasia, were similar but different. Without a doubt, Marie was the biggest flirt in the family and attracted the attention of many suitors. The youngest grand duchess, Anastasia, was the exact opposite of her sisters, especially Olga and Tatiana. If the elder two were passionate and pensive, and Marie was flirtatious, Anastasia was a tomboy. She made her unique mark by being the joker of the family. "Forever in the shadow of her more glamorous sisters," wrote one historian, "Anastasia came into her own through her gift of mimicry. Never shy, always game for a good joke, Tsarina Alexandra's youngest daughter was the very antithesis of her reserved mother."[50] Anastasia's antics endeared her to many of her relatives. Her Aunt Olga nicknamed her *schwipsig*, a German expression meaning "merry little one."[51] Perhaps more than her other daughters, Alexandra kept Anastasia under a close eye. As a young girl, she nearly drowned in the Gulf of Finland in a freak accident when she was swept underwater by a massive rogue wave, driving the air out of her lungs. As a consequence, the empress took special care of Anastasia, much in the same way she did for Alexei. For Alexandra, her two youngest children were her babies.

The Russian aristocrats saw Alexandra's Victorian, bourgeois values as abnormal. She did not believe that her daughters should grow up used to royal extravagance. The grand duchesses were unaccustomed to formality in their homes. Servants and courtiers were instructed to refer to them by their names rather than their titles, a practice that would have been unthinkable in Potsdam or Vienna. To combat indulgence, the girls slept on folding military beds—a tradition dating back almost a century—in rooms decorated with simple stuffed furniture, chintz, icons, and favorite watercolors and photographs. Alexandra wanted her daughters to learn how to endure the elements. Their rooms were heavily ventilated, even in the winter, causing them to grow largely insensitive to the cold. In the mornings, they took cold baths. Each evening concluded with a warm bath, in a solid silver tub, at which point they were allowed one of their few luxuries: scented bath mixes imported from Paris. Between the four sisters, rose, jasmine, lilac, and violet could be smelled in the hallways of the palaces on any given day.

With Olga and Tatiana now in their late teens, they began to replace the tsarina at court functions. The empress had become so insular that, when she appeared in Saint Petersburg in 1913 for the Romanov tercentennial celebrations, it was her first official public appearance since 1905. "They must get accustomed to replace me," Alexandra wrote to her old governess, "as I rarely can appear anywhere, and when I do, am afterwards long laid up—over-tired muscles of the heart."[52] Her health continued to get worse, making it far more difficult for her to appear in public. Alexandra's children were consumed with worry over their mother's worsening health. "O, if you knew, how hard Mama's illness is for us to bear," Tatiana told Rasputin in 1908.[53] Alexandra reiterated this in a letter written in 1913: "My children are growing up so fast & are such real little comforters to us—the older ones often replace me at functions & go about a great deal with their father—they are all 5 touching in their care for me—my family life is one blessed ray of sunshine excepting the anxiety of our Boy."[54]

Russia's imperial family lived in unimaginable wealth. Exact numbers differ depending on the source, but it is generally agreed that the tsar and his family were worth hundreds of millions of dollars. Nicholas was, more or less, the wealthiest monarch in the world. That wealth was not purely in money alone; it also came from copious assets. The imperial family owned "huge timber and mineral reserves in Siberia and the Caucasus; five yachts and two private trains; hundreds of horses, carriages, and new motorcars; accounts stocked with gold bullion in Moscow, London, and Berlin; thousands of works of art, including important paintings by Van Dyke, Raphael, Rembrandt, Titian, and da Vinci; crowns, tiaras, necklaces, and a fortune in jewelry; and a priceless collection of objets d'art and Easter eggs by famed jeweler Peter Karl Fabergé."[55]

Along with these assets, Nicholas, Alexandra, and their family divided their time among more than thirty breathtaking palaces. In Saint Petersburg, they stayed at the Winter Palace. Designed in the classical Baroque style, its interiors contained more than fifteen hundred rooms. During the reign of Tsar Nicholas I between 1825 and 1855, the palace could accommodate four thousand occupants. Its interiors were dazzling, with "polished marquetry floors, crystal chandeliers, marble and granite pillars and staircases, gold-inlaid ebony door, huge vases of spectacular green malachite, and lapis lazuli decorated furnishings."[56] In the summer, the Romanovs moved their court to Livadia, their Crimean palace on a remote peninsula on the north coast of the Black Sea. Livadia was much more exotic in design than many of the other imperial estates. Built from white Crimean granite, its unique neo-Renaissance design looked more Arabian than European, though its overall idea was inspired by the buildings Nicholas and Alexandra had seen on a state visit to Italy. The palace grounds included patios in both Middle Eastern and Italian designs, a Florentine tower, and a chapel modeled after the Byzantine style. It was here at Livadia that the imperial family was truly in their element. Alexandra's daughter Olga once remarked, "In St Petersburg we work, but at Livadia we live."[57]

One of the family's lesser-used homes was Spala, an old hunting lodge in Poland. Anna Viroubova described it as one "of the dampest, gloomiest palaces I have ever seen."[58] It was here that a simple accident threatened Alexei's life, cementing the tsarina's relationship with the insalubrious Gregory Rasputin. Alexei was playing when he slipped and fell. At first, the swelling seemed to go down, and life returned to normal. Two weeks later, when the family was out for an automobile ride, Alexei shrieked in pain with every bump in the road. "Every movement," Anna Viroubova recalled, "every rough place in the road, caused the child the most exquisite torture, and by the time we reached home, the boy was almost unconscious with pain."[59] An examination revealed a hemorrhage in his leg, causing blood to seep into his body. Alexei's sufferings multiplied when the swelling began pressing on nerves in his upper left thigh and abdomen, causing excruciating pain. Upon examination, doctors discovered a tumor that showed signs of becoming septic as well. Ordinarily, surgery would have been the only answer, but Alexei's hemophilia made that impossible.

The situation quickly became perilous. A heartrending drama unfolded on October 21 when Alexei developed a dangerous fever as the blood filled his tiny body. Bloodcurdling screams pierced the long halls of Spala as Alexei lay curled up on his bed, writhing in agony. The torturous screams became so horrific that the lodge's staff begged for something with which to cover their ears. The heavy doses of morphine Alexei was given a few days later barely dulled the pain. His suffering was made especially poignant by the feigned jovial atmosphere at Spala during the daytime. It was the middle of the hunting season, and aristocrats came from miles around expecting to be entertained by the tsar. Nicholas played the role of the dutiful host admirably, never allowing any of his guests to fathom the internal grief he was experiencing. Alexandra made only fleeting appearances at the dinner table. She relied heavily on her sister Irene, who was visiting with her son Sigismund, to act as hostess and offer apologies to the guests for her absence. With the exception of Nicholas, Princess Irene was the only person who truly understood Alexandra's pain. She too was a hemophilia carrier and had passed the disease to two of her sons, Waldemar and Henry. "Like Alexandra," wrote one Romanov historian, Irene "had endured the agonies of uncertain days and nights, watching helplessly as her sons suffered without relief.... This shared pain, this maternal guilt, created a bond between Alexandra and Irene that came to the fore at Spala that autumn, providing the desperate empress with an ally who shared her agony."[60]

When Alexandra was required to appear before the guests, she could not even fake a smile. It was as if her very soul was being wrenched from her body. She was forced to watch helplessly as her exhausted little boy wailed and thrashed in his bed, his forehead covered in sweat, slipping in and out of delirium. Workers at Spala were so moved that they begged the local priest to hold daily masses to pray for him. For eleven days, Alexandra sat at her son's bedside, going with almost no sleep for five of those days. Her dark hair became tinged with noticeable streaks of white. Tears streamed down her cheeks as she looked at his face, "absolutely bloodless, drawn and seamed with suffering, while his almost expressionless eyes rolled back in his head." For Nicholas, it was all too much to bear. When he came into the room, "seeing his boy in this agony and hearing his faint screams of pain, the poor father's courage completely gave way and he rushed, weeping bitterly, to his study."[61]

In Alexei's few rare moments of lucidity, Alexandra could hear him begging, "Mamma, help me!" It devastated the empress that there was nothing she could do but wait and pray. It broke her heart when he asked her, "When I am dead, it will not hurt anymore, will it, Mama?"[62] Eventually, Dr. S. P. Fedorov, the attending physician, pulled Nicholas and Alexandra aside to give them the grave news that Alexei's stomach was hemorrhaging, increasing the already high risk of blood poisoning and peritonitis. Fedorov had little recourse but to prepare them for the possibility that Alexei would soon die. Two bulletins were issued, each one day apart, preparing the public for the awful news that Alexei had passed away. Both notifications were carefully worded to give no indication of how he died. An Orthodox priest came to perform the last rites. Witnesses recalled the heartrending sight of what they believed to be Alexei's final hours: "It was as if he had already passed from life into another realm at the threshold of death, his body already corpselike in its whiteness, his breath already beginning to cease as, lacking the energy to scream or cry, he murmured his prayer for divine mercy and whispered his mother's name."[63]

In her desperation, Alexandra could think of only one thing to do. She asked her friend Anna to send a telegram to Father Gregory. Why she waited so long before contacting him remains uncertain, but faced with the imminent death of her son, the tsarina was willing to try anything. After all, had not Alexei been a divine answer to prayer? And was not Father Gregory the answer to the question of Alexei's hemophilia? Alexandra's faint hope in Rasputin can be traced not to her faith in him as a man but to her faith in God. The Russian Orthodox Church believes in the existence of *staretz* ("a holy man"). The modern interpretation is that a *staretz* is a venerated elder of the Russian Orthodox faith sent by God to advise and teach. Some were known to do miracles, most were ascetics, and all knew the Holy Scriptures inside and out. A *staretz* was never officially appointed but is recognized by the people as being imbued with the power of the Holy Spirit. In general, there is little doubt that Gregory Rasputin was a charlatan. He drank, caroused with women, and was more lecherous than even the most pernicious aristocrats. Yet he also had a believable quality and managed to convince many, including Alexandra Feodorovna and Anna Viroubova, of his God-given ability to heal, prophesy, and guide. That this supposed *staretz* was a man of the world was no secret to anyone, including the tsar and tsarina, but they faithfully believed he was a repentant sinner. According to Grand Duchess Olga Alexandrovna, "to Nicky and Alix he remained what he was—a peasant with a profound faith in God and gift of healing."[64]

Because of all these factors, when Alexandra received a reply at Spala from Rasputin, it was all she needed. Rasputin stated, "God has seen your tears and heard your prayers. Do not grieve. The Little One will not die. Do not allow the doctors to bother him too much."[65] Telegram in hand, a pale and exhausted Alexandra entered her son's room and declared "in a calm voice" to the people gathered, "I received a telegram from Father Grigory and it has reassured me completely."[66] As if it had all been planned, Alexei began to recover almost instantaneously. There was not a single face that was not shocked—and relieved. Olga Alexandrovna recalled how "within an hour my nephew was out of danger."[67] Although his life was spared, it would be a long time before Alexei was back to normal. It took almost a year before he could walk properly again, and even that was accompanied by a leg brace.

Alexandra was never the same after the Spala episode. In a letter to the bishop of Ripon, she expressed some deeply candid feelings about what her family had just experienced.

I have been so ill again with my heart—the months of phisical [*sic*] & moral strain during our Boy's illness brought on a collapse—for some years I suffer from the heart & lead the life [of] an invalid most of the time. Thank God our Darling is getting on so well he has grown very much & looks so strong, & we trust before long to see him on his legs again running about.

It was a terrible time we went through, & to see his fearful suffering was heartrending—but he was of an angelical [*sic*] patience & never complaining at being ill, he would only make the sign of the cross & beg God to help him, groaning & moaning from pain. In the Orthodox Church one gives children Holy Communion, so twice we let him have that joy, & the poor thin little face with its big suffering eyes, lit up with blessed happiness as the Priest approached him with the Holy Sacrement [*sic*]. It was such a comfort to us all & we too had the same joy,—*without* trust &

faith implicit in God Almighty's great wisdom & ineffable love, one could not bear the heavy crosses sent one.[68]

Those who were detractors of Rasputin were dismayed at the level of credibility the Spala episode brought him. This latest incident solidified indefinitely in Alexandra's mind the importance of Rasputin to the survival of her son. He was destined by God, she reasoned, to save Alexei's life. Olga Alexandrovna admitted that "never did my brother or Alicky believe that the man was endowed with any supernatural powers. They saw him as a peasant whose deep faith turned him into an instrument of God to use—but only in the case of Alexis." She also sharply pointed out, "Alicky suffered terribly from neuralgia and sciatica, but I never heard that the Siberiak helped her."[69] This was not entirely true. Alexandra and Nicholas did receive temporary relief from their headaches upon first meeting Rasputin.

Dr. Fedorov, one of the most preeminent physicians in Russia, was at an utter loss to explain how Rasputin effected Alexei's miraculous healing. When discussing the phenomenon, he once admitted that Alexandra could hardly be blamed for believing in the *staretz*. "Rasputin would come in, walk up to the patient, look at him and spit," he said. "The bleeding would stop in no time.... How could the empress not trust Rasputin after that?"[70] For nearly a century, experts have tried to debunk Rasputin's abilities. In the words of one historian,

> the secret or source of Rasputin's ability to "cure" the tsarevitch has been examined relentlessly. There appears to be no real consensus as to how he came about his "miracles." Explanations range from coincidence at Rasputin's timing to mysterious Tibetan herbs used on the imperial family to palace accomplices effecting his work, and also to his ability to calm the tsarina and so, by extension, Alexei. Then there is the theory that some sort of hypnotic ability might have been the root of his "powers." Rasputin's magnetic eyes play a major role in promoting this idea. But there is little doubt that people privy to the imperial family's troubles were mostly at a loss to explain how the monk from Siberia managed to pull off his conjuring tricks.[71]

Whatever the explanation may be, Rasputin's influence with Alexandra Feodorovna was undeniable. In the course of only a few short years, that influence would help destabilize one of the most powerful monarchies in history, with tragic consequences for Alexandra, her family, and Russia.

13

The Gathering Storm

(May–June 1914)

At Hetzendorf, Archduchess Zita enjoyed a measure of tranquility interspersed with public functions and royal duties. As the wife of the heir presumptive and being born of royal blood, she was expected to accompany Franz Joseph on occasions that, had circumstances been different, would have fallen to Franz Ferdinand's wife, the Duchess of Hohenberg. Zita attended state dinners, her hair coiffed up and covered in diamonds. In her iconic white muslin dress and wide hat, she inspected the troops on the arm of the emperor. On other occasions, with her son in tow, she made visits around Vienna. Wherever she went, Zita's grace and simplicity charmed the people she met.

In the two brief years that Zita and Charles had been married, the couple grew closer together, strengthening their loving bond. They "shared the same deep faith, the same simple tastes, the same love of home and—not so far behind these three in enduring value for a marriage—the same sense of humour."[1] Zita's popularity grew again on January 3, 1914, when she gave birth at Hetzendorf to her second child, a little girl called Adelhaid. Like Alexandra of Russia, Zita considered her family life to be truly blessed. She and her husband passed many hours together in the company of their young children. They took long walks in the parks around Hetzendorf, played games with the children, prayed together, and visited the sick and poor.

So amiable was the young couple that they became frequent companions to Franz Ferdinand and Sophie. Zita and the Duchess of Hohenberg were a study in contrasts. Where Zita was quiet and demure, Sophie was driven and ambitious. But even a decade after her controversial wedding to Franz Ferdinand, tensions over their union remained high. Conservatives labeled the archduke and duchess as pariahs, who held their own little court at their Vienna home, Belvedere Palace. Few high-ranking individuals associated with the couple for fear of earning the emperor's enmity, but rank never mattered much to Zita or her husband, who enjoyed spending time in the company of "Uncle Franzi" and "Aunt Sophie." But in the early months of 1914, Zita noticed a change in Uncle Franzi. The normally gregarious archduke became withdrawn and pensive. This change came about when, after a heated audience, the emperor decided to send him and Sophie to the Bosnian capital of Sarajevo to preside over troop maneuvers in June. On the surface, it should have been just another military exercise, since Franz Ferdinand was the inspector-general of Austria's armed forces, but "the archduke was gripped by [such] an inexplicable unease about the journey ... that he even considered tackling the emperor to have it cancelled."[2]

Franz Ferdinand's anxiety over the upcoming Bosnia trip was not unfounded. Over the past thirty years, the Balkans, nicknamed the powder keg of Europe, had become a hotbed of revolutionary, antimonarchist sentiments. Countries like Serbia, Bosnia, Montenegro, and Albania had fought long, bloody struggles for their freedom from the Ottoman Empire in the eighteenth century. But now, they found to their horror that Austria-Hungary's borders were encroaching on their own like a gathering storm. Desperate to never again be oppressed by any foreign power, terrorist groups popped up across the southern Balkans in droves, stretching from Belgrade to Sarajevo. They were determined to liberate the Slavs living under the Habsburgs—approximately 60 percent of Austro-Hungarian subjects were ethnic Slavs. Attacks on royals and government officials became bolder and bolder with each passing year. Imperial gubernators were attacked or even assassinated, buildings were bombed, and demands were made for total Austrian withdrawals from the Balkans.

All this and more was racing through Franz Ferdinand's mind in the days leading up to the long, hot summer of 1914. In the meantime, he prepared for the worst. In an interview held years later, Zita recalled a particularly tense evening.

> At the beginning of May 1914, we were in Vienna and uncle Franz Ferdinand rang up one evening asking us to come over to the Belvedere for supper. It was just a small family meal with the heir-apparent, his wife and children, and ourselves as the only guests.

Everything passed off normally – indeed quite gaily – until after supper, when the Duchess of Hohenberg went to take the children up to bed. After his wife left the room, the Archduke Franz Ferdinand suddenly turned to my husband and said:

"I have something to say but I must say it quickly as I don't want your aunt to hear anything of this when she comes down. *I shall soon be murdered*. In this desk are papers which concern you. When it happens, take them. They are for you."

My husband protested: "Surely, you must be joking." But his uncle replied: "No, I am serious. After all, everything is ready. The crypt in Arstetten is now finished."

Before anything more could be said, the Duchess reappeared and we all did our best to pass the rest of the evening as though nothing out of the ordinary had happened.[3]

Charles and Zita left Belvedere that night speechless. It was only after they returned home that they discussed in greater detail Franz Ferdinand's disturbing prophecy. In a later interview, Zita shared her thoughts on what had transpired that night.

Uncle Franz-Ferdinand obviously had reasons for believing what he told us. He had had serious threats from nationalist and anarchist groups. Obviously the police had been informed of them and took them very seriously. To tell the truth, the instigators were known to be inaccessible. They mingled and moved in a half-light, and in the political demi-world, between Turin, Paris, and Scotland. They also haunted Belgrade. It was already known at the time that, if an assassination attempt were committed, the authors of it would only be agents manipulated by a "big brother."[4]

Zita's statement reflects the general mentality of most members of the Habsburg dynasty at this time. The acts of the Nihilists in Russia, the burgeoning terrorism in the Balkans, and the murder of the Portuguese king and crown prince in 1908 showed that acts of violence against royals were on the rise. But it is doubtful anyone, even someone as politically astute as Archduchess Zita, could have predicted what would take place in just a few weeks.

In the spring, there were unmistakable signs that instability was sweeping Europe. Over the past decade, the facade of royalty's immutability had been stripped away, prompting its enemies to strike. In Germany, the growing power of the Socialists and other Leftist parties in the Reichstag were decisive blows against the Hohenzollern monarchy. Although Empress Augusta Victoria remained above reproach in the eyes of her people, the emperor had become an object of scorn, ridicule, and even resentment. It was a similar story in Russia, where the Duma, now nearing its tenth anniversary, was failing in its mission to bring reform to the tsarist empire. Nicholas II had dissolved and reformed the parliamentary body a frustrating four times, stalemating the democratic process. Russia was also paralyzed with thousands of workers' strikes from Ukraine to Siberia. At the Lena goldfields in northeast Siberia, soldiers shot and killed some five hundred miners who had gone on strike to protest their working conditions: sixteen hour days, an accident rate of seven out of every ten workers, and food that was usually rotten or inadequate. Despite its alliance with Britain, episodes like the Lena Massacre inflamed the British people's resentment toward the Russian autocracy, embodied by Nicholas II and Alexandra.

Britain was not immune from the seeds of discontent. The king was dejected that he was being forced to confront separatist causes in his own dominions. In May 1912, the Liberals in the House of Commons struck a blow against the British Empire by putting forth a home rule bill for Ireland. The ebbing Conservatives pressured the king to veto the bill, something not done by an English monarch since 1708. In the end, the indecisive and timid George chose not to interfere. "Whatever I do I shall offend half the population," he scribbled in a memo. "No Sovereign has even been in such a position."[5] Although he chose not to interfere in the elected process, George was a committed imperialist who, perhaps even more than his father, was determined to preserve the British Empire as it existed during Queen Victoria's reign. This was something he shared with Wilhelm II and Nicholas II: a commitment to passing onto his son the same empire that was passed on to him. Although the English throne was the most stable in Europe, Britain's once-great overseas empire was beginning to dwindle. Irish home rule, rising Indian independence movements, and self-determination for Canada and Australia were evidence of this.

To combat his feelings of vulnerability on the throne, King George followed his father's example by looking for good international relations to be fostered between monarchs. This proved difficult when it came to Britain's ally, France. Being a republic for nearly half a century, it was the bastion of democracy in Europe, free from monarchical constraints. "France is, and always will remain, Britain's greatest danger," said Lord Salisbury as early as 1867.[6] It was also a sore point in French republican pride that almost every deposed French dynasty since 1848 had sought refuge in England. Eighty-eight-year-old Empress Eugénie was still living quietly in the English countryside. With Germany's growing antagonism toward Britain, it was more imperative than ever that George and Mary strengthen their bonds with France. To that end, in April 1914, they took a much-anticipated trip to Paris. It was the first foreign city that the king and queen visited since their accession.

The Anglo-French relationship was one of the oldest rivalries in Europe. This was unchanged for centuries until Queen Victoria and Prince Albert visited France as guests of Emperor Napoleon III and Empress Eugénie in 1855. The visit was a lukewarm success at best, but when the gregarious Edward VII returned in 1903, it changed everything. After a series of effusive speeches and official engagements, Edward became a smash hit and was cheered with cries of *"Vive le Roi! Vive l'Angleterre!"*[7] When President Émile Loubet of France visited London a few months later, he was greeted just as enthusiastically. The friendship that Edward VII established with France led to the grand alliance, the Entente Cordiale of 1904, uniting England and France for the first time in history, thanks to the diplomatic efforts of Lord Landsdowne and Paul Cambon.

When George and Mary arrived in Paris, they were an instant sensation. There were crowds "milling round the carriage.... Wonderful reception & crowds of people.... Crowds in the street in spite of late hour.... Crowds in the streets both coming and going," were some of the entries Mary made in her diary. She added that all this enthusiasm "shows that the French people wish to be on good terms with us."[8] According to the French people, in the queen's eyes they saw "the prettiest frankness" and insisted that "her smile was full of a delicate kindness and sincerity." The Parisians, ever conscious of the latest fashions and styles, were full of praise for her wardrobe: "The whiteness of the aigrettes beneath her hat exactly suited the gracious face beneath."[9] The queen knew "how to wear with grace and dignity the dresses of gold, silver, and silk which Court etiquette insists upon; but her heart is not in vain outward show."[10] For their final night in Paris, a gala party was held at the Elysée Palace topped off by an emotional speech from the French president, Raymond Poincaré.

Outside her official duties and foreign trips, Queen Mary had a number of hobbies she pursued. One about which she was passionate was decorating. She loved sprucing up Buckingham Palace, Sandringham, Windsor Castle, and Balmoral. Whether personal properties or owned by the Crown, the Georgian architecture and style of these residences greatly appealed to the queen. She set about decorating her homes with gusto, creating interiors that were neatly ordered and well designed. Mary adored antiques, especially ones with a slight German feel to them. Most of her early homes had been furnished with wedding presents, but Windsor Castle was in desperate need of redesign. The queen eagerly went shopping for furniture and artwork. Delighted with her prowess, she took a special interest in each of her homes and the furniture within them. "For then they become somehow so much more interesting," she once quipped.[11] David Duff, one of the queen's biographers, ascribed several driving forces to Mary's love of antiques and possessions in general. The most significant, he argued, was financial. "Throughout her childhood, the Tecks had been haunted by poverty," he wrote. "Presents from rich relations, such as jewelled snuffboxes, meant security—their only way of obtaining it. The more diamonds that sparkled on the bosom of Mary Adelaide, the more credit could she obtain from the tradesmen. Thus events such as birthdays and confirmations were looked forward to. As she grew older this nightmare of poverty reappeared before Queen Mary and her possessions became more important to her."[12]

This compulsive fear of poverty that drove the queen to acquire possessions may have driven her to some extremes. Some authors and historians have claimed her "antiquing" bordered on kleptomania. On more than one occasion, when Mary was a guest somewhere and became enamored with an object, she talked the owner into giving it to her as a gift. In the rare instances when a host was unobliging, the queen reportedly was known to respectfully abscond with the object, which was promptly returned by her ladies-in-waiting with a note of apology for the "misunderstanding." The queen could not always feign guilelessness. When she saw a clock she adored at Kensington Palace that belonged to George's aunt the Duchess of Argyll, she "made her way towards … the mantelpiece, her admiration all too transparent." Louise then placed herself between the clock and the queen and firmly declared, "The clock is here, and here it remains."[13]

The queen's passions were not limited only to decorating and gardening. She was also interested in the royal genealogy surrounding the previous owners of her homes. When it came to the Georgian era—the reigns of George I, II, and III—she was an incomparable expert. She could tell anyone the stories behind almost every piece of furniture or antique that had belonged to any of the kings George. She once astounded a lady-in-waiting who inquired about a golden cannon on an Italian yacht. Excited by the question, Mary enthusiastically described how King George III had given the pair of golden cannons to the king of the Two Sicilies as a present in 1787.

Within a year of her daughter Sissy's wedding, another of Dona's children was making plans to get married, although these nuptials would embroil the Hohenzollerns in controversy, the likes of which the dynasty had not seen since 1853. Prince Oscar fell in love with a commoner—Countess Ina von Bassewitz-Levetzow. Like Eitel-Fritz and Lotte, Oscar and Ina had met after Willy and Cecilie's wedding. Ina came to Berlin with her father, the premier of Mecklenburg-Schwerin, who was the chief minister of Cecilie's brother, the grand duke. Although the Mecklenburgs were very unpopular in Berlin, Dona took an instant liking to Ina, whom she appointed one of her ladies-in-waiting. Within a few months, the empress had forged a close bond with the countess, who filled the void in Dona's life that was created when her daughter married and moved away. As a regular fixture at court, Ina was a high-society favorite with her beautiful singing voice. She became well acquainted with all of Dona's sons but was won over by Oscar's endearing awkwardness and quiet personality, which stood out all the more next to his more conceited, egotistical brothers. The relationship remained a secret for several years, until one evening when the frequently drunk Eitel-Fritz attacked Ina. Hearing Ina's scream, Oscar came to her rescue, knocking his brother onto the floor. In the aftermath, as Oscar tried to calm Ina down, he declared to his mother and brothers that he loved her, wanted to marry her, and if he could not, he would go into exile.

Dona suspected for some time that Oscar and Ina had feelings for one another. Ordinarily, the empress would never have considered allowing a royal prince to marry morganatically. Throughout most of her life, she was obsessive about the sanctity of royal marriages. When her brother Duke Ernest Günther of Schleswig-Holstein announced in 1896 that he wanted to marry the daughter of a German count, she declared that "if he entered into a marriage with a lady who was not of the appropriate rank," she would "*never ... receive her*."[14] Oscar's case was different. He was one of Dona's favorite children, and she decided not to oppose his marriage.

At the young couple's request, Dona approached Wilhelm to obtain his permission for them to wed. As expected, he flew into a fit of white-hot rage, yelling at Dona "that she was a fool to think of it," and that Ina "would be given exactly one hour to clear out of Berlin." Ina promptly departed, but Dona and Oscar stood resolute against Wilhelm. Every day for the next several weeks, the empress and her husband "went through wordy battle,... urging, pleading, supplicating, and even threatening."[15] After months of haranguing, Wilhelm finally acquiesced. His daughter, the Duchess of Brunswick, had a hand in changing his mind. According to one account, "when William II. arrived at Brunswick for the christening of his daughter's first-born child, and asked her what present he could give, he received the reply that all she craved was permission for Prince Oscar to marry the lady of his heart." In the end, "William II. could not resist this appeal."[16] The betrothal was publicly announced on May 26.

The news that one of the emperor's sons was marrying morganatically "created a considerable scandal, and led to much talk among those select circles of Court society where the sayings and doings of every member of the Imperial family are watched with keen interest."[17] Even in the far away United States, the wedding generated considerable interest. "The Kaiser at first resolutely opposed his son's breach of the dynasty's tradition and a marriage below his rank, but the Kaiserin interceded successfully on Prince Oscar's behalf," reported the *New York Times*. "When the marriage takes place the Kaiser, in accordance with tradition will confer a special name and title upon his daughter-in-law, which will give her higher rank than that which she now enjoys, although she will never be entitled to call herself a Princess of Prussia or enjoy the privileges of a member of the royal family."[18] With the official announcement made, plans went ahead for another Hohenzollern wedding later in the year.

The summer of 1914 was proving to be one of the hottest in recent memory as the sun beat down on the many visitors who had come to Vienna for a holiday. Eager to escape the heat and clamor of the capital, Charles and Zita took their children for an extended holiday to Villa Wartholz. Aside from the usual squabbles between the Great Powers, most of Europe was preparing for "a particularly enjoyable year."[19] After a respite at Wartholz, Charles and Zita planned to visit Saint Cecilia's, the abbey on the Isle of Wight where Zita had studied and where her sister Francesca was now a nun.

On the sunny afternoon of June 28, the couple was enjoying lunch outdoors when Zita noticed an exceptionally long pause between the serving of the next course. A moment later, one of the servants came running out with a telegram. It was from Baron Rumerskirch in Sarajevo, Franz Ferdinand's aide-de-camp. "Deeply regret to report that His Imperial Highness and the Duchess were both assassinated here today," the telegram stated with surprising indifference. That moment remained forever engrained in Zita's memory. Decades later, she described her husband's reaction: "Though it was a beautiful day, I saw his face go white in the sun."[20] Overwhelmed with grief, the couple sat in stunned silence for a while. Eventually, Charles went into the house to contact the emperor to confirm if it were true.

Gavrilo Princip, a Bosnian assassin, gunned down the archduke and duchess in the middle of their tour of the city. Sophie was dead by the time they reached a nearby hospital. The archduke slipped into unconsciousness and died shortly thereafter. In his trial, Princip stated he acted "to kill an enemy of the South Slavs" and that Franz Ferdinand was "an energetic man who as ruler would have carried through ideas and reforms which stood in our way."[21] A number of individuals were involved in the plot to murder the archduke. Princip and all of his accomplices were ethnic Bosnians, making them all Austro-Hungarian subjects. They had been provided with six pistols and six bombs from the Serbian State Arsenal, which were smuggled into Bosnia by Serb accomplices. Although the plot had been devised in Belgrade, it was done so without the involvement of the Serbian government.

Franz Joseph was at his summer retreat, Bad Ischl, when the terrible news broke. With his usual cold style, he wired back to Charles that the unthinkable had indeed taken place. The truth was that the emperor was actually somewhat relieved to hear his nephew had been shot. It was widely known that the two men did not like one another. Nonetheless, he realized that the assassinations would have far-reaching consequences. He immediately returned to Vienna, where Charles met him at Hietzing, the closest train station to Schönbrunn Palace where Zita had gone on ahead to meet them. That afternoon, as the emperor and his new twenty-six-year-old heir rode in an open carriage to the palace, crowds lined the streets in stunned silence. In England, Queen Mary and King George called the assassination a "great shock" and a "horrible tragedy."[22] When Emperor Wilhelm II was told while aboard the *Hohenzollern II*, he remarked, "The cowardly detestable crime ... has shaken me to the depths of my soul."[23]

The Prussian court immediately went into mourning, led by Dona's sons, who had been great admirers of Franz Ferdinand. That night, violent mobs formed across Sarajevo. Croatian supporters of the monarchy turned on ethnic Serbians, who were widely blamed for the murders. As buildings were vandalized, Croatians sung out Austria-Hungary's imperial anthem. In Vienna, an eerie calm prevailed as Franz Ferdinand's and Sophie's bodies arrived at the Hofburg Palace to lie in state. Charles and Zita attended a candlelit service in which the cardinal archbishop blessed the coffins with holy water and prayers were sung for the dead. They were later buried in their private crypt at Artstetten Castle in Lower Austria.

In Russia, Franz Ferdinand's assassination barely registered with the Romanovs, who were in the throes of their own series of tragedies. Alexandra and her family were on the *Standart*, cruising down the Baltic coast, when Alexei fell from a ladder, twisting his ankle. Within a few hours, another Spala was taking shape as he cried in agony while the joints in his leg swelled and filled with blood. To make matters worse for the tsarina, her *staretz* was nowhere to be found. Rasputin was back in Russia, convalescing after being attacked by a knife-wielding woman. Even once Alexei was out of danger and on the mend, the imperial family took little interest in the death of an Austrian archduke and his commoner wife. Although unfortunate, no one realized the significance these murders would have. After all, only a few years earlier, the king of Portugal and his son had been assassinated with nothing close to a total war resulting.

Despite being only a heartbeat away from the throne, Charles and Zita found that very little was expected of them in the tense weeks of July and August of 1914. They spent most of that time at Wartholz, left out of the planning and war councils that the emperor was holding. There was little doubt that factions in the imperial court would soon take over. The voices calling for swift and decisive action held the emperor's ear, drowning out the few moderates who insisted on less drastic measures. Blame for the murders was placed squarely on Serbia's shoulders. Crowds surrounded the foreign ministry "waving black and yellow flags and cheering any officer in uniform with wild enthusiasm."[24] Austria was so determined to wipe this fledgling kingdom off the map forever that they conveniently disregarded the fact that the murders were the work of a terrorist group—the Black Hand—and not the Serbian nation as a whole.

Wilhelm II knew immediately what would happen. He wrote to the Austrian foreign minister Count Berchtold, "If His Majesty the Emperor Franz Joseph makes a demand, the Serbian government must obey. If not, Belgrade must be bombarded and occupied until his wish is fulfilled. And rest assured that I am behind you and ready to draw the sword wherever your action requires."[25] During that tense summer, the German foreign ministry wrote to their embassy in London.

> Austria is now going to come to a reckoning with Serbia.... We have not at the present time forced Austria to her decision. But neither should we attempt to stay her hand. If we should do that, Austria would have the right to reproach us with having deprived her of her last chance of political rehabilitation. And then the process of her wasting away and of her internal decay would be still further accelerated. Her standing in the Balkans would be gone forever.... The maintenance of Austria, and in fact of the most powerful Austria possible is a necessity for us.... That she cannot

be maintained forever I willingly admit. But in the meanwhile we may be able to arrange other combinations.[26]

There was little doubt Austria would strike against Serbia. The fact that the Habsburg Empire perceived Serbia as a dangerous threat and wanted to wipe it off the map for years was widely known in political circles. In 1914, the Kingdom of Serbia was a nation still coming into its own. After wrestling its independence from the Turks in the nineteenth century, it doubled in size after the Balkan Wars of the early 1910s. The source of the poor Austro-Serbian relationship was the latter's ongoing fiat of liberating Slavic groups living under foreign governments. The Serbian government proclaimed for years its intention of liberating all Slavs living under Austrian rule to form a southern Slavic state, or Yugoslavia, as it was called in Serbian. When Franz Ferdinand died, the general consensus was that Austria would attack Serbia while Europe was on its summer vacation, thereby slipping under the radar and failing to gain too much attention. In the end, Austria sent Serbia a carefully worded ultimatum on July 23 that was so constricting that the government in Belgrade would have no choice but to refuse, thereby opening the door for a military strike. Serbia had forty-eight hours to respond. The world held its breath to see what would happen next.

PART 3

The Great Tragedy

(1914–18)

14

The Call to Arms

(July–August 1914)

The response from Serbia came swiftly. Ten demands were set forth by the Austrians. Of those ten, Serbia agreed to two unconditionally, three with some conditions, four more were evaded with vague responses and diplomatic double-talk, and only one—in which Vienna would oversee investigating and adjudicating the archduke's assassination—was rejected. Europe's politicians were amazed by how conciliatory Serbia's reply had been. "An excellent result for a forty-eight-hour [ultimatum]," Wilhelm inscribed on his own copy of the Serbian reply. "This is more than we could have expected! A great moral victory for Vienna."[1]

Just as amazing was Austria's refusal to accept the reply. Franz Joseph and his government declared Serbia's response to be unsatisfactory even though most European diplomats considered it a massive success for Austrian foreign policy. Franz Ferdinand's assassination was just the excuse the emperor needed to attack Serbia in an effort to protect Austria's imperial status. Austria hoped that they would be able to issue their ultimatum and invade Serbia before the other Great Powers could intervene. Austria, it seemed, completely failed to realize how complex the series of alliances were that bound together the Great Powers.

As soon as Austria-Hungary set its sights on punishing Serbia for the murder of the Archduke Franz Ferdinand and his wife, the diplomatic and military alliances that bound the various monarchical powers to aid one another kicked into effect. With astonishing rapidity, the powers of Europe found themselves ready to wage war. Vienna's determination to make Serbia pay compelled Serbia's ally, Russia, to aid its Slavic neighbor. Imperial Germany bore down upon the Russian Empire for aiming its sights on Austria-Hungary. With Russia under threat from Germany, England and France were not far behind themselves in lockstep with their faraway ally, Russia. It was a fast-moving, complicated chess game involving the Great Powers for the highest stakes.[2]

The decision to declare war was not taken lightly by Nicholas II. The Slavophiliac tsar was compelled to honor Russia's promise to defend Serbia. "As for ourselves, it is impossible to sit quietly and see Serbia being strangled like a kitten by a huge dog," the tsar wrote to his maternal first cousin Prince Nicholas of Greece. He added, "We cannot afford to lose this war, as the triumph of Prussian militarism would mean the end of all liberty and civilization."[3] On the evening of July 25, the Russian General Staff initiated its official war preparations that allowed for military measures along frontier regions to be put in place.

Three days later, on July 28, the state press in Vienna released its "final and irrevocable" declaration: "The Royal Government of Serbia has not given a satisfactory reply to the Note presented to it by the Austro-Hungarian Minister in Belgrade on July 23rd, 1914, the Imperial and Royal government of Austria-Hungary finds it necessary to safeguard its rights and interests and to have recourse for this purpose to force of arms. Austria-Hungary therefore considers itself from this moment in a state of war with Serbia."[4]

Queen Mary was dumbstruck by the news. "Austria has declared war on Servia!" she wrote. She was under no illusions about the consequences of declaring war. She wrote to her aunt Augusta in Neustrelitz, "God grant we may not have a European war thrust upon us, & for such a stupid reason too, no I don't mean stupid, but to have to go to war on account of tiresome Servia beggars belief."[5] What began as an isolated problem in southeastern Europe became a political crisis that stretched across the continent and eventually around the world.

Within twenty-four hours, Russia upgraded from military preparations to a partial mobilization. In the hopes of deterrence through intimidation, Berlin wired a telegram to Saint Petersburg on July 30 stating that any further Russian military action would be met with an equal response from Germany. Emperor Wilhelm took Russia's mobilization as perfidiousness from Nicholas II. Although Britain remained uncommitted at this point, Wilhelm and

Dona were adamant that King George V would throw Britain's lot in with Nicholas and Russia against them. In his telegrams to both men, Wilhelm made grandiose pronouncements of friendship and fidelity, but to his wife and ministers, he accused the king and tsar of colluding against Germany. He claimed they were manipulating the situation to destroy the German Empire. He denounced King George and the English as "a mean crew of shopkeepers revealed in their 'true colours.'" Furthermore, he accused the king's foreign minister of proving George to be "a liar.... At that, it is a matter of fact a threat combined with a bluff, in order to separate us from Austria and to prevent us from mobilising, and to shift the responsibility for the war."[6] The emperor wrote a chilling memo to Gottlieb von Jagow, his foreign minister, describing how deeply betrayed he felt.

> So the celebrated encirclement of Germany has finally become an established fact, and the purely anti-German policy which England has been pursuing all over the world has won the most spectacular victory. England stands derisive, brilliantly successful; her long-mediated purely anti-German policy, stirring to admiration even him who it will utterly destroy! The [legacy of the] dead Edward [VII] is stronger than I who am still alive ... Our agents and all such must inflame the whole Mahommedan [Islamic] world to frantic rebellion against this detestable, treacherous, conscience-less nation of shopkeepers; for if we are to bleed to death, England shall at all costs lose India.[7]

At midnight, the whole of the Russian army was mobilized. On an intimate level, Wilhelm II seethed with hatred. Politically, he was required to uphold his military alliance with Franz Joseph in the face of Russian aggression. Their two empires, along with Italy, formed the Triple Alliance, also known as the Central powers. On July 31, the German ambassador in Moscow was informed that total Russian mobilization took place the night before. At 1:00 p.m. that afternoon, Wilhelm ordered a full mobilization of German armed forces. It was only a matter of hours until a formal declaration of war was forthcoming.

That night, Wilhelm presided over another important matter, one that had important dynastic implications for the Hohenzollerns. Since the beginning of May, Dona had been planning Prince Oscar's wedding to Countess Ina, but the outbreak of war changed all that. As an officer in the military, Oscar knew that, with his regiment now mobilized, he would have to take up his command at the front lines. Those in the Prussian court who were against Oscar and Ina's marriage—led by the petty, vindictive Eitel-Fritz—sought to have the prince shipped out to the forward mobilization zone immediately. Oscar knew that if he did not act quickly, he might never get his chance to marry the woman he loved—or worse, she could become a casualty of the war. On July 31, Ina returned to Berlin. That night, she and Oscar were married in a last-minute wedding before the prince joined his regiment. It was a very small, private ceremony at Bellevue Palace, in the central Tiergarten area of Berlin. Wilhelm upheld the traditions which were so dear to him and elevated his newest daughter-in-law to the rank and title Countess von Ruppin, thereby giving her greater precedence at court, though he still refused to raise her to a princess.

Any hopes for a peaceful resolution to this international crisis were smashed the next day when the German Empire declared war on Russia. All eyes were on the imperial family, who were still at sea aboard their yacht, the *Standart*. When a pale-looking Nicholas II broke the news that they were at war, Alexandra was deeply shaken. She "began to weep, and the Grand-Duchesses likewise dissolved into tears on seeing their mother's distress."[8] Alexandra telephoned her old friend Sophie Buxhoeveden with the news.

"Good heavens!" Sophie said. "So Austria has done it!"

"No, no," Alexandra replied. "Germany. It is ghastly, terrible—but God will help and will save Russia."[9]

On August 2, the tsar, tsarina, and their daughters arrived in Saint Petersburg aboard their yacht. Upon their arrival, they received "a thunderous ovation." The masses shouted, "*Batiushka, Batiushka*, lead us to victory!"[10] That afternoon, all the Romanovs, their courtiers, officials, and aristocrats converged on the Winter Palace for the tsar's public declaration of war against Germany. More than five thousand people assembled in one of the palace's massive halls. Nicholas II's aunt Grand Duchess Marie Pavlovna vividly recalled the war congress at the Winter Palace that day. "Hands in long white gloves nervously crumpled handkerchiefs," she saw as she entered the hall, "and under large hats ... many eyes were red with crying. The men frowned thoughtfully, shifting from foot to foot, readjusting their swords, or running their fingers over the brilliant decorations pinned on their chests."[11] Afterward, the imperial family attended a *Te Deum* before appearing on the palace balcony where "a scene of almost mythic proportions unfolded." An estimated quarter of a million people fell on their knees crying out "God save the Tsar!" One witness recalled that to "those thousands of men on their knees at that moment, the Tsar was really the autocrat appointed of God, the military, political and religious leader of his people."[12] The Duma professed its undying loyalty to the tsar. They even went so far as to pass an exorbitant budget to finance the war effort. A misleading, inflated sense of euphoria swept Russia, the likes of which had not been seen since Napoleon invaded in 1812. At some point that day, Nicholas sat down to send a note to King George: "In this solemn hour I wish to assure you once more that I have done all in my power to avert war."[13]

The next day, August 3, Germany declared war on France. That same day, Dona's son Adalbert married his second cousin Princess Adelaide of Saxe-Meiningen, whom he had courted for several years. Adalbert was not married in Berlin in the presence of his family. Instead, he and Adelaide were married in the chapel at the German naval base of Wilhelmshaven in Schleswig-Holstein. Adalbert was one of the most decorated members of the Prussian royal family. He was a lieutenant on board the SMS *Luitpold* at the time. When he was informed that war broke out and he would be sent into combat, he was eager to make Adelaide his wife as quickly as possible. Their simple military wedding was attended by a few officers and was performed by the Wilhelmshaven chaplain. Unlike with Ina, both Wilhelm and Dona heartily approved of Adalbert's royal wife.

Patriotic fervor surged across the German Empire. The anti-Wilhelmine Left and Socialist parties silenced themselves. At a gathering in the throne room of the Stadtschloss, the Reichstag transferred its power to the Bundesrat. Wilhelm and the council of German princes now had direct control over the empire. They were even allowed to levy taxes to fund the war effort if needed, typically a highly controversial issue. At the time, Wilhelm and Augusta Victoria were at the Neues Palais in Potsdam, but on August 4, the royal family made the short journey in open motorcars to the Stadtschloss in Berlin. Hundreds of thousands of cheering people took to the streets. "It was a scene of the wildest enthusiasm," wrote a South African doctor who was in Berlin at the time. "The picture of the Emperor is a vivid memory. He did not bow once in acknowledgment of the shouts of the crowd. The Crown Prince nodded, and his wife nodded and smiled continually, but the Emperor sat with one hand at his golden helmet, stern and inscrutable, a figure of destiny. There was not during the whole time the faintest flicker of a smile."[14] Once they arrived at the palace, Wilhelm, Dona, and the crown prince appeared on the balcony, where the enthusiasm of the crowds continued. Standing there, Wilhelm announced to the people gathered below, "When it comes to war, all [political] parties cease and we are all brothers. If this or that party has attacked me in peace time, I now wholeheartedly forgive them."[15]

Despite the emperor's magnanimous words, some historians have commented that most of the people were cheering for Dona who, by 1914, was the "most loved member of the royal family."[16] Her unpretentious upbringing and simple, traditional values allowed the people to feel connected with their empress. One of the Potsdam courtiers asserted that "of the crowned heads of Europe of the present day the Empress Augusta Victoria is, perhaps, the most popular with her subjects, with the exception of Queen Mary of England."[17] Even in the United States, Dona was highly regarded. A special article published in the *New York Times* in 1913 sang her praises: "No Other Consort of a Prussian Ruler Ever Wielded Such a Beneficent Influence Over Her Husband, or Made Such an Impression Upon the People, by Whom She Is Regarded with Profound Affection."[18]

On the day the royal family rode into Berlin, the city reached "a state of feverish excitement." The train stations were congested with troops leaving for the front. One witness described it as nothing short of "an armed camp, and the platforms were packed with departing troops, accompanied by their families and relations." Anti-Russian and anti-British sentiments were running high. When the imperial train transporting Dowager Empress Marie Feodorovna back to Russia from England arrived, a frightening scene unfolded as "near chaos broke out." Mobs of people began shouting insults and obscenities. After Minnie pulled all the blinds down over her compartment windows, the crowds began attacking the train, breaking windows, and tearing parts off the exterior. Only quick thinking on the part of local police prevented the dowager empress from being harmed. Emperor Wilhelm could not detain Minnie in Germany, but he did refuse "to give passage to the Imperial train, ordering it to leave German soil by the shortest route—to be diverted to the Danish frontier."[19] This situation only deepened the Russian imperial family's antipathy not only for Wilhelm but for all things German.

As scenes played themselves out in Berlin with the Hohenzollerns and the dowager empress, German troops invaded Belgium and Luxembourg in a plan to sweep in and seize Paris as quickly as possible. Great Britain had been a guarantor of Belgian neutrality since 1839. Its invasion forced the British to serve Germany with their own ultimatum. Queen Mary wrote gravely on August 4, "At 12. we sent an ultimatum to Germany & at 7 p.m. she declared war on us. It is too dreadful but we could not act otherwise. We went on to the [palace] balcony at 8 p.m. & again at 11.15. after the news of war having been declared was out."[20] Britain had been slow to involve itself because it considered the conflict a continental war that would have little impact on British imperial interests. Most of the prime minister's cabinet was against the war because they erroneously believed that a European conflict would be fought mostly on land; there had not been a major naval conflict among the Great Powers since the Crimean War of 1853–56. In 1914, Britain's standing army numbered only seventy thousand men, compared to Germany's or Russia's, which were in the millions. It was only after Belgium's neutrality was violated that public opinion turned unanimously in favor of war. When George V signed the declaration, he did so on behalf of Britain's vast empire and its more than four hundred million inhabitants. In the span of only a few days, the British army swelled into the millions also.

Once Britain and Germany were at war, most of the affection Wilhelm felt for his maternal homeland died. Like his grandfather the prince consort, he truly believed in maintaining international diplomacy through personal relationships between royals. With Britain and Russia's declarations of war against Germany, the emperor took it as a personal knife in the back. "As it turned out," wrote Wilhelm's nephew Sigismund, "family relationships—or friendships between the European Monarchs for that matter—proved quite useless. The secret groups who pulled the strings of global politics were so powerful that familial influences were quite incapable of stopping them, however hard they tried."[21] There forever remained a small part of him that held affection for Britain, but he would never idolize it again. Bernhard von Bülow, who served as chancellor of Germany from 1900–09, recalled the emperor exploding in a rant against Nicholas and George: "History showed no greater perfidy.... God would punish them some day!... The Tsar's ingratitude was revolting: he had always been the Tsar's close friend. As for 'Georgie,' all the emperor had to say was that Queen Victoria, their grandmother, must have turned in her grave at the spectacle of her English grandson flinging down the gauntlet to the German."[22] Nicholas II perceived the depth of Wilhelm's antipathy when he admitted, "I felt that all was over forever between me and William."[23]

Europe's four imperial dynasties were to find themselves as much the victims of what would become the Great War as any of their subjects. Many have compared this titanic struggle to the opening of Pandora's box, releasing an evil upon Europe's crowned heads that could never be repealed. In four years' time, Augusta Victoria, Alexandra, and Zita would be toppled from their thrones, each with far-reaching consequences for themselves and their families. Only Queen Mary would emerge victorious, but even her imperial luster would begin to dwindle.

Blame for the continent's first total war in a century was placed upon Germany and the Hohenzollerns. Augusta Victoria's American physician— Dr. Arthur Davis—recalled that she was profoundly affected by the gravity of what was going on. He believed "that she was bitterly opposed to the war," but that "if that were indeed the case, she must have masked her feelings very effectually to preserve harmony in the royal household."[24] Once the war began, she was busy with a flurry of activity. Properly understanding her role as *Landsmutter*, she made a public appeal to the women of Germany to step up and assume their rightful positions as contributing members of society during this difficult time.

Obeying the summons of the Emperor our people are preparing for an unprecedented struggle which they did not provoke and which they are carrying on only in self-defense.

Whoever can bear arms will joyfully fly to the colors to defend the Fatherland and his blood.

The struggle will be gigantic and the wounds to be healed innumerable. Therefore, I call upon you women and girls of Germany, and upon all to whom it is not given to fight for our beloved home, for help. Let everyone now do what lies in her power to lighten the struggle for our husbands, sons, and brothers. I know that in all ranks of our people without exception the will exists to discharge this high duty, but may the Lord God strengthen us in our holy work of love, which summons us women to devote all our strength to the Fatherland in its decisive struggle.

The organizations primarily concerned, to whom our support is above all things needful, have already sent out notices as to the mustering of volunteers and the collection of gifts of all kinds.

Auguste Victoria

Berlin, August 6, 1914[25]

The first week of August saw the commencement of the First World War. For Dona, this served as an epic backdrop for the discreet weddings of her two sons. Afterward, those of her sons who were on active duty in the German military departed for the front lines. Berlin was "swept along in a sudden rush of patriotism." Exhilarated crowds formed throughout the city every day, clogging the streets and blocking traffic. They celebrated and cheered on the troops that marched down Unter den Linden on their way to the front lines while the German national anthem played triumphantly in the background. "Life in the Germany of today," recorded one witness, "seems to move to the rhythm of this tune. Every day troops pass by my window on their way to the station, and as they march along to this refrain, people rush to the windows and doors of the houses and take up the song so that it rings through the streets, almost like a solemn vow sung by these men on their way to death."[26]

⁘

The world now faced a perilous road, according to Tsarina Alexandra. "It will be a terrible, monstrous struggle; humanity is about to pass through ghastly sufferings," she told Pierre Gilliard, her children's French tutor. When it came to searching for the cause of the war, she looked no further than her cousin Wilhelm and Germany. "I have never liked the Emperor William, if only because he is not sincere," she said. "He is vain and has always played the comedian. He was always reproaching me with doing nothing for Germany … He will never forgive me this war!"[27] The tsar shared his wife's views that blame for the war rested with the contemptible kaiser. "He could have stopped the war had he wanted to!" he told Prince Nicholas of Greece.[28]

Not only did the war set nation against nation, it also divided Europe's extended royal family. It was not hyperbolic to say the First World War was a macrocosmic family feud. The rulers of the continent's monarchical powers were first cousins, grandchildren of Queen Victoria: King George V; Emperor Wilhelm II; Tsarina Alexandra; Queen Victoria Eugenie of Spain; Queen Maud of Norway; Queen Sophie of Greece; Crown Princess Marie of Romania (queen after 1916); and Crown Princess Margaret of Sweden.[29] The family hardships imposed by the war went far beyond these reigning (and future) monarchs and consorts. Alexandra was cut off from her sister Irene in Kiel. Her brother the Grand Duke of Hesse was required to side with Germany since he was a member of the Bundesrat. This was very painful for Alexandra, who had always been close to her brother. Her greatest worry was that Wilhelm would send Ernie to fight along the Russian front, against her own forces. A few months later, she learned Ernie refused to serve in the German military. A similar situation played out when Irene's husband, Wilhelm II's brother, was made an admiral in the German navy. Alexandra wrote to her sister Victoria shortly after the war began, "One's heart bleeds, thinking of all the misery everywhere and what will be afterwards!"[30] Many of the other Romanovs were affected as well. Almost every living member of the dynasty had a German parent or had married a German spouse.

This schism of Europe's royal houses was perhaps even more hurtful in England. The queen was cut off from her beloved aunt Augusta who, although a British princess by birth, became a German citizen in 1843 when she married the hereditary prince of Mecklenburg-Strelitz. King George V's cousin the Duke of Brunswick—Dona's son-in-law—held British titles but was declared an enemy combatant when the war started. George's other cousin Charles Eduard became the Duke of Coburg in 1900. Like the Duke of Brunswick, he had been forced to side with the Germans. As far as the British were concerned, he was dead. There were also a number of royals living in England in 1914 with strong German connections. Almost all of them had been naturalized English citizens since childhood, but that did not immunize them from the anti-German xenophobia that was sweeping Great Britain. Prince Louis of Battenberg, one of George and Mary's favorite cousins, was deeply wounded by the rising Germanophobia. Not only was he married to Tsarina Alexandra's sister Victoria, he was also one of the most decorated officers in the Royal Navy. He was made First Sea Lord in 1912 after forty-six years of distinguished service, but in October 1914, he was forced to resign because he was German. His titles were German, he had a home in Germany, he spoke German, and even members of his personal staff were German nationals. His wife, Victoria, blamed George V for not doing more on her husband's behalf. "The King is a nobody," she declared angrily.[31] The hostility shown toward the Battenbergs at the start of the war was both sadly misguided and ironic, since the family was staunchly pro-British. Louis and Victoria's son, later styled as Lord Louis Mountbatten, became "the most honored British soldier of World War II."[32]

There was even outrage when the king and queen met with some of their Greek cousins that summer. According to the ultraconservatives, Queen Sophie of Greece was Emperor Wilhelm II's sister and therefore must be pro-German. Ignored was the fact that Sophie had long been at odds with Wilhelm and Dona and that they barely spoke by the outbreak of the First World War. Sophie and her husband, King Constantine, were further condemned for opting to remain neutral during the war, rather than side with the Britain and France. This was just more evidence, the critics claimed, to support the fact that the Greek monarchs were German at heart.

Of the four great empires that went to war in 1914, Russia suffered the most when the first volleys were fired. Within a matter of months, Nicholas II's armies were in retreat. Germany had proved her military might from the outset. Russian troops soon pulled out of Poland altogether for the first time in nearly 150 years. Nearly three million men were lost before Poland was finally surrendered. Sadly, Russia was in no shape to wage war. In 1914, there were "a million fewer rifles in her arsenal than the number of men who were mobilized, and the same arsenals proved to be almost 600 million rounds of rifle ammunition short. There was only about one machine gun for every six hundred infantry ... [and] the entire Russian army had only 60 batteries of heavy artillery with which to face the Austrians and the Germans, while the Germans alone had 381 to direct against the Russians."[33]

As Nicholas II was forced to deal with Russia's shattering defeats on the battlefield, he also had to contend with the return of Rasputin to his family's life. The *staretz* was one of the most vocal opponents of the war, even going so far as to send Nicholas a telegram warning him, "Let Papa not plan war for with war will come the end of Russia and yourselves and you will lose to the last man." The tsar was so outraged by Rasputin's note that he tore it up the moment he read it.[34] Within a year, Rasputin became a regular personage in the tsarina's entourage. "The mad monk," as he was derisively known, was a master manipulator who used Alexandra's fears over Alexei's health to his advantage. He recounted that, once, during an argument with the tsar and tsarina, "I threatened to go away and leave them to their fate; they then agreed to everything."[35] The *staretz* spread many stories about his relationship with Alexandra. "Many tales are told of the Empress and me," he told a diplomat. "I know this. It is infamous. Yesterday I went to see her. The poor little thing; she too is in need of being able to speak frankly with some one. She suffers much. I console her. I talk to her of God, and of us peasants and she becomes calm. Ah! It is but yesterday she went to sleep on my shoulder."[36] Rasputin knew exactly how to twist and pull Alexandra as he desired. Preying upon her darkest fears, he once declared, "Remember that I need neither the Emperor nor yourself. If you abandon me to my enemies it will not worry me. I'm quite able to cope with them. The demons themselves are helpless against me.... But neither the Emperor nor you can do without *me*. If I am not there to protect you, your son will come to harm."[37]

In declaring war on the Central powers, Great Britain faced a daunting task. It faced the obstacle of transporting troops and supplies across the English Channel to the front lines in France. The risk of convoys being attacked by German submarines was ever present. But King George V refused to be intimidated; so too did his wife. Queen Mary took a leading role in getting the British people behind the government and the war. In August, she met with Lady Bertha Dawkins, one of her ladies-in-waiting, to begin planning relief for the soldiers. "We must have everything ready," she said. "I do not want to have the state of things which prevailed during the Boer War, with everybody just sending what they liked, without relation to the real needs of our soldiers, without organisation. It entails too much waste, and too great loss of time."[38] The queen was instrumental in organizing the "monstrous regiment of women" who took over many of the responsibilities on the home front when the men went off to war. Determined to keep the public morale afloat, she devoted herself to visiting hospitals and encouraging the troops. According to one of her biographers, Mary's "whole life now seemed to have been a preparation for [this,] her finest hour."[39]

She took it upon herself to mobilize England's vast group of unemployed women. She organized entire manufacturing sectors, especially munitions, with only women workers. These groups later formed the Women's Legion, which in turn became the Women's Army Auxiliary Corps. By the end of the summer, she was furiously working to get women workers the equality and respect they deserved. After haranguing much of the government, she was thrilled when the Central Committee on Women's Employment was formed in 1914. Included on the roster was Margaret Bondfield, the first female cabinet minister in British history.

Along with organizing help for the war effort, the queen took special delight in bringing comfort and compassion to those whom society had neglected. Shortly after the war began, Mary was at Sandringham when she heard about an elderly widow in a nearby village who had fallen ill with a serious disease. The townspeople were too frightened of catching the illness to visit her, so she was alone. A few days later, onlookers were stunned when they saw Queen Mary go into the woman's house and march straight up to the bedroom with her arms filled with flowers—which she picked herself—to visit the woman. In caring for others, Mary did not limit her time to just to the sick and wounded. She sought to inspire all her subjects.

Throughout that summer of 1914, Mary would sit by her window at Buckingham Palace and watch one regiment after another marching to the train station bound for Dover, and beyond that, France. This sight gnawed at her heart, especially because two of her sons were on active duty. The Prince of Wales was serving with the Grenadier Guards in France, and Bertie was an officer in the Royal Navy. Deeply moved by the sight of so many young men ready to give their lives for king and country, the queen issued a heartfelt letter addressed to "the Men of Our Army, Navy, and Air Force." Reminiscent of Dona's letter to the women of Germany, Mary's note touched on national pride and the honor that the troops were rendering to Britain.

> I send this message to tell every man how much we, the women of the British Empire at home, watch and pray for you during the long hours of these days of stress and endurance.
>
> Our pride in you is immeasurable, our hope unbounded, our trust absolute. You are fighting in the cause of Righteousness and Freedom, fighting to defend the children and women of our land from the horrors that have overtaken other countries, fighting for our very existence as a People at Home and Across the Seas ...

We, on our part, send forth, with full hearts and unfaltering will, the lives we hold most dear ...

... I know that I am expressing what is felt by thousands of wives and mothers when I say that we are determined to help one another in keeping your homes ready against your glad home-coming.

In God's Name we bless you and by His help we too will do our best.[40]

⬦

War brought upon Austria-Hungary a cataclysm it was unprepared to face. Its army, though large, was a hodgepodge of different ethnicities that did not even share a common language. Once fighting broke out, the empire suffered serious defeats on the battlefield, though not nearly as badly as those that had befallen Russia. The invasion of Serbia, expected to take only a matter of days, came to a screeching halt despite Austria's forty-eight infantry divisions, compared with Serbia's eleven. At the Battle of Cer in August 1914, the Austrians suffered the loss of 27,500 men compared to the Serbians' 16,500. When it became obvious that Austria could not conquer Serbia so easily, imperial forces were sent north against the Russians, but that too failed. Despite their defeat in Poland, the tsarist armies quickly overran Galicia, making it as far west as the Carpathian Mountains. Part of the reason for Russia's success was that they were in possession of Austrian mobilization schedules, thanks to Alfred Redl, an Austrian colonel who was selling state secrets to Russia. Austrian attempts to reclaim Galicia failed dismally, with more than 350,000 soldiers killed in the process. In the aftermath, Ukrainian citizens in Galicia suspected of being disloyal to Austria were executed. Only the defeat of the Russian army at Tannenberg by the German Eighth Army, which cost another 250,000 lives, slowed their advance into Hungary. By the end of the year, "some 82 percent of the original infantry complement of the Habsburg armed forces were casualties. About a million men were dead, wounded, or sick. The rest of the war would be fought by reserves, civilians, and officers just completing their training."[41]

Emperor Franz Joseph believed the causes of the war were just and righteous. Throughout his sixty-year reign, he had watched as one territory after another was ripped away from his empire. Lombardy, Venice, and parts of Switzerland, Germany, Poland, and Romania had all belonged to the Habsburg monarchy at one time or another, but military defeats had forced the emperor to surrender them. He believed this war was an attack on Austria's imperial sovereignty, and for this cause, Franz Joseph refused to back down, even if it meant the destruction of his empire. But he was also a pragmatist; every war of his reign had ended in a defeat for Austria. When Austria achieved a victory in one of its early battles in the fall of 1914, Zita congratulated the emperor, who forlornly and prophetically replied, "Yes it is a victory, but that is the way my wars always begin, only to end in defeat. And this time it will be even worse. They will say that I am old and cannot cope any more, and that after that revolutions will break out and then it will be the end."[42]

Archduchess Zita, who was raised partly in Austria and spoke German, might easily have chosen to side with the emperor's views about the war being an attack on Austria's sovereignty. Her real inclinations, however, lay with France, the country she considered her true home. Not long after war was declared, she became a target of criticism "because she had the courage to proclaim her French sympathies and to express her indignation at the unwarranted attack against Serbia with which Austria inaugurated the long struggle which ... she was to become one of the principle victims."[43] It was painful for her to watch as France, the land she loved so much, was invaded by Germany. She was also deeply saddened by the conquest of Belgium, whose king was married to Zita's cousin Elisabeth.

The war was causing Zita deep personal grief as well because the conflict divided her close-knit family. At the end of August, Charles rejoined his regiment in Galicia and was sent to Przemysl on the eastern front to fight the Russians. The impact of a total war on both the Habsburgs and Austria-Hungary weighed heavily on Charles and Zita, who recalled taking a walk together at Schönbrunn before the archduke returned to the front.

> There were of course many family and personal matters that had to be settled before his departure and we went through those first. Then my husband suddenly turned to the political situation and said:
>
> "I leave with a heavy heart because when this war is over, whatever happens in it, this Austria-Hungary that I know and love will no longer exist. Either there will be two purely German Empires in the heart of Europe with a big Slav group alongside them. Or, more likely, the Slav group will be pulled to Russia and we in turn will be swallowed up by Prussia."[44]

With Charles gone and Zita well into her third pregnancy, Hetzendorf Castle was closed down, and the archduchess took her two children to live with the emperor at Schönbrunn Palace. The war was also burdening her Bourbon-

Parma relatives. Four of Zita's brothers enlisted to fight. Princes Felix and René had lived most of their lives in Austria and were glad to take up arms to defend the Habsburg Empire. Zita's other brothers Sixtus and Xavier were Frenchmen through and through. They enlisted to fight for France on behalf of the Bourbon family. They only discovered later that, as members of the former ruling dynasty, French law forbade them from serving in the armed forces. After appealing to their cousin the queen of the Belgians, they were allowed to serve in the Belgian military. The stance Sixtus and Xavier took caused Zita great distress. Since they were in Munich at the time they enlisted, and because they identified themselves first and foremost as Frenchmen, they were behind enemy lines and could be captured as prisoners of war. It took personal appeals from both Zita and Charles to spare Xavier and Sixtus from imprisonment. "I can understand that they only want to do their duty," Franz Joseph remarked as he signed the order granting the princes temporary amnesty.[45]

On August 20, Zita and her family gathered together one last time before her relatives were expelled from Austrian territory. Prince Xavier recalled the emotional meeting: "A somewhat moving farewell. But Zita is very, very brave. She has tried to let us see nothing of her feelings ... Charles said that just as it was his duty to join the army, so it was our duty to return to France. Where now are the days of Frohsdorf and Schwarzau?"[46] They paid one last visit to their beloved Schwarzau near Vienna before her brothers left for Belgium via France. In the coming weeks, Schwarzau would be turned into a field hospital presided over by the Duchess of Parma, who was taking up a commission as a Red Cross nurse. At every doorway, in every courtyard, there were happy memories waiting to overflow in their reminiscences. In his diary, Xavier wrote about that last visit: "Mother acts just like Zita and tries not to show her feelings but it must be absolutely terrible for her.... And yet, sad as the evening was on the terrace at Schwarzau, we felt, as never before, how closely we belong together, bound to each other by indestructible ties."[47]

As Europe marched headlong into war, Xavier could not deny that it was the bonds of family that held them all together, especially Charles and Zita. "That was how we felt then, when Charles and Zita married," he remarked. "We swore then ... to try and build a ring around them to protect them in these dreadful times, for we sensed what was coming. Now it is upon us ... No more; tomorrow we set out."[48]

15

"I Am an Officer with All My Body and Soul"

(1914–15)

By 1915, the Entente was buckling under the onslaught of the Central powers. Though the Austro-Hungarian military failed in its early attempts to invade Serbia, the German war machine was finely tuned and highly effective. At the Battle of Tannenberg in East Prussia, German forces quickly routed their unqualified Russian counterparts. In the west, more French soil was being conquered every day. German troops succeeded in annihilating more than 230,000 French and British combatants in the first year alone. When German military forces drove the Russians out of East Prussia in February 1915, thanksgiving services were held in churches across Berlin. Wilhelm, Dona, and the Duke and Duchess of Brunswick attended a special service in the great Berlin Cathedral, located in the Cölln region of the old city. During the trip to the church, "the Emperor and Empress were enthusiastically cheered."[1] The truth of German successes, however, was less attributable to Wilhelm's personal military leadership than to his generals. Shortly after the war began, the emperor was forced to surrender his powers as supreme warlord of the German military to Chief of the General Staff Helmuth von Moltke, a power-hungry bureaucrat who had been itching for war. Dona was horrified when she discovered Moltke had effectively stripped her husband of his prerogatives, turning him into a figurehead who merely represented the German war effort. By the second year of the war, Wilhelm had very little to do with the day-to-day combat planning.

The intoxicating patriotism that had swelled in Berlin in August 1914 dwindled as "the inevitable effects of conflict had slowly, invidiously crept across the German capital." In the winter of 1914/15, Berlin's citizens were forced to endure food rationing and fuel shortages. One Reichstag member was deeply worried by the menacing din that was taking hold: "A deep-seated discontent animated the masses of the population throughout the first winter of the war." One city resident went even further in describing the enveloping sense of gloom and hopelessness. He wrote that Berlin was "enveloped in an impenetrable veil of sadness, gray in gray, which no golden ray of sunlight ever seems able to pierce, and which forms a fit setting for the white-faced, black-robed women who glide so sadly through the streets, some bearing their sorrows [for loved ones killed in the war] proudly as a crown to their lives, others bent and broken under a burden too heavy to be borne."[2]

With Germany's men being conscripted by the hundreds every day, the empire's infrastructure began to suffer. Unlike Austria-Hungary, which had numerous ethnic groups to conscript into fighting, Germany (like Russia) was forced to glean its soldiers from all corners of society. This left essentials like transportation, municipal and federal services, and manufacturing sectors dangerously undermanned. Empress Augusta Victoria once again turned to the women of Germany to step forward and assume their role as valued, contributing citizens of the empire during this time. "Every German woman," the government declared, "is a soldier in this economic war." The burdens the people carried began to erode the Prusso-German national identity that had existed since 1871. For the first time in decades, the German military had not marched to a swift, resounding victory over its enemies. The existentialism of the monarchy's link with the military led to a permanent shift in the attitudes of the German people toward the Hohenzollerns. Normal "events such as the 500th anniversary of the Hohenzollern house on 21 November 1915 and the normally well celebrated birthdays of the Kaiserin and Kaiser in October and January, respectively, received very little press, either in advance of the festivities or afterward."[3]

Being left behind in Berlin's maelstrom while the emperor was at the front was almost too much for Dona to bear. The sight of watching her people suffer gnawed at her constantly. The petitions she received from charities, church parishes, and hospitals increased exponentially. With Wilhelm gone, it was up to Dona to be the public face of the monarchy at home. One of the first things she did was to move her family out of the cavernous Stadtschloss into the more subdued Bellevue Palace, allowing the empress to save money on utilities, staff, and upkeep. Dona felt it was her responsibility to set an example for a more conservative, less lavish lifestyle while the war continued. The move to Bellevue also afforded her the chance to spend more time with her son Willy's family, who were living in permanent residence there while the crown prince was commanding the Fifth Army. Their support proved vital in September 1915 when tragedy struck the Prussian royal family. Prince Adalbert's wife, Adelaide, gave birth to a daughter on September 4. Named Victoria Marina, the princess died only a few hours later. This was a crushing blow for the empress, who could not bear to see any child suffer or die, let alone her own granddaughter.

The grief of Victoria Marina's death, the separation from her husband, and the burdens imposed by the war overwhelmed Augusta Victoria. Added to this dangerous mix was her poor health. In private, she suffered from bouts of anxious depression. She also began showing symptoms of heart disease, yet another malady that ran in her family; her sister Calma suffered severely from heart disease for many years. Dona's worsening health meant that her doctors were being called to Bellevue on a regular basis. They could see "that she had been suffering considerable pain and loss of sleep." These very real pains in her heart and back, her increasing fits of anxiety, and the strain the war was placing on her marriage aged the empress well beyond her fifty-six years. Arthur Davis, her American physician, noted, "her hair had turned white many years before. It was commonly said, indeed, that the change had been brought about rather suddenly as a result of certain [drugs] she had taken in an effort to avert a tendency to avoirdupois [be overweight] which had developed."[4] Dona's physical appearance was under constant scrutiny from her husband. He made sure she had a regular supply of diet pills to keep her figure trim because he loathed plump women. The diet regime proved successful if misguided. Dona's slim waistline was legendary in royal circles. "Who would believe," Wilhelm often asked, "that that woman had [seven] children."[5] Wilhelm was so concerned about her appearance that he maintained control of her wardrobe. He even designed many of her dresses himself, which he insisted she wear along with opulent rows of diamonds, wide hats he himself picked out, and sparkling jewels. In this way, he could control almost every aspect of the way Dona looked.

The war's progression meant Dona was required to take on greater responsibilities than she had previously. She was almost solely responsible for managing the imperial residences, which at one point included fifty-six palaces and castles in the Berlin-Brandenburg region alone. She was also forced to contend with an increasingly unstable husband. Once he lost his title as supreme warlord, Wilhelm "veered between euphoria, fury and dramatic lows. One moment he would demand that his soldiers take no prisoners; the next he would declaim with his old grandiosity that if one German family starved as a result of the British blockade, he would 'send a Zeppelin over Windsor castle and blow up the whole royal family of England.' Then he would be plunged into depression and knock back sleeping pills. The entourage and Dona, committed to protecting the Kaiser and the senior generals, determined to stop him interfering and colluded to shield him from bad news and keep his faux pas to a minimum."[6] Each day, Wilhelm was still briefed on the war effort, but only on plans that had already been carried out. He was never informed of upcoming missions. Within two years, the war was barely mentioned to either the emperor or empress, who was growing desperate to see her husband spend less time at his military headquarters at Spa, near Liège in eastern Belgium.

To appease the empress as she helped the generals manage her husband, and to combat Wilhelm's restlessness, the emperor was packed off between the front lines and Berlin. When Wilhelm was at home, Dona watched his moods change suddenly, usually for the worst. One member of the court felt that she too "often remained silent when she should have spoken her mind." During lunch one afternoon, Dona took special care to have one of Wilhelm's favorite meals prepared. When it was served, the emperor complained of the "monotony" at his palaces. Dona remained silent, while the household staff was forced "to bear the brunt of the Imperial displeasure."[7]

On February 8, 1915, Archduchess Zita gave birth at Schönbrunn Palace to her third child. When the newest Habsburg child, a son, was christened two days later in the gold-and-marble Maria Theresa Apartments, he was given the name Robert after Zita's father. Franz Joseph beamed through the entire ceremony, a sign of how proud and relieved he was to know that the Habsburg dynasty would live on after him through this next generation of healthy archdukes and archduchesses. Robert's birth and christening came at a bittersweet period in Zita's life. In March 1915, the Russians fought their way to a resounding victory by breaking through Austrian lines at Przemysl, which had been regarded as a veritable fortress. In addition to food, medical supplies, and ammunition, nearly 126,000 prisoners were captured. That week, Nicholas II made a surprise appearance at Przemysl to triumphantly congratulate his troops for their success.

More devastating for Zita on an intimate level was the news that, on April 15, Italy abrogated its alliance with the Central powers and joined the Triple Entente. The move came after the signing of the London Pact which, should the war end in a victory for the Entente, promised Italy the Trentino, South

Tyrol, and much of present-day Slovenia. Many politicians and diplomats were not surprised by Italy's decision because the country had long desired to claim Austrian territory. Eager to finally step up and claim its prizes, Italy declared war on Austria on May 23, 1915; they would not declare war on Germany for another fifteen months. In Vienna, there was a swift reaction. Public feeling turned sharply against Italy as Austria prepared to open a new front to the southwest. A few days later, Archduke Charles was sent to command troops of the Twentieth Army Corps on the front lines in an effort to stall an Italian invasion through what is now Slovenia.

Archduchess Zita now found to her dismay that her loyalties were even more divided than when the war began. She would forever be committed to Charles and Austria, but she could not deny her love for her native Italy, as well as her loyalty to France—before her marriage, she always signed her name as "Zite de Bourbon, Princesse de Parma."[8] The acute internal struggle she began to wage was perhaps even more difficult for her than the division within her own family. Ties with family could be mended, she reasoned; she and her brothers understood each other and remained inwardly loyal. But as the wife of the heir to the Austrian throne, who had brothers fighting for the enemy, Zita found herself accused of malfeasance. Around Vienna, she was slanderously called "the Italian woman." When the Italians halted a major Austrian offensive in the Soca River Valley of Slovenia, people reasoned it must be because of the scheming Italian wife of their heir apparent. The ensuing retreat and trench warfare—known historically as the Isonzo front—continued for another two years, costing more than three hundred thousand lives. According to the rumors, Zita, "being Italian by origin, had undoubtedly betrayed the Central Powers by selling plans of battle and defense to the enemy; the retreat on the Isonzo and the disaster of the Piave [River] could be explained in no other fashion."[9] Of course, the facts that the archduchess was both a descendant of the Austrian imperial dynasty and was utterly devoted to her husband and adopted country were completely forgotten.

So too was an incident in September 1915, when the archduchess was visiting a military hospital in Innsbruck. According to the Italian newspaper *Idea Nazionale*, Zita stopped at the bedside of a wounded Italian soldier. After speaking for a few minutes to him in Italian, the soldier—who did not recognize the archduchess—asked her if she was from Italy. "I was born in Italy," she replied, "where I lived until I was married, but as an Austrian I have nothing in common with a country which has lost her honor." Incensed, the soldier pulled himself up in the bed and shot back, "We had enough honor left to declare war on Austria!" Zita's reaction to the man's statement is not known, but when he was later castigated for "having been disrespectful to the wife of the Austrian heir apparent," he replied with equal indignity, "The Archduchess was disrespectful to the Italian nation, which was worse."[10]

The right-wing conservatives in Austria believed the empire needed to form a closer military and political alliance with imperial Germany. They saw Zita as a dangerous threat despite her conspicuous loyalty to her adopted country. They falsely accused her of having an affair with a French member of her mother's household. In a masterful display of doughtiness, Zita threw herself more than ever into the cause of supporting the Habsburg Empire. She made almost unending visits to field hospitals. Starting in Vienna, she went on a tour across the empire, taking her as close to the front lines as she could possibly get in an effort to bring hope and joy to the wounded soldiers and their families. Cardinal-Archbishop Friedrich Gustav Piffl of Vienna called her "the guardian angel of all those who suffer."[11] In recognition for her service, Franz Joseph proudly awarded her the service medal of the Red Cross in August 1915.

The departure of Italy from the Central powers was soon offset when Bulgaria and the Ottoman Empire joined their alliance. As far as Bulgaria was concerned, this was not just a military alliance. Zita's eldest sister, Maria Louisa, had been the first wife of the king of the Bulgarians, Ferdinand I, the self-styled "tsar." Melodramatic, farcical, and obnoxious with grandiose ideas about himself, the rotund Ferdinand was notoriously annoying but possessed a brilliant mind. Through personal avocation, he was reputed to be the most accurate royal genealogist in Europe. Franz Joseph was willing to overlook Ferdinand's many eccentricities, since Bulgaria's support for Austria on the Balkan front brought much-needed relief to the imperial troops.

As Zita's war work increased, she saw her husband less than ever. He was since promoted to commanding the First Hussar Regiment at the front. His return visits to Vienna were few and far between. Charles was under no illusions about what his position as an army officer meant, and he was by no means optimistic about this. "I am an officer with all my body and soul," he told Zita, "but I do not see how anyone who sees his dearest relations leaving for the front can love war." The bloody scenes Charles was seeing at the front made a profound impression on him. One eyewitness recalled the archduke surveying the troops at Gmunden before shipping out: "I remember vividly the visit of the new heir to the throne, the young Archduke Charles, who inspected the troops going to the front. There was a solemn high Mass said in the parish church, a rather beautiful late Gothic building. Many of the congregation cried. There was no wild enthusiasm when we accompanied the young soldiers, their caps decorated with green twigs, to the railway station."[12]

When the war began, Charles was initially stationed at the Russian front, but "after the first opening skirmishes it was decided that the Heir Apparent ought not to be exposed to daily peril, since in the event of his death Austria would have been hard put to appoint a fourth Crown Prince."[13] He was reassigned to the High Command in Vienna, though he still traveled around to different command centers as the emperor's representative. Franz Joseph's goal was to train his great-nephew to take over the reins of power at any moment. Charles's new post with Imperial High Command afforded him the opportunity to meet Emperor Wilhelm II for the first time in January 1915 at a German military base at Charleville. The meeting was more for show than anything else. They "achieved little in the all-important matter of establishing some clear war aims and working directly and specifically for the long-term objective of peace," though it is recorded that Charles and Wilhelm got along well "on a personal level."[14]

While her husband was away visiting military installations, Zita was left at Schönbrunn with their children. To occupy her time, she started accepting invitations from the emperor for her and the children to spend more time with him. The family started seeing the emperor almost every day. This brought a great deal of joy to Franz Joseph. "In this [*sic*] serious and exciting days it was both a comfort and a recreation for the old sovereign to pass an hour or two in the company of the young Archduchess and her merry family," wrote a member of the emperor's court.[15] They took meals together, and she accompanied him on his walks in the afternoon. Zita's role as wife and mother soon expanded to include advisor and confidante. On more than one occasion, the emperor confided his hopes and fears to his great-niece. Zita recalled that Franz Joseph "never assumed that everything was assured for all time." He confessed to her "a feeling that, ever since 1848, the empire was like [a] volcano which was uneasily sleeping. This was not only because he saw it threatened by nationalist movements and the growth of parliamentary pressure but because its future depended on alliances with all their uncertainty and weakness. And, of course, Austria-Hungary was not the old Holy Roman Empire which was, for him, his real homeland."[16]

Not content to be seen only on the emperor's arm, Zita went about making her own personal contribution to the war effort. Portraits of the imperial family were taken and made into postcards, proceeds from which went to the Red Cross. One portrait, labeled "Three Generations," showed the emperor seated in his customary dress uniform, along with Charles and Otto, who clutched his father's leg. Another one, which bore the caption "God save our Beloved Kaiser," was of Franz Joseph in a similar position, wearing the same uniform, with only Otto at his side. Even a century later, this image would become one of the most famous ever taken of the tiny archduke and his great-great-uncle.

❦

The strain that Bulgaria and the Ottoman Empire placed on the war effort was felt the most acutely by Russia, who shared borders with both nations, meaning the country was cut off from the south. Further triumphs by the Germans in the Baltic cut Russia off from Western aid altogether. After only a year, Russian losses were staggering. The problem was compounded by an inadequate support system to fuel the war effort.

> Hampered by insufficient weapons and supplies and poor food rations, Russia's armies fought on, but the losses sustained by the empire were enormous. By August 1915, a staggering 450,000 Russians a month were dying at the front. This brought the total loss of life since the previous year to 1.5 million men. For the year 1915 alone, an astounding 2 million men were captured, wounded, or killed, and the whole Russian front had for all intents and purposes crumbled.[17]

Ammunition was in such short supply that soldiers were told to limit themselves to ten bullets a day. One British observer noticed that when a group of eighteen hundred new recruits arrived at the front lines, they were unarmed. They were later told to wait until enough soldiers had died to supply themselves with guns and ammo. The Russian army as a whole was comprised of fifteen million mobilized men. This was disastrous for the country's infrastructure. Farmers, factory workers, and laborers were marched off to the front lines, leading to a falloff in Russia's fragile economy. A recession soon took hold. This meant trouble for the empire, which had been tottering on the brink of instability for many years.

Tsarina Alexandra was deeply moved by the suffering of her people. She wrote to the bishop of Ripon, an old friend, "We can only trust & pray that this terrible war may soon come to an end—The suffering around is too intense. You, who know all the members of our family so very well, can understand what we go through—relations on all sides, one against the other."[18]

The setbacks his country was enduring weighed heavily on Nicholas II. Deeply committed to his role as *Batiushka Tsar*, he believed that the only way for Russia to be victorious on the battlefield was to lead the troops himself. He relieved the commander in chief of the armed forces, his highly respected cousin Grand Duke Nicholas Nicholaievich, who was made viceroy of the Caucasus. Rumors began to spread that Nikolasha's shocking dismissal was pushed for by the empress, since the grand duke was an outspoken critic of Rasputin. There was universal agreement that this was a terrible idea. Nicholas's Council of Ministers, long accustomed to the tsar's poor decisions, fell silent in shock when he announced he was leaving for Russian military headquarters. Incredulous, they composed a long letter begging him to reconsider. The tsar's cousin Grand Duke Andrei visited the dowager empress shortly after Nicholas announced his decision and found her "in a terribly worried state." He confided in his diary Minnie's great anxiety over the whole situation.

> She was especially excited over the question of Nicholas Nicholaevich. She thinks that his removal will be the ruin of N. [the tsar] because it will never be forgiven him. She exonerated Niki [the tsar] in all this and laid all the blame on Alix. When Niki came to see her before going she [Minnie] begged and begged him to think over everything carefully and not lead Russia to ruin. To her pleas he replied that everybody deceived him, that he must save Russia, that it was his duty. It was in vain that she pleaded with him that he was poorly prepared for this hard task and that State affairs required his presence at Petrograd. He remained unpersuaded and would not even promise to deal kindly with Nicholas Nicholaevich.... Aunt Minny, as she related to me all this, was so excited, so stirred up, that I was frightened. She kept repeating the question: "What are we coming to, what are we coming to? That is not at all like Niki— he is lovable, he is honest, he is good—it is all her [Alexandra's] work.[19]

Ignoring all entreaties, Nicholas took over full command of the Russian military at their headquarters, Stavka. Originally located at Baranovichi in Belarus, it was moved to Mogilev, on the Dnieper River, five hundred miles away from the capital. Although the tsar left, he did return home from time to time. In some instances, when he left for Stavka from Saint Petersburg, he took Alexei with him. The times that the tsarevitch accompanied his father were difficult for Alexandra to cope with. She was anxious for her son's welfare, and rightly so. In 1915, Alexei nearly died when he slipped and fell at Stavka. On another occasion, the boy had a sneezing fit, which led to a nosebleed, which led to another hemophilia attack. The only hope, Alexandra reasoned, was Rasputin. "Thanks be to God!" the *staretz* wrote in a telegram. "He has given me your son's life once more."[20] And without delay, Alexei pulled through.

292

This latest episode only served to further inculcate into Alexandra the way Rasputin was tied to her son's fate like a double helix.

In Saint Petersburg, Alexandra spent hours writing letters to Nicholas at Stavka, exhorting him to hold fast to absolutism. "Forgive me, precious One," she wrote in one letter, "but you know you are too kind & gentle—sometimes a good loud voice can do wonders, & a severe look—do my love, be more decided & sure of yourself ... You think me a medlesome [*sic*] bore, but a woman feels & sees things sometimes clearer than my too humble sweetheart ... a Sovereign needs to show his will more often."[21] With her husband away from Saint Petersburg for months at a stretch, Alexandra was left to rule in his absence. Within a week, the empress gave Russia what she considered a crash course in autocracy. She took an equally hard-line approach in the capital. She systematically sought out the ministers who opposed the tsar's departure to Stavka and had them dismissed. She also shut down the lines of communication between the government and the Duma. Sadly for Alexandra, her ability to rule was as wanting as her faith in Rasputin was misplaced. She appointed and dismissed ministers based solely on the *staretz*'s opinions. The governing of Russia came to a standstill because her constant shuffling of ministers handicapped the administration. This was not a new concept in Russia, though. Nicholas II had once admitted to always having replacements ready should he need to sack his ministers at any given time.

Anger against the empress began boiling over in Moscow and Saint Petersburg. Many viewed her with distrust, thinking she was a German spy. The same way Dona's mother-in-law was labeled *Die Engländerin* ("the English woman"), so too was Alexandra being slanderously called the *Nemka* ("the German woman"). In the newspapers, she was openly slandered as "Alix Rasputin." This was a mirror image of the same innuendo that had befallen Queen Victoria during her—platonic—relationship with the Scottish gillie John Brown. The more time the queen had spent with the gillie, the more she was snidely called "Mrs. Brown." But there was never any notion of eliminating Queen Victoria's influence in the same way most people wanted Alexandra removed. There was soon talk of her being sent packing to a convent in faraway Siberia or back to Germany like the traitor she supposedly was.

Alexandra's ultraconservative rule struck an ironic chord. Had Russia and Germany been at peace at the time, she and Dona may have come to respect one another. This tendency to the political Right was something both empresses shared, but in Britain, the tsarina did not win any friends. Public opinion dramatically shifted to the Left over the last two decades, with increasing criticism in the British press of Russia's autocracy. When Alexandra took the reins of power in 1915–16, many liberal politicians in London cringed. Despite being allies with Russia, the English people held little esteem for Alexandra or Nicholas, who was now being looked upon as a weak failure of an emperor.

Although British opinion was against them, Nicholas and Alexandra maintained cordial ties with the royal family. A number of Romanovs took up residence in England away from the fighting, prompting closer communications on tactical plans between London and Saint Petersburg. In particular, Dowager Empress Marie and Queen Alexandra remained in close contact. "Aunt Alix [Queen Alexandra] wires to say they know for certain that the Germans intend to attack Warsaw this week and she hopes we are aware of it," Minnie wrote in February 1915.[22] She later wrote to Nicholas II, "I have just had a telegram from aunt Alix who wires in despair that they have lost six battleships. But I do *hope* the German losses are even *heavier*."[23]

Like Mary of England, Dona of Germany, and Zita of Austria, Alexandra of Russia was devoted to caring for wounded soldiers. It was the expected role of a reigning consort during times of war. Similarly to Queen Mary, Tsarina Alexandra was instrumental in taking a leading role in these hospitals. Russia's attrition rate in the war was extremely high. Mikhail Rodzianko, the president of the Duma, recalled seventeen thousand wounded soldiers being left on a train in Warsaw because there was nowhere for them to go. Many wounded were sent back to Saint Petersburg. The city was incapable of dealing with such a throng of human suffering, leading the tsarina to convert a number of palaces into field hospitals. By 1916, more than eighty-five hospitals in Saint Petersburg were under her aegis.

In the times when Alexei was in good health, Alexandra—with Olga and Tatiana by her side—was a familiar face in many of the hospitals. "To some it may seem unnecessary my doing this, but help is much needed and my hand is useful," she said.[24] She even went so far as to earn her certification as a Red Cross nurse. "As you know," she told her friend Princess Marie Bariatinsky, "I am *of* the preacher type. I want to help others in life, to help them to fight their battles and bear their crosses."[25]

The day she graduated after two months of nurse training was arguably the proudest moment of Alexandra's life. Anna Viroubova recalled, "I think I never saw her happier than on the day, at the end of our two months' intensive training, she marched at the head of the procession of nurses to receive the red cross and the diploma of a certified war nurse." Her position as empress did not shield Alexandra from the full horrors of the war. She experienced many of her people's hardships firsthand. She was seen in the hospitals on a daily basis, dressed in her white nurse's uniform, going from one ward to the other, comforting the soldiers or praying with them. Her day usually lasted from early morning until midnight. She would see men covered head to toe in burns or with limbs missing. Sometimes she would even assist during surgeries. Anna Viroubova often accompanied Alexandra while she was "assisting in the most difficult operations, taking from the hands of the busy surgeons amputated legs and arms, removing bloody and even vermin-infected dressings, enduring all the sights and smells and agonies of that most dreadful of all places, a military hospital in the midst of war." It was not uncommon for men who were about to have limbs amputated to be heard crying out, "Tsaritsa! Stand near me. Hold my hand that I may have courage."[26] It was not enough for Alexandra simply to care for the soldiers' physical needs. She was also deeply concerned about comforting them spiritually, so she made sure that every package bound for soldiers on the front lines included Bibles or copies of the Psalms. In the words of one historian, "she demonstrated the same deep levels of compassion for the sick and wounded that her own mother had shown before during the Franco-Prussian War of 1870–1."[27]

The empress took great joy in her work. She wrote to Nicholas at Stavka, "My consolation when I feel very down & wretched is to go to the very ill & try & bring them a ray of light & love."[28] She later admitted to the bishop of Ripon, "It does one no end of good being with those brave fellows—how resignedly they bear all pain & loss of limbs."[29] The sad irony of Alexandra Feodorovna's life was that so few people ever saw this humble, loving side to her. In the public eye, she was all too easily branded a German traitor who shared a bed with Rasputin. These rumors would gain such momentum in the coming years that they were soon to topple the monarchy forever.

16

Apocalypse Rising

(January–December 1916)

After thirty years of marriage and two years of war, Emperor Wilhelm II found himself relying on his wife more than ever. The strain of the war, combined with the marginalized role of a figurehead he was expected to play, was beginning to erode the turgid emperor. As he began a plunge into personal crisis, it was Dona who continued to be the strength behind the throne. She buttressed as many problems for her husband as possible. In public, Wilhelm propagated the myth of a powerful, confident *paterfamilias*, with Dona in the role of the *kleines hausfrau*. The truth was somewhat different. Behind the emperor's verbose facade was a man plagued by insecurities and prone to emotional instability. Conversely, Dona, having weathered her fair share of emotional storms in life, became his rock. Gone were the days of her acrimonious fits of hysteria or jealousy. In supporting her husband during the war, she found a new raison d'être that tapped into a wellspring of strength and fortitude.

In her efforts to make Wilhelm's burden as light as possible, Dona kept in regular contact with his ministers. A letter she once wrote to her mother's cousin Prince Chlodwig of Hohenlohe-Schillingsfürst, who had served as German chancellor from 1894 to 1900, encapsulates Dona's lifelong effort to shore up her husband.

> If you[,] dear Prince[,] are willing to help the emperor along ... I
> am certain that everything will turn out all right. I have always

wanted the emperor to have older more experienced friends who would help here and there with a calm word or good advice. For despite his exceptional gifts—I as his wife say this with pride, there probably is at present no other monarch in Europe as gifted as he—he is still [relatively] young, and in his youth one is apt to act spontaneously.... You may be surprised about my frankness, but I know I can rely on your discretion.[1]

In another letter, she expressed similar feelings: "You know that I do not meddle in politics, but if I see how difficult the ministers are sometimes making things for the emperor, I cannot help trying to smooth things out."[2]

On an international scale, Wilhelm became a symbol of monstrous villainy. He alone was blamed for the war. Never mind that Franz Joseph of Austria had actually started the war. Never mind that Wilhelm had rushed to stop the outbreak of hostilities. The culpability was declared to be his alone. From London to Saint Petersburg, he was accused of ordering the indiscriminate killing of women and children in Belgium. Even within Germany, he began receiving criticism for leading the empire into a war that was requiring too much money, taking too long, and costing too many lives. It was a different story for Dona. The empress continued to represent to all her people the paragon of German womanhood. Princess Catherine Radziwill observed that Dona "was thoroughly German in everything she did, from the manner in which she pinned her hat upon her head to the serious interest she took in all matters connected with the welfare of Germany, and particularly that of the poorer classes."[3] She was perhaps best summed up with the expression *kinder, kuche, kirche* ("children, kitchen, church")—a devotion to her family, her home, and her religion. Crown Prince Willy paid tribute to his mother: "I say with ardent pride: she is the very pattern of a German wife whose best characteristics are seen in the fulfilment [*sic*] of her duties as wife and mother."[4] And in the words of another contemporary, "Every housewife, every mother, looks to her as to a model, knows that she is satisfied to excel in her purely domestic duties, and that she does not strive to render herself superior to her sex by intellectual brilliancy and scientific attainments."[5]

The task of keeping a simple domestic routine for her family in Berlin was an onerous one for Dona as the war continued without any visible sign of a conclusion. She spent her evenings by the fire, knitting clothes for soldiers, making arrangements to care for the wounded or the widowed, or taking tea with her ladies. On the occasions when her husband returned from Spa, she worked to entertain him and his entourage. But even those instances were becoming few and far between. As much as Wilhelm loved his wife and valued her calming influence, it was no secret that he preferred to spend his leisure hours in the company of men—soldiers, ministers, or other princes. "In the Kaiser's militarily dominated, ultra-chauvinist Second Reich, a Prussian soldier's life was built around male bonding and the Spartan ideal of soldierly companionship," wrote one author. "Women were generally considered to be useful for breeding, cooking and polishing a chap's spurs: for real friendship, one looked to one's fellow officers."[6] This was largely due to the "dissatisfaction that the Emperor feels in the narrow circle of his home." Despite Dona's best efforts, "the presence the Empress and her *entourage* imposes on him make him uncomfortable."[7] This dichotomy Wilhelm experienced in his relationship with his wife was not a luxury he could afford much longer. Necessity would soon force him to rely on Augusta Victoria like never before.

As the leader of Germany, Wilhelm II served as head of state and commander in chief of armed forces belonging to the empire's twenty-five constituent states. By this point in the war, however, Dona was adept enough to notice that a shift in Germany's power base had occurred. Wilhelm seemed to have less influence in military matters than ever. When a series of attacks backfired that the emperor planned, governing authority began to move into the hands of his chief of the general staff Paul von Hindenburg and his deputy Erich Ludendorff, two men who had assisted in planning the successful Battle of Tannenberg. Germany was transitioning from a federated empire to a military dictatorship under Hindenburg and Ludendorff. To secure their hold on the civilian government, the two men threatened to resign unless Wilhelm forced Theobald von Bethmann-Hollweg, his chancellor, to resign. With his generals taking control, Wilhelm II began to lose his grip on reality. His famously quixotic moods became almost unstable. Dona watched anxiously from one day to the next as her husband alternated between a sense of total despair and deluded dreams of victory over the Entente.

The trials Dona was faced with became too much for the fifty-eight-year-old empress. Emotionally, she may have had a wellspring of fortitude to draw on, but physically, she began to suffer. Like Alexandra of Russia, Dona's health was worsening with each passing year. She was weak, had trouble walking or standing for any length of time, and suffered from worsening heart disease. She did everything she could to take her mind off her failing health. One of the ways she coped was by keeping a close eye on her children. Her sons followed in the tradition of the Prussian royal family, and each took up commissions in the military. Unfortunately, the princes possessed little combat expertise. Shortly after the war began, Auwi's poor judgment led to a serious automobile crash. His driver was killed, and both of the prince's legs were each fractured in twelve places.

Crown Prince Willy had become famous for his blundering command decisions. He expended nearly a million soldiers trying to capture the fortress at Verdun, which ultimately failed and resulted in a French victory. In the ensuing aftermath, Willy was captured by Russian troops. Knowing that Dona would be desperate for news of her son, Alexandra took the time to send her a personal note. Sent through the tsarina's cousin Crown Princess Margaret in neutral Sweden, she assured Dona "that her son was safe and well." When Alexandra told Nicholas about the letter, she admitted it was only the act of "a mother pitying another mother."[8] The crown prince was later released into the custody of the German military.

In watching over her children, Dona was always especially concerned for her youngest son, Prince Joachim. Much to his father's resentment, Joachim had always been a sickly, weak-willed child who frequently clung to the empress. Dona worried about him in much the same way Tsarina Alexandra fretted over Alexei. But as he grew older, the emotionally volatile Joachim chafed under his mother's constant presence and sought his own independence. His first step was joining the military. His second step was getting married. He developed a friendship with Prince Eduard of Anhalt, who commanded a Prussian cavalry regiment on the Belgian front. It was a propitious meeting, because Eduard's daughter Princess Marie-Augusta was looking for a husband. It did not take Joachim long to propose to this attractive, young princess. The match was something of a throwback to older, arranged marriages—Joachim was twenty-five, and Marie-Augusta had just turned eighteen. Earning a brief reprieve in his duties for his wedding, Joachim returned to Berlin in March 1916, along with the Anhalts and his family. The ceremony at Bellevue was a simple Lutheran service with only a few guests. Dona beamed with pride, but the emperor was noticeably absent. Wilhelm argued that his duties at Spa were too pressing for him to return home for a "simple wedding." Both Joachim and Dona were deeply hurt by Wilhelm's effrontery, but they did not let it ruin the day. In their article about the wedding, the London *Times* conspicuously noted that the "Emperor William was not present."[9]

Along with visiting soldiers and working to improve morale, the queen of England was resolute that her own household should be in order. This took several forms. It was vitally important to the king and queen that their family be actively involved in the war effort. On the home front, Princess Mary made her own rounds to hospitals and factories. She spearheaded a campaign to support British servicemen and their families. For Christmas 1914, she developed the Princess Mary's Christmas Gift Fund, which sent more than £100,000 in gifts to soldiers and sailors that year.

Economizing within the monarchy was a top priority. The queen believed it was of the utmost importance to do away with all royal extravagance. This was partly prompted by a food shortage in England. German submarines had succeeded in destroying supply lines to Great Britain, cutting it off from continental help. With little option left, food began to be rationed. The queen anticipated this latest hardship long before it began. She instituted a rationing system for all the royal residences months before the crisis unfolded. She personally planted and harvested her own vegetables at her country estate, Frogmore, near Windsor Great Park. "Over and above the vision," said one of Mary's friends, "the Queen acutely felt the horrors and hardships of the soldiers in the trenches, and, at all times deprecating extravagance, even comfort now seemed to her almost criminal."[10]

In the queen's personal wartime economy, frivolous expenses were the first things on the list to go. This came somewhat naturally to the queen who, since her family's humiliating exile to Florence in 1883, had learned to develop parsimonious spending habits when money was in short supply. At Buckingham Palace, the king and queen cut the heat to almost every room in the building. Their hot water supply was rationed, meaning George could only have a hot bath once a week. The rest of the time, he and Mary bathed in cold water. Meals were another place where the king and queen saved money. Mutton replaced lamb, pink blancmange was consumed instead of mousses and sorbets, and alcohol was strictly prohibited—though this one vice the social elite were unwilling to give up. Thanks to the royal family's budgeting, the king and queen were able to return £100,000 to the national treasury. The queen's willingness to share in her people's hardships, combined with the fact that she easily mixed with people of all classes, made her almost as iconic as Queen Victoria.

⟱

While Nicholas was away at Stavka, Alexandra was determined to rule with a firm hand. In her letters, she was obstinate that Nicholas must rule harshly: "Play the Emperor! Remember you are the Autocrat. Speak to your Ministers as their Master.... Be like Peter the Great.... Crush them all. No, don't laugh, you naughty child. I so long to see you treat in this way those who try to govern you, when it is you who should govern them."[11] Unlike Queen Mary's and Empress Augusta Victoria's influence on their husbands, which was sometimes encouraged, Alexandra's attempts to govern Nicholas were misguided and faulty. Alexandra's growing number of enemies claimed her meddling was the direct result of Rasputin's influence. Rasputin actually had little to do with the appointments and dismissals of ministers that the empress was making at this point. Most of these decisions were now made by the tsarina alone. She even went as far as shuffling the tsar's cabinet. According to one estimate, between 1915 and 1917, "Russia had four prime ministers, five ministers of the interior, four ministers of religion, four ministers of justice, three ministers of agriculture, three foreign ministers, and four ministers of war. Twenty-six men held these seven positions over a twenty-four month period."[12]

Alexandra's ineffective rule was not only damaging Russia; it was even beginning to hurt the Romanovs' close relationship with the British royal family. Marie Feodorovna regularly sent updates to Queen Alexandra at Marlborough House about the situation in Saint Petersburg. The tsarina "is ruining both the dynasty and herself," Minnie wrote around the time her daughter-in-law started shuffling ministers.[13] Queen Alexandra, who was loyal to her sister above all else, later told King George, "I am sure she [the tsarina] thinks herself like their Empress Catherine [the Great]."[14]

This game of musical chairs in the government could not have come at a worse time for Russia. By 1916, the war had changed from a European conflict into a crusade, a holy war, against Germany. The name of Russia's capital, Saint Petersburg, was deemed to be too German sounding and was changed to the more Slavic Petrograd. The London *Times* reported that "this war is holy to every one, and its motto is—getting rid of the German spirit of life."[15] German successes on the battlefield gave rise to fears that an invasion of Russia was imminent. Even Russo-Baltic aristocrats with German-sounding surnames and titles were forced to produce documents proving their Slavic ethnicity.

The Germanophobia in Russia struck particularly close to home for Alexandra, who was now not only accused of ineptitude and adultery but treason and insanity as well. Contemporaries claimed she was insane as a way of explaining her otherwise inexplicably bizarre decisions. One historian commented on the pitfalls of ascribing insanity to rulers: "A further problem arises from the fact that the 'madness' of sovereigns has sometimes been a political rather than a strictly medical category. As Janet Hartley has observed, British ambassadors and statesmen were prone to regard Tsar Alexander I of Russia as deranged, but generally only when they suspected him of acting against British interests." Explanations for Alexandra's behavior have been as varied as the years since her life have been long. More often than not, popular trends in society have influenced analyses not only of Alexandra but numerous other monarchs as well. In the 1890s, immediately before and after she married Nicholas, Alexandra was labeled as having bad nerves or nervous anxiety. In the first two decades of the twentieth century, when republicanism was on the rise after the First World War, Alexandra was the product of failing dynasties, corrupted and degenerate. Those who took on the task of examining her life in the 1920s filtered their analyses through newly popularized psychological paradigms established by experts like Freud or Jung. The tsarina, so went some arguments, must have suffered from neurosis or some repressed sexuality. With breakthroughs in science and medicine in the last thirty years, neurology and genetics became the focus of studying Alexandra and the Romanovs—inbreeding must have led to genetic mutations, diseases, and so on.[16]

Many Russians noticed striking similarities between the much-maligned empress and history's most ill-fated German queen, the archduchess Maria Antonia of Austria, more famously remembered as Marie Antoinette of France. The parallels were undeniable. Both were German-born princesses, both married into the most extravagant monarchies in the world at that time, and both came to be the scapegoats for their nations' problems. Even the way in which the tsarina and her family lived in semiseclusion at Tsarskoe Selo echoed "the simplistic charade enacted by Marie Antoinette in Le Hameau at Versailles before the Terror swept the Bourbons from their throne."[17] Alexandra was fascinated by Marie Antoinette and all deposed queens in general. She owned a number of items that had once belonged to the French queen, including a series of paintings and tapestries that had once adorned the walls of Versailles and Marie Antoinette's private château, the Petite Trianon. It is doubtful Alexandra was aware of her similarities to Marie Antoinette, but the very notion of her being a German spy made her angry beyond words. Despite being a Hessian princess and a cousin of the most hated man in Europe, Alexandra was as anti-German as anyone could be. King George V said of her, "I have known her all my life, and pro-German that she is not."[18] Even when her brother, Ernie, tried to contact her through an old servant in Austria, she refused his communiqué. Nicholas II's brother-in-law Sandro was one of the tsarina's greatest supporters. He wrote that she "was far above all her contemporaries in fervent Russian patriotism. Raised by her father, the Duke of Hesse-Darmstadt, to hate the Kaiser, she dreamed all her life to see the day of Prussia's debacle, and next to Russia her admiration lay on the side of Great Britain."[19]

Sandro's comments also touched on another important point for Alexandra. After her loyalty to Russia, she was a fervent Englishwoman. Maurice Paléologue, the French ambassador to Russia during the war, confirmed his belief in Alexandra's patriotism in his diary: "Alexandra Feodorovna is German neither in mind nor spirit and has never been so...."

In her inmost being she has become entirely Russian … I have no doubt of her patriotism.… Her love for Russia is deep and true. And why should she not be devoted to her adopted country which stands for everything dear to her as woman, wife, sovereign and mother?"[20] Unfortunately—like with her nursing—most people never saw the tsarina's patriotic side. Prone to glowering and infirmed with heart trouble and pain in her back and legs, she often retreated into her palaces at Petrograd or Tsarskoe Selo. This only added to the rumors swirling about her. Her charity work, her duties as a Red Cross nurse, and her role as a devoted Christian mother did little to help her. She was openly sneered as the *Nemka*.

In spite of her critics, Alexandra continued to be adamant that Russia needed strength and resolve in order to be ruled. Though she was neither despotic nor a tyrant, she was not in favor of granting reforms that gave more power to the masses. As a by-product of Queen Victoria's court, she believed that conservatism, traditionalism, and royalty remaining separated from the people were the proper ways to rule an empire. She failed to grasp the nature of Britain's highly successful constitutional monarchy that was now being presided over by her cousin George.

Alexandra's fierce determination was also fueled by a desire to see her son inherit the same empire that belonged to his father. She wrote to Nicholas in 1916, "I feel cruel worrying you, my sweet, patient Angel—but all my trust lies in our friend [Rasputin], who *only thinks of you*, Baby [Alexei] & Russia.—And guided by Him we shall get through this heavy time. It will be hard fighting, but a Man of God's is near to guard yr. boat safely through the reefs—& little Sunny [Alix] is standing as a rock behind you, firm & unwavering with decision, faith & love to fight for her darlings & our country."[21] This type of thinking from Alexandra, coupled with her devotion to Rasputin, played right into the hands of her enemies. The political situation in Petrograd became especially precarious later that year when the tsarina's new criteria for appointing government ministers was only "their ineptitude and for their association with Rasputin."[22]

With Nicholas II away at Stavka and Alexandra playing musical chairs in Petrograd, disturbing signs hinted at the tempest gathering over Russia. Outcries against the monarchy in general became widespread as the accusations against Alexandra continued to mount. She refused to acknowledge any of it, however. Her lifelong obduracy made her myopic to the grim reality of the situation. French ambassador Maurice Paléologue met with Alexandra around this time. He recalled that she tried to be pleasant but "said little, as usual." She struck Paléologue as a kind of "automaton. The fixed and distant gaze made me wonder whether she was listening to me, or indeed heard me at all. I was horrified to think of the omnipotent influence this poor neurotic woman exercised on the conduct of affairs of State!"[23]

She slowly became disconnected from reality, refusing to acknowledge the criticism directed at her and defending Rasputin against anyone who questioned him, including other members of the imperial family. Her greatest opponents within the imperial family were Nicholas II's aunt and cousins—Grand Duchess Marie Pavlovna and her children—who had long held ambitions for the throne. Even Alexandra's mother-in-law, Minnie, was soon an unwelcome guest because of her criticism of her daughter-in-law and the *staretz*. Minnie and Alexandra had always been at loggerheads, but there was never so much animosity as after Rasputin came on the scene. The same was true for Nicholas II's sister Olga Alexandrovna. A devoted friend to Alexandra and a loving aunt to the grand duchesses, Olga was stunned by the way Alexandra shut her out of her life when she began criticizing Rasputin.

The last straw came when Alexandra's own sister Ella, the most respected royal in Russia, arrived at Tsarskoe Selo to try and talk some sense into the tsarina. Ella had been living in near seclusion at a convent since her husband's murder in 1905. When the rest of the Romanovs heard that the highly respected Ella was venturing to Tsarskoe Selo, everyone held their breaths. Upon coming face-to-face with her sister, she cut straight to the point.

"Rasputin is exasperating society," she said. "He is compromising the imperial family and leading the dynasty to ruin."

"Rasputin is a great man of prayer," Alexandra replied, unmoved by her sister's plea. "All these rumors are slanders."[24]

Sadly, the meeting went downhill from that point, and both sisters walked away angry and resentful. Ella later recounted the meeting to Prince Felix Youssopov, the tsar's nephew. "She dismissed me like a dog," Ella reported with tears in her eyes and trembling with emotion.[25] Their meeting marked the last time Alexandra and Ella would ever see each other. The dowager empress soon joined the chorus of voices in the Romanov family speaking out against Alexandra. During an audience with the historian Paul Miliukov, she ominously predicted, "My unhappy daughter-in-law does not understand that she is ruining both the dynasty and herself. She sincerely believes in the holiness of some rogue [Rasputin] and we are all helpless to avert misfortune."[26]

By late 1916, no one could deny the dangerous revolutionary storm that was gathering over Petrograd. Grand Duchess Marie Pavlovna, one of Nicholas II's many relatives, was disturbed by the fact that

[People were] speaking of the Emperor and Empress with open animosity and contempt. The word "revolution" was uttered more openly and more often [than ever before]; soon it could be heard everywhere. The war seemed to recede into the background. All attention was riveted on interior events. Rasputin, Rasputin, Rasputin—it was like a refrain; his mistakes, his shocking personal conduct, his mysterious power. This power was tremendous; it was like dusk, enveloping all our world, eclipsing the sun. how could so pitiful a wretch throw so vast a shadow? It was inexplicable, maddening, baffling, almost incredible.[27]

When Ella failed to convince her sister to abandon Rasputin, the imperial family decided to take matters into their own hands. The plan was masterminded by Prince Felix Youssopov, who had married the tsar's niece in 1914. The Youssopovs, despite being nonroyals, were unimaginably wealthy. Their estate in the Caucasus—one of several dozen throughout Russia—was so vast that it covered 125 miles along the shore of the Caspian Sea. Felix's wealth meant that he was very popular in Saint Petersburg. He developed a long-standing friendship with Nicholas II's cousin Grand Duke Dmitri Pavlovich, whom he had fought with for Irina's heart. When Felix decided to take action against Rasputin, he recruited Dmitri with ease. Joining the conspirators in their plot were Vladimir Purishkevich, a verbose, outspoken, monarchist member of the Duma, and a relatively low-ranking military doctor named Lazovert.

Late on the night of December 29, 1916, Rasputin was lured to Youssopov's Petrograd home, the Moika Palace. He was promised a meeting with Felix's wife, Irina, who was in the Crimea at the time. At Moika, he and his would-be assassins dined on cake and a bottle of Madeira. What the *staretz* did not realize was that his food was heavily poisoned by Dr. Lazovert. Shockingly, he continued to eat and eat, showing no signs of succumbing. Desperate, Felix shot Rasputin. Assuming he was dead, the group left his body in the basement and went to drink off their crime. What happened later still defies explanation almost a century later. Late that night, Felix stumbled downstairs to examine the body. He "felt for a pulse; there was none. Then, in a burst of rage, he seized the corpse by the shoulders and shook it violently. He threw the body back against the floor, then again knelt down beside it. Suddenly, the left eye twitched and opened."[28] According to author Karl Shaw, on his deathbed, Dr. Lazovert confessed "that he had completely lost his nerve and hadn't in fact poisoned anything at all."[29] This deathbed confession has never been confirmed independently, but the fact that Lazovert fainted at least once that night lends credence to its plausibility.

Trapped in a horrific nightmare, Felix watched in disbelief as the crazed Rasputin, blood dripping from his lips, rose to his feet and attacked him.

"Felix! Felix!" Rasputin cried. "I will tell the Tsarina everything!" Hearing the commotion, Dmitri and Vladimir came running down the stairs.

"Purishkevich, shoot!" Felix frantically shouted at Vladimir. "Shoot! He's alive! He's escaping!"

As Rasputin made his way across the palace courtyard, Vladimir shot him for the last time in the back of the head. His ostensibly lifeless corpse dropped to the ground. Certain that the *staretz* was finally dead, the group disposed of his body in the freezing Neva River, where he died from drowning. Without even realizing, Felix had fulfilled an eerie prophecy Rasputin had spoken about him earlier. Anna Viroubova recalled, "The Holy Man told me that Felix Youssoupoff has the strangest destiny, but he sees blood on his hands."[30]

Rasputin's murder did not solve any problems in Russia. At first, the people were exuberant. "I clearly remember," wrote Grand Duchess Marie Pavlovna, "the unprecedented excitement at the hospital" where she worked as a nurse when news of Rasputin's death was made public. The news, she noted, "was met everywhere with a joy bordering on hysteria; people in the streets embraced each other as they did at Easter, and women cried."[31] The joy people felt at Rasputin's death was quickly consumed by the drama that was created within the imperial family when Nicholas and Alexandra learned that their own relatives had been involved in the murder. Alexandra wanted the murderers punished. "I cannot get over it," she exclaimed to Dr. Eugene Botkin, the family's physician. "Dimitriy, whom I have loved as my own son, conspiring against my life! And Youssoupoff—a nobody who owes all he has solely to the mercy of the Emperor! It is terrible."[32]

Dmitri and Felix were arrested shortly thereafter. Bertie Stopford, a member of the British embassy in Saint Petersburg, noted that "all the Imperial family are off their heads at the Grand Duke Dmitri's arrest."[33] Punishments were quickly meted out. Vladimir Purishkevich, who escaped arrest by rushing to the front lines, was absolved of guilt. Dmitri and Felix were not so fortunate. Prince Felix was banished to his palatial estate in central Russia. Dmitri was ordered to serve with the army at the Persian front. Nicholas II received a petition for clemency on Dmitri's behalf from nearly two dozen Romanovs. The first person to sign was Olga, the queen dowager of Greece, a former grand duchess and Dmitri's grandmother.

> Your Majesty,
> We all, whose names you will find at the end of this letter, implore you to reconsider your harsh decision concerning the fate of the Grand Duke Dmitri Pavlovich.

We know that he is ill and quite unnerved by all he has gone through. You, who were his Guardian and his Supreme Protector in infancy and boyhood, well know how deeply he loved You and Our Country.

Most heartily do we implore Your Majesty, in consideration of his weak health and his youth, to allow the Grand Duke to go and live on his own estates, either at Oncova or Illinskoe.

Your Majesty must know the very hard conditions under which our troops live in Persia—without shelter and in constant peril to health and life.

To have to live there would be for the Grand Duke almost certain death, and in the heart of Your Majesty surely a feeling of pity will be awakened towards this young man who from childhood had the joy of living in your house, and whom you loved and to whom you used to be like a father.

May God inspire you and guide you to turn wrath into mercy! Your Majesty's most loving and devoted,

Olga, Queen of Greece:

[et al] ... [34]

Queen Olga handed the petition to the tsar herself, who then handed it back to her, refusing his family's plea. "No one has the right to kill, and I am astonished that the family should address itself to me with such requests," he scrawled angrily into the margins of a memo to his relatives.[35] This crisis severed the ties once and for all between the tsar, tsarina, their children, and the rest of the imperial family. From this point on, the palace gates were closed to the rest of the Romanov clan, cutting Nicholas and Alexandra off from a vitally important support group. "I believe in no one but my wife," Nicholas told Sandro, his sister Xenia's husband and Prince Felix's father-in-law.[36]

Rasputin's murder was a mortal wound to Alexandra's soul. The only person she believed could save her son was now gone. Pierre Gilliard, the tutor to Alexandra's daughters, remembered "how terribly she was suffering. Her idol had been shattered. He who alone could save her son has been slain. Now that he had gone, any misfortune, any catastrophe, was possible."[37] Queen Alexandra told George V, "the wretched Russian monk caused a tremendous sensation in the world! but [is] only regretted by poor dear Alix who might have ruined the whole future of Russia through his Influence."[38] Rasputin's body was buried at Tsarskoe Selo in a quiet, tearful ceremony attended by the empress, her daughters, and a few close friends. As the coffin was lowered into the ground, Alexandra and the grand duchesses dropped in letters and holy icons that each of them had signed. Rasputin's death heralded a new, dark page in Russia, one that he himself had foreseen. Before his death, he wrote a letter entitled "The Spirit of Gregory Efimovich Rasputin-Novykh of the village of Pokrovskoe." It was an eerily accurate warning that was revealed after the funeral.

> I write and leave behind me this letter at St. Petersburg. I feel that I shall leave life before January 1. I wish to make known to the Russian people, to Papa [Nicholas], to the Russian Mother [Alexandra] and to the Children, to the land of Russia, what they must understand. If I am killed by common assassins, and especially by my brothers the Russian peasants, you, Tsar of Russia, have nothing to fear, remain on your throne and govern, and you, Russian Tsar, will have nothing to fear for your children, they will reign for hundreds of years in Russia. But if I am murdered by *boyars*, nobles, and if they shed my blood, their hands will remain soiled with my blood, for twenty-five years they will not wash their hands from my blood. They will leave Russia. Brothers will kill brothers, and they will kill each other and hate each other, and for twenty-five years there will be no nobles in the country. Tsar of the land of Russia, if you hear the sound of the bell which will tell you that Gregory has been killed, you must know this: if it was your relations who have wrought my death then no one of your family, that is to say, none of your children or relations will remain alive for more than two years. They will be killed by the Russian people.... I shall be killed. I am no longer among the living. Pray, pray, be strong, think of your blessed family.
>
> Gregory[39]

Mystics have long held the strange accuracy of this letter to be proof of Rasputin's supernatural abilities. If anything, it betrays how truly politically savvy Rasputin was. The subtext of this letter reveals a man fully aware of Russia's impending implosion, a man who knew that should there be any kind of action against the monarchy, he would be one of the first targets. To a careful eye, this last appeal from Gregory Rasputin, seemingly from beyond the grave, is little more than the emotional blackmail he continually exercised over the Romanovs.

17

"May God Bless Your Majesty"

(December 1916)

The optimism in Austria-Hungary that Bulgaria's and Turkey's entries into the war brought was ephemeral as imperial casualties mounted. According to one report submitted to Franz Joseph, "the Monarchy had lost 2,083,000 men killed or permanently disabled by the end of 1915."[1] News of Austria's losses was quickly followed by a series of events that marked a turn of the tide against the Habsburg Empire. The first blow came in August 1916 when, after two years of floundering neutrality, Romania came into the war on the Entente side. This was a bitter blow to both Franz Joseph and Wilhelm II, since King Ferdinand of Romania was a member of the House of Hohenzollern.

Romania's entrance into the war coincided with the birth of Zita's next child, a son, on May 31, 1916. She named the infant Felix after her dear brother. A book commemorating his birth was soon published, highlighting that he had arrived "in the sight of victory" after a series of successes in the Tyrol.[2] Within months of Felix's birth, there was little doubt that Franz Joseph was dying. He had been battling suffocating bronchitis for months. His final breaking point came when he heard the outcome of the Brusilov Offensive. A Russian victory on the eastern front had shattered Austria's armies, resulting in the deaths of 1.5 million soldiers, with only 350,000 Russian soldiers killed or captured. The historian Richard Charques observed about the campaign, "Relatively well nourished, the onslaught achieved swift and dramatic gains on both flanks. Brusilov's feat, assisted in part by the half-heartedness of the

Slav elements in the enemy ranks, was indeed remarkable and demonstrated in striking fashion the Russian power of recovery."[3] The defeat crushed the emperor, the most die-hard believer in the cause of the war. Archduke Charles was commanding the Twentieth Army Corps near Schässburg when he was recalled to Schönbrunn.

On November 17, Franz Joseph's condition became critical. An official announcement was made declaring that Charles would now govern alongside the emperor. Over the next several days, Franz Joseph was uncompromising in his self-discipline. He continued to work all day at his papers and only made the most minor concessions to his health. Too weak to kneel when he said his daily prayers, he acquiesced to his doctors' orders and prayed seated in his desk chair instead. The morning of November 21 marked the last day in the life of Emperor Franz Joseph of Austria. In the morning, he summoned Charles and Zita into his room where he was working on army recruitment papers. By the evening, "it was clear that he was slipping away."[4] Too weak to continue working, he took to his bed, where he died a few hours later, surrounded by Charles, Zita, his daughters Valerie and Gisela, and his ministers. Reportedly, he died singing "God Save the Emperor."[5] Afterward, the stunned group filed into an anteroom to compose themselves. "No one knew what to say or what to do," Zita remembered.[6] A few moments later, the court chamberlain Prince Lobkowitz walked up to Charles and, with tears in his eyes, made the sign of the cross on his forehead, saying, "May God bless Your Majesty." Zita later recalled, "It was the first time we heard the imperial title used to us."[7] At the age of twenty-nine, Zita's husband was now Emperor Charles I of Austria.

Twenty-four-year-old Zita was now the youngest-reigning consort in Europe. Her husband was the head of an empire that stretched from the Vorarlberg on Lake Constance in Switzerland to the Carpathian Mountains of Transylvania. Austria-Hungary's northern border reached more than sixty miles past Prague to the banks of the Elbe River, while its southernmost point touched the tip of Albania on the Adriatic Coast. Zita, along with being empress of Austria, was also now queen consort of Hungary, Bohemia, Croatia, Slavonia[8], Dalmatia, Lodomeria, Galicia, Illyria, and Jerusalem. These core territories gave Austria its essence as an empire, and its imperial status was inextricably linked with the union of these thrones with the Habsburg monarchy.

The day after his accession, Emperor Charles I composed an emotional letter to the Austrian people.

I am compelled to occupy the throne of my ancestors in troubled times.... I am one with my peoples in the firm determination to seek peace and the survival of our country....

In invoking the blessing of Heaven for my House and my Peoples I swear before God that I will be a loyal steward of the heritage of my ancestors. *I shall do all in my power to end the horrors and sacrifices of war at the earliest possible moment, and to restore the blessings of peace as soon as honor, the interest of our Allies and the co-operation of our Enemies will permit.*[9]

At two o'clock in the afternoon on the cold, gray day of November 30, 1916, tens of thousands of mourners lined the streets of Vienna, stood on balconies, or perched themselves on windows to bid farewell to Emperor Franz Joseph. After Louis XIV of France, he is the longest-reigning monarch in European history, lasting sixty-eight years and 355 days. "For us, personally, the old Emperor's death meant the loss of a good, fatherly friend," recalled Dona's daughter, Sissy. "Aside from our grief we feared for the future of the two allies in a war in which both Germany and Austro-Hungary faced hitherto inconceivable consequences."[10]

At the funeral, the new emperor and empress, who were holding the hands of four-year-old Crown Prince Otto, solemnly walked behind the coffin as it moved through the packed streets. Following the imperial couple were the kings of Bulgaria, Bavaria, Saxony, and Württemberg and nearly one hundred other visiting royals. The imperial couple—especially the boyish-looking Charles—marked a strong contrast to the visiting kings, all of whom were seasoned, middle-aged men. The funeral at Saint Stephen's Cathedral was officiated by Cardinal-Archbishop Piffl of Vienna, four other cardinals, ten bishops, and forty-eight priests. After the service was finished, the funeral procession made its way to the imperial crypts deep beneath the Capuchin Church, located near the Hofburg. Charles was dressed in a simple general's uniform, but it was Zita who drew all eyes. The grief-stricken empress looked ethereal in a black dress with a full-length veil over her face.

So many people had filled the streets that Zita's son Otto recalled years later, "It was like walking among sky-scrapers."[11] For many people, the funeral of their previous emperor provided them with the first glimpse of their new one. The imperial family made a vivid impression on the masses. Charles I seemed "a modest young man, looking boyish in field-gray, his head bared, and between him and the slim figure of his wife, entirely draped in black from head to toe, walked his son Otto, in his skirts, sash, white socks and golden ringlets." The writer of these words concluded, "In a world fast disintegrating, it was a reassuring symbol of the bourgeois security which in fact Vienna and the Empire would never know again."[12]

Upon becoming empress, Zita found herself in similar circumstances to both Alexandra of Russia and Dona of Germany. Had Charles become emperor under different circumstances, he undoubtedly would have made an admirable ruler. The reality of the situation was quite different, though. Having succeeded so suddenly, he had formed no councils, trusted no ministers, and failed to establish his own identity outside of his great-uncle's shadow. Even worse for him and Zita was the decaying state of their empire at the end of 1916. Under the duress of war, Austria-Hungary was literally tearing itself apart. Its many ethnic groups raised a chorus of voices calling for independence for the different nationalist parties. It was a sad reality that, despite Charles's kindness, empathy, and gentility, events beyond his control were already engineering his downfall.

Most of Europe seemed ambivalent toward Charles and Zita's accession, but in Britain, the news was greeted with vitriolic remarks. Forgotten was Charles's visit to London in 1911 for King George and Queen Mary's coronation. Instead, he was now the emperor of a country who was at war with Britain. The *Times* was scathing in its opinion of the new emperor.

> There is no reason whatever to suppose that the young ruler will rise in character or in statecraft above the somewhat low average of Habsburg rulers.... When Francis Joseph succeeded to his uncle's throne in his 19th year, he had already shown qualities that seemed to render him not unfit to his task. He was a young man, but a man. The Archduke Charles Francis Joseph not only in his 19th but even in his 25th year was a boy, and in some respects a young boy. Two years of war may have hardened and sobered him, but great surprises would be felt by those who knew him between 1908 and 1913 if he were to show in any respect the qualities of a great monarch.[13]

Surprisingly, the same article was more optimistic in its assessment of Zita: "The Empress Zita is a simple, unaffected woman of great charm and attractive appearance."[14] In the United States, the *New York Times* was equally flattering in its description of the new empress: "From her early days she has been studious, and is an accomplished musician and well versed in literature, history, and philosophy. She is also fond of society and is a graceful dancer."[15]

The subdued court that Empress Zita presided over came as a jarring shock to many of the imperial hangers-on in Vienna. Many of their contemporaries had expected Zita and Charles to embrace a more fashionable, if not more sybaritic, court lifestyle that embraced extravagance and wealth. What they realized instead was that the emperor and empress were deeply attached to the simple things in life. They also remained committed to each other. Like Nicholas II and George V, Charles I was wholeheartedly faithful to his wife and their wedding vows. Zita never had to worry about any mistresses parading in and out of her husband's bedroom. She always knew where his heart rested. Charles and Zita also possessed an innate goodness that annoyed some of the older, more cynical courtiers. In a combination of faith and character, they both made it a point to give people the benefit of the doubt and extended trust whenever possible.

Many were surprised by the strange mix of Empress Zita's personality. At times, she quietly submitted to her husband, obeying his decisions, but in other moments, she exerted a decisive tenacity that Charles happily embraced. One of the emperor's senior military advisers remembered Zita's daily presence at the military briefings held each evening. "She was habitually seated, reading a book or writing letters," he recalled. "Her presence was purely passive. She sometimes asked me for information on such or such an event, but it was never about important affairs. It was rare that she permitted herself a remark while the Emperor was discussing political questions with me, but when she did so, the question was always judicious and never beside the point."[16]

Even after their accession, the couple continued to devote themselves first and foremost to God. Each day began with Mass and prayer. They abstained from alcohol, cigarettes, and the other vices for which they were criticized by Vienna's smart set. The pair made it a point to let their Christian faith influence every area of their lives. Charles insisted on using Biblical principles as the basis for his reign, which led him to insist on taking milder measures on the war front. The older generals were sometimes frustrated by the pacifistic attitude of the young ruler, earning him the epithet *Friedenkaiser*—the Peace Emperor. But with Zita by his side, it did not bother Charles. Instead, he embraced the title.

As empress, Zita was now the head of a number of charitable organizations in Austria, mostly children's welfare societies and women's volunteer groups. The people that she worked with in these organizations were deeply impressed by the new empress. At a meeting of the Christian Women's League of Austria, one of the participants said of Zita, "I didn't have the feeling I was talking to the highest-ranking woman in the Monarchy, but rather with a personality whose thoughts and aspirations are completely devoted to the well-being of her fellow man. With every word the Empress spoke, one noticed that it came from the heart."[17] She spent many hours each day answering letters from people asking for her help. One woman, the wife of a coach driver, wrote to

Zita asking for help for her seriously ill daughter. Another woman asked her to assist in finding a school for an unfortunate child who possessed a stutter. Someone else hoped the empress could help her find a medicinal spa for her mother who was gravely sick.

It certainly could not have been easy to preside over a tottering empire at such an obstreperous period, but Zita earned the respect of everyone with whom she came into contact. Lieutenant General Albert von Margutti, a member of the imperial court, received an audience with the empress in January 1917 and was impressed with her: "This time I was again fascinated, not only by the charm that emanated from her august person and by the unrivalled grace of her manners, but more by the turns of her alert and pleasant conversation, sparkling with intelligence and vivacity." Margutti may have been charmed by Zita, but their audience was anything but lighthearted. It fell to Margutti to address with the empress a number of serious issues facing Austria-Hungary, including "the implacable determination of the Germans,... the danger of events precipitating the fall of Nicholas II and rebounding into that of William II and the Habsburgs."[18]

From the moment they ascended the throne, Emperor Charles I and Empress Zita would not know a moment's peace or tranquility in their reign. At the time of Franz Joseph's death, Austria's political system was suffering a breakdown. Count Stuergkh, the prime minister, had prorogued the Reichsrat, the Austrian parliament, saying with unsettling coldness, "Parliaments are a means to an end, where they fail, other means must be employed."[19] Stuergkh was later shot to death while he was having lunch in a Vienna restaurant by a young socialist named Friedrich Adler, who yelled out, "Down with absolutism! We want peace."[20] Horrified by such a senseless act of violence, Charles reconvened the Reichsrat in the spring of 1917.

In addition to the political crisis and the overwhelming business of the war effort, the imperial couple was confronted with a matter that was integral to the stability of the dual monarchy. The issue revolved around Hungary, the ancient kingdom that had made up the backbone of the Habsburg Empire for six centuries. The Hungarian people were adamantly against the war. Hungary's prime minister, Count Stefan Tisza, was the man who represented his country at Franz Joseph's Crown Council of 1914 that voted to declare war. He had been the only council member against attacking Serbia. Tisza believed that by going to war, Austria-Hungary was signing its own death warrant. It was up to the new sovereigns to convince Hungary to rally behind the continuing war effort. The Hungarians had mixed feelings about Charles and Zita. Franz Joseph enjoyed a measure of loyalty from the Magyars because they were doggedly loyal to the memory of Empress Elizabeth.

As far as the Hungarians were concerned, Charles and Zita were untried and untested. To help solidify the bond between Hungary and the new sovereigns, Charles and Count Tisza arranged for his coronation as king of Hungary. It was traditional to not have a coronation in Austria, but the crowning of a new king of Hungary was a deeply numinous event that tied the people to their sovereign. Hungarian law also stated that Charles could not reign until he was crowned, making a speedy coronation imperative. Zita shared her account of planning the coronation with her biographer Gordon Brook-Shepherd.

> Count Tisza stressed to the Emperor that, according to Hungarian law, he was only *Erbkönig* or hereditary king of Hungary until he was crowned and that, as such, he could neither promulgate nor even prolong certain basic laws. Some of these laws, including economic ones vital for the war, were due to expire at the end of the year. Hence the hurry: not even the full six months could, in these special circumstances, be allowed to pass.
>
> The Emperor consulted on the spot his experts. They all upheld Tisza's argument and all declared the matter to be urgent. At this, the Emperor agreed, and the legal point explains the date chosen for the coronation, 30 December 1916, almost the eve of the new year.
>
> The Emperor knew what he was doing and he knew the formal effect this would have on his reform plans. But the legal arguments were unassailable and the need for haste was there. He agreed in order to be able to bring the war to a rapid end. The Hungarian problem he hoped to sort out after the war.
>
> In one sense, of course, the friction between the Hungarians and the other nationalities under them was the Empire's biggest handicap. But these – we thought – were questions which must be left for peacetime. In war, Hungary was a pillar of the Dual Monarchy, and Tisza was the man of iron who carried that pillar.[21]

Like a medieval display lifted from the pages of Hungary's past, the coronation took place on December 30, 1916. It would be the last official ceremony for the Habsburgs as a reigning dynasty. It would also be the last imperial pageant that Europe would ever see. Budapest was transformed into a frozen wasteland by the painfully harsh winter that year. In spite of the cold, hundreds of thousands of people lined the route that Charles and Zita's carriage took to the gothic Cathedral of Mathias Corvinus. The wildly cheering throngs of people pressed so heavily against the procession to catch a glimpse of the new king and queen that it took them four hours to reach the cathedral. That day remained forever engraved on Zita's memory. "From the Suspension Bridge over the half-frozen Danube we detected the outlines of the Royal Castle emerging from the mist, lit up like a burning torch," she recalled years later. "I wondered if those lights, so seldom seen in Budapest, would go on burning all through the reign of the new monarch, or would the palace return to its usual gloom?"[22]

The coronation lasted for more than three hours. Once the Crown of Saint Stephen was placed on Charles's head and the sound of trumpets heralded him as the new king, Cardinal-Archbishop Johannes Csernoch proceeded to anoint Zita. Dressed in a white brocade gown embroidered with gold and covered with roses and other emblems, she was led by Csernoch to the seat next to her husband, who simply brushed her right shoulder with the ancient Hungarian crown. "Receive this crown of glory," he declared, "so that you know you are the King's wife and are charged always to care for the people of God." This simple act and declaration made Zita the crowned queen consort of Hungary. Zita's son Otto watched the ceremony from the balcony of the cathedral, seated next to his eccentric uncle King Ferdinand of the Bulgarians. Decades later, he still vividly remembered his parents' coronation: "In Vienna, I had been hemmed in as part of the proceedings [of Franz Joseph's funeral]. But in Budapest I was an observer. I travelled separately to the coronation church where I could watch everything from a loge. I remember being particularly struck by Count Tisza for, like all Hungarian Calvinists, he was wearing a costume in black which stood out among the vivid colourful dresses of the majority of the Catholic nobility."[23]

The day's events made a deep impression on the twenty-four-year-old Zita. "What impressed both of us most about the whole ceremony was the moving liturgical side of it all, especially the oaths taken by the king before his anointing to preserve justice for all and strive for peace," she said. "This sacred pledge given in the cathedral was exactly the political programme [*sic*] which he wanted to carry out from the throne. We both felt this so strongly that hardly any words were necessary between us."[24] The ceremony was followed by only a brief dinner at the palace in Budapest. Zita noted that her husband "felt that festivities were simply not appropriate to wartime, when every day so many were dying on the battlefields."[25] The only formal portrait that was taken to commemorate the occasion shows the mustachioed Charles looking uncomfortable under the weight of his dark, heavy coronation robes and the jeweled Crown of Saint Stephen. It is Zita who draws all eyes to her. Seated with her arm around four-year-old Otto, the new queen-empress was the epitome of majesty and grace with her embroidered dress and long, flowing train. Her neck was adorned with strings of pearls, and atop her head sat her diamond-studded crown, which was even larger than her husband's.

As soon as the couple returned to Vienna, Charles immediately left for Austria's military headquarters at Baden bei Wien, located a few miles south of Vienna. Following in Nicholas II's footsteps, Charles took personal command of Austria's armed forces, relieving Archduke Frederick, his older relative. The emperor moved his command center to Baden from Teschen to distance himself from Emperor Wilhelm II and Wilhelm's dictatorial advisers. Unlike other commanders, Charles wanted his family with him on his long visits to military headquarters. But unlike Nicholas II, Charles did not leave his wife to govern in his stead, although it is likely Zita would have done infinitely better than Alexandra.

At Baden, Zita and Charles strove to give their family as normal a life as possible. They purchased an old, two-story, yellow house that they named the Kaiservilla, located near the center of town. It was a simple building, with a sitting and dining room, a few living quarters, and two small rooms for the children to play in. The emperor "had to spend most of his days here and he wanted his young family to be there with him." During the days, Zita was often left to oversee life at the Kaiservilla while Charles visited military bases to discuss the war with his generals. As often as possible, she encouraged Charles to take little Otto with him. Dressed in a little white suit, the tiny crown prince could be seen returning the salutes of the soldiers as he walked by. Years later, Otto recalled those times he spent at headquarters: "My sister Adelheid usually came with me when we travelled to these different places. We were already at that time, I would almost say, a team, as we remained ever afterwards, and I particularly remember our visits to the air force base near Wiener Neustadt. My father decorated some of the officers who had done an outstanding job. Meanwhile we were shown the aeroplanes which impressed me very much."[26]

As the war continued for another interminable year, Queen Mary remained as indefatigable as ever, despite the fact that she felt the strains of the last two years as deeply as any of her subjects. In a letter to Lady Mount Stephen in 1916, she wrote, "The length of this horrible war is most depressing. I really think it gets worse the longer it lasts."[27]

While her husband visited France and met with his ministers from dawn until dusk, forty-nine-year-old Mary lost none of her determination. She personally oversaw almost every aspect of the home front, which included hospitals, nursing, munitions, and needlework for the troops. Workers were stunned to see their queen inspecting dirty factories and labor conditions, usually dressed like any ordinary person. When she was not in the factories, she was making the unenviable rounds at the hospitals for wounded soldiers that had been established across the country. Aristocratic families were patriotically turning their castles into field hospitals. One residence-turned-hospital that was particularly famous for the quality of care given to wounded soldiers was Glamis Castle in Scotland, home of Queen Mary's future daughter-in-law Lady Elizabeth Bowes-Lyon. One author made the following remark in a recent book about the British royal family: "During the First World War, the redoubtable Queen Mary was forever in and out of hospitals—sometimes three or four in an afternoon—visiting the wounded. It was on one of these tours that another and much younger family member being dragged around in her wake complained, 'I'm tired and I hate hospitals.' The queen's reported response encapsulated the attitude of modern monarchy. 'You are a member of the Royal Family. We are NEVER tired and we LOVE hospitals!"[28]

The hospitals that were in place still fell dreadfully short in caring for the volume of soldiers returning from the front lines. There were simply not enough beds and supplies to go around. Fed up with seeing so many brave men coming back and receiving pitiful care, the queen founded her own hospitals in and around London. One of the more famous ones, the Queen's Hospital in Roehampton, was designed specifically for soldiers who had lost limbs in combat. The hospital treated an estimated twenty thousand amputees during the war, but even that was believed to be only half of the men who had lost limbs between 1914 and 1918. Mary said it broke her heart to see "so many men without arms, legs, etc, etc." Her hospitals created a sense of solidarity between the people and their queen. Many people saw her as *Regina Mater*, their mother-queen. When one member of Parliament was returning from visiting his daughter at the Queen's Hospital at Stratford East, he bumped into the Prince of Wales, who asked where he had been. "To your Ma's place, of course," he replied. For the rest of Mary's life, her hospitals would always be known as "Ma's place."[29]

As devoted as she was to her cause, Mary's work took a heavy toll on her emotions; her appearance of temperance and dignity had a high price. She internalized all of her emotions since her father's stroke in Florence. True to form as a child of the Victorian era, she did not know how to release them. She never flew into dramatic rage like her father or threw fits of high drama like mother-in-law, Queen Alexandra; and she did not know how to sink into her grief and tears like Queen Victoria did after Prince Albert's death. For Mary, one form of relief was knitting. The stress and horror she absorbed was released as she worked her needles and yarn. Needlework had always been a hobby she enjoyed, ever since she became the patron of the London Needlework Guild in 1897. It was later renamed Queen Mary's Needlework Guild in 1914 in her honor. One observer at Windsor Castle noted how "when the Queen spoke of a poison-gas victim whom she had visited her needles clicked faster and faster as she bit back her emotions."[30] Those overwhelming emotions the queen felt were closer to home than most people realized. Many forgot that Mary had two sons in the war and—like any loving mother—was worried sick about their safety. The Prince of Wales was notorious for living on the edge. He made a regular habit of dashing off to the front lines on his bicycle. He was never intentionally placed in harm's way, but he created a believable illusion of sharing in the soldiers' suffering. It earned him tremendous popularity from the people, who enjoyed the thought of their heir to the throne in the trenches with the common man. David's brother Bertie saw more combat during the war. Having joined the Royal Navy, he served in the Battle of Jutland.

Added to this worry over Mary's sons were concerns her husband's well-being. It was no secret that the king did not have the strongest constitution. His immediate family seems to have inherited a number of health issues from his Danish relatives. Queen Alexandra was partially deaf and walked with a limp, the result of rheumatic fever. His brother Eddy had been sickly for most of his life. Even his sister Queen Maud of Norway suffered from "delicate health," which made it necessary for her "to make prolonged visits to England, whose temperate climate suited her better than the harsh Scandinavian winters."[31] Of his immediate family, George seemed the most robust, but that was only relative. The time he spent inspecting British forces did not help his stamina. At Hesigneul in 1915, he was thrown from his horse, which afterward fell on him. It took four days for doctors to diagnose the king with a fractured pelvis and broken ribs. "I still have to walk with a stick," he wrote to Nicholas II a year later. "A horse is a very heavy thing to fall on you and I suffered a great deal of pain, as I was badly crushed and bruised." Those around the king could see the effect it had on both his nerves and his temperament. "Very often I feel in despair," he later wrote to Nicholas.[32]

In the winter of 1916, one of the greatest tragedies in Queen Mary's life struck. On December 5, her beloved aunt Augusta, the stalwart Grand Duchess of Mecklenburg-Strelitz, died at the age of ninety-four. The two women had stayed in touch during the war thanks to the intermediary efforts of George's cousin Crown Princess Margaret of Sweden. In one of Augusta's last letters to Mary, which she composed on her deathbed, she wrote, "Tell the King, that it is a stout old English heart that is ceasing to beat." When the end finally came a few days later, the elderly grand duchess uttered only one word with her final breath: "May!"[33] When the news reached Mary on December 6, she and George were in the midst of a cabinet crisis that ended with David Lloyd George being elected prime minister. Mary confided in her diary that night, "I heard that my most beloved Aunt Augusta died yesterday morning after a month's illness which I had known of. She suffered little pain, only great weakness and slept much. A great relief to me, having been devoted to each other."[34] During her life, the "old autocrat" Augusta had taken on "the role of second mother to her niece," and "had exerted a powerful influence on Mary. Above all she showed her the best in two disparate ways of life, the English and the German, and it was the Grand Duchess's fierce patriotism that kindled in the Queen a love of Britain and the British that glowed to the end."[35] It pained the queen deeply that she was unable to attend the funeral because of the war. Although Mary and George were devoted to one another, the queen took special delight in confiding certain things to her aunt, woman to woman.

18

Imperial Endgame

(January–March 1917)

Russia had finally reached its breaking point. By mid-January 1917, plots to get rid of Alexandra and replace Nicholas were widespread, even among members of the imperial family. Even Minnie and Xenia talked about appealing to the tsar to have Alexandra removed to a convent. Minnie, deeply worried by the deteriorating situation, wrote to her daughter Xenia.

> All the bad passions seem to have taken possession of the capital. The hatred augments daily for her [Alexandra] that is disastrous, but doesn't open eyes yet. One continues quietly to play with the fire ... What my poor dear Nicky must suffer makes me mad to think! Just everything might have been so excellent after the *man's* [Rasputin's] disappearance and now it was all spoiled by her rage and fury, hatred and feelings of revenge!... so sad.... Alexandra Feodorovna must be banished. I don't know how but it must be done. Otherwise she might go completely mad. Let her enter a convent or just disappear.[1]

Petrograd descended into anarchy after Rasputin's murder because it showed the people that the power was within their own hands to take hold of what they wanted through force. The city's salons became so rife with talk of revolution that General Henry Wilson, a member of the British delegation, noted incredulously, "Everyone—officers, merchants, ladies—talks openly of the absolute necessity of doing away with" the tsar and tsarina.[2] The historian Bernard Pares recalled in his memoirs how a prominent member of Russian society had warned him, "Do not wish for a Russian Revolution! It will be far more savage than the French."[3]

By the early months of 1917, Petrograd was almost entirely under the control of the revolutionaries, who had armed themselves with tens of thousands of machine guns and other handheld weapons. In January, a mob of 150,000 starving people took to the streets demanding food. "Children are starving in the most literal sense of the word," reported one police officer.[4] By March, Petrograd was at a standstill, as most of the city's workers went on strike. A mob of angry women from a textile factory flooded Nevsky Prospect demanding bread. City transportation shut down, and the newspapers stopped printing. Frightened citizens huddling inside their homes could hear the mobs crying out for revenge against Alexandra and the government. Soldiers ordered to suppress the crowds shot and killed two hundred people, but after a few days, most of the soldiers stood down, refusing to take orders from their officers.

Desperate to stop the growing revolution, Mikhail Rodzianko, the head of the Duma, telegraphed to Tsar Nicholas II begging him to return immediately from Stavka. He warned that the garrison troops and reserve battalions were now in open revolt and that if they managed to secure the loyalty of the army, all would be lost. Within twenty-four hours of Rodzianko sending his telegram, buildings across Petrograd were flying the revolutionary red flag. Unspeakable acts of violence were carried out against anyone who had shown loyalty to the imperial family. The tsar's brother Grand Duke Michael was hunted by roaming bands of rioters as he tried to flee Petrograd for his home. He managed to evade the mobs, but not everyone was so lucky. Nicholas Stolypin, the imperial court chamberlain, and the procurator of the Holy Synod were both arrested. One of Nicholas II's military commanders—General Staekelberg—was murdered when a mob stormed his home.

The situation in Russia caused great alarm across Europe. Queen Marie of Romania, Alexandra and Nicholas's mutual cousin, was terrified at the prospect of a Russian revolution. She noted the following in her diary in 1917:

> Their [the Russians'] hatred of the Empress has reached a terrible pitch; they consider her a misfortune for the country and there is no one to-day who would not gladly get rid of her by any means. How dreadful! I cannot imagine anything more ghastly than to be hated by one's own people, and after all it is not so very difficult to

make yourself beloved if you are Queen, in Russia especially where the Tsar and Tsarina are almost sacred figures.[5]

Fleeing the unrest in Petrograd, Alexandra took her family into seclusion at the Alexander Palace in Tsarskoe Selo. She seemed calm and demure to the people around her, but she was deeply worried about the future of Russia. To make matters worse, her children were gravely ill with the measles. Dressed in her Red Cross nurse's uniform, Alexandra pushed herself to the brink of physical collapse nursing them, as well Anna Viroubova, who was also ill. Count Benckendorff, the chief marshal of the imperial court who was no fan of the tsarina, even admitted, "She is great, great … But I had always said that she was one of those people who rise to sublime heights in the midst of misfortune."[6]

Alexandra may not have fully understood the gravity of the situation, but she was very much aware that there was a power struggle being fought beyond the walls of Tsarskoe Selo. In what may have been the last letter Alexandra ever wrote to her husband as empress, she poured out her grief but also her continuing support.

> My own beloved, precious Angel, light of my life,
>
> My heart breaks, thinking of you all alone going through all this anguish, anxiety & we know nothing of you & you neither of us … you who are alone, no army behind you, caught like a mouse in a trap, what can you do? Thats [*sic*] the lowest, meanest thing unknown in history, to stop ones sovereign.… Two currents—*Duma* & revolutionists—two snakes who I hope will eat off each others heads.… Heart aches very much, but I don't heed it.… Only suffer too hideously for you.… God bless & protect you—send His angels to guard & guide you … this is the climax of the bad. The horror before our Allies!! & the enemies joy!!—Can advise nothing, be only yr. Precious self. If you have to give into things, God will help you to get out of them. Ah my suffering Saint. I am one with you, inseparably one
>
> Old Wify[7]

Giving in was exactly what Nicholas II was forced to do. As the heavily armored imperial train lumbered its way toward Petrograd with the anxious tsar on board, it was halted on March 3, 1917, at Pskov near the Estonian border. Waiting there to board the train were M. Guchkov and V. V. Shulgin, two of the Duma's highest-ranking officials. Desperate to restore order, they confronted Nicholas and forced an ultimatum upon him. He could both rally as many loyal troops as possible and march on the capital, plunging Russia into a bloody and violent civil war, or he could abdicate. Without a second thought, Tsar Nicholas II immediately abdicated. He himself wrote out the order of abdication, which included this statement: "I invite all the loyal sons of my country to fulfill their sacred duty which is to obey the Emperor in these difficult moments, and to help him, as well as the representatives of the nation, to lead Russia to victory, success, and glory. May God help Russia!"[8] Much like the similarly fated King Louis XVI of France, Nicholas refused to shed the blood of his people for the sake of keeping his throne. "Thus, with the simple stroke of a pen, Nicholas II put an end to the three-hundred-year Romanov dynasty," wrote one historian. "With his reign ended, so too ended his wife's position as empress."[9]

When he heard of the tsar's decision, Emperor Charles immediately sent a letter to Wilhelm II. He did not mince words about the gravity of the situation: "We are fighting against a new enemy which is more dangerous than the Entente: international revolution, which finds its strongest ally in general starvation. I beseech you not to overlook this portentous aspect of the matter and to reflect that a quick finish to the war even at the cost of heavy sacrifice gives us a chance of confronting this coming upheaval with success."[10]

In England, King George was shaken by what was happening. "Bad news from Russia," he wrote in his diary. "Practically a revolution has broken out in Petrograd, and some of the Guards Regiments have mutinied and killed their officers. This rising is against the Govt. not against the war." A few days later, his suspicions as to the cause of the revolution were confirmed: "I fear Alicky is the cause of it all and Nicky has been weak … I am in despair."[11] At the same time that Nicholas II's reign was coming to an end in March 1917, a new, highly dramatic, opulent play called *Masquerade* premiered at the Imperial Alexandrinsky Theater in Petrograd. The Russian historian Edvard Radzinsky remarked that this "paean to the Palace proved to be a requiem for a world that, beyond the walls of the theater, was dying."[12]

At the same time as Russia was undergoing an existential supernova, the pattern of victory the Central powers were enjoying began to disintegrate. In April 1917, the United States entered the war on the side of the Entente, which informally changed its name to the Allies. The move had been in the works since a German submarine sank the *Lusitania*, a British cruise liner, in May 1915. More than one thousand civilians were killed, including a number of Americans. "No gentleman would kill so many women and children," Wilhelm II embarrassedly told the American ambassador.[13] In Austria, Emperor Charles I was under no illusions about what the entry of the Americans into the war meant. He told his wife, "Now it's the end. If America comes in we are finished for good."[14] Along with their munitions and supplies, the Americans contributed nearly four million additional troops to the war effort. Within a few months, ten thousand new soldiers were arriving in France daily.

The sinking of the *Lusitania* and the subsequent entry of the United States into the war led to major political crisis in Germany. Chancellor Theobald von Bethmann-Hollweg was forced to resign after coming under fire from the Reichstag's Peace Resolution, a coalition of the Social Democrats, Progressives, and Centrists. Bethmann-Hollweg's replacement was Georg Michaelis, Germany's first nonaristocratic chancellor. He remained in office for only four months. On October 31, 1917, he too was forced to resign for his unwillingness to support the Reichstag's peace initiatives. He was replaced by seventy-five-year-old Count Georg Hertling.

Emperor Charles had known since he was still an archduke that unless something was done to end the war, the damage to Austria-Hungary and the rest of Europe could be irreparable. As early as January 29, 1917, Zita's two brothers Sixtus and Xavier met with their mother, the Duchess of Parma, in Switzerland to make preliminary and unofficial peace overtures. The emperor sent his old friend, Count Erdödy, to represent him at the meeting. In the Austrian foreign ministry there was some apprehension at the idea of Austria-Hungary pursuing a separate piece, since the alliance that bound it with the other Central powers was very close-knit. But the growing danger against monarchism, fueled by events in Russia, meant that peace might be the only way to save Austria-Hungary from its own revolution. In April, his foreign minister penned a prophetic note explaining that if "the monarchs of the Central Powers are unable to conclude peace in the next few months, the peoples will do so over their heads, and then the waves of revolution will sweep away everything for which our brothers and sons are still fighting and dying today."[15]

The appeals Charles made for peace through the usual diplomatic channels had failed. The only alternative he and Zita could think of to find a peaceful solution was to use the empress's brother in the Belgian army— Prince Sixtus—to open the lines of communication with France. With his intellectual prowess, erudition, and reputation as a Renaissance man, Sixtus was the natural choice to act as a conduit between Vienna and Paris if there was to be any hope for peace. Raymond Poincaré, the French president, expressed interest in an article Sixtus had published in a French magazine that called for peace via Charles and Zita. The ensuing episode, which would ultimately help to topple Charles from the throne, would come to be known infamously as the Sixtus Affair.

In early 1917, Charles ordered his military attaché in Switzerland to look into making contact with Sixtus "in order to sound out the readiness for peace on the other side."[16] The emperor and empress of Austria's peace initiatives were motivated not only by a desire to preserve their empire from any further losses but also to ally Austria with France and Britain against Germany. A British intelligence report from June 1917 cited that the "Emperor and Empress are entirely pro-French and pro-English. They are strongly anti-German and hate (a) the Kaiser (b) Prince Rupprecht [of Bavaria] both on political and private grounds. The Kaiser insulted the present Empress when she was young: Prince Rupprecht is a course [*sic*] dissolute Prussianised atheist who bullies the Emperor and Empress for their religious and moral principles."[17]

A memorandum written by Philippe Pétain, the French general in chief, to Paul Painlevé, the minister of war, shows that—at least at first—the French were willing to talk peace. The memo, dated August 4, 1917, highlights the desire on France's part to limit German power in the postwar era.

> The only enemy of France, the one danger in Europe is Prussia. The amendments to the constitutions of the other [German] governments are secondary factors as long as Prussia is not entirely and definitely vanquished and reduced to impotence. The Entente must therefore create an irremediably hostile power next to Prussia. It [the Entente] can achieve this through the Habsburgs by forming, with a bond of the personal union, a federation with a majority of Slavic states ...[18]

Once it became apparent that the French were on board and using the Duchess of Parma as a go-between, the empress convinced her brother to come to Laxenburg, a palace outside Vienna, for a secret meeting; Charles was uninvolved in the initial contact to give himself plausible deniability if needed. When Sixtus arrived on behalf of President Poincaré, he set the tone for the meeting by asking Charles Salomon, Poincaré's political adviser, to join him. At the meeting, Sixtus pulled out a folded piece of paper from his pocket. It listed four points from the French government that were nonnegotiable for the peace talks to go forward. In no uncertain terms, if Austria wanted peace, France demanded the return of Alsace and Lorraine from Germany, which had been seized in the Franco-Prussian War; the restoration of Belgium's independence; the guaranteed independence of Serbia; and the handover of

Constantinople to Russia. Years later, Prince Sixtus wrote in his memoirs his impression of the initial peace negotiations.

> The young Emperor was innocent of his predecessor's faults and had come to the throne with only one desire, which was to put an end to the universal slaughter. He wished to play an untrammeled [*sic*] game, face to face with his associates and face to face with his enemies, in order to provoke a possibility and a necessity for peace. The Emperor Charles would have gone on further, for his duty clearly showed him that he could not uselessly sacrifice his people to the obstinacy of an ally [Germany] whose pride was causing his coming destruction.... a separate peace with Austria would have realised the principle object of the war. It would have brought about invincibly the submission of Bulgaria and Turkey. The facts of 1918 have proved how easy it would have been after 1917 to come to an understanding with these two powers. The war would have been concentrated on the French front and brought about the results obtained eighteen months later. The lives of thousands, nay millions of men would have been saved.[19]

Upon leaving that first meeting, Sixtus obtained a guarantee from Count Ottokar Czernin, the Austrian foreign minister, that he was fully committed to the peace process. Ambitious, underhanded, tall, and with a gaunt face and deeply recessed eyes, Czernin was a vocal Germanophile who was committed to Austria-Hungary's military alliance with the Hohenzollern Empire. There were even rumors that he was a German spy. All of these things made Sixtus very skeptical of his assurances, but he trusted Zita and Charles implicitly. It was enough for the peace process to go to stage two: examining the feasibility of France's terms. Empress Zita recalled her husband's reaction to the demands.

> The return of Alsace-Lorraine was of course a French interest. But it was also one of the Emperor Charles's, who was the head of the House of Lorraine. This family link of his with Lorraine was one reason why President Poincaré, who came from that province himself, had so much personal sympathy with the Emperor.
> The four points that [were taken] back to Switzerland were personally drafted by the Emperor. It was still too early in his reign for him to have formed any close circle of advisers around him. As for the South Slav kingdom idea, I remember that he had pondered on this—and discussed it with several advisers and

friends including my brothers—while he was heir-apparent and even earlier, before the war.... It was envisaged by the Emperor as part of his overall federalist solution.[20]

Once Sixtus returned to France, a flurry of letters flew back and forth between him and Zita, to whom Charles had asked to speak on his behalf. It spoke volumes to the deep love the emperor and empress had for one another that Charles was able to trust his wife implicitly to speak for him. It was also hoped that should these negotiations ever be made public, it would appear as a woman asking her brother for help, not the emperor of Austria suing for peace.

After taking time to consider his options, and advised by his loving wife, Emperor Charles wrote Sixtus a long and thoughtful letter in response to the four points the prince had brought with him on behalf of the French government.

My dear Sixtus,

The third year of this war that has brought the world so much mourning and sorrow is coming to an end....

I beg you to let the President of the French Republic, M. Poincaré, know in a secret and unofficial way that I shall support the just claims of France to Alsace-Lorraine in every way and with all my personal influence.

Belgium must be re-established as a sovereign state, retaining all its African possessions.... The sovereignty of Serbia will be re-established and, as a token of our good-will, we are inclined to guarantee her an equitable and natural access to the Adriatic, and far-reaching economic concessions. Austria-Hungary, on the other hand, will demand as an indispensable condition that the Kingdom of Serbia dissociates itself from, and suppresses the tendency for the disintegration of the Monarchy,... that it shall faithfully and by all means in its power stop that kind of agitation in Serbia and outside her frontiers, and that it will make a pledge to that effect under the guarantee of the Entente Powers.

The recent events in Russia oblige me to withhold comment on that subject until the final formation of a legal government.

Hoping that this way we shall soon be able, on both sides, to put an end to the suffering of so many millions of men and of so many families that live in sorrow and anxiety.

I beg you to believe in my kindest and most fraternal regards,

Karl[21]

In spite of the best efforts made by Zita's husband, the peace process was mired by one struggle after another. German military command had been sounded out regarding peace but had not been told about the emperor's meetings with Sixtus. The Germans refused to even consider most of France's Four Points. Charles found himself making little progress convincing Wilhelm II or even his own foreign minister, Count Czernin, who was acting as an intermediary between the two emperors. The fact that Wilhelm was willing to negotiate was obvious, but so too was the fact that his generals, specifically those in favor of the war, were actually in control.

In an effort to appeal to Wilhelm in person, Charles and Zita arranged to meet with the German emperor during his visit to the military base at Homburg in 1917. Officially, Charles had arranged the visit so Zita could meet Augusta Victoria for the first time. At the peace talks between the two emperors, Charles conspicuously failed to mention Alsace-Lorraine and a unified Slavic state to Wilhelm. He also failed to mention the fact that the go-between was Sixtus, how far along the peace process was, or even how closely the Austrian monarchs were working with the French. Years later, Zita described the meeting between the two emperors.

The purpose of the Homburg meeting was not to break the news to the German Emperor that we had made a move to the other side, for this *we had already told him*. When Emperor William was in Vienna in February 1917 my husband had confided to him that he had taken an opportunity to make contact with the *Entente* to find a possible solution to the war.

The German Emperor immediately asked for the name of the intermediary. My husband replied firmly: "That's something I cannot tell you, but I can guarantee his discretion." Emperor William accepted this and said: "All right, go ahead. I agree."[22]

Though Wilhelm may have been open to the idea of peace negotiations, the final word came from his generals, who were clearly opposed to the idea. The difference in attitudes between the Austrians and Germans can be seen in a confrontation between Zita and Henning von Holtzendorff, one of Wilhelm's generals, at a lunch party at Homburg. When the general commented that Zita sounded against the war, she replied that indeed she was, "as every woman is who would rather see joy than suffering." Angered, Holtzendorff shot back bellicosely, "Suffering? What does that matter? I work best on an empty stomach. It's a case of tightening your belt and sticking it out."[23] It quickly became obvious to both Charles and Zita that the German military leaders could not be reasoned with.

Although the Homburg visit failed to gain German support for the Sixtus peace initiative, it gave Empress Zita the first and only opportunity she would ever have to meet Dona. Since her husband's accession, the two women had kept up an amiable correspondence, but they had never met until now. A photograph of the two empresses taken at the time paints a vivid picture. Both look regal in dark dress suits adorned with pearls, wide hats, and parasols, but it is obvious that the women represented different things. Dona, conservative and dignified, symbolized traditionalism and the past, while Zita, with her more stylish ensemble, embodied liberality and the future of monarchy. During one of the receptions at their meeting in Homburg, Zita brought up a subject with Dona that had disgusted her. Zita had been shocked to learn that, twice a year, German bombers were attacking the home of the king and queen of the Belgians on their name days.

"Just imagine if France or England knew of this meeting taking place and bombed the building!" Zita remarked.

Dona was horrified—as Zita had hoped—and replied, "Don't worry. I am sure the English would not bomb because they would know there are ladies present." Zita managed to calm the German empress until she made her point.

"But I am told that the Queen of the Belgians *is* being bombed by German pilots," she said. Zita later recounted to a friend that Dona "was incredulous and, to my delight, called over [General] Hindenburg ... who said he had never heard of these attacks, but would go into the matter immediately. And the fact was that, from that time on, the bombings stopped."[24]

When news of Germany's resistance reached Paris, Raymond Poincaré brought the negotiations to a screeching halt. The British, who had at one time been interested in talking peace, were no longer on board once Austria expressed resistance to granting Italy unwarranted territorial concessions carved out of present-day Slovenia and Croatia. Prince Sixtus explained Charles's position on Italy: "The Emperor stated that he was prepared to make [only] the necessary sacrifices to Italy, but that these must be no more than was strictly fair, confined, that was, to territories [that were] Italian in speech and sentiment."[25] The British government became extremely critical of Zita at this time, blaming her for the breakdown of the peace process, similar to the way they vilified Alexandra of Russia. Still latently anti-Catholic, the British foreign ministry accused Zita of scheming and made veiled references to "Bourbon intrigues." Prince Sixtus staunchly defended his sister's role.

> Legend says that my sister the Empress played a principal part in these negotiations. Too feudal to love intrigue for the pleasure of it, she was content to write me this charming letter as a woman and as a sovereign, begging me to come to Vienna: "Do not let yourself be held by considerations which in ordinary life would be justified. Think of all the unfortunates who live in the hell of the trenches and die there every day by the hundreds, and come!"[26]

But by June, even Sixtus became frustrated, mostly by Italy's refusal to participate unless it received most of the Austrian Balkans. Italy's recalcitrance brought what was left of the peace talks to a standstill. With little accomplished, and without the support of France or Britain, Sixtus gave up on the peace process and returned to his regiment in the Belgian army. By the summer, Emperor Charles and Empress Zita were continuing their labors to find a peaceful end to the war. Russia had begun to cannibalize itself, and there was growing unrest in Germany and Austria. "In World War I Emperor Charles of Austria, King of Hungary, tried desperately to end the bloodshed with a constructive peace," Archduke Otto wrote decades later of his father's efforts. "Many are the reasons why he could not succeed. It staggers the imagination if one considers what would have happened had this man of peace been successful in his endeavours."[27] Sadly, the Sixtus Affair would not be successful. On the contrary it would serve to break the foundations of the entire Austro-Hungarian monarchy in just over a year. In the process, Europe's last imperial remnants would be swept away forever.

19

Hated, Humbled, Rejected

(March–November 1917)

O nce Alexandra's husband abdicated his throne, there was a heated debate over what would happen to the government in Russia. The Duma had no immediate plans to abolish the monarchy, since they expected young Alexei to be named tsar with a state-appointed regent. But that plan fell through because Nicholas knew that if his son became tsar, he would be separated from his family, and Nicholas was unwilling to let that happen. He could not bear the thought of his close-knit family being broken up. Such a move would devastate Alexandra.

With Alexei taken out of the succession, Nicholas passed the throne directly to his brother Michael, who some royalists hailed as Tsar Michael II. "We have judged it right to abdicate the Throne of the Russian State and to lay down the Supreme Power," Nicholas declared in his formal abdication. "Not wishing to be parted from Our Beloved Son, We hand over Our Succession to Our Brother the Grand Duke Michael Aleksandrovich and Bless Him on his accession to the Throne."[1] But so unstable was the monarchy's position now that, upon learning of his accession when he awoke the next morning, Michael declined to take the throne. He renounced his claim in the presence of Mikhail Rodzianko and the Duma officials who had come to his apartment at Gatchina Palace to meet him.

At Tsarskoe Selo, Alexandra was racked with anxiety. The overthrow of the government in Petrograd led to a collapse of the most basic services. Electrical lines were cut, water was shut off, and the railways were blocked.

Rumors circulated that mobs of armed soldiers were making their way to Tsarskoe Selo to kill the empress or capture the tsarevitch, neither of whom knew anything of Nicholas's abdication. In a last-ditch attempt to keep order, the Alexander Palace guard regiment—some fifteen hundred soldiers who had remained staunchly loyal to the Romanovs—blockaded the palace's courtyard with artillery and snipers. For a sleepless night, they kept their vigil, until it became clear that no armed troops were en route, at least not at the moment. Inside the palace, Alexandra was struggling to maintain her calm veneer. She paced back and forth in her room while she waited to hear any news from her husband. The waiting came to an end late that night when Grand Duke Paul Alexandrovich, Nicholas's uncle, arrived at the palace with the earth-shattering news. After the meeting, a speechless Alexandra stumbled into another room where her friend Lili Dehn was waiting. Falling lifelessly onto a nearby couch, she cried out, *"Abdiqué!"* A few moments later, she turned to Lili and muttered, "the poor one ... all by himself ... oh my God, what has happened! And I cannot be near him to comfort him."[2]

When the moment finally came, and Alexandra realized her position as Empress of All the Russias was at an end, there was no anger or bitterness. "It's for the best," she said. "It's the will of God. God will make sure that Russia is saved. It's the only thing that matters."[3] She did not reproach her husband for abdicating but instead was overcome with grief for what he must be feeling in the moment. That night, Alexandra sat down at her desk and penned an emotional letter to her husband, giving him her support.

> I *fully* understand yr. action [in abdicating], my own heroe [*sic*]! I *know* that [you] could not sign [anything] against what you swore at yr. coronation. We know each other through & through—need no words—as I live, we shall see you back on yr. throne, brought back by your people, to the glory of your reign. You have saved yr. son's reign & the country & yr. saintly purity.... I hold you tight, tight in my arms & will never let them touch your shining soul, I kiss, kiss, kiss & bless you & will always understand you.
>
> *Wify*[4]

The overthrow of the greatest autocratic dynasty in modern history sent shockwaves across Europe. Queen Marie of Romania was frightened at what was taking place in Russia.

> What an hour for that woman [Alexandra] ... she who would listen to no one except Rasputin, and separated herself little by little from

all members of the family, then from the whole of society, never showing herself any more, shutting herself up either in Tsarskoe or in the Crimea....

What may her feelings be to-day? How does she bear it, separated, as she is from her husband, he not able to get to her and all her children down with measles. A ghastly situation. I sit and ponder over it and to me it seems tragic and fearful beyond words.[5]

As Alexandra waited at Tsarskoe Selo for Nicholas to return, she and Lili Dehn spent their time destroying letters, diaries, and other documents that they were afraid would fall into the hands of the revolutionaries. Most of the papers were harmless enough; love letters between Nicholas and Alexandra or correspondences with Queen Victoria, but Alexandra could not take the chance of her personal thoughts being used as propaganda against her family.

At the end of March, soldiers arrived at Tsarskoe Selo with orders from the new, officially named Russian Provisional Government. Alexandra and her children were placed under house arrest. The palace staff was told they could leave immediately and go free or share in the Romanovs' captivity. In an unseemly display of loathsome cowardice, many of the servants abandoned the helpless Alexandra to her captors. Only Lili Dehn and a handful of loyal servants stayed with the family.

From the day the soldiers arrived, the atmosphere at the Alexander Palace was thick with tension. The occupying soldiers began hurling insults on the former empress. The grand duchesses were still bedridden, and Alexandra had all but locked herself away in her Mauve Boudoir. Her only companion continued to be Lili, who promised the girls she would not leave their mother's sight. The days waiting for Nicholas were whittled away in quiet prayer and reading, but the nights were insufferably long. Alexandra barely slept. Outside the palace, the sounds of gunfire rang out as drunken soldiers caroused throughout the village grounds. Every so often, Alexandra would pull the drapes aside and look out anxiously, hoping to catch a glimpse of Nicholas returning. From the next room where she slept, Lili could hear her pacing back and forth, the only sound a faint cough brought on by stress and fatigue. The ex-tsarina counted the minutes until her husband returned. It was the last time the couple would ever be separated. They would remain together until the bitter end.

When Nicholas finally reached Tsarskoe Selo, he dejectedly made his way past dozens of angry soldiers who hurled insult after insult upon "Citizen Nicholas Romanov." In front of his family's captors, he refused to show any emotion, but when he and Alexandra entered her Mauve Boudoir alone, he fell to the ground, his face bathed in bitter tears. Alexandra took her husband into her arms. Overcome herself, she found it hard to find the words to comfort him. According to Lili Dehn, Alexandra assured Nicholas that "the husband and father [were] of more value in her eyes than the Emperor whose throne she shared."[6]

The next few months proved taxing on the former imperial family. They remained under house arrest at the Alexander Palace while the Russian Provisional Government decided what should be done with them. Determined to live normal lives, Nicholas, Alexandra, and their family continued their daily routines when possible. Very much the outdoorsman, Nicholas insisted on physical activity by maintaining the palace grounds himself. Guards were surprised to find the former tsar and autocrat of All the Russias chopping wood and shoveling snow. The guards watching could not help but sneer at Nicholas, "Well, well, Nicolouchka (Little Nicholas), so you are breaking the ice now, are you? Perhaps you've drunk enough of our blood? … And in summer, when there's no more ice—what'll you do then, *Goloubchik nach* (our darling)? Perhaps you'll throw a little sand on the walks with a little shovel?"[7] Along with his daughters, Nicky—who was now known simply as Nicholas Alexandrovich Romanov—planted a vast vegetable garden of beans, turnips, lettuce, squash, and some five hundred heads of cabbage.

Alexandra was unable to move around as freely as her husband. Her fragile health completely collapsed. Her dark hair became filled with gray. Her face, once praised as the most beautiful in all of Europe, had aged well beyond its forty-five years. Her heart trouble and the pain in her back, legs, and head meant she could barely walk. The woman who had once ruled a sixth of the world's landmass was now confined to a wheelchair most of the time. But Nicholas and their daughters happily pushed her around the village grounds. On some afternoons, when the weather was pleasant enough, Alexandra sat outdoors with one of her daughters or her lady-in-waiting, Baroness Sophie Buxhoeveden. It was on one such afternoon that a particularly vulgar guard sat next to Alexandra, accusing her of hating Russia. Her calm, rational answers to the soldier's accusations began disarming him. The conversation eventually turned to matters of politics, religion, and family. The guard was especially surprised to learn that, despite being born German, the former empress was a Russian "with all her heart." When the officer on duty arrived, the guard stood to his feet. Taking her hand, he said, "Do you know, Alexandra Feodorovna, I had quite a different idea of you? I was mistaken about you."[8]

The captivity at Tsarskoe Selo lasted six long months. During that time, the Romanovs were forced to endure repeated interrogations from Alexander Kerensky, the justice minister of the Russian Provisional Government. One of his first acts at the palace was to have Lili Dehn, the last of Alexandra's friends, sent back to Petrograd. "I am the Procurator-General, Kerensky," he told Nicholas and Alexandra upon meeting them in the palace's schoolroom. "The queen of England asks for news of the ex-tsarina."[9] It was the first time Alexandra had been addressed that way, prompting her face to turn red. She told Kerensky that, as usual, her heart was troubling her. He then spent hours questioning her about her political agenda. After a grueling interview, Kerensky admitted to Nicholas, "your wife does not lie."[10] He was also forced to admit, "I had imagined her differently. She is very sympathetic. She is an admirable mother. What courage, what dignity, what intelligence and how beautiful she is!"[11]

The fate of the former imperial family was brought up around the time of Kerensky's visit. One of the first foreign requests for the Romanovs' freedom came from Wilhelm and Dona. Though Russia and Germany were technically enemies, Wilhelm offered his cousin and her family exile in Berlin. Wilhelm later said, "I ordered my Chancellor to try and get in touch with the Kerensky government by neutral channels, informing him that if a hair of the Russian Imperial family's head should be injured, I would hold him personally responsible if I should have the possibility of doing so."[12] But Alexandra could never forgive Wilhelm his failings, and she could never give up her antipathy for all things German. When she was told of the possibility of escaping to Germany, she was indignant, saying, "after what they have done to the Tsar, I would rather die in Russia than be saved by the Germans."[13] When the plan failed, Wilhelm admitted, "The blood of the unhappy Tsar is not at *my door*; not on *my hands*."[14]

Another possibility that presented itself was sending the family to England. After all, King George V and Nicholas were first cousins through their mothers. George and Alexandra were first cousins, since both were grandchildren of Queen Victoria. King George and Queen Mary were "deeply distressed" by the Romanovs' situation, and working through their prime minister, David Lloyd George, they made overtures to invite the imperial family to spend the rest of their days in Britain.[15] But this plan was doomed from the start. Public opposition began to take hold in England. The government was deeply concerned over who would be paying the family's bills. Although previous Romanovs had been known for their exorbitant spending, there was a misconception that Alexandra and her family were the same way. In reality, they were among the most frugal, down-to-earth royals Europe had known in recent years. The British government ultimately insisted that if the Romanovs wanted to come to England, it was up to Alexander Kerensky, the newly appointed prime minister of the Russian Provisional Government, to cover their expenses.

From there, the plan began to dissolve on both ends. The Russian Provisional Government was unwilling to pay anything on the Romanovs' behalf. And in Britain, public opinion had long steered against the Romanov dynasty's autocracy in favor of England's more liberal, parliamentary monarchy. King George received letters from different classes of British society imploring him not to give the tsar and his family refuge. "Every day, the King is becoming more concerned about the question of the Emperor and Empress coming to this country," wrote Baron Stamfordham, George's private secretary. "His Majesty receives letters from people in all classes of life, known or unknown to him, saying how much the matter is being discussed, not only in clubs by working men, and that Labour Members in the House of Commons are expressing adverse opinions to the proposal."[16] Even the *Times* was hostile toward the idea, especially when it came to the ex-tsarina. "How can we tolerate this friend of Germany in our midst?" one reporter wrote.[17] At Buckingham Palace, the fate of Nicholas and Alexandra gnawed at Queen Mary, who was "harbouring guilt along with her anxiety. If any tragic fate befell them, she knew she would always feel a measure of the responsibility."[18]

The fact that Alexandra had been practically raised by Queen Victoria seems to have all but been forgotten. Lord Francis Bertie, the British ambassador to France, was particularly scathing in his opinion of the former tsarina. Reflecting the drastic misconception the public had about her, he wrote in 1917, "The Empress is not only a Boche [German] by birth but in sentiment. She did all she could to bring about an understanding with Germany. She is regarded as a criminal or a criminal lunatic and the ex-Emperor as a criminal from his weakness and submission to her promptings."[19] Alexandra was not oblivious to the accusations being made against her in the foreign press. She poured out her frustration in a letter to a patient she had met at Tsarskoe Selo, when some of the other buildings had been converted into field hospitals earlier in the war: "When they write filth about Me—let them, they started tormenting me long ago, I don't care now, but that they slander Him [Nicholas], throw dirt on the Sovereign Anointed by God, that is beyond the bearable."[20]

Bowing to pressure both from the people and his government, the king had no choice but to withdraw his offer of asylum to his cousins and their family. One night, while the king and queen were having tea with the Prince of Wales at Buckingham Palace, a telegram arrived. It asked that, in light of the current pressure against harboring the Romanovs, "would there be any objection from the Palace if a destroyer was not sent to Russia and asylum not offered." Upon reading it, the queen declared simply, "No." The king agreed. "To say no was not a callous act," wrote one historian. "The Queen, conceiving it her prime duty to protect the English throne, was aware that it could not be put at risk even for dear cousins."[21] Shortly thereafter, the Foreign Office issued a statement: "His Majesty's Government does not insist on its former offer of hospitality to the Imperial Family."[22] But the king's decision did not abate the criticism that both he and the queen were facing at this time. The German Imperial Air Service had just bombed London. Leading the attack had been the new heavy bomber, the Gotha G.IV. In the aftermath of the attack, the British monarchy was faced with a public relations nightmare. The official name of the royal family was Saxe-Coburg-Gotha. This commonality between their monarchs and the Germans proved too much for some people in British society. Ugly rumors began to permeate Britain that George and Mary were pro-German; the fall of the once-mighty Romanovs only fueled republican sentiments elsewhere. A week after Nicholas abdicated, crowds gathered at the Royal Albert Hall to celebrate the end of the tsarist regime. In a letter to the *Times*, the celebrated author H. G. Wells asserted that "the time has come to rid ourselves of the ancient trappings of throne and sceptre."[23] The very notion of hereditary monarchy was under assault.

The king and queen's critics believed that evidence of their German sympathies was obvious and came by way of the fact that a number of their relatives were German royals. Then there was George himself, whose grandfather Prince Albert was from the German dukedom of Saxe-Coburg-Gotha. As such, all the members of the British royal family had inherited Prince Albert's German titles. As for Queen Mary, who had been born and raised in England, her brothers Dolly and Alge were the duke and prince of Teck, respectively, making them part of the Württemberger monarchy.

According to the rumors, the king and queen were supposed to be in league with their extended family, namely the other children and grandchildren of Queen Victoria and Prince Albert. As far back as 1871, the British court had been sneered as little more than an arcane "pack of Germans."[24] Though harsh, this was not inaccurate. Six of Queen Victoria's nine children married Germans, giving rise to two generations of British royals who were princes and princesses of Hesse-Darmstadt, Battenberg, Teck, or Schleswig-Holstein. This did not include Queen Victoria's grandchildren (by birth or by marriage) from Prussia, Hohenlohe-Langenburg, Saxe-Coburg-Gotha, Saxe-Meiningen, Hesse-Cassel, Schaumburg-Lippe, and Anhalt. Officials at Buckingham Palace were heard remarking that the king and royal family were more German than Wilhelm. By 1917, the British court was made up of so many foreign royals that H. G. Wells once called it "alien and uninspiring," to which King George famously replied, "I may be uninspiring, but I'll be damned if I'm an alien."[25] These protestations on the king's part seemed to go unnoticed by the British public. During a dinner party at Buckingham Palace in May 1917, Lady Maud Warrender mentioned to the queen that London was rife with rumors that the king and queen must be pro-German since their family names were German. George was sitting nearby and overheard the remark. Growing pale, he abruptly left the table, looking shaken and disturbed. There was little recourse but to take drastic action.

On June 19, 1917, a special session of the Privy Council was called by the king at Buckingham Palace. At the meeting, the king announced that he was ready to support British nationalist opinions and cut the monarchy's ties with its German past. Under the advice of his Privy Counsellors, George issued an order-in-council formally changing the name of the British royal family. A list of historic English surnames were reviewed by the king, queen, Prince Louis of Battenberg, George's uncle the Duke of Connaught, and Lord Stamfordham. The names Lancaster, York, Plantagenet, Tudor-Stewart, England, D'Este, and Fitzroy were all considered and unanimously voted down. Only after Lord Stamfordham suggested a name that once belonged to Edward III did the king and queen agree. No longer known as the German-sounding House of Saxe-Coburg-Gotha, the royal family would be henceforth known as the House of Windsor. One of Queen Mary's biographers observed that for her, "there was a sense of great pride at her new name and in the fact that she was to be the matriarch of a new dynasty—the Royal House of Windsor."[26]

The king went even further than just changing the family name. He issued letters patent that revoked the titles of his and Mary's German relatives living in Britain, replacing them with English ones. Officially, the king only "requested" that his relations voluntarily surrender their titles, although the "request was in effect a command."[27] The king "deemed it desirable in the conditions brought about by the present war that those Princes of his family who are his subjects and bear German names and titles should relinquish these titles and henceforth adopt British surnames."[28] Prince Louis of Battenberg wrote to his daughter Louise in June, "It has been suggested that we should turn our name into English, viz: Battenhill or Mountbatten. We incline to the latter as a better sound ... of course we are at his [the king's] mercy. We are only allowed to use our German title as the Sovereign has always recognized it, but he can refuse this recognition [at] any moment."[29] The Tecks and the Battenbergs became the Cambridges and the Mountbattens. In his official statement, King George V announced the following:

> Now, therefore, We, out of Our Royal Will and Authority, do hereby declare and announce that as from the date of this Our Royal Proclamation Our House and Family shall be styled and known as the House and Family of Windsor, and that all descendants in that male line of Our said Grandmother Queen Victoria who are subjects of these Realms ... shall bear the said Name of Windsor:
>
> And do hereby further declare and announce that We for Ourselves and for and on behalf of Our descendants of Our said Grandmother Queen Victoria who are subjects of these Realms relinquish and enjoin the discontinuance of the use of the Degrees, Styles, Dignities, Titles, and Honours of Dukes and Duchesses of Saxony and Princes and Princesses of Saxe-Coburg and Gotha, and all other German Degrees, Styles, Dignities, Titles, Honours and Appellations to Us or to them heretofore belonging or appertaining.[30]

Between September and November 1917, two generations of English-born royals found themselves stripped of their rank and titles. Even Queen Victoria's daughters Helena and Beatrice reverted to their premarital English titles. The rest were forced to adopt English peerages that placed them on par with the country's aristocracy. Louis of Battenberg's wife and Tsarina Alexandra's sister Victoria was now the Marchioness of Milford Haven. She wrote to her lady-in-waiting that she regretted the loss of her royal rank: "I am unduly influenced by the recollection of brewers, lawyers, bankers [and other] Peers."[31]

Following this declaration came the equally bold Enemy Princes Bill—also known as the Titles Deprivation Act—passed by Parliament later that year. The controversial document stripped all German royals of any British titles or privileges. Eight Knights of the Garter, England's highest honor, had already been stripped of their order in 1915 and declared "enemy knights."[32] Among the disavowed members of the order were Wilhelm II, his son Willy, and his brother Prince Henry; King Wilhelm II of Württemberg ("Uncle Willie"); Grand Duke Ernie of Hesse; Charles Eduard, Duke of Coburg; and Ernest Augustus, Duke of Brunswick. Uncle Willie aside, all of these men were George's cousins.

The foreign press was soon united in covering Britain's severing of all ties with its German heritage. One tabloid cartoon showed King George, covered in coronation robes and wearing the imperial crown, furiously sweeping away a dust ball that spelled out the words "Made in Germany." The reaction on continental Europe was just as biting. Wilhelm II was outraged by his cousin's actions. He immediately stripped King George of all the German military honors that had been bestowed upon him. He also destroyed many of the pictures and mementos that the two cousins had acquired over the years. Later, speaking to one of his staff, Wilhelm caustically remarked that he planned to see a performance of Shakespeare's play, *The Merry Wives of Saxe-Coburg-Gotha*.

At the same time that King George was reforming the British monarchy, his wife was living through an exceptionally difficult time. For a number of years, their youngest son, John, was plagued by violent seizures accompanied by extended periods of anxiety and disorientation. Even as an infant, his nurses observed that he had trouble sitting upright. He was eventually diagnosed with epilepsy in an advanced stage. Research conducted in the past several years has indicated that Prince John also suffered from a debilitating form of autism. So severe was his condition that he was the only member of the royal family to not attend the king and queen's coronation in 1911. The feelings Mary associated with John's illness remain unclear. She made no mention of him in her letters or diary entries. Even her letters to Aunt Augusta, her closest relative, lack any reference to John, his illness, or their impact on the family. According to her biographer David Duff, there was a marked difference in the way Queen Mary treated John compared to her other children. "His mother loved him," he wrote, "spent much time with him and treasured his quaint little sayings, but he was an everlasting worry to her."[33]

Like Tsarevitch Alexei, Prince John's seizures kept him incapacitated for long periods. The difference in the lives of Alexandra's and Mary's sons came by way of the fact that Alexei suffered through his illness with his family. By contrast, in 1917, John was given a separate establishment of his own, Wood House, on the grounds of the royal estate at Sandringham where the prince led a quiet life surrounded by a team of devoted nurses led by the lovable Charlotte Bill. Queen Mary was harshly criticized for sending John to Sandringham, but the young prince thrived at Wood House. He led a happy life where he received a well-planned education from his tutor, Henry Peter Hansell, and enjoyed trips into the Norfolk countryside with his equerry, Thomas Haverly. Although Mary did not visit her son as frequently as her other children, she was able to see him regularly when she was at Sandringham. As spring turned to summer and little John settled in at Wood House, the strain of the last year began to take its toll on the queen. She was plagued by severe pain in her right arm and shoulder, and her hair became tinged with gray. "I have never in my life suffered so much *mentally* as I am suffering *now* and I know you are feeling the same," she wrote to George.[34] It did not help that she was soon forced to turn her attentions back to the war, which was set to take an important turn. The wholesale, internecine destruction of Europe over the past three years had blinded many—including George and Mary—to the fact that the First World War had eroded the foundations of the continent's two remaining empires, which were set to collapse at any moment.

20

Into the Abyss

(November 1917–May 1918)

I n the summer of 1917, the Russian Provisional Government took a major step against the former imperial dynasty by confiscating their personal properties. It was reported that as early as May, the government had taken estates belonging to Nicholas that were valued at $700 million at the time. A commission was also set up to determine whether or not the properties owned by various grand dukes and duchesses, "worth about $210,000,000 should be seized for the benefit of the public."[1] This seizure of the Romanovs' former homes coincided with their permanent relocation. Officially, the Kerensky government claimed that because Tsarskoe Selo was so close to the capital, the specter of violence against them was an ever-present danger.

To ensure their continued safety, and with the possibilities of exile abroad now gone, the Russian Provisional Government decreed that the family was to leave Tsarskoe Selo for Tobolsk, a town in far-flung Siberia. Nearly seven hundred miles from Moscow, Tobolsk was a community of twenty thousand people, situated on the banks of the Tobol and Irtysh rivers. Although the town boasted the first school, theater, and newspaper in Siberia, it was a barren region with desolate hinterland stretching in every direction as far as the eye could see. "I chose Tobolsk," Alexander Kerensky later said," because it was an out-and-out backwater...had a very small garrison, no industrial proletariat, and a population which was prosperous and contented, not to say old-fashioned. In addition...the climate was excellent and the town could

343

boast a very passable Governor's residence where the Imperial family could live with some measure of comfort."[2]

When Alexandra and her family left Tsarskoe Selo, they did so for the last time. "The sunrise that saw us off was beautiful," Nicholas wrote in his diary. "We left Tsarskoe Selo at 6:10 in the morning. Thank God we are all saved and together."[3] At dawn on August 13, after a night of standing and waiting in one of the palace's semicircular halls, the Romanovs and the forty-two courtiers who chose to remain with them entered a series of automobiles. Surrounded with armed escorts, the caravan headed to a nearby train station. The train that transported them had its windows blacked out, shades pulled down, and was disguised with Japanese flags. It left for Siberia on August 13, the day after Alexei's thirteenth birthday. It took several days to reach Tobolsk. They traveled by train to Tiumen and then took the steamship *Rus* upriver to Tobolsk. Along the way, they passed Rasputin's native Pokrovskoie. When they arrived, the family and their paucity of retainers were forced to reside in the Governor's Mansion, a dilapidated two-story edifice with barred-up windows and a fenced-in courtyard. The building was in such bad shape that they could not move in immediately. It took another week for the house to be made livable, which meant the Romanovs had to spend the time aboard the cramped old steamer that had brought them upriver. Aboard ship, Alexandra's family suffered greatly. Marie had a cold, Pierre Gilliard contracted painful boils on his arms and legs, and Alexei had suffered an injury in his arm, which was bleeding internally. Night after night, his cries echoed through the ship's empty corridors, keeping his depressed family awake. The Duchess of Coburg, Nicholas and Alexandra's aunt, wrote to her daughter Queen Marie of Romania of the imperial family's plight. She explained that they had been "bundled off in the middle of the night to some unknown destination! May God have mercy on them!"[4]

When they were finally allowed to settle in at the Governor's Mansion, the family and their court made efforts to rebuild something of their life from Tsarskoe Selo. They decorated their rooms with photographs, paintings, and other souvenirs they brought with them. Their personal belongings added to the sense that they still had some semblance of freedom. Most important of all were the $14 million in diamonds, pearls, sapphires, emeralds, rubies, and gold that were carefully hidden among their possessions. These assets were intended to sustain them abroad if escape from Russia would be necessary. Once the Romanovs were settled in, Alexandra sent a letter to her sister-in-law Xenia, who had taken refuge at Ai-Todor in the Crimea with most of the other Romanovs, including the dowager empress.

My darling Xenia, My thoughts are with you, how magically good and beautiful everything must be with you—you are the flowers. But it is indescribably painful for the kind motherland, I cannot explain. I am glad for you that you are finally with all your family as you have been apart.... Everybody is healthy, but myself, during the last 6 weeks I experience nerve pains in my face with toothache. Very tormenting ...

We live quietly, have established ourselves well [in Tobolsk] although it is far, far away from everybody. But God is merciful, He gives us strength and consolation ...[5]

Alexandra's letter made it sound like Xenia and the other Romanovs were leading still relatively normal lives, but other members of the imperial family were suffering too. Minnie and the relatives who were with her at Ai-Todor lived under a sort of liberal house arrest. They were surrounded by revolutionary guards, but they had the freedom to come and go. Other Romanovs were not so fortunate. Many of the grand dukes and duchesses who were unable or unwilling to flee were left penurious. Grand duchesses were forced to sell their priceless treasures just to buy bread and potatoes. The dowager empress was not immune from these hardships. She wrote to Nicholas in Tobolsk detailing her difficult situation.

My Dear Nicky

You know that my thoughts and prayers never leave you—I think of you day and night and sometimes feel so sick at heart that I believe I cannot bear it any longer. But God is merciful—He will give us strength for this terrible ordeal.... Who could have thought ... of all that was in store for us, and what we should have to go through. It is unbelievable. I live only in my memories of the happy past and try as much as possible to forget the present nightmare....

... we are always hungry. It is so difficult to get provisions, white bread and butter are the things I miss most, but sometimes I get some sent by kind people ...

I am very glad to get those dear letters from Alix and my granddaughters who all write so nicely. I thank and kiss them all ... I long for news ...

On December 6th [the day of the tsar's patron saint] all my thoughts will be with you, my dear darling Nicky, and I send you my warmest wishes. God bless you, send you strength and peace of mind ...

I kiss you tenderly. May Christ be with you.—Your fondly
loving old

Mama[6]

Other Romanovs suffered from equally difficult circumstances. The tsar's cousin Grand Duke Nicholas Constantinovich died in poverty in Tashkent, Uzbekistan. Others were living under self-imposed house arrest for their own safety. Queen Olga of Greece, who had returned to her native Russia after her husband's death in 1913, had not left her home, Pavlovsk Palace, for two months.

Without a doubt, the circumstances of the immediate imperial family were the worst. But the Romanovs at Tobolsk were somewhat relieved when they discovered that they still had some freedom. They attended Mass regularly, where they were greeted by people who were still loyal to the monarchy. Ordinary citizens crossed themselves or dropped to their knees when the imperial family passed by on their way to Mass. It comforted them that people still addressed them as "Your Imperial Majesties." In the weeks that followed, Alexandra was able to contact some of her friends and relatives scattered throughout Europe. In her letters, she nursed a growing belief that the Russian people would soon realize they were deceived by the communist ideals of the revolution and restore the monarchy. "Many already recognize that it [the revolution] was all—a Utopia, a chimera," she wrote to Madame Syroboyarsky, whom she befriended when Syroboyarsky's son was injured in the war. "Their ideals are shattered, covered with dirt and shame, they didn't achieve a single good thing for Russia." She believed that, before long, more of the people would "awake, the lie will be revealed, all the falsity, for not all the people have been spoilt, they were tempted, led astray."[7]

Her faith in God also continued to be a source of great comfort to her, which she mentioned in many of her letters. "Ah God! Still He is merciful and will never forget His crown," she wrote to Anna Viroubova. She also became increasingly preoccupied with the afterlife. In the same letter to Anna, she went on to say, "Great will be their reward in Heaven. The more we suffer here the fairer it will be on that other shore where so many dear ones await us."[8] Her unwavering faith would sustain Alexandra as her life entered its final, sad year.

Throughout the course of 1917, Russia continued to cannibalize itself in bloody revolution. Alexander Kerensky and the government of the newly proclaimed Russian Republic had been moderate and somewhat sympathetic to the former tsar and his family. But Kerensky's administration was undermined by choosing to keep Russia in the war. Amid this growing unpopularity, Kerensky and his government were overthrown by one of the most notorious revolutionaries in history—Vladimir Ilyich Ulianov. More commonly known as Vladimir Lenin, he and the ruthless Bolsheviks began their overthrow by taking control of key places in and around Petrograd. The government, which had retreated to the Winter Palace, finally conceded defeat after Russian warships, now under control of pro-Bolshevik sailors, began shelling the palace. Once in power, Lenin turned his attention to the captive Romanovs. He made it his mission to make life for them as unpleasant as possible. While Alexander Kerensky was determined to keep the family isolated but safe, Lenin's rise to power signaled a dangerous threat against their lives.

As Siberia descended into a winter of endless night and bitter cold, the living conditions at the Governor's Mansion in Tobolsk became unbearable. Nicholas, Alexandra, and their family were provided with little or no heat for the handful of rooms into which they were crammed. The windows were terribly thin and lacked insulation, offering no protection from the dangerous subzero temperatures outside, which plunged as low as -40°C on some days. Alexandra felt the cold worse than anyone else; her hands and feet nearly froze. "We shiver in the rooms, and there is always a strng [*sic*] draught from the windows," she wrote to Anna Viroubova before Christmas. "Your pretty jacket is useful. We all have chilblains on our fingers."[9] Gleb Botkin, son of the family's physician, Dr. Eugene Botkin, who had joined the family in Tobolsk, noted how "the Siberian winter held us, by that time, completely in its icy grip ... one can only sit in despair and shiver ... one no longer lives during the Siberian winter but merely vegetates, in a sort of frozen stupor."[10]

During this difficult period in Alexandra's life, it was her daughter Anastasia who kept the family's spirits afloat. Throughout the long, dark Siberian winter, Anastasia entertained her family with "amateur theatricals" and performing tricks with Jimmy, Tatiana's dog that she brought from Tsarskoe Selo. Alexandra's youngest daughter "was absolutely fearless and refused to be cowed by misfortune and the restrictions of imprisonment."[11]

The overthrow of the Russian Provisional Government did nothing to improve Russia's fortunes in the war. Many became disillusioned when the Bolsheviks were unable to lead the army to victory on the battlefield. Desperate to preserve his hold on power, Lenin made the decision to pull his country out of the war. In March 1918, Russia signed a peace accord with the Central powers known as the Treaty of Brest-Litovsk. The treaty brought peace to Russia, allowing Lenin to concentrate his full efforts on the fragile government, but the price was high.

> Lenin conceded huge tracts of land and large swathes of population in a humiliating and harsh agreement imposed by Germany and its allies. Russia gave up Finland, Poland, the Ukraine, the Baltic States, and most of Byelorussia. Not only had Russia lost much land and a good many people to the Central powers, it had also let down the Entente side by withdrawing from the war. Nicholas was devastated by the news. "Had I known it would come to this," he dejectedly told Dr. Botkin, "I would never have abdicated."[12]

Alexandra was just as aghast at the news. For her, it amounted to nothing short of treason. "What infamy!" she exclaimed, "that the Lord God should give peace to Russia, yes, but not by way of treason to the Germans." And she later wrote to Anna Viroubova, "What a nightmare it is that it is Germans who are saving Russia (from Communism).… What could be more humiliating for us? With one hand the Germans give, and with the other they take away. Already they have seized an enormous territory. God help and save this unhappy country. Probably He wills us to endure these insults, but that we must take them from the Germans almost kills me."[13]

The war's unpopularity in Vienna took a meteoric rise as food became scarce. "Many workers seemed to be living mainly off sour cucumbers," one eyewitness said. A meager flour ration of 165 grams per day was instituted. Elderly women waited in line for hours to board trains to take them to the provinces to trade clothes and shoes for bread and potatoes. The Austrian economy crumbled under the weight of sustaining total warfare. Money soon became worthless. Austria-Hungary—like Russia in the last days of the Romanov monarchy—was engulfed in waves of paralyzing strikes, demonstrations, and work stoppages. Factory workers in Wiener-Neustadt, twenty-five miles from Vienna, walked off the job and laid siege to the nearby town hall. According to one estimate, within "forty-eight hours, nearly 100,000 men were out on strike in Lower Austria alone." By the end of January 1918, a poisonous cloud of unrest had consumed provinces across Austria-Hungary. Fueled by starvation, Upper Austria, Styria, the Tyrol, Moravia, and western sections of Hungary rose up against the monarchy.[14]

Unrest was not confined solely to the empire's core territories. In February, the flagship of the Imperial Fifth Fleet, anchored in the Gulf of Kotor off the coast of Montenegro, began flying the red flag of revolution. At midday, the sailors sang "La Marseillaise." Within an hour, the entire fleet—comprised mainly of Croatian and Czech sailors—had mutinied. "The Emperor was not really surprised by the Kotor mutiny," Zita admitted. "He told me that he had for a long time feared that something of the sort might happen. Our navy had been forced into idleness by the *Entente* blockade of the high seas and the Fifth Fleet, who were relatively well fed, had been cooped up for months in the same harbour."[15] Things were just as bad in the east. After Austro-Hungarian forces overran and occupied Ukraine, a state of anarchy ensued. Desperate to feed the empire's starving population, the government ordered Ukraine to produce more than a million tons of food by the summer. The Ukrainian peasants, who themselves were starving, hid as much of their grain as possible. When quotas were not met, whole villages were burned to the ground. As a result, the Ukrainians began launching a guerilla warfare campaign against the Austro-Hungarians. When they succeeded in assassinating two officers, imperial troops retaliated by executing thirteen villagers. According to an Austrian intelligence report, by August 1918, the "murder of landowners, policemen, and officials and other enemy acts of terrorism against the troops of the Central Powers were the order of the day."[16] Over the course of the summer, the violence escalated to horrific proportions.

As Austria-Hungary's fortunes took a turn for the worse, Empress Zita's close association with her family in Italy and France laid her open to more accusations of treachery. The German ambassador to Austria wrote in a telegram sent to Berlin that the "Empress is descended from an Italian princely house ... People do not entirely trust the *Italian* [author's italics] and her brood of relatives."[17] The German government began its own campaign to discredit Zita, whom they perceived as a threat to German influence in Austrian domestic affairs. "It was difficult for them to attack the Emperor directly," wrote one historian. "They thus chose another target: Zita. Her French ancestry, in the bellicose speeches of the pan-Germanists, would serve as the pretext for a campaign of disparagement of the Empress. In Germany, she was called '*the Frenchwoman*,' and in Austria, '*the Italian woman*.' Within a few months, some would be accusing her of treason."[18]

The way that Zita was slanderously referred to as "the Italian woman" mirrored the way Alexandra of Russia was labeled "the German woman." No one seemed to notice, or chose not to notice, that because of Zita's position as the Austrian empress, her family's homes in Italy were confiscated by the government. Villa Pianore and several other homes were turned into naval hospitals. The *New York Times* reported on the rising anti-Austrian sentiment in Italy: "After the last discussion in the [Italian] Parliament Premier Orlando initiated a stricter policy against subjects of the Central Powers. Several arrests were made, many Austro-Germans were interned, and hotels managed by Germans were closed. The public, however, has been complaining that nothing was being done to sequestrate the beautiful villas and palaces belonging to German and Austrian royalties."[19]

One British newspaper could not help but notice the parallels between the way Tsarina Alexandra and Empress Zita were depredated.

> The latest instance is the agitation now being made in Vienna against the Austrian Empress, who is declared to be responsible for the Piave disasters owing to her protest against [the] destruction of Italian towns, and against other forms. Her masculine critics are also adopting another old device, where women are concerned, by making imputations against her character.... The Empress Zita is not the first Royal consort to be blamed for a country's ills. The ex-Czar's wife was said to be mainly responsible for her husband's downfall ... Queens are rarely, if ever credited by men with their countries' triumphs.[20]

Zita tried not to dwell on the problems that plagued her and her husband. One bright spot in the midst of all the turmoil surrounding the empress's life was her family. On March 10, 1918, she delivered a son named Carl Ludwig. To celebrate, Charles offered amnesty to a number of people charged with political crimes, reinforcing his sobriquet as "the Peace Emperor." He believed that the happiness experienced by the pardoned prisoners would mirror the "joyous event of the delivery by my wife the Empress and Queen."[21] This was not the first time the emperor had shown clemency to enemies of his government. On July 2, 1917, some two thousand political prisoners—mostly Czechs—were set free in a broad amnesty. But the happiness Zita and Charles enjoyed over this latest addition to their family was short lived. The war's climactic final stage was set to begin and would shatter the lives of not only Zita and her family but of Dona of Germany and the Hohenzollerns as well.

Ground zero for this theatrical endgame was the Austro-Hungarian foreign minister, Count Ottokar Czernin, who had represented the empire at the Brest-Litovsk negotiations. At the conference, when he was asked about the greatest obstacle to lasting peace, he replied that it was none other than Georges Clemenceau, the French prime minister. According to the count, "I was willing [to negotiate over peace] and that, as regards to France, I could see no obstacle to peace apart from the French desire for Alsace-Lorraine. The response from Paris was that negotiation on this basis was not possible."[22] Czernin "blamed France for failing to grasp the opportunity to prevent the slaughter on the Western front, and in particular pointed to Clemenceau ... as an obstacle in the way of peace."[23] Czernin later declared that the emperor had been fully aware of his remarks and supported them, but in her diary, the empress painted a very different picture: "H.M. received it [notification of Czernin's remarks] so late that he could not deal with it in time."[24]

Czernin's statements were followed by a scurrilous exchange of attacks that flew back and forth between Czernin and Clemenceau. The day after the controversial remarks were made, Clemenceau barked with rage, "Count Czernin is lying."[25] Angry beyond words, Clemenceau focused his ire squarely at Czernin and Austria. "For it was actually the Emperor Karl who, in an autographed letter of March, 1917, gave his definite support to the just claims of France relative to Alsace-Lorraine," Clemenceau said. "The only thing left for Count Czernin to do is to make a full admission of his guilt."[26] Attempting to protect his own interests, Czernin forged a number of low-level documents supporting his claims, which he made available to the public and included the letter Charles had sent to Sixtus in March 1917. Zita remembered her and Charles's reaction to the release of the letter: "As events were now more than a year old and had anyway been written off, we could not reconstruct them exactly from memory.... we had no means of proving or disproving the exact words quoted by Clemenceau."[27] Realizing he did not have the support of the emperor and empress, Czernin went into a mad frenzy, forging and reforging documents that made him appear innocent.

The backlash was immediate and dangerous. Propaganda painted Zita as an intriguing harlot who was using her brother to fuel her quest for power. Allied planes dropped leaflets on Czech, Hungarian, and Slovenian troops claiming Zita was giving away their military secrets. Like Nicholas II, Charles was portrayed as docile, weak willed, and dominated by his wife. Some of the more hurtful rumors included Charles being a secret alcoholic who was on the verge of divorcing his wife. The campaign of vilification against them was an undeniable mirror of the same sad circumstances that faced Nicholas and Alexandra. In a letter to the British statesman Arthur Balfour, the foreign secretary Sir Horace Rumbold empathized with the imperial couple. "No one could blame the Emperor, that is, to say, the Empress, for trying to make peace after her own fashion: she could not be expected to realise that the days are long gone by, when women and priests could sway the destinies of nations," he wrote in May 1918. "It seems strange however, that the Entente, one of the planks whose democratic platform is the abolition of secret diplomacy, should have availed themselves readily for her services."[28]

The Austrian monarchs now faced a political crisis. Wilhelm II felt betrayed by Charles, who had no choice but to send an emergency telegram to Wilhelm denying the letter's authenticity, saying, "At a time when Austro-Hungarian cannon [*sic*] are thundering alongside German guns on the Western Front proof is scarcely needed that I am fighting and will continue to fight for your provinces as though I were defending my own."[29] Wilhelm warily accepted Charles's explanation, but not before the latter was forced to travel immediately to German military headquarters at Spa for an emergency meeting face-to-face. After an audience that lasted hours, Charles regained Wilhelm's support—but at the cost of "the closest military, political and economic union which the two empires had hitherto concluded."[30] The cost of Ottokar Czernin's irresponsible remarks was Austria-Hungary's now total dependence on Germany. The famed Habsburg historian Edward Crankshaw summarized the calamity of the situation this way:

> When Clemenceau published the Sixtus letter in 1918 as a retort to Czernin's blustering.... Austria found her last escape route closed. William II was not unnaturally indignant when he discovered that Karl had pledged himself to back France's demand for Alsace-Lorraine. Karl was summoned to the German Emperor's headquarters at Spa, there to explain, to apologise and to suffer his inheritance to be tied indissolubly to the Hohenzollern destiny: therefore the great Empire, already subservient to Berlin in all matters concerning the higher conduct of the war, was in every way a German satellite.[31]

In May 1918, Charles traveled by train to Berlin to sign the official documents binding Austria-Hungary into a closer alliance with Germany. Wilhelm was satisfied to have the agreement signed, but Dona forced Charles to submit to her "wrath" for having betrayed Wilhelm.[32]

Empress Zita was forced to personally bear the consequences of Czernin's indiscretion. Threats were made on the life of her brother Sixtus. She confided to her diary, "The brothers [Sixtus and Xavier] are in great danger of being shot." Count Czernin claimed that the only way for Charles and Zita to save her brothers' lives was to announce that the emperor "suffers from periodic mental lapses." He insisted that Charles "must withdraw from government on the grounds that it was during one of these fits that he wrote the letter Clem. has published."[33] Not surprisingly, Charles refused to consider abdicating over this crisis of Czernin's making. In an uncharacteristic outburst of anger, he leveled the foreign minister.

"It's out of the question," he declared. "What shall we come to once we start declaring monarchs to be lunatics?"[34] Desperate to save face, Czernin then turned to Zita, imploring her to use her influence to encourage Charles to accept Czernin's solution.

"The honour of a gentleman," she calmly replied, "is to protect his sovereign."[35] The Sixtus Affair finally came to an end on April 14, 1918, at a Crown Council presided over by both Emperor Charles and Empress Zita. "Dreadful scene with Czernin," the empress wrote in her diary that night. "He again tries to persuade the emperor to step down and when that doesn't succeed, he has a nervous breakdown, weeps, and suddenly offers his resignation, which H.M. immediately accepts."[36]

Throughout the entire ordeal, Zita had been skeptical of her husband's foreign minister. Rumors abounded that Czernin himself had been responsible for the threats against the empress's brothers. Another rumor claimed that he was engineering a German-backed overthrow of the Habsburgs. Although none of these accusations were ever proven, they certainly lend credence to why Czernin was so adamant that he could only save Sixtus and Xavier by forcing Charles to abdicate. What everyone failed to realize was that the Sixtus Affair and Ottokar Czernin's fall from grace were only the beginning. Time was ticking for Europe's empires as they stood upon the brink of an abyss. The weeks and months to come would prove to be the most difficult in the lives of Charles and Zita of Austria-Hungary.

21

The House of Special Purpose

(May–July 1918)

After four years of fighting, imperial Germany was beginning to erode under the increasingly successful attacks of the Allies. German military leaders were crushed by the news that their forces were defeated in the Battle of Amiens in August 1918. It proved to be "the largest tank battle of the First World War—and Germany's enemies had all of the tanks."[1] German casualties soared beyond thirty thousand, with thousands more of their soldiers surrendering en masse. Within a matter of weeks, Allied forces captured fifty thousand additional German soldiers. Tensions were escalating between the Hohenzollerns and the Habsburgs, whom they believed were not doing enough to help the war effort compared to German sacrifices. The Allied victory at Amiens brought about the final collapse of the western front, prompting Emperor Charles and Empress Zita to head to Spa for a few days for an emergency summit with Wilhelm, who described the tense visit as "unwelcome." By this point, any pretense of friendliness that Wilhelm felt for the Austrian monarchs had been discarded. It was by now widely known that the emperor "disliked Karl and his empress, Zita of Bourbon-Parma." Wilhelm believed Charles "was the creature" of his wife, whom he described as "spiteful" and "anti-Hohenzollern." When Charles and Zita arrived at Spa, "the Kaiser found the royal couple untrustworthy and detestable."[2]

After Charles and Zita left Spa, Wilhelm made a brief visit to Berlin before returning to military headquarters. When he arrived in the capital, he was shocked by how unbearable life there had become. There were visible shadows of the revolution in Petrograd from the year before. The British blockade of Germany, along with its recent defeats, devastated the Prusso-German economy. Starving people sliced cuts of meat off horses that had died from the cold or from exhaustion when bread, potato, and turnip rations ran out. Heating in Berlin was not consistent, and electricity was spotty at best. Thousands of people "stood in food lines through the night, through rain and snow, suffering from cholera and typhus that swelled into epidemics."[3] Protesters marched on government buildings. In the Reichstag, there was a heated debate over reclaiming its powers from the Bundesrat. The Socialists called for an end to the war, accompanied by Wilhelm's abdication. Chancellor Georg Hertling sought help from Empress Augusta Victoria. In a meeting with her, Hertling insisted that the government would have to start granting concessions to the public if they hoped to avoid further unrest. He hoped that she would be willing to convince her husband to take a more liberal political stance. As an ultraconservative monarchist, the empress was furious at such an idea. "I am prepared to suffer the worst, before I will tolerate that any right of the crown is curtailed," she told Hertling.[4]

There were few options left by the summer months. Wilhelm's generals were forced to admit that a military victory for the Central powers was no longer possible. Dona had since moved to her favorite summer residence, the Wilhelmshöhe Palace in Kassel. She acutely felt these latest trials her husband was facing. Helpless as Wilhelm slipped into depression, and weak from overstrained nerves and heart disease, the empress suffered a massive heart attack in mid-August. Dona's recovery at Wilhelmshöhe was slow, but thanks to the highly skilled team of doctors at her service, her condition was quickly stabilized. She was confined to her bed for weeks and was placed on a strict diet of cold foods. Wilhelm was on his way to Spa from a tour of the naval shipyards at Kiel and interrupted his journey to visit his convalescent wife. The growing unpopularity of both the war and the monarchy in Germany did not diminish the affection the people had for their empress. During an appearance at the Krupp factories in Essen on September 18, the emperor noticed the genuine sympathy of the people for "his bedridden spouse."[5]

This display of support for the monarchy was fleeting and could not prevent the great trials that were set to be unleashed. With Wilhelm's greatest helpmate removed from his daily life while she slowly recovered, and overwhelmed by the cataclysm surrounding him, the emperor suffered another nervous breakdown at Wilhelmshöhe shortly after appearing at Essen. He was placed on a similar regimen as his wife and was ordered to stay away from war business for several weeks. True to her selfless nature, the moment Dona was told of Wilhelm's condition, she forced herself out of bed and rushed to his side. She spent days with him, nursing him and restoring his confidence and strength. The fact that his wife was endangering her own health for his sake touched a chord with Wilhelm. He developed a new love and respect for Dona devoid of his previous condescension. A new level of total intimacy entered their marriage that had not existed before.

At the end of September, Wilhelm was back on his feet at Spa, where he felt he was better equipped to deal with the growing unrest across the empire. On September 29, Count Hertling resigned. His departure marked a turning point in German politics. The emperor was now hard-pressed to find a new chancellor, since few people were willing to take up the mantle of such an unstable government. Wilhelm was forced to admit that things were going to get worse before they got better. He was also deeply anxious about what effect Germany's mounting problems would have on his frail wife. The night that Hertling resigned, Wilhelm sat down and penned a brief note to Dona, preparing her for the difficult days to come: "We are approaching grave days and important measures will have to be sought to find internal rest and unity as well as external peace. God help us in this work and our heroes, too."[6]

The next day, he sent his adjutant General Friedrich von Gontard to Wilhelmshöhe to personally update the empress on everything that was happening. "Your Majesty must be strong, for I bring no good news," Gontard told her when he arrived. It took over an hour for Gontard to deliver his detailed report. He explained to the empress the crisis in the Reichstag with Hertling's departure, the decisive setbacks for Germany in the war, and the growing unpopularity of the monarchy. Once Dona dismissed the general, she sat alone in her apartments for hours contemplating everything she had just heard. When she finally summoned her trusted friend and lady-in-waiting Countess Mathilde Keller, the countess was in awe of her composure. "She stood like a heroine before me," Keller later told Gontard, "terribly sad, fully aware of the gravity of the situation, but there was no wailing and moaning. Her composure was remarkable!" That same day, Wilhelm sent Dona another letter from Spa, adding his personal voice to Gontard's visit.

> Gontard will already have told you how serious it is for us. Our brave army, in glorious defiance, is daily smashing back the overwhelming attacks by the enemy masses. But we, too, are suffering losses and our troops are steadily being reduced. Domestically, there's nothing but discord, wrangles and vexation! So it was decided at yesterday's conference, 1: In order to restore domestic peace, there will be an enlargement of the government by some men from the different parties who will assume responsibility, 2: To sue for peace and an armistice. Old Count Hertling has asked to be relieved. [Friedrich]

Berg [Chief of the Civil Cabinet] and I are once again looking for a successor.

God has not allowed us to achieve the goal we had hoped for; He has decided on a path of pain and sorrow. We yield to His Holy Will and go to Him with the hope and prayer that He will be willing to give us the strength of His Spirit to pass through this difficult time in the belief that He will lead us to our best way even if His way is also difficult and appears to us to be obscure. May He strengthen our faith, all of us, and not abandon my poor people and the Fatherland, but be a Saviour in need. Without His help it would have been worse for us. I will continue to do my duty to Him and to the Fatherland, with all my strength, as long as God allows me!

[Postscript]

The Chancellor has gone in order to make room for new men: noble, distinguished and quite without personal consideration for himself. It will be bitterly hard for me to part from this admirable man. Who could follow him? God help us![7]

The question of who was finally answered a few days later. On October 3, the patriotic Prince Max of Baden—the same Max of Baden who had once courted Alexandra of Russia—was appointed to the German chancellorship. Many hoped that the liberal Max would be able to grant concessions to the republicans, successfully negotiate peace with the Allies, and preserve the monarchy.

As winter loosened its grip on Siberia, life became precarious for Alexandra Feodorovna. In April, Alexei was felled by another crippling attack of hemophilia brought on by sliding down a flight of stairs on a sled and made worse by whooping cough. A few days later, his upper abdomen filled with blood, and he had a soaring fever. He stopped eating for days, growing pale and thin as a result. The boy was forced to endure unbearable pain, but this time there were no teams of doctors—or even simple comforts—to ease his suffering. All that the poor child had was his family, their physician Dr. Botkin, and one vial of morphine that was to be used for the entire family in only the worst emergencies. "I would like to die, Mama," Alexei muttered;

"I'm not afraid of death, but I'm so afraid of what they might do to us here."[8] The situation became even more heartrending for Alexandra when her captors insisted on transferring Nicholas from Tobolsk to Ekaterinburg, deep in the Siberian frontier, only fifty miles from the border dividing Asia from Europe.

The news made Alexandra's heart sink because it was widely known that Ekaterinburg was home to the most fanatically radical group of Bolsheviks in all of Russia. Terrified for her husband's life, she was torn between accompanying Nicholas and staying with her son. It was a devastating decision for a wife and mother, and she came to an impasse. The person who finally made the decision for Alexandra was the resolute Tatiana. "You cannot go on tormenting yourself like this," she told her mother. Alexandra chose to join her husband and leave Alexei in the care of his loving sisters and Dr. Botkin. "It is the hardest moment of my life," she admitted to her maid. "You know what my son is to me, and I must choose between him and my husband. But I have made up my mind. I must be firm. I must leave my child and share my husband's life or death."[9] The decision was also made easier when they were allowed to bring Marie and several of their servants with them.

The night before Nicholas, Alexandra, and their group departed, tea was served to the family in Alexandra's room. It was a solemn scene where no one tried to feign happiness. The next day, there was nothing but tears at the Governor's Mansion: "With superhuman effort Alexandra tore herself from the house where her sick son, Alexei, could be heard crying wildly: 'Mother, mother.'"[10] The long, arduous journey was made on carts covered with straw and mattresses. Alexandra had to be lifted onto the back of the only hooded cart because she had been suffering chest pains and had not slept the night before. On April 30, the three Romanovs were delivered into the custody of Alexander Beloborodov, chairman of the Ural soviet. "In one of Russian history's more frightful gestures," a receipt was issued for the acquisition of the three captives:

1. The former tsar, Nicholas Alexandrovitch Romanov.
2. The former tsarina, Alexandra Feodorovna Romanova.
3. The former Grand Duchess Marie Nicholaievna Romanova.
All to be kept under guard
in the city of Ekaterinburg.[11]

Weeks of uncertainty passed for the children who remained at Tobolsk because they received no word from their parents since they had left. When they finally received the news that their parents and sister had arrived in Ekaterinburg, the girls and Alexei were ecstatic. "We were so terribly glad to receive news, we kept on sharing our impressions!" Anastasia wrote to Marie. "I am always with you dears in my thoughts. It's so terribly sad and lonely. I just don't know what to do. The Lord helps and will help."[12]

Fearful that monarchist forces would try to liberate the Romanovs still in Tobolsk, the Bolsheviks decided to relocate them to Ekaterinburg as well. They were reunited with their parents at 2:00 a.m. on the morning of May 23. Their arrival in Ekaterinburg was harrowing. An angry mob formed as their train pulled into the station, demanding to see the Romanovs and crying out for them to be hanged. It was a hatred the likes of which Alexandra's children never knew before. The "petty humiliations and uncertainties endured by [the children] in the year since their father's abdication must have been replaced by the first very real fears for their lives."[13] If they had thought the conditions in Tobolsk were restrictive, they were wholly unprepared for what awaited them at their new home, the Ipatiev House, along Voznesensky Prospect. Originally belonging to a local businessman named Nicholas Ipatiev, the house was seized by the Bolsheviks, who gave the owner twenty-four hours' notice to vacate. They unnervingly renamed it "the House of Special Purpose." It was turned into a prison with a stockade, high fence, and seventy-five armed guards on duty twenty-four hours a day. As with so much else in the lives of Alexandra and her family, the selection of the Ipatiev House was both fateful and ominous. The Romanov dynasty began in 1613 at the ironically though coincidentally named Ipatiev Monastery at Kostroma on the Volga River, when the sixteen-year-old Michael Romanov became the first tsar. Three centuries later, the dynasty would end at the Ipatiev House.

At Ekaterinburg, the family's last bit of dignity was stripped away. Nearly all of their servants were sent away, save for Dr. Botkin; the maid Anna Demidova; the cook Ivan Kharitonov; the footman Ivan Sednev and his twelve-year-old nephew Leonid, the kitchen boy; and the valets Alexei Trupp and Terenty Chemodurov. The family's personal belongings, packed into suitcases at Tobolsk, were torn open, and most of their goods were stolen by revolutionary soldiers. "So far we have had polite treatment and men who were gentlemen but now,…"[14] Alexandra remarked when their belongings were stolen. The only two pieces of jewelry that she continued to wear were bracelets given to her by her uncle the Duke of Albany, which she could no longer get off her wrists. Inside the house, the Romanovs were crammed into three small rooms on the south side of the upper floor; Alexei was initially given his own room but was eventually moved in with his parents. Alexandra's four daughters shared a single room, sleeping on camp beds. Their servants were forced to sleep on pieces of furniture in hallways, kitchens, or closets. There were almost no furnishings, save for a few wardrobes, mirrors, and several military beds. The windows were completely whitewashed to prevent them from looking outside or signaling anyone on the street. Alexandra took these latest indignities in stride, but she was terribly anxious for the fate of Russia. "Although we suffer horribly still there is peace in our souls," she wrote.[15] She later wrote to Anna Viroubova, "I suffer most for Russia ... it is the sufferings of the innocent which nearly kills us."[16]

The summer heat proved to be just as suffocating as the winter had been bone-chillingly cold. The intense heat waves were punctuated only by occasional, violent thunderstorms. In either weather, the guards refused to give the family permission to open the windows to let some of the heat out. The Romanovs had reached their nadir. They spent the long days and nights almost entirely in their tiny rooms, reading the Bible, praying softly, or playing bezique (a card game popular among royals). Alexandra settled into as much of a daily routine as she could. She awoke between eight and nine every morning and gathered with her family in one of the more comfortably furnished drawing rooms for prayer. Each day, she wrote her activities in her beloved diary. She never confided her innermost thoughts, hopes, or fears, knowing full well that the guards would read her entries. The diary had been a gift to her from Tatiana the previous Christmas, which she had sewn together by hand—on the first page was a handwritten inscription from the grand duchess: "To my sweet darling Mama...May God's blessing be upon you and guard you for ever. Your ever loving girl, Tatiana."[17] On rare occasions when weather permitted, the family was allowed to take exercise in the gardens after breakfast and later in the afternoon. Alexei and Nicholas loved the chance to take in the fresh air. Alexei, though, was still recuperating from the hemophilia attack he suffered during their last weeks in Tobolsk and could not walk yet and had to be carried by his father. More often than not, Alexandra was too ill to join her family. The pain in her back, legs, and head were crippling. One of her daughters, usually Olga or Tatiana, stayed with her, pressing a cold compress to her head or reading to her from the Psalms. In the evenings, Nicholas often read aloud to his family, or they occasionally sang hymns. By eleven o'clock, everyone was usually in bed.

Alexandra's four daughters continued to be an invaluable, if not the only, source of strength for her. She was immensely proud of the Christian morality they displayed. A priest who was summoned to take confession for the family during their confinement noted of the Romanov girls, "Lord, let all children be morally upright as the children of the former tsar. Such mildness, restraint, obedience to their parents' wishes, such absolute devotion to God's will ... and complete ignorance of worldly filth—either passionate or sinful—amazed them."[18] Even the soldiers on duty at the Ipatiev House could not help but be impressed by the family's quiet dignity and grace under fire. Analoy Yakimov, one of the guards, admitted how his feelings had changed once the Romanovs arrived: "After I had seen them several times I began to feel entirely different toward them. I began to pity them. I pitied them as human beings ... I kept on saying to myself, 'Let them escape, or do something to allow them to escape.'"[19] Hope for escape was something Alexandra held on to during this desperate period. A number of well-meaning monarchist groups planned but never carried out rescue attempts. Rescue seemed so real in late 1917 and early 1918 that Alexandra drew up plans of the Ipatiev House and had them smuggled out. "The friends sleep no longer, and hope the hour so long awaited has arrived," she wrote cryptically to a sympathizer at the end of June 1918. "The revolt of the Czechoslovaks menaces the Bolsheviks more and more seriously. Samara, Cheliabinsk and the whole of Siberia, eastern and western, are under the control of the provincial national government [the White, monarchist government]. The army of the Slavic friends is eighty kilometers from Ekaterinburg."[20]

Throughout the last weeks of June, a sense of hope gripped the Romanov family. A public announcement was made that Nicholas's brother Grand Duke Michael escaped Russia with the help of monarchist armies. The ghastly truth was that, on the night of June 13, the Bolsheviks executed Michael in the forest near Perm. A week later, Alexandra received a letter signed by "An Officer of the Russian Army," who wrote explicit instructions for the family's rescue: "Be ready all the time, day and night. Make a sketch of your two rooms, the places of the furniture, of the beds. Write exactly when you all go to bed. One of you should not sleep between two and three o'clock all the following nights." From then on, the family changed their routine. They began packing away clothes when the guards were not looking. Following their instructions, one member of the family stayed awake each night listening for a signal. A second letter informed them that the signal would be a whistle in the night. Once they heard it, they were to barricade the door to their room and then escape out the window. "The means for getting away are not lacking and the escape is surer than ever," the mysterious officer wrote. June 27—Marie's nineteenth birthday—arrived, and there was still no sign of their rescuers. That night, the entire family lay awake in their clothes, sweating from the intense heat, anxiously listening for a whistle. It never came. The sun began to rise, and Nicholas and Alexandra realized there would be no escape. "The waiting and uncertainty were torture," Nicholas wrote in his diary.[21] Only years later was it revealed that there was no rescue plan. The letters had been concocted by the Soviet secret police, the Cheka, to gain evidence of the family's supposedly traitorous motives. Nicholas and Alexandra had no way of knowing that all of their letters to their would-be rescuers were being received by the Cheka at their headquarters, the Hotel America, a few streets away.

By July 1918, Ekaterinburg was turning into a war zone. The White Army—made up of loyal army officers, monarchists, and conservatives—led by the Czechoslovaks was less than fifty miles away and advancing on the city. In response, the Bolsheviks fortified Ekaterinburg with weapons and artillery. Infantry comprised of Austrian prisoners of war were brought in to bolster the Bolsheviks' ranks. When a seemingly uneventful change of guards took place a few days later, the family had no way of knowing that their new captors were the brutally violent Cheka, the same group who had sent the false rescue letters the previous month. Along with the Cheka came a new commandant of the Ipatiev House, the ruthless Jacob Yurovsky. Under this new dictator, the Romanovs' freedoms became nonexistent. Outdoor exercise was forbidden, and the few personal belongings the family had left were taken by Yurovsky and locked away. He "made us show all our jewels we had on," Alexandra wrote in her diary, "and the young one [Yurovsky's assistant] wrote them all down in detail and then they were taken from us (where to, for how long, why?? don't know)."[22]

They heard Mass on Sunday, July 14, when a priest named Father Ivan Storozhev and a deacon were brought to the house in what was unknowingly to be the last rites of Alexandra Feodorovna and her family. All the while, Yurovsky stood in a corner of the room watching. Storozhev later recalled his experience at the Ipatiev House:

> It seemed to me that on this occasion, Nicholas Alexandrovich and all of his daughters were—I won't say in depressed spirits—but they gave the impression just the same of being exhausted.... According to the liturgy of the service it was customary at a certain point to read the prayer *Who Resteth with the Saints*. On this occasion, for some reason, the Deacon, instead of reading this prayer, began to sing it, and I as well, somewhat embarrassed by this departure from the ritual. But we had scarcely begun to sing when I heard the members of the Romanov family, standing behind me, fall on their knees. After the service everyone kissed the Holy Cross.... As I went out, I passed very close to the former Grand Duchesses and heard the scarcely audible words, "Thank you."[23]

After the service, as Storozhev took his leave, Jacob Yurovsky made the bone-chilling comment, "Well, they've said their prayers and unburdened themselves."[24] Later, the deacon remarked to Storozhev upon leaving the house, "You know, Father Archpresbyter, I think something must have happened there."[25]

The day after this poignant service, two nuns from a local convent arrived with provisions for the family. Later in the morning, four women were brought in from the Ekaterinburg Union of Professional Housemaids to clean the family's rooms. When they arrived, the Romanovs were playing cards at the dining room table. The women noticed that the grand duchesses seemed happy and vibrant, with little sign of worry or anxiety. After welcoming the maids with warm smiles, the girls accompanied them upstairs to help with the cleaning. The ominous Yurovsky stood at the door listening to the maids' conversations with the girls. Anastasia became so fed up with him that when he turned and walked away, she stuck her tongue out and thumbed her nose at him. All eight women broke out laughing.

The morning of Tuesday, July 16, was a gray, cloudy one remarkable for its excessive humidity. In the afternoon, when the clouds disappeared and a clear blue sky emerged, Nicholas and the children were allowed to walk in the gardens surrounding the house. Alexandra sat inside with Tatiana, reading from the Old Testament, specifically the prophets Obadiah and Amos. In the evening, the temperature was warm but comfortable. There seemed to be sympathy toward the family from the Cheka. Yurovsky even visited his prisoners to ask if there was anything they needed. When Nicholas asked for some simple medical supplies, eggs, dairy, and a little meat, Yurovsky said he would have them brought as quickly as possible. In her diary that night, Alexandra recorded the details of what was—unbeknownst to her—the last day of her life.

> July 3 (16). Tuesday. Irina's [Princess Irina Youssopov, the tsar's niece] 23rd BD. 11 [a.m.]. Gray morning, later lovely sunshine. Baby has a slight cold. All went out ½ hour in the morning. Olga and I arranged our medicines. T[atiana]. read. 3[p.m.] rel[igious] readings. They went out. T. stayed with me and we read the b[ooks] by pr[ophet]. Amos and pr. [prophet] Avdiy [Obadiah]. Talked. Every morning the superint. comes to our rooms, at last after a week brought eggs again for Baby. 8. Supper.....Played bezique with N. 10½ to bed. 15 degrees.[26]

Around 2:00 a.m., the Romanovs were startled awake by Dr. Botkin. Yurovsky ordered him to assemble the family in the basement. They were ostensibly being moved to another location ahead of the monarchist White Army, which was only a matter of days away from capturing Ekaterinburg. The girls hastily dressed themselves while Nicholas carried a groggy Alexei downstairs. Accompanying the family was Dr. Botkin, the valet Alexei Trupp, the maid Anna Demidova, and the cook Ivan Kharitonov. The kitchen boy

Leonid had been sent away the day before under the pretense he was joining his uncle Ivan, who had been removed from the Ipatiev House six weeks earlier. Unbeknownst to any of them, Ivan Sednev had already been executed.

The group was led to the ground floor, through the courtyard, and back inside where they reached the staircase and entered the basement. In the damp, leaky room, Alexandra immediately protested the conditions. "Aren't there even any chairs?" she asked, her face wincing from the pain in her legs. "Can we not sit down?"[27] She insisted that there should be at least three chairs: one for herself, Nicholas, and Alexei, who was still weak from his recent hemophilia attack. With no questions asked, three were brought in. Behind Yurovsky, one of his guards muttered under his breath that the "heir wanted to die in a chair. Very well then, let him have one."[28] For nearly an hour, they waited in silence with no further explanation from the gruff soldiers guarding them. At three o'clock, a truck outside began running its engine as loudly as possible. No one seemed to notice that it drowned out all the other sounds from the area, including those from inside the house. A few minutes later, Yurovsky ordered the Romanovs to assume the positions for a formal photograph, which he insisted needed to be taken to prove to the Soviets that they had not been kidnapped by the White Army. Yurovsky left the room, presumably to get a camera, but when he returned, flanked by guards, there was no camera in sight. His face was pale, and his hands were clammy.

"Well, here we all are," Nicholas told Yurovsky, thinking his family was still going to be moved after taking a photograph. "What are you going to do now?" Yurovsky raised his voice to be heard more clearly.

"In view of the fact that your relatives in Europe continue their assault on Soviet Russia," he said, glaring straight at Nicholas, "the presidium of the Ural Regional Soviet has sentenced you to be shot."[29]

In a moment of grim realization, Nicholas rose to his feet. His face was blank with shock. He barely had the chance to utter the word *what* before Yurovsky pulled out a pistol and shot him in the chest at point-blank range. Out of instinct, Alexandra and Olga crossed themselves, trembling with fear. At that moment, a hail of bullets rained down on the unsuspecting family. Alexandra had just enough time to make the sign of the cross again before she was killed by a single bullet. The guards were alarmed when their bullets ricocheted off the wounded grand duchesses. Long before their date with destiny, the girls, at Alexandra's insistence, had sewn their multi-million-dollar collection of jewels into their corsets. Now, realizing that their shots would be ineffective, the guards used bayonets to murder the four sisters. Miraculously, the one person who survived the horrific attack was Alexei, who, "still in his father's arms, somehow managed to show signs of life as his hand began to clutch his father's coat. Yurovsky took his gun and fired into the young boy's head. The family's ordeal was ended." It took twenty minutes to end the life of the last emperor and empress of Russia. Even though they were gone, victims of "one of history's grisliest political assassinations," the legacy of Tsarina Alexandra and her family would live on for decades.[30]

Eight days later, Ekaterinburg fell to the White Army. Rushing to the Ipatiev House, White soldiers discovered that the occupants had vanished. All that was left were a few pieces of clothes left on the ground, and a bullet-riddled, bloodstained wall in the basement.

22

The Fall of Eagles

(July–November 1918)

With the collapse of the western front and the push of British, American, and Canadian troops into Germany, there was little doubt that the Great War would end in a victory for the Allies. For the first time in nearly four years, Queen Mary felt that she could finally exhale. On Saturday, July 6, 1918, she and George celebrated their twenty-fifth wedding anniversary. The day began with a thanksgiving service at Saint Paul's Cathedral, followed by celebrations at the Guildhall, London's Gothic-inspired city hall. There, surrounded by hundreds of friends and family, the royal couple received a "humble address" from Parliament expressing their deepest gratitude for the king and queen's "unfailing devotion to duty in this time of stress." George and Mary insisted that the traditional gifts of silver be donated to the Red Cross on behalf of the war effort.[1]

The celebrations surrounding the silver wedding anniversary were overshadowed by the news that Nicholas, Alexandra, and their family were murdered at Ekaterinburg. On Sunday, July 21, the king and queen were preparing to have lunch with Princess Helena, George's aunt, and her two daughters, the princesses Marie Louise and Helena Victoria. At around 1:00 p.m., Helena and her daughters were waiting in the corridors at Windsor Castle for the king and queen "who were—for the first time in anyone's memory—a half-hour late." When they finally appeared on the landing, both looked grave and deeply upset. The king looked so grief-stricken as he and

Mary descended the staircase that Helena assumed it must have been a major German victory on the battlefield.

"Oh, George, is the news very bad?" she asked.

"Yes, but it is not what you think," he replied. "Nicky, Alix, and their five children have all been murdered by the Bolsheviks at Ekaterinburg."[2]

Mary cancelled lunch with Aunt Helena. She spent the rest of the afternoon in solitude grieving with Nicholas's aunt Queen Alexandra and the tsarina's sister the Marchioness of Milford Haven. That night, the queen confirmed in her diary that the sad news had arrived: "The news were confirmed of poor Nicky of Russia having been shot by those brutes of Bolsheviks last week, on July 16th. It is too horrible & heartless ... terribly upset by the news."[3] Some twenty years later, Queen Mary would still be "sorely conscience stricken" over the Romanovs' fate. Dona's grandson Fritzi would report that, even in 1936, the queen was "still haunted by the fate which befell the Tsar and his family."[4]

On July 25, the king declared a month of official mourning for the imperial family. Later that day, he and the queen attended a memorial service at the Russian church on Welbeck Street in London. Members of the royal family wore black armbands as a sign of support for the Romanovs. This practice was abruptly stopped when the tsar's mother Minnie sought refuge in England, since she believed that her son and family were still alive. Early reports claimed only Nicholas had been killed. But for more than a month, information coming out of Russia was scarce. It was not until the end of August that the grisly details emerged that the entire family had in fact been executed as well. "I hear from Russia that there is every probability that Alicky and the four daughters and little boy were murdered at the same time as Nicky," George wrote. "It is too horrible and shows what fiends those Bolshevists [*sic*] are. For poor Alicky, perhaps it was best so. But those poor innocent children!"[5] From the British public, though, there seemed to be a general lack of sympathy for the tragic fate of the Romanovs. Lord Stamfordham, the king's private secretary, wrote an indignant letter to the British statesman Lord Esher:

> Was there ever a crueler murder and has this country ever before displayed such callous indifference to a tragedy of this magnitude: What does it all mean? I am so thankful that the King and Queen attended the memorial service. I have not yet discovered that the PM ... [was] even represented. Where is our national sympathy, gratitude, common decency ... Why didn't the German Emperor make the release of the Czar and his family a condition of the Brest-Litovsk peace?[6]

Mary's son David never forgot the impact the Romanov murders had on his father. Years later, David recalled, "The Russian Revolution of 1917 with the murder of the Tsar Nicholas II and his family had shaken my father's confidence in the innate decency of mankind."[7]

~≈~

The murder of the Russian imperial family was met with reactions of horror in every corner of Europe. The tsar's dramatic downfall had been enough of a shock, but to learn that he and his entire family had been brutally murdered proved too much for many of the continent's crowned heads. Dona was "haunted" by the massacre.[8] Her Russian antipathy was widely known, but the execution of an anointed monarch and his innocent children overwhelmed the highly sensitive empress. In the words of one historian, "That the once powerful Romanov dynasty should be toppled by the people meant that other thrones were in danger of succumbing to the same fate."[9] With the eruption of the Russian Revolution in 1917, Charles and Zita's fates looked increasingly bleak because the overthrow of the imperial family in Russia emboldened the Austrian imperial family's enemies—the political and nationalist parties within Austria-Hungary—to seek a similar outcome for the emperor and empress.

When the imperial couple left Vienna in May 1918 on an official visit to Bulgaria, their critics accused them of running. The truth was that King Ferdinand of the Bulgarians, Zita's brother-in-law, insisted they make an appearance in Sofia to rally support for the alliance between their two countries. It also afforded Zita the rare opportunity to visit her nieces and nephews, the children of her sister Maria Louisa and King Ferdinand, who were only a few years younger than the empress.[10] The visit seemed a success. The Bulgarians cheered Charles and Zita, threw parades for them, and lit fireworks off at night. But the enthusiasm of the crowds was misleading. The five days they spent in Bulgaria masked a growing feeling among the Central powers of the war's futility. It was a similar feeling when they visited Constantinople later that year to shore up relations between Austria-Hungary and the fraying Ottoman Empire.

Over the summer, Zita and her family slipped away from Vienna for a much-needed respite at their beloved Villa Wartholz. When they returned to Vienna, the empress was overcome with worry and deep sadness over the country's worsening predicament. Vienna was in the grips of turmoil, prompting Zita to dejectedly ask her husband as they pulled up to Schönbrunn,

"Is this all a dream?"[11] In Austria, the emperor's enemies allied to topple the monarchy. When the Reichsrat convened in July, one of the members of the Czech delegation stood up and shouted out, "We regard Austria as a centuries' old crime against humanity … It is our highest national duty to betray Austria whenever and wherever we can. We shall hate Austria, we shall fight against her, and God willing, we shall in the end smash her to pieces."[12] Of all the ethnic groups that comprised the Austro-Hungarian Empire, the Czechs had created the greatest problems for the monarchy. For decades, the Crown had been in constant negotiations with the Czechs over one issue or another. As a Slavic people who comprised the largest portion of the empire's population—Germans and Hungarians combined only amounted to half the total population—they were determined to receive equality. When that failed, they wanted total independence. This problem was inflamed by the exiled Czech nationalist Thomas Masaryk, who, living mostly in the United States at the time, rallied hundreds of thousands of people to his cause of total Czech independence from Austria-Hungary.

By August 1918, the perfidy of the nationalist parties reached new proportions. The Reichsrat nearly dissolved after the Poles, Ukrainians, Italians, and Slavs all declared their desire for independence. Their mission to dismantle Austria-Hungary was further fueled when the Allied forces, led by President Woodrow Wilson of the United States, acknowledged the new nation-state of Czechoslovakia. Declaring itself an independent country, Czechoslovakia forged itself from the eight-hundred-year-old Kingdom of Bohemia, one of the traditional backbones of the Habsburg monarchy. Shortly thereafter, the Allies acknowledged Thomas Masaryk as the head of the Provisional Government of Czechoslovakia—on November 14, he would formally be elected its first president by the National Assembly in Prague.

This latest crisis in Austria-Hungary came as the Allies began their final assault into Central Europe. On August 8, British forces smashed through the German lines at Amiens. Later joined by the French, they conquered six miles of trenches and captured nearly sixteen thousand German and Austrian prisoners of war. Nearly sixty years later, Empress Zita still remembered her husband's reaction to the news of the Allied advance. "The Emperor Charles had been skeptical all along of the victory boasts which the German supreme command had been making throughout the spring and summer about its offensive in the west," she said. "So, when the news of the 8 August defeat reached us … his first words to me were simply: 'Well, so now here we are.'"[13]

There was little doubt that the Austrian Empire was facing its greatest crisis, but unlike in Russia and Germany, the imperial family was not universally reviled. Charles, and especially Zita, still enjoyed some measure of popularity. One incident that shows this is a charity ball held at the end of summer 1918. The event was organized to raise money for those who had been wounded in the war. A number of members of the imperial court warned the empress against going for fear that "she would be booed" and the resulting "scandal would be tremendous." Ever defiant in the face of adversity, Zita declared both she and Charles would attend. When they arrived at Vienna's newly built Konzerthaus, they were both apprehensive about what they might encounter. When they entered the densely crowded Großer Saal, they were met with dead silence. After a moment of this, the crowds erupted into "frenetic applause." The rest of the evening passed smoothly. After the performance, the emperor and empress mingled freely with all the guests. The French journalist and historian Jean Sévillia described the sad irony of what took place that night: "In all the provinces of the Empire, in the State, the Church, at the levels of the population, vigorous forces remained faithful to the monarchy. The voice of this silent majority was not heard however: no effort was made to make it speak."[14]

The Konzerthaus ball at the end of August was followed almost immediately by the collapse of the Central powers. It began with the surrender of Bulgaria on September 25, 1918. Bulgaria's capitulation came as no surprise to Charles and Zita, who received the telegram announcing it at 7:30 p.m. on September 25. According to the empress, King Ferdinand had been "looking for a way out."[15] King Ferdinand had proved an ineffective wartime leader and had no choice but to capitulate. Defeated and humiliated, Ferdinand departed Bulgaria aboard his train bound for his native Coburg. With Austria's southern European ally vanquished and the Central powers cut off from Turkey, the tide continued to turn against them. Romania and Serbia, who had been conquered by the Central powers, reentered the war with a vengeance. Once the Balkan front collapsed, Zita knew that it "made it even more urgent to start peace talks with the Western Powers while there was still something to talk about."[16]

By the beginning of October, Austria-Hungary began its descent into near anarchy. The Czechoslovak nationalist party had control of Prague, the Hungarian Magyars were succumbing to Bolshevik propaganda filtering in from Russia, and soldiers from Slovenia and Croatia were in open revolt. Like Tsar Nicholas II, Emperor Charles did not want civil war to erupt, prompting him to acknowledge the different nation-states within the empire. Upon meeting with his Crown Council, Charles's ministers presented him with a People's Manifesto, but the emperor made it clear he would not sign an act of abdication. For the better part of a day, his ministers hounded him incessantly to sign the manifesto, following him from one room of Schönbrunn to the next. Fed up, Charles turned to his minister of the interior, who was holding the document, and said, "If you won't even let me *read* it, how do you expect me to *sign* it?" When he finally read the document, Charles handed it to his wife for her opinion. Zita mistook it for an abdication. In one of the rare emotional outbursts of her life, she flew into a frenzy.

"A sovereign can never abdicate," she said. "He can be deposed and his sovereign rights declared forfeit. All right. That is force. But abdicate—never, never, never! I would rather fall here at your side. Then there would be Otto. And even if all of us here were killed, there would still be other Habsburgs!" The ministers still pressed for a signature.

"The country will be reduced to the utmost misery," Zita declared. "Who will be concerned for the country if it is no longer led by the one man who is above party interests, and cares only for the future of all?"[17] When one of his ministers told Charles that it was not an abdication—that he was not surrendering his role as emperor—he sat silently for a moment then said, "Madness reigns today and a madhouse is no place for a sovereign."[18] With that, Emperor Charles I affixed his signature in pencil. His ministers hurriedly grabbed the document and rushed over to the Reichsrat.

The parliamentary delegations decried the manifesto. The Czechs boycotted it, the Slovenians and the other Slavs walked out of the assembly, the Germans refused to accept it, the Ukrainians outright denied its existence, the Poles were in abstention, and the Italians refused to believe it applied to them. Protests broke out in Vienna and the economy "came to a standstill; [there was] no coal, no food, no direction, no control. Prisoners of war returning from Russia brought with them Bolshevik ideas, or at any rate the contempt for 'authority' which had inaugurated the Russian Revolution."[19]

Near the end of October, Charles sent Wilhelm II a telegram stating that he intended to ask for peace from the Allies "within twenty-four hours." Charles declared he was ready "without awaiting the result of the other negotiations, to enter into negotiations upon peace between Austria-Hungary and the states in the opposing group, and for an immediate armistice upon all the Dual Monarchy's fronts."[20]

A few days later, riots broke out in Hungary. Charles and Zita hurried to Budapest to assess the stability of the monarchy there. "We must show the people, that we are where our duty commands," Zita said.[21] The Hungarians had shown the couple moving demonstrations of loyalty at their coronation. Now, they hoped that those same people would support the entire empire in its hour of despair. Charles, Zita, and their children arrived by motorcar in Budapest on October 24. They took up residence at Gödöllö Palace, one of the largest royal residences in Central Europe. Built in a double-U shape, Gödöllö boasted eight wings in addition to the residential apartments, as well as a church, theater, riding hall, greenhouse, and orangery. As soon as the children were settled in, Charles and Zita faced the daunting task of consolidating the government. They appointed a new prime minister named Michael Karolyi. Descended from a wealthy aristocratic family, Karolyi believed he was destined to play a part in ruling Hungary. He had been opposed to Austria's involvement in the war but managed to convince Charles that his appointment as prime minister would strengthen the ties between Hungary and Austria. This proved to be a fatal mistake. When the emperor sounded out Karolyi's government a few days later for support, he was alarmed to learn that they were abandoning the monarchy in favor of turning the country into a republic. Knowing he had been beaten, Charles released Karolyi and his government from their oaths of loyalty. The death knell of the Habsburg monarchy had been sounded.

Throughout the rest of the empire, the situation completely fell apart. From October 24 to November 3, the Battle of Vittorio Veneto was fought along the Austro-Italian border. The Italian army inflicted demoralizing casualties on the Austro-Hungarian forces—more than four hundred thousand soldiers were captured, wounded, or killed. The defeat marked the collapse of the Italian front and the first dissolutions in the Austro-Hungarian military. This disastrous outcome precipitated the total collapse of the Austro-Hungarian Empire.

On October 29, the Croatian parliamentary body, the Sabor, met in Zagreb where they severed all ties with Austria-Hungary. The Habsburg kingdoms of Croatia and Dalmatia declared themselves independent from the empire. They proclaimed themselves the Common Sovereign National State of the Slovenians, Croatians, and Serbs. On the same day, students, factory workers, and their supporters revolted in Vienna. By the next day, the military had joined the revolution and were marching through the streets with an army of soldiers numbering in the tens of thousands. Later that day, the head of Austria's National Council, Franz Dinghofer, declared that the legislative body "would take over the whole administration of the country, 'but without the Habsburgs.'" Within a few days, the eastern empire was dissolving. The Polish National Council took the reins of administration, as did the Ukrainians, who proclaimed the West Ukrainian Republic at Przemysl. On October 31, the empire's Romanian subjects declared their independence.

At Gödöllö, Charles and Zita were shocked and saddened by the reports flooding in, but the situation would continue to go from bad to worse. The next day, Charles was forced to surrender his sovereign powers in the Balkans by a delegation representing the newly formed State of Slovenes, Croats and Serbs. This nation would join with Serbia on December 1, changing its name to the Kingdom of Serbs, Croats, and Slovenes. It would informally be known as Yugoslavia, a name that would not become official until 1929.

In the east, the Ukrainians founded their own national republic. This was especially bittersweet since the leader of the Ukrainian nationalist cause was a Habsburg—Archduke Wilhelm. Once it was obvious that Hungary, the Balkans, and the eastern realms were beyond hope, Charles and Zita left Budapest, worried about the deteriorating political situation in Austria. In spite of the revolts, Gödöllö was still considered safer than any place in Vienna. The empress made the difficult decision to leave her children at the palace under the care of her brother Prince René, the court chamberlain, Count Hunyády, and the staff. Zita explained the reasons for her decision this way:

> It was a dreadful decision to have to take but we did it deliberately. It was the only way to show the Hungarian people that their King and Queen did not intend to flee Hungary for good. It would have been the last straw had that idea spread about! But our children were not left there as hostages against our will. Nobody asked that they should stay. It was our decision and it was helped by two things. First, at that particular moment, the situation in Vienna looked if anything even more dangerous than in Budapest. We were not moving from trouble into peace but from one storm into another. Second, our children were by now so used to their parents being continually on the move that they were in no way anxious or frightened at being left alone.[22]

When the imperial couple arrived at Schönbrunn Palace late on the night of October 30, Vienna was eerily calm, as if it could explode at any moment. There was little doubt that night that the age of empires was about to meet its climactic end. If Zita expected their first night back in Vienna to be calm, she was mistaken. No sooner had they returned to Vienna than Budapest exploded into violent revolution. Crowds looted, plundered, and murdered innocent people, but their greatest animosity was directed against the Habsburgs. "The emperor had not got to bed in Schönbrunn until long after midnight on 30 October," Zita recalled. "In the small hours, just as he had fallen asleep, an urgent telephone call came through for him from Budapest. It was General Lucacics, the commander of the garrison there, who told me, beside himself with agitation, that revolution had broken out in the city and that he simply had to speak to the emperor." Zita, in her usual direct manner, cut straight to the heart of the issue: "I was naturally very worried about the safety of my children."[23]

As soon as she hung up the phone, Zita called Gödöllö to raise the alarm. The chaos in the streets was making its way up to the palace. The children and their attendants were bundled up in the night and set off in a cavalcade of automobiles for Vienna, where they arrived many hours later. To speed up their journey and keep the children safe, the imperial crests on the sides of the cars were painted over. As morning dawned on October 31, the republicans had full control of Budapest. Michael Karolyi telegraphed to Berlin, "Revolution in Budapest. National Council has taken over the government. Military and police acknowledge National Council completely. Inhabitants rejoicing."[24] With each hour that passed, the Habsburgs' empire unraveled more and more. Kingdoms, grand duchies, principalities, and whole ethnic groups declared their independence, leaving the monarchy without a leg to stand on. From Prague in the north to Sarajevo in the south, protests, riots, and revolutions were breaking out everywhere.

On November 1, 1918, Emperor Charles I contacted President Woodrow Wilson without any conditions for negotiations. Austria-Hungary, or what was left of it, was now agreeing to the Allies' terms unconditionally, which included national self-determination for all of the empire's ethnic groups. In all but name, the First World War had ended. Charles had no choice but to finally concede defeat. All of the empire's territories had broken away, creating half a dozen ethnically diverse nations spread across central and southern Europe. Charles issued another manifesto in which he did not abdicate but, instead, renounced his participation in government. Upon signing the order, he ended six hundred years of Habsburg rule in Austria. His reign was the shortest in Habsburg history, lasting just under two years. Though he could have fought to the bitter end, he announced, "Filled, now as ever, with unwavering devotion to all my peoples, I do not wish to oppose their growth with my own person ... The people, through its representatives, has taken over the government. I renounce all participation in the affairs of state."[25] Not wishing to vanish from the public eye completely, Emperor Charles opted to leave Vienna but remain within Austria's borders.

The next day, November 2, was a depressing one at Schönbrunn. Beginning with the Hungarian Battalion, one regiment after the other abandoned the imperial family. Zita explains the last day her family spent at the palace as follows:

> Our own life guard troops were also disappearing, but it was the departure of the Hungarian battalion which first created a really dangerous situation. The whole palace was now open. There were not even sentries at the main gates. The only people permanently at Schönbrunn from now on – apart from the Emperor and myself and our children – were about half-a-dozen ladies-in-waiting and

aides, a few remaining servants and retainers and the life guards officers who stayed behind after their men left.[26]

That night, Charles, Zita, and their children fled Schönbrunn Palace. Before their departure, they attended a special Mass to pray for their safe return soon. Unsettling echoes of the Russian imperial family's dramatic fate haunted the Habsburgs. The empress later said that the "whole day was a nightmare."[27] As they packed everything they could take, shouts could be heard outside calling for the imperial family's blood. Later that evening, the emperor and empress entered the Hall of Ceremonies, where the loyal staff who had stayed with them was dismissed in a series of emotional embraces. Charles and Zita took the time to shake hands with every person there, offering each of them a personal farewell. As Zita and her family left the palace, they marched down the long stairwell to the inner courtyard. Flanking them on either side in full honor guard were cadets from the nearby Maria Theresia Military Academy, who had unexpectedly shown up earlier that evening to defend the imperial family. According to the empress, the young men, many of whom were teenagers, stood there "with tears in their eyes, but still perfectly turned out and guarding us to the end."[28] As they reached the bottom of the stairs, Erich Mann, one of the cadets, snapped to attention and saluted the emperor and empress. Although Zita understood the magnitude of their situation, Charles did not. One witness observed that even though the emperor "was in fact leaving for good, and was never to recover even one of the several crowns he had been forced to abandon, he did not realize the finality of the occasion."[29]

Amid a flood of tears, the family finally entered their automobiles bound for the imperial hunting lodge at Eckartsau, near the Hungarian border. Decades later, the memory of their flight from Schönbrunn remained fresh in Zita's mind: "It was dark by now, and a misty autumn night. The emperor and I and all the children except Karl Ludwig squeezed into the back of one car with Count Hunyády at the front. In the next one came the infant Karl Ludwig and the children's nurses … I did not risk driving out of the main gate in front of the palace. Instead we continued parallel with the main building along the broad gravel path that leads to the eastern side gate. We slipped out of this and left the capital by a special route. Late that night—without any trouble or incidents—we arrived at Eckartsau."[30]

Arguably, the fall of the Habsburgs created more shock than any other dynasty deposed at the end of the First World War. They had reigned the longest, the fiercest, and the proudest of any of Europe's modern dynasties. A British newspaper described theirs as "the oldest and most eminent dynastic name in European history."[31] One Habsburg historian poignantly summarized their downfall with these words:

> For centuries, Christians regarded the Holy Roman Empire, ruled by the Habsburgs, as the opposite of a sign of the apocalypse: so long as it existed, the world would not end. In the early nineteenth century the Holy Roman Empire had been dissolved, but the Habsburgs, under Franz Josef, had recovered and endured, throwing a grey cloak of timelessness over the shuddering body of a continent changing itself from within. Now, with empires destroyed and dynasties dethroned, progressive time began. It was socialist time, the promise of new beginnings for oppressed classes at the end of a feudal age; national time, the conviction that peoples could move forward from a dark past of imperial oppression into a brighter future of state independence; or liberal time, the confidence that new republics would create the conditions for lasting peace in Europe and the world.[32]

As a symbol of their nearly millennium-long reign, the Habsburgs had chosen a black, double-headed eagle as their crest. The day that the Habsburgs were forced to vacate their throne would be forever remembered as the fall of eagles.

⟶⟶

In Germany, the appointment of a new government headed by Prince Max of Baden did not solve any problems. Like Vienna and Petrograd, a dangerous cloud of anarchy swirled. Streets were empty because there was no fuel for automobiles. The sidewalks were crowded with "heart-broken women," who had deprivation written across their "faces like masks, blue with cold and drawn with hunger." The protests outside government buildings earlier in the year were replaced with bellicose demonstrations in city squares. Bands of mounted police were now forced to patrol the capital day and night. They looked on the people uneasily but were unable to act against their growing hostility.[33] Despite his claims of bridging the gulf between the monarchy and the Leftist groups, Prince Max immediately sounded out the Allies for peace terms. Their demands were steep. On top of already harsh political and economic reparations, President Wilson issued a series of notes declaring that the German Empire must become a full democratic republic devoid of its emperor. The most inflammatory of the notes, sent to the German government on October 14, referred to the "destruction of every arbitrary power anywhere that can [...] disturb the peace of the world" and added that "the power which has hitherto controlled the German nation is of the sort described here. It is within the choice of the German nation to alter it."[34]

"It aims directly at the fall of my house, and above all at the abolition of the monarch!" Wilhelm angrily declared when he saw Wilson's note.[35] Dona was equally outraged, decrying "the audacity of the parvenu across the sea who thus dares to humiliate a princely house which can look back on centuries of service to people and country."[36] When word of Wilson's terms leaked out to the public, political rallies sprang up everywhere. As the people gathered, they cried out, "Down with the Kaiser."[37] Berlin descended into being a city on the brink, with riots on a scale it had not seen in seventy years. The people's fury, held in check for so long, was set to erupt, fanned into a flame by the dissolution of the Austro-Hungarian Empire.

The collapse of the German Empire began in the north with the imperial navy, whose sailors revolted on the night of October 29. Some forty thousand sailors and soldiers succeeded in taking Germany's two largest seaports, Wilhelmshaven and Kiel, after the commanding officers ordered a final kamikaze mission against Allied naval forces. Thousands of sailors took to the streets of Kiel singing "La Marseillaise." By the first week of November, the empire's outer territories were engulfed in the sea of revolutionary fever that was sweeping across eastern and central Europe. Hanover, Frankfurt, and Munich were firmly in the hands of the revolutionaries, who were calling themselves the Workers and Soldiers Councils. On November 7, public services in Berlin came to a standstill. Railway lines were cut to prevent monarchists from sending for reinforcements. In Brunswick, Wilhelm's son-in-law Ernest Augustus abdicated his ducal throne, ending his daughter Sissy's role as Duchess of Brunswick. The dukedom of Brunswick had been a particular hotbed of revolutionary activity. Throughout the war, protestors had taken to the streets outside the Brunswick Palace chanting for reform. Once the German Revolution began, the people of Brunswick were among the first to rise up. Within two weeks, German revolutionaries managed to force the abdication of every one of the empire's royal rulers. By the end of the week, the Stadtschloss in Berlin was flying the revolutionary flag. Dona was personally offended when her brother-in-law Prince Frederick Leopold hoisted the revolutionary banner above his hunting lodge at Glienicke. "The red flag floated over the palaces, while royal mottoes vanished from the courts, the newspapers and the commercial world," wrote Ralph Haswell Lutz in his study *The German Revolution*.[38] Violent riots broke out as monarchist and rebel forces exchanged cannon fire across Berlin.

At the time, Dona was still recuperating from her heart attack. Upon her return from Wilhelmshöhe, it was deemed too unsafe for her to return to Bellevue in Berlin, so she returned to the Neues Palais in Potsdam. It was here in October 1918 that Dona was reunited with her husband. It was the first time they had been together since Wilhelm's nervous breakdown, recovery, and subsequent departure for Spa. Given the revolutionary atmosphere in Berlin, it was decided the emperor needed to return to face the oncoming storm in person. As much as Wilhelm II was being faced with the most difficult moment of his reign, many people were closely watching Empress Augusta Victoria. To the people around her, she exhibited a calm, grave exterior, but the voices that were now crying out for her husband's abdication both angered and frightened her. She was worried about Germany and the effect that Wilhelm's possible abdication would have on the country. Princess Ina Luise of Solms-Baruth, one of Dona's ladies-in-waiting, wrote to Princess Daisy of Pless, "About the Emperor, I hope and pray he will be firm, and won't abdicate; they were quite resolved to be firm, and the Empress told me to say everywhere that she stands firm."[39]

With the revolution spreading, Wilhelm decided to leave Potsdam for his military command at Spa on October 29. When the uprisings began, and before they spread to the rest of the empire, it made sense for the emperor to be closer to the epicenter. But once it was clear this was more than an isolated revolt, Wilhelm and his advisors felt the greatest place of strength from which he could preserve his reign was military headquarters. The decision to leave Potsdam was not one the emperor came to easily. It required heavy prodding from both his advisers and his wife. Dona loathed being parted from her husband, but she believed that if he had any chance of restoring order, he would have to appeal to the army and hope to trigger an uprising in favor of the monarchy. When Wilhelm found his wife to say good-bye, she collapsed into tears. "This is the end," she sobbed; "now I have no more hope."[40] It was the last time Augusta Victoria would lay eyes on the man who was both her husband and the German emperor. The next time she saw him, he would simply be Wilhelm Hohenzollern.

As soon as Wilhelm reached Spa, he sent Dona two letters. The first, written on November 7, never made it to Potsdam because the postal stations nearby had been seized by the revolutionaries. His second letter, written and sent the next day, made it through but contained the direst reports.

> My letter of yesterday did not come through as there is insurrection in Cologne and the station is occupied. The people have all gone insane! They have proclaimed a republic in Munich, as the King [of Bavaria] is supposed to have abdicated. I don't know if this

letter will reach you. God be with you and us. I am gathering all the troops from the front together, so as to march on Berlin with them as soon as an armistice has been declared. Our sons must take over your defence until we can come to your help from here. If it's no longer safe for you in Potsdam, then you must go with the children to Königsberg or Rominten if necessary. I cannot judge matters from here. All connections are so uncertain ...[41]

With the emperor out of the capital, Prince Max again received pressure from the Allies on November 9 that the only way to ensure peace would be if Wilhelm abdicated. Knowing that he would never willingly abdicate, Max took it upon himself to force the emperor's hand. He composed a personal letter calling on the emperor to step down.

> Your abdication has become necessary if civil war in Germany is to be avoided ... The great majority of the people believe that you are to blame for the present situation ... Today I can no longer hold my protecting hand before the wearer of the crown ... We are heading straight for civil war ...
>
> There are two possibilities. First, abdicate, nomination of a deputy and the summoning of a National Assembly. Second, abdication and renunciation of the succession by the Crown Prince and a Regency for his son. Whichever course is chosen, it must be acted on with the utmost speed ... This is the final hour ... If abdication does not follow today, then I can no longer carry on [in the Reichstag], nor can the German princes protect their Emperor any further....
>
> A voluntary sacrifice must now be made if your good name is to be preserved in history ...[42]

At Spa, Wilhelm was promptly joined by the crown prince, whose chief of the general staff read the letter to the emperor. Indignant, Wilhelm shot back, "You, a Prussian official, who have sworn the oath of fealty to your king, how can you venture to come before me with such a proposal!"[43] Wilhelm also declared that if he must abdicate as German emperor, he was unwilling to abandon the Prussian throne. He may have to renounce the federated imperial throne, but he refused to give up the crown which the Hohenzollerns had worn for centuries. What he failed to realize was that the abdication was all encompassing. There could be no thrones left in Germany if there was to be peace with the Allies.

His first reaction after being told that his abdication must be total was to immediately set into motion his earlier plan of rallying the army to march on Berlin, except instead of simply restoring order, he would be fighting to preserve his divine right to rule. This was rather ambitious, since most of the railway lines had already been cut, which would mean marching the army for nearly three weeks on foot to reach Berlin. Although the emperor was willing to see his plan to completion, it was doomed to failure. General Wilhelm Groener, the deputy chief of the general staff, informed the emperor that the troops were now in full revolt. "The army will return home in good order under the command of its chiefs, but not under the orders of Your Majesty," Groener told him. "The army is no longer behind Your Majesty."[44] Fearing for the future of Germany, Wilhelm finally capitulated. He shriveled into his chair and accepted the abdication, both for him and his son Crown Prince Willy, who described his father as looking "so sallow and emaciated" that day.[45] In a single moment, Emperor Wilhelm II was forced from the throne that his ancestors had sat upon for more than five hundred years since first being chosen as rulers of Prussia in the fifteenth century. By those standards, the German Empire's lifespan was fleeting. It existed for forty-seven years, nine months, and twenty-one days.

Wilhelm opted to leave the country as quickly as possible, since his safety could no longer be guaranteed. The one concession he forced his ministers to agree to was that he would not sign the abdication until he was safely outside of Germany. One of the last letters he ever wrote on German soil was to Dona back in Potsdam.

If I am not allowed to stay in the midst of the remaining faithful [officers], then I must go with you to a neutral State, Holland or elsewhere, where merciful heaven may permit us to eat our bread—in exile. God's hand lies heavily upon us! His Will be done! So, on Hindenburg's advice, I am leaving the army, after fearful mental struggles. As God wills, *auf Wiedersehen*. My lasting gratitude for your faithful love—
Your deeply mortified husband.[46]

In England, the queen was relieved to hear that Wilhelm was no longer in power. "Heard that William had abdicated & his son renounced his right to the Throne," she wrote in her diary on November 9. "What a downfall, what retribution to the man who started this awful war."[47] King George described Wilhelm's abdication with added poignancy in his own journal.

We got the news that the German Emperor had abdicated, also the Crown Prince. "How are the mighty fallen." He has been Emperor just over 30 years, he did great things for his country, but his ambition was so great that he wished to dominate the world and created his military machine for that object. No one man can dominate the world, it has been tried before, and now he has utterly ruined his Country and himself and I look upon him as the greatest criminal known for having plunged the world into this ghastly war with all it's [*sic*] misery.[48]

The day after George wrote this, Wilhelm implemented his decision and went into exile. Since it was imperative that he leave immediately, and since most of his family was back in Potsdam, he had no choice but to go without them. "My wife stays, and they want me to leave," Wilhelm exclaimed to his aides. "It would look like fear."[49] The emperor received assurances that because his wife was still widely respected, she would be protected from harm. At 4:30 a.m., Wilhelm and his entourage boarded his personal train. Their destination upon leaving Spa was the Netherlands, where Wilhelm's cousin Queen Wilhelmina had invited him into exile. But once reports reached Spa that several of the rail crossings were now controlled by revolutionaries, the emperor was transferred to a black car, with the imperial insignia scratched off to avoid drawing attention. The atmosphere as Wilhelm departed Spa in the foggy dampness was highly charged, but the send-off was very formal without any fanfare; the German press printed only a short byline about his departure.

Once he reached the border, Wilhelm boarded a train again, bound for a nearby Dutch village. He saluted each of his generals, thanking them for their service. When he boarded the train, a message from Dona was there waiting for him. She reported "that she was in good spirits"—most likely a lie—and that her thoughts were with him. He spent most of the journey alone in his private coach, pacing up and down across the floor. Periodically, he stopped to stare at a photograph hanging on the wall that depicted him having tea with Queen Victoria at Osborne House. In England, King George V wrote in his diary, "William arrived in Holland yesterday. Today has indeed been a wonderful day, the greatest in the history of this Country."[50] Crown Prince Willy arrived in the Netherlands two days later. It was equally imperative that he get out of Germany as quickly as possible, since his behavior over the years had made him universally hated by his people. Instead of joining his father, with whom he had always had a difficult relationship, Willy found a home on Wieringen Island in North Holland. Empress Zita was hardly surprised by the outcome and later remarked, "The emperor Charles was not surprised ...

including the choice of Holland, though, to put it mildly, it wasn't considered exactly an inspiring example. But as we always knew that he was under the thumbs of his generals, this, after all, seemed the natural end. They had just packed him off."[51]

With the German emperor's abdication and exile in November 1918, the Allies accepted the unconditional surrender of the Central powers. The end of the war saw the fall of the eagles, as Europe's imperial powers were known. Tsarist Russia fell to the Bolsheviks in 1917, followed a year later by imperial Germany and Austria-Hungary. Of Europe's imperial monarchs, only King George V and Queen Mary remained on the throne. Nicholas and Alexandra were dead, Wilhelm went into exile while Dona lingered on in Potsdam, and Zita and Charles had driven off into the night, leaving Vienna forever.

When it came to Great Britain, however, November 1918 was a time unparalleled in the nation's history. Despite their casualties between 1914 and 1918—which included 750,000 killed from Great Britain alone, as well as another 200,000 from across the empire—one historian noted that the country "had triumphed through the long years of attrition, and her monarchy, alone of the major monarchies which ruled Europe before the war, had emerged not only intact but thriving."[52] November 11, 1918, was declared Armistice Day. The king, the queen, and the Prince of Wales appeared on the balcony of Buckingham Palace. The scene that unfolded was awe inspiring. A crowd numbering more than one hundred thousand had gathered in the great round courtyard beyond the palace gates, cheering on the royal family and holding up their portraits. In the center, rising above everyone, was the Queen Victoria monument that had been dedicated by George and Wilhelm seven years earlier. Accompanying the king and queen that day was David Lloyd George, Britain's long-suffering, redoubtable prime minister, who shrunk into the balcony's doorway so as not to pull attention away from the royal family. Queen Mary wrote simply in her diary of that day, "dull first, rain in the afternoon." But even she could not help but describe the joy at seeing the end of "this ghastly war," and considered Armistice Day "the greatest day in the world's history."[53] In a speech at the Palace of Westminster, the king declared, "May goodwill and concord at home strengthen our influence for concord abroad. May the morning star of peace, which is now rising over a war-worn world, be here and everywhere the herald of a better day, in which the storms of strife shall have died down and the rays of an enduring peace be shed upon all nations."[54]

The news of the armistice may have brought a feeling of relief that was "indescribably intense," but it was bittersweet for George and Mary. Their German relatives, many of whom they had been close with before the war, were now suffering in defeat. Mary's cousin the Grand Duke of Mecklenburg-

Strelitz—Aunt Augusta's grandson—committed suicide by shooting himself in February. "Uncle Willie," the king of Württemberg, abdicated on November 30. So too did George's cousin the Duke of Coburg. This tiny, central German dukedom had been the ancestral home for the entire British royal family. The young duke's life "was a tragic example of the royal family's divided loyalties during the war. As an Eton schoolboy of fifteen, having inherited his father's title upon his early death, Queen Victoria had insisted the boy, who had never been out of Britain, be sent to Germany to prepare for his reign in his duchy. Now, he was *persona non grata* in both countries."[55]

Exuberant crowds in London danced around bonfires until the small hours of the morning. In the week that followed, the king and queen rode throughout the city in an open carriage five times. A photograph taken of Mary en route to an armistice celebration with her husband and Queen Alexandra shows her beaming with a wide, toothy smile that radiated warmth and exuberance. Everywhere the royal couple went, they were met with crowds exploding with enthusiastic patriotism for king and country. The *Times* reported "the wonderful popularity with Londoners—as we are convinced, with the whole country—of THEIR MAJESTIES the KING and QUEEN ... this signal outburst of loyal feeling is born of the conviction that the CROWN, well-worn, is the symbol and safeguard of unity, not only here in England, but in the free dominions overseas, and in India."[56] Mary wrote to her son Harry, "It has been very wonderful and gratifying that after all these 4 years of ghastly warfare the people did crowd here to *us* the moment they knew the war was practically over."[57] It is uncertain whether even Queen Victoria was as popular as George and Mary were at the end of the First World War.

In the days following the signing of the armistice, a subdued, gravely ill Dona was alone at the Neues Palais, save for a few faithful retainers. She was joined by some family members a few days later, including several of her sons, daughters-in-law, and grandchildren. The day that Emperor Wilhelm fled Germany, the empress sent a letter to her daughter, Sissy, who had taken refuge with her in-laws at their private estate at Gmunden in Austria.

> I'm still here in our old home, but for how long? With me I have some of my boys, some daughters-in-law and grandchildren and their love does me good. I worry so much about beloved Papa! He is so alone in his misfortune and I am not with him to help him bear

it, he who has always wanted and done his best for the Fatherland. May God grant that I should be reunited with him once more.... God grant that we shall see each other again.[58]

The *New York Times* reported that "Wilhelm II's wife, Auguste Viktoria, and the former Crown Princess Cecilie and her children have remained at the New Palace in Potsdam under the protection of the local soldiers and workers' council. Auguste Viktoria has expressed her thanks to the council for her family's protection."[59]

The end of the war brought speculation over Dona's fate. Those loyal to the monarchy suggested she remain in Germany. Since there were no immediate threats against her life, and since most of the German people still held her in high regard, many hoped that, by remaining in the country, she could serve as a rallying point for monarchists. The most ardent royal supporters even hoped that her presence would pave the way for an eventual restoration of the monarchy. But when asked about what course of action she would take, the empress was unequivocal: she would join her husband in exile. The newly formed Council of People's Commissars granted her permission to travel safely to the Netherlands now that her husband had promised to abdicate. For Dona, "there was never any choice in this matter. For one thing, Queen Wilhelmina of the Netherlands wished her to join William to give his stay in Holland a more private character." On a deeper, more personal level, "she could not have born [*sic*] the thought of being separated from William at a time when he needed her more than ever."[60] As soon as the decision was made to go into exile, Dona frantically began packing as many belongings as she could take with her. The idea of common thieves appropriating her personal treasures almost overwhelmed her, prompting her to pack everything from clothes and jewels to cutlery and knickknacks. Her daughters-in-law offered the stoical empress support, but she demurred, choosing instead to be left alone. Even the presence of her eldest grandchild, Prince Wilhelm, failed to cheer her up.

The tide of events in Germany shifted drastically at the end of November, as Marxist Communists began fighting with the more moderate republicans for control of the government. Berlin and its environs became war zones, making it imperative for Dona to leave soon. Violence against the monarchy was escalating. Two attempts were made on the life of Wilhelm's brother Henry and Wilhelm's nephews. In Potsdam, small bands of rioters barged into the Neues Palais. The small detachment of bodyguards that Wilhelm had left to protect Dona was unable to adequately defend the palace. The empress was unharmed, but everyone's nerves were sufficiently jolted. Eitel-Fritz finally persuaded his mother to relocate to his home, the more secure

Villa Ingenheim, in southwest Potsdam. Within hours of vacating the Neues Palais, crowds broke in and ransacked the ground floor. Thieves made off with antiques, furniture, and clothes, including one of Dona's nightgowns. But Ingenheim proved just as vulnerable as the palace. The guards assigned by Eitel-Fritz to protect her openly supported the revolution by wearing red cockades in their hats. But unlike many of the guards who abandoned Tsarina Alexandra at Tsarskoe Selo to join the revolution, those at Ingenheim still did their best to protect Augusta Victoria.

On the first night she spent at her son's home, a group of bibulous sailors broke into the building and easily overpowered the guards. While the sailors tore room after room apart looking for Dona's diaries and letters, she was questioned by their officer. The empress faced bravely them, showing great strength during her interrogation, despite still being very ill. When the officer suggested she would be more comfortable if she sat down, she defiantly retorted, "*I* am accustomed to sit down only when I feel like it."[61] Dona's courage lasted through the hours of questioning. In the end, it was by the "sheer force of her character she had subdued them, and afterwards she had been left in peace."[62]

At the Villa Ingenheim, Dona remained in almost total seclusion under the protection of the small handful of guards who were still committed to her safety. The terrifying ordeal involving the drunken sailors further undermined her poor health. Suffering from continual heart pain and fatigue brought on by stress, she spent long hours in bed. The only thing that eased her suffering was the presence of her sons Eitel-Fritz, Oscar, Auwi, and their wives and children, along with Crown Princess Cecilie and her family. Missing from the family group now gathered at Ingenheim were Crown Prince Willy, who was by that time settled on Wieringen Island, and Prince Adalbert, who was in Kiel. When the revolution began, Adalbert fled to his personal yacht, which was manned by a crew still loyal to him. His wife, Adelaide, and their daughter attempted to reach Kiel but were blocked by revolutionaries. They found safety near Munich, taking refuge with the Bavarian royal family; husband and wife were eventually reunited and made their way safely to Switzerland.

At the end of November, the time had come for Dona to leave Germany and join her husband in exile in the Netherlands. The night before her departure, she packed as many things as she could, including a few jewels, clothes, and personal items. Most of her crown jewels had been spirited away with Wilhelm's cousin the queen of Sweden, who was in Carlsruhe at the time. Before dawn on the cold, wintry morning of November 27, 1918, Augusta Victoria, wearing a long black dress and a matching hat that partially covered her face, left Potsdam. Accompanying the empress was a small group comprised of her ever-faithful friend Countess Mathilde Keller, her beloved dachshund Topsy, and one or two attendants. Noticeably absent from the traveling party were Dona's daughters-in-law, most of whom chose to stay in Germany, and most of whom now chose to live separately from their husbands. With the exceptions of Oscar's wife, Countess Ina, and Adalbert's wife, Princess Adelaide, whom those princes had married for love, all four of her sons' wives were forced to endure unfaithful, bigoted husbands who had shown time and again that their military careers were more important to them than their marriages. Crown Prince Willy proved to be a particularly brutal husband who hit Cecilie on more than one occasion. When Willy became too insufferable, Cecilie fled abroad, usually with the emperor's consent, while Dona cared for her young grandchildren.

Upon leaving Ingenheim, Dona was driven by Cecilie to the Charlottenburg station—the same train station where, thirty years before, she and Wilhelm experienced a very different scene. Back then, during the howling winter, the couple had met Wilhelm's parents upon their return from San Remo when they had just ascended the throne, making the young couple the new crown prince and princess of Germany. This time, the emotional scene that took place was very different. There were no imperial officials, no crowds paying their respects. The Berlin of November 1918 was a far cry from the Berlin of 1888. Absent were outbursts of loyalty to the monarchy or the military on parade in imperial livery. City life hardly seemed to notice the passing into shadow of the empress or her family. On the platform of the station, Dona and Cecilie shared a last, tearful embrace. The only other people there were gray-coated soldiers returning from the front lines, none of whom acknowledged Dona. The only light that illuminated the platform was from the train conductor's lantern. Cecilie noted that, despite the pain of her departure, Dona maintained "the placidity of her temperament."[63]

Dona and her group left for the Netherlands in a specially prepared black train. To ensure the empress's safety, the government provided her with an escort—the First Guards Regiment—to accompany her to the border and then disembark. But even this benevolent gesture was tainted by political undertones. Instead of wearing the traditional dress uniform in the presence of the empress, they wore civilian clothes. The journey through German territory was performed at breakneck speed. This was necessary to ensure the empress quitted the country while public opinion was still in her favor. With great relief, the train arrived at Amerongen the next day. In spite of the uncertainty of what lay ahead, Dona conducted herself during the journey with great dignity and restraint. Her companions chatted and played cards, but Dona isolated herself at the back of the train, attended only by Countess Keller. Those on board both pitied and were impressed by the empress, who, in spite of her great misfortune, carried herself well. That same regal bearing—the one she had shown as a child—was almost all that Dona had left for her years of exile.

PART 4

Twilight and Shadow

(1918–89)

23

The Edge of Night

(November 1918–April 1919)

Wilhelm arrived in Amerongen to a disheartening welcome. Half a dozen or so Dutch military officers confiscated most of his military property and ordered the majority of his staff back to Germany. The Dutch officers escorted him to his new home, Amerongen Castle, a four-story brick building located a few miles outside the town, belonging to the "phenomenally obliging" Count Bentinck.[1] "Now," Wilhelm said to his aide upon arriving, rubbing his hands together, "give me a cup of real good English tea!"[2] The next day, he wrote a self-pitying note to Dona: "My reign is ended, my dog's life is over, and has been rewarded only with betrayal and ingratitude."[3] Though incredibly small by the standards of Wilhelm's former homes, Amerongen was still luxurious compared to what many deposed royals were now experiencing. The castle was large enough that it was surrounded by two moats, requiring entry through a medieval-style drawbridge.

On November 28, men dressed in long black coats arrived at Amerongen from Berlin. They were representatives of the new German government, the Weimar Republic. They had come to secure Wilhelm's signature on the abdication order, ending the reign of the Hohenzollerns once and for all. Unlike other abdications, this one was simple yet exacting.

> I hereby for all the future renounce my rights to the Crown of Prussia and my consequential rights to the German Imperial Crown.

At the same time I release all officials of the German Empire and Prussia, as well as all the officers, non-commissioned officers, and men of the Navy, of the Prussian Army, and of the federal contingents, from the oath of fealty, which they have made to me as their Emperor, King and Supreme Commander....

Given under our hand and our Imperial seal,

Wilhelm

Amerongen, November 28, 1918[4]

Later that same day, Dona arrived by train at the Amerongen station. She was met with a similar bare-bones welcome to what Wilhelm had received. Looking "worn and ill"[5] according to one witness, she half smiled at the aide-de-camp who was sent to meet her at the station. She was reunited with Wilhelm in the castle gardens. The ex-emperor was standing alone on the bridge over the moat surrounding their new home, leaves from the golden trees fluttering on the surface of the water. The mist that rose from the river created an almost dreamlike quality to the scene. When Wilhelm finally looked up and saw his long-suffering wife, he snapped to attention and gave her a military salute. Then, with tears in her eyes, she ran over to her husband and embraced him, reportedly for the first time in public. A week later, she wrote to her daughter, "Reunited with Papa eight days ago, praise God!"[6]

The Austrian imperial family found refuge in the town of Eckartsau, taking up residence at the old imperial hunting lodge nearby. Within a few days of their departure from Vienna, the new government of German-Austria, as it was calling itself since becoming a republic on November 12, confiscated almost all of the imperial family's assets, including their former homes. Eckartsau had the advantage—besides being remote—of being privately owned by the Habsburgs, but compared to their former palaces, it was terribly spartan. Overnight, Zita's family lost almost everything. At their new home, they were "without fuel for the heating stoves or more than the barest necessities in the royal pantry."[7] As Zita recalled, "Food supplies were supposed to be sent out to us from Vienna but the lorries arrived irregularly and, more than once, they were attacked and picked clean on the way. Everything else was in short supply ... The electricity was more off than on and some everyday essentials like matches were missing altogether."[8] The problem of their difficult living conditions came down to the fact that "the court exchequer had been dismissed and the new authorities in Vienna cut off the allowance for the upkeep of the dynasty."[9] Despite the family's hardships, Zita's children found Eckartsau "extraordinary but still very beautiful."[10]

For the next few weeks, delegations from the remnants of the Austro-Hungarian Empire trickled into Eckartsau. Charles met with each of them, showing his usual characteristic calm and respect for each individual. Zita's task during this time was equally daunting. It was up to her to care for her five children, all under the age of six, while being pregnant for the sixth time. The few free minutes she had each day were spent turning the barely livable hunting lodge into a home.

Security was also an issue. Sentiments against the monarchy were rising, and there were only a handful of guards to protect the family. Their entourage, which only a number of weeks before had numbered in the hundreds, had dwindled to less than fifty. The empress feared for the safety of her family, especially after angry crowds were spotted outside the gates. To make matters worse, the drafty, damp climate at Eckartsau played havoc with the health of the emperor and the children. By Christmas, Zita was the only person in the household who had not fallen ill. "Christmas 1918 was a rather sombre festival," she recalled, "especially as the emperor, who was anyway suffering from repeated heart attacks and overstrain, had gone down with a severe attack of Spanish influenza ten days before and was now really ill. All the children caught it as well ... Charles Ludwig, for example, who was then barely eighteen months old, very nearly died."[11]

The empress was determined to give her children as happy a Christmas as possible, despite being nearly destitute from having had all their assets seized. She had a tree brought in from the forest and decorated. On Christmas Eve, she spread out a pile of tiny gifts for everyone. She recalled how they were able to provide gifts: "We had found at Eckartsau a trunk we had once used on our official journeys which was nearly full of minor presents and this came in most useful."[12] For the servants who were with the Habsburgs, Zita gave each of them specially wrapped up scraps of chocolate that she had been saving. By Christmas Day, the emperor was dangerously sick. His fever skyrocketed. Zita's eldest son, Otto, remembered that his father "got up for the occasion but was so weak that [he] had to remain seated in an armchair and retired again to bed immediately afterwards."[13]

⋯

The end of the Great War brought with it the end of Old Europe. Almost every monarchical power was overthrown, replaced by republics or dictatorships.

The Habsburgs, Hohenzollerns, and Romanovs had been dethroned, exiled, or executed. The federal monarchies that had made up the German Empire were dissolved and reformed into the Weimar Republic. The diverse ethnic groups that belonged to the Habsburgs for six hundred years all broke away. What had been one great empire were now half a dozen smaller nations that included Czechoslovakia, Yugoslavia, and a unified Romania. But it was perhaps the former empire of Tsar Nicholas II and Tsarina Alexandra Feodorovna that was the most tragic of all, whose rich past was now washed away in violence and bloodshed.

In Britain, whatever popularity George and Mary enjoyed in 1914 had exploded four years later. The king and queen were more popular than ever and planned on settling down to a quiet, retiring life to enjoy peace they had not known for years. But as the rest of the world struggled to move past the horror of the last four years, the British royal family was hit by a personal tragedy. At 5:30 a.m. on January 18, 1919, the queen received a telephone call informing her that Prince John, her youngest son, died during the night when a severe seizure caused his heart to fail. The thirteen-year-old prince had led a retiring life at Wood House; however, despite her son's isolation, Mary suffered his death like any loving mother. She wrote to her old childhood friend, Emily Alcock.

> For him it is a great release, as his malady was becoming worse as he grew older, & he has thus been spared much suffering. I cannot say how grateful we feel to God for having taken him in such a peaceful way, he just slept quietly into his heavenly home, no pain, no struggle, just peace for the poor little troubled spirit which had been a great anxiety to us for many years, ever since he was four years old—The first break in the family circle is hard to bear but people have been so kind & sympathetic & this has helped us much.[14]

The private funeral for Prince John was conducted on January 21 at the church in Sandringham. Mary confided her memories about the service to her diary that night: "Canon Dalton & Dr. Brownhill conducted the service which was awfully sad and touching. Many of our own people and the villagers were present. We thanked all Johnnie's servants who have been so good and faithful to him."[15]

The queen did not have much time to mourn the loss of John because only a few months later came the Paris Peace Conference to settle the fate of Europe after the war. Never before in history had there been the precedent of reconstruction after such wholesale devastation. In soldiers alone, there was "an awesome loss of lives. The British Empire had lost 767,000 men; France 1,383,000; the United States 81,000; Italy 564,000; Germany 1,686,000; and Russia 1,700,000. At least 1,000,000 men were missing in action, and over 12,000,000 had suffered serious injury, many maimed, blinded, or mentally unbalanced."[16] It was estimated that Austria-Hungary had lost more than 17 percent of its active male population.[17] The humanitarian crisis that ensued after the war was equally devastating. In Russia, the hardships imposed by the war and the Bolsheviks' brutal regime left somewhere between five and ten million people dead from starvation between 1918 and 1922.[18] One of the most pressing concerns at the time of the peace conference was the rampant Spanish influenza sweeping the globe. Despite its name, this deadly pandemic was believed to have originated somewhere in the central United States. The death toll, estimated somewhere between fifty and one hundred million, easily dwarfed those caused by the war.

At the peace conference to rebuild postwar Europe, Britain was expected to play one of the leading roles. Representing Great Britain at the bargaining table was David Lloyd George, its irascible prime minister. The conference was expected to bring together some of the greatest statesmen of the early twentieth century, including Woodrow Wilson of the United States and Georges Clemenceau of France. Germany was forced to take responsibility for the war. Austria-Hungary, though, suffered the worst breakup. It lost all of its territories that did not have a majority of ethnic Germans. The new state of German-Austria (which was renamed the Republic of Austria a few months later) was reduced to less than half of its former size with no access to the Adriatic Sea. Semiautonomous regions were absorbed into neighboring Allied nations, such as Italy and Romania. Despite the meager portions that some of the smaller Allies received, Great Britain emerged victorious as Europe's only remaining imperial power. In addition to its own overseas territories, the empire received Germany's colonies in Africa. With the defeat of the Ottoman Empire—the Porte would completely disintegrate in 1922—Britain also became the dominant power in the Middle East. Over the course of the next twenty-five years, British foreign policy in places like Iran and Palestine would fundamentally shape global events well into the twenty-first century.

During the conference, Mary and George played host to an old friend— Queen Marie of Romania, another granddaughter of Queen Victoria and the king's first cousin. Marie used her stay at Buckingham Palace to launch a whirlwind campaign to gain British support for war-ravaged Romania. Marie remarked about the "tremendous emotion" of arriving in London after so many years away, where she was "greeted at the station by George and May, with a crowd of officials and many, many friends."[19] Her visit to London lasted only a few days before she returned to Paris for the remainder of the conference, which had become mired in petty squabbles among the delegates. The stalled peace process weighed heavily on Queen Mary's mind. "Alas," she wrote to an old American friend, "the end of the war seems to have brought great unrest behind it, it seems such a pity that all classes had worked so well during the war, it is not possible now to work for the reconstruction of the world—it would have been a splendid opportunity to have come together."[20]

With much of the world's attention fixed on the high-stakes negotiations taking place in Paris, few noticed that the British Empire was beginning to crumble, despite its territorial acquisitions at the bargaining table. The high mortality rate of conscripted Indian soldiers during the war led to a resurgence of anti-British activity in India, which was only made worse by the brutal, almost dictatorial rule that the British colonial government established in 1918. Complete press censorship, arrests without warrants or trials, and martial law turned British India into a powder keg that exploded in 1919 after the massacre in the city of Amritsar in northwestern India. What began as anti-British demonstrations turned violent when five Englishmen were killed. An English female missionary who just happened to be riding her bike nearby was violently assaulted. The retribution a week later by the British government was brutal. As tens of thousands of people crammed into a public garden known as the Jallianwala Bagh near the Golden Temple, British officers opened fire on the crowds at point-blank range. Terrified people literally trampled one another to death as they desperately fought to reach the exits; some were shot as they tried climbing over the garden wall. After six minutes of horrific bloodshed, 379 people were dead, with another 1,500 wounded. The loss of life and the attacks Britain received from the world were harsh reminders that, although the British monarchy was the strongest in the world, in the postwar years, its empire was being shaken to its very foundations.

The New Year brought little relief to Empress Zita of Austria and her family. In spite of her best efforts, Christmas had been exceptionally gloomy. It was becoming obvious that the hunting lodge at Eckartsau was by no means a permanent home. Its damp climate became inhospitable as the temperature outside plummeted. It was also becoming increasingly difficult to heat the building, forcing the young children to huddle together for warmth.

Any hope that Charles and Zita may have had of permanently settling their family abroad was dashed when Swiss authorities went back on a previous offer of total asylum. Instead, the most they would offer the family were traveling visas. In February 1919, the need to get out of the country became more pressing when the first democratic elections were held in Austria. The result was an overwhelming majority for the Socialists, who were antagonistic toward the members of the Habsburg family. A few weeks later, the government passed the Habsburg Law of 1919, forbidding any Habsburgs from entering Austria without renouncing their imperial titles. The government went a step further and confiscated all the land belonging to the members of the imperial family. Estimates at the time placed the worth of these estates at well into the hundreds of millions of dollars. Years later, Archduke Otto wrote that everything, even "all the data of the family including the family archives have been taken from us by the Republic of Austria so that we have none."[21]

Internationally, the emperor and empress continued to come under fire, but unlike the slanders against Nicholas and Alexandra (which had some elements of truth), those being made against the Habsburgs were totally unfounded. One American newspaper ran a story in February 1919 claiming "that former Austrian emperor Karl is contemplating seeking a divorce from his wife, Zita, on the grounds that she assisted Italian victories" during the war.[22] Those who knew the emperor and empress refused to acknowledge such slander since divorce completely went against what they both believed about marriage. Their continued devotion to one another through their trials also helped dispel the divorce rumors.

The safety of Zita's family seemed to be in danger until help arrived on February 15. Strangely enough, that help did not come from the Austrians, the Hungarians, or even the Swiss. Instead, the two people who took up the cause of the Austrian imperial family were none other than King George V and Queen Mary. George had very strong feelings when it came to Charles. According to Empress Zita's official biographer Gordon Brook-Shepherd,

> the King nursed a distinctly uneasy conscience over his reluctance to support a rescue bid for his cousin, Tsar Nicholas, the year before. The butchery of the Russian Emperor and his family at Ekaterinburg by Bolshevik thugs had brought soul-searching as well as shock. There was no blood tie between the houses of Windsor and Habsburg and, moreover, they had fought for four bitter years in opposite camps. But the King had not forgotten that, as Archduke Karl, newly-engaged to his Bourbon Princess, the beleaguered squire of Eckartsau had attended his coronation in London (indeed, for the procession, he had been placed in the carriage immediately in front of those carrying the British royal family). But the events of the summer of 1918 rather than those of the summer of 1911 were uppermost in the King's mind now. When

told that Eckartsau could easily become a second Ekaterinburg, he hastily arranged for emergency military protection.[23]

Zita's brother Sixtus had visited Buckingham Palace to seek help for his sister and her family. In a meeting with the king and queen, Sixtus gravely explained the danger of the situation, alluding to the massacre at Ekaterinburg. Queen Mary was deeply troubled by what she heard. Turning to her husband, she said, "What Sixtus has told us is very serious." The king was equally concerned. "We will immediately do what is necessary," he said. According to Gordon Brook-Shepherd and Queen Elizabeth II's personal librarian, Sir Robin Mackworth-Young, the exact details of this meeting were never recorded, but it was enough to spur the British monarchs into action.[24] George deployed two British colonels to Eckartsau in an effort to relieve some of the family's burdens. The officers in question were Colonel Sir Thomas Cunningham, Britain's military representative to the Allied Mission in Vienna, and Colonel Summerhayes, a member of the Royal Army Medical Corps. They were ordered to "endeavour by every means ... to ameliorate the conditions of life of the Emperor and Empress and give them the moral support of the British government."[25]

The family at Eckartsau was informed that Summerhayes and Cunningham would be arriving in February 1919 to be of service. Zita described how her husband was "astonished and overwhelmed with gratitude and relief and also [was] deeply touched by this gesture of solidarity from one monarch to another across all the barriers of war." With Zita's help, Charles drafted a short thank-you note for the king of England.

Majesty,

I am happy to be able to thank Your Majesty for the delicate attention in sending Colonel Summerhayes. I am very touched by this courteous act and at the same time am very grateful. The Colonel is a charming man who fulfills his mission with great tact and amiability. The situation in the world is very difficult for us sovereigns. May God have pity on humanity's suffering and soon give them the rest they need!

Your Majesty's good brother and cousin,

Charles

Eckartsau, 21 February 1919[26]

After a few weeks, a third officer—Colonel Edward Strutt—arrived on the scene to relieve Cunningham and Summerhayes. A fluent linguist from an aristocratic background with a deep Catholic faith, Strutt developed a strong rapport with Zita and Charles. He recorded his impression of the emperor in his diary. "It was impossible to avoid liking him," Strutt wrote; "an eminently lovable if weak man, by no means a fool, and ready to face his end as bravely as his ancestress, Marie Antoinette."[27] Strutt was also struck by the empress, whom he described as having "extraordinary strength of character." Colonel Strutt noted that there was a determination "written in the lines of her square little chin, intelligence in the vivacious brown eyes, intellect in the broad forehead half hidden by masses of dark hair."[28] He was deeply moved by the empress's strength, believing that if she had the chance, she alone could have carried the Austrian monarchy. It was his opinion that Zita "must always share with the Queens of the Belgians and Rumania the honour of being one of the three great royal women of the war."[29] The colonel made just as strong an impression on the family as they did on him. Otto, Zita's eldest son, recalled decades later, "I still think with great respect and great gratitude toward him. Recently, an English person asked me whether I was not full of resentment against the British for the way they had treated my father later on in his exile. I replied: 'But after all, there was Colonel Strutt.'"[30]

By March, anger in Austria toward the monarchy was at an all-time high. Soldiers belonging to the new government made regular assaults on the grounds surrounding the hunting lodge. One particularly violent incident occurred when a cart loaded with food, clothing, and medicine bound for Eckartsau was intercepted by a group of young officers who proceeded to destroy and then light the cart and its contents on fire. When the badly beaten cart driver arrived at Eckartsau, he was carrying a note from a lieutenant addressed to "Mr. Karl Habsburg." With the army now clearly against them, it became imperative for Zita and her family to get out of Austria as quickly as possible. On March 15, the British War Office received intelligence suggesting the family was in imminent danger. They sent a note to their mission in Vienna, saying, "Most desirable to get the Emperor out of Austria without delay. All possible steps to be taken to expedite departure."[31] It was now up to Colonel Strutt to get the family safely out of the country, but Charles was implacable. He refused to leave Austria under any circumstances. The colonel realized his best chance was to appeal to the empress. He met with her alone, making a passionate speech saying that, from everything he could see, the country was entirely against them. He would get them out of the country somehow, he said, without Charles having to abdicate. For a moment, Zita fell silent.

"A dead Habsburg is no good to anyone, whereas a live one, with a family, may yet be," Strutt finally told her. It was enough. She smiled and took his hand.

"I will do all I can to help," she replied. "We will leave under your orders and arrangements and trust you to avoid Karl's having to abdicate."[32]

The options for the family's exile were limited, since most countries wanted nothing to do with the deposed dynasty. The years after World War I saw the birth of a number of national republics that had once been monarchies, and most of those wanted to distance themselves from royalty as much as possible. With much of Europe out of the question, the only real possibility left for the Habsburgs was Switzerland. When the moment came for Colonel Strutt to tell Charles he had no choice but to go into exile, the emperor looked him directly in the face and asked, "Only promise me that I shall leave as emperor and not as a thief in the night." His face gravely serious, Strutt replied, "Sir, I promise."[33]

After an exhausting political chess match, Strutt managed to secure a promise from Austrian chancellor Karl Renner that the Habsburgs could leave Austria unconditionally. On the afternoon of Sunday, March 23, Zita, Charles, their family, and a handful of retainers left Austria. At 10:00 a.m., the imperial family attended Mass in the chapel at Eckartsau. The deeply moving service was performed by the court bishop Seydl with Otto serving as altar boy. Once the Mass ended, the entire congregation broke out into the imperial anthem. This was especially poignant because it was "destined to be the last time it was sung before an Austrian Emperor, who sat with his family in the gallery."[34] By the end of the song, everyone in the chapel was reduced to tears. The rest of the day was rife with emotion. As the children gathered their belongings, Zita packed her family's most treasured possessions, which included a trunk of dazzling jewels. One of the most precious pieces the empress was taking with her was a six-row pearl necklace and chain of diamonds that had once belonged to Empress Maria Theresa.

At 6:35 p.m., Charles and Zita, locked arm in arm, descended down the grand staircase at Eckartsau to bid farewell to the last home their family had in Austria. Gathered on the ground floor for a tearful good-bye were the many servants, groundskeepers, and townspeople who had remained loyal to the imperial family throughout their struggle. At the sight of the emperor and empress, everyone fell to their knees in hushed reverence. Colonel Strutt observed in his journal that the "dignity of the Imperial couple at so heart-rending a moment was superlative."[35] The family filed into the automobiles for the twenty-minute drive to the train station at Kopfstetten.

Many of the Austrian people were deeply saddened by the departure of their imperial family. Joining the family in exile were a small group of servants and a number of Zita's relatives, including her brothers, who had fought for Austria in the war, and her mother, the Duchess of Parma. When the motorcade arrived at Kopfstetten, Zita and her family were met by a crowd of nearly two thousand people, all in tears, waiting in the rain. Deeply moved, the emperor and empress took the time to shake hands with as many people as they could before Colonel Strutt implored them to board the train. There were twenty-five people in total aboard the train that night. As it lumbered its way through Austria, the reality of her family's situation came crashing down on the empress. "My family has been exiled from France, Italy and Portugal," she muttered to Strutt. "When I married I became an Austrian subject, and now I am an exile from Austria. Colonel Strutt, tell me to what country do I belong now?"[36] There came no reply.

Nearly a day later, the train pulled into the station at Buchs in Switzerland. The first stop after disembarking was Wartegg, an old castle on Lake Constance that had once belonged to Zita's father after his own exile from Parma. Waiting to greet Zita and her family were many of her Bourbon relatives, including her brothers Felix and Sixtus. From Wartegg, Charles sent a message to King George V.

> My dear brother,
> We have arrived on the hospitable soil of Switzerland with the military escort that the Government of Your Majesty has kindly placed at my disposal, I desire to express to you directly and without delay my feelings of gratitude which makes me feel the support and generosity of the British Empire in these cruel circumstances that I believe are only temporary.... I have nothing but praise, especially for the steps taken by Colonel Strutt, who has accompanied me thus far and whose character is full of fortitude and has been greatly appreciated by me.
>
> Charles
> Wartegg, 11 April 1919[37]

Wartegg offered the family a modicum of safety, but it was incredibly cramped. The castle became a rallying point for dozens of Habsburgs and Bourbons. The emperor's mother, brother, and cousins arrived. Most of Zita's family came too, including many of the half-siblings from her father's first marriage. Every floor of the castle, including the attic, was occupied by exiled royals. The servants and staff who accompanied the imperial family were forced to find housing in nearby villages and hotels.

Crowded though Wartegg may have been, Zita was pleased to have so many relatives around. Her children had the chance to once again play in the castle gardens and enjoy life away from political upheaval. One visitor even played in the snow with the children and helped them build a snowman.

Charles was offered the chance to take a moment to exhale after the tumult of the last year. As spring returned to Europe, the Habsburgs found their spirits temporarily lifted. But within a few weeks, the Swiss government began pressuring Charles to relocate his family further west, deeper within the country. The Swiss authorities were worried because Wartegg was just across the border from Austria. "From the balconies of Wartegg, the mountains of Vorarlberg seemed almost close enough to touch," wrote one Habsburg biographer.[38] The Swiss government had also received pressure from the Austrians who, on April 3, ratified the Habsburg Law. Designed to secure the country's new republicanism, Charles and Zita were now forbidden from ever returning to Austria. The law also stripped them of their sovereignty and titles and forbade any members of the imperial dynasty outside of the immediate imperial family from setting foot on Austrian soil unless they formally renounced all their titles, styles, and claims to the throne.

Not wanting to aggravate the country that harbored them, Charles and Zita relocated their family to Villa Prangins on the shores of Lake Geneva. Their new home was an eclectic mixture of "Venetian-style watchtowers, French-style conical domes and Tudor-style chimney stacks."[39] Inside, it offered them more space than Wartegg. The family took over use of the entire ground floor. The second floor was used by the members of their court: Bishop Seydl, the family's priest; Count Ledochowski, the emperor's aide-de-camp; Zita's ladies-in-waiting, the countesses Bellegarde and Kerssenbrock; and the court secretaries, barons von Schonta and Werkmann. The other two wings housed the domestic staff, consisting of a cook, a footman, and the maids.

The family moved into Prangins at the end of May 1919. On September 5, Zita went into labor with her sixth child, a son. Acknowledging their new humble circumstances, Charles and Zita named the boy Rudolf. The name was chosen in honor of Rudolf IV, the Swiss count who founded the Habsburgs: "The imperial family were returning to their humbler roots; this symbolised their new lifestyle, one in which, to all outward appearances, Karl was leading the existence of any prosperous Swiss country gentleman."[40] After Rudolf's birth, the family settled down to a quiet life they had not known in years. Circumstances seemed to ease for Charles and Zita, but changes were in store. The political upheaval that would sweep across the former Austro-Hungarian empire was set to engulf the emperor and empress yet again. Once it was all over, their exile would be final and would mark the closing chapter of their life together.

24

The Quest for the Crown

(1919–20)

At Amerongen Castle in the Netherlands, Augusta Victoria was a shell of her former self. Her only consolation was being with her husband again. If Empress Zita was more like Queen Mary in her response to adversity, then Dona was a mirror of Tsarina Alexandra's more melancholy personality in times of hardship. The former German empress's health and psyche were shattered by her country's revolution and the toppling of her family from the throne. Wilhelm became worried about his wife, who had more difficulty accepting their circumstances than anyone else at Amerongen. Dona lacked the faculty to adapt to new situations the way her husband could. Wilhelm "realized that, having originally come from humbler surroundings than Potsdam, she could not reconcile herself to living modestly again in Holland." In the end, it was her pride, which was "nourished by her position as one of the great ladies of Europe" that "prevented her from accepting with resignation the topsy-turvydom" of postwar, republican Europe.[1]

From the day she arrived at Amerongen, Dona sequestered herself in the small suite of rooms that had been set aside for her use on the castle's upper floor. Initially, the only person admitted into her presence was her lifelong friend and lady-in-waiting, Countess Keller. Somber, morose, and perennially depressed, the former empress and queen refused to participate in the little bit of court life that went on at Amerongen. Even when she ate her meals, she did so alone. One of the few pastimes she did partake in was letter writing. She wrote most often to her daughter, Sissy, who was still living with her in-laws at Gmunden. The former Duchess of Brunswick recalled that despite the difficult circumstances facing her mother, Dona wrote often and "always pleasantly." But Sissy added gravely, "I could read between the lines the pressure she was under." For the most part, letter writing was Dona's sole activity. "Perhaps I would get some strength back if I had something to do in my own home," she admitted. "Here, I always have melancholy thoughts and, at the most, letters to write."[2] Aside from continuing her correspondence, one activity she began to occupy herself with was knitting. She hand made hundreds of articles of clothing to be sent to children living in the poorest parts of Germany. These were later distributed by the Red Cross, of which she had once been the head. Only a handful of people ever saw her from day to day, and that was usually limited to her husband or Countess Keller, who continued to bring Dona her meals. The only visitors she received—beyond her family and staff—were children from the nearby village of Zuiderzee. Dona was always intrigued by these children, who often wore traditional, old-fashioned Dutch country attire.

While other royals who found themselves deposed after the war were enduring hardship and poverty, Wilhelm and Dona were afforded a degree of luxury. In addition to nearly fifty live-in servants who waited on them at Amerongen, over a hundred courtiers joined them in exile. Not all of them did so from honorable motives. Many accompanied the former monarchs out of fear of falling into insignificance with the collapse of the monarchy. Wilhelm and Dona were permitted to keep twenty-five train carts sent by the German government full of personal belongings, including furniture, an automobile, and a boat. In a surprisingly magnanimous gesture, the Germans also agreed to acknowledge a number of the Hohenzollerns' privately owned properties in Berlin that were worth more than $2 million at the time. Wilhelm also had nearly $12 million tied up in stocks and bonds, though these would not be liquidated until 1926. When Wilhelm died years later, he was estimated to be worth 14 million German reichsmarks, or more than $62 million in today's money.[3] The assets that the Hohenzollerns brought with them into exile helped fund the semicontinuation of their daily routines. Meals were attended by no less than twenty people, Wilhelm and his aides took afternoon walks in the parks around Amerongen, and courtiers insisted on having all their expenses paid. Wilhelm and Dona made no effort to be optimistic about their circumstances. This was supremely ironic given the level of comfort they received, compared to Nicholas and Alexandra or Charles and Zita.

Dona's bleak frame of mind led to her suffering from deep depression, which she blamed on the "catastrophe" that had befallen her family. According to one of the hangers-on at Amerongen, the overthrow of the Hohenzollerns "had been infinitely more shattering to her than to" Wilhelm.[4] "The revolution broke the Empress's heart," Wilhelm wrote in his memoirs. "She aged visibly from November, 1918, onward, and could not resist her bodily ills with the strength of before."[5] He reiterated this to their daughter: "She suffers dreadfully and her condition often makes me despair, especially when the pain overcomes her."[6] Her son Willy wrote that "she suffers severely, is physically ill, but will not give way; she knows only one thought, namely, the welfare of my father and of us all, and has only one wish, which is to lighten for us what we have to bear."[7] Wilhelm's doctor made regular visits to examine her, but at nearly sixty two years old, Augusta Victoria was never again healthy after her heart attack. Courtiers at Amerongen knew their matriarch was not long for this world. One such individual who saw Dona on a handful of occasions left her reminiscences of the ex-empress in exile.

> She was, as everyone knows, more interested in the hidden domestic life than in the public political one. She believed that the role [*sic*] of her husband was divinely ordained, and when the foundations of this her world were scattered she could only think it was because malign forces had triumphed. Thus *her* plight at least seemed pathetic to the onlookers at [Amerongen], and for a woman, distressed in mind and destitute of state, there was only human sympathy.[8]

As his wife glowered and shrank, Wilhelm became immersed in bitter resentment, blaming everyone around him for his failed reign. Writing to August von Mackensen, one of his former generals, he grandiosely decried his abdication as "the deepest, most disgusting shame ever perpetrated by a person in history, [which] the Germans have done to themselves."[9] Wilhelm's behavior and growing victim mentality made him nearly unbearable to his own staff. Even his loyal aide-de-camp General Hans von Plessen wrote in his diary, "The Emperor has a cold heart towards everyone, even towards his children. He is ungrateful, had always acted, but never applied himself. He had never done any serious work."[10]

By mid-1919, public attention shifted back to the Hohenzollerns. Perhaps because of Wilhelm's very visible role during the war, he and his family became the subject of scrutiny and curiosity. Legal, political, and academic circles all began putting the former emperor, and also his eldest son, under a microscope. Numerous studies evaluating Wilhelm's mental stability and fitness to rule were released, including *The Madness of Wilhelm II*, *Kaiser Wilhelm Periodically Insane!*, and *Wilhelm II as Cripple and Psychopath*.[11]

On the international stage, there were constant demands by foreign governments for Wilhelm's extradition so that he could be tried for war crimes.

This became an official objective during the Paris Peace Conference, with Article 227 of the final treaty stipulating that the "Allies and associated Powers publicly indict Wilhelm II von Hohenzollern, former Emperor of Germany, for the gravest violation of the international moral code and the sanctity of treaties."[12] A special international court to hear the case for extradition was to be convened, presided over by representatives of the United States, Britain, France, Italy, and Japan. David Lloyd George "suggested he be hanged."[13] The British press ran the headlines HANG THE KAISER! and MAKE GERMANY PAY![14] One newspaper showed a cartoon depicting a rope tied between the Eiffel Tower and Cleopatra's Needle in London with Wilhelm suspended by his wrists. Lloyd George's demands for Wilhelm's extradition may have been, at least partly, only rhetoric. Britain was in the midst of an election at the time, and Lloyd George, determined to stay in office, found Germany an easy scapegoat. G. S. Viereck, an American journalist who became acquainted with Wilhelm and Dona in 1921, believed that "Lloyd George's electioneering campaign was a daily torture to the Kaiserin and a chief cause of her ultimate death."[15]

Other Allied leaders were going a step further in seeking accountability for the war. They demanded more than a thousand Germans be handed over and tried for war crimes, including Wilhelm's eldest son and the infamous Crown Prince Rupprecht of Bavaria. Others wanted to see the former emperor exiled permanently to Africa or South America, similar to the way Napoleon was exiled to Saint Helena. Dona was now more protective of her husband than ever. She knew that if he were extradited to Paris or London, he would almost certainly be executed. She was greatly relieved when Queen Wilhelmina refused to give him up, citing Dutch neutrality in the war and the fact that handing Wilhelm over "would have compromised Dutch sovereignty."[16] Wilhelm took public opinion toward him very personally. He considered visiting a plastic surgeon to have his appearance altered and later escaping unnoticed into the night. He thought about smuggling himself back into Germany to live out his days hiding on the country estate of his friend Princess Maria Christina of Salm-Salm. He also contemplated committing suicide. This last possibility resonated with the increasingly fatalistic Dona, who told him, "William, then we'll go together into the beyond."[17]

By January 1920, Wilhelm's defeatist phase seems to have passed; so too did efforts to extradite him. On March 24, David Lloyd George washed his hands of the ex-emperor and declared he and his wife were solely the responsibility of the Netherlands. Wilhelm realized it was time to make a more permanent home, since Amerongen was intended to be only a temporary lodging while Wilhelm's fate was decided. He bought a new home, Huis Doorn, three miles outside Amerongen. It belonged to Baroness Ella van

Heemstra, the mother of Hollywood actress Audrey Hepburn. Doorn was an eighteenth-century manor house with its own tower and almost sixty hectares of forest surrounding it. What appealed to Wilhelm and Dona most, besides its rustic beauty, was that it offered them a level of privacy they had not experienced since they arrived in the Netherlands. Amerongen was full of curious spectators who were eager to catch a glimpse of the ex-emperor and his reclusive wife. The funds for the purchase of Doorn came from the sale of a number of the Hohenzollerns' private yachts, including Dona's beloved *Iduna*, upon which she had spent so much time traveling the Greek Isles.

While Wilhelm made the arrangements for their eventual move, Dona took charge of furnishing their new home before they moved in. For a brief period, she seemed to be her old self again. Perhaps the greatest contributing factor to this reprieve in her long illness was Sissy's arrival for a visit in March 1920. The journey from Gmuden to Amerongen was a perilous one, the result of the increasing violence of the German Revolution. During a brief stop in Potsdam to visit her former homes, heavy fighting between monarchists and republicans in the streets made the city unsafe. Sissy's husband was forced to return to Gmunden with their children for their own safety. "The journey was gruesome, for the revolt had spread westwards and I thought I would never see my husband and children again," Sissy admitted in her memoirs. "However, the thought of my seriously ill mother drove me on." When she finally arrived at Amerongen, Sissy wrote that the "joy of reunion with my parents was indescribable, but I was upset to see how … my mother's illness had changed her imposing appearance."[18]

By the time of her daughter's visit, Dona was so weak that she could no longer climb the stairs at Amerongen and had to have a lift installed to allow her to move between floors. The presence of her daughter and the time she spent finding and placing furniture in Huis Doorn helped somewhat to reinvigorate Dona's broken spirit. It also afforded her the opportunity to focus on something other than her family's mounting problems. Her eldest son, Willy, had settled on Wieringen Island on the Baltic Sea where he took up a job as a tradesman. His wife, Cecilie, refused to join him, using the overthrow of the monarchy as the excuse she needed to finally separate from her adulterous husband. The marriages of Dona's other sons, who had stayed in Germany as private citizens, collapsed. The childless Eitel-Fritz and Lotte were under constant scrutiny from both their family and the foreign press for lecherous affairs the couple was known to have. Early in their marriage, Wilhelm and Dona were furious when Lotte openly took a lover. Lotte, who had long since drifted apart from her mother-in-law, was called as a witness in a divorce trial where she announced of the accused, "our intimate relations continued even after my marriage to the Kaiser's son."[19] By March 1919, the *New York Times* was reporting that Eitel-Fritz had begun the process of divorcing Lotte. The article also alleged that "the former Prince attempted to begin proceedings before the war [but] his father vetoed the plan."[20]

In March 1920, Auwi divorced his wife, Alexandra Victoria, after a long and bitter separation. "This marriage," wrote Sissy, "which was greeted with such joy by the two mothers [Dona and Calma], alas, did not live up to their expectations."[21] In the divorce proceedings, Auwi won sole custody of their only child, Alexander. Alexandra Victoria eventually remarried to a commoner and later told reporters she was infinitely happier as a commoner's wife than living as a princess of Prussia. Like Eitel-Fritz, Auwi and his son settled in Potsdam near the Neues Palais. Auwi continued to cause his parents grief by taking an active role in the German socialist movement, which eventually paved the way for the rise of Adolf Hitler's Nazi party in the 1930s. Of Dona's six sons, the only two who caused her little difficulty were Adalbert and Oscar. Adalbert, along with his wife, Adelaide, and their two young children, settled down to a quiet life in La Tour-de-Peilz, on Lake Geneva in Switzerland. Oscar's life remained devoid of scandals as well—though, eventually, he too would join the Nazi ranks. He and his wife, Ina, were raising three children, whom the ex-empress doted on. Since his abdication, Wilhelm had grown so close to Oscar that he forgave his morganatic wedding. This may not have been a great leap, since Ina was reportedly Wilhelm's favorite daughter-in-law. Using his authority as the head of the House of Hohenzollern, Wilhelm, under the witness of Cardinal Brandr Beekman-Ellner, bestowed upon his daughter-in-law the style and title of Her Royal Highness the Princess of Prussia, although since the monarchy no longer existed, this was purely a courtesy title.

Reports of unrest in Hungary had been mounting since the end of the war. The country's loss of two-thirds of its territory at the Paris Peace Conference triggered turmoil amongst all classes. The people soon turned their anger on Prime Minister Michael Karolyi. By 1919, his government was overthrown by a Communist coup d'état led by the insidious Bela Kun. But Kun's own junta failed after only six months, when Hungary was humiliated in a short-lived war with Romania. The National Assembly of Hungary soon proclaimed that the country should restore the monarchy—but without asking Emperor Charles I to return as king. In March 1920, with the National Army in control of the Hungarian Parliament Building, the assembly voted Nicholas Horthy, a Hungarian admiral, as regent. An ambitious man with a thirst for power, Horthy served in the imperial navy and had been an aide-de-camp to Emperor

Franz Joseph. During the war, one of the archdukes had recommended that Charles promote Horthy to commander in chief of the navy. Upon becoming regent, Horthy's first condition was that he be granted expanded executive powers and personal equality for him with the position of king.

In Switzerland, Charles and Zita were alarmed by the chain of events in Budapest. At first, "Horthy immediately sent protestations of loyalty to [Charles at] Prangins but, as the months passed, he became more evasive as Karl pressed him over handing back the throne." Horthy made the Royal Palace in Budapest his new home, but what was most difficult for Charles and Zita to accept was when "Horthy declared himself, as Regent, to be a [royal] Duke and started receiving foreign ambassadors as 'His Serene Highness.'"[22]

Prompted by his family and other royalists, Charles traveled to Hungary. He only agreed to go on the condition that Zita accompany him, but when she announced to everyone that she was pregnant for the seventh time, the entire plan fell into doubt. Charles and his advisors wanted a postponement, but Zita would not hear of it. "Every minute counts!" she exhorted her husband.[23] After a long discussion, she convinced him to go. He first traveled to Strasbourg, where he met one of his followers who supplied him with a train ticket and a forged Spanish passport. Dressed in an ordinary gentleman's suit with a walking stick, Charles arrived in Hungary on March 26, 1921—Easter weekend—to reinstate himself as the rightful king. Having shaved his trademark mustache and using forged passports, Charles slipped across the Austro-Hungarian border and traveled directly to the home of Count Janos Mikes, a well-known Hungarian monarchist who was in favor of Charles's restoration.

At Mikes's palace, the emperor called a secret meeting of his Privy Council, which included Horthy's minister of education and his military advisor Colonel Antal Lehar, who pledged Hungarian troops to support Charles. "But I don't want to take Hungary with soldiers," Charles replied quietly. "I am not *usurping* a throne, you know. And there is to be no fighting."[24] But when attempts to negotiate with Prime Minister Pal Teleki failed at 2:00 a.m., Charles decided to confront the regent himself. On March 27, Charles—dressed in a military cadet's uniform that his aide found at the last minute—arrived unannounced at Horthy's country estate, Kenderes, as he and his wife were sitting down to Easter dinner. The two men sequestered themselves in Horthy's office—the same office that had once belonged to Charles. The two-hour meeting was exhausting. The regent would later describe it as one of "the most difficult moments in my entire life" and a "thoroughly odious" experience. Charles told him the time had come to hand over power.

"This is a disaster," Horthy replied. "In the name of God, Your Majesty must leave at once and return to Switzerland, before its too late and the

[Allied] Powers learn of your presence in Budapest." The emperor spent the rest of the time locked with Horthy in a battle of wills, using every argument he could think of to induce the regent to surrender the crown. Exhausted from having been awake for more than two days, Charles reached the end of his rope.

"I stick by my position. I'll give you five minutes to think it over," he told Horthy.[25]

Horthy and Charles eventually agreed to a three-week political cease-fire so both men could strengthen their positions, but it soon became clear that the odds were stacked against the emperor. At the end of March, both Yugoslavia and Czechoslovakia declared that they would be willing to start another war if the Habsburgs were restored to the throne. The Allies, led by France, were unwilling to recognize a Hungarian kingdom led by Charles. By April 6, Charles was forced to concede defeat. Not only was the army still loyal to Horthy, but Hungarian support for the monarchy had all but evaporated. Most of the people were apathetic at the sight of the last emperor. Depressed and suffering from a severe cold he caught on his first night in Hungary, Charles dejectedly returned to Switzerland no closer to reclaiming the throne. The foreign press quickly jumped on the chance to show yet another failed endeavor on the emperor's part. In England, one newspaper wrote drily,

> the outcome of the interview between Karl and the Regent is best demonstrated by the fact that the ex-King was forced to leave Budapest immediately for Szombathely.
>
> Soon thereafter it became known that Regent Horthy had minced no words in informing Karl that the ill-timed visit was detrimental to the best interests of Hungary, since the country needed nothing so much as peace and time for recovery.
>
> The Regent further assured His Majesty of his, Horthy's, unchanging loyalty and devotion, explaining nonetheless that the mandate placed upon him by the Nation could not be laid down except by parliamentary procedure.
>
> At half past five the ex-King left Budapest in the company of Prime Minister Teleky, Count Sigray and the commanding officer of the Hussars, Captain Gjörgy ...[26]

The first Hungarian power play had ended with a resounding victory for Nicholas Horthy. But what Charles did not realize was that in less than a year, another opportunity would present itself to reclaim the throne of Hungary, with permanent consequences for the House of Habsburg.

25

The Last Journey

(1920–21)

It took nearly a year, but eventually Dona and Wilhelm were able to move into their new home at Huis Doorn. When they relocated, their court numbered nearly fifty people, more than half of whom were servants. Many of the other courtiers remained in and around Amerongen, making the commute to Doorn when needed.

By the time the estate was ready, Dona's health was barely hanging on. Suffering from a failing heart, arthritis, and high blood pressure, she was confined almost entirely to a wheelchair or her bed. Many of her friends and family were afraid "that the empress, terminally ill, would not live to warm her new house."[1] The prospect of moving into her new home, surrounded by its bucolic forests and rolling hillsides, sustained Dona. When they finally moved in on May 15, 1920, it was the happiest Wilhelm had seen his wife since they left Germany. To help her feel more at home, he had an elaborate rose garden planted near her rooms. Of all her life in Germany, it was the beautiful gardens at the Neues Palais in Potsdam that Dona said she missed the most. The garden at Doorn included a species of rose, the Kaiserin Auguste Viktoria, which had been named in her honor in 1890. With the burdens of state no longer on his shoulders, Wilhelm took an almost selfless devotion to caring for his wife. Once the garden was finished, he had a small greenhouse built so that fresh roses could be grown and delivered daily to her room.

The Hohenzollerns' fortunes seemed to be improving as more of their family came from Germany to visit. Their son Willy was a regular guest, though his movements on Wieringen Island were strictly monitored. He could only leave the island and visit his parents with the permission of the Dutch authorities. During one of Willy's first visits to Doorn, he and Dona were sitting in the gardens outside. In one of the rare moments of her life, Dona confided her great depression to her son when he remarked of the natural beauty surrounding them. "My boy," she said, "yes, it is beautiful here, but oh! it is not my Potsdam, the New Palace, my little rose-garden, our home. If you only knew how homesickness often gnaws at me. Oh, I shall never see my home again."[2]

In mid-June, Dona's youngest son, Joachim, visited from his home in Switzerland, where he had bought a villa after the war. He had spiraled into a tailspin of grief and depression and was never able to accept life as a commoner after the end of the monarchy. The idea of having to work for a living and being just like everyone else, without the extravagant comforts of royalty, proved too much for the thirty-year-old former prince. Though Dona was happy to see him, it was not a pleasant reunion between father and son. Wilhelm never forgave Joachim for what he considered cowardice and weakness. In the sitting room at Doorn, Joachim told his parents that his marriage to Marie-Augusta was over. Theirs had never been a happy marriage, "but an arrangement." According to one contemporary source, Joachim "suffered from depression and other mental health issues, and may have been an abusive husband. The princess fled the marital home"[3] once already. Joachim had since become addicted to gambling, and his wife left him a second time. He filed for divorce, winning custody of their only child, Karl Franz (b. 1916). Wilhelm was furious and ordered his son out of the house. In a tearful embrace, Dona said good-bye to her son. She would never see him again.

The arrival of the Duke and Duchess of Brunswick on July 15, 1920, greatly lifted the mood at Doorn following Joachim's bitter parting from his father. When they arrived, Sissy immediately received a report on her mother's health from her physician Dr. Hähner before going in to greet her.

> The day before yesterday Her Majesty suffered a heart spasm which, thanks to treatment, was alleviated. On this account, Her Majesty must keep to her bed and will, therefore, have to greet Your Royal Highness from her bed … The consequences of this attack have not yet been completely overcome, though the strength of the heart itself has improved, but there is nevertheless an increased breathlessness … I hope that if no unforeseen troubles arise, good progress will be made.[4]

Trouble did indeed arise. Instead of returning to Switzerland after leaving the Netherlands, Joachim traveled to one of his family's old homes, Villa Liegnitz, in Potsdam. Three weeks later, he was dead. On the afternoon of July 18, 1920—three days after Sissy arrived at Doorn—Joachim shot himself. He died a few hours later at Saint Joseph's Hospital in Potsdam. The Berlin correspondent for the *New York Times* reported that Joachim "had been suffering from great mental depression, according to those intimates of the Hohenzollerns who had seen him." When the reporter questioned Eitel-Fritz "as to the motive of his brother's suicide, [he] declined to make any statement, referring ... to the official announcement that Joachim was suffering from 'a fit of excessive dementia.'"[5]

When the news arrived at Doorn, Wilhelm was the first to be told. Overcome by emotion, he collapsed into a nearby chair, holding his head between his hands in shock. That afternoon, as he gazed silently out the window in despair, he summoned the household together and told them. The empress must never be told the truth, he said. With her condition deteriorating, he knew that her youngest son taking his own life would most likely kill her. Everyone therefore agreed to keep up the facade that Joachim had been killed in a hunting accident. On that sunny afternoon when Wilhelm broke the news to his wife, she "took the news calmly and with the usual composure she exhibited when fate dealt her severe blows, but there was no doubt of the pain the news had caused her."[6] Although she accepted her husband's explanation and never wavered in her outward calm, everyone around her believed that she knew the truth about her son. In their grief, Wilhelm and Augusta Victoria were denied permission to return to Germany for their son's funeral. In his memoirs, Willy described his brother's death: "our parents and we children have suffered a heavy blow: my brother Joachim, utterly broken down, has passed out of this life. Immediately on receipt of the news, I travelled to Doorn, in order to be with my mother in, at any rate, the first and severest hours of her sorrow. What a deal of suffering destiny has heaped upon this poor and sick maternal heart."[7]

The presence of Willy and Sissy brought Dona comfort. Another relative she delighted in was her grandson Karl Franz. Following Joachim's death, Wilhelm issued an edict declaring Eitel-Fritz was to take sole custody of the boy, who was promptly sent to Doorn for extended visits with his grandparents—a German court would rule a year later that Wilhelm had no legal authority to issue such an edict, and the boy was returned to Marie-Augusta. Little Karl Franz brought "an atmosphere of gaiety and insouciance to a house where the outlook is often sombre." One witness observed that Wilhelm "delights in the child's prattle."[8] As a living link with Dona's beloved dead son, Karl Franz had a special bond with his grandmother. But unlike her husband, she could not run and play with him. Her time with Karl Franz was limited to her sitting in a wheelchair at lunch or watching him play in the garden. In the autumn months, Karl Franz was joined by his cousins, Willy and Cecilie's children. For the first time since their exile, Wilhelm and Dona were surrounded by most of their children and grandchildren, who had largely been spared the horrors of the war and abdication. Wilhelm felt reinvigorated hearing his grandchildren laughing and playing in the halls at Doorn.

The leitmotif of Dona's family could not hide the truth: she was dying. It was only a matter of time. On October 22, 1920, the Hohenzollerns celebrated Augusta Victoria's sixty-second birthday, but it was a somber occasion. Her son Willy poignantly recalled sitting with his mother on her birthday.

> It was on the 22[n]d, the anniversary of my mother's birthday.—They were quiet, sad days in Doorn; for it cannot escape the eye of any one who loves her that my mother's strength is waning, that sorrow is eating her up. The wound made in her maternal heart by the death of my brother Joachim has never healed; he was the weakest of us boys and claimed a greater share of her motherly care.
>
> On the birthday itself, she had kept to her bed. I could only sit beside her, hold her hand in mine and talk to her. I told her a number of amusing and harmless little anecdotes concerning my island household; and it was a pleasure to see a faint smile light up her kind features every now and then; but it was only a short flicker of sunshine, that was gone again almost instantly. And when she is up and walks through the rooms and her tired eyes wander caressingly over all the old furniture and mementos of her Berlin and Potsdam days, it is as though she were bidding them all a silent farewell.[9]

Within a month, Dona was at death's door. Newspapers across Europe and North America were on standby to release her obituary. The former empress was suffering from repeated heart attacks, which were complicated by the formation of blood clots. This left her so weak that during the last half of November, she was only semiconscious on all but a few days. It became even more difficult to treat her when she developed a fever of 104 degrees. So often was Dona expected to pass away before the end of the year that her son Willy was summoned to Doorn half a dozen times. On December 1, the *New York Times* ran the headline GERMAN EMPRESS NEAR DEATH. The article went on to say that Dona's "death is expected at any moment." One member of the household at Doorn told reporters, "Her Majesty, realizing the seriousness of her condition, is quite resigned, and actually longs for the end of her sufferings, which began in 1918."[10] Miraculously, she rallied and made it to Christmas 1920.

Dona's final months were made even more unbearable by sinister threats on her husband's life. Plots abounded claiming that the former imperial couple would be kidnapped and murdered. Dona became obsessively paranoid about her and Wilhelm's safety. She rarely slept because she was awoken by every noise in the night, terrified that it was someone coming to kidnap them. "They are coming for him," she would scream and then burst into tears.[11] A few poorly planned kidnap attempts were made on the couple as early as 1919, when a group of American officers based in Luxembourg managed to break into Amerongen Castle, but they were easily thwarted. It was enough to prompt Wilhelm to consider arranging a police guard for himself.

Dona believed that the British were responsible for all the threats against them. Even in her twilight years, her antipathy for Britain had not subsided. She was so convinced of her final fate that she wrote a farewell letter to her family in the event she and Wilhelm were captured or murdered: "In case Papa and I, by God's Will, never see you again, this letter brings you our final greetings and out blessings ... I know, my dear children, that you will, with God's help, be brave. It is bitterly hard to say goodbye, but our warm love for you transcends the grave. And now, God protect you until we meet again with God."[12] She also assured her children that neither she nor Wilhelm "would permit themselves to be delivered to the enemy, but even if that fate was avoided, there was no certainty as to where they could wile away their old age."[13]

The frail Hohenzollern matriarch spent Christmas 1920 surrounded by her children and grandchildren. She made few appearances during the festivities, being unable to walk even a few steps without needing her wheelchair. By the spring of 1921, there was little doubt that the end was near. She spent most of her time in bed, but she rarely slept in peace. She was restless, spoke in her sleep, and suffered delusions that caused her to think she was surrounded by absent family, especially Joachim. "What she said was often surprising, almost clairvoyant," Sissy recalled. "One night, when my brother August Wilhelm was keeping vigil [at her bedside], she bade us children goodbye in her sleep. Shattered, Auwi told us later what he had heard."[14]

On February 22, Dona's controversial brother Ernest Günther, Duke of Schleswig-Holstein, died at Primkenau at the age of fifty-seven. "According to the doctors who are treating the Kaiserin," reported the *New York Times*, Dona was not "informed about her brother's death, due to the frailty of her own health."[15] A week later, a faint glimmer of gaiety appeared at Doorn as Dona and Wilhelm commemorated their fortieth wedding anniversary. The former empress barely noticed the milestone because was she so ill she could only remain conscious for a few hours each day. It was the last occasion the Hohenzollerns celebrated as a family. In mid-March, Augusta Victoria's death vigil began. Her five sons dutifully arrived at Doorn, but the instability in Germany and Austria prevented Sissy from arriving in time. Willy recalled that Dona "was so feeble that she could scarcely speak; and yet the slightest attention was received with 'Thank you, my dear boy'; and then she gently stroked my hand."[16] Along with Wilhelm, each of the princes took turns holding the vigil at Dona's bedside. In one of her last conversations with her husband, Dona told him in her typical selfless fashion, "I must live, because I cannot leave you alone."[17]

Spring came early that year, and the warmer weather made Dona more comfortable. Wilhelm and Eitel-Fritz spent the most time at her bedside, but these were long hours passed in silence since even simple conversation exhausted her. Occasionally, on days when Dona showed strength, she was propped up next to her window where she enjoyed looking out into the garden with its flowers and budding trees. Her physician, Dr. Hähner, kept her pain to a minimum by giving her frequent hypodermic injections of a heart stimulant. By the predawn hours of April 11, 1921, her breathing had become extremely labored. At 5:00 a.m., Dr. Hähner, Countess Keller, and the nurse moved Dona into a position they hoped would make it easier for her to breathe. Over the next hour, her pulse grew weaker and weaker. Wilhelm and Adalbert were both summoned to her bedside where, at 6:00 a.m., Augusta Victoria died from massive heart failure. She was sixty-two years old. Sissy, who had been en route back to Doorn, was unaware that her mother had died. She received the news during a stopover in Nuremberg, where placards had been posted announcing the empress's death.

The tributes that poured into Doorn were heartfelt. They amounted to some ten thousand messages of condolence, "a mark perhaps more of the respect with which Dona had been regarded in Germany than real enthusiasm for" Wilhelm.[18] Even American newspapers paid tribute to "the life of the once beautiful Empress and Queen of Prussia, Augusta Victoria who, for nearly 40 years had been the most beloved hausfrau of the German people."[19] It stung Wilhelm deeply that no message of condolence arrived from King George V or the British royal family.

Dona's body rested at Doorn with a round-the-clock vigil provided by her husband and sons, who were dressed in full Prussian military uniforms. Scattered throughout the room were pine-scented wreaths and bundles of flowers. Willy spent the first night after his mother died seated next to her coffin. He was struck by how much her passing reminded him of Queen Victoria's. He had great difficulty coming to terms with his mother's death. He wrote in his memoirs, "I was unable to grasp the idea that she would no more speak to me, that her kind eyes would no more be turned upon me. She was the magnet which attracted us children, wherever we might be, toward the parental home. She knew all our wishes, our hopes, our cares. Now she had been taken from us forever."[20]

In a gesture of sympathy, the Allied Mission in Berlin and the German government allowed the empress's body to be buried in Potsdam, in accordance with her wishes. "I will sleep in my own homeland,"[21] she once told her daughter. But there were stipulations. To avoid arousing monarchist sentiments, the train carrying the coffin and its caretakers was required to travel without any fanfare or official ceremonies at any point on German soil until it reached Potsdam. The German government took great pains to keep many of the details of Dona's funeral a secret in the hope of attracting as little attention as possible. The publicly announced date for the funeral was changed without warning just for this reason. The final, most important condition was that Wilhelm must not accompany his wife's coffin. This was deeply painful for the former emperor, since "it meant he would never be able to stand at his wife's grave."[22] In the end, it would fall to his sons to escort Dona to her final resting place; Auwi and Eitel-Fritz immediately left for Germany to begin funeral preparations, while Oscar and Adalbert decided to accompany the coffin on its last journey.

Rather than have a funeral at Doorn, the Hohenzollerns chose to have a small memorial for Dona at the train station at Maarn, five miles away. On the dark, misty night of April 17, Dona's coffin, decorated in the traditional Prussian style with pine fronds and covered with the Standard of the Queen of Prussia, was taken to the dimly lit Maarn station in a specially modified automobile. Mourners stood along the entire route, their heads bare and bowed low in silent respect. The only sound that could be heard was the clattering of hooves from the horses pulling the coffin. Following close behind was a procession of black automobiles. The first was filled with bouquets and funeral wreaths. The second contained Ernst von Dryander, the court chaplain, wearing his black clerical robes. The third bore members of the former imperial court. Ten minutes after these vehicles arrived at Maarn, a fourth, large motorcar pulled up. Oscar and Adalbert stepped out, both wearing the uniform of the Prussian Guards, complete with iconic, black, spiked helmets and gray capes over their shoulders. Wilhelm's attire was that of a general of the Brandenburg Infantry, which was one of the last uniforms he would ever be seen wearing. Sissy and the other women wore the traditional mourning black. Their long black dresses were in such stark contrast to the resplendent military uniforms that some witnesses thought they were nuns.

Along with Dona's husband and children, the service at Maarn was attended by a surprisingly impressive group of former courtiers, government officials, and representatives sent on behalf of Queen Wilhelmina and the kings of Spain and Sweden. When it was time for the service to begin, Dr. Dryander had everyone assemble on the train platform around the coffin, where he said a few words, "his voice vibrating with emotion." Reporters at the scene noted that the ex-emperor "wept bitterly" over his wife's coffin. After the brief service, Adalbert, Oscar, and the other male members of the court loaded their mother's casket into the last of three dark-green compartments attached to the funeral train, which was scheduled to depart before dawn the next morning. Sleeping on the train that night in the second compartment outfitted with beds were the two princes, Dr. Dryander, and the empress's ladies-in-waiting, who were permanently returning to Germany after the funeral. In the morning, they would accompany the coffin back to Potsdam. Willy asked the Dutch government for permission to go but was told if he did, he would not be permitted to reenter the Netherlands. Accompanied by Sissy, father and son boarded the train for a final good-bye. Afterward, Wilhelm proceeded into the travel car to thank those who were sleeping on board for their devotion to the late empress in accompanying her body to Potsdam. When Wilhelm emerged a few minutes later, according to the *New York Times* reporter on the scene, his "figure was that of a man broken by sorrow."[23] Without any words, he and Sissy got into their automobile and drove back to Doorn. Willy, Sissy's husband, and the rest of their courtiers who were remaining in the Netherlands followed shortly thereafter.

At 7:45 a.m., the funeral train left Maarn. News reports from that day imply Wilhelm had planned to return to see the train off. However, the Associated Press reported that he "suffered all through the night from severe nervous depression" and could not bring himself to return to Maarn when the "funeral train departed with the body of his wife, Auguste Viktoria."[24] The Dutch government paid their respects by flying their flags at half-mast at all the stations through which the train passed on its way out of their country. The Dutch people were no less reverent. Thousands of ordinary citizens, most of whom had never even laid eyes on Dona, lined the train tracks. When the train crossed into Germany at 10:00 a.m., the outpouring of affection for the country's last empress was even more heartfelt, despite the best efforts of the republican government. The entire journey from Maarn to Potsdam—more than three-hundred-and-seventy miles–was lined in "an unbroken human chain" of tens of thousands of mourners who had come to pay their last respects.[25] All along the way, the people echoed the same words: "The Kaiserin is coming!" So many people lined the railway tracks that the train was forced to delay its arrival in Potsdam. A number of towns forced the train to stop at their stations to allow their citizens the chance to mourn. Hundreds—and in some cases, thousands—of people surrounded the train at different stations. Dressed in black, they dropped to their knees and prayed. In other towns, church bells tolled, choirs sang, and bands played hymns. "A whole people were mourning their beloved Empress," wrote Sissy.[26]

The train pulled into Wildpark Station near Potsdam during the predawn hours of April 19; the funeral would take place later that day. So many thousands of people had defied the orders of the German government and paid their respects en route that by the time the coffin reached Potsdam, it was completely covered in wreaths. When the passengers disembarked, they were met by Eitel-Fritz, Auwi, several dozen royals, and former imperial officials. Dr. Dryander recited prayers as each person came to pay his or her personal respects. Once the ceremony was over, the two military regiments that had been Dona's personal units, the Pasewalker Cuirassiers and the Eighty-Sixth Schleswig-Holstein Infantry, formed an honor guard and stood watch over the coffin for the rest of the night.

As dawn broke that morning, Augusta Victoria was buried. The funeral cortège was surrounded by hundreds of people in the procession from Wildpark Station to Dona's final resting place: the Antique Temple, the great domed mausoleum built by Frederick the Great at Sanssouci Park. The pallbearers were four knights of the Order of the Black Eagle, the highest chivalric order in the old Prussian kingdom of which Dona and her mother-in-law, Vicky, were the only female members. Immediately behind the pallbearers came Oscar, Eitel-Fritz, Adalbert, and Auwi, along with Ina and Adelaide, all with heads bowed low. The *New York Times* wrote that "the most unparalleled crowds" came out to watch the spectacle. Estimates placed the number of spectators between two hundred thousand and three hundred thousand, all of whom stood in respectful silence as the procession moved through the streets. "So intense was the silence that you could hear the plashing of the fountains playing in front of the various palaces," wrote one witness.[27] Sissy had been kept apprised of the entire spectacle. She wrote of how awe-inspiring the funeral was: "The crowd was immense, more than 200,000 appeared, perhaps a quarter of a million, at the funeral, reverently quiet. No one spoke aloud, there was no noise of any kind, no pushing and shoving. A veritable sea of flowers and wreaths had been laid all round the circular, ivy-covered edifice of the Temple of Antiquity. After the coffin had been placed in front of the altar in the mausoleum, my brothers took over the vigil, their swords drawn, while Pastor Dryander gave the funeral oration."[28] Dryander praised "the ex-Empress as mother and woman, one who placed duty above everything else."[29] The funeral service concluded when the pastor read an excerpt from the Gospels. Dona's casket was then placed in the Antique Temple, next to that of her son Joachim.

For Wilhelm, the loss of his wife affected him very deeply. The day of the funeral was understandably painful, but he was surrounded by stalwart companions, especially his eldest son, his daughter, and his brother Henry, who came to be at his side. Of the four imperial couples who ruled Germany, Austria-Hungary, Britain, and Russia, Wilhelm held the dubious distinction of being the only husband to outlive his wife. The weeks and months that followed Dona's death were almost unbearable for him. "My loneliness was indescribable," he recalled.[30] He was heard repeatedly telling those around him, "It will be quiet in the house," and that Dona had been such "a splendid person!"[31] He later turned his wife's bedroom into a shrine devoted to her memory, with a cross of flowers draped across her bed. Once a week, for the rest of his life, he would retire to his wife's room, mourning her memory and missing her constant, unwavering support.

⤙⤚

At Villa Prangins in Switzerland, Charles was deeply disturbed by Nicholas Horthy's growing political ambitions. In the months since the emperor's departure from Budapest, the regent had tightened his grip on power by curtailing the powers of Hungary's National Council and Parliament. He also began a campaign aimed at convincing the Allies to permanently forbid the Habsburgs from ever reclaiming the Hungarian throne.

While her husband met with advisors and monarchists, Empress Zita came to the realization that if her family ever had a chance to return to politics, it would not be in Austria.

> She well remembered that in Hungary lay the family's sole hope for return to royal rank and power, since, despite the Versailles dictum, Hungary remained constitutionally a kingdom without a king. Therefore Karl, Zita and the children must become "Magyarized," not only in speech but also in habit and manner, against that day when a summons from Budapest would call them back. They must give up their Viennese dialect and study the difficult Magyar tongue.
>
> This imposed considerable hardship on the family circle where up to then only Austrian—German with a southern accent—had been spoken. But Zita was adamant in her resolve. Having attained a throne by marriage, she did not intend to lose it through sheer negligence.[32]

Zita took it upon herself to teach her six children how to be Hungarian, from the way they dressed to how they spoke. She even started translating their names into Hungarian. This made a lasting impression on Otto, who would develop a deep love and appreciation for Hungary and its people.

The arrival of summer brought many changes for Zita's family. Upon the emperor's return to Prangins, the empress presented him with their seventh child, a daughter she had named Charlotte. Soon thereafter, the Swiss authorities, upset by Charles's blatant political activity, revoked the family's visas. There were few countries willing to harbor them. As Empress Zita recalled, "Norway and Denmark could not be considered, as the general feeling in both countries at the time was too hostile. For little Luxembourg we would have been too big a weight. Italy was impossible and Portugal too remote from the Emperor's lands to be practicable.... From England and Sweden we received firm refusals; from Holland an evasive reply and from Spain only a long silence." With exile abroad not an option, Charles was granted an emergency one-year lease on an old Swiss castle, Hertenstein, near Lucerne. As Zita noted, "we got an extension of our time in Switzerland, not at our own request, but at that of the Spanish and Hungarian Governments."[33] For the fifth time in four years, the Habsburgs moved to a new home, but for the first time, a genuine sense of hopelessness crept into their lives. The children—who slept on spartan military cots for lack of better beds—spent their nights listening "in awe to the disconsolate conversations between King and Queen. Presently Otto and his brothers spoke solemnly of a 'homelessness' they did not understand, and of their own sacred obligation to protect Papa and Mama against a wicked world." But in a strange way, their "grief itself served to knit the family more closely together."[34]

By October, Charles and his legitimist supporters, encouraged by Empress Zita, felt the time was right for a second attempt to reclaim the Hungarian throne. But this time, Zita—who was now at the beginning of yet another pregnancy—insisted on taking an active role in the restoration bid. She planned most of the campaign herself, sending postcards (since letters from the family were forbidden by the Allies) to her brothers Sixtus and René asking for help. She also stated unequivocally that she would join her husband this time, despite her accouchement. When one of the family's aides tried to dissuade her from going, she responded with her characteristic fortitude, "Do not try to change my mind. I am quite determined to fly as well. Nothing will happen to our children here in Switzerland, as they are in safe hands. But the Emperor faces danger and thus my duty as a wife becomes greater than my duty as a mother.... So do not even attempt to describe those dangers—that would only strengthen me in my decision.... I am the Queen of Hungary and if the King goes back there, my place is at his side."[35]

After writing and sealing their wills, Charles and Zita left Hertenstein on the morning of October 20. The children were left in the care of their parents' relatives from both the Bourbon and Habsburg families, but at first they did not know the truth.

> As part of the deception plan, the children had been told that their parents would be returning that same evening, so Otto and the others ran alongside the car as it left the drive[way] as though seeing them off for a family day trip. There was no return that evening nor during any of the evenings that followed. As the days grew into weeks and the mood among the castle staff darkened, it gradually became clear to the older children that this had been no routine journey, nor was it to have a normal ending. Indeed, everything about this second—and fatally decisive—restoration bid was extraordinary.[36]

Using the names "Mr. and Mrs. Kovno," the imperial couple traveled to an airfield at Dübendorf outside of Zurich where they chartered a six-seat Junker monoplane bound for Hungary. Never before had either of them ever sat in an airplane. "The Emperor and I were seated right at the back of the plane, behind the wings, and both of us felt somewhat giddy," Zita recalled. "But neither that, nor the seriousness of the occasion, could take away the novelty of a first flight in such beautiful weather."[37] As they flew past the Bavarian Alps and over Austria, Charles and Zita looked out the window longingly. "Descend!" Zita cried suddenly over Vienna. "Oh, let me see Schönbrunn."[38] For their long voyage, the couple traveled with almost nothing in their possession. They had no money, luggage, passports, travel papers—nothing, except the hope of their restoration to the throne. After four hours and a near-death crash over Bavaria when the engine died, the tiny plane landed at Dénesfa in Hungary, the country estate of Count Cziraky, one of the emperor's supporters. Years later, on the spot where Charles and Zita's plane landed, Hungarian legitimists erected a chapel with the inscription, "He came to his own and his own received him not."[39]

Unlike his first attempt in March, Charles had no intention of meeting with Nicholas Horthy. Instead, he and Zita headed directly for the town of Sopron, near the Austro-Hungarian border. When they arrived, the emperor immediately formed his own provisional government complete with prime minister and ministers of the interior, foreign affairs, finance and industry, defense, and education. On October 21, Charles and his supporters prepared a group of armored trains to ferry their army of two thousand soldiers to

Budapest, 120 miles away. Zita looked on the date as a good portent. It was their tenth wedding anniversary.

The journey to the capital was insufferably slow. Instead of plowing forward at full speed, the train plodded along, making stops at every village along the way so that the citizens could take the oath of loyalty to the king-emperor. Though it was touching to see so many people still loyal to Charles and Zita, this cost them precious time. On the first day alone, it took nearly ten hours to cross fifty miles. The time delay notwithstanding, everything seemed to be going swimmingly at first. Towns all along the train's route joined the loyalist side. In Budapest, the army began deserting Horthy's government en masse. Within two days, almost none of the regent's generals were willing to lead an army against Charles, and enough soldiers from outside Budapest could not reach the city in time. Signs that the Horthy regime may be crumbling emerged when, out of desperation, one of his supporters formed a ragtag army of four hundred university students, who were told that it was the much-hated Czechs, not their own countrymen, who were en route to the capital.

A Hungarian civil war seemed inevitable by October 23. Martial law was declared in Budapest. With Charles and his loyalists a mere twenty miles from the capital, the international community took action. The Allies declared they would never acknowledge a Habsburg restoration. The Little Entente—Czechoslovakia, Romania, and Yugoslavia—all announced that Charles's return to the throne was a casus belli. They later signed an agreement to take any action necessary to prevent the Habsburgs from ever returning to the throne. Thomas Hohler, the British envoy to Hungary, sent a telegram to London stating that "all is lost" for the Horthy regime.[40] Holher later sent Horthy a message insisting that he "proclaim without delay the dethronisation [*sic*] of the ex-King Karl."[41] When word reached Budapest that the Czechs were ready to invade the moment Charles was restored, the tide turned against the royalists. Riding on horseback in his black admiral's uniform with gold tassels and glittering medals, the broad-faced Horthy made a dramatic speech to his small band of troops. He warned them that a restoration of Charles and Zita would revive the old empire, ending forever the notion of Hungarian independence.

When Charles and Zita's train arrived on the outskirts of Budapest, it came under heavy fire from the newly reenergized Hungarian army. Their move toward the city came to a halt when the troops under the emperor's command were forced to fortify their position. Once the fighting began near the suburb of Budaörs, Horthy's generals—the same ones who only days before refused to fight against their legitimate king—sprung into action. In what became known as the Battle of Budaörs, fourteen Hungarian soldiers and five loyalist officers were killed. By the end of the day, it was obvious to Zita that she and her husband would never reach Budapest. Determined never to shed any of his people's blood, Charles agreed to a cease-fire with Horthy's troops. "I'll have no massacre of Hungarians," he declared. "For or against me, they must be compelled to lay down arms."[42] When negotiations started at a nearby train station the next morning, it was clear that Charles had lost. The regent demanded that he order his troops to stand down and surrender all equipment and weapons. In return, everyone except the emperor, empress, and their "agitators and ringleaders" would be granted amnesty. He also offered a personal guarantee for the imperial couple's safety. The negotiations nearly exploded a few moments later into another firefight when a stray bullet whizzed past Charles's ear and pierced the armor of the royal train. Believing they were betrayed, the emperor's military commanders called for a "last stand" and "a fight to the last drop of blood." But like Nicholas II, Charles would never consider plunging his country into a civil war. "I forbid any more fighting!" he declared. "It's all quite senseless now."[43] He ordered an immediate surrender of all his troops.

Humiliated and dispirited, Charles and Zita withdrew from Budapest, dismissing the officers, ministers, and ordinary citizens who remained loyal to them. They relocated to the town of Tata, forty-three miles northwest of Budapest, at the home of their old friend Count Moric Esterhazy. On the evening of their arrival in Tata, Zita and Charles spent a tense, dismal night at Esterhazy's palace; Count Moric kept a twenty-four-hour vigil, watching over them. All was still and calm until a group of marauders broke into the palace in the middle of the night in a fit of bloodlust, determined to kidnap Charles. Only the quick thinking of Esterhazy, who threw one of the attackers off a second-story balcony, saved the emperor's life.

In the days that followed, Admiral Nicholas Horthy reasserted his control over the country with a vengeance. At the end of October, Zita and Charles heard the shocking news that several of Hungary's most respected royalists were arrested. They were equally stunned when armed guards arrived at the Esterhazy Palace a few days later with orders from Horthy to take them into military custody. They were held at the monastery at Tihány while the regent decided what to do with them. Charles and Zita were confined to two narrow rooms on the second floor. The monks at Tihány made every effort to make their stay as easy as possible by donating furniture and warm clothes. Their internment at Tihány showed unmistakable echoes of the last days of Tsarina Alexandra and her family. The emperor and empress were watched by a regiment of guards who were ordered to keep them under surveillance at all times. Indignant at the way he and his wife were being treated, Charles uncharacteristically goaded his captors, "Why don't you finish your task? Why don't you put me in chains?"[44]

The Allies were now determined to send Charles and Zita into permanent exile; returning to Switzerland was now out of the question. The Swiss authorities washed their hands of the emperor and his meddling. The decision was made to exile the couple off continental Europe to the Portuguese island of Madeira, though Charles and Zita were never told of their final destination until they were near Gibraltar.[45] After nearly two weeks of incarceration at Tihány, they left for the port of Baja, a Renaissance-era city with a small port on the Sugovica River, where a British ship would take them to the Danube and out to the Mediterranean. Groups of peasants waited all night in the bitter cold to say good-bye. Once there, the emperor and empress were treated to scenes of small devotion with bouquets of flowers. Zita had to ask permission from her escort to collect the flowers, which she was allowed to do. The chauffeur who had driven them said of the emperor, "Whatever people say, he's a very pleasant gentleman."[46] Zita boarded the British monitor *Glow-Worm* first, followed by her husband, who was dressed in a fur coat to guard against the cold morning.

The *Glow-Worm* traveled down the Sugovica into the Danube. After a week, the ship made a rendezvous with the five-thousand-ton cruiser HMS *Cardiff*, onto which the emperor and empress were transferred for the remainder of their voyage. Zita wrote in her diary, "We transferred ship at eight in the evening for supper on the *Cardiff*. I was given the Admiral's cabin, the Emperor that of the Commander."[47] A British officer on board recalled seeing the couple for the first time: "a strong military escort lined the way from the train to the vessels. Then came the ex-King in Field Marshall's uniform, and Queen Zita in a blue costume.... as he went on board the ex-King showed a cheerful countenance and was extremely gracious to everybody." But the observer also added, "He set his face from the beginning against receiving any representative of the Hungarian government on the grounds that the government was in rebellion against him."[48] During the voyage, they were told the ship would not be sent to retrieve their seven children back at Herteinstein. Zita nearly collapsed when she was told: "The children! Are we to be carried off without our children?"[49] A few days later, she was able to report, "Joyous news this afternoon: I received a telegram from Colonel Strutt in London that all is well with the children. Our first news of them for eighteen days."[50] Zita's pregnancy made the journey especially hard on her, and Charles suffered from seasickness. "The Emperor and I are both dreadfully sea-sick," Zita wrote in her diary. "I go over twice to his cabin to see how he is – and pay dearly for it. The Emperor also comes twice over to me – and removes himself hastily."[51]

The *Cardiff* spent nearly three weeks traveling down the Danube and across the Mediterranean. They had no possessions with them, no money, not even a change of clothes. Their plight was poignantly summed up by an Austrian observer who was onboard: "They journeyed down the Danube into exile, to a destination still unknown to them, separated from their children, their country, without any means, completely destitute."[52] The greatest comfort the couple received on the voyage was the opportunity to hear Mass and receive Communion, but even the empress's steely nerves were tested on the arduous journey. "Terribly bad sea," she wrote in her diary. "One could hardly sleep for being thrown about so much. The Emperor is dreadfully ill. This *would* have to be the day when the clocks are put back an hour so it all lasts longer."[53] Zita's comment about the clocks be put back was a reference to daylight saving time, which had only come into effect three years earlier and was taking some getting used to.

With great relief, the couple disembarked almost a month later at the town of Funchal on Madeira. Zita reported in her diary that day, "The Lord be praised. We have arrived at Funchal ... Despite the fact that the Portuguese had deliberately announced the wrong time for our landing, quite a large crowd had gathered in the pouring rain to give us a welcome.... Journey's end."[54] Their departure on board the *Cardiff* signaled the final exit of Emperor Charles I from the political scene. There was now no doubt of the permanence of this exile. There would be no return visits to their former territories for Charles and Zita. They had taken their last journey into exile together. It would be their last journey as husband and wife.

26

"I Can't Go On Much Longer"

(January–April 1922)

Permanently exiled from continental Europe, Emperor Charles I was a broken man. He and Empress Zita, now refugees, were forced to settle in the Madeiran town of Funchal, at the Villa Victoria, an annex of the famous Reid's Hotel. Christmas 1921 was especially gloomy. The couple spent the day in quiet prayer, reflecting on their misfortunes. Since the Allies had decreed that none of their former staff could join them in exile, they were entirely alone, save for a Portuguese nobleman named Dom João d'Almeida. A kindhearted man, Dom d'Almeida "volunteered his services as an aide-de-camp and now represented all the 'court' they possessed."[1]

In January 1922, Empress Zita's second son, Robert, came down with painful appendicitis and needed an immediate operation. Zita rushed to Zurich, where her son was convalescing at a nuns' hospital. The Allies took her return to the continent with significant gravitas because they were afraid she would make another attempt to reclaim the Hungarian throne. An article that appeared in the *New York Times* on January 13 described the precautions being taken in Zurich: "The Swiss papers state that Zita, who is considered an intriguer and the real head of the Hapsburg restoration movement in Europe, must be watched closely during her short stay in the country in order that the Swiss government may not be fooled for the third time by her intrigues." When Zita, dressed in plain traveling clothes so as not to attract any attention, arrived at the train station in Zurich, she was "delighted" to find several of her children, who had come from Hertenstein to greet her.[2] The moment

Zita walked into her son's ward, his face lit up in such a way she could not describe it. The Swiss authorities watched Zita's movements constantly. On the days she was at the hospital, every nun leaving the building was forced to submit to a police search and have her veil lifted to ensure it was not the empress trying to escape in disguise.

While she was in Zurich, Zita sought out a lawyer named Bruno Steiner. In November 1918, Charles had entrusted a priceless array of jewels—which included the empress's diamond crown; a collection of Lorraine jewels; eight golden fleeces; the famed Florentine diamonds; and various other jewels, gemstones, and brooches—to Steiner for safekeeping. Some of the single stones themselves were estimated to be worth nearly fifty thousand francs. When Zita managed to locate Steiner's residence, she was dismayed to find that he was gone. Her brother Xavier began a search for him, eventually tracking him to a hotel in Frankfurt. The prince confronted the shocked lawyer, who insisted that the jewels were safe in a nearby bank. When Xavier returned to the hotel at 7:00 a.m. the following morning to collect the items, Steiner was gone, presumably with the jewels, never to be heard from again.

True to form, the empress never allowed her children to see how frightened and panicked she must have been by Steiner's treachery, nor did she have much time in Zurich to ponder this disaster. Two weeks after Robert's operation, Zita was forced to leave Switzerland. She managed to secure permission from the Allies to bring her children back with her. Robert remained in Zurich, recovering under the care of an old family friend, and he would be sent to Madeira when he was well enough to travel. As Zita and her children arrived in Funchal by boat on February 2, she was enthusiastically welcomed home by her husband, who had tears streaming down his face at the sight of his family.

The Roaring Twenties marked the beginning of Great Britain's true entrance into the new century. The Great War was left behind as a casualty of the previous decade, and there was a great expectancy of the new wealth, glamour, and extravagance that would flood in from the United States. On the front lines of this new modern epoch were Queen Mary's children—David, Bertie, Mary, Harry, and George—who had grown into attractive, popular socialites. David in particular had a reputation as a playboy. As much as the king and queen loved their son, they did not understand him. They felt an insuperable chasm separated them, forged in the early years of the twentieth century. The king and queen were anachronisms of the old system of royalty whose hallmarks had been conservatism, duty, and propriety. At court, the king was determined to hold on to the traditions of the past. He insisted on everyone wearing Victorian fashions, with properly matching coat, tails, and hat. Years later, David recalled his father's hatred of change: "He disapproved of Soviet Russia, painted finger-nails, women who smoked in public, cocktails, frivolous hats, American jazz and the growing habit of going away for the weekends."³ Sadly for George and Mary, the postwar world eagerly forgot the era whose values and traditions they fought to preserve. Many people blamed the old system of royalty for the war, since many of the leading participants were grandchildren of Queen Victoria.

The twenty-eight-year-old Prince of Wales symbolized everything that the new generation craved. His love of pleasures and women, of which he made no secret, disturbed his parents. His mother chalked it up to a certain "restlessness" he felt from living at Buckingham Palace. To find relief, David became a familiar face on London's social scene. The king wrote to his wife, "I see David continues to dance every night & most of the night too. What a pity they [reporters] should telegraph it every day, people who don't know, will begin to think that he is either mad or the biggest rake in Europe, such a pity!"⁴ To help their son shed his playboy image, the king and queen sent him on a world tour shortly after the war. Everywhere he visited, David was met with rapturous acclaim. "We are much looking forward to the return of our dear son after his triumphal (I think I may say this without being vain) tour for such it has been," the queen wrote to an old friend. The list of places on the royal visit included Japan, Australia, and India in the east, and both Canada and the United States in the west. Mary wrote happily after David's stop in Canada, "he really is a marvel in spite of his 'fads' & I confess I feel very proud of him."⁵

King George had particular difficulty accepting his sons as grown men, even though he would grant each of them peerages. Bertie, following in his father's footsteps, became the Duke of York in 1920—the traditional title given to the next heir after the Prince of Wales; Harry was named Duke of Gloucester in 1928; and George inherited the title that had last belonged to Queen Victoria's father, Duke of Kent, in 1934. In exchange for these honors (which also increased the princes' allowances), King George expected his sons to fall in line with a minimum of fuss.

The king and queen's daughter, Princess Mary, was not like her brothers. There was little doubt that she was her parents' favorite child, and when she announced in 1921 that she wanted to get married, the queen gave her heartiest approval. King George did not acquiesce so easily. The prospect of losing his only daughter saddened him deeply. With some prodding from his wife, he eventually gave his consent. In England, the marriage of the monarch's eldest daughter—traditionally known as the Princess Royal, though Mary did not receive this title formally until 1932[6]—was a serious affair that commanded a certain degree of respect and dignity. The title of Princess Royal was first used by King Charles I in the seventeenth century for his eldest daughter. Over the centuries, it became a significant honorific, though it did not elevate the bearers' rank or status constitutionally. The most famous Princess Royal was Augusta Victoria's mother-in-law, Vicky, the Empress Frederick. Her marriage to the then Prince Frederick Wilhelm of Prussia in 1858 was intended to cement a new alliance between England and Prussia. Naturally the question everyone wanted to know was, would Princess Mary follow suit and contract a glittering dynastic marriage?

Prior to the war, the queen had hoped to see her daughter paired off with a Hanoverian prince, but the war's outcome drastically reduced the pool of acceptable royal candidates. By 1921, the only thrones left in Europe, aside from Britain, were Italy, Belgium, the Netherlands, Bulgaria, Yugoslavia, Romania, Albania, Denmark, Norway, and Sweden. Of those that remained, most were discounted for reasons of religion and politics. But what of the many royal princes from elsewhere in the world? A British princess marrying into a dynasty from another continent—Asia or the Middle East—was regarded as unthinkable. In 1958, after divorcing his second wife, Queen Soraya, the shah of Iran hoped to marry Princess Alexandra of Kent, one of George and Mary's future granddaughters. The idea was not even considered, and the shah was forced to look elsewhere for a wife.

Being a forthright young woman, devotedly English, it is almost certain Princess Mary would never have considered marrying outside Europe. As such, it came as no surprise that she forsook any possibility of an arranged union and chose to marry for love. The man she set her heart on was a nonroyal, Viscount Henry Lascelles. This made her one of only a handful of modern English princesses to marry a commoner. Queen Victoria's fourth daughter, Princess Louise, married the Marquess of Lorne (who became the Ninth Duke of Argyll in 1900). The king's sister Louise of Wales married the Earl (and later the First Duke) of Fife in 1889. The marriages of the two princesses Louise helped prepare the English people to accept their royal family marrying commoners. Before Princess Louise married the Marquess of Lorne, no English princess had married one of their own countrymen since Henry VIII's sister married the Duke of Suffolk in 1515.

As for Princess Mary's fiancé, Lascelles was the "immensely rich"[7] son of the Earl of Harewood, a business tycoon from the Yorkshire area. He was also fifteen years her senior. The age difference between the couple raised more than one eyebrow, but he was accepted as a member of the royal family with some ease. He had been a friend of the king's for years, and as a member of the aristocracy, he would not be taking the princess off to live in some foreign court. That her daughter's breaking with tradition did not bother Queen Mary can be seen in her diary: "At 6.30 Mary came to my room to announce to me her engagement to Lord Lascelles!... Of course everybody guessed what had happened & we were very cheerful & almost uproarious at dinner—We are delighted."[8] It helped that the queen thought highly of Lascelles, not to mention that her daughter was clearly in love. "They are both very happy & Mary is simply beaming," she wrote to her brother Dolly, now the Marquess of Cambridge. "We like him very much ... *I* personally feel quite excited as you can imagine."[9]

The wedding took place at Westminster Abbey on February 28, 1922. One of Mary's bridesmaids was her friend Lady Elizabeth Bowes-Lyon, who would later marry her brother Bertie and eventually become queen of England. In their February 28 issue, the *Times* reported, "Everybody knew beforehand that only one thing could possibly be wanting to make Princess Mary's wedding day a perfect one, and that was sunshine. The sun shone brightly, and so it was perfect."[10] The king and queen were deeply saddened by their daughter's departure from their close-knit family circle at Buckingham Palace. After the wedding reception, George admitted that "it was terribly sad to think that she was leaving us.... I went up to Mary's room & took leave of her & quite broke down.... Felt very low & depressed now that darling Mary has gone."[11] The queen made a similar comment shortly after the wedding in a letter to her son David, who was in India at the time.

> The wonderful day has come & gone, & Mary is married & has flown her home leaving a terrible blank behind her as you can well imagine. Papa & I are feeling very low & sad without her ... Nothing could have gone off better than the wedding did, a fine day, a beautiful pageant from start to finish, a fine service in the Abbey, Mary doing her part to perfection (a very great ordeal before so many people).... Enormous crowds everywhere & a great reception when we stepped on to the Balcony [of Buckingham Palace] ... Mary & Harry L. drove off at 3.45 – Papa & all of us throwing rice & little paper horse shoes & rose leaves after them. Papa & I felt miserable at parting, poor Papa broke down, but I mercifully managed to keep up as I so much feared Mary wld break down. However she was very brave & smiled away as they drove off in triumph to the station.[12]

The queen's remark about stepping out onto the balcony refers to the iconic tradition for members of the British royal family to appear on Buckingham

Palace's balcony after the ceremony to greet the cheering masses. This much-loved tradition was in place as early as 1858, when Queen Victoria's daughter Vicky married Fritz. Since that time—with the notable exception of the prolonged court mourning for Prince Albert after 1861—almost every royal couple has followed suit and made the appearance.

After their daughter's marriage, George and Mary shrank from public life. Now in middle age, the couple who had fallen in love during the reign of Queen Victoria now had trouble understanding the new generation that was taking control of the Roaring Twenties. Mary and George preferred quiet evenings spent at Buckingham Palace reading, knitting, or sipping tea. Although they continued their official duties with enthusiasm, "in private the King and Queen preferred dignified seclusion, eating alone with each other, protected by the walls of their palaces from the post-war kaleidoscope of socialism, jazz and fast young women."[13] Their son Bertie was particularly concerned about his parents. He wrote to his brother David the day of their sister's wedding.

> Things will be very different here, now that Mary has left & Papa & Mama will miss her too terribly, I fear, but it may have a good effect in bringing them out again into public. I feel that they can't possibly stay in & dine together every night of their lives & ... I don't see what they are going to do otherwise, except ask people here or go out themselves. But we shall know more about this as days go on.[14]

The days came and went, but there was little sign that the king and queen were changing their ways. Their comfortable domestic routine from their years as newlyweds was resurrected at Buckingham Palace. It would serve them well for many years as additions to their family arrived. But in only a few short years, this bliss would be shattered and would threaten the British monarchy with its greatest crisis in modern history.

Once Archduke Robert was reunited with his family in Funchal, the Habsburgs moved out of Reid's Hotel into a more permanent home. A local banker offered them the use of his estate, the Villa Quinto, perched nearly two thousand feet high on a mountainside overlooking Funchal. Constantly damp and plagued with mildew, it was barely livable for a young family. There was no electric lighting, and the only running water was on the first floor and in the kitchen; most of the time, it was freezing cold. To conserve the little bit of hot water they did have, Zita washed her children's clothes only once a week. She made it a habit to dress them in dark fabrics so that dirt would not be as noticeable. Communication was also a constant problem. Charles and Zita wanted to keep abreast of events in Austria and Hungary, but the only way they could contact the outside world was to send letters down the mountain into Funchal via automobiles or ox carts, but this was something they could not afford.

Lack of money was perhaps the greatest crisis facing the Habsburgs. There was a heated debate among the Allied powers over what the imperial family would do for money. Colonel F. B. Mildmay—a British member of Parliament who was no fan of the Habsburgs—unexpectedly took up their cause. In a memo to Lord Cecil Harmsworth, the undersecretary of state for foreign affairs, Mildmay explained why Britain had a responsibility to Zita and her family:

> I am not out to sympathize with the fallen rulers of enemy countries, but I am anxious to know whether, directly or by implication, the British government, in common with those of our Allies, made itself responsible at [the 1919 peace conference of] Versailles for receipt by the family of the late Austrian Emperor of the bare means to live. I am told, on authority which to me is unquestionable, that if any responsibility does lie with us, and with the powers who signed at Versailles, are open to a charge of culpably ignoring it....
>
> I suggest, but I may be quite wrong, that the powers banished the Emperor to this far island and then washed their hands of him, not troubling as to how he was to live.... The Austrian Government then seized their private fortune and property, and ever since 1918 the family has been living on the proceeds of the Habsburg family jewellry[*sic*] which is not very valuable. When they got to Madeira, little was left, so that real want and distress compelled their acceptance of the free house...at which moment [the emperor,] his wife and six or seven children had nothing but starvation to contemplate....
>
> I am under the impression that they are still left without means of any kind, and that the [family is] all but destitute.[15]

Mildmay's letter was enough to get the attention of the British government. Lord Curzon, the foreign secretary, used his influence to push through a final annual income for the Habsburgs. The sum of £20,000 per year was settled upon. The Entente decided that the money would come in equal shares of

£5,000 from the four successor states to the Austro-Hungarian Empire: Czechoslovakia, Hungary, Yugoslavia, and the now-unified Romania. This amount would have made the Habsburgs reasonably comfortable, but the four countries refused to pay a single pound, leaving them with almost no source of income.

The lack of money meant the food situation was dire. The Habsburgs lived almost entirely off of vegetables and puddings or jams that Zita made herself. The journey into Funchal was so long and expensive that they could not afford to get meat for the children, who were beginning to languish. Added to this perilous situation was Zita's eighth pregnancy, which was in its third trimester. Since the empress and her family could not afford the basic necessities of meat and hot water, there was no possibility they could pay for a doctor to care for Zita during this critical time. The only help she could expect during the delivery was from the children's maid, who was not trained in childbirth. Zita tried to make the best possible life in exile for her young family. She filled her days with household work, cooking, washing, ironing, and patching the few pieces of clothes they had left. When she was not occupied by these duties, she supervised her children, who divided their time between studying and crafts. Quinto's garden provided foliage for artwork that the children made to pass the hours.

Particularly important for the empress was a makeshift chapel that she built in one of Quinto's rooms adjoining the main hall for the family to pray in each day. For help constructing it, Zita appealed to the Funchal authorities, who "fervent Catholics themselves, could not refuse so pious a wish."[16] The government supplied the Quinto chapel with a small altar and an image of the Sacred Heart. Father Zsamboki, the priest who came with the Habsburgs into exile, conducted the daily Catholic services. In the midst of such dire circumstances, Zita's faith never wavered. "Even if we have failed in everything," she said, "we have to thank God, for His ways are not our ways."[17]

A Portuguese maid who volunteered to serve the family was moved to tears by their plight. "I just cannot bear that these two innocent people should be left so long in this completely inadequate house," she wrote. "Someone ought to lodge a protest!... Sometimes we do get very low and depressed, but when we see how patiently Their Majesties accept all these ills, we carry on again courageously."[18]

Outwardly, Charles tried to wear a brave face during his exile, but the people around him could see that he was but a shell of his former self. In March 1922, accompanied by Otto and Adelhaid, he made the long pilgrimage down into Funchal. For weeks, he and Zita had saved every penny to buy some toys for their son Carl Ludwig, who was about to turn four. Someone ran after the emperor to offer him a warm overcoat, but he declined to take it. Though it was sunny that day, the air was cold and damp. Charles, who had always been plagued by a weak constitution, soon fell ill with bronchitis and a fever of 104 degrees. For the next two weeks, his condition worsened. On March 25, pneumonia set in. Out of desperation, he was injected with turpentine to draw the infection away from his lungs. By the end of the month, his body was covered in sores, blisters, and lesions from countless unsuccessful treatments. A priest was brought in to lead the family in a special Mass of intercession, to take the emperor's confession, and to offer him Holy Communion.

Charles refused to allow his children into his sickroom at first. This was a long-standing rule upon which he insisted in order to prevent contagion. This became moot when Felix and Carl Ludwig came down with pneumonia anyway; Robert was suffering a postoperative gastric infection; and the household staff members were beginning to contract influenza. Late on the night of March 27, after the emperor partook of the Holy Sacraments, he summoned Otto to his bedside for some time alone between father and son. The next day, Charles said: "The poor boy. I would gladly have spared him that yesterday. But I had to call him to show him an example. He has to know how one conducts oneself in such situations—as Catholic and as Emperor."[19]

When his condition became critical, a crucifix was brought before him. The heavily pregnant Zita, sitting next to the sickbed, held it as her children sat in hushed reverence. "I must suffer like this so my peoples can come together again," Charles told his wife, his eyes fixed on the cross.[20] Charles lingered on for days, slowly suffocating. His face pale, covered in sweat, he repeatedly kept telling his wife how much he loved her. "Oh, why do they not let us go home," he asked Zita. "I want so much to go home with you." By March 31, he was drifting in and out of consciousness. Looking around his room, he called each of his children by name. "Protect their bodies and their souls," he muttered to his wife. At 12:23 p.m. on April 1, he was ready to surrender his life. Looking over at Zita, who was still sitting next to him with the crucifix in her hands, he managed to mutter, "I can't go on much longer ... Thy will be done ... Yes ... Yes ... As you will it ... Jesus!"[21] A few moments later, Charles I of Austria died in his wife's arms. He was only thirty-four years old. Zita, his eight-month-pregnant widow, was thirty. A few minutes after the emperor died, his devastated family and their small staff assembled in a nearby room. Dropping to their knees, they hailed ten-year-old Otto as "His Majesty." Otto later recalled how odd that moment was: "I thought this was somehow wrong. His Majesty had always been my father. That was surely still my father."[22] Had the Habsburgs not been dethroned, Otto would have taken on the mantle of emperor, with Zita acting as regent. Otto was now hailed as the rightful heir to the Austrian throne, though he did not assume the title of emperor, and he did not begin exercising his authority as head of the House of Habsburg. That would remain Zita's domain until he came of age.

Five days later, the emperor's body was taken in a simple, two-wheeled handcart to the church of Nossa Senhora do Monte for a funeral service. Several thousand people lined the route the pitiful funeral procession took. A deep silence prevailed as a sign of respect for the imperial family. Empress Zita had hoped to obtain permission to bury her husband in the Habsburg crypt in Vienna, but the Austrian government refused. She instead had the body buried in the cemetery at Nossa Senhora. One of the bouquets placed at the grave had written on a small band tied around it, "TO THE MARTYR KING."[23] An Austrian woman who witnessed the funeral was deeply impressed with how Zita carried herself.

> This woman is really to be admired. She did not for one second lose her composure, nor did the children. I saw no tears from any of them. They only looked very pale and sad. When she came out of the church, she greeted the people on all sides and then spoke to those who had helped with the funeral. They were all under her charm ... But what will now become of this poor family?[24]

The foreign press could not deny the significance of the emperor's passing. One Austrian newspaper recorded that "his death on a distant and remote island must bring a pang of nostalgia to all those who recall what we had lost, lost through relentless fate but also, in part, through him."[25] In Vienna, a requiem mass performed at Saint Stephen's Cathedral was interrupted by cries of "Down with the Republic!" by monarchists. Empress Zita received numerous heartfelt condolences. "The whole Hungarian people mourns alongside Your Majesty," the Hungarian prime minister Count Bethlen telegraphed. "I would like you to accept the expression of my deepest sympathy in the name of the royal Hungarian government."[26] By all accounts, the condolences offered by the Hungarian government were sincere. The London *Times* reported the reaction in Budapest to Charles's death.

> The Regent, Admiral Horthy, and the Prime Minister, have sent heartfelt condolences to the Queen. The Government has ordered all public buildings to fly a flag at half-mast. Theatre performances and music are all forbidden. The wedding of the Regent's daughter has been postponed. Church bells are tolling. The Cardinal Primate will personally celebrate the Requiem Mass. It is, at any rate, agreed that Hungary must by united expressions of mourning fulfil its

chivalrous duties towards the Monarch banished by foreign decree. An imposing manifestation of mourning is expected ...[27]

The passing of Emperor Charles I brought to the fore the tremendous changes that had taken place in the former crown lands of the Austro-Hungarian Empire. "Along with the Habsburgs had fallen their ambitions," wrote one historian. "Ukraine was Soviet; Poland was a republic; Austria was stripped of empire; Hungary had rejected its Habsburg king."[28]

In less than a decade, Empress Zita of Austria was crowned, deposed, arrested, exiled, and widowed, all by the time she was thirty. The loss of her husband marked the most pivotal turning point in her life the same way her father's death did in 1907. She was now solely responsible for the care of seven—soon to be eight—children, all ten years of age and younger. Following in the tradition of Queen Victoria and her own ancestor Empress Maria Theresa, the last empress of Austria wore only widow's black for the rest of her life to mourn the loss of her beloved Charles, the man who had been hailed as the Peace Emperor during his reign of less than two years.

27

Return to Grace

(1922–28)

Within two months of her husband's death, Zita was forced to move her family yet again, since the widowed empress did not want her last child to be born in near poverty on Madeira. Less than a month after the emperor's death, help for the family finally arrived from King Alfonso XIII of Spain, who was partially prompted by the compassion of his wife, Queen Victoria Eugenie ("Ena"). Upon his deathbed, Charles had placed the hope for his family's future in the Spanish king. "He is chivalrous," he told Zita, "he has promised me."[1] Alfonso unequivocally told the Allies that he was now going to help Habsburgs. The king was a natural proponent, since he and Charles I's father were second cousins—his mother, Queen Maria Cristina, was an Austrian archduchess.

In May 1922, the Spanish warship *Infanta Isabel* arrived at Funchal to take Zita and her family to live in Spain. It was an emotional departure because, for the first time, they felt that they were really saying good-bye to Charles. As Zita watched Madeira shrink on the horizon, her "heart throbbed with a piercing ache. There, on that island, she was leaving behind her other self—that which had been most precious in her life."[2] In Spain, Empress Zita, her children, and their tiny staff disembarked from the *Infanta Isabel* in Cadiz where they boarded a train bound for the Puerta de Atocha Station in Madrid.

Looking somber and dignified in her black, widow's dress, the empress waved to the tens of thousands of people who greeted her with shouts of

"*Viva la Emperatriz!*" The king, the queen, and their highest-ranking officials amassed to greet Zita and the awestruck archdukes and archduchesses. When they arrived at the Royal Palace in Madrid, one witness recalled a conversation between Alfonso and Zita about her husband's last illness.

> King Alfonso related to her, how in the night before the death of the Emperor Charles, he was overcome with a feeling that, in the event of the Emperor's death, if he, the King, would not take his widow and the children under his protection, his own wife and his own children would suffer one day the same fate. He only found peace, after he had firmly resolved to give the bereaved family a home in Spain, as the death of the Emperor seemed to be certain. King Alfonso was not less overcome than the Empress Zita, when she then told him what the Emperor Charles had said before his death [about Alfonso being chivalrous].[3]

Zita's life of widowhood began in the Spanish capital, but within a few days, she and her family relocated to the palace of El Pardo in the Madrid suburb of Fuencarral-El Pardo. A luxurious palace, El Pardo was built as a hunting lodge in 1406 but had been refurbished numerous times over the centuries. The bright and cheery El Pardo was much better maintained than Eckartsau or Quinto, providing the most comfortable home that Zita and her family had known since their escape from Schönbrunn in November 1918. It was at El Pardo that Zita gave birth to her eighth and final child, a daughter, on May 31, 1922. Her family's luggage had not even been delivered to the palace rooms when the contractions began. Unlike her previous deliveries, this one was long and difficult. The exhausted empress was in labor for nearly a day before finally giving birth to the tiny infant. The posthumous daughter of the last emperor of Austria was named Elisabeth, after Franz Joseph's wife.

Little Elisabeth was sickly, and many did not expect her to live long. King Alfonso pressed for the archduchess to be baptized immediately. After a few days, her health improved. Zita's postnatal recovery was not so quick. Her eighth delivery in almost as many years took its toll on the normally robust empress. She was bedridden for two weeks before she even showed a glimpse of recovery. But the sight of her newborn daughter beginning to thrive reinvigorated her spirits. So too did frequent visits from the Spanish royal family. Alfonso and Ena made regular trips to see the archdukes and archduchesses playing happily in their nursery at El Pardo. The queen also had her personal physician regularly check on Zita.

El Pardo soon became an appealing pseudocourt in Spain. A bevy of guests began frequenting the palace. The king was a regular face. So too was his mother, Queen Maria Cristina, who usually came with freshly picked lilies and violets for the empress. Everyone was surprised when Zita was paid a visit by Archduke Wilhelm, a member of the extended Habsburg family who had caused the dynasty no end of embarrassments. A vocal socialist with nationalist sympathies for Ukrainians, Wilhelm had spent much of the war years lobbying Emperor Charles for the creation of an independent Ukraine within the monarchy, with him as its king. After the fall of the dynasty, Wilhelm continued to cause controversy with his socialist sympathies and constant requests to Charles for money. When his own fortunes plummeted in 1922, he made for the royalist safe haven in Madrid under the protection of his relative the king. While in Madrid, Wilhelm sought to heal many of the wounds between his branch of the Habsburgs and Zita's.

Another individual who visited Zita on an almost daily basis was Alfonso XIII's wife, Queen Ena. Descending on El Pardo with characteristic calm and dignity, very much a Victorian paradigm like Queen Mary, Ena was eager to embrace Zita as a friend. After her father, Prince Henry of Battenberg, died at a young age, she was raised entirely by her mother, Princess Beatrice, and her grandmother Queen Victoria. All her life, she embodied the traits of ideal an English queen. By contrast, King Alfonso was a fickle, passionate man whose behavior was unpredictable at best. As young adults, the mismatched couple fell passionately in love, but their life together was marred by one misfortune after another. At their wedding in 1906—which had been attended by Ena's favorite cousins Prince George and Princess May—the couple was nearly killed in a botched assassination attempt. Not long after that, their marriage began to fall apart when it was discovered that Ena—like her cousin Alexandra of Russia—had introduced hemophilia into the Spanish royal family. Unable to reconcile himself to the fact that the woman he had once loved so much had unwittingly helped to weaken the Bourbon dynasty, Alfonso sought comfort in the arms of as many women as he could find.

The days at El Pardo became uncomfortable when Alfonso began visiting the Habsburgs without his wife. The king, who was driven by his emotions, used his audiences with the empress to air his grievances about Ena. Zita, however grateful to the king for his charity, could see the impact this was having on her family and started looking for a home away from Madrid. The king pleaded with her to stay in the capital. Offering the family permanent use of El Pardo as an incentive, he encouraged the empress to send her children to school in the city. Zita's friend and biographer Gordon Brook-Shepherd explained why she could not accept such an offer: "But however grateful she was for the rescue, Zita would have none of all this. Madrid was already in political ferment, hardly the educational background for Habsburg children, who anyway spoke no Spanish. What their mother needed was a home of their own, where she could supervise the academic programme [*sic*] herself, through house tutors whom she would select. Above all, she wanted to be closer to France, the home of her ancestors."[4]

The political situation in Spain during the 1920s was one of the biggest contributing factors to Zita's decision to take her family away from the capital. The government was led by the politically ambiguous General Miguel Primo de Rivera, whose administration was characterized by its emulation of Benito Mussolini's Fascist Italy. During the first half of the decade, Madrid was seized by work stoppages and industrial impediments. Writing to Queen Mary, Queen Ena expressed her concerns: "I am sure you must all be anxious about the coal-strike & I do hope that this fearful catastrophe may still be avoided. Really what hateful times we are living in."[5] Having endured enough political turmoil in the last five years, Empress Zita was eager to take her eight young children out of the maelstrom that was engulfing Madrid. Thus her search began. Out of her element in Spain, Zita appealed to Alfonso and Ena for help.

"We do not need a palace," she told the king. "Is there not a house in some small village?" After thinking about it for some time, he replied that there was an old palace called Uribarren in the Basque region.

"It is the draughtiest house in Spain, because it is made up of windows. But it can be had for a song," he sallied.[6]

So in June 1923, Zita settled her family into their permanent home at the Uribarren Palace, in the Basque region of northeastern Spain. Uribarren was a medieval palace complex in the fishing village of Lequeitio, on the sandy shores of the Bay of Biscay. Whenever they wanted, the children could run and play along the beach or go swimming. The three-story, thirty-room palace provided the empress with everything she needed. It was commodious enough to accommodate her entire family. There was a chapel for them to pray in and read from the Bible. Its location was warm enough that they did not have to worry about dampness or catching a chill. For the first time since she ascended the throne, Empress Zita could finally breathe a sigh of relief. Her children were safe. They could finally move on with their lives in peace and quiet.

The residents of Lequeitio quickly took the imperial family into their hearts. It was these local residents that came to the Habsburgs' rescue in early 1923. Count Torregrossa, Uribarren's first owner, arrived in Lequeitio without warning, saying he wanted his palace back and evicting Zita and her children. The family spent the winter at the nearby resort of San Sebastian. The townspeople were so outraged by Torregrossa's actions that they formed a committee and convinced him to sell them the palace, which they promptly turned over to Zita, rent-free, for as long as she needed it. When they returned in early 1924, Lequeitio's four thousand residents assembled in front of the palace, cheering as they welcomed them back. The entire town had been draped in the Habsburg flag with Zita's portrait hanging in almost every window. This outpouring of affection was testimony to the strength and power of Empress Zita's character.

⤝⤞

In the postwar era, instability was not confined to Hungary or Spain. The 1920s was a decade of considerable unrest for Britain's imperial interests, both domestically and abroad. Owing to its close ties to other royal families, the British monarchy found itself increasingly called upon to be the savior of unlucky royals throughout Europe. In 1922, King George's cousin King Constantine I of Greece was overthrown in a coup d'état after fifteen thousand soldiers marched on Athens. Constantine told the people he was "happy that another opportunity has been given me to sacrifice myself once more for Greece."[7] The rest of the Greek royal family was not immune from the political turmoil sweeping the nation. F. O. Lindley, the British ambassador to Greece, wrote on October 1, 1922, suggesting that "a British man-of-war be sent for since the lives of the Royal Family were in danger."[8] The British Royal Navy cruiser HMS *Calypso* was sent on an emergency mission to Greece to evacuate Constantine's brother Prince Andrew and his family, who were in danger from the antimonarchist military junta. Andrew's mother, Queen Olga, wrote George a letter of gratitude for rescuing her son and his family: "Words fail me to express all my gratitude to you for all you did to save my beloved Andrea! I can only say 'God bless you.'"[9] The rescue of Prince Andrew by the king of England would ultimately prove fortuitous, since Andrew's son Philip would one day marry George's granddaughter—Elizabeth II, the future queen of England.

At home, civil unrest threatened to destabilize all of Great Britain. At the same time as the *Calypso* was evacuating members of the Greek royal family, two events took place that, together, toppled the government of the wartime prime minister David Lloyd George. The first crisis revolved around Ireland. Though it had been part of the British Empire since 1704, the island nation had been striving to achieve its independence for decades. In July 1914, Britain came perilously close to civil war over this problem. The idea of creating an independent Ireland gained enough momentum that Dona's son Joachim was considered for the kingship of the country in 1916. But the Irish independence controversy was overshadowed and soon forgotten by the outbreak of the First World War. Now, nearly ten years later, it came boiling to the surface again after Ireland held general elections, forming its own parliament. In response, Lloyd George ordered his administration to launch a guerilla warfare campaign against the Irish. The situation nearly exploded when English officers opened fire on Irish citizens, killing many. Only a direct appeal from the king stopped further violence. In the end, the country was partitioned into the Irish Free State, with the British-allied Northern Ireland acting autonomously from the rest of the country.

The flashpoint of the second crisis was the Chanak seaport in the Dardanelles, which was guarded by French and British troops against Turkish aggression. The fraying Ottoman Empire had been emboldened by a recent victory over Greek forces at Smyrna, leading to the abdication of King Constantine and the exile of Prince Andrew. This prompted them to launch an attack on Chanak. Britain threatened to declare war if Turkey did not withdraw, but public opinion was against the Lloyd George government. The people were not ready to face the hardships imposed by another costly war, and the empire's territories were not willing to defend the motherland for a conflict on the other side of the world. Leading the chorus of voices crying out against war in the Dardanelles was Canada. Traditionally a vital organ of the British army, Canadian forces refused to participate. They rightly claimed that they were not directly involved in the conflict and therefore had no business going to war against Turkey. With Canada refusing to pledge her troops, support for an offensive at Chanak fell apart, and Britain withdrew its threat of war.

His government's handling of the Irish and Chanak crises cost David Lloyd George his post as prime minister. His position had been undermined for years, ever since he nearly caused a revolution in Ireland during the war by introducing conscription there. His political opponents were able to discredit him further by going public with the news that he had been selling knighthoods and peerages—which could only be bestowed by the monarch—for money. With Great Britain's reputation damaged and its empire suffering, David Lloyd George was defeated in the House of Commons in October 1922. He was replaced by Andrew Bonar Law, but even that was short lived. Over the next thirty years, Queen Mary would see the rise and fall of no less than eight prime ministers. The fall of Lloyd George had a significant impact on the future of the British monarchy, which had long been admired as one of the greatest imperial powers in history. Under Lloyd George's government, the British Empire began to crumble. When Canada refused to support Chanak, it became Canada's first step toward independence from Britain. Seeds of separatism had already been sown at the Paris Peace Conference when Britain's imperial dominions—the colonies specifically populated by Caucasians and Europeans—were declared autonomous within a new Commonwealth of Nations. No British monarch could ever again declare war on behalf of the

British Empire, whose many realms felt they had fought and won their right to autonomy. It also served as a rallying cry for the empire's overseas territories. The sun began to set on the British Empire, and by the time Queen Mary's son would ascend the throne, it would fade to a dim memory.

After weathering the crises at Chanak and in Ireland, the queen showed no signs of slowing down. During those turbulent events, she continued to greatly impress the British people with her "self-assured calm throughout all her public engagements."[10] When she celebrated her fifty-fifth birthday in May 1922, it proved to be a memorable one. She and George made a state visit to Belgium, where they stayed as guests of King Albert I and Queen Elisabeth. It was the first state visit by a British sovereign in seventy years. Mary deeply enjoyed the visit, touring famous historic sites throughout the country, including the battlefield at Waterloo. She also visited the cemeteries of British soldiers who were killed in Belgium and laid a wreath at Edith Cavell's tomb. An English nurse in Belgium during the war, Cavell evacuated two hundred Allied soldiers from the country when it came under German occupation. When she was discovered in 1915, Cavell was executed. Although the queen had looked forward to the trip, she was exhausted at the end of it. "Felt rather tired," she wrote in her diary, but "I enjoyed my Belgian stay very much indeed."[11]

Belgium was followed that year by a state visit to Italy. Writing to her friend Emily Alcock, Mary could not contain her excitement at the prospect of returning to Italy, which she had not seen since her childhood: "We are looking forward to going to Rome in May, on our State visit to their Italian Majesties.... I have never been to Rome so I must try & see something of its beauties."[12] The Italian state visit raised more than a few eyebrows, since by that time the country was firmly under the control of Fascism. Victor Emmanuel III, the king of Italy, had appointed the notorious Benito Mussolini as his prime minister, leading to an uneasy alliance between the monarchy and the government. Victor Emmanuel argued that if they left each other alone, the arrangement would be fine. Lord Curzon, the British foreign secretary, was adamant that George and Mary's visit was devoid of any political underpinnings. The king and queen stayed in Rome during their visit. Despite the political instability—Mussolini had led his forces in a march on the city only the previous year—the visit went off without a hitch. George and Mary socialized well with the king and his wife, Queen Helen. The royal couple was also well received by the Italian people, who were in awe of Mary's grace and dignity.

Once they returned from their visit to Rome, the queen and king were excited to announce a new addition to their family. In February 1923, they became grandparents when Princess Mary gave birth to a son, George, at her London home, Chesterfield House. The birth of Mary's grandson was followed by the much-anticipated wedding of her second son, Bertie. The queen considered it a stroke of good fortune for her son, who was mild-mannered and suffered from a significant speech impediment. Bertie's struggle with and overcoming of his speech impediment was so impacting that it inspired the critically acclaimed 2010 film *The King's Speech*. In his shyness, Bertie took after his great-grandmother Queen Victoria, who, later in life, shuddered at the very notion of being out in public. It did not help Bertie's shyness that he had knock-knees and was left-handed, a condition that was classified as a medical disorder at the time. In spite of his shortcomings, the Duke of York had earned a name for himself as an excellent soldier during the war, whose commitment to honor, duty, and tradition made his parents proud.

There could be no greater contrast than between David and Bertie. Though he was sociable and very charming, the Prince of Wales chafed under his parents' influence, making them worry about his future as king. Bertie, on the other hand, greatly admired his brother and possessed a chronic awareness of his failings and no sense of his strengths. When Bertie fell in love with Lady Elizabeth Bowes-Lyon[13], the king and queen were not so concerned that she was not a royal. They were happy their son had found someone he genuinely loved and who returned that love, meekness and all. They also saw the marriage as a sign of the times. With only a handful of monarchies left intact after the war, the British royal family had to accept that there were few royal candidates left for their children to pick from. Along with this realization, George and Mary accepted the fact that their children may have to marry British citizens out of necessity. Traditionally, royals were forbidden from marrying their own countrymen, since they could never be the same rank as their royal spouses. Evidence that the king and queen accepted this fact early on comes from one of George's journal entries from during the war: "I also informed the [Privy] Council that May and I had decided some time ago that our children would be allowed to marry into British families. It was quite an historical decision."[14]

Bertie and Elizabeth courted for nearly two years before she accepted his proposal. It was a widely known fact that she was unwilling to give up her freedom for the duties of a royal life. But when she finally did accept, everyone was ecstatic. Queen Mary sent her the following note:

> The King and I are delighted to welcome you as our future daughter in law and we send you our warmest congratulations. The news has

come as a great surprise and we feel very much excited!... I hope you will look on me as a "second mother" and that we shall become great friends. May God bless you both, my beloved children, is the heartfelt prayer of your loving future mother in law, Mary R.[15]

Bertie was the first British prince in several hundred years to marry a nonroyal with the consent of the monarch. On Saturday April 21, Elizabeth lunched with the king and queen, who bestowed upon their future daughter-in-law their gifts for the wedding. From the king, Elizabeth received a tiara and complete suite of diamonds. From the queen came a stunning sapphire necklace. The wedding took place at Westminster Abbey on April 26, 1923. An estimated one million people lined the procession route from the palace to the church. The choice of Westminster Abbey was significant, since it was only the third royal wedding to be held there since the union of Richard II and Anne of Bohemia in 1382. For the ceremony, Elizabeth wore a dress of cream chiffon moiré, a long silk net train, and a point de Flandres lace veil, all of which were lent by the queen. Queen Mary looked radiant in a silver-and-blue-aquamarine dress. Accompanying the royal family to the wedding was the king's seventy-eight-year-old mother, Queen Alexandra, and her sister Dowager Empress Marie Feodorovna.

Although George and Mary responded quite differently to their sons' marriages than they did their daughter's, like any mother, the queen deeply missed her son once he moved out of Buckingham Palace. His new home with Elizabeth was at 17 Bruton Street in the central London area of Mayfair. "I hope you will not miss me very much," the Duke of York wrote to his mother after the wedding, "though I believe you will as I have stayed with you so much longer really than the brothers."[16] On June 6, the Duke and Duchess of York moved into the queen's childhood home, White Lodge, which the queen decreed was "in excellent order."[17] It was a difficult transition for Mary when her daughter-in-law began redecorating it, as the queen had such fond memories of the house. The queen also caused her son and daughter-in-law some frustration by insisting that she be in charge of the changes to the building. Of course, Mary knew that many of the changes Elizabeth was making were necessary upkeep, but she still had to put on a brave face at the sight of her beloved White Lodge being renovated. By 1923, White Lodge was not the same private country home it had been during Mary's childhood. The estate had become notoriously expensive to maintain. It also became a tourist destination for thousands of eager spectators who arrived weekly to catch a glimpse of the Yorks.

During this period in her life, the queen of England spent much of her spare time redecorating her own homes, a habit she had enjoyed since her youth. She feverishly oversaw changes at Buckingham Palace, Windsor, Balmoral, and on rare occasions, Holyrood Palace in Edinburgh. She took particular delight in creating interiors in the style of King George II, who ruled Britain from 1727 to 1760. The fruits of her labors were a tasteful mix of modern and traditional English styles. She also had a keen eye for minor details—a new painting here, some rearranged knickknacks there. One of the more unique objets d'art she owned was a handcrafted, custom-made dollhouse presented to her by George's cousin Princess Marie Louise of Schleswig-Holstein-Sonderburg-Augustenburg. Marie Louise had a professional architect draw up the plans, which included a Georgian facade and interior apartments modeled after those lived in by the king and queen. Mary, delighted with some changes she made to Buckingham Palace in 1925, wrote to her brother Dolly, "There are 2 or 3 things in the Palace I should like to show you, small alterations I think you will approve of."[18] Her decorating at Buckingham Palace, along with her numerous official duties, were inspired in large part by a tremendous desire to remain active. It was also a means of keeping her from worrying too much over her playboy son David, who showed no signs of giving up his bachelor lifestyle.

That same year, Queen Alexandra's health gave her family cause for concern. In March, she wrote to Queen Mary, "I feel *completely* collapsed—I shall soon go." That year, the aging queen dowager had suffered a stroke, slurring her speech. Alexandra, who had long been plagued by deafness, stopped making any effort to lip read. Even Mary was forced to admit that "it is difficult to understand what she says."[19] George and Mary were with the queen dowager at Sandringham on the afternoon of November 19, 1925, when she passed away after suffering a heart attack. Queen Olga of Greece, George's aunt, wrote a letter of sympathy to the king: "My heart *aches* for you and I only wish words could express all one feels ... yr darling, beloved motherdear, how terribly you must be missing her!"[20] The day after Alexandra died, the royal family attended a small remembrance service before the state funeral. Mary wrote that her mother-in-law "looked so lovely & young with pink draperies & flowers round her."[21] At the funeral in London, thousands stood in hushed silence outside Westminster Abbey. Mourning alongside the royal family were the king's sister Queen Maud of Norway and her family, who looked dignified in black. Queen Alexandra was buried in the Memorial Chapel at Windsor Castle. "Now darling Mama lies near Eddy," Mary wrote.[22]

As the 1920s moved forward, the queen of England was the undisputed matriarch of a rapidly growing royal dynasty, by now the most stable, most prominent royal house in the world. Shortly before Queen Alexandra's death, the Windsors received an addition with the birth of Princess Mary's second son, Gerald. The following year, public attention turned again to the monarchy when the Duchess of York gave birth. The infant, a daughter, was the first British royal to be born of a new generation. The queen recorded the happy event in her diary: "We were awakened at 4 a.m. by Reggie Seymour who informed us that darling Elizabeth had gotten a daughter at 2.40. Such relief and joy."[23] This was the first granddaughter for the king and queen, who promptly arrived from Windsor by motorcar the next morning.

As the first princess of the next generation, the baby's baptism on May 29 was carried out with stately dignity. Held in the private chapel of Buckingham Palace and performed by Cosmo Lang, the archbishop of York, the baby girl was baptized with water from the Jordan River while wearing a satin cream gown of Honiton lace that had been worn by Queen Victoria's eldest child, Vicky, at her baptism in 1841. During the ceremony, at which the queen was asked to be the godmother, the infant was named Elizabeth Alexandra Mary for her mother, great-grandmother, and grandmother. The arrival of grandchildren was a source of deep joy for the queen. She was not an affectionate, tactile grandmother the way her mother-in-law, Queen Alexandra, had been to Mary's own children. "We did not talk of love and affection and what we meant to each other," said one of the queen's grandsons, "but rather of duty and behaviour and what we ought to do."[24]

The birth of Princess Elizabeth in 1926 punctuated an exceptionally bleak period in Queen Mary's life. It began with the death of Queen Alexandra and continued with the death of her sister Minnie, the dowager empress of Russia, in 1928. In a letter to the queen, Minnie's daughter Xenia expressed what she and her sister, Olga, were going through: "You know how much we loved our mother & how we clung to her always & how in these cruel years of exile more than ever. She was *all* that was left to us—everything was centered in her—our home, our country, all the dear past … The light of our life is gone."[25] Minnie's life since the Russian Revolution had been a sad one, having lost two of her sons, her grandchildren, and numerous other relatives to the Bolsheviks' murderous rampages. She had settled in England for a time, staying with Queen Alexandra, though this eventually led to strained nerves between the dowager empress and the British royal family. She eventually decided to spend her last years in semiseclusion at Hvidøre, a seaside villa in Denmark. Upon her departure from England, she wrote to the queen, "I am more than sorry that I might have caused involuntary trouble to you, but I hope & trust that my absence will help to calm everyone. Everyone has only been kind to me & I have never even heard an unkind insinuation of any kind. With God's help things will blow over and I will return. I promise faithfully not to go near Buckingham Palace as long as my presence there might be misconstrued."[26] When she died, her famous jewels—which were estimated to be worth possibly as much as £500,000 at the time—were sold to help her daughters' financial situations.

The queen, a consummate lover of jewels and antiques, contributed to the auction by purchasing some of Minnie's most famous pearls. She later turned them into her famous pearl-drop tiara, which became one of the British royal family's most prized crown jewels. Princess Diana was a particular fan of it during the 1990s. Minnie was not the only person from whom Mary received jewels. Upon the death of Grand Duchess Marie Pavlovna in 1920, Mary acquired her famous loop diamond and pearl tiara. This piece became a particular favorite of her granddaughter, the future queen Elizabeth II. When George's aunt the Duchess of Coburg also died in 1920, she bequeathed "a chain with sapphires and a brooch to match" to the queen. The duchess's daughter Queen Marie of Romania wrote that she hoped Mary would "think of my sad old Mama sometimes when she wears" the jewels.[27]

The deaths of Alexandra and Minnie in relatively quick succession seemed overwhelming for Mary and George. Shortly after Minnie's death, George fell ill in the winter of 1928 after a weeklong hunting party at Sandringham. The king caught a dangerous chill. In no time, streptococcal infection set in. For the next several weeks, his condition grew worse. No sooner was the infection identified than blood poisoning flooded his body. There was little doubt that George was near death. In the meantime, stories were flying about the future of the monarchy. According to one story, the king had in fact died, and the queen was in league with Bertie to usurp the throne from the Prince of Wales, who was on his way back from safari in Africa. Bemused by such stories, Bertie half jokingly wrote to his brother, "In the event of anything happening to Papa I am going to bag the Throne in your absence!!! Just like the Middle Ages."[28] It was a cruel story, not only since the king was still alive, but also because Bertie had no desire whatsoever to rule.

A special council of six advisers led by the queen was appointed to rule during George's illness. Though Mary took a leading role on the council, she nursed her husband with unfailing devotion. But even the indefatigable queen could not maintain her characteristic calm. "G. was very ill in the evening as the heart began to give out," she confided to her diary. She ended with the ominous words, "Terribly anxious."[29] When the king's condition became critical, he was moved from Sandringham to Buckingham Palace where the family could be closer to London's medical community. Outside the palace, hordes of people stood crowded around the Queen Victoria Memorial in stunned silence, reading the bulletins posted on the gates. Churches nationwide were opened twenty-four hours a day to allow people to pray for the king. On December 12, an operation was performed to save his life. His chances of survival were slim, but without the surgery, the certitude of death was absolute. It took nearly three months, but the crisis passed; the king had been spared. Later, after her first real conversation with her husband during his recovery, Mary was so moved that she recorded, "After tea G. sent for me, he was perfectly clear & we had a talk for 20 minutes which cheered me much after not having spoken to me for practically 6 weeks."[30] Once it was obvious the king was on the mend, his cousin Queen Sophie of Greece sent him a relieved letter: "It was the greatest joy—to see your picture in the papers again to see you up about & about. It all brought you, if possible, still nearer to your people who showed such touching loyalty. It was splendid."[31]

After his brush with death, the king showed signs of his age. Just shy of his sixty-fourth birthday, George's health was never the same. His convalescence was long and arduous, and even after he was deemed healthy, it appeared he had lost most of his hearing. This latest illness showed everyone just how fragile the king had become. It also revealed how close to the throne David really was, leaving everyone to wonder whether or not the playboy prince would be able to handle being king. George was deeply worried about the future of the monarchy in his son's hands. Speaking about the Prince of Wales, he ominously declared, "After I am dead, the boy will ruin himself within 12 months." George knew that the hope of the dynasty rested with the Yorks: "I pray to God my eldest son will never marry and have children, and that nothing will come between Bertie and Lilibet [Elizabeth] and the throne."[32] Time would soon show just how prescient King George's words would be.

28

The Tinge of Sunset

(1928–36)

The six years that Empress Zita and her family had spent at Uribarren Palace in Lequeitio were among the calmest they had known since their brief time at Wartegg. "Such a quaint place, so bracing and wholesome!" was how Zita described it.[1] The family's financial situation also improved. Revenues started coming in from two of the Habsburgs' personal properties in Hungary, an estate at Rackeve, and an apartment house in Budapest. These were augmented by vineyards in the Rhineland and South Africa. King Alfonso also insisted on providing for the family. With the help of an anonymous group of Spanish grandees, he raised a small fortune to help the Habsburgs improve their standard of living.

Like Tsarina Alexandra of Russia, Zita took delight in raising her children herself, though it was a responsibility she did not take lightly. "I have one great political duty, and perhaps only that one," she said in an interview. "I must raise my children according to the mind of the Emperor, to make of them good men who fear God, and above all to prepare Otto for his future. None of us knows what that is."[2] From her perspective, Zita was not only caring for her children; she was maintaining the future of the dynasty. All of her children were scholarly like their mother and became her students in history and languages over the years. In appearance, the archduchesses— Adelhaid, Charlotte, and Elisabeth—shared similarities with their brothers, the archdukes Otto, Robert, Felix, Carl Ludwig, and Rudolf. Whereas Otto, Charlotte, and Adelhaid, with their fair hair and blue eyes, resembled their father, the other five children inherited their mother's dark, exotic features. The Archduchess Adelhaid, more studious and intellectual than her sisters, was close to her eldest brother, the robust Archduke Otto.

At Uribarren, Otto was given a stricter education than his siblings; naturally, the youngest children had the lightest workloads. This was mostly because, if there was ever a restoration of the Habsburgs, it would be Otto who would be placed on the throne. The other children were aware of their brother's vaunted position. When the children played, the moment the empress stepped into the room they snapped to attention, saluting both her and Otto. King Alfonso treated Otto as if the monarchy still existed, emphasizing his role as the lawful imperial heir. The king frequently invited the archduke to formal events in Madrid, where he was given the place of honor next to the royal family. But Otto's vaunted position never got the best of him. When he was once confined indoors for two days because his only pair of shoes was being repaired, his mother remarked, "he will understand the poor and will really be their king!"[3] As the eldest child, he was sensitive of his family's uneasy position, vividly remembering when his parents were deposed and exiled. Rather than being spoiled or difficult, Otto's circumstances had shaped him into a thoughtful young man who cared deeply for his family and his responsibilities.

Whenever Otto returned to Uribarren after his visits to the king and queen in Madrid, a disciplined atmosphere prevailed. Under his mother's supervision, the fifteen-year-old archduke typically began his day at 6:00 a.m., followed by nearly thirteen hours of studying or bookwork. The money that the empress had received from King Alfonso allowed her hire a number of tutors to instruct her children in German, French, English, and the classics. Zita's other sons thrived at Lequeitio. Robert, Felix, Carl Ludwig, and Rudolf grew into obedient children who adhered to their mother's wishes. They also inherited her fervent patriotism for Austria, along with the hope that the monarchy would one day be restored. None of the children seemed to inherit the weak constitution that had plagued Emperor Charles. With the exception of Archduchess Elisabeth at birth, all eight of the children were in excellent health, suffering rarely from serious illnesses.

Unfortunately, the tranquility at Uribarren did not last. By the late 1920s, Spain was beginning to succumb to its political woes. The king's mother, Queen Maria Cristina, was a regular visitor to Uribarren Palace and kept the family abreast of current politics. Archduke Otto recalled one of the last meetings between the empress and the queen: "She told my mother about her anxiety about the future of Spain. During her time as Queen it was she, rather than her husband who had kept up personal contact with all the left-wing leaders … who were later to proclaim the republic. She warned that if she were to die, she was very much afraid that the monarchy in Spain would come to an end within the next six months."[4] The deteriorating atmosphere in Spain galvanized the thirty-eight-year-old Zita, who had been preparing to send her older children off to reputable universities. For the second time in less than a decade, the empress was forced to find a new home for her family.

> But where? That was the problem facing the young matriarch with the heavy Habsburg mantle on her shoulders. For her, France would have been ideal; but the republic, having got rid of its own Bourbons, might not take kindly to the Regent of another banished dynasty settling there, especially in view of the unabashed monarchist activities of her two brothers in Paris. England, the Netherlands and the Scandinavian countries all still had monarchies, but their Protestant reigning houses had no family links with the Habsburgs. A strong link did exist with Luxembourg, for Felix, another of Zita's many brothers, had married Charlotte, the reigning Grand Duchess. They now stood eager to help in any way ... but the principality was simply too tiny to bear the weight of Zita's burgeoning ambitions. Mussolini's Italy was out of the question. Portugal, for all the official friendliness shown in Madeira, had deposed her own mother's dynasty and was, in any case, too far away from Europe's centre of gravity.[5]

In 1930, Zita chose to relocate her family to politically neutral Belgium. It was an ideal choice, since its proximity to France, Luxembourg, Austria, and Germany meant the Habsburgs could be closer to their numerous relatives. King Albert I and Queen Elisabeth, the Belgian monarchs, offered the family an invitation to stay in their country indefinitely.

In September, the empress rented a small villa from the Marquis de Croix called Hams Castle. Located near the town of Steenokkerzeel, it was roomy enough to house Zita, her family, and their small entourage of servants that had steadily grown since Lequeitio. The location was exactly what the empress had been looking for. It was close to Brussels, and it was on the direct road to the Catholic University of Louvain, one of the most reputable Catholic universities in Europe. Surrounded on three sides by a lake, visitors to Hams Castle were greeted by a medieval gate overgrown with ivy. Inside, carpeted stone and oak stairwells dominated the first floor. Throughout the castle were numerous reminders of Charles I, from photographs and paintings to trinkets he had owned.

Shortly after the family settled in at Hams, they were informed that the monarchy in Spain had been overthrown. King Alfonso, Queen Ena, and their family escaped into exile in Paris. As soon as she heard the news, the empress "penned a touching note, assuring her former hosts of a warm welcome as well as a share in what scant means she possessed" should they join them at Hams Castle.[6] This sad reminder of the fickle lives of royalty had been preceded by a bittersweet family milestone for the Habsburgs. On November 20, 1930, Otto turned eighteen. Since he had now reached his age of majority, he was declared the formal head of the House of Habsburg. For the many royals in exile, Otto was now the physical embodiment of all their hopes for a restoration. He and his mother agreed, however, that until he completed his studies at Louvain, the empress would continue to oversee dynastic affairs.

A few days after Otto's birthday, the first momentous gathering of the Habsburg dynasty in exile took place. In the Grand Salon at Hams Castle, Empress Zita—wearing only the glittering diamond-studded brooch of the Star Cross Order to enliven her widow's dress—declared in front of more than eighty archdukes, archduchesses, princes, and nobles assembled that, in keeping with the late emperor's last wishes, Otto has "in his own right" become "sovereign and head of the reigning house."[7] Empress Zita then knelt before her son and kissed his hand. She then affixed her signature to the official proclamation, followed by her son Robert, the emperor's brother Max, and her mother-in-law, the Archduchess Maria Josepha. A delegation led by Stefan Rakovsky even arrived from Hungary to sign the proclamation on behalf of his country's royalist community.

During her years in exile, Empress Zita never completely lost hope that the monarchy would someday be restored in Austria, though she naturally believed that Otto would take on the mantle of emperor. By the mid-1930s, disillusionment against the republic in Austria was running high, leading many to wonder whether a restoration was imminent. Zita's brother Sixtus met with King Alfonso XIII in June 1933. In a letter to the empress, Sixtus conveyed the message Alfonso had given him upon returning from Austria: "Vienna feels it stands on the threshold of the restoration."[8] Optimism about a possible Habsburg restoration progressed so far that Zita's supporters planned to bring Otto to London to meet King George and Queen Mary in the hopes of securing British support. The plan, devised mostly by Sixtus and King Alfonso, had Otto accompanying the king on his private visit to England that year. Alfonso wrote to Zita himself, saying he planned "to present Otto to King George V and to various people in power as well as organise a military tour of arsenals and barracks." Encouraged by the idea, Zita quickly sent off a letter to King George on June 22. She asked if he felt Alfonso's invitation to bring Otto to London "would be acceptable," which would make her "happy if he could be received at court." To avoid arousing any negative public opinion in England, she assured the king that Otto would travel incognito as the Duke de Bar. She signed herself, "Your Majesty's very affectionate sister and cousin."[9]

Although King Alfonso assured Zita that George and Mary thought the idea of Otto's visiting their court was "magnificent," it did not take long for the king's government to voice concerns about having a deposed imperial heir being received at Buckingham Palace. Sir Clive Wigram, George's private secretary, wrote a candid letter to Sir Robert Vansittart, the permanent undersecretary at the Foreign Office, about the problems that could arise if Otto were to visit. "I fancy," he wrote at the end of the letter, "that King Alfonso was under the impression that he could bring the Duc de Bar to this country absolutely privately, but this, of course, would be impossible as to all intents and purposes he [Otto] is a pretender."[10]

Once again, King George V was forced to bow to the pressure being placed upon him by his government. In the same way that he withdrew the offer of asylum for the Romanovs in 1918, so too did he retract, albeit politely, his support for Otto's being received at court. In a letter dated June 29, the king explained to Zita the difficult position he was in:

> It would have been a pleasure to the Queen and Myself to have met the Archduke Otto but I am advised that if he were to visit England in the existing unsettled condition of Central Europe, his presence in this country would inevitably give rise to speculation and rumour which would be embarrassing not only to my government, but possibly also to you and your son ...[11]

Although George showed Zita the utmost courtesy by addressing her as "Her Imperial Majesty, the Empress Zita,"[12] it was now clear that if the Habsburgs wanted foreign support for a restoration bid, they would have to look elsewhere.

Both Zita and Otto understood that time was of the essence if they hoped to see a Habsburg restoration in Austria. At the same time as the empress was corresponding with King George V, a new German Socialist party was gaining more influence in politics. Officially listed as the *Nationalsozialistische Deutsche Arbeiterpartei* (National Socialist German Workers' Party)—but more commonly known as the Nazis—and led by the bellicose Adolf Hitler, the party came to national power in 1933 with Hitler's election as chancellor of Germany. The devastating military and economic reparations that the Allies forced on Germany after the war made Hitler's rise to power possible. The inter-war period that gave birth to the Nazis had been "a hotbed of radical politics and a cauldron of economic distress. Industrial production faltered, unemployment soared and the currency collapsed. The nation lost its established leaders, the middle classes lost their savings and large sections of the public lost all hope. The vacuum was filled by wild radicals from both the Right and the Left. Fascist and Communist Party gangs battled each other in the streets."[13] The Nazis were self-determinationists "run wild, perverted by a defeat misunderstood, poisoned by racial mysticism."[14] In the Netherlands, ex-emperor Wilhelm was greatly alarmed by events in Germany, especially Hitler's violent treatment of the Jews. For the first time since World War I, Wilhelm wrote directly to Queen Mary. "For the first time I am ashamed to be a German," he wrote in indelible pencil.[15]

By the mid-1930s, Nazi Germany's aggression was unmistakable. There was little doubt that Hitler's ambitions would not be confined solely to his own country. Despite the growing tensions in Germany and Austria created by the Nazis, Empress Zita was eager to present all German peoples with a symbol of hope against Hitler. In September 1934, she announced her plan to return to Austria as quickly as possible in an effort to rally support for a Habsburg restoration to counterbalance Nazism. Her actions were even attracting attention in the United States, where the one newspaper reported, "Zita's friends in Belgium said that she expects to be living in Austria by Christmas. It was said she would bring with her Archduke Otto, her son, claimant of the throne." But even after so many years, some of the European governments were still anxious about Zita's presence in Austria. "It was feared by many political observers here that if her coming is a prelude to re-establishment of the Hapsburg monarchy, Austria, Hungary and the nations of the little entente [*sic*] will be confronted with new problems which will lead to more bloodshed, involving middle Europe, and possibly the entire continent, in a war." The countries that were most at risk from Nazi aggression like France "indicated that a restoration would be tolerated ... if that restoration would strengthen the Austrian opposition to the Nazis."[16] In 1935, Hitler introduced military conscription, created a German air force, the Luftwaffe, for the first time since 1918, and massively increased the size and scope of Germany's army, which had been reduced to a fraction of its prewar size. In London, many perceived that Hitler was determined to see Europe dominated by Germany. Winston Churchill prophetically warned Parliament that Great Britain was entering "a corridor of deepening and darkening danger" in regards to Nazi Germany "along which [the country] should be forced to move, perhaps for months, perhaps for years."[17]

Now finished his studies at Louvain, Archduke Otto began making regular, secret trips to Berlin to see exactly the extent of Hitler's control.

On more than one occasion, he only narrowly missed being arrested by the Gestapo, who viewed him as a serious threat to growing dreams of Nazi ascendancy in Austria. During his visits to Germany, Otto was unnerved to find that Augusta Victoria's sons had joined the Nazis. Willy, the former crown prince, published a number of articles in the British media supporting Hitler. Even more unsettling were reports that Dona's sons Eitel-Fritz and Oscar had joined the Sturmabteilung. More commonly known in English as the Brownshirts, these were Hitler's elite paramilitary storm troopers. Many Hohenzollerns joined the Nazi ranks throughout the 1930s with the hope that Hitler would restore their dynasty to the throne. Hitler "hoped, by associating himself with the old ruling family, to strengthen his credentials as the legitimate successor to Prussia-Germany's monarchical tradition."[18] Auwi was more devoted to the Nazi party than any of his brothers. In 1933, he became a pro-Nazi, Prussian member of the Reichstag. Around the same time, American newspapers announced that Hitler had chosen Auwi's twenty-one-year-old son, Alexander, to be his eventual successor as head of the Third Reich. By 1939, Auwi had worked his way up to become second in command of one of Hitler's secret police units, the Obergruppenführer. Otto recalled a particularly pointed meeting with Auwi and the impression he made.

> Prince August Wilhelm was, in my eyes, a convinced Nazi but all the Hohenzollerns shared the illusion that Hitler would reinstate the monarchy once in power. I was certain that Hitler was only using them as a means to attract monarchist voters. I had seen how the Crown Prince had already supported Hitler against President Hindenburg and that fundamentally he wanted to do exactly the same thing with me as regards the Austrian voters. I had the great advantage of having already read *Mein Kampf* from start to finish and knew what his aims were. All this only reinforced my refusal to meet him ... On the other hand, it would have been an interesting experience. In fact, this was the only interesting conversation I ever avoided in my life.[19]

There was royalist attention aimed at Hams Castle from all across Europe in the late 1930s. Many were wondering if Zita's family would follow the Hohenzollerns and join the Nazis. If there was any doubt, Otto, using his authority as head of the family and with his mother's support, published a letter making their position clear.

> I absolutely reject [Nazi] fascism for Austria and see the solution only in a constitutional monarchy along democratic lines similar

to that in England. I hope the Hapsburg law will soon be revoked by emergency decree, but I consider that the moment for a successful restoration is not yet ripe.... I refuse to be drawn into any adventurous *Putsch* [restoration] attempts....

An un-Austrian movement [Nazism] has lately been created which promises everything to everyone, but really intends the most ruthless subjugation of the Austrian people....[20]

Perhaps as a way to ensure Habsburg loyalty against Nazism, the Allied forces, led by France and Britain, restored to the Habsburgs a number of wealthy estates that had been seized under the Habsburg Law of 1919. Even the ban on certain members of the imperial family entering Austria was lifted. For the first time in nearly twenty years, the Habsburgs could afford to live comfortably once again.

Now that her son had come of age, Zita found she was not carrying as much political weight as she had in years gone by. Though she continued to be active, she found that, for the first time in years, she had the opportunity to pursue personal interests. An intelligent woman, she possessed a cultivated mind that could easily match wits with any scholar. Now in her forties, she had also become an avid reader. The shelves at Hams Castle were always being replenished with books the empress had purchased when she had the money. Not surprisingly, Zita's literary tastes did not gravitate toward popular fiction or mainstream novels. Among her favorite topics were biographies and memoirs. She also occasionally enjoyed reading the classics by Homer, Aristotle, and Dante. This love of reading was something that Zita shared with Alexandra of Russia, who once lamented that she could not spend more time reading: "Alas I have not much free time, but when I find a spare moment I sit down and read. I am so fond of 'Boehme' and many of the German & Dutch theosophists of the 15th & 16th cent."[21] A love of literature was something Alexandra shared with her husband, Nicholas. In the days of the tsarist empire, the imperial librarian would bring in twenty new books each month from around the world for Nicholas and Alexandra to read. But one area where Zita and Alexandra held different views was periodicals. Zita detested them, believing that newspapers were "committed to the task of keeping humanity on edge and in a dyspeptic dither with the constant expectation of disaster."[22]

The worsening global economic situation that helped give ascendancy to Nazism in Germany was also being felt in Britain. The Great Depression was causing unemployment to skyrocket, forcing the Labour Party government to deal with a crisis of extraordinary proportions. Conditions became so bad that the royal family cut short its summer holiday and returned to London, where King George forged a coalition of three political parties to form a national effort to combat the Depression. This coalition of the Conservative, Labour, and Liberal parties went on to win the 1931 election. George managed to avert a national disaster but at a high price. Exhausted from stress, the king fell ill with severe bronchitis, forcing him back on bed rest.

One of the last highlights in the denouement of King George's reign was in May 1935, when celebrations were held in honor of his Silver Jubilee, marking twenty-five years on the throne. Twelve other English monarchs had reigned just as long, but none of them had marked the occasion. According to tradition, only golden anniversaries were celebrated. The special nature of this milestone led to the creation of the Jubilee Trust, set up by the monarchy, to raise money for charity. Within a few weeks, £1 million was raised. Across the British Empire, festivities were held in honor of the last reigning king-emperor and queen-empress in the world. "I had no idea I was so popular," the king told Australian prime minister Robert Menzies.[23] Contemporaries noted that the occasion was "the biggest money-spending festival since the war."[24] The celebrations in London brought together one of the last major gatherings in history of Old Europe's surviving royals. The guest list included Queen Maud and King Haakon VII of Norway, George's sister and brother-in-law, and his cousin and old flame Queen Marie of Romania.

On May 6, the royal family and visiting dignitaries attended a service of thanksgiving at Saint Paul's Cathedral. The British politician Henry ("Chips") Channon watched the procession of royals depart from Saint James's Palace. Recalling the scene, Channon was in raptures over Queen Mary: "All eyes were on the Queen in her white and silvery splendour. Never has she looked so serene, so regally majestic, even so attractive. She completely eclipsed the King. Suddenly, she has become the best dressed woman in the world."[25] The queen did indeed look supremely majestic in her silver-and-white gown covered by a long cape with a high white collar. In place of her usual diamond tiara was a simple white hat with a high aigrette. "For them it was a wonderful experience," wrote one of the queen's biographers. "They realized at last they stood where Victoria and Edward and Alexandra had stood before them, high in the estimation of the people. Perhaps it meant more to Mary than it did her husband. Little May of Teck, the poor relation, the morganatic Princess, had made it to the top."[26] Mary recorded the memorable day in her journal for posterity.

> Our Silver Jubilee. Crowds in the parks & streets quite early—At 10 we went downstairs & saw all the members of our family who were to take part in the various carriage processions. We left at 5 to 11 in the big open carriage with 6 grey horses—We had a marvellous reception from the crowds of people all the way to St Pauls [*sic*] Cathedral & back—The thanksgiving service at 11.30 was beautiful—Back before 1 & we all went on to the Balcony where the crowds cheered us—After luncheon we had to go on to the Balcony again…. After dinner we had to go out on the balcony again—A wonderful day.[27]

The monarchy in Britain had become so popular that the king and queen appeared on the balcony of Buckingham Palace every night for a week to greet the patriotic crowds. Even in the streets of London's East End, which was famous for its socialist and republican views, George and Mary were cheered wildly by the people. Every day, they were driven in an open coach through the streets of London. Even in the poorest suburbs, they were met with excited crowds filled with flag-waving children and smiling faces. On May 9, the royal family assembled at Westminster Hall, where the king received a loyal address. The two thousand people who were gathered there sang the national anthem. Queen Maud, who had always been devoted to her beloved England, was thrilled to be back in London. Upon returning to Norway after the jubilee celebrations, she wrote to Queen Mary,

> I was *very* sad leaving "Home" and you *all*, but I was *so* delighted to have been present at the Jubilee, I *loved* the enthusiasm and devotion which the people have for dear George and you, it is *so* touching—and in no other country I am sure it is like that! One is *proud* to be *British*. I was glad to have been in London for G[eorge]'s birthday and could see you *all* once more.—I do hope both you and George are not *too* tired, with all you have to do. It *is* wonderful, all you have got through.[28]

The excitement that followed the king and queen's Silver Jubilee was followed by one encouraging event after another. The birth of Mary's fourth grandchild, Princess Margaret, to the Duke of York meant the continuation of the British royal family.

Two family marriages took place between 1930 and 1935. Mary's son George, Duke of Kent—who became the first member of the royal family to work in the civil service when he took up a post at the Foreign Office—married, as did his brother Harry, Duke of Gloucester. George was the only one of Queen Mary's children to marry a royal—Princess Marina of Greece. Consequently, she was the last foreign princess to marry into the British royal family. Marina was a granddaughter of the king's uncle George I of Greece, making her and the Duke of Kent second cousins. They first met in 1923 when Marina came to Buckingham Palace for a visit with her mother, who had been evacuated from Greece in 1922. "She has not a cent," King George remarked of Marina, but this was quickly forgiven because of her "charm and beauty."[29] The queen had hoped Marina would hit it off with the Prince of Wales, but she and the Duke of Kent became smitten with one another. The queen wrote to her husband before the wedding, "I am sure we shall like Marina & that she will be a charming addition to the family."[30] At their wedding reception, the queen had a seemingly innocuous meeting with a young woman who was a friend of David's named Wallis Simpson. "I want to introduce a great friend of mine," he told his mother.[31] Mary shook Wallis's hand graciously, thinking nothing of it. At the time, she could not have fathomed that Wallis would soon threaten to destabilize the entire British monarchy.

On November 6, 1935, Harry followed in his brother Bertie's footsteps by marrying a British woman—Lady Alice Montagu-Douglas-Scott, daughter of the Seventh Duke of Buccleuch, an old friend of the king's. The duke died shortly before the wedding, so it was celebrated very quietly in the chapel at Buckingham Palace. The princesses Elizabeth and Margaret were bridesmaids. The queen was greatly pleased by the match, since Alice possessed a suitably grand lineage. She was a descendant of King Charles II through his illegitimate son the Duke of Monmouth; her father had served with King George when he was a cadet in the Royal Navy; her paternal grandmother had been Mistress of the Robes to Queen Alexandra; and her maternal grandmother had been one of Queen Mary's own ladies-in-waiting during her days as Duchess of York. "Now all the children are married but David," the king wrote.[32] A few days later, the queen's sister-in-law Princess Alice, Countess of Athlone, wrote to Mary, "This is indeed good news & I congratulate you on settling another son & upon getting what I know to be a really splendid daughter-in-law. If only David would follow suit. He seems to have missed his best chances. But never mind, one must look on the blessings one has & be thankful for them."[33] Within two months, a new tragedy struck, cutting straight to the heart of the British royal family.

Never again healthy after his brush with death in 1928, King George V was plagued by failing health in the last decade of his life. In January 1936, the king and queen moved to Sandringham for a brief rest, but Mary was disconcerted to see that her husband was a shadow of his former self. Suffering from emphysema, bronchitis, and congestive lung disease, the king was slowly suffocating. Within a few weeks, it was obvious that he was dying. Mary almost became a prisoner at Sandringham because of the numerous reporters and photographers that had descended on the country estate. Between George's bouts of consciousness, his children kept their mother occupied. "G. about the same, sat with him from time to time," she wrote in her diary. "Did not go to Church as the place was surrounded by reporters & photographers, too heartless—Walked with Mary morning & afternoon ... Georgie arrived at 7—also Archbishop of Canterbury—David and Bertie left but will return tomorrow—"[34]

These opportunities gave Mary the chance to reflect on her forty-two-year marriage to her beloved George. She thought about everything they had gone through together—their accession to the throne, the outbreak of the First World War, and the numerous political crises they had weathered—and could not bear to think that their life together was over. Queen Mary was not ready to see her husband relinquish the crown to the forty-one-year-old Prince of Wales. Leaving the throne to David at this stage, when he had still failed to prove his worthiness to take on the royal mantle, would surely spell trouble for the nation. The Labour Party, with its socialist ideas on governing, might be tempted to call for abolishing the monarchy once and for all. On January 18, the king's Privy Counsellors arrived at Sandringham to gain his imprimatur on the formation of a Council of State, comprised of the queen and their four sons. After sitting in the king's bedroom in silence for about ten minutes, George faintly whispered his approval. Lord Dawson, the king's doctor, handed him the official document for his signature. Exhausted, George took a pen in his hand and, accompanied by Lord Dawson, marked two little crosses for his signature. As he did this, "[t]ears filled King George's eyes," because he "understood that this effort would be his last act as King."[35] Many of the Privy Counsellors also had tears in their eyes.

It pleased the queen greatly that her husband was able to spend his last days at Sandringham, the place he loved most. He cherished the estate where he had spent many happy years as a child with his parents and siblings. For a man such as the king, who enjoyed peace, quiet, and simplicity in life, Sandringham was ideal with its rolling hillsides, snow-covered trees, and picturesque waterways. It therefore seemed appropriate that it was here that he died on January 20, 1936, surrounded by his family. Just before the end, according to Lord Wigram, David "became hysterical, cried loudly and kept on embracing the Queen."[36] To ease the king's suffering in his final hours, he was given a lethal dose of cocaine and morphine. After the king breathed for the last time, Mary, her face bathed in tears, took David's hand in hers. Kneeling, she kissed it and hailed him as king in a strong, resolute voice, followed by each of her children. "I could not bring myself to believe that the members of my own family or indeed anyone else, should be expected to humble themselves before me in this way," David later wrote.[37] In her diary that night, Mary wrote, *"Am brokenhearted ... *at 5 to 12 my darling husband passed peacefully away—my children were angelic."[38] Later, in a rare outpouring of grief, she admitted about her husband, "The sunset of his death tinged the whole world's sky."[39] The death of the man she loved was a feeling that was all too familiar to Mary. King George died in the same bed as his brother Eddy had nearly forty-five years earlier. She admitted in her typical calm fashion, "Such a sad day. It is curious my having been present in this house at the death beds of 2 brothers Eddy & George."[40]

When the news of the king's death was announced, the demonstrations of grief were sincere not only across the British Empire but the whole world. King George V had been a bastion of strength throughout the long, difficult years of the Great War, and the people of the world mourned his loss. For a week before the funeral, Queen Mary appeared throughout London to show her gratitude to the people for their heartfelt condolences. Dressed in black with a long veil covering her face, she was surrounded by the women of the royal family. Witnesses stood in awe of Queen Mary, the Princess Royal, the duchesses of York and Kent, her sister-in-law Queen Maud of Norway, and George's aunt Princess Beatrice as they moved through the city in an ethereal mixture of mourning and dignity. The draped coffin containing the king's body was laid in the church at Sandringham, resting beneath the bas-relief gold altar and stained glass window that extended nearly the entire height of the church. Queen Mary's sons took turns holding an almost round-the-clock vigil over their father's coffin. The queen's memory was forever ingrained with that sight. "Went to the Church after luncheon," she wrote. "It all looked very peaceful—but so sad—My sons returned also Harry & Alice & Elizabeth. Did business with David who was most helpful and kind."[41]

From the Wolferton train station near Sandringham in Norfolk, King George V's body was taken to London on Thursday, January 23. Upon arrival, the new king and his brothers followed their father's coffin on foot to the Palace of Westminster for the lying in state. During the procession, the Maltese cross on top of the diamond-covered Imperial State Crown, which had been sitting on the coffin, came loose and crashed on the ground. Everyone saw it as a bad omen for the new reign. They would not be mistaken.

During the lying in state at Westminster, more than a million souls gathered to pay their last respects to the man who had ruled the British Empire for twenty-five years. For all his unflinching traditionalism, George also demonstrated an ability to be forward thinking. He had been "the first British sovereign to recognize that the royal family needed to be popular to survive. He was the first King to hire a public-relations officer, the first to make use of the talking cinema newsreel, the first to make use of the Christmas radio broadcast to the nation, and the first to insist that his relatives do something to make themselves look slightly more useful to help justify their gilded existences."[42] Coupled with his legacy of stability for the institution of monarchy was the fact that he was also the longest-reigning king of England since George III, who reigned from 1760 to 1820—though from 1811 his eldest son acted as regent. In *Life* magazine's special 2010 royalty issue, the king received an apt epitaph describing the challenges he faced in his long reign.

> [King George V] was suited like his father for a Victorian or an Edwardian time, but that's not what the world would offer. He was a man of stamp collecting and game hunting, but socialism was on the rise—communism and fascism too—during his relatively long reign from 1910 to 1936. Meantime, the Great War ensued, the Great Depression hit, and the world was altered mightily. During World War I, he was the one who was compelled to shed his family's Germanic name (Saxe-Coburg and Gotha) and adopt a British-sounding one (Windsor). He coped as he could, but when he died, his country—and the world—was on the verge of an Armageddon like no other.[43]

The emotional funeral was held at Windsor Castle on the damp, misty morning of January 28. Chips Channon noted that the queen looked "more magnificent than ever."[44] Her four sons walked behind the gun carriage bearing the king's body to Westminster Hall. The silence in the streets was overwhelming. The whole of London seemed to come to a standstill.

The funeral for King George V marked the final gathering in history of Old Europe's royals, most of whom had reigned or been deposed during the First World War. Along with the kings of Norway, Denmark, Bulgaria, and Belgium were royal representatives of Italy, Yugoslavia, Sweden, Greece, Egypt, Luxembourg, France, Spain, Albania, and Russia. In a surprise move that suggested a decline in anti-German sentiments in Britain, the funeral also brought together a number of deposed German royals, including the Grand Duke of Hesse, the Duke of Brunswick, and perhaps most poignantly the middle-aged, arthritic, English-born Duke of Coburg who arrived wearing a German military helmet. The funeral was also the last time that the ex-emperor Wilhelm contacted his British cousins. He penned a note of condolence to

Mary, and sent his grandson Fritzi—Crown Prince Willy's fourth son—to the funeral. Afterward, the queen gave Fritzi—who would later marry a British woman and become a naturalized citizen—a gold box from George's writing desk as a gift for Wilhelm. "Deeply moved by the kind thought that prompted you to send me this gift as a souvenir," he wrote to Mary, signing the letter as her "devoted cousin."[45] After King George V was laid to rest, Queen Mary wrote: "We left him sadly, lying with his ancestors in the vault. We returned to London by train & got home by 3.30."[46]

In the days and weeks that followed George's death, his grieving widow was overwhelmed by the "wonderful crowds of sorrowing people mourning their dear King."[47] What truly took Queen Mary by surprise was the outpouring of affection toward her. She had long believed that her popularity was tied directly to being the king's wife. But when he died, her own popularity continued. It touched a deep chord in her heart when she realized that the British people loved her for who she was, not for whom she was married to. In Parliament's tribute to the late king, the government expressed its sincere gratitude that "even in her sorrow Queen Mary is spared to the people who love her."[48]

29

For the Love of a Woman

(1936–53)

The death of King George V marked the passing from the world stage of one of the last great monarchs of the Old World. Born during the reign of his grandmother Queen Victoria, and raised in an era when the sun never set on the British Empire, George played a key role in world affairs and shaped the course of history. But now, the accession of the playboy king—who took the name Edward VIII—ushered in a new period in England's history, for many expected great things from him. In a mixture of hope and grief, Edward, dressed in an admiral's uniform and accompanied by his brother Bertie, was solemnly proclaimed Britain's new monarch by the Accession Council in "a fleeting, brilliant ceremony" the morning after his father died[1]—Edward arrived at the ceremony in London from Sandringham by airplane, making him the first British monarch to ever travel by air.

For the first time in a quarter century, Mary was not at the center of the British monarchy, though she remained its highest-ranking woman since Edward VIII had no queen. On the first Easter after George V's death, Mary moved into Royal Lodge at Windsor Great Park with the Yorks, where she stayed for several weeks. "I feel that the Family, as a family, will now revolve around you," the Duchess of York wrote to Queen Mary. "Thank God we have all got you as a central point, because without that point it might easily disintegrate."[2] On May 25, Queen Mary participated in her first semiofficial public engagement since her husband's death. Accompanied by her entire family, she traveled to Southampton at the invitation of the Cunard White

Star Company to inspect their newest ocean liner, the RMS *Queen Mary*, which was scheduled to embark on its maiden voyage to New York two days later. The visit greatly boosted Mary's spirits. The next day, May 26, the royal family assembled again, this time at Buckingham Palace, to celebrate Mary's sixty-ninth birthday.

Queen Mary spent the months that followed working on her late husband's affairs, managing his will, and planning her eventual move back to Marlborough House—the traditional residence of the Prince of Wales or, should there be no incumbent, the queen dowager. She considered this of the highest priority, since Buckingham Palace was the home of the sovereign. She resolved to make the transition as smoothly as possible and was determined not to be a thorn in the new king's side the way Queen Alexandra had been in hers and George's.

In July, Queen Mary returned to Sandringham for the first time since George's death. This was when the reality of her loss struck her, causing her to fight back sobs. Filled with compassion for his grieving mother, the king came to visit Mary often during the summer months. She wrote to Edward after one such visit.

> I fear I was very quiet today when you came to see me but I feel sure you realized that I felt very sad at leaving those comfortable rooms which have been my happy Home for twenty-five years, and that I was terribly afraid of breaking down—It was dear of you to come and see me off and I thank you with all my heart … It is very nice here and peaceful and I am sure I shall like it, but I miss dearest Papa quite dreadfully, even more than in London, and his rooms look so empty and deserted without him: I forced myself to go in and look round but felt very sad.[3]

With the arrival of autumn, so too came time for Mary's permanent departure from Buckingham Palace for Marlborough House. The move on October 1 was a monumental undertaking for the sixty-nine-year-old queen dowager, who was bringing with her a personal suite of sixty-five staff, servants, and household workers. The night before she left Buckingham Palace, the queen made a telling entry in her diary: "Sad to think that this is my last day in the old Home of twenty-five years—*Toute passe, tout casse, tout lasse!*"[4]

As Queen Mary did her best to settle down to a retiring life at Marlborough House, and just as the nation seemed to come to terms with George's death, a new and disturbing crisis arose. King Edward VIII had defied all sense of propriety and declared his desire to marry a commoner. The king's decision would make him "arguably the blackest sheep in 300 years of royal-family history" in England.[5] The object of Edward's affections was none other than the woman he had introduced to Queen Mary at a family wedding, Wallis Simpson, wife of the American businessman Ernest Aldrich Simpson.

At the time of his accession, Edward was forty-one years old. He was a handsome, clean-cut man with deep blue eyes, a defined jawline, and blond hair. His love interest could not have been more different. The dark-haired, dark-eyed Bessie Wallis Simpson was a thirty-nine-year-old American from Baltimore. Despite her more feminine sounding first name, she preferred to go by Wallis because she claimed "Bessie ... sounded too much like a cow."[6] Edward and Wallis's backgrounds drew a stark contrast to one another. Wallis, whose father died when she was young, spent her life relying upon the charity of other relatives. To make ends meet, her mother opened up their Baltimore apartment on East Biddle Street as a makeshift restaurant by cooking extravagant meals for the building's other tenants. Despite her humble surroundings, Wallis "behaved like a genuine Southern belle, with an overdeveloped sense of entitlement, and somehow she managed to receive just about everything she demanded." Eventually, she made her way to London, where she became popular in the social circles of the 1930s. Unlike many working-class Americans at the time, she was an excellent connoisseur of wine and a talented chef; thanks to her, British society was introduced to the concept of hot hors d'oeuvres. She was also the first person to coin the phrase "You can never be too rich or too thin."[7] What made Wallis's relationship with the king so unthinkable was not that she was a commoner but that she was once divorced and still married to her second husband. Up until the mid-twentieth century, divorce was a strict social taboo—King Edward VII once described divorce as an unseemly subject that should not even be discussed in front of women. Court cases involving divorce required witnesses to come forward and, as happened to many aristocrats, lawsuits were filed against adulterers.

Like many royal mistresses before her, Wallis moved in court circles, thanks largely to her charm, joie de vivre, and nonchalance about her social status. It was only a matter of time before she caught Edward's eye. The two met at a house party at Melton Mowbray in Leicestershire on January 10, 1931, when they were introduced by Edward's then mistress Lady Thelma Furness, the American wife of the head of the Furness Withy shipping corporation. The king "was the open sesame to a new and glittering world," Wallis would later reflect. "Yachts materialized; the best suites in the finest hotels were flung open; airplanes stood waiting ... It was like being Wallis in Wonderland."[8]

But unlike so many other royal dalliances throughout history, Edward and Wallis's romance would eventually lead to the altar. Most accused Simpson of being a philandering gold digger who was anxious to be a queen. When asked by her son why she would not receive Mrs. Simpson, Queen Mary answered, "Because she is an adventuress."⁹ But Wallis Simpson's supporters held to the belief that she never wanted to be queen but instead would have been happier as Edward's official mistress. "I told him I didn't want to be queen," she insisted. "All that formality and responsibility ... I told him that if he stayed on as king, it wouldn't be the end of us. I could still come and see him and he could still come and see me. We had terrible arguments about it. But he was a mule. He said he didn't want to be king without me, that if I left him he would follow me wherever I went."¹⁰

Edward invited Stanley Baldwin, the British prime minister at the time, to Buckingham Palace in November 1936 for a special meeting. The king defied the country's constitution and the laws governing the monarchy by announcing his intention to marry Wallis. Despite comprehensive coverage of their romance in the foreign press, the British media had remained eerily silent on the matter. So when Edward told Baldwin of his plans, the dumbfounded prime minister stammered out that the woman who marries the king "becomes the Queen of the country. Therefore in the choice of a Queen the voice of the people must be heard."¹¹ Edward put forward the idea of a morganatic marriage, a union in which the couple was legally married but the wife did not share her husband's royal title. Impossible, Baldwin replied. There was no precedent in English history for the wife of the king to be anything but a queen. Undaunted, Edward intended to go forward with his plan of marrying Wallis Simpson. His shocking announcement caused a quintuple crisis in Great Britain: societal, religious, legal, moral, and constitutional.

From a societal perspective, the king had offended many of his subjects who were still members of the aristocratic system. Many of the monarchy's strongest supporters felt snubbed by his disdain for tradition. Edward VIII was the first monarch in British history that wanted to marry a divorcée. The uninformed have often asked why could Edward VIII not marry the divorced Wallis Simpson if Henry VIII was able to marry six times? The answer is simple: Henry never divorced any of his wives. Upon forming the Church of England, he had four of his marriages annulled—declared invalid, as if they never happened.¹² Since Wallis Simpson's first marriage was terminated in a legal divorce, and it was expected her second marriage to Ernest Simpson would follow likewise, Edward VIII was in unchartered—and unfriendly— waters. His Cabinet refused to sanction the marriage to Wallis. So too did the British territories. According to the 1931 Statute of Westminster, "any alteration in the law touching the succession of the Throne or the Royal Style and titles shall hereafter require the assent as well of the Parliament *of all the Dominions* as of the Parliament of the United Kingdom." Canada, Australia, and South Africa unanimously declared they would not accept an American divorcée as their queen. From a religious stance, Edward, as the king, was also the head of the Church of England, and for him to marry a divorcée was completely against what the church taught. From a legal point of view, Wallis's divorce was only considered valid in the United States. In England at that time, the only legal cause for divorce was adultery, and since this was not the case for Wallis, her divorce could be considered invalid and therefore throw her potential marriage to the king in jeopardy, creating a dynastic crisis. Edward's decision also had profound moral and ethical consequences. The Privy Council, royal family, and many of the social elite knew Wallis to be very licentious in her behavior. It was a known fact that she had many lovers. With such actions, it was impossible for her to ever be queen. Finally, and arguably most significantly, Edward's decision created a constitutional crisis when Stanley Baldwin threatened to resign if the king married Wallis. Such a move would require the Privy Counsellors to resign as well, forcing the king to form a new government from ministers who would accept his marriage. Since few, if any, sanctioned Edward's relationship with Wallis, the prime minister's resignation would cause the government to collapse, threatening the very foundations of the British Empire. Clearly the king could not "both remain on the Throne and marry Mrs. Simpson."[13] There was no choice. He would have to abdicate.

Although British public opinion "was solidly against his marrying Mrs. Simpson," thousands of letters from the poor and working classes poured into Buckingham Palace "voicing their approval of his relationship with Wallis." Some historians believed that Edward never saw these letters, "or he may not have been so hasty to abdicate." Only in 2003 were letters from the Royal Archives made public that showed just how much of the British population emphatically supported the king's desire to marry the woman he loved. According to one biographer, the idea that Wallis "became queen or some other form of consort—was overwhelmingly endorsed by the working classes, by former servicemen who admired Edward's courage during the Great War, and by most British subjects under the age of fifty."[14] Of course, none of these people knew about British Secret Intelligence Service reports that Wallis had been a drug courier in China—a fact that is still disputed by historians and biographers today—or that she was a proponent of Fascism and the Nazi Party.

This unprecedented crisis affected Queen Mary on a deeply personal level. Years later, she still found it hard to discuss the incident in detail, though she described Edward's actions as a "shock" that "grieve me beyond words."[15] Not only did the king's actions offend her sense of reverence for the institution of the monarchy, but the fact that the epicenter was her own son was at times too much to bear. Unwilling to do nothing while Edward undermined the credibility of the royal family, Queen Mary made sure to be seen out in public presenting an image of calm strength. As often as possible, she was out visiting exhibitions, museums, and the many Christmas festivities that were under way.

In early December, she was at Marlborough House with Bertie when Edward arrived to inform them of his decision to abdicate. Upon being announced, the king walked across the room, kissed his mother's hand, and apologized for calling at so late an hour. He had something important to say, he told them. They were curious about what he might say, his mother replied. Taking a sip of whiskey, Edward, standing with his back to a roaring fire, blurted it out.

"Mama, I find I cannot live alone as King, and I must marry Mrs Simpson." Still calm and collected, Mary asked him what he was going to do.

"I shall abdicate," he told them. "Mrs Simpson is everything in my life, and all that matters is our happiness." Queen Mary stood silent for a moment.

"No, you are mistaken, David," she replied in one of the rare angry moments of her life. "All that matters is our duty. Consider the millions of young men who sacrificed their *lives* for their country in the Great War. And you will not even give up for your country a twice-married woman who is not even yet free to marry you!"

"No, Mama, all that matters is our happiness. That is all," the king shot back again.[16]

No longer able to be silent, Bertie chimed in, his voice stuttering with emotion. And what of Elizabeth? he asked. What of his family? What about the sacrifices Edward was expecting everyone else to make for the sake of his happiness? The king merely shrugged off his brother's remarks, flippantly telling him he would make a good king. Then, as quickly as he entered, Edward kissed his mother's hand and darted out of the room, leaving the pair stunned.

"He is wrong in almost everything he is doing," Mary told Bertie, "and only right in one thing."

"What is that, Mama?" Bertie asked.

Turning to her son, she replied, "In his belief that you'll make a very good king. And as Papa always said, Elizabeth will make a wonderful Queen."[17]

The next day, Mary sent Edward a letter which he appears to have mistaken for acceptance of his decision: "As your mother I must send you a letter of true sympathy on the difficult position in which you are placed. I have been thinking so much of you all day, hoping you are making a wise decision for your future."[18] The king sent his mother a warm reply: "I feel so happy and relieved to have at last been able to tell you my wonderful secret, a dream which I have for so long been praying might one day come true. Now that Wallis will be free to marry me in April it only remains for me to decide the best action I take for your future happiness for the good of all concerned."[19] In a letter to her daughter-in-law Elizabeth, Queen Mary was more candid about her feelings. "I am more worried than I can say at what is going on." Throughout the crisis, she felt very lonely and isolated. "There is no one I can talk to about it, except you two [Elizabeth and Bertie] as Mary is away & one can't discuss that subject with friends," she wrote to Elizabeth. "What a sad mess to have got into & for such an unworthy person too!!!"[20]

At 10:00 a.m. on December 10, 1936, the official announcement was made. Queen Mary wrote how "the paper" was "drawn up for David's abdication of the Throne of this Empire because he wishes to marry Mrs Simpson!!!!! The whole affair has ... been very painful—It is a terrible blow to us all."[21] King Edward VIII became the first English monarch in history to voluntarily give up the throne. Later that day, Prime Minister Baldwin finally revealed the intimate details of the abdication crisis to the House of Commons. In her diary that night, Queen Mary recorded that this "was received in silence & with real regret. The more one thinks of this affair the more regrettable it becomes."[22] The next day, Edward formally abdicated in the presence of his three brothers. He was forty days shy of having reigned for just one year. This gave him the dubious distinction of being the shortest-reigning monarch in British history and the fifth shortest in English history. That day, he made a radio broadcast informing the people of his choice: "You must believe me when I tell you that I have found it impossible to carry the heavy burden of responsibility and to discharge my duties as king as I would wish to do, without the help and support of the woman I love."[23] He also said that to avoid further scandal, he would be leaving the country immediately.

That night, the now ex-king met with his family to say their farewells at Royal Lodge, in Windsor Great Park. Queen Mary and the Princess Royal were the first to drive back to London after saying a "dreadful goodbye." The queen confided that "[t]he whole thing was too pathetic for words."[24] At the stroke of midnight, Edward and Bertie said an emotional good-bye. Edward bowed to his brother, hailing him as his new king, and the pair parted company. As part of Edward's abdication, it was agreed that he and Wallis would never again reside in England, though in the future they would fight to have this decision reversed. When someone asked Queen Mary when her son might return to his homeland, she replied, "Not until he comes to my funeral."[25] The relationship between the queen and her eldest son would remain estranged for the rest of their lives, despite the fact that they would continue to write to each other on a regular basis. After his mother's death, Edward's attitude toward her would grow decidedly more hostile. "My sadness was mixed with incredulity that any mother could have been so hard and cruel towards her eldest son for so many years and yet so demanding at the end without relenting a scrap," he wrote in a private letter to his wife. "I'm afraid the fluids in her veins have always been as icy cold as they are now in death."[26] In an interview with the *Daily Express* years later, Edward admitted his true feelings about the abdication: "But make no mistake, it is the circumstances, not the decision itself, that I regret. If twenty years were to be erased and I were to be presented with the same choice again under the same circumstances, I would act precisely as I did then."[27]

Edward VIII's abdication and subsequent marriage to Wallis Simpson in June 1937 had far-reaching consequences and set a dangerous precedent. In the years that followed, kings and rulers around the world found themselves under fire from commoner mistresses who demanded they follow Edward VIII's example and renounce their thrones for love. In Britain, the abdication crisis threatened the Windsor dynasty, already weakened by King George V's death and the monarchy's connection to Germany during the war. But in spite of everything, Queen Mary continued to enjoy unbridled popularity. Whenever she appeared in public, she was met with thunderous applause. One afternoon, the sight of her on the street prompted all the witnesses to cry out, "Thank God we've still got Queen Mary."[28] In October 1936, Elizabeth wrote to Mary, "In these anxious & depressing days you are indeed 'a rock of defence' darling Mama, & I feel sure that the whole country agrees."[29] Regardless of his mother's unimpeachable character, Edward's actions had repercussions.

On December 12, the day after the abdication became official, Bertie became King George VI, making his wife Elizabeth the queen consort. Bertie chose to take his father's name to create a sense of continuity and traditional values from George V's reign. Their ten-year-old daughter, Princess Elizabeth, was now heir apparent. George VI and his Privy Council sprung into action to limit the damage done to the monarchy by his brother. Edward was given the title Duke of Windsor and the style of Royal Highness. "Furthermore, my first act on succeeding my brother will be to confer on him a Dukedom and he will henceforth be known as H.R.H. The Duke of Windsor," George VI announced.[30] This honor, however, was deemed inappropriate for Wallis and was therefore denied to her or any children they might have. "Is she a fit and proper person to become a Royal Highness after what she had done in this country, and would the country understand it if she became one automatically on marriage?" George VI asked. "I and my family and Queen Mary all feel that it would be a great mistake to acknowledge Mrs. Simpson as a suitable person to become Royal. The Monarchy has been degraded quite enough already."[31] Queen Mary unequivocally agreed with the king: "It is unfortunate that he [Edward] does not understand our point of view with regard to the HRH and that this rankles still, but there is no doubt you must stick to this decision as it wld make great difficulties for us to acknowledge her [Wallis] as being in the same category with Alice & Marina."[32]

There was a particular lack of sympathy from foreign courts for Edward or his American bride. Queen Maud of Norway was particularly scathing in her opinion of the whole affair. "Where is She? *Do* wish something *could* happen to prevent them from marrying," she wrote to Queen Mary. "*How* sad it all is, that he has ruined his life, fear later he will be sorry what he has done and given up." Queen Marie of Romania was just as dumbfounded over the news, since she had attached the highest hopes to Edward VIII's accession. "Personally, I am too royal not to look upon David as a deserter," the flamboyant queen admitted. "There is too much poetry in my heart and soul to be touched by this love story. She [Wallis] is an uninteresting heroine.... I could weep over him."[33]

To secure Wallis's divorce from her second husband, Edward secretly paid Ernest Simpson an estimated £100,000 "partly to compensate him for the theft of his wife, and partly to get him to appear to be the adulterer in the subsequent divorce proceedings."[34] Once it was official, Wallis and Edward rushed off to get married at the Château de Candé, a Renaissance manor house in France. Huddled outside the château's fences were anxious paparazzi hoping to capture photographs of the ceremony. As expected, the highly controversial wedding was small—only sixteen guests were in attendance. The Church of England refused to sanction it, and no members of the royal family attended. "I suppose you get endless letters as I do," Mary wrote to George VI, "imploring us not to go out for the wedding as it wld do great harm, especially after the terrible shaking the Monarchy received last Dec[embe]r."[35] The only mention of the wedding that Mary made was a brief note in her diary: "Alas! the wedding day in France of David & Mrs Warfield ... We all telegraphed to him."[36] Edward took the absence of his family as an "unforgivable snub." Shortly after the ceremony, he wrote to his mother, "I was bitterly hurt and disappointed that you virtually ignored the most important event of my life. You must realize by this time, that there is a limit to what one's feelings can endure, this most unjust and uncalled for treatment can have had but one important result; my complete estrangement from you all."[37]

The abdication of Edward VIII was soon followed by the coronation of the new king and queen on May 12, 1937—the date planned for Edward VIII's coronation. It was expected to be even larger in scale than the 1935 celebrations for King George V's Silver Jubilee. In one of the rare moments of her life, Queen Mary broke with tradition by attending the coronation. Even the etiquette-insensitive Queen Alexandra had retired to Sandringham for George V's crowning. This tradition dictating that a queen dowager was forbidden from attending the coronation of her husband's successor predates the Plantagenet dynasty in the fifteenth century. But in light of the events surrounding George's accession, everyone felt Mary's presence was a necessity.

By dawn on coronation day, some fifty thousand people had flooded Pall Mall. Another two million people poured into London that day. Those invited to be in the congregation at Westminster Abbey had to be in the church around 7:00 a.m. The guest list included George VI's aunt and uncle Queen Maud and King Haakon VII of Norway; his second cousins the kings Christian X of Denmark and George II of Greece; King Yeta III of Barotseland (part of present-day Zambia); the prince-regent of Yugoslavia; Prince Chichibu of Japan; and Crown Princess Juliana of the Netherlands and her husband, Prince Bernhard. Departing from Buckingham Palace, Maud and Mary led the procession to Westminster Abbey in a glass coach escorted by a troop of mounted Horse Guards. As they proceeded down Piccadilly, thousands of voices cheered, "Queen Mary! Queen Mary!"[38]

Upon arriving at Westminster, the various royals processed down the abbey. After the Kents and Gloucesters took their seats, Queen Mary entered with Queen Maud at her side. "As Queen Mary's noble figure appeared against the sombre woodwork of the choir-entry the impression was such as to give me a catch in the throat of my memory," wrote one observer. "She was ablaze with large diamonds the size of beans, and she wore around her silvered head the circlet of her former crown with the 4 arches removed. But it was not alone the glory of her personal appointments, but the majesty and grace of her bearing that made everyone hold their breath."[39] The two elderly queens were seated together in a special pew with the princesses Elizabeth and Margaret. "Maud and I processed up the Abbey to the Royal Box," Queen Mary recalled. "I sat between Maud and Lilibet, and Margaret came next. They looked too sweet in their lace dresses and robes, especially when they put on their coronets. Bertie and E. looked so well when they came in and did it all too beautifully. The service was wonderful and impressive—we were all much moved."[40] During the service, little Margaret fidgeted incessantly. Mary eventually settled the princess by giving her a pair of opera glasses to look through. Later, along with the queen of Norway and the rest of the royal family, Mary posed with the newly crowned monarchs for the formal portrait. Queen Mary looked majestic in her famous diamond-and-pearl crown, red royal sash, and flowing ermine-lined robe. Queen Maud later admitted of her nephew, "Thank goodness dear Bertie and Elizabeth are so devoted to each other, and great help to each other, and they are *so* popular, and so are the darling little children."[41]

Just before midnight on coronation day, Queen Mary wrote to the newly-crowned king and queen: "I cannot let this day pass without once again telling you both how beautifully & reverently you carried out this most beautiful impressive service, I felt <u>so</u> proud of you both, & I felt beloved Papa's spirit was near us in blessing you on this wonderful day. I could not help feeling what that poor foolish David has relinquished for nothing!!! but it is better so & better for our beloved Country."[42]

The outpouring of affection for the monarchy at this time touched the royal family deeply. Queen Mary received thousands of letters from the people offering her their prayers and support after everything she had endured in the last year. Moved by "the kind letters" she had received, Mary asked the king's permission to issue a message of thanks to the British people. He immediately gave his consent, saying, "It will be such a great help to me." Cosmo Lang, the archbishop of Canterbury since 1928, composed the message on Queen Mary's behalf. Direct and uncontroversial, the message tried to give some credit to Mary's eldest son, while begging for support for George VI. She "declared that her heart had been filled with distress when her dear son laid down his charge." She concluded by saying, "I commend to you his brother, summoned so unexpectedly and in circumstances so painful to take his place ... With him I commend my dear daughter-in-law who will be his Queen. May she receive the same unfailing affection and trust you have given to me for six and twenty years."[43]

Any tranquility that was hoped for after the abdication crisis was marred by talk of war in Europe again. After less than eighteen months on the throne, King George VI was confronted with the greatest trial of his life. On March 12, 1938, the Nazis invaded Austria in a forced union they called the *Anschluss*. At Hams Castle in Steenokkerzeel, Zita and her family were deeply distressed by the annexation of their beloved homeland through Hitler's fait accompli. The next day, the empress spent hours in the private chapel of her castle praying "for a miracle to save Austria for the Hapsburgs." Acting on his authority as head of the family, Otto "was reported bound to consult friendly statesmen of France and Britain on Reichsfuhrer Hitler's Austrian coup."[44] The union between Germany and Austria was a cause for alarm in Europe, but few governments were willing to take a stand against Adolf Hitler. It was a mistake the world was about to regret.

Before the unthinkable happened, Queen Mary's life was marred by further heartache. Her favorite sister-in-law and childhood friend Queen Maud died on November 20, 1938. The queen of Norway had come to England for a visit. While she was there, she checked herself into hospital after she began feeling unwell. An x-ray revealed Maud was suffering from an abdominal obstruction, prompting doctors to operate. The night before her surgery, Mary sat with Maud, keeping her company. Things seemed to be going well after the surgery until Maud suffered a sudden heart attack during the night and died. Her death came as a deep loss to Mary. The pair had grown up together, became close friends, and eventually sisters-in-law. Queen Mary confided that she "felt stunned at the tragic news."[45] In a last act of friendship to the queen of Norway, Mary asked that her body be allowed to lie in state in the chapel of Marlborough House. It was a fitting choice, since Maud had been christened in the very same chapel sixty-eight years earlier. King George V and Queen Maud's uncle the Duke of Connaught sent Queen Mary a heartfelt note the day Maud's body arrived at Marlborough House: "My thoughts are with you today when dear Maud will be brought back to her old home to rest in the Chapel in which she was christened previous to her crossing the seas to the land of her adoption [Norway]."[46] After three days at Marlborough House, Queen Maud's body was taken aboard the RMS *Royal Oak* bound for Norway. Assembled at the train station to bid an emotional last farewell to independent Norway's first queen was Mary and the rest of the British royal family, including Queen Victoria's three surviving children—the Duchess of Argyll, the Duke of Connaught, and Princess Beatrice.

Any lingering hopes of a Habsburg restoration in Austria came to an abrupt end after the *Anschluss* with Germany in March 1938. Hitler was so worried about a Habsburg restoration that he gave the *Anschluss* the cryptonym "Operation: Otto" in the hopes of preventing the archduke from being placed on the Austrian throne. Zita and Otto, who were by now visibly anti-Nazi, could never consider a restoration under Hitler's banner. "The great European powers," Zita once wrote, "must be made well aware that, if they are against an Anschluss, then they must support the restoration."[47] These seemed like such hollow words once Germany invaded.

Once the Nazis were firmly in control of Austria, Zita and her family took a very public stand against Hitler and his agenda. On the day of the *Anschluss*, Otto—with Zita's endorsement—released a declaration from Steenokkerzeel condemning the invasion. In his statement, Otto announced that he spoke as "their heir to a dynasty which, for 650 years, has presided over the greatness and prosperity of Austria and is now the spokesman of the ardent patriotic feelings of millions of Austrians." He called on all people worldwide to condemn the "violent annexation" of Austria and to "support the Austrian people in their unquenchable will for liberty and independence."[48] It did not take long for Otto's declaration to receive a response from the Nazis. On April 19, the Ministry of Justice in Vienna issued a warrant "for the arrest of Otto Habsburg for the crime of high treason." German authorities claimed that the order for Otto's arrest "marked the well-deserved end of a charlatan who, for years, has used the great wealth of his house to foment unrest." Rudolf Hess, Hitler's deputy at the time, gave orders that Otto was to be executed if caught. Nazi reprisals against the Habsburgs were not limited to Otto. Though they did not seek to detain Zita, they were determined to curtail her influence in Europe. It was their hope that Otto's arrest would draw "a final line under the Legitimist adventures of Zita of Habsburg-Parma-Bourbon."[49] For the moment, Otto and Zita were beyond Nazi reach in Belgium, but not every Habsburg was so lucky. The Gestapo rounded up and imprisoned a number of archdukes, including Franz Ferdinand's two sons, Max and Ernest.

In September 1939, the situation in Europe collapsed completely when Germany invaded Poland. Great Britain, as a leading member of the Allies and a guarantor of the 1919 Treaty of Versailles that ended World War I, could not remain idle. With the consent of his empire and the Commonwealth, King George VI declared war on Nazi Germany, igniting the Second World War. On the morning of Sunday, September 3 Prime Minister Neville Chamberlain (who replaced Stanley Baldwin in 1937) announced to all of Great Britain that they were once again at war. Queen Mary, who was at Sandringham at the time, was at church that morning when the broadcast was made. The rector set up his wireless in the church's nave so the parishioners could all listen. That evening, Queen Mary—with tears in her eyes—sat next to the radio and listened as her son made his now-famous radio address to the nation and the Commonwealth. She remarked that the king's voice reminded her of her husband's.[50]

Over the next six months, events moved forward at a staggering pace. By April 1940, Germany had conquered Denmark, Norway, and Sweden. Of all the Scandinavian countries, Norway held out the longest, launching a resistance movement against the Nazis that lasted nearly two months. In the end, defeat was inevitable, prompting Queen Mary's brother-in-law King Haakon VII to flee to London. Hitler soon set his sights on Western Europe.

On May 9, 1940, Empress Zita's family gathered together to celebrate her forty-eighth birthday at Hams Castle. That night, German troops swooped down on Belgium as a prelude to an all-out invasion of France. Armed paratroopers landed only a mile away from Steenokkerzeel. There was now no choice. Zita and her family had to immediately flee Hams, their home of ten years, before Nazi troops could arrest Otto and his relatives. Only a few hours after they evacuated, German dive-bombers fired on the old castle, collapsing part of the roof.

Using the pseudonym Duchess de Bar to conceal her identity, Zita, her children, and their entourage fled to a villa in southwest France called Lamonzie-Montastrue. Owned by the empress's sister-in-law Grand Duchess Charlotte of Luxembourg and guarded by French Moroccan soldiers, the family found refuge here after more than a month of traveling under forged French passports and dodging German invasion forces. The Habsburgs used Lamonzie as a staging point for the rest of their escape. It was clear that Nazi troops were pressing farther west, leaving Zita with only Spain and Portugal as possible destinations for refuge. With the assistance of French troops, the family made it to the Spanish border, where one of the patrol guards recognized Zita and her group. The officer had been a fisherman in Lequeitio and vividly remembered the kind, generous woman whom the town had affectionately named "Our Empress of Lequeitio." With the officer's help, the group made it safely into Spain, just beyond Hitler's reach.

From Spain, the Habsburgs had few escape routes open to them. Portugal was no longer a safe haven, since over the past decade the Nazis had built up a noticeable presence in Lisbon. Escaping to London was also out of the question, since most of the air and sea routes to Britain had been cut off by Germany. Zita's son Felix advised his mother to evacuate to the United States, where President Franklin D. Roosevelt had made the family an offer of asylum. Zita was left with no choice. She had difficulty coming to grips with saying good-bye to Europe, since she did not know if she would ever return. Thus, in 1940, the empress, her children, and a small group of servants left Europe to join Felix, who was already in Washington DC. It was the second time in her life that Zita was flying in an airplane. Unlike that first flight in 1922, though, she had no husband and was not fighting to reclaim her throne. The forty-eight-year-old empress was fleeing for her life. She was also caught off guard by her accommodations. Unlike the tiny Junker monoplane that had barely carried her and Charles into Hungary, this new transatlantic, Pan American *Dixie Clipper* was spacious and equipped with all the latest amenities, though their journey was not without difficulties. Their plane experienced mechanical trouble over the Azores, where they were forced to make an emergency landing and await replacement parts. After a few days, they resumed their journey and landed at New York's LaGuardia Airport on July 20. Some fanfare accompanied their arrival because one of the other passengers onboard was William C. Bullitt, the American ambassador to France. After landing, Zita issued a bold public statement against the Nazis. It was the first time she ever released such a politically charged declaration in her own name.

The empress, who holds firmly to the cause of democracy in Europe, is convinced that freedom and Christianity will triumph over barbaric totalitarianism. Her ideas about the future of Europe are the same as those expressed by Archduke Otto. She believes that a Central European confederation of states, based on democratic principles, should be formed in the Danube area after the defeat of Nazism. Such a group of states could form a bulwark against any future aggression of pan-Germanism or Bolshevism.[51]

It was in North America that Empress Zita of Austria would spend the tumultuous 1940s. True to form, she would not be idle. Now in middle age, she was faced with the daunting task of settling her family on a new continent.

Britain faced an overwhelming challenge in dealing with a second world war. As one of the few countries in Europe that had not fallen to Germany, it became a stronghold for governments in exile. Monarchs like King Haakon VII of Norway, King Peter II of Yugoslavia, and Queen Wilhelmina of the Netherlands fled to London in an effort to preserve their legitimate governments following Nazi invasions.

For King George VI, the prospect of having his seventy-four-year-old mother so close to harm was deeply distressing. With no small effort, he managed to convince Queen Mary that it was safer for her to leave London along with the three million children and elderly who were being evacuated into the countryside. Her presence at Marlborough House would only cause everyone anxiety, he explained. Sandringham was quickly ruled out as a wartime residence since the king feared that with Norfolk being so close to the coast, his mother may be bombed or even kidnapped by the Germans.[52] Mary, long accustomed to facing adversity head-on, disliked the idea but eventually agreed. In the company of her staff from Marlborough House—some sixty-three people and seventy pieces of personal luggage—she left London at 10:00 a.m. on September 4, 1939. Her destination was Badminton House, a villa on the west coast in Gloucester owned by her niece the Duchess of Beaufort, her brother Dolly's daughter. During the journey, Mary passed through Peterborough and Oundle, followed by a stop in Althorp for lunch. It was here that an ironic twist of fate ensued. Queen Mary was received for lunch by the Seventh Earl Spencer and his wife. Their future granddaughter

Lady Diana Spencer who would one day become Princess of Wales. "How fascinated would Mary have been if she could have known that it was from this household that would come the next Princess of Wales," remarked biographer David Duff.[53]

Mary's home for the next six years, Badminton House was a comfortable old estate in Gloucester that was designed in the Palladian style, mimicking the buildings of Venice. Its massive, yellow Cotswold stone walls were surrounded by nine miles of verdant green forests. It was also a place that was familiar to Queen Mary. As a young woman, she had visited Badminton House for prolonged visits in the 1880s with her mother, the Duchess of Teck. At Badminton, Mary felt out of touch and isolated from her family, whom she missed deeply. Sensing his mother's restlessness, George VI asked that the Foreign Office send daily news reports to his mother so that she could keep up to date with all the latest information about London and the ongoing war. Arthur Penn, Mary's treasurer and old friend, also made arrangements to come from his regiment to Badminton a few times a week to act as her private secretary.

Queen Mary was not exempt from the hardships of her people while she was at Badminton. She found herself eating meals made up of rations, interspersed with vegetables grown in the gardens of the house or brought from the nearby village of the same name. Even worse were the scenes in London as the city's residents subsisted on meager rations of unpalatable morsels. The pitiful supplies of food and fuel were soon rationed. Food rations were not the only hardship the people of London were forced to endure during the war. In September 1940, the German Luftwaffe began bombing the city directly, showing no regard for civilians and noncombatants; Buckingham Palace was a regular target. On September 13, the king and queen were nearly killed when German bombers emerged low from the clouds and dropped a stick of bombs directly onto Buckingham Palace. In a long letter to Queen Mary, Elizabeth described the horrific attack.

> My darling Mama
> I hardly know how to begin to tell you of the horrible attack on Buckingham Palace this morning [*sic*] Bertie & I arrived there at about ¼ to 11, and he & I went up to our poor windowless rooms to collect a few odds and ends.... At this moment we heard the unmistakable whirr-whirr of a German plane. We said, "ah a German", and before anything else could be said, there was the noise of aircraft diving at great speed, and then the scream of a bomb. It all happened so quickly, that we had only time to

look foolishly at each other, when the scream hurtled past us, and exploded with a tremendous crash in the quadrangle.

I saw a great column of smoke & earth thrown up into the air, and then we all ducked like lightning into the corridor. There was another tremendous explosion, and we & our 2 pages who were outside the door, remained for a moment or two in the corridor away from the staircase, in case of flying glass. It is curious how one's instinct works at these moments of great danger, as quite without thinking, the urge was to get away from the windows. Everybody remained wonderfully calm, and we went down to the shelter. I went along to see if the housemaids were alright, and found them busy in their various shelters.[54]

A few days later, German bombers led another raid, this time to London's East End, which was one of the hardest hit areas of the city. The queen was horrified by the senseless destruction. "The damage is ghastly," she told Queen Mary.

I really felt as if I was walking in a dead city, when we walked down a little empty street. All the houses evacuated and yet through the broken windows one saw all the poor little possessions, photographs, beds, just as they were left. At the end of the street is a school which was hit, and collapsed on the top of 500 people waiting to be evacuated – about 200 are still under the ruins. It does affect me seeing this terrible and senseless destruction – I think that really I mind it much more than being bombed myself. The people are marvellous, and full of fight. One could not imagine that life *could* become so terrible. We *must* win in the end.

Darling Mama, I do hope that you will let me come & stay a day or two later. It is so sad being parted, as this War has parted families.

With my love, and prayers for your safety, ever darling Mama, your loving daughter in law Elizabeth

PS Dear old BP [Buckingham Palace] is *still standing* and that is the main thing.[55]

While her son and daughter-in-law fought to keep London functioning during the bombing campaign that came to be known as the Battle of Britain, Queen Mary once again threw herself into causes on the home front. She spearheaded a number of campaigns to salvage supplies. She spent days on end in the village of Badminton with a team of scrappers going from street to street searching for anything that could be reused. In her diary, she described her efforts: "We began the Salvage ... for old bottles, old tins, & scrap iron, we were most successful & filled over a wheelbarrow full—We are doing this at the request of the Ministry of Supply—& I hope to start it in villages in the neighbourhood."[56]

Throughout the war, Queen Mary continued to be the embodiment of the Mother of the Nation, though she was now the queen dowager. One person who came to look upon her as a second mother was Empress Zita's son Robert, who took up residence in London during the war instead of joining his family in North America. Mary was very impressed by the young archduke who was "battling on almost alone in wartime London." She took it upon herself "discreetly to 'adopt' him." Shortly after Robert's flat at 59 Saint James's Street was bombed, Queen Mary sent him a letter from Badminton House.

> I hope you realise how much I feel for you being cut off from your family and friends at this anxious moment, and that is why I asked you whether I could call you R. and you should call me Aunt because I should like you to feel that you have someone in England to whom you can write sometimes if you feel like when you feel rather lonely. I know so many members of your family personally or by name. I have always felt very Austrian at heart because my father served in the Austrian army until he married my mother in 1866 and he had so many Austrian and Hungarian friends.[57]

Empress Zita was immensely touched by the concern Queen Mary was showing to her son. It prompted her to send a letter to Mary via her son Felix, who was going to England to visit Robert. It was the first and only time Zita and Mary would ever have direct contact. Written in French, Zita addressed the letter to her "Dear Cousin, Her Majesty the Queen-Mother of England." Along with her "gratitude," Zita assured Mary of her "constant and fervent prayers for the victory of Christianity over paganism, and for our poor Europe to be saved from complete moral, intellectual and physical destruction."[58]

However concerned she was for Archduke Robert, it could not compare with the close eye Queen Mary kept on her own children. During the early 1940s, she made weekly visits to London to check up on her family. Her son the Duke of Kent appeared to be headed for a promising life, enrolling in the military and being promoted to the rank of admiral during the war. But tragedy struck in the summer of 1942, when he died in a plane crash in Scotland. The news arrived on the evening of August 25. Lady Cynthia Colville, one of the queen's ladies-in-waiting, was reading aloud to her when the king's private secretary Sir Eric Miéville arrived with the news and told

Colville privately. When she returned, Mary asked her if something had happened to the king.

> When Lady Cynthia, much shaken, returned to tell the Queen, Queen Mary rose from her chair. "What is it? Is it the King?" she asked.
>
> "No, Ma'am, I am afraid it is the Duke of Kent, there was an air crash. He was killed instantly."
>
> Queen Mary's face went white and she lowered herself slowly back into her chair. "I must go to Marina tomorrow," she said in a quiet voice.[59]

In her grief, Queen Mary was touched to receive a "most dear telegram" from the Duke of Windsor, who was asking for details about the accident. Mary replied in an eight-page letter that gives a rare insight into her deep grief: "Most darling David, In this terrible hour of grief at the passing of our darling precious Georgie, my thoughts go out to you, who are so far away from us all, knowing how devoted you were to him." She ended the letter with the words, "I send a kind message to your wife who will help you to bear the sorrow."[60] The duke later wrote to the king that their mother "is certainly a most courageous and noble person and it is hard that in her later years, she should have yet another great and bitter blow to bear. Her fortitude is indeed an example to us all."[61] Four days later, she watched disconsolately with her family as George was buried at Windsor Castle. His coffin was placed next to two other royal princes who died young: the Duke of Albany, Queen Victoria's hemophiliac son; and the Duke of Clarence, Queen Mary's first love. After the funeral, Queen Mary returned to Badminton House, except this time she was accompanied by the Princess Royal.

After nearly six years of fighting, Britain and her allies once again emerged victorious after Nazi Germany surrendered in 1945. Queen Mary, who had spent nearly all of that time at Badminton House, looked forward to returning to Marlborough House in London. To her own surprise, when the time came to take leave of Badminton and her niece the Duchess of Beaufort, Mary's eyes filled with tears. "Oh, I *have* been happy here," she said as she handed gifts to the Badminton staff.[62] She had forged a bond with the tiny Gloucester town. They had seen each other through the darkest days of the war. Now, Mary was sad to be parted from them. This deep affection and bond that Queen Mary of England had with her people would be one of her most endearing legacies.

With her return to London, Queen Mary once again lived at Marlborough House. Now entering her twilight years, she still insisted on making regular visits to hospitals, factories, and other public venues. Many of the people who saw or accompanied her on these visits "were impressed, sometimes embarrassed, by the thoroughness with which she undertook her tasks." She made it very clear that "she was not there to be seen but to see, and she insisted on seeing everything. Her questions, the result of her habit of serious reading, especially of social history, showed that she understood the background." But even at this point in her life, Mary still had a reputation for sometimes being "forbidding, and, on occasion, a stickler for etiquette. But this was all part of her rigid schooling and her Hanoverian ancestry."[63]

With her life in London being much as it had been before World War II, Queen Mary found herself being able to spend more time with her grandchildren, whose numbers had multiplied. During the war, she became a grandmother twice more when the Duchess of Kent gave birth to a son, Michael, just weeks before his father was killed. The second birth was to the Duke and Duchess of Gloucester. Alice delivered a healthy son in 1944 who they named Richard.

As time went on, it became clear that Mary's granddaughter Elizabeth would inherit the throne one day, since the king and queen never had a son.[64] This meant that when she came of marriageable age, there was great excitement in London. As early as 1944, Queen Mary had "wondered if an Englishman, through and through, might not be more popular with the people of Britain."[65] One frontrunner at the time was Hugh Euston, heir to the Duke of Grafton. In the end, Princess Elizabeth gave her heart to a man of her own choosing. In 1947, she married Prince Philip of Greece, a man she had been enamored with for more than ten years. It has been observed that theirs was truly an enduring love match. More than sixty years later, Elizabeth and Philip would be described as "one of the great love stories of the British monarchy."[66] As a small child, Prince Philip had been invited to take tea with Queen Mary, whom she described as "a nice little boy with very blue eyes."[67] The only son of King George V's cousin Prince Andrew, Philip renounced his Greek titles as a young man. He opted instead for the surname Mountbatten and embarked upon a successful career in the Royal Navy. Unlike in previous generations, however, nearly 40 percent of the British people were against the marriage on the grounds that Philip was a foreigner. The fact that his deaf, mute mother had cloistered herself as a nun and his destitute father had died in exile did not endear Philip to his future subjects—and the fact that he had no wealth, and at least two of Philip's sisters had married German princes who were devout Nazis, did not help. In the end, it was decided that none of Philip's sisters should be invited to the wedding.

The day before the wedding, King George made Philip an English prince, with the peerage Duke of Edinburgh. As a wedding gift—which was added to the twenty-five hundred the bridal couple received—Queen Mary gave Princess Elizabeth the diamonds that Queen Victoria had given at her wedding to George in 1893. One gift the princess received earned Queen Mary's antipathy: a piece of cloth hand woven by Mohandas Gandhi. She resented Gandhi for his activism on behalf of Indian independence from Britain, declaring his present "an indelicate gift" and "a horrible thing."[68] Elizabeth and Philip, however, respected Gandhi and were grateful for the gift.

Despite the excitement for the wedding, it was still a difficult event to plan. As with any family, squabbling was unavoidable. The Princess Royal refused to attend, ostensibly for reasons of poor health. She later admitted it was a protest over the fact that her brother—the former Edward VIII—had not been invited. The wedding also had strong national implications. England was still struggling to recover from the war. As such, Elizabeth was forced to use ration coupons to buy the material for her dress. Nonetheless, Mary's granddaughter looked every inch a royal bride in her white satin wedding dress adorned with garlands of orange blossoms, lilacs, and jasmine. The Westminster Abbey ceremony on November 20 was attended by two thousand people, including six kings and seven queens. The ceremony was broadcast by BBC Radio to two hundred million people worldwide. One witness at Westminster Abbey noted how "Queen Mary looked supremely happy ... For the first time in many years I saw the old radiance in her smile."[69] Winston Churchill described the wedding as a "bright ray of color on the hard gray road we have to travel."[70] After the ceremony, only a small crowd of 150 were invited to attend a reception at Buckingham Palace. The highlight of the reception was a nine-foot-high wedding cake. However, guests were only served from one of its four tiers. The remaining three were given to schoolchildren who were required to live on food rations after the war.

The royal wedding was followed by the birth of a son, Prince Charles, to the Duke and Duchess of Edinburgh at Buckingham Palace on Sunday, November 14, 1948. The duchess's pregnancy and delivery were followed with excitement throughout Britain. When the baby arrived, the official notice of his birth was posted on the gates outside Buckingham Palace. Mary "was rather surprised" by how many people gathered outside the palace awaiting the news "with sandwiches, like a film queue!"[71] "I am delighted at being a great grandmother!" Mary declared. At Charles's christening in the Music Room at Buckingham Palace on December 15, the elderly Queen Mary gave the infant a very special gift: "I gave the baby a silver gilt cup & cover which George III had given to a godson in 1780—so that I gave a present from my g[rea]t grandfather, to my great grandson 168 years later."[72] After lunch on the day of the christening, Queen Mary invited everyone to sit down and study Queen Victoria's old photo albums to see which of his ancestors Charles resembled the most. Mary decided it was Victoria's husband, Prince Albert.

The year 1947 also brought with it one of the most important colonial issues in British history: the independence of India. Since the Paris Peace Conference of 1919, the British Empire had been in decline, especially once the former imperial body had been reformed into a Commonwealth of Nations that allowed each territory to have its own self-autonomy. Britain's dwindling influence was evident to the new rising power of the twentieth century, the United States. Dean Acheson, the US secretary of state from 1949 to 1953, described the Middle East and Asia as "the last remaining bulwark of British solvency."[73] The last jewel in the imperial crown, India, had been slowly slipping from British hands. The massacre at Amritsar gave rise to two major Indian independence movements: the Indian National Congress and the Muslim League.

In Britain, Indian independence and the dismantling of the empire could not have taken place if not for the 1945 election of Clement Attlee and his Labour Party. When the Royal Indian Navy revolted in 1946, Attlee had no choice but to offer India its independence. The plan had been to transition to Indian autonomy by 1948, but the growing risk of an Indian civil war prompted the Labour Party to vote forward independence on August 15, 1947. With this act of Parliament, Britain's imperial title over India came to an end; so too did its empire. The British Empire as an imperial power essentially came to an end after World War I, replaced instead with the Commonwealth. But over time, even the Commonwealth "was fractionalizing as more and more countries—Jamaica, Kenya, Fiji—gained real-world autonomy while remaining 'loyal' to the Crown. Others—South Africa, Pakistan, Ceylon (which added to the indignity by changing its name to Sri Lanka)—chose, as had India, not to stay formally loyal, even if they remained friendly."[74]

Although Queen Mary was allowed to retain her status as empress of India, King George VI was forced to surrender the title. He was allowed to continue using the courtesy title king of India for another three years. Technically, George's wife, Elizabeth, was the last empress (and eventually queen) of that country, though she was never crowned in a *durbar*. Mary was the last empress to be invested with the crown in India and, unlike her daughter-in-law, she was allowed to keep the coveted imperial title for the rest of her life without being downgraded to queen of India. The loss of India from the British Empire was extremely difficult for Mary to accept. After receiving George's first letter after India's independence, Mary wrote on the back of the envelope, "The first time Bertie wrote me a letter with the I [imperator,

Latin for emperor] for Emperor of India left out, very sad."[75] Like Augusta
Victoria of Germany, Alexandra of Russia, and Zita of Austria, Mary's family
was stripped of its imperial titles by independence movements within their
empire. But unlike Russia, Germany, and Austria-Hungary, the last days
of the British Empire had not been marked by total revolution. And unlike
her imperial counterparts, Mary was still a British queen who enjoyed the
unparalleled affection of her people.

For the first time since World War II ended, the lives of Queen Mary
and her family seemed to be settling down. She was a doting grandmother
who was excited with the birth of another great-grandchild. In 1950, the
Duchess of Edinburgh gave birth to a daughter, Anne. The king and queen
had emerged from the war more popular than ever. Winston Churchill had
once written to the king that "Yr Majesties are more beloved by classes and
conditions than any of all princes of the past. I am indeed proud that it
[should] have fallen to my lot and duty to stand at Yr Majesty's side as First
Minister in such a climax of the British story."[76]

Mary was the last of Europe's queen-empresses who still enjoyed her
position, having ruled on the same tier as Augusta Victoria, Alexandra, and
Zita. It remains uncertain whether or not she thought of herself in those
terms. What is certain, however, is that like these other women, her life was
not devoid of heartache. At this stage of her life—she was now nearly eighty-
five—she expected things to settle down to a measure of tranquility. She
would not get her wish. In January 1952, the Duke and Duchess of Edinburgh
embarked on a tour of Australia by traveling through Kenya. Queen Mary,
the king, the queen, and the rest of the royal family all went down to Victoria
Station to see the couple off. The king, who had undergone surgery the year
before to treat lung cancer, was slowly returning to his duties, while Queen
Mary returned to her hospital visits and audiences with old friends. At the
end of January, George VI wrote his mother a touching letter that ended
with "Best love to you, I remain, Ever, Your very devoted son, Bertie." On
the back of the envelope, she would later write in tiny letters, "Bertie's last
letter to me."[77]

On the morning of February 6, 1952, Mary was working at her papers
in her sitting room at Marlborough House when Lady Cynthia Colville, her
Mistress of the Bedchamber, arrived, visibly shaken. The unenviable task had
fallen to her of telling Mary that King George VI died suddenly during the
night at Sandringham from a coronary thrombosis. He was only fifty-two.
Queen Mary recorded in her diary that night, "I got the dreadful shock
when Cynthia asked to see me at 9.30, after breakfast, to tell me that darling

Bertie had died in his sleep early today ... The news came out about *10.30.* Later letters kept arriving & flowers from kind friends."[78] That same day, Mary sent her newly widowed daughter-in-law Elizabeth a touching letter, in which she wrote "about the great affection between our darling Bertie and us *all.* I cannot get over the fearful shock you must have had when you realised that he had died in his sleep. You have been such a wonderful wife to him in 'weal & woe' & such a prop when things were a little difficult and he was upset, this must be a comfort to you in your great grief and I feel this very much indeed."[79]

Mary's twenty-five-year-old granddaughter was now Queen Elizabeth II, who immediately rushed back from Nairobi to London at 4:00 p.m. For the first time in more than fifty years, Great Britain was once again ruled by a queen, the same as during Mary's childhood. The afternoon that Elizabeth II arrived, Queen Mary insisted on hurrying to Clarence House to pay homage to her as the new sovereign. "Her old Grannie and subject must be the first to kiss her hand," she said.[80] When Queen Mary entered the room at Clarence House where her granddaughter was waiting, Elizabeth gently rose to her feet and extended her hand for Mary to kiss. With simple gestures, she kissed the new queen's hand and declared loudly, "God save the Queen."[81] One witness noticed that "Elizabeth's eyes pricked with tears as she accepted her grandmother's obeisance."[82] The new queen looked dignified and regal in a slim, simple black dress accented by a single row of pearls. Although Elizabeth II was young, Mary praised her for having "a fine steadfast character, & will I know always do her best for our beloved country and her people all over the world – and dear Philip will be a great help."[83]

Grief in Britain at the king's death was deep and sincere. Theaters across the country were closed, and the BBC cancelled all their television programming except for the news. The immediate mourning that was ordered was deemed proper by Prime Minister Winston Churchill. "We cannot at this moment do more than record the spontaneous expression of grief," he said. Outpourings of grief were not limited to Great Britain. The United States Congress adjourned out of respect for the king. President Harry Truman eloquently described where this deep grief was coming from: "He shared to the end of his reign all the hardships and austerities which evil days imposed on the brave British people. In return, he received from the people of the whole Commonwealth a love and devotion which went beyond the usual relationship of a king and his subjects."[84] Some three hundred thousand people filed past the king's coffin as it lay in state at Westminster Hall. At the rain-soaked funeral for King George VI on Friday, February 15 Queen Mary, accompanied by her daughter-in-law and Queen Elizabeth II, was dressed all in black, with a full-length veil covering her face. Chips Channon recorded the poignancy of the king's funeral and lying in state.

> The Great Hall was cold, splendid and impressive ... a few paces behind [George VI's coffin] the royal family followed, walking in measured paces like figures in a Greek tragedy. First walked the young Queen, all in black but wearing fresh-coloured stockings; behind her, to the right, was the Queen Mother—unmistakable with her curious side-ways lilting walk. On her left, was Queen Mary, frail and fragile, I thought, with her veil and her black umbrella and steel-coloured stockings. I was very sorry for her as she must have known and realised that she is next.[85]

After lying in state at Westminster for three days, the king's body was buried at Windsor Castle, along with his brothers Johnnie and George. On the day of the funeral, her old friend the Countess of Airlie wrote of her impressions as she observed Mary watching the procession of the king's body on the gun carriage: "As the cortège wound slowly along, the Queen whispered in a broken voice, 'Here *he* is,' and I knew that her dry eyes were seeing beyond the coffin a little boy in a sailor suit. She was past weeping, wrapped in the ineffable solitude of grief. I could not speak comfort to her. My tears choked me. The words I wanted to say would not come. We held each other's hands in silence."[86]

The funeral was significant for many reasons. It was the first time that a royal event was ever broadcast over live television. It was the first time in modern history that three English queens were alive at the same time. It also was the third time that Mary had outlived one of her children. Queen Mary never recovered from the loss of her son George VI, and she was never fully reconciled to the Duke of Windsor, whose abdication she blamed for bringing on the king's premature death. Mary's life has often been looked upon as a royal triumph, which to many it was, but it was also marked by tragedy and loss. The deaths of her husband and three sons were insidious distinctions that neither Dona, Alexandra, nor Zita were forced to endure to such a degree. Fate, it seemed, was exacting a high price for Mary's successful life.

The king's death was a crushing blow to his mother's spirits. Within a matter of months, the eighty-five-year-old queen dowager's health began to collapse. In the winter of 1952/53, she began suffering breathing problems and chest pain. She was diagnosed with high blood pressure accompanied by a hardening of her arteries. For the first real time in her life, she took to her bed and for nearly five weeks. It was also the first time that pages in her diary, which she had kept meticulously since youth, were left blank.

Speaking to her old friend Lady Shaftesbury, she asked poignantly, "I suppose one must force oneself to go on until the end?"

"I am sure that Your Majesty will," Shaftesbury replied.[87]

For Christmas that year, the royal family gathered at Sandringham as usual. Queen Mary spent much of the time up in her room, coming down only occasionally to join everyone for tea. In the new year, Mary was anxious to get out into London, especially to see the preparations being made at Westminster Abbey for the coronation of Elizabeth II, planned to take place in June. In the spring, an examination by Mary's doctors revealed that her breathing difficulty and chest pain were caused by lung cancer in an advanced stage, undoubtedly the result of being a social smoker, as well as a lifetime married to a heavy smoker. With the end near, the Duke of Windsor received permission to come from Florida to visit his mother. In February, Mary took her last drive through London. The bitter winter cold devastated her health, forcing her to take to her bed again at Marlborough House. But even in her last weeks, she refused to give up her most beloved habits. On March 24, 1953, Mary was resting in bed when she asked one of her ladies to read aloud from a book about her beloved India, the land that lived in her heart for so many decades. Later, a number of relatives, including the Duke of Windsor and Queen Elizabeth II, visited her bedside. That evening, as she fell asleep, Queen Mary of England, the last empress of India, slipped into a coma. Late in the night, Prime Minister Winston Churchill, trembling from emotion, informed Parliament that she died at 10:35 p.m.: "Mr. Speaker, I rise to move adjournment of the House. I have with great regret to make the announcement that Queen Mary has died."[88] The entire House, which had been in session late into the night, erupted in cries of grief, especially from the Leftist Socialists. A few blocks away at Marlborough House, an attendant posted the news of the queen dowager's death on the gates outside. Mary's last wish was that Queen Elizabeth II's coronation not be postponed in the event of her death. It was a difficult request, but the young queen acquiesced to her beloved "Grannie's" desire for duty above all else.

The people of Great Britain deeply mourned the loss of Queen Mary. She had lived through the careers of more monarchs than any other queen consort in English history, spanning the entire reigns of George V, Edward VIII, and George VI, and ending at the beginning of Elizabeth II's reign. Millions of people identified with her in a way not usually seen with queen consorts. It may have had something to do with the fact that she was the first English queen consort to be born and raised in country since the time of Henry VIII in the sixteenth century. She became a symbol of hope and perseverance for her people throughout the cataclysmic first half of the twentieth century. "Queen Mary was loved as no Queen before her had been loved," wrote one newspaper.[89]

When the time came, the people whom Mary had served for decades gave her a fitting funeral. On March 29, her coffin—draped in her red, gold, and blue standard—was taken by gun carriage from the Queen's Chapel at Marlborough House to Westminster Hall for the lying in state. On the day of the funeral, drums beat mournfully as tens of thousands of soldiers followed the casket on its long march through the streets of London. Thousands more lined the streets to pay their last respects to the woman who had been "the people's queen" for forty-five years. Several prominent foreign royals came to pay their respects, including the Duke and Duchess of Brunswick, the king of the Belgians, the queen of the Netherlands, and the crown prince of Norway. The coffin was taken by train from Paddington Station in London to Windsor Castle. Along the entire route, thousands of people stood silent and bareheaded as her coffin was taken "slowly and majestically" away.[90] Her body was buried beside her husband, King George V, at the Memorial Chapel. In death, she rejoined her fiancé, her husband, and her three sons.

30

The Last Empress

(1940–89)

The death of Queen Mary meant that of the four imperial matriarchs who had once ruled Europe, Empress Zita was the only one left. She spent the duration of the horrific Second World War in relative safety in North America, but these were not idle years for her or her family. Her older sons Otto, Robert, and Felix became familiar faces in Washington as they fought for Austrian interests in the postwar era. They had even managed to convince President Roosevelt to develop an elite Austrian liberation unit of the armed forces. Referred to as the Free Austria Movement, but officially designated the 101st US Infantry Battalion, the team disbanded on its first day from lack of interest from the recruits, who were mostly composed of Austrian exiles and émigrés.

In keeping with her kinetic lifestyle, Zita, her children, and their staff moved around frequently. During the first years of the war, they took up residence at Royalston, the Massachusetts country estate of the wealthy New York banker Calvin Bullock, who was a friend of Felix's. But Zita did not believe Royalston was a suitable home to raise her younger children, Charlotte, Carl Ludwig, Elisabeth, and Rudolf. At the end of the summer of 1940, she made the decision to relocate her family to Quebec. This was a move made out of necessity, since her younger children were still not fluent in English, but French was a language they had nearly mastered. It was a hard decision for Zita, since their new home, the Villa Saint-Joseph, was a dilapidated old house long since abandoned. Located at 239 Chemin Saint Louis, it belonged to the Sisters of Joan of Arc, a local Catholic order of nuns. After moving in on October 1940, one of the first tasks Zita undertook was the conversion of one of the house's rooms into a chapel, so that the family could have Mass every day, presided over by a local Canadian priest.

This was a difficult time for the family. In 1941, Hitler used his personal authority to strip Zita, her children, and their relatives of their European citizenship. This made them essentially stateless. During this period, their finances were more strapped than ever. An increase in the size of their household was also a problem when Zita's younger sister—the mentally disabled Princess Isabella—and their mother, the seventy-nine-year-old Duchess of Parma, arrived. Even the food they ate was barely palatable. Zita was forced to make meals from the foliage growing around the house. "Almost every day we make salad and spinach dishes from dandelions," Zita told a friend, "and we've tried to gather and bring home more and more of them because we consume such quantities ourselves that there is nothing left over for the servants."[1] One of the visitors to Saint-Joseph during this time was Queen Mary's sister-in-law Princess Alice, whose husband, the Earl of Athlone, was the governor-general of Canada during World War II.[2] Alice recalled her meeting with Zita.

> Zita still wore the same [*sic*] dress as she did when she became a widow—down to the ground, right up to her hands and up to her chin, with no ear-rings or any bit of jewellery [*sic*].
>
> In contrast, she was very talkative, well-informed and cultivated.... She had her old mother with her, who was much more worldly.
>
> We sat down to a typical German tea of *Butterbrod* and little square cakes and biscuits. Only Ariel [Alice's lady-in-waiting] and I were allowed cups of tea—the others drank tumblers of water ... I thought they seemed very poor.[3]

The end of the war brought many changes with it—not only for the world, but for Zita and the Habsburgs as well. For the first time, her family unit began breaking apart as the older children struck out on their own. Otto and Adelhaid, both of whom had earned their doctorates, returned to Europe. They obtained passports courtesy of Monaco, thanks largely to the efforts of Charles de Gaulle. Otto returned to Europe to work on behalf of Austria in the political jockeying for power, and Adelhaid went to Paris to help the wounded and injured from the war. Felix also left, traveling to Mexico where he started his own business. In 1948, Otto and Robert embarked on an extensive tour of the Middle East, Pakistan, India, Vietnam, China, the Philippines, and the Pacific speaking on the postwar reconstruction and the need for European unity as a means to securing future peace. It was while speaking in these exotic countries that the archdukes first began working for a paycheck.

Zita opted to remain at Saint-Joseph for the time being but found herself being drawn back to Europe. She spent several years after the war touring Canada and the United States, soliciting aid for war-torn Austria. At the top of her list of goals was to have Austria declared as one of the countries occupied by Hitler and not allied with him. If she succeeded, Austria would be the recipient of much-needed aid. In 1948, the empress was invited to speak at a special gathering of the wives of the members of the United States Congress. Her passionate words made an impact. Austria was accepted as a beneficiary of the Marshall Plan, the American program designed to rebuild Europe through monetary support. With her sons now taking up the imperial mantle, many saw this as "the last political act of Zita."[4]

With the reconstruction of Europe proceeding, and with the sun setting on her own political influence, Zita naturally turned her attention to the future of her family. As her children grew older, she eagerly followed their marriage prospects. The late 1940s and early 1950s saw a series of family weddings, one quickly after the other. The youngest of the Habsburg brood, Elisabeth, was the first to marry. She fell in love with Prince Heinrich of Liechtenstein, and they were married in May 1949 at the Château de Lignières, a property owned by Prince Xavier of Bourbon-Parma, the bride's uncle. The following year, the empress returned to Europe once again for Carl Ludwig's wedding to Princess Yolande de Ligne. She was the daughter of the prominent French ambassador Eugène, the Eleventh Prince de Ligne. She was also a descendant of the famous Prince Charles-Joseph de Ligne, who had served at the Court of King Louis XVI and Queen Marie Antoinette in the 1770s and 1780s.

Time did not diminish Zita's belief that the Austrian monarchy might one day be restored under the Habsburgs, but the issue of the dynastic succession was still unresolved, since none of the empress's sons had any children of their own yet. Once Elisabeth and Carl Ludwig married, all eyes naturally shifted to Otto. At first, he expressed little interest in finding a wife. His name had been connected to Princess Maria Francesca of Italy, the daughter of King Victor Emmanuel III, but the rumors of their engagement in the 1930s came to naught. It was not until a chance meeting in 1950 that the archduke met the woman with whom he would spend the rest of his life. Princess Regina of Saxe-Meiningen was a young nurse working at a refugee camp in Bayreuth, where Otto had set up a small villa as his base of political operations. "It was in the summer of 1950 at a camp refugee centre in Munich that I met Regina for the first time," Otto recalled.[5] Both were children of exiled royals. Regina's father had been taken prisoner by the Russians during the war and died at a POW camp in Siberia. Both had their property and income confiscated, and both were politically ambitious people with a drive to see Europe restored to greatness.

The young royals soon fell in love and were married six months later. Their wedding on May 10, 1951, was held at the Church of the Cordeliers in Nancy, the capital of the province of Lorraine, which had been ruled by the Habsburgs since Maria Theresa's marriage in 1737. In charting a course for his dynasty's future, Otto paid homage to the shared imperial ties between Austria and Britain. Along with his brother Robert, Otto had grown close to Queen Mary, whom he began calling his "Dear Aunt." Shortly before the queen dowager died, Otto wrote to her with the news of his upcoming wedding, "knowing the deep friendly feelings which Your Majesty has always shown to my family and myself." In one of her last direct communications with another royal family, Mary sent Otto and Regina a "magnificent wedding present."[6]

The wedding was a true imperial pageant. Deputations arrived from across the former Austro-Hungarian Empire—at least, from those states on the western side of the Iron Curtain. Regina's long lace veil had been worn by one of Maria Theresa's daughters at her wedding in the 1760s. Atop her head sat the same glittering diamond crown that Emperor Franz Joseph had presented to Zita in 1911. The myrtle blossoms in her bouquet came straight from the gardens at Schönbrunn. The service was presided over by nearly three dozen clergy from Austria and Hungary and was attended by more than two hundred royals. So many people attended that the large church was literally packed from wall to wall, with many guests standing in the aisles and along the back wall. Empress Zita, who celebrated her sixtieth birthday the day before the wedding, was seated in the front row and looked somber but simplistically majestic. Like Queen Victoria, she too wore a black dress and long veil to her son's wedding, though her ensemble was accented by a row of flawless pearls, the glittering Star Cross Order, and the imperial sash. After a nuptial mass performed by the bishop of Nancy, the newlyweds and their relatives made a triumphal procession through the crowded streets of Nancy. Excited well-wishers cheered the family and threw their hats in the air as a sign of respect. So many people had flooded into the streets, onto balconies, and on rooftops that the Nancy police found themselves unable to restrain the crowd's wild enthusiasm.

With her children now married, Empress Zita took the opportunity to return to Europe permanently.[7] She made a home for herself in the tiny nation of Luxembourg, which was ruled by her sister-in-law Grand Duchess Charlotte. This afforded Zita the opportunity of being near her aged mother, the Duchess of Parma, who lived at her brother Felix's home, Berg Castle. After the duchess celebrated her ninetieth birthday in November 1952, Zita took it upon herself to care for her mother personally. When the duchess passed away at the remarkable age of ninety-seven in 1959, the empress began a quest to find a private home for her own twilight years.

In 1963, she found a small castle called Saint Johannes in Zizers, Switzerland, which was maintained by the kindly Johannes Vonderach, bishop of Chur. Zita's suite of four rooms was barely enough to house herself, her sister Isabella, and a lady-in-waiting, but it was simple enough for the unpretentious empress. She especially valued the private chapel that was part of her suite, allowing her to continue her daily routine of Mass and prayer each morning. At Saint Johannes, Zita received regular visits from her family living nearby in Austria, Liechtenstein, France, and Italy. By the mid-1960s, she could proudly boast of having more than thirty grandchildren. Zita's friend and biographer Gordon Brook-Shepherd noted the following:

> Otherwise, by the start of this Zizers era, Elisabeth had already borne her Liechtenstein husband five children (four of them boys); Yolanda had given birth to four for [Carl Ludwig] (two of them boys); Robert and Margherita had five (two of them girls); while Xenia had also borne Rudolf four children (only one girl). Felix and Anna proved the most prolific of all, producing no fewer than seven children between 1953 and 1961, of whom four were sons. That left the head of the family [Otto], on whom the succession initially rest. From the strictly dynasty point of view (though from no other) Regina caused some concern by bearing five daughters (Andrea, Monika, Michaela, Gabriela and Walburga) in rapid succession between 1953 and 1958. Then, in 1961, came Charles, the first of the couple's two sons, and the direct heir was in place.[8]

As Zita entered her twilight years, resistance in Austria toward the imperial family started declining. In 1968, the Austrian government announced that all Habsburgs born after April 10, 1919, when the dynasty was formally deposed, could return to their homeland. For the first time, the door of opportunity was open for Zita's grandchildren to visit, but she was still denied entry. This policy was particularly painful for the empress in 1971, when her daughter Adelhaid died suddenly in Pöcking, Bavaria. The circumstances surrounding her death have never been made public. The archduchess was buried in Tulfes in the Tyrol, but her mother was denied permission to attend the funeral because of the Habsburg Law. Otto, who had always been close to Adelhaid and had finally been issued an Austrian passport to travel within Austria on October 31, 1966, represented his family at the funeral—Otto received an

Austrian passport and citizenship on February 8, 1957, under the condition that he accept the name Dr. Otto von Habsburg instead of his imperial titles. Ironically, his Austrian passport was valid in every country except Austria.

The late 1960s and early 1970s engendered a resurrection of sorts of monarchy in Europe. In 1975, history was made when the Spanish monarchy was restored under the old Bourbon dynasty. In the last years of his life, Spain's Fascist leader General Francisco Franco showed growing interest in seeing a return of monarchy. He developed an unusual relationship with the last queen and Empress Zita's old friend, Queen Ena—King Alfonso, after leaving his wife, had died in exile in Rome in 1941. Through mutual cooperation and interest in the welfare of Spain, these two astute political figures paved the way for the queen's grandson Prince Juan Carlos to become king upon Franco's death. Sadly, Ena died in 1969, but the return of a deposed monarchy—especially one that had strong Habsburg links—was a moment of great hope for royals across Europe. In an interesting twist, King Juan Carlos's wife, Queen Sofía, was a great-granddaughter of Empress Augusta Victoria through her daughter the Duchess of Brunswick. For Empress Zita, this restoration gave her tremendous hope for the future. But like Queen Ena, Zita knew that the sun had long set on her life in politics. She began to look to the future.

With all of her surviving children now entering middle age, Zita found herself surrounded by several dozen grandchildren, many of whom had already entered adulthood. This inevitably led to a number of happy family milestones, as Zita's grandchildren began marrying. Carl Ludwig's son Christian became the subject of a media frenzy when he married Marie Astrid of Luxembourg, one of Europe's most beautiful princesses, in 1982. Marie Astrid had garnered her fair share of attention, since she was one of the few eligible princesses from a reigning European house. Her name had also been mentioned as a possible wife for Queen Elizabeth II's son Prince Charles. Two years after this royal wedding was yet another, in 1984, when Robert's son Lorenz married the wealthy Princess Astrid of Belgium. Such family triumphs were undoubtedly gratifying for Zita, who had watched as her family was blacklisted by the surviving royal houses of Europe after World War I.

By the 1980s, Zita's health continued to generally be good, which was a testament to the longevity of her ancestors. When she celebrated her ninetieth birthday in May 1982, the elderly empress continued to look regal in her simple widow's dress, which she had accessorized over the years with white lace and the string of pearls she had kept since her coronation. During her birthday celebration at Saint Johannes, an official photograph of the imperial family was taken. In it, Zita is surrounded by no fewer than seventy-five of her children, grandchildren, and great-grandchildren. "My ninetieth birthday was a great joy for me for two reasons," Zita told a family friend. "First, all my children, the majority of my grandchildren and twelve of my great-grandchildren had gathered here together ... for the occasion. The oldest of these great-grandchildren had the same birthday as I did, and was all of five years old!"[9] Upon reaching this milestone, Zita became—along with Queen Mary's daughter-in-law Elizabeth—one of the longest-lived royal consorts in European history. Many media outlets around the world could not help but wax sentimental. One British newspaper described "Zita, the last Empress of Austria" as "the last contemporary survivor of those royal houses of Europe that flourished up to the First World War." The article also touched a continuing painful issue for the empress.

> Unlike her son Otto, who renounced his claim to the Habsburg throne 20 years ago, Zita is no abdicator. She is still the Empress, and will not have it otherwise. She would like now to return to Vienna, and the Austrian Government would be willing to accommodate her, but for a couple of stumbling blocks. One of these is her own formidable insistence on her ancient status; the other is the Habsburg Law, passed in 1919, which denies entry in Austria of all those members of the Franz-Joseph clan who have not formally renounced their claim to the throne.[10]

A few days after her birthday came the exciting news that Zita had been waiting decades for: the Austrian government finally granted her and the family permission to return from exile—it was speculated that King Juan Carlos was a driving force in repealing the law. On May 16, 1982, Empress Zita of Austria got into a car with her daughter Elisabeth, her son Robert, and his wife, Margharita, bound for their homeland. As their car reached the Austrian border, Zita could hardly contain her excitement. When they arrived at Tufles in the Tyrol on that warm May morning, Zita stepped out of the car to an unexpected sight. The border guards who had assembled snapped to attention, offering the empress a salute. Along with them were a group of dignitaries and government officials who had come to greet, or rather supervise, her. Dressed in her typical black dress and matching hat, the nonagenarian empress made only the slightest wave, since she wanted to avoid attention as much as possible.

The highlight of the visit was her arrival at the burial site of her daughter Adelhaid. "I went straight to Tulfes," she wrote a month later, "to pray at the grave of my daughter Adelhaid, and also to give thanks to God in the dear little Tyrolean church there for my return home." Everyone was entranced by the diminutive empress as she prayed at her daughter's grave; she finally had the chance to say good-bye. The last stop for the day was to her grandson Archduke Lorenz, who was studying nearby at the University of Innsbruck and who had invited his grandmother for a small meal. The brief trip into Austria lasted only a single day. By that evening, Zita and her family were back at Saint Johannes in Zizers. Afterward, Zita wrote a telling letter to a friend about the experience: "We drove early, without any problems, across the border and into the Tyrol, where, for the first time in sixty-three years of exile, I trod on the soil of the homeland again.... It was for me a great, unforgettable day ..."[11]

Over the course of the next seven years, Zita made a number of trips back to Austria. Much to the republican government's chagrin, she created quite a spectacle. Curiosity about Europe's last living imperial consort exploded. But owing to her tremendous strength of character and sense of Christian integrity, she surprised many people by her humble, kindly nature. She held a series of interviews with the Austrian newspaper *Kronen Zeitung* and also made a number of appearances on national television, but there were no grudges or recriminations against the country that had exiled her. In one such interview, she took a rare moment to look back on her life and those who impacted it.

> All those who preceded me, left their mark on my life, and all those who were and are with me, above all the Emperor who gave meaning and fullness to my existence. Without those who have gone before us, we would be nothing. Whatever happened, whatever I have done, I have done it for those who lived before us. Certainly we have made mistakes, but good will presided over all our enterprises.[12]

This quiet dignity she possessed won over the hearts of the Austrian people, who, on her next visit, unreservedly addressed her as "Your Majesty."

During a visit in November 1982, Zita made two very poignant stops. The first was to the church of Mariazell, the famous pilgrimage site where the statue of the Virgin Mary was said to perform miracles. The last time she had been there was on her honeymoon. Upon hearing that the empress had arrived, nearly twenty thousand people flooded to Mariazell to catch a glimpse of her. The second location she visited was especially emotional not only for Zita but for the entire imperial family. At Saint Stephen's Cathedral, the largest church in Vienna, nearly ten thousand parishioners turned out to offer their respects to the Habsburg family at a special Mass commemorating their struggles over the last seven decades. There was little doubt that "Zita had become news. The world's press and television looked in on the spectacle of republican Vienna coming to terms with its imperial past."[13]

By 1988, the ninety-six-year-old empress's health gave cause for concern. It started as cataracts in her eyes. With a tinge of sadness, she told a friend, "It's too silly, but, alas, I can't see a thing."[14] She was eventually totally blind, forcing her to replace her wristwatch with a room clock that announced the time. The other residents at Zizers noticed little change in the empress's lifestyle, although she was now attended by a nurse and an Italian maid. She continued her daily routine almost uninterrupted. She knew the corridors of the building so well that she rarely needed help getting around. The biggest noticeable difference was that, now, the empress in black carried a long white walking stick. In the summer, she went to visit her daughter Elisabeth at Waldstein in Austria where she fell ill with pneumonia. Not until the end of August was she well enough to return to Zizers. There, she spent the fall and winter bedridden, except for brief periods when she sat up in an old armchair near her bed.

By February 1989, no one could deny the truth: the last empress was dying. At the beginning of March, she telephoned Otto at his home in Pöcking, Bavaria, with the message, "I am dying. Come and see me."[15] She spent her final two weeks in her sparsely decorated room at Saint Johannes, surrounded by her many children and grandchildren. Each of her sons and daughters took turns sitting with her night and day. She stopped taking any food or water for nearly all that time. Zita surprised her family by her lack of nostalgia at the end. She did not share any reminiscences of the extraordinary life she had led but was instead only concerned with the future of her beloved Europe. Otto later told a family friend, "In the last talks we had she did not once mention things past. Instead, she asked me about what was happening now, about the latest situation in Eastern Europe and in the European Community."[16] On March 13, the curtain descended on the life of the last matriarch of the Habsburg Empire. That day, a special blessing arrived from Pope John Paul II, which was read to the empress by her old friend Bishop Vonderach. Just after 1:00 a.m. on March 14, 1989, Zita died peacefully in the presence of a nurse and her daughter-in-law Regina.

One of the residents at Saint Johannes remembered how "we were all invited up to see her in her room. There she was in just a nice dress, with her pearls around her neck. They were not just any pearls—they were the kind you don't see today, the kind only royalty use to have."[17] Austrian chancellor Franz Vranitsky ordered national mourning and granted the long-suffering empress perhaps the greatest possible tribute: an imperial state funeral in Vienna—the first since Franz Joseph's in 1916. The return of almost the entire Habsburg family to Vienna in 1989 was a moment of profound significance for Austria, which was beginning to move on from the horrors of the early twentieth century. Empress Zita's funeral was symptomatic of the country's eagerness to take pride in its rich imperial history once again. Tony Judt, the Pulitzer Prize-nominated author and expert on European history, was in Vienna in 1989 and recalled the atmosphere in the former Habsburg capital.

> Vienna in 1989 was thus a good place from which to "think" Europe.... the very streets of the Austrian capital bore witness to the chasm of silence separating Europe's tranquil present from its discomforting past. The imposing, confident buildings lining the great Ringstrasse were a reminder of Vienna's one-time imperial vocation—though the Ring itself seemed somehow too big and too grand to serve as a mere quotidian artery for commuters in a medium-sized European capital—and the city was justifiably proud of its public edifices and civic spaces. Indeed, Vienna was much given to invoking older glories.[18]

Austria's desire to "invoke older glories" may be one of the reasons that, perhaps more than any of her imperial counterparts, Empress Zita's funeral was the most steeped in the rich, vibrant traditions of the past. The arrangements were on such a grand scale that the funeral was estimated to cost £200,000. In keeping with tradition, Zita's heart was interred in Switzerland at the Muri Abbey—the first church ever built by the Habsburgs, in 1027. From Zizers, her coffin, upon which was placed Austria's medieval archducal crown, was taken to the Klosterneuburg Abbey overlooking Vienna on March 29. For a day and a half, tens of thousands of people filed past the draped coffin to pay their last respects to the woman who had held on to the dream of Austria's glory for nearly three-quarters of a century. One mourner said, "I vote Socliast and I'm no monarchist, but she was our Empress and I wanted to pay my respects."[19] One of her biographers summed up the significance that her death had across the continent: "She had been the last tangible link with the vanished Europe that had existed two world wars before. The photo-portrait taken of her as a young princess of Bourbon-Parma on her engagement to the heir of the Austro-Hungarian Empire gazed out from magazines and newspapers across Europe and America."[20] On the evening of March 30, the coffin was transported to the inner courtyard of the Hofburg Palace for a small service before it was moved by a torchlight procession to Saint Stephen's Cathedral.

The emotional funeral at Saint Stephen's was held at 3:00 p.m. on April 1, 1989, sixty-seven years to the day since Emperor Charles I died in Funchal on Madeira. The primary mourners included two hundred members of the Habsburg and Bourbon families, accompanied by another six hundred guests from other royal houses from around the world. More than six thousand people attended the service, while thousands more lined the streets outside— panegyrists claimed there were around four hundred thousand spectators, while conservative estimates placed it as low as forty thousand. Millions more watched the funeral on television. So many people arrived from across the former Austro-Hungarian Empire that the service was read aloud in German, Hungarian, Slovenian, Croatian, Czech, Polish, and Italian. The four-and-a-half hour funeral mass was conducted by two archbishops and four bishops.

When the service was completed, the funeral procession moved from Saint Stephen's to the Church of the Capuchins less than two miles away, where the Habsburg family crypt is located. It was here, among 144 Habsburgs— including twelve emperors and sixteen empresses—that Zita was laid to rest. The final delivery of her coffin was a moment deeply immersed in Austria's imperial traditions. The master of ceremonies at the head of the funeral procession knocked three times on the church's door. The first time, the guardian monk asked who was seeking entry. The queen of Bohemia, Croatia, Slavonia, and so on, the master of ceremonies declared. He did not know her, the monk replied. After a second knock, the monk again asked who was seeking entry. Zita, the empress of Austria and queen of Hungry, the master of ceremonies announced. Again, the monk answered he did not know her. On the third knock, after the monk asked who was seeking entry, the master of ceremonies said it was Zita, a mortal sinner. The door opened wide and the pallbearers placed the coffin in the crypt.

The *New York Times* sent one of its staff to report on the funeral, which was described in vivid detail in its April 2 issue.

> Old Vienna dusted off its imperial finery today to lay to rest Austria's last Empress, paying a regal tribute to a woman who remained quietly true to her lost crown and to the late Emperor through seven decades of exile. For the first time since the 600-year Austro-Hungarian monarchy was dissolved in 1919, the ornate black imperial catafalque – borrowed from the Museum at Schonbrunn Palace – rolled past the old palaces and baroque temples of central Vienna to the imperial burial vault. There, under the Capuchin Church, Zita, Empress of Austria and Queen of Hungary, was laid to rest among the richly decorated caskets of the Hapsburgs.[21]

More than twenty years later, Zita's life, death, and legacy are still felt, especially in Roman Catholic circles, whose faith she so devotedly defended. As recently as 2010, a Catholic periodical published an article about Zita, giving her a moving epitaph.

> Following the example of Charles, whose memory she kept alive, she never abdicated her rights, and it was as Empress of Austria and Queen of Hungary that she was interred on April 1, 1989, in the Crypt of the Capuchins in Vienna. The popular fervour of which she was the object in the course of this ceremony [her funeral] showed an astonished world that, after seventy years of the republic, Zita remained in Austria the *Landesmutter*, the "mother of the country," a terrestrial image of Her who is venerated at the sanctuary of Mariazell in the heart of the former Empire under the title of *"Magna Mater Austriæ, Magna Domina Hungarorum, Mater Gentium Slavorum."*[22]

Empress Zita's death at Saint Johannes and funeral in Vienna in 1989 brings to a close the final chapter in the lives of these four very special women, each of whom reigned as consorts of the last European emperors. Raised in an era where responsibility, commitment, sacrifice, and duty before self were elevated as the highest ideals, they embraced their new lives, adapted, and came to love their countries and peoples. They gave all they were for their husbands, their families, and ultimately, their empires.

Epilogue

Recent events in Central and Eastern Europe and the collapse of the Soviet empire built in Yalta...have drawn attention once more to the historical events which have led to the present situation. We must go back to their roots, which lie deep down, especially to the affairs of World War I and their consequences. Had different decisions been taken then the tragedies of our continent, whether Hitlerism or Communism, could perhaps have been avoided.[1]

—Dr. Otto von Habsburg, 1990

The impressive state funeral of Empress Zita of Austria was a fitting tribute to Europe's last imperial consort, who also had the distinction of being the longest-living monarch—reigning or consort—in Austrian history. Her funeral brought the memory of the imperial era into the modern world and put a face on the profound impact of a very special group of royal women. As the gothic black funeral catafalque wound its way through the crowded streets of Vienna, one of the most important eras in European history came to a symbolic end.

Empress Zita never lived to see her dearest wish come true, the restoration of the Habsburg dynasty to the Austrian throne. She did, however, proudly live to see Otto take his place on the world stage. In 1979, he became the first Habsburg to return to an active role in politics when he became a member of the European Parliament, which paved the way for the formation of the European Union. Otto worked as a senior member of that parliament for thirty years, advocating the development of former Habsburg territories like Croatia, Hungary, and Slovenia that suffered under decades of Communism. He remarked in 2007, "we are a politically very engaged family so that for instance I arrived today from Hungary, where I had several meetings and shall leave the day after tomorrow for Croatia for a series of meetings there, too." Even at the age of ninety-five, he maintained a "strong engagement in the political action" of twenty-first-century Europe.[2] Otto's two youngest daughters, Gabriela and Walburga, have followed in his footsteps and taken up careers in politics. Gabriela is the current Georgian ambassador to Germany, and Walburga is a member of the Swedish Parliament.

Archduchess Regina died in February 2010. Otto died the following year, on July 4, 2011, at the age of ninety-eight. Otto's death came shortly after the decision by the Austrian government that now allows members of the Habsburg family to run for the presidency of Austria. Along with King George VI, the Duke of Windsor, and the Grand Duchess Anastasia, Otto von Habsburg was one of the most politically and historically significant of the twenty-six children born to the four empresses.[3] His six-hour funeral on July 16 was a mirror reflection of Zita's funeral twenty-two years earlier, presided over by diplomats, politicians, and crowned heads of Europe. Otto was laid to rest in the imperial crypt alongside his mother. His heart was embalmed in Budapest, the city that lived in his heart for decades. Otto and Regina had seven children and twenty-two grandchildren. The remains of Emperor Charles I continue to reside in the cemetery in Funchal where he was buried in 1922. His heart was later exhumed and moved next to his wife's at the Muri Abbey in Switzerland. The Habsburg family's requests for a state funeral in Vienna have been denied.

Zita's second son, Robert, inherited the Habsburgs' possessions in Italy when he was declared Archduke of Austria-Este, a title that was last held by the ill-fated Franz Ferdinand. Archduke Robert died in 1996. He was survived by his wife, Margherita, their four children, and eighteen grandchildren. Archduke Felix remained actively involved in Austrian politics, lobbying the government to return all of the Habsburg family's possessions that were seized in 1919. He lived in Mexico City until his death in September 2011, only two months after Otto. Carl Ludwig, Zita's fourth son, died in Brussels in 2007. He was buried next to his mother in the Habsburg family vault in Vienna. Archduke Rudolf, the empress's first child born in exile, worked as a Wall Street broker and a banker for many years. His wife, Xenia, died in a car crash in 1968. In 1971, he married for the second time, to Princess Anna von Wrede, with whom he had a daughter. He died in Switzerland on May 16, 2010.

Empress Zita's two surviving daughters each married into royal families. Charlotte, who had married the Duke of Mecklenburg in 1956, worked as a welfare worker in Manhattan's East Harlem for many years. She sometimes used the name Charlotte de Bar in honor of the alias her mother used when they fled France during the Second World War. She died in a car crash in Munich four months after her mother in 1989. She and her husband, George, had no children. The youngest Habsburg, Elisabeth, married Prince Heinrich of Liechtenstein. She died in Graz, Austria, in 1993.

Following her death, Augusta Victoria's legacy continued to live on in Germany. Women, especially those belonging to the Right Wing, cherished her memory. They made pilgrimages to her tomb at the Antique Temple where they laid wreaths, prayed, and sang songs in her honor. They praised her "as the passive sufferer, the compassionate mother of her children and 'her' people, the self-sacrificing wife, the charitable and religious woman—in short: the incarnation of German women's loyalty and selfless grandeur."[4]

In the Netherlands, the former Emperor Wilhelm II continued to live at Huis Doorn. In 1922, he married for the second time, to the impoverished Princess Hermine of Schönaich-Carolath.[5] Eighteen years younger than Wilhelm, Hermine was the fifth child of Prince Henry XXII of Reuss-Greiz. At the age of twenty, she married the older, unimportant Prince Johann Georg of Schönaich-Carolath, who died unexpectedly in 1920. Although the Hohenzollerns and German monarchists protested the marriage, Wilhelm was happy with his second wife, to whom he granted the courtesy title of German empress. She insisted upon being addressed this way, even though her husband had long since abandoned using his own titles. Hermine's relationship with Dona's children was not easy, but she assured Sissy that she would "in piety and reverence uphold the memory of the dear, irreplaceable Kaiserin and respect the inner and essential ties between father and children [existing because of] the death of the noble Kaiserin."[6] In an effort to ingratiate herself with her stepchildren, Hermine hung Dona's portrait in her boudoir. She later suggested that a biography of the late empress be commissioned. Wilhelm's second marriage lasted almost twenty years, until his death from a series of heart attacks at Doorn on June 4, 1941. In an interesting twist, a second link between Wilhelm and Hermine took place when Wilhelm's grandson Karl Franz married Hermine's daughter Princess Henriette. The couple married in 1940 and had three children before divorcing in 1946.

Contrary to the hopes of the Hohenzollerns, the monarchy in Germany was never restored under Adolf Hitler. Any possibility of a Hohenzollern restoration in Germany ended forever in January 1934 when Hitler outlawed all monarchist organizations. In Wilhelm's eyes, Hitler's actions were tantamount to a declaration of "war against the house of Hohenzollern."[7] That did not stop any of his sons from continuing to serve the Nazis. After the Second World War, Auwi was arrested by American authorities and charged with war crimes. He was sentenced to two years of hard labor. Augusta Victoria of Germany and Alexandra of Russia were already connected by their respective marriages. Two generations later, the descendants of these two empresses were again united when Dona's great-grandson Franz Wilhelm— the son of Prince Karl Franz and Princess Henriette—married the Grand Duchess Maria Vladimirovna, the current claimant to the Russian throne (though her claim is highly disputed by the various surviving branches of the Romanov dynasty).

At the time of Queen Mary's death in 1953, only three of her children were still alive. The Duke of Windsor lived in exile with Wallis for the rest of his life. During World War II, he scandalized his family by expressing pro-Nazi sympathies. "I have not one drop of blood in my veins which is not German," he reportedly boasted in the 1930s.[8] In response, he was made governor-general of the Bahamas and thus sent far away from Britain where he could not cause any further trouble for the monarchy. In the 1950s, the Duke and Duchess of Windsor returned to France, where they died in 1972 and 1986, respectively. Queen Mary was never fully reconciled with Edward, even though he did attend her funeral, and she never met Wallis face-to-face again. The couple had no children. Throughout the remainder of her life, Princess Mary, Countess of Harewood (as she was styled after 1932) remained an honorary member of the British Armed Forces. In 1965, she died from a massive heart attack. The queen's last surviving son, the Duke of Gloucester, served as governor-general of Australia. He died in 1974. His wife, Alice, survived him by thirty years, dying in 2004 at the age of 102. At the time of her death, she was the oldest person in history to be part of the British royal family.

Queen Mary's granddaughter Elizabeth II has reigned since 1952. On May 12, 2011, she became the second-longest-reigning sovereign in English history—the first continues to be Queen Victoria. Should Elizabeth be on the throne in 2015 at the age of eighty-nine, she would not only surpass Queen Victoria but would also become the longest-reigning female monarch in history. In June 2012 she celebrated her Diamond Jubilee. An estimated 1.2 million people arrived in London on June 3 to watch as a flotilla of one thousand boats paraded down the Thames to pay tribute to the queen and the royal family. The 2012 Diamond Jubilee surpassed even Queen Victoria's in 1897.[9] The queen and Prince Philip have been married for sixty-five years. Her mother, Elizabeth, was styled as the queen mother until her death in 2002 at the age of 101. Mary's great-grandson Charles remains heir apparent and Prince of Wales. Now sixty-two years old, Charles—like his mother—reached a milestone of his own in 2011: he is currently the longest-serving heir to the throne in British history. His personal life has been buffeted by many scandals, especially his highly publicized wedding to Lady Diana Spencer in 1981, from whom he was divorced in 1996. Their equally publicized, vitriolic separation "was the single most important event in the history of the British monarchy since the abdication of Edward VIII in 1936."[10] In 2005, Charles married Camilla Parker-Bowles, who is styled as HRH the Duchess of Cornwall.

In Russia, the grisly murders of Nicholas, Alexandra, and their family at Ekaterinburg in 1918 were, sadly, only the beginning of the Bolsheviks' murderous rampage against the House of Romanov. In the weeks and months that followed, seventeen members of the imperial family—cousins, aunts, and uncles of the tsar—were rounded up and brutally executed. Alexandra's sister Ella was arrested by the Cheka on Lenin's orders. The grand-duchess-turned-nun was dragged out in the middle of the night, blindfolded, and thrown into an abandoned iron mine in Alapaevsk with other Romanovs and political prisoners. The group was killed by two hand grenades and a brushwood fire. It was later reported by some of the killers that, up until the end, Ella and the others could be heard singing hymns from the bottom of the dark mine shaft.

The shroud of secrecy and misinformation that surrounded the deaths of Alexandra Feodorovna and her family led to decades of speculation over their fate. In June 1920, Count Benckendorff, the former grand marshal of the imperial court, reported in his diary, "I am still without definite news with regard to the fate of the Emperor, Empress and their children."[11] Much of the misinformation can be traced to the fact that not all of the bodies were buried together; an error on the part of the murderers meant that two bodies were buried separately from the rest. Those that were buried together were placed in a hidden grave deep in the Koptyaki Forest. It was not until 1920, after three official investigations, that some of the details came to light regarding the ultimate fate of the Romanov family. Even the official reports were based on conjecture and circumstantial evidence, all of which was cast into doubt a few years later by an event that would precipitate one of the greatest royal mysteries in history.

In February 1920, a woman appeared in Berlin who was eventually believed to be Alexandra's youngest daughter, Grand Duchess Anastasia. The woman, who took the name Anna Anderson, convinced many royalists that she was the grand duchess, having escaped execution in Siberia. Not everyone was convinced. Grand Duchess Olga Alexandrovna, Anastasia's aunt, had no doubt this woman was an imposter. Tsarina Alexandra's siblings Princess Irene of Prussia and Grand Duke Ernest Louis of Hesse concurred. Anderson generated enough interest that several plays and films romanticizing her life—including the Academy Award winning *Anastasia* starring Ingrid Bergman—have been created. When she died in Virginia in 1984, state authorities made a surprising and unexpected de facto acknowledgment of her identity in her death certificate. The document listed her given names as Anastasia Nicholaievna, her parents as "Czar Nikolai" and "Alix of Hesse-Darmstadt," her place of birth as Peterhof, and her occupation as "Royalty."[12] In keeping with her wishes, her remains were cremated.

Following the rise of Mikhail Gorbachev's *glasnost*, statements made by several former guards from the Ipatiev House led to the discovery in the Koptyaki Forest of the remains of nine individuals believed to be Nicholas, Alexandra, three of their five children, and their retainers. In 1992, a year after the fall of the Soviet Union, two of the skeletal remains recovered from Koptyaki were conclusively identified as those belonging to Nicholas and Alexandra. The confirmation came by testing their mitochondrial DNA against samples provided by several of their surviving relatives. In 1994, a series of similar tests was performed to compare Anna Anderson's DNA from a preserved strand of hair and some tissue with that of the tsar and tsarina. There were enough discrepancies to rule out the possibility of relation. Additional analyses comparing Anderson's mitochondrial DNA with the Duke of Edinburgh—whose grandmother Victoria was Tsarina Alexandra's sister—confirmed the impossibility that Anna Anderson was in any way related to the Romanovs. It was later revealed she was a Polish-born German factory worker named Franziska Schanzkowska.

After nearly nine decades of searching, the bones of the missing Romanovs were found in 2008. Tests later identified the two missing bodies as belonging to Grand Duchess Anastasia and Tsarevitch Alexei. It had previously been believed the remains were those belonging to Marie. Since the fall of Communism in 1991, sentiment toward the imperial family in Russia has been on a meteoric rise. On July 17, 1998—the eightieth anniversary of their deaths—the family's bodies were exhumed and brought back to Saint Petersburg for an epic state funeral in Catherine's Chapel at the Saints Peter and Paul Fortress. Their coffins were draped in the yellow flags of the Imperial House of Romanov.

Alexandra, Nicholas, and their family were later canonized in the Russian Orthodox Church amid the sounds of the *Panikhida*, the Orthodox requiem for the dead. The Ipatiev House was later torn down and replaced by the onion-domed Cathedral of the Blood, built in their honor. The Romanovs were not the only imperial family to be revered as saintly. On October 3, 2004, the Roman Catholic Church beatified Emperor Charles I, whom they have since named Blessed Charles of Austria. Since that time, a number of miracles have been attributed to him, paving the way for his being named a saint. Zita's beatification process began in 2009.

The lives and legacies that Augusta Victoria, Mary, Alexandra, and Zita left have proved timeless. The stories of their lives, their romances, and their fates have captivated audiences worldwide for decades. Whole new generations are being drawn to the stories of these four remarkable women. Nearly a century has passed since December 1916, when these four women reigned concurrently, but even now, in the twenty-first century, their legacies are rising again like a phoenix from the ashes. In 2011, descendants of both Mary and Dona were married in elaborate, traditional ceremonies that evoked strong images of Europe's royal past. In April, the wedding of Queen Elizabeth II's grandson Prince William to Catherine Middleton brought a tremendous resurgence of popularity for the House of Windsor. In August, Dona's great-great-grandson was married in a church on the grounds of the Neues Palais in Potsdam, marking the first major dynastic wedding for the Hohenzollerns in over forty years. "People are longing for things they don't get out of the republic," said one of the broadcasters at the wedding. "People are looking for little princes and princesses who are born and will be of some importance for the rest of their lives."[13]

Decades have passed since these women graced Europe's last four imperial thrones. Yet for everything that is known about their lives, there are still so many issues that divide historians, academics, and general readers. Was Queen Mary a totally inept mother, or was her parenting more dictated by her husband's wishes? Was Augusta Victoria a xenophobic, pruddish bigot or caring, compassionate *Landesmutter*? Is it possible she was both? This book has humbly tried to—if not answer—at least shed some light on these questions. Were these women perfect? Certainly not. One only has to do a cursory review of their lives to discover the criticisms and accusations leveled against them. What can be said for certain, however, is that during their tumultuous lives, Augusta Victoria, Mary, Alexandra, and Zita faced criticism, persecution, poverty, and death, but they resolved to meet their challenges with dignity, grace, and courage. Driven by duty, they accepted their lives as their own, taking whatever came their way. Devoted, dutiful, and committed to the imperial cause above all else, the lives of these four royal women were a requiem to the age of empires.

Endnotes

Introduction

1. Miranda Carter, *George, Nicholas and Wilhelm: Three Royal Cousins and the Road to World War I* (New York: Knopf, 2009), p. 65.
2. Abbas Milani, *The Shah* (New York: Palgrave Macmillan, 2011), pp. vi–vii.

Part 1: Unlikely Empresses (1858–94)

1:   Imperial Forge

1. The title *hereditary prince* was commonly used to denote the heir of a sovereign dukedom, the ducal equivalent of a crown prince. On more than one occasion it was used for the heir to a kingdom when the succession was in question.
2. John Van der Kiste, *Queen Victoria's Children* (Stroud, Gloucester: The History Press, 2009), p. 27.
3. Prince Ernest was one of many sovereign princes who were mediatised, or dispossessed of his realm, when Napoleon reorganized Europe in 1806. Ernest I and others like him were allowed to hold on to their titles and rank, but they no longer actually had a sovereign territory to govern.
4. Queen Victoria to Princess Feodora of Leiningen, January 6, 1853, in *Queen Victoria: A Personal History,* Christopher Hibbert (London: HarperCollins, 2010), p. 263.
5. David Bagular, *Napoleon III and His Regime: An Extravaganza* (Baton Rouge: Louisiana State University Press, 2000), p. 218.
6. Princess Michael of Kent, *Crowned in a Far Country: Portraits of Eight Royal Brides* (New York: Touchstone Books, 2007), p. 116.
7. Gillian Gill, *We Two—Victoria and Albert: Rulers, Partners, Rivals* (New York: Ballantine Books, 2009), pp. 95–96.
8. Hibbert, *Queen Victoria*, p. 281.
9. Gill, *We Two*, p. 98.
10. Robert K. Massie, *Dreadnought: Britain, Germany, and the Coming of the Great War* (New York: Ballantine Books, 1991), p. 57.

11.   Daphne Bennett, *Vicky: Princess Royal of England and German Empress* (London: Collins & Harvill Press, 1971), p. 212.

12.   Prince Francis of Teck to Princess Amélie of Teck, December 4, 1867, in *Queen Mary: 1867–1953* (London: Alfred A. Knopf, 1960), James Pope-Hennessy, p. 7. The date given by Pope-Hennessy (*above*) may be a typo, since he claims it was written in the April before Princess May was born.

13.   Statement of Dr. Arthur Farre and Edward H. Hills, May 27, 1867, in *Her Royal Highness Princess Mary Adelaide Duchess of Teck: Based on Her Private Diaries and Letters* (New York: Charles Scribner's Sons, 1900), ed. C. Kinloch Cook, vol. 2, p. 1.

14.   David Duff, *Queen Mary* (London: Collins, 1985), p. 26.

15.   Pope-Hennessy, *Queen Mary*, p. 23.

16.   Kathleen Woodward, *Queen Mary: A Life and Intimate Study* (London: Hutchinson, n.d.), p. 18.

17.   Letter of Princess Mary Adelaide of Cambridge, undated, in *Her Royal Highness*, Cook, p. 415.

18.   On its own merits, the request had precedent. When Queen Victoria's third daughter, Princess Helena, was married in 1866 to Prince Christian of Schleswig-Holstein-Sonderburg-Augustenburg (Dona Holstein's uncle), the queen elevated the groom to the rank and style of Royal Highness from the vastly inferior Serene Highness; and their children bore the style of Highness. In Francis Teck's case, the queen rightly feared that an elevation would set a dangerous precedent. Any of her numerous relatives could marry without concern for the monarchy or foreign policy and then expect the queen to elevate their spouses in the same way she may have elevated Francis.

19.   Queen Victoria to Princess Mary Adelaide of Teck, May 18, 1866, in *Queen Mary*, Pope-Hennessy, p. 25.

20.   The calculation is based upon http://www.measuringworth.com/calculators/exchange/result_exchange.php (viewed on April 14, 2011). It is also interesting to note that Queen Victoria, upon the marriage of her daughter Louise a few years later, requested she receive a stipend of only £6,000 per year.

21.   Queen Victoria to Crown Princess Victoria of Germany, April 15, 1874, in *Queen Mary*, Pope-Hennessy, p. 29.

22.   Viktoria Luise, Duchess of Brunswick and Lüneburg, Princess of Prussia, *The Kaiser's Daughter*, trans. and ed. Robert Vacha (Englewood Cliffs, NJ: Prentice-Hall, 1977), p. 53.

23.   The formation of the German Empire did not inherently elevate the Hohenzollerns to the status of an "imperial family." While the emperor and crown prince bore imperial rank and style, the rest of the Hohenzollerns continued to only be entitled to use the royal titles of Prussia. Going forward, the Hohenzollerns as a whole will be referred to as the Prussian royal family, distinguishing them from the emperor, empress, crown prince, and crown princess.

24.   Christopher Clark, *Kaiser Wilhelm II: A Life in Power* (Kobo desktop version, 2009: retrieved from http://www.kobobooks.com), chap. 2, para. 1.

25.   The Ernestine duchies are a number of Saxon states whose founders were the numerous sons of Ernest, Elector of Saxony (1441–86). There had been almost two dozen Ernestine duchies since the fifteenth century, but by 1871 only four still existed: Saxe-Altenburg, Saxe-Meiningen, Saxe-Coburg-Gotha, and Saxe-Weimar-Eisenach. The word *Saxe* is the French form of *Saxony* (the German being *Sachsen*). Since the language of royalty until the nineteenth century was French, the German rulers identified themselves using French titles (i.e. Saxe-Coburg instead of Sachsen-Coburg).

26.   Clark, *Kaiser Wilhelm II* (Kobo desktop version), chap. 2, para. 4.

27.   Hesse was known after 1816 as Hesse and by the Rhine. Up until 1866, it was also more commonly referred to as Hesse-Darmstadt to distinguish it from the northern state of Hesse-Cassel.

28.   Matthew Dennison, *The Last Princess: The Devoted Life of Queen Victoria's Youngest Daughter* (London: Weidenfeld & Nicolson, 2007), p. 50.

29.   Hibbert, *Queen Victoria*, p. 441.

30.   Robert K. Massie, *Nicholas and Alexandra* (New York: Atheneum, 1967), p. 29.

31.   Sophie Buxhoeveden, *The Life and Tragedy of Alexandra Feodorovna, Empress of Russia* (London: Longmans, Green, 1928), p. 15.

32.   Catrine Clay, *King, Kaiser, Tsar: Three Royal Cousins Who Led the World to War* (New York: Walker, 2006), p. 111.

33.   Princess Alice of Hesse to Queen Victoria, undated, 1873, in *Alice, Grand Duchess of Hesse, Princess of Great Britain and Ireland* (New York: G. P. Putnam's Sons, 1885), ed. Karl Sell, p. 313.

34.   Van der Kiste, *Queen Victoria's Children*, p. 28.

2:   "Sleeping Beauty!"

1.   Geoffrey Wakeford, *Three Consort Queens: Adelaide, Alexandra & Mary* (London: Robert Hale, 1971), p. 158.

2.   Gelardi, *Born to Rule*, p. 8.

3.   Woodward, *Queen Mary*, p. 52.

4.   Dennison, *The Last Princess*, p. 51.

5.   David Duff, *Hessian Tapestry* (London: Frederick Muller, 1967), p. 121.

6.   Massie, *Nicholas and Alexandra*, p. 29.

7.   Coryne Hall, *Little Mother of Russia: A Biography of Empress Marie Feodorovna* (Teaneck, NJ: Holmes & Meier, 2001), p. 151.

8.   Princess Alice of Hesse, to Queen Victoria, March 23, 1877, in *Alice, Grand Duchess of Hesse*, ed. Sell, pp. 359–360.

9.   Princess Alice of Hesse, to Queen Victoria, June 6, 1877, in ibid., p. 362.

10.   Van der Kiste, *Queen Victoria's Children*, p. 107.

11.   Julia P. Gelardi, *In Triumph's Wake: Royal Mothers, Tragic Daughters, and the Price They Paid for Glory* (New York: Saint Martin's Press, 2008), p. 292.

12.   Packard, *Victoria's Daughters*, p. 167.

13.   Mary Adelaide, Duchess of Teck, to the Countess of Hopetown, December 17, 1878, in *Her Royal Highness*, Cook, vol. 2, p. 105.

14.   Queen Victoria to Princess Victoria of Hesse, December 14, 1878, in *Advice to a Grand-daughter: Letters from Queen Victoria to Princess Victoria of Hesse* (London: Heinemann, 1975), ed. Richard Hough, p. 9.

15.   Gelardi, *Born to Rule*, p. 8.

16.   Mary Adelaide, Duchess of Teck, to the Dowager Countess of Aylesford, January 17, 1879, in *Her Royal Highness*, Cook, vol. 2, p. 105.

17.   Princess Beatrice to Mary Adelaide, Duchess of Teck, January 22, 1879, in *The Last Princess*, Dennison, p. 120.

18.   Mary Adelaide, Duchess of Teck, to Lady Elizabeth Biddulph, February 25, 1879, in ibid., p. 107.

19.   Buxhoeveden, *Alexandra Feodorovna*, pp. 8, 12.

20.   Carolly Erickson, *Alexandra: The Last Tsarina* (New York: Saint Martin's Press, 2001), p. 18.

21.   Buxhoeveden, *Alexander Feodorovna*, p. 111.

22. Packard, *Victoria's Daughters*, p. 286.
23. Peter Kurth, *Tsar: The Lost World of Nicholas and Alexandra* (Toronto: Madison Press Books, 1998), p. 28.
24. Buxhoeveden, *Alexandra Feodorovna*, p. 110.
25. Gelardi, *Born to Rule*, p. 13.
26. Marie Bothmer, *Sovereign Ladies of Europe* (London: Kessinger, 2005), p. 198
27. Marguerite Cunliffe-Owen, *Imperator et Rex: William II. of Germany* (New York: Harper & Brothers, 1904), p. 52.
28. Axel von Schwering, *The Berlin Court Under William II* (London: Cassell, 1915), p. 57.
29. Bothmer, *Sovereign Ladies*, p. 199.
30. Ibid.
31. Hibbert, *Queen Victoria*, p. 443.
32. Urusula von Eppinghoven, *Private Lives of the Kaiser and Kaiserin of Germany: Secret History of the Court of Berlin* (New York: Henry W. Fischer, 1909) , vol. 1, pp. 180–181.
33. Crown Princess Victoria of Germany to Prince Wilhelm of Prussia, May 7, 1878, in *Young Wilhelm: The Kaiser's Early Life, 1859–1888*, trans. Jeremy Gaines & Rebecca Wallach (New York: Cambridge University Press, 1998), John C. G. Röhl, p. 330.
34. Cunliffe-Owen, *Imperator et Rex*, pp. 53–54.
35. Prince Wilhelm of Prussia to Frederick VIII, Duke of Schleswig-Holstein, undated, 1879, in *Young Wilhelm*, Röhl, p. 337.
36. Röhl, *Young Wilhelm*, p. 349.
37. Karl Shaw, *Royal Babylon: The Alarming History of European Royalty* (Kobo desktop version, 2011: retrieved from http://www.kobobooks.com), chap. 5, para 42.
38. Diary entry of June 1, 1880, in *Gone Astray: Some Leaves From An Emperor's Diary* (New York: John Lane, 1918), Wilhelm II, German Emperor and King of Prussia, pp. 92–93.
39. Empress Augusta of Germany to Princess Augusta Victoria, February 20, 1880, Parcel No. 14, Hohenlohe Letters, Langenburg Hausarchiv.
40. Lance Salway, *Queen Victoria's Grandchildren* (London: Collins & Brown, 1991), p. 13.
41. Georg Hinzpeter to Princess Augusta Victoria, February 7, 1882, Rep. 53A, Brandenburg-Preussischen Hausarchiv, Berliner Hauptarchiv.
42. Princess Augusta Victoria to Prince Wilhelm of Prussia, September 23, 1880, in *Young Wilhelm*, Röhl, pp. 360–361.
43. Princess Augusta Victoria to Prince Wilhelm of Prussia, undated, 1880, in ibid., p. 361.
44. Princess Augusta Victoria to Prince Wilhelm of Prussia, undated, January 1881, in ibid.
45. Thomas August Kohut, *Wilhelm II and the Germans: A Study in Leadership* (New York: Oxford University Press, 1991), p. 63.
46. *New York Times*, February 26, 1881.
47. Bothmer, *Sovereign Ladies*, p. 204.
48. Crown Princess Victoria of Germany to Queen Victoria, February 27, 1881, in *The Letters of Empress Frederick* (London: Macmillan, 1928), ed. Sir Frederick Ponsonby, p. 214.
49. Diary entry of February 27, 1881, in *Gone Astray*, Wilhelm II, p. 94.
50. Crown Princess Victoria of Germany to Queen Victoria, March 21, 1880, in *The Letters of Empress Frederick*, Ponsonby, p. 210.

51. Gelardi, *In Triumph's Wake*, p. 295.
52. Carter, *George, Nicholas and Wilhelm*, p. 9n.
53. Princess Charlotte of Saxe-Meiningen to Dr. Ernst Schweninger, undated, 1903, in *Young Wilhelm*, Röhl, p. 109.
54. Röhl, *Young Wilhelm*, p. 354.
55. Paul-Louis Hervier, *The Two Williams: Studies of the Kaiser and the Crown Prince* (London: Eveleigh Nash, 1916), p. 111.
56. Anonymous, *The Real Crown Prince: A Record and An Indictment* (London: George Newnes, n.d.), p. 9.
57. Diary entry of May 6, 1881, in *Gone Astray*, Wilhelm II, p. 94.
58. Nine months after the wedding, Frederick Ferdinand succeeded his father and became the Duke of Schleswig-Holstein-Sonderburg-Glücksburg. He inherited the title Duke of Schleswig-Holstein in 1931 when the Augustenburg line became extinct.
59. Gelardi, *In Triumph's Wake*, p. 300.
60. Dennison, *The Last Princess*, p. 160.
61. Pope-Hennessy, *Queen Mary*, pp. 52–53.
62. Sarah Bradford, *King George VI* (London: Weidenfeld & Nicolson, 1989), p. 20.
63. The calculation is based upon http://www.measuringworth.com/calculators/exchange/result_exchange.php (viewed on April 14, 2011).
64. Pope-Hennessy, *Queen Mary*, p. 97.
65. Letter of Mary Adelaide, Duchess of Teck, June 6, 1883, in *Her Royal Highness Princess Mary Adelaide*, Cook, p. 125.
66. Woodward, *Queen Mary*, p. 74.
67. Duff, *Queen Mary*, p. 47.
68. Ibid., pp. 47–49.
69. Woodward, *Queen Mary*, p. 76.
70. Gelardi, *Born to Rule*, p. 17.
71. Packard, *Victoria's Daughters*, p. 224.
72. Queen Victoria to Princess Victoria of Battenberg, June 27, 1884, in *Advice to a Grand-daughter*, Hough, p. 67.
73. Hibbert, *Queen Victoria*, p. 409.
74. Gelardi, *From Splendor to Revolution*, p. 107.
75. Kurth, *Tsar*, p. 28.
76. Tor Bomman-Larsen, *Kongstanken: Haakon & Maud—I* (Oslo: J. W. Cappelen, 2002), p. 119.
77. Clay, *King, Kaiser, Tsar*, p. 102.

3: Ninety-Nine Days

1. Duff, *Queen Mary*, p. 52.
2. Diary entry of Princess May of Teck, May 25, 1885, in ibid., p. 58.
3. Cook, *Her Royal Highness Princess Mary Adelaide*, vol. 2, p. 165.
4. Hibbert, *Queen Victoria*, p. 428.
5. Ibid.
6. Pope-Hennessy, *Queen Mary*, p. 151.
7. Princess May of Teck to Emily Alcock, July 25, 1887, in ibid.
8. E. J. Feuchtwanger, *Albert and Victoria: The Rise and Fall of the House of Saxe-Coburg-Gotha* (London: Hambledon Continuum, 2006), p. 202.
9. Hibbert, *Queen Victoria*, p. 430.

10. Ibid.

11. Wilhelm, German Crown Prince, *Memoirs of the Crown Prince of Germany* (New York: Charles Scribner's Sons, 1922), p. 34.

12. Hibbert, *Queen Victoria*, p. 430.

13. Cook, *Her Royal Highness Princess Mary Adelaide*, vol. 2, p. 177.

14. Pope-Hennessy, *Queen Mary*, p. 190.

15. Mary Adelaide, Duchess of Teck, to the Marchioness of Salisbury, April 18, 1889, in *Her Royal Highness*, Cook, p. 189.

16. Hibbert, *Queen Victoria*, p. 543.

17. Gelardi, *In Triumph's Wake*, p. 332.

18. Carter, *George, Nicholas and Wilhelm*, p. 130.

19. Ibid., p. 21.

20. Tyler-Whittle, *The Last Kaiser*, p. 76.

21. Ibid., p. 78.

22. Bennett, *Vicky*, p. 215.

23. Röhl, *Young Wilhelm*, p. 362.

24. Pakula, *An Uncommon Woman*, p. 536.

25. Röhl, *Young Wilhelm*, p. 315.

26. Crown Princess Victoria of Germany to Queen Victoria, May 25, 1886, in *Letters of Empress Frederick*, Ponsonby, p. 231.

27. Eppinghoven, *Private Lives*, vol. 2, p. 311.

28. Catherine Radziwill, *The Royal Marriage Market of Europe* (New York: Funk & Wagnalls, 1915), p. 32.

29. Hervier, *The Two Williams*, p. 112.

30. Christopher Clark, *Kaiser Wilhelm II: A Life in Power* (London: Penguin Books, 2009), p. 31.

31. Diary entry of March 9, 1888, in *Gone Astray*, Wilhelm II, pp. 146–147.

32. Empress Victoria of Germany to Queen Victoria, March 9, 1888, in *Letters of Empress Frederick*, Ponsonby, p. 287.

33. Charles Lowe, *The German Emperor William II* (London: Bliss, Sands, & Foster, 1895), p. 59.

34. Ibid., p. 60.

35. Gelardi, *In Triumph's Wake*, p. 310.

36. Empress Victoria of Germany to Queen Victoria, March 16, 1888, in *George, Nicholas and Wilhelm*, Carter, p. 75.

37. Hibbert, *Queen Victoria*, p. 436.

38. Diary entry of Queen Victoria, April 26, 1888, in ibid., p. 437.

39. Ibid.

40. Gelardi, *In Triumph's Wake*, p. 315.

41. Ibid., p. 316.

42. Queen Victoria to Princess Victoria of Battenberg, July 4, 1888, in *Advice to a Granddaughter*, Hough, p. 95.

43. Clark, *Kaiser Wilhelm II* (Kobo desktop version), chap. 2, para. 1.

44. Pakula, *An Uncommon Woman*, p. 498.

45. Gelardi, *In Triumph's Wake*, p. 319.

46. Ibid., p. 334.

47. Pakula, *An Uncommon Woman*, p. 536.

4: **"Bitter Tears"**

1. Clay, *King, Kaiser, Tsar*, p. 156.
2. Gelardi, *From Splendor to Revolution*, p. 51.
3. Clay, *King, Kaiser, Tsar*, p. 156.
4. Ibid., p. 157.
5. For more information on the theories regarding Eddy, refer to Andrew Cook, *Prince Eddy: The King Britain Never Had* (Stroud, Gloucester: The History Press, 2011).
6. Queen Victoria to Princess Victoria of Battenberg, March 31, 1889, in *Advice to a Grand-daughter*, Hough, p. 100.
7. Queen Victoria to Princess Victoria of Battenberg, October 30, 1889, in ibid., p. 105.
8. Erickson, *Alexandra*, p. 36.
9. Prince Albert Victor of Wales to Prince Louis of Battenberg, October 7, 1889, Southampton University archive MB1/T77/f2, in Cook, *Prince Eddy* (Kobo desktop version, 2012; retrieved from www.kobobooks.com), chap. 7, para. 116-17.
10. Queen Victoria to the Empress Frederick, May 7, 1890, in *Matriarch: Queen Mary and the House of Windsor* (London: Hodder & Stoughton, 1984), Anne Edwards, p. 24.
11. Queen Victoria to Princess Victoria of Battenberg, July 15, 1890, in *Advice to a Granddaughter*, Hough, p. 106.
12. Queen Victoria to Princess Victoria of Battenberg, December 19, 1890, in *Queen Victoria in Her Letters and Journals* (New York: Viking Penguin, 1985), ed. Christopher Hibbert, p. 318.
13. Erickson, *Alexandra*, p. 43–44.
14. Tyler-Whittle, *The Last Kaiser*, p. 129.
15. Shaw, *Royal Babylon* (Kobo desktop version), chap. 5, para. 2.
16. John C. G. Röhl, *Wilhelm II: The Kaiser's Personal Monarchy, 1888–1900* (New York: Cambridge University Press, 2001), p. 129.
17. Gordon Brook-Shepherd, *The Last Habsburg* (London: Weidenfeld & Nicolson, 1968), p. 3.
18. Queen Emma of the Netherlands was the second youngest. She was a mere three months and ten days older than Dona. Her title as the youngest reigning consort was short-lived, lasting only fourteen months. On October 19, 1889, King Charles I ascended the Portuguese throne. His wife, Queen Amélie, was twenty-four.
19. Clay, *King, Kaiser, Tsar*, p. 139.
20. Röhl, *Wilhelm II*, p. 625.
21. Lamar Cecil, *Wilhelm II: Emperor and Exile, 1900–1941* (Chapel Hill: University of North Carolina Press, 1996), pp. 3–4.
22. Carter, *George, Nicholas and Wilhelm*, p. 96.
23. Feuchtwanger, *Albert and Victoria*, p. 95.
24. Carter, *George, Nicholas and Wilhelm*, p. 88.
25. Ibid., p. 97.
26. Diary entry of March 15, 1890, in *Gone Astray*, Wilhelm II, p. 200.
27. Gelardi, *In Triumph's Wake*, p. 325.
28. Diary entry of July 5, 1890, in *Gone Astray*, Wilhelm II, pp. 204–205.
29. Schwering, *Berlin Court Under William II*, p. 56.
30. Clark, *Kaiser Wilhelm II* (Kobo desktop version), chap. 3, para. 11.
31. Shaw, *Royal Babylon* (Kobo desktop version), chap. 5, para. 51.
32. Cecil, *Wilhelm II*, p. 4.
33. John Van der Kiste, *Kaiser Wilhelm II: Germany's Last Emperor* (Gloucestershire: Sutton Publishing, 1999), p. 79.

34. Pakula, *An Uncommon Woman*, p. 539.

35. Gelardi, *Born to Rule*, pp. 25–26.

36. Arthur Gould Lee, ed., *The Empress Frederick Writes to Sophie, Her Daughter, Crown Princess and Later Queen of the Hellenes: Letters 1889–1901* (London: Faber & Faber, 1955), p. 76.

37. Pakula, *An Uncommon Woman*, p. 539.

38. Empress Frederick, to Crown Princess Sophie of Greece, undated, 1890, in *The Empress Frederick Writes to Sophie*, ed. Gould Lee, p. 74.

39. *Spokane Falls Daily Chronicle*, December 18, 1890.

40. Pakula, *An Uncommon Woman*, p. 540.

41. Tyler-Whittle, *The Last Kaiser*, p. 145.

42. Pakula, *An Uncommon Woman*, p. 537.

43. Ibid., p. 540.

44. Princess Marie Louise of Schleswig-Holstein-Sonderburg-Augustenburg was a first cousin to both Wilhelm and Augusta Victoria. Her mother, Princess Helena, was Queen Victoria's daughter; and her father, Prince Christian, was Fritz Holstein's younger brother. Marie Louise's mother and Wilhelm's mother were sisters, and Marie Louise's father and Augusta Victoria's father were brothers.

45. Carter, *George, Nicholas and Wilhelm*, p. 129.

46. Eppinghoven, *Private Lives*, vol. 2, p. 295.

47. Röhl, *Wilhelm II*, p. 361.

48. Queen Marie of Romania, *The Story of My Life* (London: Cassell, 1934), vol. 2, p. 227.

49. Diary entry of Empress Augusta Victoria, undated, September 1892, in *The Kaiser's Daughter*, Viktoria Luise, p. 1.

50. Diary entry of Queen Victoria, December 5, 1891, in *Queen Victoria in Her Letters*, Hough, p. 320.

51. Augusta, Grand Duchess of Mecklenburg-Strelitz to George, Duke of Cambridge, December 25, 1891, in *Queen Mary*, Pope-Hennessy, p. 207.

52. Hibbert, *Queen Victoria*, p. 541.

53. Pakula, *An Uncommon Woman*, p. 556.

54. Queen Victoria to the Empress Frederick, undated, November 1891, in *Queen Mary*, Pope-Hennessy, p. 172.

55. Duff, *Queen Mary*, p. 75.

56. Queen Victoria to the Empress Frederick, December 16, 1891, in *Queen Mary*, Pope-Hennessy, p. 204.

57. Ibid., p. 41.

58. Queen Victoria to the Empress Frederick, November 19, 1891, in ibid., p. 196.

59. Gelardi, *In Triumph's Wake*, p. 332.

60. Pope-Hennessy, *Queen Mary*, pp. 198–199.

61. Queen Victoria to Princess May of Teck, December 13, 1891, in *Matriarch*, Edwards, p. 41.

62. Princess May of Teck to Augusta, Grand Duchess of Mecklenburg-Strelitz, December 16, 1891, in *Queen Mary*, Pope-Hennessy, p. 208.

63. Gould Lee, *The Empress Frederick Writes to Sophie*, p. 103.

64. Edwards, *Matriarch*, p. 42.

65. Duff, *Queen Mary*, p. 77.

66. Augusta, Grand Duchess of Mecklenburg-Strelitz, to Mary Adelaide, Duchess of Teck, December 7, 1891, in *Matriarch*, Edwards, p. 42.

67. Cook, *Prince Eddy* (Kobo desktop version), chap. 11, para. 27.

68. Interview of Lady Frederick Willens by James Pope-Hennessy, 1958, ibid., ch. 12, para. 24.

69. Gyles Brandreth, *Philip and Elizabeth: Portrait of a Royal Marriage* (London: W. W. Norton, 2004), p. 53.

70. Mary Adelaide, Duchess of Teck, to Queen Victoria, January 14, 1892, in ibid., pp. 51–52.

71. Princess May of Teck to Queen Victoria, undated, January 1892, Z95/6, Queen Mary Papers, the Royal Archives in *Queen Mary*, Pope-Hennessy, p. 215.

72. Diary entry of Queen Victoria, January 14, 1892, in *Queen Victoria in Her Letters*, Hibbert, p. 321.

73. Pope-Hennessy, *Queen Mary*, p. 213.

74. Princess May of Teck to Emily Alcock, February 13, 1892, in *Matriarch*, Edwards, p. 53.

5:   A Touch of Destiny

1. Robert's maternal grandmother, Princess Caroline of Naples and Sicily, was the half sister of Maria Pia's father, King Ferdinand II of the Two Sicilies.

2. Arturo Beech and David McIntosh, *Empress Zita of Austria, Queen of Hungary (1892–1989)* (Eurohistory: North Pacific Heights, 2005), p. 2.

3. Henry's death left the Bourbons without any direct, male-line heirs to the French throne. This prompted them to formally renounce their claims to the throne. This renunciation made the Orléans branch of the royal family the official pretenders to the throne.

4. Beech and McIntosh, *Empress Zita of Austria*, p. 2.

5. Thomas de Notre-Dame du perpétual secours, "Empress Zita, French Princess, Empress and Regent of Austria-Hungary," *The Catholic Counter-Reformation in the XXIᵉ Century: He is Risen!*, no. 28, (February 2010), p. 1.

6. Empress Zita to Gordon Brook-Shepherd, April 22, 1968, in *The Last Empress: The Life and Times of Zita of Austria-Hungary, 1892–1989* (London: HarperCollins, 1991), Gordon Brook-Shepherd, p. 7.

7. Brook-Shepherd, *The Last Habsburg*, p. 17.

8. Princess May of Teck to Prince George of Wales, January 14, 1893, in *Matriarch*, Edwards, p. 64.

9. Gould, *Empress Frederick Writes to Sophie*, p. 140.

10. Wakeford, *Three Consort Queens*, p. 162.

11. Queen Victoria to George, Duke of York, undated, May 1892, AA 10/39, King George V Papers, the Royal Archives, quoted in *Queen Victoria*, Hibbert, p. 728. The "not very agreeable associations" of which the queen wrote had been her uncle Frederick, Duke of York (1763-1827), a thoroughly profligate, unpopular man who was one of the many lecherous sons of George III.

12. George, Duke of York, to Princess May of Teck, March 29, 1892, in *King, Kaiser, Tsar*, Clay, p. 151.

13. Julia P. Gelardi, *From Splendor to Revolution: The Romanov Women, 1847–1928* (New York: Saint Martin's Press, 2011), p. 140.

14. Queen Victoria to George, Duke of York, April 6, 1892, in *George V* (London: Weidenfeld & Nicolson, 2000), Kenneth Rose, p. 25.

15. Diary entry of Princess May of Teck, May 29, 1893, in *Queen Mary*, Pope-Hennessy, p. 250.

16. Diary entry of Queen Victoria, May 3, 1893, in *Queen Victoria in Her Letters*, Hibbert, p. 324.

17. Alexandra, Princess of Wales, to Princess May of Teck, May 13, 1893, in *Matriarch*, Edwards, p. 66.

18. Clay, *King, Kaiser, Tsar*, p. 152.

19. Princess May of Teck to George, Duke of York, July 6, 1893, in *Queen Mary*, Pope-Hennessy, p. 257.

20. Edward J. Bing, ed., *The Letters of Tsar Nicholas and Empress Marie* (London: Ivor Nicholson & Watson, 1937), p. 72.

21. Woodward, *Queen Mary*, p. 116.

22. Diary entry of Queen Victoria, July 6, 1893, in *Queen Victoria in Her Letters*, Hibbert, p. 325.

23. Diary entry of Lady Geraldine Somerset, July 6, 1893, in *Matriarch*, Edwards, p. 77.

24. Carter, *George, Nicholas and Wilhelm*, p. 195.

25. Edwards, *Matriarch*, p. 83.

26. Carter, *George, Nicholas and Wilhelm*, p. 247.

27. Erickson, *Alexandra*, p. 45.

28. Hibbert, *Queen Victoria*, p. 540.

29. Erickson, *Alexandra*, pp. 99–100.

30. Ibid., p. 34.

31. Gelardi, *Born to Rule*, pp. 42, 44.

32. Van der Kiste, *Queen Victoria's Children*, p. 92.

33. Princess Alix to Tsarevitch Nicholas, November 8, 1893, in *A Lifelong Passion: Nicholas and Alexandre, Their Own Story* (London: Weidenfeld & Nicolson, 1996), eds. Andrei Maylunas and Sergei Mironenko, pp. 32–33.

34. Princess Alix to Grand Duchess Xenia of Russia, November 8, 1893, in ibid.

35. Massie, *Nicholas and Alexandra*, p. 28.

36. E. M. Almedingen, *The Empress Alexandra, 1872–1918: A Study* (London: Hutchinson, 1961), p. 20.

37. E. P. P. Tisdall, *Marie Feodorovna: Empress of Russia* (New York: John Day, 1957), p. 178.

38. Tsarevitch Nicholas to Empress Marie Feodorovna, April 10, 1894, in *Tsar Nicholas and Empress Marie*, Bing, p. 75.

39. Diary entry of Lady Lytton, April 19, 1894, in *Lady Lytton's Court Diary* (London: Rupert Hart Davis, 1961), ed. Mary Luytens, p. 65.

40. Massie, *Nicholas and Alexandra*, p. 34.

41. Kurth, *Tsar*, p. 41.

42. Diary entry of February 6, 1901, in *Gone Astray*, Wilhelm II, p. 215.

43. Tsarevitch Nicholas to Empress Marie Feodorovna, April 10, 1894, in *Lifelong Passion*, Maylunas and Mironenko, p. 49.

44. Princess Alix to Queen Victoria, April 10/22, 1894, in *George, Nicholas and Wilhelm*, Carter, p. 117.

45. Carter, *George, Nicholas and Wilhelm*, p. 116.

46. Massie, *Nicholas and Alexandra*, pp. 35–36.

47. Erickson, *Alexandra*, p. 60.

48. Gordon Brook-Shepherd, *Royal Sunset: The Dynasties of Europe and the Great War* (London: Weidenfeld & Nicolson, 1987), p. 194.

49. Gould Lee, *Empress Frederick Writes to Sophie*, p. 170.

50. Carter, *George, Nicholas and Wilhelm*, p. 159.

51. Princess Alix to Grand Duchess Xenia of Russia, undated, April 1894, in *Lifelong Passion*, Maylunas and Mironenko, p. 45.
52. Gelardi, *From Splendor to Revolution*, p. 142.
53. Gelardi, *Born to Rule*, pp. 50–51.
54. Almedingen, *Empress Alexandra*, p. 24.
55. Gelardi, *Born to Rule*, p. 51.

Part 2: The Age of Empires (1894–1914)

6: "A Little Scrubby Hessian Princess"

1. Hall, *Little Mother of Russia*, p. 156.
2. Queen Victoria to Princess Victoria of Battenberg, October 21, 1894, in *Advice to a Grand-daughter*, Hough, p. 126.
3. Carter, *George, Nicholas and Wilhelm*, p. 116.
4. Gelardi, *From Splendor to Revolution*, pp. 56–57.
5. Carter, *George, Nicholas and Wilhelm*, p. 50.
6. Penny Wilson and Greg King, *The Resurrection of the Romanovs: Anastasia, Anna Anderson, and the World's Greatest Royal Mystery* (Hoboken, NJ: John Wiley & Sons, 2011), p. 40.
7. Kurth, *Tsar*, p. 8.
8. Even until after the birth of the Soviet Union, the titles *tsar* and *emperor* were used interchangeably. Most Romanov monarchs since Peter the Great used the title *emperor*, but the Slavophilic Nicholas II preferred *tsar*.
9. Carter, *George, Nicholas and Wilhelm*, p. 51.
10. Clark, *Kaiser Wilhelm II* (Kobo desktop version), chap. 2, para. 11.
11. Princess Alix to Tsarevitch Nicholas, April 26, 1894, in *Lifelong Passion*, Maylunas and Mironenko, p. 60.
12. Massie, *Nicholas and Alexandra*, p. 39.
13. Edwards, *Matriarch*, p. 86.
14. Massie, *Nicholas and Alexandra*, p. 40.
15. Nigel Cawthorne, *Kings and Queens of England: A Royal History from Egbert to Elizabeth II* (London: Arcturus Publishing, 2009), p. 185.
16. Duff, *Queen Mary*, p. 94.
17. Carter, *George, Nicholas and Wilhelm*, p. 117.
18. Massie, *Nicholas and Alexandra*, p. 41.
19. Gelardi, *Born to Rule*, p. 54.
20. Vladimir Poliakoff, *The Tragic Bride: The Story of Empress Alexandra of Russia* (New York: D. Appleton, 1928), p. 62.
21. Brook-Shepherd, *Royal Sunset*, p. 194.
22. Massie, *Nicholas and Alexandra*, p. 44.
23. May, Duchess of York, to George, Duke of York, November 1, 1894, in *Queen Mary*, Pope-Hennessy, p. 300.
24. Edwards, *Matriarch*, p. 87.
25. Gelardi, *Born to Rule*, p. 55.
26. Grand Duke Alexander, *Once a Grand Duke* (New York: Garden City Publishing, 1932), p. 168.
27. Carter, *George, Nicholas and Wilhelm*, p. 112.

28. Grand Duchess Elizabeth to Queen Victoria, October 24/November 5, 1894, in *Grand Duchess Elizabeth of Russia* (Redding, CA: Nikodemos Orthodox Publication Society, 1991), Lubov Millar, p. 81.
29. Massie, *Nicholas and Alexandra*, p. 45.
30. Ibid., p. 47.
31. Hall, *Little Mother of Russia*, p. 167.
32. Queen Victoria to the Empress Frederick, November 13, 1894, in *Born to Rule*, Gelardi, p. 55.
33. *New York Times*, November 27, 1894.
34. Kurth, *Tsar*, p. 50.
35. Tsarina Alexandra to Grand Duchess Elizabeth, November 14, 1894, in Edwards, *Matriarch*, p. 88.
36. *New York Times*, November 27, 1894.
37. Gelardi, *From Splendor to Revolution, p. 147.*
38. George, Duke of York, to Queen Victoria, November 28, 1894 in *George, Nicholas and Wilhelm*, Carter, pp. 122–123.
39. Massie, *Nicholas and Alexandra*, p. 48.
40. Gelardi, *Born to Rule*, p. 57.
41. Charlotte Knollys to Mrs. Archibald Knollys, November 25, 1894, MSS 21M69/25/2. Knollys Papers, Hampshire Record Office, quoted in *Born to Rule*, Gelardi, p. 57.
42. King, *The Last Empress*, p. 76.
43. Frederic Hamilton, *The Vanished World of Yesterday* (London: Hodder & Stoughton, 1950), p. 475.
44. Carter, *George, Nicholas and Wilhelm*, p. 182.

7:   **"Only Give Me a Chance"**
1. Catherine Radziwill, *Nicholas II: The Last of the Tsars* (London: Cassell, 1931), p. 89.
2. Tsarina Alexandra to Prince Louis of Battenberg, January 10, 1895, in MSS MB1/T95, Broadlands Archives, Hartley Library, University of Southampton, quoted in *Born to Rule*, Gelardi, p. 58.
3. Gelardi, *Born to Rule*, pp. 62–63.
4. *Daily Telegraph*, November 16, 1895.
5. Gelardi, *Born to Rule*, pp. 62-63.
6. Erickson, *Alexandra*, p. 107.
7. Gelardi, *From Splendor to Revolution*, p. 150.
8. Kurth, *Tsar*, p. 58.
9. Gelardi, *From Splendor to Revolution*, p. 155.
10. Kurth, *Tsar*, pp. 58-59.
11. Gelardi, *Born to Rule*, p. 69.
12. Empress Marie Feodorovna to Queen Louise of Denmark, May 16/28, 1896, in *From Splendor to Revolution*, Gelardi, p. 156.
13. Erickson, *Alexandra*, p. 109.
14. Empress Marie Feodorovna to Queen Louise of Denmark, undated, 1896, in *From Splendor to Revolution*, Gelardi, p. 157.
15. Maylunas and Mironenko, *Lifelong Passion*, p. 151.
16. Queen Marie, *The Story of My Life*, vol. 2, p. 73.
17. Erickson, *Alexandra*, p. 113.
18. Ibid., p. 115.

19. Hibbert, *Queen Victoria*, p. 509.
20. Carter, *George, Nicholas and Wilhelm*, p. 168.
21. Hibbert, *Queen Victoria*, p. 509.
22. Gelardi, *Born to Rule*, p. 73.
23. Hibbert, *Queen Victoria*, p. 509.
24. Diary entry of Queen Victoria, October 3, 1896, in *The Letters of Queen Victoria: Third Series, A Selection From Her Majesty's Correspondence and Journal Between the Years 1886 and 1901* (London: John Murray, 1932), ed. George Earle Buckle, vol. 3, p. 88.
25. Gelardi, *Born to Rule*, p. 73.
26. Woodward, *Queen Mary*, p. 120.
27. David Sinclar, *Two Georges: The Making of the Modern Monarchy* (London: Hodder & Stroughton, 1998), p. 107.
28. Mark Logue and Peter Conradi, *The King's Speech: How One Man Saved the British Monarchy* (Toronto: Penguin Canada, 2010), p. 47.
29. Mary Adelaide, Duchess of Teck, to Prince Alexander of Teck, December 20, 1895, in *Three Consort Queens*, Wakeford, p. 165.
30. Hibbert, *Queen Victoria*, p. 332.
31. Diary entry of Queen Victoria, December 14, 1895, in *Queen Victoria in Her Letters*, Hibbert, p. 331.
32. John Wheeler-Bennett, *King George VI: His Life and Reign* (New York: Macmillan, 1958), p. 7.
33. Diary entry of Queen Victoria, December 16, 1895, in ibid.
34. Bradford, *King George VI*, p. 2.
35. This wedding was yet another example of the complex intermarriages of Europe's royal families. Princess Alexandra of Edinburgh was a first cousin of Wilhelm II. Prince Ernest of Hohenlohe-Langenburg was a first cousin of Augusta Victoria's.
36. May, Duchess of York, to Mary Adelaide, Duchess of Teck, April 15, 1896, in *Queen Mary*, Pope-Hennessy, p. 318.
37. Wakeford, *Three Consort Queens*, p. 165.
38. Duff, *Queen Mary*, p. 97.
39. Hector Bolitho, *King George VI* (New York: J. B. Lippincott, 1938), p. 18.
40. Duff, *Queen Mary*, p. 100.
41. Richard Hough, *Born Royal: The Lives and Loves of the Young Windsors* (London: Bantam Books, 1988), p. 11.
42. This statute has been in effect ever since, although Queen Elizabeth II announced in 2011 that she planned to repeal this law.
43. England was unified with Scotland by the Treaty of Union in 1707, which was ratified by the Acts of Union that same year. The unification of these realms created the Kingdom of Great Britain. It was under King George III in 1800 that Ireland was brought under the crown by another Act of Union, thus creating the United Kingdom of Great Britain and Ireland.
44. Diary entry of May, Duchess of York, June 22, 1897, in *Queen Mary*, Duff, pp. 100–101.
45. Marfa Mouchanow, *My Empress* (New York: John Lane, 1928), p. 91.
46. *Boston Evening Post*, August 9, 1897.
47. Erickson, *Alexandra*, p. 240.
48. Ibid., p. 118.
49. Carter, *George, Nicholas and Wilhelm*, p. 177.
50. Wakeford, *Three Consort Queens*, p. 166.

51.   Alexandra, Princess of Wales, to Augusta, Grand Duchess of Mecklenburg-Strelitz, undated, 1897, in *Matriarch*, Edwards, p. 95.

52.   May, Duchess of York, to Augusta, Grand Duchess of Mecklenburg-Strelitz, November 3, 1897, in ibid.

53.   Queen Victoria to Princess Victoria of Battenberg, November 17, 1890, in *Advice to a Grand-daughter*, Hough, pp. 139–140.

54.   Wakeford, *Three Consort Queens*, p. 149.

55.   Duff, *Queen Mary*, p. 92.

56.   Hough, *Born Royal*, p. 50.

57.   Gelardi, *In Triumph's Wake*, p. 331.

58.   Gelardi, *Born to Rule*, p. 85.

59.   Diary entry of Queen Victoria, undated, September 1897, in *George, Nicholas and Wilhelm*, Carter, p. 195.

60.   Wakeford, *Three Consort Queens*, p. 167.

61.   Queen Victoria to Princess Victoria of Battenberg, April 1, 1899, in *Advice to a Grand-daughter*, Hough, p. 144.

62.   Isabel V. Hull, *The Entourage of Kaiser Wilhelm II 1888–1918* (Cambridge: Cambridge University Press, 1982), p. 19.

63.   Carter, *George, Nicholas and Wilhelm*, p. 222.

64.   *Daily Mail*, November 22, 1899.

65.   Gould Lee, *The Empress Frederick Writes to Sophie*, p. 325. Vicky's reference to Adelaide being three years older than her is a strange error. It was a widely known fact that Adelaide was five years older than the Empress Frederick.

66.   Hibbert, *Queen Victoria*, p. 543.

67.   Boston Women's Health Collective, *Our Bodies, Ourselves: Pregnancy and Birth* (New York: Touchstone Books, 2008), pp. 489–491.

68.   Clark, *Kaiser Wilhelm II* (Kobo desktop version), chap. 1, para. 40.

69.   Cecil, *Wilhelm II*, p. 3.

70.   *New York Times*, November 26, 1900.

71.   Röhl, *Wilhelm II*, p. 627.

72.   Ibid., p. 626.

73.   Hull, *Entourage of Kaiser Wilhelm II*, p. 19.

74.   Massie, *Dreadnought*, p. 671.

75.   Hull, *Entourage of Kaiser Wilhelm II*, p. 19.

76.   Massie, *Dreadnought*, p. 671.

77.   Van der Kiste, *Kaiser Wilhelm II*, p. 106.

78.   Brook-Shepherd, *The Last Habsburg*, p. 4.

79.   David James Smith, *One Morning in Sarajevo: 28 June 1914* (London: Weidenfeld & Nicolson, 2008), p. 68.

80.   Eppinghoven, *Private Lives*, vol. 2, p. 254.

81.   Tyler-Whittle, *The Last Kaiser*, p. 128.

82.   Massie, *Dreadnought*, p. 296.

83.   Diary entry of Queen Victoria, July 31, 1900, in *Queen Victoria*, Hibbert, p. 346.

84.   Carter, *George, Nicholas and Wilhelm*, p. 128.

85.   Ibid., p. 129.

86.   King Edward VII to the Empress Frederick, February 1, 1901, in *Edward VII: Prince and King* (London: Collins, 1979), Giles St Aubyn, p. 314.

87.   Diary entry of George, Duke of York, January 22, 1901, in *George, Nicholas and Wilhelm*, Carter, p. 229.

88.   Massie, *Dreadnought*, p. 296.

89. Gelardi, *Born to Rule*, p. 89.
90. Diary entry of May, Duchess of York, January 22, 1901, in *Queen Mary*, Pope-Hennessy, p. 347.
91. Edwards, *Matriarch*, p. 104.
92. Hough, *Born Royal*, p. 27.
93. Massie, *Nicholas and Alexandra*, p. 75.

8: The Weight of the World

1. Gelardi, *Born to Rule*, p. 111.
2. Edwards, *Matriarch*, p. 110.
3. May, Duchess of York, to Hélène Bricka, January 26, 1901, in *Queen Mary*, Pope-Hennessy, p. 348.
4. May, Duchess of York, to Augusta, Grand Duchess of Mecklenburg-Strelitz, February 3, 1901, in ibid.
5. Arthur Balfour, First Earl of Balfour, to King Edward VII, February 6, 1901, in *King George V: His Life and Reign* (London: Constable, 1952), Harold Nicolson, pp. 67–68.
6. Hough, *Born Royal*, p. 30.
7. George, Duke of York, to Queen Alexandra, undated, 1901, in *King, Kaiser, Tsar*, Clay, p. 210.
8. M. C. Carey, *Princess Mary* (London: Nisbet, 1922), pp. 15–16.
9. John C. G. Röhl, *Kaiser Wilhelm II: New Interpretations—The Corfu Papers* (Cambridge: Cambridge University Press, 1982), p. 98.
10. Hull, *Entourage of Kaiser Wilhelm II*, p. 26.
11. Röhl, *Wilhelm II*, p. 623.
12. Schwering, *Berlin Court Under William II*, p. 61.
13. Röhl, *Wilhelm II*, p. 626.
14. Giles MacDonogh, *The Last Kaiser: William the Impetuous* (London: Weidenfeld & Nicolson, 2000), p. 252.
15. Schwering, *Berlin Court Under William II*, p. 62.
16. Röhl, *Wilhelm II*, p. 639.
17. MacDonogh, *The Last Kaiser*, p. 252.
18. Carter, *George, Nicholas and Wilhelm*, p. 186.
19. MacDonogh, *The Last Kaiser*, p. 256.
20. Clark, *Kaiser Wilhelm II*, p. 126.
21. *New York Times*, March 25, 1905.
22. Gelardi, *In Triumph's Wake*, p. 337.
23. Diary entry of Grand Duchess Xenia, June 5, 1901, in *Lifelong Passion*, Maylunas and Mironenko, p. 206.
24. *Daily Mail*, June 19, 1901.
25. Gill, *We Two*, p. 289.
26. Georgina Battiscombe, *Queen Alexandra* (London: Constable, 1969), p. 254.
27. Erickson, *Alexandra*, p. 145.
28. Grand Duchess Marie of Russia, *Education of a Princess: A Memoir* (New York: Viking Press, 1931), p. 56.
29. George, Prince of Wales, to Tsar Nicholas II, December 21, 1901, in *George, Nicholas and Wilhelm*, Carter, p. 198.
30. Gelardi, *From Splendor to Revolution*, pp. 174–175.
31. Erickson, *Alexandra*, p. 127.

32. Hall, *Little Mother of Russia*, p. 192.
33. Gelardi, *From Splendor to Revolution*, p. 209.
34. Duff, *Queen Mary*, p. 117.
35. Woodward, *Queen Mary*, p. 139.
36. Duff, *Queen Mary*, pp. 117–118.
37. Woodward, *Queen Mary*, p. 142.
38. Joseph Pope, *The Tour of Their Royal Highnesses the Duke and Duchess of Cornwall and York Through the Dominion of Canada in the Year 1901* (Ottawa: S. E. Dawson, 1908), p. 64.
39. Ibid., pp. 73–74.
40. George, Duke of York, to Queen Alexandra, undated, 1901, GV/PRIV/AA 36/53, King George V Papers, the Royal Archives, in *Queen Mary*, Pope-Hennessy, pp. 362–363.
41. Pope, *The Tour of Their Royal Highnesses*, p. 80.
42. Clay, *King, Kaiser, Tsar*, p. 210.
43. Royal address of George, Duke of York, November 3, 1901, in *The King to His People: Being the Speeches and Messages of His Majesty George V as Prince and Sovereign* (London: Williams & Norgate, 1911), King George V of Great Britain, p. 79.
44. Carter, *George, Nicholas and Wilhelm*, p. 196.
45. Duff, *Queen Mary*, p. 120.
46. Clay, *King, Kaiser, Tsar*, p. 207.
47. The calculation is based on http://www.measuringworth.com/calculators/exchange/result_exchange.php (viewed on April 14, 2011).
48. Thomas, "Empress Zita," *The Catholic Counter-Reformation*, p. 1.
49. James and Joanna Bogle, *A Heart for Europe: The Lives of Emperor Charles and Empress Zita of Austria-Hungary* (London: Gracewing, 1990), p. 32.
50. Robert George, *Heirs of Tradition: Tributes of a New Zealander* (Manchester, NH: Ayer Publishing, 1971), p. 201.
51. Ibid., p. 202.
52. Gelardi, *Born to Rule*, p. 94.
53. Ibid.
54. Paul Vassili, *Confessions of the Czarina* (New York: Harper & Bros., 1918), p. 52.
55. Carter, *George, Nicholas and Wilhelm*, p. 103.
56. Ibid., p. 270.
57. Gelardi, *From Splendor to Revolution*, p. 293.
58. Gelardi, *Born to Rule*, p. 66.
59. Kurth, *Tsar*, p. 54.
60. Erickson, *Alexandra*, p. 158.
61. Gelardi, *From Splendor to Revolution*, p. 182.
62. Gelardi, *Born to Rule*, p. 107.
63. Erickson, *Alexandra*, p. 159.
64. Mouchanow, *My Empress*, p. 155.
65. Diary entry of Tsar Nicholas II, July 30, 1904, in *A Lifelong Passion*, Maylunas and Mironenko, p. 243.
66. Rappaport, *Last Days of the Romanovs*, p. 88.
67. Diary entry of Tsar Nicholas II, September 8, 1904, in *Black Night, White Snow: Russia's Revolutions 1905–1917* (New York: Doubleday, 1977), Harrison E. Salisbury, p. 110.
68. Erickson, *Alexandra*, p. 161.

9:   A Mother's Heart

1.   German Crown Prince, *Memoirs*, p. 68.
2.   Erickson, *Alexandra*, p. 167.
3.   Brook-Shepherd, *Royal Sunset*, p. 204.
4.   Charles Hardinge, *Old Diplomacy* (London: John Murray, 1947), p. 114.
5.   Carter, *George, Nicholas and Wilhelm*, p. 187.
6.   Buxhoeveden, *Alexandra Feodorovna*, p. 109.
7.   Kurth, *Tsar*, pp. 81-82.
8.   Gelardi, *From Splendor to Revolution*, p. 188.
9.   Ibid., p. 190.
10.   Edward Crankshaw, *Shadow of the Winter Palace: Russia's Drift to Revolution, 1825–1917* (New York: Viking Press, 1976), p. 329.
11.   Tsar Nicholas II to Emperor Wilhelm II, October 20, 1904, in *The Willy-Nicky Correspondence: Being the Secret and Intimate Telegrams Exchanged Between the Kaiser and the Tsar* (New York: Alfred A. Knopf, 1918), ed. Herman Bernstein, p. 67.
12.   Gelardi, *Born to Rule*, p. 116.
13.   Brook-Shepherd, *Royal Sunset*, p. 202.
14.   Ian Vorres, *The Last Grand Duchess: Her Imperial Highness Grand Duchess Olga Alexandrova* (New York: Charles Scribner's Sons, 1965), p. 113.
15.   Schwering, *Berlin Court Under William II*, pp. 55–56.
16.   Ibid., p. 57.
17.   Eppinghoven, *Private Lives*, vol. 2, p. 335.
18.   Cunliffe-Owen, *Imperator et Rex*, p. 257.
19.   Schwering, *Berlin Court Under William II*, p. 55.
20.   Cecil, *Wilhelm II*, p. 5.
21.   Ernst von Heltzendorff and William Le Queux, *The Secrets of Potsdam: A Startling Exposure of the Inner Life of the Courts of the Kaiser and Crown-Prince* (London: London Mail, n.d.), p. 174.
22.   Viktoria Luise, *The Kaiser's Daughter*, p. 2.
23.   Anonymous, *Real Crown Prince*, p. 15.
24.   Schwering, *Berlin Court Under William II*, pp. 60–61.
25.   German Crown Prince, *Memoirs*, p. 4.
26.   Carter, *George, Nicholas and Wilhelm*, p. 274.
27.   Röhl, *Kaiser Wilhelm II*, p. 104.
28.   Cecil, *Wilhelm II*, p. 82.
29.   Bothmer, *Sovereign Ladies*, p. 210.
30.   Viktoria Luise, *The Kaiser's Daughter*, p. 6.
31.   *New York Times*, June 11, 1908.
32.   Ibid., September 5, 1904.
33.   Ibid., June 5, 1905.
34.   Viktoria Luise, *The Kaiser's Daughter*, p. 55.
35.   German Crown Prince, *Memoirs*, p. 282.
36.   Robert Zedlitz-Trützschler, *Twelve Years at the Imperial German Court* (London: Nisbet, 1924), p. 99.
37.   Mme. la Marquise Fontenoy, *Secret Memoirs of William II of Germany and Francis Joseph of Austria* (London: Hutchinson, 1900), vol. 1, p. 193.
38.   Catherine Radziwill, *The Disillusions of a Crown Princess* (New York: John Lane, 1919), p. 86.
39.   Edwards, *Matriarch*, pp.142–143.

40.   May, Princess of Wales, to George, Prince of Wales, undated, in *Queen Mary*, Pope-Hennessy, p. 386.

41.   William Shawcross, *Queen Elizabeth: The Queen Mother* (Toronto: HarperCollins, 2009), p. 106.

42.   Carter, *George, Nicholas and Wilhelm*, p. 199.

43.   Cook, *Prince Eddy* (Kobo desktop version), ch. 12, para. 7.

44.   Carter, *George, Nicholas and Wilhelm*, p. 198.

45.   Edward, Duke of Windsor, *A King's Story* (London: Cassell, 1951), pp. 24–25.

46.   Eulalia, Infanta of Spain, *Courts and Countries After the War* (New York: Dodd, Mead, 1925), pp. 111–112.

47.   May, Princess of Wales, to Hélène Bricka, September 13, 1904, in *Queen Mary*, Pope-Hennessy, p. 390.

48.   May, Princess of Wales, to Hélène Bricka, December 19, 1905, in ibid, p. 391.

49.   Edward Legge, *King George and the Royal Family*, (London: Grant Richards, 1918), vol. 1, p. 72.

50.   Royal address of George, Prince of Wales, November 18, 1905, in *The King to His People*, King George V, p. 77.

51.   Wakeford, *Three Consort Queens*, p. 170.

52.   May, Princess of Wales, to Augusta, Grand Duchess of Mecklenburg-Strelitz, April 7, 1906, in *Queen Mary*, Pope-Hennessy, p. 395.

53.   Dennison, *The Last Princess*, p. 264.

54.   Edwards, *Matriarch*, p. 157.

55.   Pope-Hennessy, *Queen Mary*, p. 400.

56.   Gelardi, *Born to Rule*, p. 141.

57.   Duff, *Queen Mary*, p. 126.

58.   May, Princess of Wales, to Augusta, Grand Duchess of Mecklenburg-Strelitz, May 31, 1906, in *Queen Mary*, Pope-Hennessy, pp. 401–402.

59.   Duff, *Queen Mary*, p. 126.

60.   Maud's husband, King Haakon VII (1872–1957), was born Prince Carl of Denmark. His father, King Frederick VIII, was the eldest son of King Christian IX—the "grandfather of Europe." King Frederick and Maud's mother, Queen Alexandra, were siblings. This meant Haakon and Maud were first cousins. As a member of the Danish royal family, Haakon was also a first cousin to King George V, Tsar Nicholas II, and King Constantine I of Greece.

61.   Pope-Hennessy, *Queen Mary*, pp. 401–402.

62.   John Van der Kiste, *Edward VII's Children* (Stroud, Gloucester: Alan Sutton Publishing 1989), p. 109.

63.   Gelardi, *Born to Rule*, p. 147.

64.   Wakeford, *Three Consort Queens*, p. 169.

65.   Hough, *Born Royal*, p. 44.

10:   Life's Unexpected Trials

1.   Norman Stone, *Europe Transformed, 1878–1919*, 2nd ed., (Oxford: Blackwell Publishing, 1999), p. 166.

2.   W. Bruce Lincoln, *In War's Dark Shadow: The Russians Before the Great War* (New York: Dial Press, 1983), p. 295.

3.   Gelardi, *Born to Rule*, pp. 117–118.

4.   Tsar Nicholas II to Empress Marie Feodorovna, October 19/November 9, 1905, in *The Letters of Tsar Nicholas and Empress Marie*, Bing, pp. 186–187.

5. Grand Duke Alexander, *Once a Grand Duke*, p. 225.
6. Elizabeth Narishkin-Kurakin, *Under Three Tsars: The Memoirs of the Lady-in-Waiting Elizabeth Narishkin-Kurakin*, ed. René Fülöp-Miller (New York: E. P. Dutton, 1931), p. 190.
7. V. N. Kokovtsov, *Out of My Past: The Memoirs of Count Kokovtsov*, trans. Laura Matveev, ed. H. H. Fisher (Stanford: Stanford University Press, 1935), pp. 130–131.
8. Grand Duke Alexander, *Once a Grand Duke*, p. 227.
9. A. A. Mossolov, *At the Court of the Last Tsar*, trans. E. W. Dickes (London: Methuen, 1935), p. 139.
10. Gelardi, *Born to Rule*, p. 119.
11. Kurth, *Tsar*, p. 85.
12. Ibid., p. 120. Anna was originally born Anna Taneyeva but was married briefly to Alexander Viroubov. In an interesting twist, Anna was a descendent of Nicholas II's great-great-grandfather Tsar Paul I. Through marriage, she and Alexandra were third cousins.
13. Ibid., p. 121.
14. Helen Rappaport, *The Last Days of the Romanovs: Tragedy at Ekaterinburg* (New York: Saint Martin's Press, 2008), p. 60.
15. William Le Queux, *Love Intrigues of the Kaiser's Sons* (New York: John Lane, 1918), p. 21.
16. Radziwill, *Royal Marriage Market*, p. 39.
17. Arthur Davis, *The Kaiser As I Know Him* (New York: Harper Brothers, 1918), p. 43.
18. Lowe, *German Emperor William II*, p. 29.
19. Anonymous, *The Kaiser's Heir*, p. 28.
20. Empress Augusta Victoria to Emperor Wilhelm II, undated, 1892, in *Wilhelm II*, Röhl, p. 623.
21. Edward Lyell Fox, *William Hohenzollern & Co* (New York: Robert M. McBride, 1917), p. 33.
22. Radziwill, *Disillusions of a Crown Princess*, p. 90.
23. *New York Times*, November 6, 1907.
24. Diary entry of George, Prince of Wales, November 13, 1907, GV/PRIV/GVD, George V Papers, the Royal Archives, quoted in *George, Nicholas and Wilhelm*, Carter, pp. 297–298.
25. Wilhelm II, German Emperor, King of Prussia, *The Kaiser's Memoirs*, trans. Thomas R. Ybarra (London: Harper & Bros., 1922), p. 117.
26. *New York Times*, November 17, 1907.
27. Van der Kiste, *Queen Victoria's Children*, pp. 185–186.
28. Carter, *George, Nicholas and Wilhelm*, pp, 297–298.
29. *New York Times*, October 22, 1908.
30. Viktoria Luise, *The Kaiser's Daughter*, p. 8.
31. Radziwill, *Royal Marriage Market*, pp. 38–39.
32. *New York Times*, November 17, 1907.
33. The calculation is based upon http://www.measuringworth.com/ppowerus/?redirurl=calculators/ppowerus/ (viewed on April 2, 2011).
34. Diary entry of George, Prince of Wales, August 2, 1909, GV/PRIV/GVD, King George V Papers, the Royal Archives, quoted in *George, Nicholas and Wilhelm*, Carter, p. 319.
35. Massie, *Nicholas and Alexandra*, p. 182.
36. Ibid.
37. Edwards, *Matriarch*, p. 172.

38.	Diary entry of May, Princess of Wales, May 4, 1910, in *Queen Mary*, Pope-Hennessy, p. 412.

39.	Packard, *Victoria's Daughters*, pp. 332–333.

40.	Diary entry of Queen Mary, May 6, 1910, in *Queen Mary*, Pope-Hennessy, p. 412.

41.	Diary entry of King George V, May 6, 1910, in *Matriarch*, Edwards, p. 180.

42.	Brandreth, *Philip and Elizabeth*, p. 56.

43.	John Van der Kiste, *Crowns in a Changing World: The British and European Monarchies, 1901–36* (London: Grange Books, 1993), pp. 71–73.

44.	Michael Farquhar, *Behind the Palace Doors: Five Centuries of Sex, Adventure, Vice, Treachery, and Folly from Royal Britain* (New York: Random House, 2011), pp. 277–278.

45.	Duff, *Queen Mary*, p. 135.

46.	Queen Mary to Augusta, Grand Duchess of Mecklenburg-Strelitz, May 15, 1910 in *Queen Mary*, Pope-Hennessy, p. 417.

47.	The scale of the funeral, up to and including the august personages in attendance, was literally unmatched in history. Nothing close to it was seen until 1971, when Iran celebrated the twenty-five-hundred-year anniversary of the Persian Empire. This celebration of monarchy remains the largest gathering of world leaders in human history. The guest list included more than two dozen monarchs, royals, and viceroys, along with another thirty presidents and prime ministers.

48.	Gelardi, *Born to Rule*, p. 170.

49.	Barbara Tuchman, *The Guns of August* (New York: Ballantine Books Presidio Press, 2004), p. 1.

50.	Empress Marie Feodorovna to Tsar Nicholas II, May 7/20, 1910, in *Tsar Nicholas and Empress Marie*, Bing, p. 254.

51.	Tuchman, *Guns of August*, p. 4.

52.	Carter, *George, Nicholas and Wilhelm*, p. 196.

53.	Wakeford, *Three Consort Queens*, p. 150.

54.	Edwards, *Matriarch*, p. 185.

55.	Hall, *Little Mother of Russia*, p. 231.

56.	Wakeford, *Three Consort Queens*, p. 150.

57.	Queen Mary to King George V, October 22, 1910, GV/PRIV/CC8/118, King George V Papers, the Royal Archives, quoted in *Queen Mary*, Pope-Hennessy, p. 424.

58.	Queen Mary to Augusta, Grand Duchess of Mecklenburg-Strelitz, December 2, 1910, in ibid.

**11:	"We Must Help Each Other Get to Heaven"**

1.	Timothy Snyder, *The Red Prince: Secret Lives of a Habsburg Archduke* (London: Bodley Head, 2008), p. 73.

2.	Carter, *George, Nicholas and Wilhelm*, p. 82.

3.	Thomas, "Empress Zita," *The Catholic Counter-Reformation*, p. 2.

4.	The term Austria-Hungary was an unofficial one. Following the formation of the dual monarchy in 1867, the formal name of the empire became the Kingdoms and Lands Represented in the Imperial Council and the Lands of the Holy Hungarian Crown of Saint Stephen. Like the empire itself, the name was oversized, vague, and verbose.

5.	Thomas, "Empress Zita," *The Catholic Counter-Reformation*, p. 2.

6.	Snyder, *The Red Prince*, p. 230.

7.	John Gunther, "Habsburgs Again?" *Foreign Affairs* (July, 1934), vol. 12, no. 4, p. 579.

8. Maria Theresa was Zita's maternal aunt, the sister of her mother, Maria Antonia. She was also Charles's step-grandmother, having married his grandfather Archduke Charles Louis in 1873.

9. Albert von Margutti, *The Emperor Francis Joseph and His Times* (New York: George H. Doran, 1921), p. 153.

10. Thomas, "Empress Zita," *The Catholic Counter-Reformation*, p. 1.

11. Brook-Shepherd, *The Last Habsburg*, p. 15.

12. Bogle, *A Heart for Europe*, p. 29.

13. Beech and McIntosh, *Empress Zita of Austria*, p. 8.

14. Margutti, *Emperor Francis Joseph*, p. 153.

15. Radziwill, *Royal Marriage Market*, p. 17.

16. *New York Times*, January 28, 1903.

17. Bogle, *A Heart for Europe*, p. 32.

18. Duff, *Queen Mary*, p. 144.

19. Bogle, *A Heart for Europe*, p. 33.

20. Edwards, *Matriarch*, p. 213.

21. Duff, *Queen Mary*, p. 145.

22. Queen Mary to Augusta, Grand Duchess of Mecklenburg-Strelitz, June 25, 1911, in *Queen Mary*, Pope-Hennessy, pp. 438–439.

23. Brook-Shepherd, *The Last Habsburg*, p. 21.

24. Duff, *Queen Mary*, p. 146.

25. Bogle, *A Heart for Europe*, p. 34.

26. Duff, *Queen Mary*, p. 145.

27. Bogle, *A Heart for Europe*, p. 35.

28. Ibid., p. 36.

29. Brook-Shepherd, *The Last Empress*, p. 19.

30. *New York Times*, December 18, 1910.

31. Carter, *George, Nicholas and Wilhelm*, p. 28.

32. Letter of Sir Henry Ponsonby, January 27, 1873, in *Queen Victoria*, Hibbert, p. 407.

33. Carter, *George, Nicholas and Wilhelm*, p. 43.

34. Shawcross, *Queen Elizabeth*, p. 106.

35. Pope-Hennessy, *Queen Mary*, p. 428.

36. Cook, *Prince Eddy* (Kobo desktop version), ch. 12, para. 7.

37. Wakeford, *Three Consort Queens*, p. 172–173.

38. Woodward, *Queen Mary*, p. 125.

39. Edwards, *Matriarch*, p. 69.

40. Anthony J. Camp, *Royal Mistresses and Bastards: Fact and Fiction, 1714–1936* (Marlborough, Wiltshire: Heraldry Today, 2007), p. 9; Gelardi, *Born to Rule*, p. 110.

41. Kenneth Rose, *George V* (London: Weidenfeld & Nicolson, 2000), p. 96.

42. John Fortescue, *Narrative of the Visit to India of Their Majesties King George V. and Queen Mary and of the Coronation Durbar Held at Delhi 12th December 1911* (London: Macmillan, 1912), p. 79.

43. Tsar Nicholas II to King George V, January 15/26, 1911, GV/PRIV/AA/43/151, the Royal Archives, quoted in *George, Nicholas and Wilhelm*, Carter, p. 329.

44. Duff, *Queen Mary*, p. 150.

45. Queen Mary to Augusta, Grand Duchess of Mecklenburg-Strelitz, December 6, 1911, in *Matriarch*, Edwards, pp. 222–223.

46. Pope-Hennessy, *Queen Mary*, p. 454.

47. The calculation is based on http://www.measuringworth.com/calculators/exchange/result_exchange.php (viewed on April 14, 2011).

48. Diary entry of King George V, December 12, 1911, in *Queen Mary*, Pope-Hennessy, p. 447.
49. *Times*, December 13, 1911.
50. Queen Mary to Augusta, Grand Duchess of Mecklenburg-Strelitz, December 13, 1911, in *Queen Mary*, Pope-Hennessy, p. 445.
51. Diary entry of King George V, December 14, 1911, GV/PRIV/GVD/AA 37/36, King George V Papers, the Royal Archives, quoted in ibid., p. 457.
52. Clay, *King, Kaiser, Tsar*, p. 294.

12: "The Little One Will Not Die"

1. Bogle, *A Heart for Europe*, p. 37.
2. *Neue Freie Presse*, November 20, 1912.
3. *Times*, June 29, 1914.
4. *New York Times*, May 15, 1911.
5. Wilhelm II, *The Kaiser's Memoirs*, p. 142.
6. Clark, *Kaiser Wilhelm II* (Kobo desktop version), chap. 4, para 37.
7. *Daily Telegraph*, October 28, 1908.
8. *Westminster Gazette*, October 31, 1908.
9. Carter, *George, Nicholas and Wilhelm*, p. 309.
10. Ibid., p. 4.
11. Ibid., p. 22.
12. Massie, *Dreadnought*, pp. 691–692.
13. Clark, *Kaiser Wilhelm II*, p. 246.
14. Viktoria Luise, *The Kaiser's Daughter*, p. 36.
15. Clark, *Kaiser Wilhelm II* (Kobo desktop version), chap. 3, para. 24.
16. German Crown Prince, *Memoirs*, p. 99.
17. Stone, *Europe Transformed*, p. 138.
18. Gelardi, *From Splendor to Revolution*, p. 274.
19. Viktoria Luise, *The Kaiser's Daughter*, p. 14.
20. Clark, *Kaiser Wilhelm II*, p. 210.
21. Viktoria Luise, *The Kaiser's Daughter*, p. 77.
22. Radziwill, *Royal Marriage Market*, p. 42.
23. German Crown Prince, *Memoirs*, p. 6.
24. Anonymous, *The Kaiser's Heir* (London: Mills & Boon, 1914), p. 26.
25. Schwering, *Berlin Court Under William II*, p. 80.
26. Viktoria Luise, *The Kaiser's Daughter*, pp. 53, 56.
27. Ibid., p. 66.
28. Ibid.
29. Ernest Augustus was the son of Princess Thyra of Denmark, whose father was King Christian IX. Thyra's sisters were Queen Alexandra and Empress Marie Feodorovna. Had Hanover not been annexed in 1866, Thyra's husband would have become king, and she would have become a reigning consort like her sisters.
30. Clay, *King, Kaiser, Tsar*, pp. 1–2.
31. Viktoria Luise, *The Kaiser's Daughter*, p. 68.
32. Legge, *King George and the Royal Family*, p. 197.
33. Viktoria Luise, *The Kaiser's Daughter*, p. 71.
34. Augusta, Grand Duchess of Mecklenburg-Strelitz, to Queen Mary, May 29, 1913, in *Queen Mary*, Pope-Hennessy, p. 479.

35.   Diary entry of Empress Augusta Victoria, May 24/25, 1913, in *The Kaiser's Daughter*, Viktoria Luise, p. 74.
36.   Tyler-Whittle, *The Last Kaiser*, p. 255.
37.   Farquhar, *Behind the Palace Doors*, p. 279.
38.   Diary entry of Queen Mary, May 27, 1913, in *Queen Mary*, Pope-Hennessy, p. 478.
39.   Queen Mary to Augusta, Grand Duchess of Mecklenburg-Strelitz, June 1, 1913, in ibid.
40.   Clark, *Kaiser Wilhelm II*, p. 254.
41.   Schwering, *Berlin Court Under William II*, p. 110.
42.   Bogle, *A Heart for Europe*, p. 43.
43.   Gelardi, *Born to Rule*, pp. 121–122.
44.   Lili Dehn, *The Real Tsaritsa* (London: Thornton Butterworth, 1922), pp. 82–83.
45.   Buxhoeveden, *Alexandra Feodorovna*, p. 153.
46.   Kurth, *Tsar*, p. 89.
47.   Wilson and King, *Resurrection of the Romanovs*, p. 46.
48.   Kurth, *Tsar*, p. 89.
49.   Wilson and King, *Resurrection of the Romanovs*, p. 46.
50.   Gelardi, *Born to Rule*, p. 187.
51.   Rappaport, *Last Days of the Romanovs*, p. 82.
52.   Erickson, *Alexandra*, p. 210.
53.   Rappaport, *Last Days of the Romanovs*, p. 73.
54.   Tsarina Alexandra to the Reverend William Boyd Carpenter, bishop of Ripon, January 24/February 7, 1913, Add. MSS 46721/244, the British Library, quoted in *Born to Rule*, Gelardi, p. 188.
55.   Wilson and King, *Resurrection of the Romanovs*, p. 40.
56.   Gelardi, *From Splendor to Revolution*, p. 101.
57.   Rappaport, *Last Days of the Romanovs*, p. 76.
58.   Kurth, *Tsar*, p. 92.
59.   Wilson and King, *Resurrection of the Romanovs*, pp. 60–61.
60.   Ibid., p. 62.
61.   Anna Viroubova, *Memories of the Russian Court* (New York: Macmillan, 1923), p. 93.
62.   C. S. Denton, *Absolute Power* (London: Arcturus Publishing, 2006), p. 575.
63.   Erickson, *Alexandra*, p. 221.
64.   Gelardi, *Born to Rule*, p. 136.
65.   Denton, *Absolute Power*, p. 575.
66.   Ibid., p. 176.
67.   Vorres, *Last Grand Duchess*, p. 140.
68.   Tsarina Alexandra to the Reverend William Boyd Carpenter, bishop of Ripon, January 24/February 7, 1913, Add. MSS 47621/244, the British Library, quoted in *Born to Rule*, Gelardi, p. 178.
69.   Vorres, *Last Grand Duchess*, p. 140. *Alexis* is the more commonly used transliteration used in Britain of the name *Alexei*.
70.   Alex De Jonge, *The Life and Times of Grigorri Rasputin* (New York: Coward, McCann & Geoghegan, 1982), p. 152.
71.   Gelardi, *Born to Rule*, p. 177.

13:   The Gathering Storm

1.   Bogle, *A Heart for Europe*, p. 40.
2.   Brook-Shepherd, *The Last Empress*, p. 26.

3. Ibid., pp. 26–27.
4. Thomas, "Empress Zita," *The Catholic Counter-Reformation*, p. 2.
5. Undated memo of King George V, PS/PSO/GV/C/K/2553/1/70, King George V Papers, the Royal Archives, quoted in *George, Nicholas and Wilhelm*, Carter, p. 351.
6. Massie, *Dreadnought*, p. xxiii.
7. Van der Kiste, *Queen Victoria's Children*, pp. 184–185.
8. Edwards, *Matriarch*, p. 238.
9. Legge, *King George and the Royal Family*, p. 149.
10. Ibid., p. 158.
11. Woodward, *Queen Mary*, p. 149.
12. Duff, *Queen Mary*, p. 131.
13. Van der Kiste, *Queen Victoria's Children*, p. 199.
14. Röhl, *Wilhelm II*, p. 657.
15. Charles Kingston, *Famous Morganatic Marriages* (London: Stanley Paul, 1919), p. 93.
16. Schwering, *Berlin Court Under William II*, p. 92.
17. Radziwill, *Royal Marriage Market*, p. 40.
18. *New York Times*, May 26, 1914.
19. Bogle, *A Heart for Europe*, p. 44.
20. Empress Zita to Gordon Brook-Shepherd, April 23, 1968, in *The Last Empress*, Brook-Shepherd, p. 30.
21. Massie, *Dreadnought*, p. 859.
22. Queen Mary to Augusta, Grand Duchess of Mecklenburg-Strelitz, July 5, 1914, in *Queen Mary*, Pope-Hennessy, p. 483.
23. Massie, *Nicholas and Alexandra*, pp. 277–278.
24. Bogle, *A Heart for Europe*, p. 52.
25. Massie, *Nicholas and Alexandra*, p. 288.
26. Ibid., p. 289.

Part 3: The Great Tragedy (1914–18)

14: The Call to Arms

1. Clark, *Kaiser Wilhelm II* (Kobo desktop version), chap. 7, para 50.
2. Gelardi, *Born to Rule*, p. 199.
3. Gelardi, *From Splendor to Revolution*, p. 273.
4. Bogle, *A Heart for Europe*, p. 53.
5. Queen Mary to Augusta, Grand Duchess of Mecklenburg-Strelitz, July 28, 1914, in *Queen Mary*, Pope-Hennessy, pp. 483–484. Servia is an out of date English word for Serbia. In some British sources, the two words are used interchangeably.
6. Carter, *George, Nicholas and Wilhelm*, p. 369.
7. Emperor Wilhelm II to Gottlieb von Jagow, July 30, 1914, in ibid., p. 370.
8. Pierre Gilliard, *Thirteen Years at the Russian Court* (London: Hutchinson, 1921), p. 105.
9. Erickson, *Alexandra*, p. 238.
10. Gelardi, *From Splendor to Revolution*, p. 271.
11. Wilson and King, *Resurrection of the Romanovs*, p. 66.
12. Gelardi, *Born to Rule*, p. 200.
13. Tsar Nicholas II to King George V, August 2, 1914, in *Crowns in a Changing World*, Van der Kiste, p. 103.
14. Anonymous, *Real Crown Prince*, p. 156.

15. Clark, *Kaiser Wilhelm II*, p. 332.
16. Ibid., p. 253.
17. Schwering, *Berlin Court Under William II*, p. 64.
18. *New York Times*, June 8, 1913.
19. Gelardi, *From Splendor to Revolution*, p. 270.
20. Diary entry of Queen Mary, August 3, 1914, in *Queen Mary*, Pope-Hennessy, p. 484.
21. Viktoria Luise, *The Kaiser's Daughter*, p. 82.
22. Farquhar, *Behind the Palace Doors*, p. 279.
23. Carter, *George, Nicholas and Wilhelm*, p. 371.
24. Davis, *The Kaiser As I Know Him*, p. 164.
25. Public statement of Empress Augusta Victoria, August 6, 1914, in *The Fall of the German Empire, 1914—1918* (Stanford: Stanford University Press, 1932), ed. Ralph Haswell Lutz, vol. 1, pp. 21–22.
26. Wilson and King, *Resurrection of the Romanovs*, p. 102.
27. Gilliard, *Thirteen Years*, pp. 107–110.
28. Gelardi, *From Splendor to Revolution*, p. 273.
29. King George and Queen Maud were children of King Edward VII. Emperor Wilhelm, Queen Sophie, and the Duchess Charlotte were the children of the Empress Frederick. Tsarina Alexandra and Grand Duke Ernest Louis were Princess Alice's children. Crown Princess Marie was the daughter of the Duke of Edinburgh (later the Duke of Coburg). Crown Princess Margaret of Sweden was the daughter of the Duke of Connaught. Duke Charles Eduard was the posthumous son of the hemophiliac Duke of Albany. Queen Victoria Eugenie was the only daughter of Princess Beatrice. Through King Christian IX of Denmark, Tsar Nicholas II, King George V, King Haakon VII of Norway, and King Constantine I of Greece were also first cousins.
30. Erickson, *Alexandra*, p. 240.
31. Brandreth, *Philip and Elizabeth*, p. 20.
32. Packard, *Victoria's Daughters*, p. 283.
33. W. Bruce Lincoln, *The Romanovs: Autocrats of All the Russias* (New York: Dial Press, 1981), p. 685.
34. Bernard Pares, *My Russian Memoirs* (New York: AMS Press, 1969), p. 355.
35. Gelardi, *From Splendor to Revolution*, p. 295.
36. Eugene De Schelking, *Suicide of Monarchy: Recollections of a Diplomat* (Toronto: Macmillan Company of Canada, 1918), p. 118.
37. Diary entry of July 24, 1915, in *An Ambassador's Memoirs* (London: Hutchinson, 1927), Maurice Paléologue, vol. 2, pp. 35–36.
38. Woodward, *Queen Mary*, p. 177.
39. Wakeford, *Three Consort Queens*, p. 176.
40. Woodward, *Queen Mary*, p. 174–175.
41. Snyder, *The Red Prince*, pp. 77–78.
42. Andrew Wheatcroft, *The Habsburgs: Embodying Empire* (London: Penguin Books, 1996), p. 287.
43. Catherine Radziwill, *Secrets of Dethroned Royalty* (New York: John Lane, 1920), pp. 163–164.
44. Brook-Shepherd, *The Last Habsburg*, p. 153.
45. Brook-Shepherd, *The Last Empress*, p. 34.
46. Ibid.
47. Diary entry of Prince Xavier of Bourbon-Parma, August 20, 1914, in ibid., pp. 34–35.
48. Ibid.

15: **"I Am an Officer with All My Body and Soul"**

1. *New York Times,* February 22, 1915.
2. Wilson and King, *Resurrection of the Romanovs,* p. 102.
3. Belinda Davis, *Home Fires Burning: Food, Politics, and Everyday Life in World War I Berlin* (Chapel Hill: University of North Carolina Press, 2000), pp. 34, 107.
4. Davis, *The Kaiser As I Know Him,* p. 167.
5. Cecil, *Wilhelm II,* p. 3.
6. Carter, *George, Nicholas and Wilhelm,* p. 384.
7. Robert Zedlitz-Trützschler, *Twelve Years at the Imperial German Court* (London: Nisbet, 1924), p. 37.
8. Brook-Shepherd, *The Last Empress,* pp. 10–11.
9. Bertita Harding, *Imperial Twilight: The Story of Karl and Zita of Hungary* (New York: Blue Ribbon Books, 1941), p. 121.
10. *New York Times,* September 14, 1915.
11. Thomas, "Empress Zita," *The Catholic Counter-Reformation,* p. 2.
12. Bogle, *A Heart for Europe,* p. 54.
13. Harding, *Imperial Twilight,* p. 69.
14. Bogle, *A Heart for Europe,* p. 58.
15. Margutti, *Emperor Francis Joseph,* p. 159.
16. Brook-Shepherd, *The Last Empress,* p. 37.
17. Gelardi, *Born to Rule,* p. 216.
18. Tsarina Alexandra to the Reverend William Boyd Carpenter, bishop of Ripon, January 20/February 2, 1915, Add. MSS 46721/246, The British Library, quoted in *Born to Rule,* Gelardi, pp. 216–217.
19. Diary entry of Grand Duke Andrei Vladimirovich, September 6, 1915, in *From Splendor to Revolution,* Gelardi, p. 281.
20. Gelardi, *Born to Rule,* pp. 217–218.
21. Tsarina Alexandra to Tsar Nicholas II, April 4, 1915, in Gelardi, *From Splendor to Revolution,* p. 283.
22. Empress Marie Feodorovna to Tsar Nicholas II, February 1/14, 1915, in *Letters of Tsar Nicholas and Empress Marie,* Bing, p. 292.
23. Empress Marie Feodorovna to Tsar Nicholas II, May 22/June 4, 1916, in ibid., p. 297.
24. Erickson, *Alexandra,* p. 243.
25. Ibid., p. 100.
26. Viroubova, *Memories,* pp. 109–110.
27. Rappaport, *Last Days of the Romanovs,* p. 67.
28. Tsarina Alexandra to Tsar Nicholas II, October 1, 1915, in *The Complete Wartime Correspondence of Tsar Nicholas II and Empress Alexandra, April 1914–March 1917* (Westport, CT: Greenwood Press, 1999), ed. Joseph T. Fuhrmann, no. 504, p. 257.
29. Tsarina Alexandra to the Reverend William Boyd Carpenter, bishop of Ripon, January 20/February 2, 1915, Add. MSS 26721/248, The British Library, quoted in *Born to Rule,* Gelardi, p. 223.

16: **Apocalypse Rising**

1. Empress Augusta Victoria to Prince Chlodwig of Hohenlohe-Schillingsfürst, July 29, 1896, in "Empress Auguste Victoria and the Fall of the German Monarchy" in *The American Historical Review* (October 1952), Andreas Dorpalen, vol. 58, no. 1, p. 22.

2.   Ibid.
3.   Radziwill, *Royal Marriage Market*, p. 32.
4.   German Crown Prince, *Memoirs*, p. 5.
5.   Fontenoy, *Secret Memoirs*, vol. 1, p. 191.
6.   Shaw, *Royal Babylon* (Kobo desktop version), chap. 5, para 47.
7.   Zedlitz-Trützschler, *Twelve Years*, p. 67.
8.   Erickson, *Alexandra*, p. 245.
9.   *Times*, March 11, 1916.
10.   Woodward, *Queen Mary*, p. 175.
11.   Edmund Walsh, *The Fall of the Russian Empire* (Boston: Little, Brown, 1928), p. 117.
12.   King, *Last Empress*, p. 245.
13.   Kokovstov, *Out of My Past*, p. 296.
14.   Queen Alexandra to King George V, undated, GV/PRIV/AA35/6, King George V Papers, the Royal Archives, quoted in *George, Nicholas and Wilhelm*, Carter, p. 391.
15.   *Times*, October 13, 1914.
16.   Clark, *Kaiser Wilhelm II*, (Kobo desktop version), chap. 1, para. 41. In his book, Clark specifically used these examples in his analysis of Emperor Wilhelm II. While Clark uses them in a specific context, they are apt in a broader sense. Like Wilhelm, there was very much a sociocultural pattern in the way Alexandra and many other royals have been evaluated.
17.   Wilson and King, *Resurrection of the Romanovs*, p. 47.
18.   Gelardi, *From Splendor to Revolution*, p. 293.
19.   Grand Duke Alexander, *Once a Grand Duke*, p. 271.
20.   Gelardi, *Born to Rule*, p. 239.
21.   Ibid., pp. 241–242.
22.   Ibid., p. 244.
23.   Gelardi, *From Splendor to Revolution*, p. 296.
24.   Hugo Mager, *Elizabeth, Grand Duchess of Russia* (New York: Carroll & Graf, 1998), pp. 302–303.
25.   Felix Yusupov, *Lost Splendour* (London: Cape, 1953), p. 157.
26.   Gelardi, *From Splendor to Revolution*, p. 310.
27.   Grand Duchess Marie, *Education of a Princess*, pp. 248–249. This was not the same Marie Pavlovna ("Miechen") who was Nicholas II's aunt and a princess of Mecklenburg-Schwerin. This grand duchess was one of the tsar's cousins.
28.   Gelardi, *Born to Rule*, p. 250.
29.   Shaw, *Royal Babylon* (Kobo desktop version), chap. 5, para 141.
30.   Gelardi, *From Splendor to Revolution*, pp. 313–314.
31.   Grand Duchess Marie, *Education of a Princess*, p. 250.
32.   Gleb Botkin, *The Real Romanovs* (New York: Fleming H. Revell, 1931), pp. 127–128.
33.   Gelardi, *From Splendor to Revolution*, p. 315.
34.   Ibid., p. 317.
35.   Princess Paley, *Memories of Russia, 1916–1919* (London: Herbert Jenkins, 1924), p. 38.
36.   Grand Duke Alexander, *Once a Grand Duke*, p. 275.
37.   Gilliard, *Thirteen Years at the Russian Court*, p. 183.
38.   Carter, *George, Nicholas and Wilhelm*, p. 395.
39.   Massie, *Nicholas and Alexandra*, pp. 402–403.

17: **"May God Bless Your Majesty"**

1. Robin Okey, *The Habsburg Monarchy 1765–1918: From Enlightenment to Eclipse* (New York: Palgrave Macmillan, 2002), p. 381.
2. Bogle, *A Heart for Europe*, p. 73.
3. Ibid., p. 60.
4. Ibid., p. 63.
5. Leslie Carroll, *Notorious Royal Marriages: A Juicy Journey Through Nine Centuries of Dynasty, Destiny, and Desire* (London: Penguin Books, 2010), p. 370.
6. Brook-Shepherd, *The Last Empress*, p. 41.
7. Beech and McIntosh, *Empress Zita of Austria*, p. 41.
8. The Kingdom of Slavonia was a province of the Habsburg monarchy and, later, the Austrian Empire. Its borders were spread across parts of northern Croatia and Serbia. Slavonia should not be confused with the modern day nation of Slovenia.
9. Harding, *Imperial Twilight*, p. 64.
10. Viktoria Luise, *The Kaiser's Daughter*, pp. 89–90.
11. Gordon Brook-Shepherd, *Uncrowned Emperor: The Life and Times of Otto von Habsburg* (London: Hambledon & London, 2003), p. 27.
12. Taylor, *Fall of the Dynasties*, p. 353.
13. *Times*, November 23, 1916.
14. Ibid.
15. *New York Times*, November 24, 1916.
16. Thomas, "Empress Zita," *The Catholic Counter-Reformation*, p. 2–3.
17. Maureen Healy, *Vienna and the Fall of the Habsburg Empire: Total War and Everyday Life in World War I* (Cambridge: Cambridge University Press, 2004), p. 296.
18. Thomas, "Empress Zita," *The Catholic Counter-Reformation*, pp. 2–3.
19. Taylor, *Fall of the Dynasties*, p. 355.
20. Okey, *The Habsburg Monarchy*, p. 384.
21. Brook-Shepherd, *The Last Habsburg*, pp. 51–52.
22. Catherine Karolyi, *A Life Together* (London: Allen & Unwin, 1966), pp. 168–169.
23. Brook-Shepherd, *Uncrowned Emperor*, pp. 28–29.
24. Brook-Shepherd, *The Last Empress*, p. 56.
25. Brook-Shepherd, *The Last Habsburg*, p. 55.
26. Brook-Shepherd, *Uncrowned Emperor*, p. 32.
27. Queen Mary to Lady Charlotte Mount Stephen, November 10, 1916, in *Queen Mary*, Pope-Hennessy, p. 504.
28. John Fraser, *The Secret of the Crown: Canada's Affair with Royalty* (Toronto: House of Anansi Press, 2012), p. 48.
29. Wakeford, *Three Consort Queens*, p. 178.
30. Ibid.
31. Gelardi, *Born to Rule*, p. 132.
32. King George V to Tsar Nicholas II, January 7, 1916, in *George, Nicholas and Wilhelm*, Carter, p. 393.
33. Wakeford, *Three Consort Queens*, p. 151.
34. Diary entry of Queen Mary, December 6, 1916, in *Queen Mary*, Pope-Hennessy, p. 503.
35. Wakeford, *Three Consort Queens*, p. 151.

18: **Imperial Endgame**

1. Hall, *Little Mother of Russia*, p. 279.
2. Grand Duke Alexander, *Once a Grand Duke*, pp. 283–284.
3. Pares, *My Russian Memoirs*, p. 361.
4. Carter, *George, Nicholas and Wilhelm*, p. 397.
5. Diary entry of January 17/30, 1917, in *The Story of My Life*, Queen Marie, vol. 3, p. 129.
6. Rappaport, *Last Days of the Romanovs*, p. 67.
7. Tsarina Alexandra to Tsar Nicholas II, March 2, 1917, in *The Fall of the Romanovs: Political Dreams and Personal Struggles in a Time of Revolution* (New Haven: Yale University Press, 1995), eds. Mark D. Steinberg and Vladimir M. Khrustalëv, pp. 93–95.
8. Abdication of Tsar Nicholas II, March 3, 1917, in *From Splendor to Revolution*, Gelardi, p. 322.
9. Gelardi, *Born to Rule*, p. 257.
10. Bogle, *A Heart for Europe*, p. 95.
11. Diary entry of King George V, March 13, 1917, GV/PRIV/GVD, King George V Papers, the Royal Archives, quoted in *George, Nicholas and Wilhelm*, Carter, p. 399.
12. Kurth, *Tsar*, p. 8.
13. Carter, *George, Nicholas and Wilhelm*, p. 385.
14. Brook-Shepherd, *The Last Habsburg*, p. 77.
15. Snyder, *The Red Prince*, p. 87.
16. Brook-Shepherd, *The Last Empress*, p. 66.
17. Memorandum of W. Gugoy, June 3, 1917, FO 371-3134, London Public Records Office.
18. Memorandum of Philippe Pétain to Paul Painlevé, August 4, 1917, in "Empress Zita," *The Catholic Counter-Reformation*, Thomas, p. 3.
19. Bogle, *A Heart for Europe*, p. 80.
20. Brook-Shepherd, *The Last Habsburg*, pp. 67–68. The Habsburgs' ties to Lorraine stretched back two hundred years to when Maria Theresa, the heiress to the Austrian throne, married Francis Stephen, Duke of Lorraine. The title had been passed down to Austrian emperors ever since. Since that time, the official name of the Austrian imperial family has been Habsburg-Lorraine.
21. Emperor Charles I to Prince Sixtus of Bourbon-Parma, March 24, 1917, in *The Fall of Eagles* (New York: Crown Publishers, 1977), C. L. Sulzberger, pp. 337–341.
22. Brook-Shepherd, *The Last Habsburg*, p. 74.
23. Bogle, *A Heart for Europe*, p. 82.
24. Brook-Shepherd, *The Last Habsburg*, pp. 74–75.
25. Ibid., pp. 85–86.
26. Bogle, *A Heart for Europe*, pp. 89–90.
27. Ibid, p. iii.

19: **Hated, Humbled, Rejected**

1. Tsar Nicholas II, March 3, 1917, State Archive of the Russian Federation 601/2100, in *Michael and Natasha: The Life and Love of the Last Tsar of Russia* (London: Weidenfeld & Nicolson, 1997), Donald and Rosemary Crawford, p. 288.

2.   Gelardi, *From Splendor to Revolution*, p. 325. The original quote, translated by the author, was written in French: *"le pauvre ... tout seul là bas ... oh, mon Dieu, par quoi il passé! Et je ne puis pas être près de lui pour consoler."*

3.   Buxhoeveden, *Alexandra Feodorovna*, p. 262.

4.   Gelardi, *Born to Rule*, pp. 257–258.

5.   Queen Marie, *The Story of My Life*, vol. 3, pp. 151–152.

6.   Dehn, *The Real Tsaritsa*, pp. 190–191.

7.   Paley, *Memories of Russia*, p. 87.

8.   Erickson, *Alexandra*, p. 306.

9.   Ibid., p. 310.

10.   Buxhoeveden, *Alexandra Feodorovna*, p. 282.

11.   Gelardi, *From Splendor to Revolution*, p. 327.

12.   Carter, *George, Nicholas and Wilhelm*, p. 410.

13.   Gilliard, *Thirteen Years*, p. 257.

14.   Carter, *George, Nicholas and Wilhelm*, p. 410.

15.   Massie, *Nicholas and Alexandra*, p. 495.

16.   Arthur Bigge, Baron Stamfordham, to Arthur Balfour, April 6, 1917, LG/F/3/2/19, Parliamentary Archives.

17.   Rappaport, *Last Days of the Romanovs*, p. 151.

18.   Edwards, *Matriarch*, p. 264.

19.   Massie, *Nicholas and Alexandra*, p. 496.

20.   Alexandra Feodorovna Romanova to Alexander Syroboiarsky, May 29, 1917, in *Fall of the Romanovs*, Steinberg and Khrustalëv, pp. 150–152.

21.   Tyler-Whittle, *The Last Kaiser*, p. 285.

22.   Carter, *George, Nicholas and Wilhelm*, p. 403.

23.   Edwards, *Matriarch*, p. 266.

24.   Hibbert, *Queen Victoria*, p. 382.

25.   Nicolson, *King George V*, p. 308.

26.   Edwards, *Matriarch*, p. 270.

27.   Dennison, *The Last Princess*, p. 277.

28.   Legge, *King George and the Royal Family*, vol. 1, p. 287.

29.   Prince Louis of Battenberg to Princess Louise of Battenberg, June 6, 1917, in *The Last Princess*, Dennison, p. 277.

30.   Royal Proclamation of King George V, July 17, 1917, in *King George and the Royal Family*, Legge, vol. 1, pp. 294–295.

31.   Dennison, *The Last Princess*, p. 277.

32.   Legge, *King George and the Royal Family*, vol. 1, p. 297.

33.   Duff, *Queen Mary*, p. 134.

34.   Queen Mary to King George V, March 27, 1918, in *Matriarch*, Edwards, p. 271.

20:   Into the Abyss

1.   Report from the Associated Press, May 25, 1917 (published June 30, 1917).

2.   Kurth, *Tsar*, p. 164.

3.   Ibid., p. 166.

4.   Gelardi, *From Splendor to Revolution*, p. 338.

5.   Coryne Hall and John Van der Kiste, *Once a Grand Duchess: Xenia, Sister of Nicholas II* (Phoenix Mill: Sutton Publishing, 2002), p. 121.

6.   Empress Marie Feodorovna to Nicholas Romanov, December 21, 1917, in *From Splendor to Revolution*, Gelardi, p. 340.

7. Erickson, *Alexandra*, p. 319.
8. Viroubova, *Memories*, p. 298.
9. Erickson, *Alexandra*, p. 324.
10. Botkin, *Real Romanovs*, p. 165.
11. Rappaport, *Last Days of the Romanovs*, p. 83.
12. Gelardi, *Born to Rule*, p. 268.
13. Ibid.
14. Brook-Shepherd, *The Last Habsburg*, p. 121.
15. Ibid., p. 125.
16. Snyder, *The Red Prince*, p. 99.
17. Beech and McIntosh, *Empress Zita*, p. 36.
18. Thomas, "Empress Zita," *The Catholic Counter-Reformation*, p. 3.
19. *New York Times*, January 15, 1918.
20. *Ashburton Guardian*, July 11, 1918.
21. Healy, *Fall of the Habsburg Empire*, p. 296.
22. Diary entry of Empress Zita, April 2, 1918, Habsburg Family Archives, Cassette No. 22, File 128, in *The Last Empress*, Brook-Shepherd, p. 93.
23. Bogle, *A Heart for Europe*, p. 91.
24. Diary entry of Empress Zita, April 2, 1918, Habsburg Family Archives, Cassette No. 22, File 128, in *The Last Empress*, Brook-Shepherd, p. 93.
25. Brook-Shepherd, *The Last Habsburg*, p. 144.
26. John Toland, *No Man's Land: 1918, The Last Year of the Great War* (Garden City, NY: Doubleday, 1980), p. 167.
27. Brook-Shepherd, *The Last Empress*, p. 96.
28. Sir Horace Rumbold to Arthur Balfour, May 9, 1918, in *A Heart for Europe*, Bogle, pp. 97–98.
29. Brook-Shepherd, *The Last Habsburg*, p. 147.
30. Taylor, *Fall of the Dynasties*, p. 358.
31. Bogle, *A Heart for Europe*, p. 95.
32. Cecil, *Wilhelm II*, p. 275.
33. Diary entry of Empress Zita, April 13, 1918, Habsburg Family Archives, Cassette No. 22, File 128, in *The Last Empress*, Brook-Shepherd, p. 101.
34. Ibid.
35. Thomas, "Empress Zita," *The Catholic Counter-Reformation*, p. 4.
36. Diary entry of Empress Zita, April 14, 1918, in *The Last Empress*, Brook-Shepherd, pp. 102–103.

21: The House of Special Purpose

1. Snyder, *The Red Prince*, p. 102.
2. Cecil, *Wilhelm II*, p. 275.
3. Wilson and King, *Resurrection of the Romanovs*, p. 102.
4. Dorpalen, "Empress Auguste Victoria," *The American Historical Review*, p. 29.
5. Clark, *Kaiser Wilhelm II*, p. 333.
6. Emperor Wilhelm II to Empress Augusta Victoria, September 29, 1918, in *The Kaiser's Daughter*, Viktoria Luise, p. 119.
7. Emperor Wilhelm II to Empress Augusta Victoria, September 30, 1918, in ibid., pp. 120–121.
8. Rappaport, *Last Days of the Romanovs*, p. 94.
9. Buxhoeveden, *Alexandra Feodorovna*, p. 329.

10.   Gelardi, *Born to Rule*, p. 269.
11.   Receipt of the Ural Regional Soviet, April 30, 1918, in Kurth, *Tsar*, pp. 184-185.
12.   Wilson and King, *Resurrection of the Romanovs*, p. 82.
13.   Ibid., pp. 83–84.
14.   King, *The Last Empress*, p. 344.
15.   Viroubova, *Memories*, p. 305.
16.   Ibid., p. 318.
17.   Kursh, *Tsar*, p. 176.
18.   Diary entry of Afansy Beliaev, March 2–31, 1917, in *Fall of the Romanovs*, Steinberg and Khrustalëv, p. 144.
19.   Gelardi, *Born to Rule*, p. 270.
20.   Erickson, *Alexandra*, p. 341.
21.   Ibid., p. 344.
22.   Ibid., p. 345.
23.   Wilson and King, *Resurrection of the Romanovs*, p. 90.
24.   Rappaport, *Last Days of the Romanovs*, p. 162.
25.   Gelardi, *Born to Rule*, p. 270.
26.   Diary entry of Alexandra Romanova, July 3/16, 1918, in Kurth, *Tsar*, p. 194.
27.   Erickson, *Alexandra*, p. 351.
28.   Rappaport, *Last Days of the Romanovs*, p. 186.
29.   Ibid., p. 188.
30.   Gelardi, *Born to Rule*, p. 271.

22:   The Fall of Eagles

1.   Rappaport, *Last Days of the Romanovs*, pp. 58–59.
2.   Edwards, *Matriarch*, pp. 274–275.
3.   Diary entry of Queen Mary, July 24, 1918, in *Queen Mary*, Pope-Hennessy, p. 505.
4.   Edwards, *Matriarch*, p. 382.
5.   Diary entry of King George V, August 31, 1918, GV/PRIV/GVD, King George V Papers, the Royal Archives, quoted in *George, Nicholas and Wilhelm*, Carter, p. 411.
6.   Lord Stamfordham to Lord Esher, July 25, 1918, in *George V*, Rose, p. 217.
7.   Massie, *Nicholas and Alexandra*, p. 498.
8.   *Lewiston Evening Journal*, April 11, 1921.
9.   Gelardi, *Born to Rule*, p. 260.
10.   Since Maria Louisa's wedding was less than a year after Zita was born, the two sisters were never close. Maria Louisa died in 1899 from pneumonia twenty-four hours after giving birth to her last child when Zita was only seven. Ferdinand did not become King of the Bulgarians until 1908, so Zita's sister was never queen consort.
11.   Brook-Shepherd, *Uncrowned Emperor*, p. 33.
12.   Taylor, *Fall of the Dynasties*, p. 358.
13.   Empress Zita to Gordon Brook-Shepherd, October 9, 1978, in *The Last Empress*, Brook-Shepherd, p. 110.
14.   Thomas, "Empress Zita," *The Catholic Counter-Reformation*, p. 4.
15.   Brook-Shepherd, *The Last Habsburg*, p. 168.
16.   Beech and McIntosh, *Empress Zita of Austria*, p. 111.
17.   George, *Heirs of Tradition*, p. 206.
18.   Toland, *No Man's Land*, pp. 586–587.
19.   A. J. P. Taylor, *The Habsburg Monarchy, 1809–1918: A History of the Austrian Empire and Austria-Hungary* (London: Hamish Hamilton, 1948), p. 265.

20. S. Miles Bouton, *And the Kaiser Abdicates: The German Revolution November 1918–August 1919* (New Haven: Yale University Press, 1921), p. 126.
21. Thomas, "Empress Zita," *The Catholic Counter-Reformation*, p. 4.
22. Brook-Shepherd, *The Last Habsburg*, p. 188.
23. Brook-Shepherd, *The Last Empress*, p. 121.
24. Bouton, *And the Kaiser Abdicates*, p. 127–128.
25. Brook-Shepherd, *The Last Empress*, p. 131.
26. Brook-Shepherd, *The Last Habsburg*, p. 205.
27. Ibid., p. 215.
28. Toland, *No Man's Lands*, p. 587.
29. Taylor, *Fall of the Dynasties*, p. 352.
30. Brook-Shepherd, *The Last Empress*, p. 132.
31. *Guardian*, July 4, 2011.
32. Snyder, *The Red Prince*, p. 108.
33. Wilson and King, *Resurrection of the Romanovs*, p. 102.
34. Clark, *Kaiser Wilhelm II* (Kobo desktop version), chap. 8, para 39.
35. Carter, *George, Nicholas and Wilhelm*, p. 412.
36. Tyler-Whittle, *The Last Kaiser*, p. 296.
37. Taylor, *Fall of the Dynasties*, p. 323.
38. Ibid., p. 325.
39. Princess Ina Luise of Solms-Baruth to Princess Daisy of Pless, November 7, 1918, in "Empress Auguste Victoria," *The American Historical Review*, Dorpalen, p. 37.
40. Dorpalen, "Empress Auguste Victoria," *The American Historical Review*, p. 33.
41. Emperor Wilhelm II to Empress Augusta Victoria, November 8, 1918, in *The Kaiser's Daughter*, Viktoria Luise, pp. 135–136.
42. Gordon Brook-Shepherd, *November 1918* (Boston & Toronto: Little, Brown, 1981), p. 357.
43. Bouton, *And the Kaiser Abdicates*, p. 178.
44. Taylor, *Fall of the Dynasties*, p. 342.
45. Brook-Shepherd, *November 1918*, p. 364.
46. Emperor Wilhelm II to Empress Augusta Victoria, November 9, 1918, in *The Kaiser's Daughter*, Viktoria Luise, p. 138.
47. Diary entry of Queen Mary, November 9, 1918, in *Queen Mary*, Pope-Hennessy, p. 507.
48. Diary entry of King George V, November 9, 1918, in *George, Nicholas and Wilhelm*, Carter, p. 413.
49. Taylor, *Fall of the Dynasties*, p. 346.
50. Carter, *George, Nicholas and Wilhelm*, p. 414.
51. Brook-Shepherd, *The Last Empress*, p. 127.
52. Clay, *King, Kaiser, Tsar*, p. 352.
53. Wakeford, *Three Consort Queens*, p. 180.
54. Shawcross, *Queen Elizabeth*, p. 96.
55. Edwards, *Matriarch*, p. 280.
56. Carter, *George, Nicholas and Wilhelm*, p. 405.
57. Edwards, *Matriarch*, p. 280.
58. Empress Augusta Victoria to Victoria Louise, Duchess of Brunswick, November 11, 1918, in *The Kaiser's Daughter*, Viktoria Luise, p. 144.
59. *New York Times*, November 13, 1918.
60. Dorpalen, "Empress Auguste Victoria," *The American Historical Review*, p. 38.
61. Viktoria Luise, *The Kaiser's Daughter*, p. 144.

62. Tyler-Whittle, *The Last Kaiser*, p. 308.
63. Radziwill, *Disillusions of a Crown Princess*, p. 213.

Part 4: Twilight and Shadow (1918–89)

23: The Edge of Night

1. Clark, *Kaiser Wilhelm II*, p. 346.
2. Norah Bentinck, *The Ex-Kaiser in Exile* (New York: George H. Doran, n.d.), p. 23.
3. Emperor Wilhelm II to Empress Augusta Victoria, November 11, 1918, in *The Kaiser's Daughter*, Viktoria Luise, p. 139.
4. Bentinck, *The Ex-Kaiser in Exile*, pp. 33–34.
5. Ibid., p. 35.
6. Viktoria Luise, *The Kaiser's Daughter*, p. 144.
7. Harding, *Imperial Twilight*, p. 129.
8. Brook-Shepherd, *The Last Habsburg*, p. 220.
9. Harding, *Imperial Twilight*, p. 129.
10. Brook-Shepherd, *Uncrowned Emperor*, p. 44.
11. Brook-Shepherd, *The Last Empress*, p. 136.
12. Ibid.
13. Brook-Shepherd, *Uncrowned Emperor*, p. 45.
14. Pope-Hennessy, *Queen Mary*, p. 510.
15. Diary entry of Queen Mary, January 21, 1919, in "Reflections on the 'Lost Prince,'" *Royalty Digest*, Charlotte Zeepvat, iss. no. 141, vol. 12, no. 8, p. 4.
16. Edwards, *Matriarch*, p. 279.
17. Martin Kitchen, *Europe Between the Wars*, (New York: Longman, 2000), p. 22.
18. Bertrand M. Patenaude, "Food as a Weapon," *Hoover Digest*, no. 1, (January 30, 2007), taken from http://www.hoover.org/publications/hoover-digest/article/6135 (viewed on July 11, 2011).
19. Gelardi, *Born to Rule*, p. 282.
20. Queen Mary to Emily Alcock, February 2, 1919, in *Queen Mary*, Pope-Hennessy, p. 511.
21. Letter of Dr. Otto von Habsburg to the author, April 28, 2007.
22. *New York Times*, February 16, 1919.
23. Brook-Shepherd, *Uncrowned Emperor*, p. 46.
24. Brook-Shepherd, *The Last Habsburg*, p. 224.
25. Brook-Shepherd, *The Last Empress*, p. 137.
26. Emperor Charles I to King George V, February 21, 1919, CV M1466/5, the Royal Archives, quoted in *The Last Habsburg*, Brook-Shepherd, pp. 224–225. The original letter was written in French: "*Majesté, Je suis heureux de pouvoir venir remercier Votre Majesté de la si delicate attention de m'avoir envoyé le colonel Summerhayes. Je suis fort touché de cet acte si courtois et ne même temps j'en suis très reconnaissant. Le colonel est un homme charmant qui remplit sa mission avec beaucoup de tact d'amabilité. La situation dans le monde entier est très difficile surtout pour nous souverains. Que Dieu ait pitié de l'humanité souffrante et lui rende bientôt le repos dont elle a si besoin! De Votre Majesté le bon frère et cousin, Charles. Eckartsau, 21 February 1919.*"
27. Diary entry of Colonel Edward Strutt, February 27, 1919, in *The Last Habsburg*, Brook-Shepherd, p. 232.

28. Brook-Shepherd, *The Last Empress*, p. 140.
29. Diary entry of Colonel Edward Strutt, February 27, 1919, in *The Last Habsburg*, Brook-Shepherd, pp. 232–233.
30. Brook-Shepherd, *Uncrowned Emperor*, p. 47.
31. Brook-Shepherd, *The Last Empress*, p. 141.
32. Diary entry of Colonel Edward Strutt, March 19, 1919, in *The Last Habsburg*, Brook-Shepherd, p. 240.
33. Brook-Shepherd, *The Last Empress*, p. 143.
34. Brook-Shepherd, *Uncrowned Emperor*, p. 50.
35. Diary entry of Colonel Edward Strutt, March 23, 1919, in *The Last Habsburg*, Brook-Shepherd, p. 244.
36. Brook-Shepherd, *The Last Empress*, p. 145.
37. Emperor Charles I to King George V, April 11, 1919, GV AA43/224, the Royal Archives, quoted in *The Last Habsburg*, Brook-Shepherd, p. 250. The original letter was written in French: "*Arrivé sur le sol hospitalier de la Suisse avec l'escorte militaire que le gouvernement de Votre Majesté a bien voulu mettre à ma disposition, je désire vous exprimer directement et sans délai les sentiments de gratitude que me fait éprouver l'appui sûr et généreux de l'empire britannique dans ces circonstances cruelles que je veux croire momentanées.… Je n'ai eu qu'à me louer, en particulier, des dispositions prises par le Colonel Strutt, qui m'a accompagné jusqu'ici et dont le caractère plein de droiture a ete hautement apprecié par moi. Charles. Wartegg, 11 April 1919.*"
38. Brook-Shepherd, *Uncrowned Emperor*, p. 53.
39. Ibid., p. 54.
40. Ibid.

24: The Quest for the Crown

1. Tyler-Whittle, *The Last Kaiser*, p. 326.
2. Viktoria Luise, *The Kaiser's Daughter*, pp. 144–145, 148.
3. Carter, *George, Nicholas and Wilhelm*, p. 419.
4. Bentinck, *The Ex-Kaiser in Exile*, p. 35.
5. Wilhelm II, *The Kaiser's Memoirs*, p. 338.
6. Viktoria Luise, *The Kaiser's Daughter*, p. 147.
7. German Crown Prince, *Memoirs*, p. 107.
8. Bentinck, *The Ex-Kaiser in Exile*, pp. 35–36.
9. Wilhelm Hohenzollern to August von Mackensen, December 2, 1919, in *The Kaiser and His Court: Wilhelm II and the Government of Germany* (Cambridge: Cambridge University Press, 1994), John C. G. Röhl, p. 210.
10. MacDonogh, *The Last Kaiser*, p. 422.
11. Clark, *Kaiser Wilhelm II*, chap. 1, para. 42. *The Madness of Wilhelm II* was written by F. Kleinschrod. *Kaiser Wilhelm Periodically Insane!* was written by H. Lutz. H. Wilm wrote *Wilhelm II as Cripple and Psychopath*.
12. Viktoria Luise, *The Kaiser's Daughter*, p. 145.
13. MacDonogh, *The Last Kaiser*, p. 422.
14. Carter, *George, Nicholas and Wilhelm*, p. 416.
15. Tyler-Whittle, *The Last Kaiser*, p. 311.
16. Clark, *Kaiser Wilhelm II*, p. 345.
17. MacDonogh, *The Last Kaiser*, p. 422.
18. Viktoria Luise, *The Kaiser's Daughter*, p. 148.
19. *New York Times*, March 11, 1922.

20. Ibid., March 17, 1919. Eitel-Fritz and Lotte divorced in 1926.
21. Viktoria Luise, *The Kaiser's Daughter*, p. 8.
22. Brook-Shepherd, *Uncrowned Emperor*, p. 55.
23. Harding, *Imperial Twilight*, p. 143.
24. Ibid., p. 173.
25. Thomas Sakmyster, *Hungary's Admiral on Horseback* (Boulder, CO: East European Monographs, 1994), pp. 95–96.
26. Harding, *Imperial Twilight*, p. 188.

25: The Last Journey

1. MacDonogh, *The Last Kaiser*, p. 426.
2. German Crown Prince, *Memoirs*, p. 283.
3. *New York Times*, October 13, 1921.
4. Viktoria Luise, *The Kaiser's Daughter*, p. 149.
5. *New York Times*, July 18, 1920.
6. Viktoria Luise, *The Kaiser's Daughter*, p. 150.
7. German Crown Prince, *Memoirs*, p. 184.
8. Bentinck, *The Ex-Kaiser in Exile*, p. 144.
9. German Crown Prince, *Memoirs*, p. 209.
10. *New York Times*, December 1, 1920.
11. Bentinck, *The Ex-Kaiser in Exile*, p. 36.
12. Viktoria Luise, *The Kaiser's Daughter*, p. 153.
13. Cecil, *Wilhelm II*, p. 296.
14. Viktoria Luise, *The Kaiser's Daughter*, p. 150.
15. *New York Times*, February 23, 1921.
16. German Crown Prince, *Memoirs*, p. 280.
17. MacDonogh, *The Last Kaiser*, p. 427.
18. Carter, *George, Nicholas and Wilhelm*, p. 419.
19. *Lewiston Evening Journal*, April 11, 1921.
20. German Crown Prince, *Memoirs*, p. 281.
21. Viktoria Luise, *The Kaiser's Daughter*, p. 151.
22. Ibid.
23. *New York Times*, April 18, 1921.
24. Report of the Associated Press sent to *New York Times*, April 18, 1921.
25. Clark, *Kaiser Wilhelm II*, p. 347.
26. Viktoria Luise, *The Kaiser's Daughter*, pp. 151–152.
27. *New York Times*, April 19, 1921.
28. Viktoria Luise, *The Kaiser's Daughter*, pp. 151–152.
29. *New York Times*, April 19, 1921.
30. Clay, *King, Kaiser, Tsar*, p. 354.
31. MacDonogh, *The Last Kaiser*, p. 427.
32. Harding, *Imperial Twilight*, p. 133. This refers to the Treaty of Versailles that was signed at the Paris Peace Conference in 1919. Signed at the Palace of Versailles, the treaty confirmed the borders of postwar Europe and stipulated that the Habsburgs and Hohenzollerns were barred from ever returning to the Austrian and German thrones, respectively.
33. Brook-Shepherd, *The Last Habsburg*, pp. 278–279.
34. Harding, *Imperial Twilight*, p. 201.
35. Brook-Shepherd, *The Last Habsburg*, p. 284.

36. Brook-Shepherd, *Uncrowned Emperor*, p. 59.
37. Brook-Shepherd, *The Last Habsburg*, p. 285.
38. Harding, *Imperial Twilight*, p. 210.
39. Thomas, "Empress Zita," *The Catholic Counter-Reformation*, p. 4.
40. Sakmyster, *Hungary's Admiral*, pp. 113–115.
41. Brook-Shepherd, *Uncrowned Emperor*, p. 61.
42. Harding, *Imperial Twilight*, p. 241.
43. Brook-Shepherd, *Uncrowned Emperor*, pp. 118–119.
44. Harding, *Imperial Twilight*, p. 248.
45. Charles and Zita would not be the last foreign monarchs to be taken into "protective custody" by the British. Even into the Second World War, rulers of less powerful countries who did not conform to the British agenda were forced to abdicate, usually by military occupation, economic sanctions, or diplomatic leverage. In almost every instance, these rulers and their relatives were taken aboard British naval vessels; it would then be implied they were being taken somewhere for their own safety. In the end—like the emperor and empress of Austria—they would always be taken to remote corners of the world in a Napoleonesque manner to remove them from spheres of influences. One of the most famous examples was the forced abdication of the Reza Shah of Iran in the 1940s, who was eventually taken to South Africa.
46. *New York Times*, November 4, 1921.
47. Diary entry of Empress Zita, November 6–7, 1921, in *The Last Habsburg*, Brook-Shepherd, p. 307.
48. Bogle, *A Heart for Europe*, p. 137.
49. Harding, *Imperial Twilight*, p. 257.
50. Diary entry of Empress Zita, November 8, 1921, in *The Last Habsburg*, Brook-Shepherd, p. 309.
51. Diary entry of Empress Zita, November 10, 1921, in ibid., p. 310.
52. Bogle, *A Heart for Europe*, p. 139.
53. Diary entry of Empress Zita, November 19, 1921, in *The Last Habsburg*, Brook-Shepherd, p. 319.
54. Ibid.

26: "I Can't Go On Much Longer"

1. Brook-Shepherd, *Uncrowned Emperor*, p. 63.
2. *New York Times*, January 13, 1922.
3. Brandreth, *Philip and Elizabeth*, p. 57.
4. King George V to Queen Mary, undated, August 1925, in *Queen Mary*, Pope-Hennessy, p. 516.
5. Pope-Hennessy, *Queen Mary*, p. 515.
6. Princess Mary did not become the Princess Royal until January 1, 1932. The title does not automatically go to the monarch's eldest daughter. The incumbent must wait until the current Princess Royal has died. In this case, Mary had to wait for the death of her aunt Louise, Princess Royal and Duchess of Fife, to inherit the title. It also must be bestowed by the monarch. King George V issued letters patent to that end.
7. Duff, *Queen Mary*, p. 174.
8. Diary entry of Queen Mary, November 21, 1921, in *Queen Mary*, Pope-Hennessy, p. 518.
9. Queen Mary to Adolphus, Marquess of Cambridge, November 22, 1921, in ibid.
10. *Times*, February 28, 1922.

11.   Diary entry of King George V, February 28, 1922, in Hough, *Born Royal*, p. 212.
12.   Queen Mary to Edward, Prince of Wales, March 2, 1922, in Edwards, *Matriarch*, p. 290.
13.   Shawcross, *Queen Elizabeth*, p. 112.
14.   Albert, Duke of York, to Edward, Prince of Wales, February 22, 1922, in Pope-Hennessy, *Queen Mary*, p. 521.
15.   Bogle, *A Heart for Europe*, p. 148.
16.   Harding, *Imperial Twilight*, p. 264.
17.   Thomas, "Empress Zita," *The Catholic Counter-Reformation*, p. 4.
18.   Karl Werkmann, *Der Tote auf Madeira* (Munich: Kulturpolitik, 1923), p. 307.
19.   Brook-Shepherd, *The Last Habsburg*, p. 328.
20.   Wheatcroft, *The Habsburgs*, p. 290.
21.   Bogle, *A Heart for Europe*, p. 144.
22.   Brook-Shepherd, *Uncrowned Emperor*, p. 70.
23.   Thomas, "Empress Zita," *The Catholic Counter-Reformation*, p. 4.
24.   Werkmann, *Der Tote*, pp. 310–311.
25.   *Die Presse*, April 2, 1922.
26.   Brook-Shepherd, *Uncrowned Emperor*, p. 72.
27.   Bogle, *A Heart for Europe*, pp. 144–145.
28.   Snyder, *The Red Prince*, p. 131.

27:   Return to Grace

1.   Bogle, *A Heart for Europe*, p. 144.
2.   Harding, *Imperial Twilight*, p. 272.
3.   Bogle, *A Heart for Europe*, pp. 150–151.
4.   Brook-Shepherd, *Uncrowned Emperor*, p. 73.
5.   Gelardi, *Born to Rule*, p. 294.
6.   Harding, *Imperial Twilight*, pp. 288–289.
7.   Gelardi, *Born to Rule*, p. 303.
8.   F. O. Lindley to George Curzon, First Marquess Curzon of Kedleston, October 1, 1922, in *From Splendor to Revolution*, Gelardi, p. 376.
9.   Queen Olga to King George V, November 23/December 6, 1922, the Royal Archives, RA GV/PRIV/AA 46/99, in ibid., pp. 376–377.
10.   Edwards, *Matriarch*, p. 311.
11.   Diary entry of Queen Mary, May 13, 1922, in *Queen Mary*, Pope-Hennessy, p. 527.
12.   Queen Mary to Emily Alcock, February 21, 1923, in ibid., pp. 527–528.
13.   According to William Shawcross, the Queen Mother's official biographer, the Bowes-Lyon family omits the hyphen from their name (Shawcross, *Queen Elizabeth*, p. 8n). The author has chosen to leave the name hyphenated to avoid confusion.
14.   Diary entry of King George V, July 17, 1917, in *Queen Elizabeth*, Shawcross, p. 113n.
15.   Queen Mary to Lady Elizabeth Bowes-Lyon, January 15, 1923, in ibid., p. 152.
16.   Albert, Duke of York, to Queen Mary, April 27, 1923, in *Queen Mary*, Pope-Hennessy, p. 529.
17.   Shawcross, *Queen Elizabeth*, p. 161.
18.   Pope-Hennessy, *Queen Mary*, p. 525.
19.   Edwards, *Matriarch*, p. 300.
20.   Gelardi, *From Splendor to Revolution*, p. 378.
21.   Pope-Hennessy, *Queen Mary*, p. 538.

22.   Duff, *Queen Mary*, p. 186.
23.   Diary entry of Queen Mary, April 21, 1926, in *Queen Mary*, Pope-Hennessy, p. 530.
24.   Brandreth, *Philip and Elizabeth*, p. 58.
25.   Gelardi, *From Splendor to Revolution*, p. 383.
26.   Ibid., p. 358.
27.   Ibid., p. 369.
28.   Albert, Duke of York to Edward, Prince of Wales, December 6, 1928, in *Queen Elizabeth*, Shawcross, p. 303.
29.   Diary entry of Queen Mary, December 2, 1928, in *Queen Mary*, Pope-Hennessy, p. 542.
30.   Diary entry of Queen Mary, January 6, 1929, in ibid., p. 544.
31.   Van der Kiste, *Crowns in a Changing World*, p. 174.
32.   Philip Ziegler, *King Edward VIII: The Official Biography* (London: HarperCollins, 1990), p. 199.

28:   The Tinge of Sunset

1.   Harding, *Imperial Twilight*, p. 293.
2.   Thomas, "Empress Zita," *The Catholic Counter-Reformation*, p. 5.
3.   Ibid.
4.   Dr. Otto von Habsburg to Gordon Brook-Shepherd, August 4, 1999, in *Uncrowned Emperor*, Brook-Shepherd, p. 74.
5.   Ibid., p. 75.
6.   Harding, *Imperial Twilight*, p. 305.
7.   Habsburg Family Archives, Cassette No. 30, File 186, in *The Last Empress*, Brook-Shepherd, p. 232.
8.   Prince Sixtus of Bourbon-Parma to Empress Zita, June 21, 1933, in *The Last Empress*, Brook-Shepherd, p. 240.
9.   Ibid.
10.   Sir Clive Wigram to Sir Robert Vansittart, June 26, 1933, in ibid., p. 242.
11.   King George V to Empress Zita, June 29, 1933, in ibid.
12.   Ibid.
13.   Norman Davies, *Vanished Kingdoms:The History of Half-Forgotten Europe* (London: Allen Lane, 2011), p. 567.
14.   Snyder, *The Red Prince*, p. 131.
15.   Tyler-Whittle, *The Last Kaiser*, p. 339.
16.   *Milwaukee Journal*, September 15, 1934.
17.   Edwards, *Matriarch*, p. 329.
18.   Clark, *Kaiser Wilhelm II*, p. 354.
19.   Memorandum of Dr. Otto von Habsburg to Gordon Brook-Shepherd, October 8, 1999 in *Uncrowned Emperor*, Brook-Shepherd, p. 80.
20.   *Manchester Guardian*, September 25, 1933.
21.   Tsarina Alexandra to the Reverend William Boyd Carpenter, bishop of Ripon, December 29, 1902/January 11, 1903, Add. MSS 46721/236, The British Library, quoted in *Born to Rule*, Gelardi, p. 243.
22.   Harding, *Imperial Twilight*, p. 321.
23.   Cawthorne, *Kings and Queens of England*, p. 184.
24.   Edwards, *Matriarch*, p. 328.
25.   Ibid., p. 331.
26.   Duff, *Queen Mary*, p. 197.

27. Diary entry of Queen Mary, May 6, 1935, in *Queen Mary*, Pope-Hennessy, p. 554.

28. Gelardi, *Born to Rule*, p. 355.

29. Duff, *Queen Mary*, p. 194.

30. Queen Mary to King George V, undated, August 1934, in *Queen Mary*, Pope-Hennessy, p. 551.

31. Edwards, *Matriarch*, p. 318n.

32. Shawcross, *Queen Elizabeth*, p. 347.

33. Noble Frankland, *Prince Henry, Duke of Gloucester* (London: Weidenfeld & Nicolson, 1980), p. 123.

34. Edwards, *Matriarch*, p. 345.

35. Ibid.

36. Shawcross, *Queen Elizabeth*, p. 351.

37. Edwards, *Matriarch*, p. 346.

38. Diary entry of Queen Mary, January 20, 1936, in *Queen Mary*, Pope-Hennessy, p. 558.

39. Shawcross, *Queen Elizabeth*, p. 351.

40. Pope-Hennessy, *Queen Mary*, p. 559.

41. Diary entry of Queen Mary, January 22, 1936, in ibid., p. 560.

42. Shaw, *Royal Babylon* (Kobo desktop version), chap. 9, para. 4.

43. Hildegard Anderson, "The Royals: An Illustrated History of Monarchy—From Yesterday to Today," *Life Books Special Edition* (December, 2010), p. 41.

44. Henry Channon, *Chips: The Diaries of Sir Henry Channon*, ed. Robert Rhodes James (London: Weidenfeld & Nicolson, 1967), p. 55.

45. Wilhelm Hohenzollern to Queen Mary, February 2, 1936, in *George, Nicholas and Wilhelm*, Carter, p. 424.

46. RA QM/PRIV/QMD/1936: 28 January, in *Queen Elizabeth*, Shawcross, p. 352.

47. Shawcross, *Queen Elizabeth*, p. 352.

48. Wakeford, *Three Consort Queens*, p. 184.

29: For the Love of a Woman

1. Channon, *Chips*, p. 54.

2. Elizabeth, Duchess of York, to Queen Mary, March 11, 1936, RA QM/PRIV/CC12/24, in Shawcross, *Queen Elizabeth*, pp. 360-361.

3. Queen Mary to King Edward VIII, undated, 1936, in *Queen Mary*, Duff, p. 204.

4. Diary entry of Queen Mary, September 30, 1936, in ibid., p. 207.

5. Shaw, *Royal Babylon* (Kobo desktop version), chap. 9, para. 81.

6. Edwards, *Matriarch*, p. 323.

7. Carroll, *Notorious Royal Marriages*, pp. 391–392.

8. Shaw, *Royal Babylon* (Kobo desktop version), chap. 9, para. 85.

9. Duff, *Queen Mary*, p. 208.

10. Carroll, *Notorious Royal Marriages*, pp. 390–391.

11. Lewis Broad, *The Abdication* (London: Frederick Muller, 1961), p. 75.

12. Tudor enthusiasts will recall that Henry VIII outlived his third wife, Jane Seymour, who died a few days after giving birth to Henry's only son. He predeceased his sixth and final wife, Catherine Parr.

13. Edwards, *Matriarch*, p. 364.

14. Carroll, *Notorious Royal Marriages*, p. 396.

15. Queen Mary to Edward, Duke of Windsor, July 5, 1938, in *Queen Mary*, Pope-Hennessy, pp. 574–575.

16. Hough, *Born Royal*, p. 285.
17. Ibid.
18. Ziegler, *Edward VIII*, pp. 323–324.
19. King Edward VIII to Queen Mary, November 20, 1936, EDW/ADD/ADD/ABD/1, the Royal Archives, quoted in ibid., p. 324.
20. Queen Mary to Elizabeth, Duchess of York, November 17, 1936, QEQM/PRIV/RF, the Royal Archives, quoted in *Queen Elizabeth*, Shawcross, p. 373.
21. Pope-Hennessy, *Queen Mary*, p. 579.
22. Diary entry of Queen Mary, December 10, 1936, in *Queen Elizabeth*, Shawcross, p. 381.
23. Cawthorne, *Kings and Queens*, p. 189.
24. Edwards, *Matriarch*, p. 368.
25. Carroll, *Notorious Royal Marriages*, p. 400.
26. Ziegler, *Edward VIII*, p. 538.
27. *Daily Express*, June 3, 1957.
28. Edwards, *Matriarch*, p. 378.
29. Elizabeth, Duchess of York, to Queen Mary, October 21, 1936, QM/PRIV/CC12/36, the Royal Archives, quoted in *Queen Elizabeth*, Shawcross, p. 370.
30. Wheeler-Bennett, *King George VI*, p. 288.
31. Farquhar, *Behind the Palace Doors*, p. 287.
32. Queen Mary to King George VI, February 4, 1937, RA GVI/PRIV/RF/11 in *Queen Elizabeth*, Shawcross, pp. 421-422.
33. Gelardi, *Born to Rule*, p. 361.
34. Shaw, *Royal Babylon* (Kobo desktop version), chap. 9, para. 87.
35. Queen Mary to King George VI, April 10, 1937, RA GVI/PRIV/RF/11, the Royal Archives, quoted in *Queen Elizabeth*, Shawcross, p. 421.
36. Diary entry of Queen Mary, June 3, 1937, in *Queen Mary*, Pope-Hennessy, p. 585.
37. Farquhar, *Behind the Palace Doors*, p. 288. Once Wallis secured her divorce from her second husband, Ernest Simpson, she resumed using her maiden name, Warfield.
38. Duff, *Queen Mary*, p. 220.
39. Shawcross, *Queen Elizabeth*, p. 401.
40. Diary entry of Queen Mary, May 12, 1937, in *Queen Mary*, Duff, p. 220.
41. Gelardi, *Born to Rule*, p. 368.
42. Queen Mary to King George VI, May 12, 1937, RA GVI/PRIV/RF/11, in *Queen Elizabeth*, Shawcross, p. 404.
43. Shawcross, *Queen Elizabeth*, p. 387.
44. *Palm Beach Post*, March 13, 1938.
45. Diary entry of Queen Mary, November 20, 1938, in *Queen Mary*, Pope-Hennessy, p. 588.
46. Pope-Hennessy, *Queen Mary*, p. 588.
47. Habsburg Family Archives, Cassette No. 20, File 502, in *The Last Empress*, Brook-Shepherd, p. 252.
48. Declaration of Archduke Otto, March 12, 1938, Habsburg Family Archives, Cassette No. 21, File 361, in ibid., p. 266.
49. *Volkzeitung*, April 20, 1938.
50. Queen Mary to King George VI, September 3, 1939, RA GVI/PRIV/RF/11, in *Queen Elizabeth*, Shawcross, p. 493.
51. Declaration of Empress Zita, July 27, 1940, Habsburg Family Archives, "New York Trunk," No. 3, File 261, in *The Last Empress*, Brook-Shepherd, p. 278.

52. The idea of Queen Mary being kidnapped by the Germans was not so far-fetched. A few months earlier, the Germans had unsuccessfully tried to capture Queen Wilhelmina of the Netherlands, who fled to safety in England.

53. Duff, *Queen Mary*, p. 229.

54. Queen Elizabeth to Queen Mary, September 13, 1940, QM/PRIV/CC12/135, the Royal Archives, quoted in *Queen Elizabeth*, Shawcross, pp. 522–523.

55. Ibid.

56. Diary entry of Queen Mary, December 19, 1939, in *Queen Mary*, Pope-Hennessy, p. 602.

57. Queen Mary to Archduke Robert, undated, 1941, in *The Last Empress*, Brook-Shepherd, p. 286.

58. Empress Zita to Queen Mary, undated, RA GVCC 45/1256, the Royal Archives, quoted in ibid., p. 287. In the original letter and in Brook-Shepherd, Zita addressed Mary as "*Chère Cousine, Sa Majesté la Reine-Mère d'Angleterre.*"

59. Edwards, *Matriarch*, p. 394.

60. Queen Mary to Edward, Duke of Windsor, August 31, 1942, RA EDW/PRIV/MAINB/156, the Royal Archives, quoted in *Queen Elizabeth*, Shawcross, p. 552.

61. Edward, Duke of Windsor, to King George VI, September 15, 1942, RA GVI/PRIV/RF/11, in ibid.

62. Edwards, *Matriarch*, p. 403.

63. "Queen Mary," *British Medical Journal*, vol. 1, no. 4813 (April 4, 1953), p. 772.

64. British succession laws required men to precede women, regardless of their birth order, to inherit the throne. Only in instances when the monarch or heir apparent had no sons (in the cases of George VI and Queen Victoria's father the Duke of Kent) could women ascend the throne. This was changed on October 28, 2011, at the biennial Commonwealth Heads of Government meeting in Australia when Queen Elizabeth II and the sixteen Commonwealth leaders agreed to give women equal succession rights with men. The new succession law is not retroactive, and the queen emphasized it only applies to the descendants of Charles, Prince of Wales. As such, should the current Duke and Duchess of Cambridge have a daughter, followed by a son, their daughter would become heiress and eventually queen regnant.

65. Queen Mary to King George VI, March 6, 1944, RA GVI/PRIV/RF/11, in *Queen Elizabeth*, Shawcross, p. 579.

66. "The Queen and Prince Philip," *Hello! Canada*, no. 217 (May 16, 2011), p. 112.

67. Brandreth, *Philip and Elizabeth*, p. 104.

68. Bradford, *George VI*, p. 560.

69. Edwards, *Matriarch*, p. 407.

70. Anderson, "The Royals," p. 52.

71. Princess Elizabeth to May Elphinstone, November 18, 1948, RA QEQM/OUT/ELPHINSTONE, in *Queen Elizabeth*, Shawcross, p. 637.

72. Pope-Hennessy, *Queen Mary*, p. 617.

73. US Department of State, *Foreign Relations of the United States of America*, 1952–1954 (Washington DC: GPO), vol. 10, p. 280. Acheson did not actually write his note regarding British solvency until November 1951, well after India's independence. At the time, Acheson was describing Britain's foreign policy toward its former imperial territories and protectorates in the Middle East, specifically Iran. The sentiment describing the end of the British imperial era is still appropriate.

74. Anderson, "The Royals," p. 59.

75. Bradford, *George VI*, p. 525.

76. Farquhar, *Behind the Palace Doors*, p. 297.

77.   Shawcross, *Queen Elizabeth*, p. 651.
78.   Diary entry of Queen Mary, February 6, 1952, in Shawcross, *Queen Elizabeth*, p. 654.
79.   Queen Mary to Queen Elizabeth, February 7, 1952, in RA QEQM/PRIV/RF, the Royal Archives, quoted in *Queen Elizabeth*, Shawcross, p. 655.
80.   Pope-Hennessy, *Queen Mary*, p. 620.
81.   Edwards, *Matriarch*, p. 414.
82.   Brandreth, *Philip and Elizabeth*, p. 216.
83.   Queen Mary to Queen Elizabeth, February 7, 1952, RA QEQM/PRIV/RF, the Royal Archives, quoted in *Queen Elizabeth*, Shawcross, p. 656.
84.   Anderson, "The Royals," p. 56.
85.   Channon, *Chips*, p. 464.
86.   Edwards, *Matriarch*, p. 415.
87.   Shawcross, *Queen Elizabeth*, p. 676.
88.   *Ottawa Citizen*, March 23, 1953.
89.   Duff, *Queen Mary*, p. 241.
90.   Shawcross, *Queen Elizabeth*, p. 676.

30:   The Last Empress

1.   Letter of Empress Zita, May 6, 1941, Habsburg Family Archives, Cassette No. 23, File 861 in *The Last Empress*, Brook-Shepherd, p. 284.
2.   The Earl of Athlone was the former Prince Alexander ("Alge") of Teck, Queen Mary's brother. Along with many other members of the British royal family, Alge renounced his German titles in 1917 and adopted the surname Cambridge along with the title Earl of Athlone. He married George V's cousin Princess Alice of Albany in 1904.
3.   Princess Alice of Albany, *For My Grandchildren: Some Reminiscences of H.R.H. Princess Alice, Countess of Athlone* (London: Evans Brothers, 1966), p. 257.
4.   Thomas, "Empress Zita," *The Catholic Counter-Reformation*, p. 6.
5.   Dr. Otto von Habsburg to Gordon Brook-Shepherd, November 1, 2000, in *Uncrowned Emperor*, Brook-Shepherd, p. 178.
6.   Archduke Otto to Queen Mary, undated, January 1951, RA GV/CC 45 No. 1708, the Royal Archives, quoted in *The Last Empress*, Brook-Shepherd, p. 315.
7.   Felix married Princess Anna-Eugénie of Arenberg in 1952; Rudolf married twice, first to the Russian noblewoman Countess Xenia Besobrasova in 1953 (she died in 1968), and later to Princess Anna von Wrede on 1971; Robert married Princess Margharita of Savoy-Aosta in 1953; and Charlotte married Georg, Duke of Mecklenburg, in 1956. Zita's eldest daughter, Archduchess Adelheid, never married.
8.   Brook-Shepherd, *The Last Empress*, p. 315.
9.   Empress Zita to Gordon Brook-Shepherd, June 28, 1982, in *The Last Empress*, Brook-Shepherd, p. 322.
10.   *Glasgow Herald*, May 15, 1982.
11.   Brook-Shepherd, *The Last Empress*, p. 322.
12.   Thomas, "Empress Zita," *The Catholic Counter-Reformation*, p. 1.
13.   Brook-Shepherd, *The Last Empress*, p. 323.
14.   Ibid., p. 326.
15.   Ibid., p. 327.
16.   Dr. Otto von Habsburg to Gordon Brook-Shepherd, December 17–19, 1990, in ibid., p. 328.

17.   Michelle Green, Ellen Wallace, and Jonathan Cooper, "Europe's Heads, Crowned and Otherwise, Bury Zita, the Last Habsburg Empress," *People*, April 17, 1989, accessed March 4, 2012, http://www.people.com/people/archive/article/0,,20120043,00.html

18.   Tony Judt, *Postwar: A History of Europe Since 1945* (New York: Penguin Books, 2005), pp. 2–3.

19.   Green, Wallace, and Cooper, "Europe's Heads, Crowned and Otherwise, Bury Zita, the Last Habsburg Empress," *People*, April 17, 1989, accessed March 4, 2012, http://www.people.com/people/archive/article/0,,20120043,00.html

20.   Bogle, *A Heart for Europe*, p. 160.

21.   *New York Times*, April 2, 1989.

22.   Thomas, "Empress Zita," *The Catholic Counter-Reformation*, p. 1.

Epilogue

1.   Bogle, *A Heart for Europe*, p. iii.

2.   Letter of Dr. Otto von Habsburg to the author, April 28, 2007.

3.   For further information on Otto von Habsburg, the Duke of Windsor, King George VI, and the mystery of Grand Duchess Anastasia/Anna Anderson, consult the bibliography that follows.

4.   Raffael Scheck, *Mothers of the Nation: Right-Wing Women in Weimar Germany* (New York: Berg Publishing, 2004), p. 11.

5.   On the Official Website of the Imperial and Royal House of Hohenzollern, her name is given as Hermione. This is somewhat modern, as most pre-twenty-first-century sources refer to her as Hermine (http://www.preussen.de/en/family/family_tree/william_ii._king_of_prussia__german_emperor.html [viewed November 1, 2011]).

6.   Cecil, *Wilhelm II*, p. 315.

7.   Clark, *Kaiser Wilhelm II*, p. 355.

8.   Shaw, *Royal Babylon* (Kobo desktop version), chap. 5, para. 19.

9.   The June 3 flotilla was the largest assemblage of boats in history. The celebrations that day were also the largest England had seen since the reign of King Charles II in the 1660s.

10.   Ibid., chap. 9, para. 109.

11.   Wilson and King, *Resurrection of the Romanovs*, p. 98.

12.   Death certificate of Anastasia Nicholaievna Manahan, February 12, 1984, Commonwealth of Virginia, certificate of death 203-256, *op. cit.* in *Resurrection of the Romanovs*, King and Wilson, p. 253. Anderson married American professor Dr. John "Jack" Manahan in 1968.

13.   *Wall Street Journal*, August 26, 2011.

Bibliography

PRIMARY SOURCES

Periodicals

Ashburton Guardian
Boston Evening Post
Daily Chronicle
Daily Express
Daily Mail
Daily Telegraph
Delo
Die Presse
Lewiston Evening Journal
Manchester Guardian
Neue Freie Presse
Newsweek Special Commemorative Issue: William & Catherine, A Royal Wedding
Ottawa Citizen
Providence News
Spokane Falls Daily Chronicle
The Glasgow Herald
The Guardian
The Lady
The Milwaukee Journal
The New York Times
The Palm Beach Post
The Times
Volkzeitung

Justin C. Vovk

UNPUBLISHED LETTERS AND DOCUMENTS

Personal Correspondence
Dr. Otto von Habsburg, letter to the author, April 28, 2007.

Austria
Vienna State Archives
Hausarchiv
Hofarchiv
Staatsarchiv

England
London Public Records Office
Parliamentary Archives
Southampton University Archives

Germany
Berliner Hauptarchiv
Brandenburg-Preussisches Hausarchiv

Langenburg Hausarchiv
Hohenlohe Letters

PUBLISHED DIPLOMATIC AND POLITICAL DOCUMENTS

MacCauley, Clay. *The Hohenzollern Dynasty; Motive and Movement.* Tokyo: n.p., 1916.
Rich, Norman and M. H. Fisher, eds. *The Holstein Papers.* Vol. 2. Cambridge: Cambridge University Press, 1957.
US Department of State. *Foreign Relations of the United States of America,* 1952-1954. Vol. 10. Washington DC: GPO.

PUBLISHED LETTERS AND MEMOIRS

Airlie, Mabel. *Thatched With Gold.* Edited by Jennifer Ellis. London: Hutchinson, 1962.
Alexander, Grand Duke of Russia. *Once a Grand Duke.* New York: Garden City Publishing, 1932.
Alexandra Feodorovna, Tsarina of Russia. *Letters of the Tsaritsa to the Tsar, 1914-1916.* London: Duckworth, 1923.

Alice, Princess of Albany. *For My Grandchildren: Some Reminiscences of H.R.H. Princess Alice, Countess of Athlone*. London: Evans Brothers, 1966.

Benson, Arthur and Reginald Brett, eds. *The Letters of Queen Victoria: A Selection from Her Majesty's Correspondence Between the Years 1837 and 1861*. Vol. 2. London: J. Murray, 1907.

Bentinck, Norah. *The Ex-Kaiser in Exile*. New York: George H. Doran, n.d.

Bernstein, Herman, ed. *The Willy-Nicky Correspondence: Being the Secret and Intimate Telegrams Exchanged Between the Kaiser and the Tsar*. New York: Alfred A. Knopf, 1918.

Bing, Edward J., ed. *The Letters of Tsar Nicholas and Empress Marie: Being the Confidential Correspondence Between Nicholas II, Last of the Tsars, and His Mother, Dowager Empress Marie Feodorovna*. London: Ivor Nicolson & Watson, 1937.

Birmingham, Stephen. *Duchess: The Story of Wallis Warfield Simpson*. Boston: Little, Brown, 1981.

Bismarck, Otto von. *Bismarck: The Man and the Statesman*. New York: Harper, 1898.

Bolitho, Hector, ed. *Further Letters of Queen Victoria: From the Archives of the House of Brandenburg-Prussia*. London: Thorton Butterwood, 1938.

Botkin, Gleb. *The Real Romanovs*. New York: Fleming H. Revell, 1931.

Buckle, George Earle, ed. *The Letters of Queen Victoria: Third Series, A Selection From Her Majesty's Correspondence and Journal Between the Years 1886 and 1901*. Vol. 3. London: John Murray, 1932.

Buxhoeveden, Sophie. *The Life and Tragedy of Alexandra Feodorovna, Empress of Russia*. London: Longmans, Green, 1928.

Channon, Henry. *Chips, the Diaries of Sir Henry Channon*. Edited by Robert Rhodes James. London: Weidenfeld & Nicolson, 1967.

Cook, C. Kinloch, ed. *Her Royal Highness Princess Mary Adelaide Duchess of Teck: Based on Her Private Diaries and Letters*. Vols. 1 and 2. New York: Charles Scribner's Sons, 1900.

Davis, Arthur. *The Kaiser As I Know Him*. New York: Harper Brothers, 1918.

De Schelking, Eugene. *Suicide of Monarchy: Recollections of a Diplomat*. Toronto: Macmillan Company of Canada, 1918.

Dehn, Lili. *The Real Tsaritsa*. London: Thornton Butterwork, 1922.

Edward, Duke of Windsor. *A King's Story*. London: Cassell, 1951.

Eppinghoven, Ursula von. *Private Lives of the Kaiser and Kaiserin of Germany: Secret History of the Court of Berlin*. Vols. 1—3. New York: Henry W. Fischer, 1909.

Ernest II, Duke of Saxe-Coburg and Gotha. *Memoirs of Ernest II, Duke of Saxe-Coburg-Gotha*. Vol. 4. London: Elibron Classics, 2005.

Eulalia, Infanta of Spain. *Courts and Countries After the War*. New York: Dodd, Mead, 1925.

FitzGerald, Desmond. *Desmond's Rising; Memoirs 1913 to Easter 1916*. Dublin: Liberties Press, 2006.

Fontenoy, Mme. la Marquise. *Secret Memoirs of William II of Germany and Francis Joseph of Austria*. Vol. 1. London: Hutchinson, 1900.

Fuhrmanm, Joseph T., ed. *The Complete Wartime Correspondence of Tsar Nicholas II and Empress Alexandra, April 1914-March 1917*. Westport, CN: Greenwood Press, 1999.

George V, King of Great Britain. *The King to His People: Being the Speeches and Messages of His Majesty George V as Prince and Sovereign*. London: Williams & Norgate, 1911.

Gilliard, Pierre. *Thirteen Years at the Russian Court*. London: Hutchinson, 1921.

George, Robert. *Heirs of Tradition: tributes of a New Zealander*. Manchester, NH: Ayer Publishing, 1971.

Hamilton, Frederic. *The Vanished World of Yesterday*. London: Hodder & Stoughton, 1950.

Hanbury-Williams, John. *Emperor Nicholas II As I Knew Him*. London: Arthur L. Humphreys, 1922.

Hardinge, Charles. *Old Diplomacy*. London: John Murray, 1947.

Heltzendorff, Ernest von and William Le Queux. *The Secrets of Potsdam: A Startling Exposure of the Inner Life of the Courts of the Kaiser and Crown-Prince*. London: London Mail, n.d.

Hibbert, Christopher, ed. *Queen Victoria in Her Letters and Journals*. New York: Viking Penguin, 1985.

Horthy, Nicholas. *Memoirs*. Edited by Ilona Bowden. Safety Harbor, FL: Simon Publications, 2000.

Hough, Richard, ed. *Advice to a Grand-daughter: Letters from Queen Victoria to Princess Victoria of Hesse*. London: Heinemann, 1975.

Karolyi, Catherine. *A Life Together*. London: Allen & Unwin, 1966.

Kokovtsov, V. N. *Out of My Past: The Memoirs of Count Kokovtsov*. Translated by Laura Matveev. Edited by H. H. Fisher. Stanford: Stanford University Press, 1935

Lee, Arthur Gould, ed. *The Empress Frederick Writes to Sophie, Her Daughter, Crown Princess and Later Queen of the Hellenes. Letters 1889-1901*. London: Faber & Faber, 1955.

Leudet, Maurice. *The Emperor of Germany at Home*. Translated by Virginia Taylor. London: Hutchinson, 1898.

Lutz, Ralph Haswell, ed. *Fall of the German Empire, 1914-1918.* Vols. 1 and 2. Stanford: Stanford University Press, 1932.

Luytens, Mary, ed. *Lady Lytton's Court Diary.* London: Rupert Hart Davis, 1961.

Marie, Grand Duchess of Russia. *Education of a Princess: A Memoir.* New York: The Viking Press, 1931.

Marie, Queen of Romania. *The Story of My Life.* Vols. 1 and 2, 1934; Vol. 3, 1935. London: Cassell.

Marie Louise, Princess. *My Memories of Six Reigns.* London: Evans Brothers, 1956.

Mossolov, A. A. *At the Court of the Last Tsar.* Translated by E. W. Dickes. London: Methuen, 1935.

Mouchanow, Marfa. *My Empress: Twenty-Three Years of Intimate Life with the Empress of All the Russias from Her Marriage to the Day of Her Exile.* New York: John Lane, 1928.

Narishkin-Kurakin, Elizabeth. *Under Three Tsars: The Memoirs of the Lady-in-Waiting Elizabeth Narishkin-Kurakin.* Edited by René Fülöp-Miller. New York: E. P. Dutton, 1931.

Nicholas II, Tsar of Russia. *Journal intime de Nicholas II.* Translated by Pierre Agrégé. Paris: Payot, 1925.

————. *Letters of the Tsar to the Tsaritsa, 1914-1917.* Translated by A. L. Hynes. London: Bodley Head, 1929.

Paléologue, Maurice. *An Ambassador's Memoirs.* Vol. 2. London: Hutchinson, 1927.

Paley, Princess. *Memories of Russia, 1916-1919.* London: Herbert Jenkins, 1924.

Pares, Bernard. *My Russian Memoirs.* New York: AMS Press, 1969.

Ponsonby, Frederick, ed. *Recollections of Three Reigns.* London: Eyre & Spottiswoode, 1951.

————. *The Letters of Empress Frederick.* London: Macmillan, 1928.

Radziwill, Catherine. *Secrets of Dethroned Royalty.* New York: John Lane, 1920.

————. *The Austrian Court From Within.* London: Cassell, 1916.

————. *The Disillusions of a Crown Princess.* New York: John Lane, 1919.

————. *The Royal Marriage Market of Europe.* New York: Funk & Wagnalls, 1915.

Schwering, Axel von. *The Berlin Court Under Wilhelm II.* London: Cassell, 1915.

Sell, Karl, ed. *Alice, Grand Duchess of Hesse, Princess of Great Britain and Ireland.* New York: G. P. Putnam's Sons, 1885.

Schench, G. *Handbuch über den Königlich Preußischen Hof und Staat fur das Jahr 1908*. Berlin: n.p., 1907.

Sixtus, Prince of Bourbon-Parma. *L'offre de paix séparée de l'Autriche (5 décembre 1916-12 octobre 1917)*. Paris: Plon-Nourrit, 1920.

Steinberg, Mark D. and Vladimir M. Khrustalëv, eds. *The Fall of the Romanovs: Political Dreams and Personal Struggles in a Time of Revolution*. New Haven: Yale University Press, 1995.

Vassili, Paul. *Confessions of the Czarina*. New York: Harper, 1918.

Viktoria Luise, Duchess of Brunswick and Lüneburg, Princess of Prussia. *My Memoirs*. London: Eveleigh Nash & Grayson, 1929.

———. *The Kaiser's Daughter*. Translated and edited by Robert Vacha. Englewood Cliffs, NJ: Prentice-Hall, 1977.

Viroubova, Anna. *Memories of the Russian Court*. New York: Macmillan, 1923.

Wilhelm, German Crown Prince. *Memoirs of the Crown Prince of Germany*. New York: Charles Scribner's Sons, 1922.

Wilhelm II, German Emperor, King of Prussia. *Gone Astray: Some Leaves From An Emperor's Diary*. New York: John Lane, 1918.

———. *My Early Life*. New York: AMS Edition, 1971.

———. *The Kaiser's Memoirs*. Translated by Thomas R. Ybarra. London: Harper, 1922.

Yusupov, Felix. *Lost Splendour*. London: Cape, 1953.

Zedlitz-Trützschler, Robert. *Twelve Years at the Imperial German Court*. London: Nisbet, 1924.

SECONDARY SOURCES

BOOKS

Almedingen, E. M. *The Empress Alexandra, 1872-1918: A Study*. London: Hutchinson, 1961.

Anonymous. *The Kaiser's Heir*. London: Mills & Boon, 1914.

———. *The Real Crown Prince: A Record and An Indictment*. London: George Newnes, n.d.

Aronson, Theo. *A Family of Kings: The Descendants of Christian IX of Denmark*. London: Weidenfeld & Nicolson, 1976.

———. *Crowns in Conflict: The Triumph and the Tragedy of European Monarchy, 1910-1918*. London: John Murray, 1986.

———. *Grandmama of Europe: The Crowned Descendants of Queen Victoria*. Indianapolis: Bobbs-Merrill Company, 1973.

Bach, Wilhelm Karl. *Kaiserin Auguste Viktoria*. Berlin: F. Hirt, 1898.

Bagulay, David. *Napoleon III and His Regime: An Extravaganza*. Baton Rouse: Louisiana State University Press, 2000.

Baier, Stephan and Eva Demmerle. *Otto von Habsburg: Die Biografie*. Vienna: Amalthea, 2002.

Battiscombe, Georgina. *Queen Alexandra*. London: Constable, 1969.

Beaven, Arthur H. *Marlborough House and Its Occupants Present and Past*. London: White, 1896.

Beech, Arturo and David McIntosh. *Empress Zita of Austria, Queen of Hungary (1892-1989)*. North Pacific Heights: Eurohistory, 2005.

Bennett, Daphne. *Vicky: Princess Royal of England and German Empress*. London: Collins & Harvill, 1971.

Benson, Frederic Edward. *The Kaiser and the English Relations*. London: Longmans, Green, 1936.

Berghahn, Volker. *Germany and the Approach of War in 1914*. London: Palgrave Macmillan, 1993.

Bocca, Geoffrey. *The Woman Who Would Be Queen: A Biography of the Duchess of Windsor*. New York: Rinehart, 1954.

Bogle, James and Joanna. *A Heart for Europe: The Lives of Emperor Charles and Empress Zita of Austria-Hungary*. London: Gracewing, 1990.

Bolitho, Hector. *King George VI*. New York: J. B. Lippincott, 1938.

Bomann-Larsen, Tor. *Kongstanken: Haakon & Maud-I*. Oslo: J. W. Cappelen, 2002.

Boston Women's Health Collective. *Our Bodies, Ourselves: Pregnancy and Birth*. New York: Touchstone Books, 2008.

Bothmer, Marie. *Sovereign Ladies of Europe*. London: Kessinger, 2005.

Bouton, S. Miles. *And the Kaiser Abdicates: The German Revolution November 1918-August 1919*. New Haven: Yale University Press, 1921.

Bradford, Sarah. *King George VI*. London: Weidenfeld & Nicolson, 1989.

Brandreth, Gyles. *Philip and Elizabeth: Portrait of a Royal Marriage*. London: W. W. Norton, 2004.

Brook-Shepherd, Gordon. *November 1918*. Boston: Little, Brown, 1981.

———. *Royal Sunset: The Dynasties of Europe and the Great War*. London: Weidenfeld & Nicolson, 1987.

———. *The Austrians: A Thousand-Year Odyssey*. New York: Carroll & Graf, 1997.

———. *The Last Empress: The Life and Times of Zita of Austria-Hungary, 1892-1989*. London: HarperCollins, 1991.

———. *The Last Habsburg*. London: Weidenfeld & Nicolson, 1968.

———. *Uncle of Europe*. London: HarperCollins, 1975.

———. *Uncrowned Emperor: The Life and Times of Otto von Habsburg*. London: Hambledon & London, 2003.

Camp, Anthony J. *Royal Mistresses and Bastards: Fact and Fiction, 1714-1936.* Marlborough, Wiltshire: Heraldry Today, 2007.

Carey, M. C. *Princess Mary.* London: Nisbet, 1922.

Carroll, Leslie. *Notorious Royal Marriages: A Juicy Journey Through Nine Centuries of Dynasty, Destiny, and Desire.* London: Penguin, 2010.

Carter, Miranda. *George, Nicholas and Wilhelm: Three Royal Cousins and the Road to World War I.* New York: Knopf, 2009.

Cawthorne, Nigel. *Kings & Queens of England: A Royal History From Egbert to Elizabeth II.* London: Arcturus Publishing, 2009.

Cecil, Lamar. *Wilhelm II: Emperor and exile, 1900-1941.* Chapel Hill: University of North Carolina Press, 1996.

Chapman-Huston, Desmond, ed. *Daisy, Princess of Pless.* London: John Murray, 1928.

Clark, Christopher. *Iron Kingdom: The Rise and Downfall of Prussia, 1600-1947.* London: John Allen Lane, 2006.

———. *Kaiser Wilhelm II: A Life in Power.* London: Penguin, 2009.

Clay, Catrine. *King, Kaiser, Tsar: Three Royal Cousins Who Led the World to War.* New York: Walker, 2006.

Clear, Celia. *Royal Children, 1840-1980.* New York: Stein & Day, 1981.

Cook, Andrew. *Prince Eddy: The King Britain Never Had.* Stroud, Gloucester: The History Press, 2011.

Crankshaw, Edward. *The Fall of the House of Habsburg.* London: Viking Press, 1963.

———. *Shadow of the Winter Palace: Russia's Drift to Revolution, 1825-1917.* New York: Viking Press, 1976.

Crawford, Donald and Rosemary. *Michael and Natasha: The Life and Love of the Last Tsar of Russia.* London: Weidenfeld & Nicolson, 1997.

Cunliffe-Owens, Marguerite. *Imperator et Rex: William II. of Germany.* New York: Harper & Brothers, 1904.

Davis, Belinda. *Home Fires Burning: Food, Politics, and Everyday Life in World War I Berlin.* Chapel Hill: University of North Carolina Press, 2000.

Davies, Norman. *Vanished Kingdoms: The History of Half-Forgotten Europe.* London: Allen Lane, 2011.

De Jong, Alex. *The Life and Times of Grigorri Rasputin.* New York: Coward, McCann & Geoghegan, 1982.

Dennison, Matthew. *The Last Princess: The Devoted Life of Queen Victoria's Youngest Daughter.* London: Weidenfeld & Nicolson, 2007.

Denton, C. S. *Absolute Power.* London: Arcturus Publishing, 2006.

Dicey, Edward. *The Schleswig-Holstein War.* Vols. 1 and 2. London: Tinsley Brothers, 1864.

Dixon, Simon. *Catherine the Great*. New York: HarperCollins, 2009.

Duff, David. *Hessian Tapestry*. London: Frederick Muller, 1967.

———. *Queen Mary*. London: Collins, 1985.

Eade, Philip. *Young Prince Philip: His Turbulent Early Life*. London: HarperPress, 2011.

Edwards, Anne. *Matriarch: Queen Mary and the House of Windsor*. London: Hodder & Stoughton, 1984.

Epton, Nina. *Victoria and Her Daughters*. London: Weidenfeld & Nicolson, 1972.

Erbstößer, Elizza. *Auguste Victoria: Die letzte deutche Kaiserin*. Waldshut-Tiengen, BW: European Media Service GTI GmbH, 2008.

Erickson, Carolly. *Alexandra: The Last Tsarina*. New York: Saint Martin's Press, 2001.

Evers, Ernst. *Auguste Viktoria: das lebensbild der deutschen Kaiserin*. Berlin: Stiftungsverlag, 1908.

Farquhar, Michael. *Behind the Palace Doors: Five Centuries of Sex, Adventure, Vice, Treachery, and Folly from Royal Britain*. New York: Random House, 2011.

Felberman, Louis. *The House of Teck: A Romance of a Thousand Years*. London: John Long, 1911.

Feuchtwanger, E. J. *Albert and Victoria: The Rise and Fall of the House of Saxe-Coburg-Gotha*. London: Hambledon Continuum, 2006.

Fiegl, Erich. *Kaiser Karl, personliche, Aufzeichnungen, Zeugnisse und Dokumente*. Vienna: Amalthea, 1984.

———. *Kaiserin Zita von Österreich nach Österreich*. Vienna: Amalthea, 1982.

Fleischmann, Hector. *Napoleon III and the Women He Loved*. Translated by A. S. Rappaport. London: Holden & Hardingham, 1915.

Frankland, Noble. *Prince Henry, Duke of Gloucester*. London: Weidenfeld & Nicolson, 1980.

Fraser, Antonia. *Marie Antoinette: The Journey*. New York: Anchor Books, 2002.

Fraser, John. *The Secret of the Crown: Canada's Affair with Royalty*. Toronto: House of Anansi Press, 2012.

Frederic, Harold. *The Young Emperor: William II of Germany*. New York: G. P. Putnam's Sons, 1891.

Fortescue, John. *Narrative of the Visit to India of Their Majesties King George V. and Queen Mary and of the Coronation Durbar Held at Delhi 12th December 1911*. London: Macmillan, 1912.

Fox, Edward Lyell. *Wilhelm Hohenzollern & Co*. New York: Robert M. McBride, 1917.

Friedman, Dennis. *Darling Georgie: The Enigma of George V.* London: Peter Owen, 1998.

Fulford, Roger. *Hanover to Windsor.* London: Collins, 1970.

Geiss, Immanuel, ed. *July 1914—The Outbreak of the First World War: Selected Documents.* London: Batsford, 1967.

Gelardi, Julia P. *Born to Rule: Five Reigning Consorts, Granddaughters of Queen Victoria.* New York: Saint Martin's Press, 2005.

———. *From Splendor to Revolution: The Romanov Women, 1847-1928.* New York: Saint Martin's Press, 2011.

———. *In Triumph's Wake: Royal Mothers, Tragic Daughters, and the Price They Paid For Glory.* New York: Saint Martin's Press, 2008.

Gill, Gillian. *We Two: Victoria and Albert—Rulers, Partners, Rivals.* New York: Ballantine Books, 2009.

Glass, D. V. and D. E. C. Eversley, eds. *Population in History: Essays in Historical Demography.* London: Arnold, 1965.

Gombás, István. *Kings and Queens of Hungary & Princes of Transylvania.* Budapest: Corvina, 2002.

Haendler, Wilhelm. *Kaiserin Auguste Viktoria.* Berlin: n.p., 1930.

Hall, Coryne. *Little Mother of Russia: A Biography of Empress Marie Feodorovna.* Teaneck, NJ: Holmes & Meier, 2001.

Hall, Coryne and John Van der Kiste. *Once a Grand Duchess: Xenia, Sister of Nicholas II.* Phoenix Mill: Sutton Publishing, 2002.

Harding, Bertita. *Imperial Twilight: The Story of Karl and Zita of Hungary.* New York: Blue Ribbon Books, 1941.

Healy, Maureen. *Vienna and the Fall of the Habsburg Empire: Total War and Everyday Life in World War I.* Cambridge: Cambridge University Press, 2004.

Hervier, Paul-Louis. *The Two Williams: Studies of the Kaiser and the Crown Prince.* London: Eveleigh Nash, 1916.

Hibbert, Christopher. *Edward VII: The Last Victorian King.* New York: Palgrave Macmillan, 2007.

———. *Queen Victoria: A Personal History.* London: HarperCollins, 2010.

Hobsbawm, Eric. *The Age of Empire, 1875-1914.* London: Weidenfeld & Nicolson, 1987.

Hopkins, J. Castell. *The Life of King Edward VII: With a Sketch of the Career of King George V.* n.p., 1910.

Hough, Richard. *Born Royal: The Lives and Loves of the Young Windsors.* London: Bantam Books, 1988.

———. *Louis and Victoria.* London: Weidenfeld & Nicolson, 1974.

Howard, Ethel. *Potsdam Princes.* New York: Dutton, 1915.

Hull, Isabel V. *The Entourage of Kaiser Wilhelm II 1888-1918*. Cambridge: Cambridge University Press, 1982.

Judd, Denis. *George V.* London: Weidenfeld & Nicolson, 1973.

Judt, Tony. *Postwar: A History of Europe Since 1945*. New York: Penguin, 2005.

Kent, Princess Michael of. *Crowned in a Far Country: Portraits of Eight Royal Brides*. New York: Touchstone Books, 2007.

King, Greg. *The Last Empress: The Life and Times of Alexandra Feodorovna, Tsarina of Russia*. London: Citadel Press, 1994.

Kingston, Charles. *Famous Morganatic Marriages*. London: Stanley Paul, 1919.

Kitchen, Michael. *Europe Between the Wars*. New York: Longman, 2000.

Kohut, Thomas August. *Wilhelm II and the Germans: A Study in Leadership*. New York: Oxford University Press, 1991.

Krieger, Bogdan. *Kaiserin Auguste Viktoria als Landsmutter im Kriege*. Berlin: Lichterfelde, 1919.

Kurth, Peter. *Tsar: The Lost World of Nicholas and Alexandra*. Toronto: Madison Press Books, 1998.

Legge, Edward. *King George and the Royal Family*. Vol. 1. London: Grand Richards, 1918.

Le Qeuex, William. *Love Interests of the Kaiser's Sons*. New York: John Lane, 1918.

Lincoln, W. Bruce. *In War's Dark Shadow: The Russians Before the Great War*. New York: Dial Press, 1983.

———. *The Romanovs: Autocrats of All the Russias*. New York: Dial Press, 1981.

Lowe, Charles. *The German Emperor William II*. London: Bliss, Sands, & Foster, 1895.

Logue, Mark and Peter Conradi. *The King's Speech: How One Man Saved the British Monarchy*. Toronto: Penguin Canada, 2010.

Ludwig, Emil. *Wilhelm Hohenzollern: The Last of the Kaisers*. Translated by Ethel Colburn Mayne. New York: Ames Press, 1970.

MacDonogh, Giles. *The Last Kaiser: William the Impetuous*. London: Weidenfeld & Nicolson, 2000.

Mager, Hugo. *Elizabeth, Grand Duchess of Russia*. New York: Carrol & Graf, 1998.

Margutti, Albert von. *The Emperor Francis Joseph and His Times*. New York: George H. Doran, 1921.

Massie, Robert K. *Dreadnought: Britain, Germany, and the Coming of the Great War*. New York: Ballantine Books, 1991.

———. *Nicholas and Alexandra*. New York: Atheneum, 1967.

Justin C. Vovk

May, Arthur J. *The Hapsburg Monarchy, 1867-1914*. New York: W. W. Norton, 1951.

———. *The Passing of the Habsburg Monarchy*. Vols. 1 and 2. Philadelphia: The University of Pennsylvania Press, 1966.

Middlemas, Keith. *The Life and Times of Edward VII*. Edited by Antonia Fraser. London: Weidenfeld & Nicolson, 1972.

Milani, Abbas. *The Shah*. New York: Palgrave Macmillan, 2011.

Millar, Lubov. *Grand Duchess Elizabeth of Russia*. Redding, CA: Nikodemos Orthodox Publication Society, 1991.

Mitton, G. E. *Austria-Hungary*. London: Adam & Charles Beck, 1914.

Mombauer, A. and W. Deist, eds. *The Kaiser: New Research on Wilhelm II's Role in Imperial Germany*. Cambridge: Cambridge University Press, 2003.

Morrow, Anne. *Cousins Divided: George V and Nicholas II*. Stroud, Gloucester: Sutton Publishing, 2006.

Newnes, George. *HRH, the Prince and Princess of Wales*. London: William Clowes & Sons, 1902.

Nicolson, Harold. *King George V: His Life and Reign*. London: Constable, 1952.

Okey, Robin. *The Habsburg Monarchy 1765-1918: From Enlightenment to Eclipse*. New York: Palgrave Macmillan, 2002.

Packard, Jerrold M. *Victoria's Daughters*. New York: Saint Martin's Press, 1998.

Pakula, Hannah. *An Uncommon Woman: The Empress Frederick—Daughter of Queen Victoria, Wife of the Crown Prince of Prussia, Mother of Kaiser Wilhelm*. New York: Simon & Schuster, 1995.

Pares, Bernard. *Fall of the Russian Monarchy: A Study of the Evidence*. New York: Random House, 1961.

Poliakoff, Vladimir. *The Tragic Bride: The Story of Empress Alexandra of Russia*. New York: D. Appleton, 1928.

Pollak, Gustav. *The House of Hohenzollern and the Hapsburg Monarchy*. New York: The New York Evening Post, 1917.

Polzer-Hoditz, Arthur. *The Emperor Charles*. London: Putnam & Sons, 1930.

Pope, Joseph. *The Tour of Their Royal Highnesses the Duke and Duchess of Cornwall and York Through the Dominion of Canada in the Year 1901*. Ottawa: S. E. Dawson, 1908.

Pope-Hennessy, James. *Queen Mary, 1867—1953*. New York: Alfred A. Knopf, 1960.

Poschinger, Margaretha von. *Life of the Emperor Frederick*. Translated by Sidney Whitman. London: Harper & Brothers, 1901.

Radzinsky, Edvard. *Alexander II: The Last Great Tsar*. Translated by Antonina W. Bouis. New York: Simon & Schuster, 2005.

Rappaport, Helen. *A Magnificent Obsession: Victoria, Albert, and the Death that Changed the British Monarchy*. New York: Saint Martin's Press, 2011.

———. *The Last Days of the Romanovs: Tragedy at Ekaterinburg*. New York: Saint Martin's Press, 2008.

Richardson, Matt. *The Royal Book of Lists: An Irreverent Romp Through Royal History from Alfred the Great to Prince William*. Toronto: Dundurn Press, 2001.

Röhl, John, C. G. *Kaiser Wilhelm II: New Interpretations—The Corfu Papers*. New York: Cambridge University Press, 1982.

———. *The Kaiser and His Court: Wilhelm II and the Government of Germany*. New York: Cambridge University Press, 1994.

———. *Wilhelm II: The Kaiser's Personal Monarchy, 1888-1900*. New York: Cambridge University Press, 2001.

———. *Young Wilhelm: The Kaiser's Early Life, 1859-1888*. Translated by Jeremy Gaines and Rebecca Wallach. New York: Cambridge University Press, 1998.

Rose, Kenneth. *George V*. London: Weidenfeld & Nicolson, 2000.

Sackmyster, Thomas. *Hungary's Admiral on Horseback*. Boulder, CO: Social Science Monographs, 1994.

Salway, Lance. *Queen Victoria's Grandchildren*. London: Collins & Brown, 1991.

Sanders, G. Ivy. *Edward Prince of Wales*. London: Nisbet, 1921.

Scheck, Raffael. *Mothers of the Nation: Right-Wing Women in Weimar Germany*. New York: Berg Publishing, 2004.

Seton-Watson, R. W. *The Southern Slav Question and the Habsburg Monarchy*. London: Constable, 1911.

Shanafelt, Gary W. *The secret enemy: Austria-Hungary and the German alliance, 1914-1918*. Boulder, CO: East European Monographs, 1985.

Shaw, Karl. *Royal Babylon: The Alarming History of European Royalty*. New York: Broadway Books, 1999.

Shawcross, William. *Queen Elizabeth: The Queen Mother*. Toronto: HarperCollins, 2009.

Shaw, Stanley. *William of Germany*. New York: Macmillan, 1913.

Sinclair, David. *Two Georges: The Making of the Modern Monarchy*. London: Hodder & Stroughton, 1998.

Smith, David James. *One Morning in Sarajevo: 28 June 1914*. London: Weidenfeld & Nicolson, 2008.

Smolle, Leo. *Kaiser Karl I, Ein Bild Seines Lebens*. Vienna: Schulbucherverlag, 1917.

Snyder, Timothy. *The Red Prince: The Secret Lives of a Habsburg Archduke*. London: Bodley Head, 2008.

St Aubyn, Giles. *Edward VII: Prince and King*. London: Collins 1979.

Stone, Norman. *Europe Transformed, 1878-1919*. Oxford: Blackwell Publishing, 1999.

Sulzberger, C. L. *The Fall of Eagles*. New York: Crown Publishers, 1977.

Taylor, A. J. P. *The Habsburg Monarchy, 1809-1918: A History of the Austrian Empire and Austria-Hungary*. London: Hamish Hamilton, 1948.

Taylor, Edmond. *The Fall of the Dynasties: The Collapse of the Old Order, 1905-1922*. New York: Garden City, 1963.

Tillett, E. D. *The Royal House of Windsor*. Edited by Frank Fox. London: Jarrold & Sons, 1937.

Toland, John. *No Man's Land: 1918, The Last Year of the Great War*. Garden City, NY: Doubleday, 1980.

Tuchman, Barbara. *The Guns of August*. New York: Ballantine Books Presidio Press, 2004.

Tyler-Whittle, Michael. *The Last Kaiser: A Biography of Wilhelm II German Emperor and King of Prussia*. New York: Times Books, 1977.

Van der Kiste, John. *Crowns in a Changing World: The British Empire and European Monarchies, 1901-36*. London: Grange Books, 1993.

———. *Edward VII's Children*. Stroud, Gloucester: Alan Sutton Publishing, 1989.

———. *George V's Children*. Stroud, Gloucester: The History Press, 2003.

———. *Kaiser Wilhelm II: Germany's Last Emperor*. Bodmin: Sutton Publishing, 1999.

———. *Queen Victoria's Children*. Stroud, Gloucester: The History Press, 2009.

Vivian, Herbert. *The Life of Emperor Charles of Austria*. London: Grayson & Grayson, 1932.

Volkov, Solomon. *Romanov Riches: Russian Writers and Artists Under the Tsars*. New York: Alfred A. Knopf, 2011.

Von Kürenberg, Joachim. *The Kaiser: A Life of Wilhelm II, Last Emperor of Germany*. Ann Arbor: University of Michigan Press, 1922.

Vorres, Ian. *The Last Grand Duchess: Her Imperial Highness Grand Duchess Olga Alexandrovna*. New York: Charles Scribner's Sons, 1965.

Wakeford, Geoffrey. *Three Consort Queens: Adelaide, Alexandra & Mary*. London: Robert Hale, 1971.

Walsh, Edmund. *The Fall of the Russian Empire*. Boston: Little, Brown, 1928.

Warwick, Christopher. *George and Marina, Duke and Duchess of Kent.* London: Weidenfeld & Nicolson, 1988.

Werkmann, Karl. *Der Tote Auf Madeira.* Munich: Kulturpolitik, 1923.

Whates, Richard. *T.R.H. The Prince and Princess of Wales.* London: George Newnes, n.d.

Wheatcroft, Andrew. *The Habsburgs: Embodying Empire.* London: Penguin Books, 1996.

Wheeler-Bennett, John. *King George VI: His Life and Reign.* New York: Macmillan, 1958.

Wickham Steed, Henry. *The Hapsburg Monarchy.* London: Constable, 1919.

Wilgus, William J. *Transporting the A.E.F. in Western Europe, 1917-1919.* New York: Columbia University Press, 1931.

Williams, Susan. *The People's King: The True Story of the Abdication.* New York: Palgrave Macmillan, 2004.

Wilson, A. N. *The Rise & Fall of the House of Windsor.* London: W. W. Norton, 1993.

Wilson, Penny and Greg King. *The Resurrection of the Romanovs: Anastasia, Anna Anderson, and the World's Greatest Royal Mystery.* Hoboken, NJ: John Wiley & Sons, 2011.

Woodward, Kathleen. *Queen Mary: A Life and Intimate Study.* London: Hutchinson, n.d.

Zieglar, Philip. *King Edward VIII: The Official Biography.* London: HarperCollins, 1990.

ARTICLES AND ESSAYS

Anderson, Hildegard. "The Royals: An Illustrated History of Monarchy—From Yesterday to Today." *Life Books Special Edition* (December, 2010).

Cecil, Lamar. "William II and His Russian 'Colleagues,'." Edited by Carole Fink, Isabel V. Hull, and MacGregor Knox. *German Nationalism and the European Response, 1890-1945.* Norman: University of Oklahoma Press, 1985.

Dorpalen, Andreas. "Empress Auguste Victoria and the Fall of the German Monarchy." *The American Historical Review.* Vol. 58, no. 1 (October, 1952).

Green, Michelle, Ellen Wallace, and Jonathan Cooper. "Europe's Heads, Crowned and Otherwise, Bury Zita, the Last Habsburg Empress." *People.* Vol. 31, no. 15 (April 17, 1989).

Gunther, John. "Habsburg Again?" *Foreign Affairs.* Vol. 12, no. 4 (July, 1934).

Hevesy, William de. "Postscript to the Sixtus Affair." *Foreign Affairs*. Vol. 21, no. 3 (April, 1943).

McLean, Roderick R. "Kaiser Wilhelm II and his Hessian Cousins: Intrastate Relations in the German Empire and International Dynastic Politics, 1890-1918." *German History*. Vol. 19, no. 1 (2001).

Mommsen, Wolfgang J. "Kaiser Wilhelm II and German Politics." *Journal of Contemporary History*, 25 (1990).

Patenaude, Bertrand M. "Food as a Weapon." *Hoover Digest*. No. 1 (January 30, 2007).

"The Queen and Prince Philip." *Hello! Canada*. No. 217 (May 16, 2011).

"Queen Mary." *The British Medical Journal*. Vol. 1, no. 4813 (April 4, 1953).

Stowell, Thomas. "Jack the Ripper – A Solution?" *The Criminologist*. Vol. 5, no. 18 (November, 1970).

Thomas de Notre-Dame du perpétual secours. "Empress Zita, French Princess, Empress and Regent of Austria-Hungary." *The Catholic Counter-Reformation in the XXIe Century: He is Risen!* No. 28 (February 2010).

Zeepvat, Charlotte. "Reflections on the 'Lost Prince'." *Royalty Digest*. Iss. 141, vol. 12, no. 8.

Index

T

U

V

5906388R00373

Printed in Great Britain
by Amazon.co.uk, Ltd.,
Marston Gate.